THE MERCHANT

Choice, Hazard and Com...

THE MERCHANT OF VENICE
Choice, Hazard and Consequence

JOAN OZARK HOLMER

MACMILLAN

72502

First published 1995 by
THE MACMILLAN PRESS LTD
Houndmills, Basingstoke, Hampshire RG21 2XS
and London
Companies and representatives
throughout the world

ISBN 0–333–52263–X hardcover
ISBN 0–333–52264–8 paperback

A catalogue record for this book is available
from the British Library

Printed in Malaysia

To my family,
for all their love and support

Contents

	List of Figures	viii
	Preface	ix
	Acknowledgements	xix
	List of Abbreviations	xxi
1	'Truth will come to light': The Historical Prism	1
2	'O me, the word "choose"': Structure and Language	40
3	'Give and hazard': Friends and Lovers	95
4	'Pardon this fault': Antonio and Shylock	142
5	'A Daniel come to judgement': The Trial	183
6	'Joy be the consequence': Union and Reunion	246
	Notes	285
	Bibliography	342
	Index	356

List of Figures

1 Diagram of structural unity   50
2 Diagram of biblical genealogy   74

Preface

In the course of this book I will embrace Hamlet's conclusion that 'the play's the thing' (2.2.604). In my focus on the play a difficult question will be debated: does Shakespeare fashion an artistic unity out of the richly varied and often contradictory elements that constitute *The Merchant of Venice*? This fundamental question, voiced in sundry ways, vexes both textual and performance criticism up to the present moment and will probably continue to do so. The more we discover about this play and its significant contexts, the more we realise we need to know about Shakespeare, sixteenth-century literature, Elizabethan England, Renaissance Europe, and ourselves. I will explore Shakespeare's artistic choices and risks, analysing how and why Shakespeare refashioned materials available to him (both old and new sources) as well as what novelties he added to create what has become his most frequently performed comedy, and for our century, what has also become his most controversial comedy. This study will attempt to demonstrate that this play possesses a profoundly *complex* dramatic unity. What most effectively prevents our appreciation of this complexity is quite simply oversimplification, whether through lack of knowledge or lack of perception, and all of us may be guilty of oversimplification to various degrees. The play's inherent dynamic energy almost attacks us as we confront the many twists and turns in the staging of its intricately interrelated plots.

Wrestling with this play over the years has confirmed for me that there shall probably never be a 'final' interpretation or any single reading or approach that does justice to the orchestrated *whole* of *The Merchant of Venice*. Perhaps the most daunting challenge that scholars, directors, actors, and teachers face is keeping the 'whole' of the play in 'play', whether in one's own mind and heart or on stage in the minds and hearts of many others. It is always easier to get a relative grip on 'parts' of the play, such as its 'economics' or the Christian–Jew issue, but the consequent danger lies in fallaciously substituting the part for the whole.

I suggest that *The Merchant of Venice* is paradoxically more than the sum of its parts. The play in its entirety is bigger, more inclusive and elusive, than any one of us, including myself, who spend countless hours in the library and in the theatre, enjoying it, wondering about it, and trying to pluck out the heart of its mystery. Therefore, this study suffers from no delusion of pretending to be 'the final word' on the play. New discoveries will always be forthcoming, and pre-existing interpretations will have to be refined to accommodate new evidence. However, any 'performance', whether of an actor or a critic, must become temporarily 'fixed' for the moment of its reception by another. Different modes of production vary in degree of fluidity; although the actor can revise a gesture in the next day's performance, the critic will have to wait considerably longer before revising in print. Therefore, this particular study of the play at this point in time is intended to explore new ways of seeing the play in light of the question of dramatic unity and therein contribute to what I see as the *ongoing* debate over this inexhaustible play and the *unending* search it provokes for me and for others.

But if we are going to focus on 'the play', what do we mean by 'the play'? The play-script as performed? The play-text as written and as read? In the past thirty years literary criticism and research have witnessed some extraordinary changes in questions asked, methods used, approaches taken, and ideas examined, proliferating sites of meaning as well as fundamental reconsideration of such formerly basic terms as 'performance', 'meaning', 'text', and 'play'. Both aspects of the play, as script and as text, necessarily complement each other, go hand-in-glove, as it were. However, script and text allow for different modes of questioning and representation of response. The greater the separation in time between the play's two historicities – the immediate era of its production versus subsequent eras of its production – theoretically the greater the need for mediation, whether that mediation concerns stage conventions, language, social customs, or ideas. In other words, Shakespeare's audiences presumably needed much less 'glossing' than we do. Although his audiences were by no means homogeneous, they enjoyed an arguably lesser degree of heterogeneity than audiences today, especially regarding differences in races, religions, politics, and languages. An actor, for example, has to find a dramatic gesture, intonation, or facial expression that will convey to a modern audience the bawdy innuendo of some word (e.g., 'ring') now no longer perceived as bawdy but whose former bawdy sense has been sufficiently glossed by

Shakespearian scholars. The actor is 'spared' the drudgery of work in the library's stacks, but the scholar is also 'spared' the actor's imaginative work of active 'translation'.

In an ideal world both should collaborate, sharing each other's wealth, and positive signs of such collaboration are increasingly visible in various guises – dramaturgs in repertory companies and actors in the classrooms. But in the real world of rehearsal deadlines and page limits we too often need to pick and choose, to become increasingly focused or specialised. As my wise mentor, Dan Seltzer, was fond of observing in class, the study of Shakespeare involves the art of amputation. No one can do it all, and some of the deliberate limitations of my book concern general theoretical debates about Shakespeare and the review of performance criticism, matters large enough and important enough to constitute separate books in their own rights. *The Merchant of Venice* already enjoys an extensive history of performance criticism, which I have not the space to review. However, James C. Bulman's recent book on the subject opens, not surprisingly, by calling attention to the 'crucial problem in staging *The Merchant of Venice*', namely 'how to balance its two distinct and seemingly unrelated plots' because 'Venice and Belmont seem to belong to different plays'.[1] This is the very problem I seek to understand here.

I, therefore, have chosen to focus on the play-text and to attempt to provide new information of an analytical and descriptive nature that could prove useful to a director, actor, or performance critic. But I try to stop short of prescribing how this information could or should be enacted on stage. Let us consider briefly one example that illustrates my rationale. One of the most exciting and provocative videocassettes to use in teaching this play derives from the 'Playing Shakespeare' series, coordinated by John Barton. In this videotape, entitled 'Exploring a Character', Patrick Stewart and David Suchet, who take turns playing Shylock, discuss with Barton how they envision the role and why they make the choices they do. Stewart and Suchet, in a workshop format, enact pivotal moments from the play, back-to-back and exchanging roles with each other. The viewer is privileged to witness simultaneously fine acting and alternative interpretations, despite identical text and essentially identical direction from Barton. In their discussion of Shylock, however, emphasis is placed on the subject of money, but virtually no emphasis is placed on *modes* of money, the importance of how money is obtained, whether by merchantry or usury. Is the subject of usury worth more than a passing reference?[2] Why did Shakespeare add it? Despite some recent critical interest in the subject, usury is probably the most underestimated, and sometimes even misunderstood, element in the play. I try to uncover and recover pertinent historical and literary contexts that elucidate Elizabethan views on usury and then try to determine if, how, and why Shakespeare is using these views in his play. But I seldom postulate dramatic correlatives for how a modern production might communicate such views on stage to a twentieth-century audience. That is another challenge.

On the other hand, I do incorporate aspects of performance theory or the phenomenology of performance whenever these are particularly appropriate for the issues being discussed: for example, the interplay of the artistic phenomena of empathy and aesthetic distance; the deployment of stage time; the use of oral and visual repetition; implicit and explicit directives in the script; verbal symbols that become visual symbols as 'props'; the placement and sequential unfolding of narrative; and the discrepancies between a character's knowledge (whether of self or others), the audience's usually (but not always) more comprehensive knowledge, and the author's omniscience. It seems to me that Shakespeare mastered every facet of his playwrighting craft, doing all things well, even in a play as relatively 'early' as *The Merchant of Venice*. For instance, a reasonably close comparison of Marlowe's *The Jew of Malta* and Shakespeare's *Merchant*, undertaken herein, reveals not only that Shakespeare is far more indebted to Marlowe than has generally been suggested, but also that Shakespeare is sufficiently independent in his deliberate departures from Marlowe, charting his own remarkably new dramatic territory. If Shakespeare is anxiously trying to contain Marlowe's ghostly influence, he succeeds wonderfully with various examples that range from assiduous assimilation to innovative imitation to confident contradiction.

The theoretical grounding for this study derives primarily from Renaissance literary critical theory, especially as articulated by Sir Philip Sidney in his *An Apology for Poetry*, and as expounded by major scholars in this field. However, this book is not intended to be another book on theory and Shakespeare. Specific arguments from a wide range of different critical approaches and methodologies – both old and new – are considered throughout the book for their explicit comments on various aspects of *The Merchant of*

Venice. The focus for critical engagement has been directed toward the concrete, particular structures of the texts discussed, not to the overarching general theory. Indeed, an effort has been made to incorporate a substantive amount of the voluminous criticism on this play, not solely to cite critical support and rebuttal but to indicate the broad spectrum of possibilities for interpretation. If one is to judge by the annals of academic in-fighting recently recorded in *PMLA*, *New Literary History*, and *Shakespeare Left and Right*, the avenues for 'valid' criticism and research seem to be narrowing into one-way or right-of-way intersections, ironically at a time when an explosion of diversity exists. With the French might we not exclaim, 'Vive la différence'? Rather than overworrying about *the* approach taken, might we not concern ourselves more with how *responsibly* the approach is pursued? As the medievalists knew in their doctrine of Egyptian gold,[3] gold is gold regardless of the camp in which it is mined.

This in turn opens Pandora's box, the problem of 'meaning' and authorial intention. Recent critical debates about Shakespearian meaning attest to how volatile this issue is, whether considered from the perspective of deconstructionist critics, for example Terence Hawkes, or from the perspective of materialist critics, for example Walter Cohen. In his earlier book, *That Shakespeherian Rag* (1986), Terence Hawkes tells us he questioned 'whether we could have any genuine access to final, authoritative or essential meanings in respect of Shakespeare's plays' and concluded that 'like it or not, all we can ever do is use Shakespeare as a powerful element in specific ideological strategies'.[4] Now, in his recent book *Meaning by Shakespeare*, Hawkes probes further the implications of his position:

> The issues at stake can be simply put. Suppose we have no access to any 'essential' meaning nestling within Shakespeare's texts and awaiting our discovery (any more, let it be said, than Shakespeare did). Then what can their purpose be? . . . the plays have the same function as, and work like, the words of which they are made. We *use* them in order to generate meaning.

Indeed we do. But didn't Shakespeare, like us, also use words to generate meaning?

With all due respect for Hawkes's provocative message, that keeps us thinking about thinking and the problem of meaning, I beg to differ regarding his tenet, parenthetically asserted, about Shakespeare's absence of intended meaning. Hawkes, as an author, intends to convey an 'essential meaning', and he succeeds in clearly stating his meaning: 'Shakespeare doesn't mean: *we* mean *by* Shakespeare.' Why should we deny to Shakespeare what we do not deny to ourselves, namely the quintessentially human pleasure and pain of cultivating and communicating symbolic meaning? As physicians and scientific researchers of the human mind remind us: 'Words, phrases, sentences, all evoke images in our minds. They all contain meaning – the driving force in human language.'[5] In scrutinising the many different meanings that information has for humans, as compared with a computer, such researchers observe the complexity of this subject: 'Meaning is always context dependent. Language isn't simply words strung together. Beneath its surface lies an implicit knowledge about the world, a shared, often intuitive insight into why people think and act the way they do.' Dr Daniel Kahneman argues, 'What makes thinking human is the search for interpretation.'

In his stimulating article on *The Merchant of Venice* Walter Cohen brings materialist criticism to bear on interpretations of the play that can be generated by linking economic history and contemporary theory within 'the framework provided by the Marxist notion of the mode of production'.[6] Cohen rightly sees the play's significant concern with the problem of usury and provides helpful historical information about Venice, but the theological and legal climate of late sixteenth-century England deserves more attention for Shakespeare's innovative use of old and new arguments about usury. Citing Marx's discussion of usury, in which he claims usury declines with the transition to capitalism, partly through the 'opposition of mercantile capital', Cohen suggests that, in England, 'once the majority of the traditional ruling class had adapted to capitalism, the issue of usury faded away'.[7] However, this seems not to be the historical case for Elizabethan-Jacobean England, as Norman Jones ably demonstrates in his historical study of usury and law.[8] In a country without banks the problem of usury does not quietly fade away as mercantile capital grows. Usury was actively debated as changes in England's economy at all levels provoked a general reassessment of usury, beginning with the economic crisis in the 1590s and culminating in the legalisation of usury by Parliament in 1624. Citing Marx's quotations from Shakespeare's *Merchant*, Cohen shows that Marx at one point identifies Shylock with 'capital' and at another point 'with labor', so that Marx succeeds in 'capturing Shylock as both victimizer and victim'.[9] But according to Elizabethan ideas of usury, Shylock probably would not be identified with labour because usury was traditionally criticised as labourless profit, and Thomas Wilson metaphorically describes usurers as idle drones who 'enrich themselves with the labor and travail of others'.[10]

Cohen emphasises that the complexity of *The Merchant of Venice* 'is a consequence of fundamental contradiction in Shakespeare's social material' so that the 'flaws' in the play are 'not signs of artistic incompetence but manifestations of preformal problems'.[11] This viewpoint tends to delimit Shakespeare's artistic role in selecting and structuring such contradiction, as he further complicates the already complex material he adapts from his literary (fictional and nonfictional), biblical, social, economic, political, and legal 'sources'. Cohen sees Shakespeare as needing 'to transform materialist problems into idealist ones (Antonio cannot very well give up commerce, but he can learn to be more merciful)'.[12] However, throughout the play Shakespeare rather interrelates than transforms materialist and idealist problems; the issue of wealth is deftly intertwined with the issue of faith. Cohen judiciously recognises the problem of mistaking part for whole in the play's criticism, but he also believes that the play fails in its 'central design to provide a completely satisfying resolution to the dilemmas raised in the course of the action'.[13]

It is precisely Shakespeare's 'central design' that I wish to reexamine. What is it? Does it fail? If it fails, where does it fail? In the theatre? Or in polemical essays? Do we need to observe more, know more, and question more in order to see 'connections' where we have previously thought there were none? How substantive is the factor of 'cohesion' for this play?

However, to accept the presence of an author's intended meaning is not the same thing as accurately defining what that intended meaning is. All attempts by an outsider to get inside an author's mind and heart in order to know his meanings are necessarily approximations. This seems especially true for a fictional work of art in which we often find directions through indirections, and the author is under no obligation to furnish consistently straightforward exposition. To know 'definitively' an author's intents one needs to *be* the author. Perhaps debate should pivot more on Hawkes's qualifier 'essential' and Cohen's 'possibilities'. Hawkes

opens his book with an example from *Hamlet*. A counter example
might be raised: if a play embodies no 'essential' meaning, why
does Hamlet disapprove of clowns who improvise nonessential,
although supposedly entertaining, material and thereby obscure
'some necessary question of the play ... to be consider'd' (3.2.42–3)?
Meaning 'by Shakespeare' might often, like Hamlet's ghost, 'coms't
in such a questionable shape' (1.4.43), but come it will. A play
can embrace a plurality of meanings, but some seem to be more
'possible' than others, or, at least according to Hamlet, more 'necessary' than others. Literary works do take on 'afterlives' in their
readers, who may find meanings the author never intended but
which might be appreciated or dismissed, by author or by reader,
if the author could be given a chance to dialogue with the reader.

Judging from twentieth-century attempts to ban productions of
The Merchant of Venice or its use in classrooms, the play, at least
for some, has lost its power 'to please'.[14] Thomas Cartelli insightfully
reminds us about the importance of pleasure in theatrical experience, going so far as to imply that pleasure, especially the pleasure of fantasy fulfilment, is what empowers meaning.[15] We might
note that Prospero, in his epilogue to the audience, claims the
purpose of his 'project' was 'to please' (ll. 12–13), yet this romance with a comedic ending has its share of suffering and tragic
potential, not unlike *The Merchant of Venice*. In the make-believe
realm of dramatic fiction the 'pleasure' derived by an audience
or a reader can paradoxically include pain because the imaginative experience is essentially vicarious. We may empathise with
a character's suffering *as if* it were our own, but in point of fact
it is not. As Touchstone might say, 'Much virtue in If' (5.4.103).
The delicate balance between empathy (our feeling for and with
another) and aesthetic distance (our knowing that art is not life;
this is but a play) allows us to experience unpleasurable emotions (fear, anger, sorrow) 'pleasurably'. But the pursuit of intellectual or conceptual meaning also falls within the perimeter of
what constitutes aesthetic pleasure. If not, we would not enjoy
the riddles, puzzles, and mysteries we find in so many plays.
Our play, in fact, opens on a note of mystery – Antonio's professed inability to know himself or to explain his strange, newfound
melancholy.

If we dismiss 'meaning' from *The Merchant of Venice*, we do so
at our own peril. Shakespeare literally inscribes a search for meaning
in this play quite explicitly in his presentation of the casket test.

Nerissa explains that the right choice depends on choosing *'his meaning'* (1.2.13, my italics), that is, the meaning intended by Portia's father and not the viewer's or reader's own self-imposed meanings on the lottery, such as those of Morocco and Arragon. But what, pray tell, is 'the meaning' of this test? Ay, there's the rub. I submit that this outside interpreter's attempt at explicating 'the meaning' of the casket test can only be an approximate endeavour at best. Critical analysis is perhaps paradoxically reductive and productive; it deconstructs a work to reconstruct an appreciation of that work on a more solid foundation. But any distillation of abstract meanings or themes should supplement, not replace, the more inclusive experience of one's own imaginative participation in the 'life' of the literary work itself, the life transmitted to the work by its author and the life generated from the work by the reader's or viewer's response to it. As modern scholarship on scholarship highlights for us, every critic has some critical assumptions, most of which are predisposed by the critic's personal history as well as the historical moment at the time of writing.[16] By now it should be clear that I assume *The Merchant of Venice* has an author; that author is William Shakespeare; he knew how to write plays and perform them; and we moderns can approximate an understanding of the play he wrote the more we know and the more we test what we think we know by constantly re-experiencing the play and discussing it with others who read, research, perform, and view the play. Put another way, the play is the thing.

But 'knowing' an Elizabethan play includes knowing the literary and historical contexts that nurture the form the play takes. For Renaissance plays the form(s) in which a play can come down to us is problematic in itself. *The Merchant of Venice*, unlike *Hamlet* or *King Lear*, mercifully has a relatively stable textual history so that comparatively little criticism has been devoted to technically textual matters. Sidney's emphasis on the epistemological principle of comparison in his definition of comedy[17] might be borrowed to enhance our appreciation of *The Merchant of Venice* through intertextuality, internally through a comparison of our play with others in Shakespeare's own corpus and externally through a comparison with other pertinent texts outside his canon. This difficult play demands multiple contexts and multiple perspectives, promoting a fuller awareness of its important sixteenth-century theatrical, literary, theological, social, and philosophical nexus. The first chapter will introduce three historical contexts – the aesthetic, the religious, and the economic – that are particularly valuable for the close examination of the play-text that follows in subsequent chapters.

Anyone who has dared to work on this play must acknowledge an enormous debt to other scholars, directors, and actors; I am deeply grateful for many earlier contributions, whether or not we end in agreement. Indeed, disagreement proves essentially thought-provoking, and I hope I have managed herein to disagree without being disagreeable. At a time when some critical debates focus our attention on whether we have in the English Renaissance a theatre of power or a 'powerless theatre',[18] I wish to focus on the power of the play.

JOAN OZARK HOLMER

Acknowledgements

I would like to thank the many colleagues, students, and friends who have taken an interest in my work and have supported me in a variety of ways. To Michael Scott I owe the impetus for this book, and I am grateful for his reading of an early draft. My department and university have kindly enabled the completion of this book through granting me a sabbatical and a leave of absence. Very special thanks go to my learned and generous colleague, Bruce R. Smith, who read parts of the manuscript and provided incisive advice. My supportive colleague, Paul Betz, has given his judicious counsel about sundry matters whenever I have sought his aid. I thank Jason Rosenblatt and Father Robert B. Lawton, S.J. who shared their expertise in Hebrew for my discussion of Shylock's name. For their interest and inspiration regarding my work in Shakespeare and Renaissance studies I will always be grateful to Thomas P. Roche, Daniel Seltzer, Earl Miner, O. B. Hardison, Franklin B. Williams, Michael J. Collins, Ray Reno, and Leeds Barroll. To the patient and talented Joan Reuss belongs a lion's share of thanks for generous and timely help in preparing the typescript. Joan Smallwood also genially gave her expert assistance in computer technology.

I owe a significant debt to my students, who have constantly energised my wrestling with *The Merchant of Venice* over the past twenty years. I am grateful to Beth Charlebois, who helped in countless ways and encouraged me with her indefatigable enthusiasm. The staffs of the Folger Shakespeare Library and the Georgetown University Library have also been extremely helpful. To earlier scholars and critics of this play I am thankful for their many contributions.

To all the members of my family, near and far, I especially owe thanks for their understanding and good wishes. I am especially indebted to my husband, Alan, for vigilantly keeping me on schedule and to my children, Scott and Joy, for goodnaturedly tolerating my long hours at the library. To my father and my mother goes a very great debt of loving thanks for painstakingly reading the entire manuscript in several drafts.

I thankfully acknowledge the following permissions I have received to reprint in this book portions of my previously published work: to the Council for Research in the Renaissance for 'Loving Wisely and the Casket Test: Symbolic and Structural Unity in *The Merchant of Venice*', *Shakespeare Studies*, **11** (1978) pp. 53–76; to the William Marsh Rice University for 'The Education of the Merchant of Venice', *Studies in English Literature, 1500–1900*, **25** (1985) pp. 307–35; and to the Associated University Presses for 'Miles Mosse's *The Arraignment and Conviction of Vsurie* (1595): A New Source for *The Merchant of Venice*', *Shakespeare Studies*, **21** (1993) pp. 11–54. In my book, spelling and punctuation in quotations taken from older works have been modernised.

List of Abbreviations

AJES	*Aligarh Journal of English Studies*
ANQ	*American Notes & Queries*
CI	*Critical Inquiry*
DNB	*Dictionary of National Biography*
E&S	*Essays and Studies*
EIC	*Essays in Criticism*
ELH	*Journal of English Literary History*
ELR	*English Literary Renaissance*
Expl	*Explicator*
HLQ	*Huntington Library Quarterly*
IJES	*Indian Journal of English Studies*
JEGP	*Journal of English and Germanic Philology*
JHI	*Journal of the History of Ideas*
JWCI	*Journal of the Warburg and Courtauld Institutes*
MLN	*Modern Language Notes*
MLQ	*Modern Language Quarterly*
MLR	*Modern Language Review*
MP	*Modern Philology*
N&Q	*Notes and Queries*
OED	*Oxford English Dictionary*
PMLA	*Publications of the Modern Language Association*
RenD	*Renaissance Drama*
RenQ	*Renaissance Quarterly*
RSR	*Reference Services Review*
SAP	*Studia Anglica Posnaniensia*
SAQ	*South Atlantic Quarterly*
SEL	*Studies in English Literature, 1500–1900*
ShakS	*Shakespeare Studies*
ShOSN	*Shakespeare Oxford Society Newsletter*
ShS	*Shakespeare Survey*
SP	*Studies in Philology*
SQ	*Shakespeare Quarterly*
TSLL	*Texas Studies in Literature and Language*
UC	*The Upstart Crow*
UTQ	*University of Toronto Quarterly*

1
'Truth will come to light': The Historical Prism

Generally applauded throughout the world today are the depth and variety of Shakespeare's perceptions in pondering the human condition and his theatrical enactment of these insights in powerful dramatic form. But if we would claim Shakespeare as our contemporary, we must in reciprocal fairness attempt to be his contemporary as well. We must travel back in time to his world, with its own language, beliefs, habits, and perceptions. We should gratefully acknowledge that scholars have written extensively about the importance of the Ptolemaic model of the universe, the idea of hierarchical order governing the macrocosm and microcosm in this great Chain of Being, and the new philosophical theories as well as scientific discoveries that develop in the late Renaissance, eventually upending the traditional model.

'Reality' – whatever it truly is – may not change much, but human perceptions and interpretations of 'reality' do change. C. S. Lewis wisely counsels us 'to regard all Models in the right way, respecting each and idolizing none. . . . No Model is a catalogue of ultimate realities, and none is a mere fantasy.'[1] Indeed, our own cherished models get discarded too. In this matter of appreciating models for interpreting ourselves and our world we might do well to recall Theseus' advice for the beneficent power of imaginative amendment: 'The best in this kind are but shadows; and the worst are no worse, if imagination amend them' (5.1.212). What does need to be stressed, however, especially at this crossroads in our own sense of literary history and changing academic curriculums, is what Charles W. R. D. Moseley cautions in his recent book on Shakespeare's history plays: 'in studying Shakespeare . . . we are making an attempt to open ourselves so as to get to grips with that unparalleled mind for what he has got to tell us rather than for what we can foist on him. . . . He

1

cannot fairly be read if we pretend he is other than he is: a man of the Renaissance, in the peculiar late form it took in England.'[2]

'THE WORLD . . . A STAGE' (1.1.77–8)

The art of drama, especially in the hybrid form it took in Elizabethan England, is exceptionally complex. Shakespeare and his contemporaries generally adhere to the Renaissance rhetorical ideal of 'imitatio', whereby the combination of old material with new is expressed in an original manner. This 'recombinant' theory of literary creativity mirrors one contemporary theory of divine creativity, namely God's creation of the world, not 'ex nihilo', but rather out of something, the four contraries (hot, cold, moist, dry), which are then combined into the four elements (air, fire, water, earth), which, in turn, are usually called in man the four humours (sanguine, choleric, phlegmatic, melancholic). For the Elizabethans this recombinant creativity produces infinite variety. The poetic feigning of images is described in the sixteenth century as a process of severing and joining things real to form things imagined, and according to Renaissance critical theory regarding the operation of the poetic imagination, the imagination's transforming or 'feigning' power is guided by reason to create art.[3] Shakespeare draws on a wide variety of literary and historical sources to create his plays. No one play is ever reducible to its 'source', although a comparative study often yields observations that then beg to be interpreted: what might the dramatist want to accomplish by the changes he makes? Shakespeare's genius in his use of sources is always transformative; he takes the raw materials of other sources and shapes them into his own artistic vision, the imaginative and fictive realm of his play.

Shakespeare manages to achieve a very high degree of artistic unity so that, as O. B. Hardison reminds us, one reason we value his plays so much is for their artistic coherence.[4] Heinrich Wölfflin's concept of 'multiple unity', explained in his *Principles of Art History*, describes the type of vision found in painting, sculpture, and architecture of the High Renaissance, and this concept is aptly applied to Shakespeare's drama by Madeleine Doran.[5] Doran explains that this 'multiple unity' is a coordination of independent parts: 'multiplicity is one of the first things that strikes us as characteristic of sixteenth-century literary art. Rabelais, Ariosto, Cervantes,

Spenser, and Shakespeare saw beauty in multiplicity of detail. Abundant variousness was a way of seeing the world in the sixteenth century that no longer had the same meaning or value at the end of the next century.'[6] According to Wölfflin, with Baroque art the emphasis shifted to a ' "unified unity" ', a 'subordination' to 'a more unified total motive', rather than a 'co-ordination of accents'.[7] Doran favourably compares Shakespeare's art with Giovanni di Paolo's painting of St John in the Desert, where 'narrative sequence' is complemented by 'dramatic emphasis to a climactic moment', and such a comparison implies that Shakespeare's version of 'multiple unity' is distinctive in his cultivation of 'dramatic emphasis'.[8]

I suggest that in *The Merchant of Venice* Shakespeare's dramatic art is rooted in 'multiple unity' characteristic of High Renaissance art but also anticipates 'unified unity' characteristic of Baroque art. The integrity of artistic vision that Shakespeare creates out of the many disparate elements in his play springs chiefly from a richly refined ideology about love, and human choices for and against wise love, that receive an even richer expression through his complex use of language. The artistic unity of many Elizabethan plays does depend on a unity achieved through diversity, that is a coordination of parts, an integration of plots, themes, and characters through the play's language and scenic sequence. Elizabethan dramatists value seeing 'interrelationships' within the play's variety of materials. This artistic interest in finding interrelationships within diversity or multiplicity is characteristic of Elizabethan intellectual habits, their model of the universe itself being grounded on seeing relationships, correspondences, within all of creation. Elizabethan emphasis on desirable amplification of language in literature finds a dramatic correlative in the emphasis in their plays on the extension, not so often the compression, of action. Dramatic narrative essentially concerns what happens to the characters and what the characters undergo in responding to these events. Shakespeare's consummate skill is to enact in the audience what has been enacted on stage. We might observe that the heart of Shakespeare's dramatic skill is that we are made 'to see it feelingly' (4.6.149), to borrow a line from Gloucester.

As M. M. Mahood notes in her edition of *The Merchant of Venice*, we moderns need to familiarise ourselves with the attitudes and assumptions that Shakespeare's first audience probably brought to this play, but at the same time we must also perceive how Shakespeare's play is the work of 'a highly individual artist'.[9] Shakespeare, as a shrewd professional in the theatre, is fully aware of his possible dramatic opportunities to play with his audience's *expectations*. Whether to laugh, or weep, or rejoice, or fear, or puzzle, or admire, the audience will be provoked by Shakespeare to *respond*, both emotionally and intellectually, certainly at least to think and to feel newly and, hopefully, more deeply and wisely about the 'problems' enacted by his players. As Lawrence Danson rightly remarks, *The Merchant of Venice*, comedy though it is, may be viewed not only as a 'problem play' (like so many others of Shakespeare's) but as 'the most scandalously problematic of Shakespeare's plays'.[10]

Shakespeare's play is rendered no less problematic when we recall the prevailing literary temper of his age, that endorsed Horace's dictum for art expressed in his *Ars Poetica*, that the poet should profit ('prodesse') and delight ('delectare') by mixing the sweet ('dulce') and the useful ('utile').[11] Hence, Edmund Spenser declared his aim for his great romance epic, *The Faerie Queene*, was 'to fashion a gentleman or noble person in virtuous and gentle discipline', and similarly Sir Philip Sidney, in his *An Apology for Poetry*, argued for the superior power of the poet as the best teacher because the poet both delights and instructs, can literally move humans to 'well doing' or *praxis*, not only 'well knowing' or *gnosis*.[12] In his *Areopagitica* Milton dares to declare 'our sage and serious poet Spenser' a better teacher than John Duns Scotus or St Thomas Aquinas because Spenser immerses his characters in 'trial, and trial is by what is contrary': 'the knowledge and survey of vice is in this world so necessary to the constituting of human virtue' that for Spenser's Guion to embody true temperance he must endure 'the cave of Mammon and the bower of earthly bliss, that he might see and know, and yet abstain'.[13] Thomas Nashe specifically defends the plays on the English stage against the contemporary accusation of corruptive influence. When the English are most idle, in the afternoon, and most likely to get into trouble, Nashe wittily argues that plays perform a genuine moral service to the state by distracting people from mischief: 'But what shall he do that hath spent himself? where shall he haunt? Faith, when Dice, Lust, and Drunkeness, and all have dealt upon him, if there be never a Play for him to go to for his penny, he sits melancholy in his Chamber, devising upon felony or treason, and how he may best exalt himself by mischief.' But Nashe, like Sidney, also stresses the educational anatomising of vice and virtue that plays achieve in their deconstruction of false appearances, a dominant theme in our play: 'In Plays, all cozenages, all cunning drifts over-gilded with outward holiness . . . all the cankerworms that breed on the rust of peace, are most lively anatomiz'd: they show the ill success of treason, the fall of hasty climbers, . . . and how just God is evermore in punishing murder.' Nashe concludes that plays are 'sower pills of reprehension, wrapped up in sweet words . . . for no Play . . . praiseth or approveth pride, lust, whoredom, prodigality, or drunkenness, but beats them down utterly'.[14]

Given the expansive genre of comedy in Renaissance drama, which embraces the romantic, tragicomic, and problematic aspects of our play, it is worth recalling Sidney's definition of comedy: 'comedy is an imitation of the common errors of our life. . . . Now, as in geometry the oblique must be known as well as the right, and in arithmetic the odd as well as the even, so in the actions of our life who seeth not the filthiness of evil wanteth a great foil to perceive the beauty of virtue.'[15] Shakespeare does effectively use the Sidneyan principle of contrastive comparisons for comedic epistemology. Although *The Merchant of Venice* has often been analysed in terms of its polar contrasts – Old Law and New Law, Justice and Mercy, Venice and Belmont – the play's opposites do not solely oppose but also temper each other, much in a spirit similar to the Christian idea of the fulfilment of the Old Law, not its destruction in the New Law. In the *Preface to Shakespeare* Dr Johnson praised Shakespeare's characters: 'His persons act and speak by the influence of those general passions and principles by which all minds are agitated, and the whole system of life is continued in motion.'[16] Whether we are attuned to Horace's pleasure and profit or to Johnson's passions and principles, Shakespeare's *The Merchant of Venice* has yielded over four centuries of infinite variety in the responses of audiences and critics. This kaleidoscopic range of response will be addressed in the subsequent chapters at appropriate points.

Although we can at best achieve only an approximate understanding of how Elizabethans experienced Shakespeare's plays, whereas we have a firsthand appreciation of our own modern experience, we do at least need to remind ourselves of some important Elizabethan literary conventions. For example, considering a firsthand (but recorded later) description of a performance of a morality play in about 1570, Arthur Kirsch notes that the moral of the play is perceived as both 'the moral of the story, as we would now say, and the story itself'.[17] This perceived fusion of meaning and narrative, so characteristic of great Renaissance works like Spenser's *Faerie Queene*, contributes to the complex texture that Shakespeare cultivates in his dramatic art. For example, when we are first introduced to the casket test, which was a death-bed inspiration of Portia's 'virtuous' (1.2.23) father to ensure her future happiness of loving 'rightly' (1.2.27), Nerissa explains that the right choice depends on choosing '*his meaning*' (1.2.13, my italics), the meaning Portia's father devised for the three chests. Indeed, what do they 'mean' – collectively and individually? How and why do all the suitors but one misperceive the meaning and therefore choose wrongly? What might Portia's father intend by 'rightly' choose and 'rightly love' (1.2.27)?

This matter is no small consideration in the light of Shakespeare's own choices. Mahood emphasises that 'first and foremost *The Merchant of Venice* is a romantic play' (p. 9). Shakespeare could have followed his main literary source for the flesh-bond plot, which includes a very different plot for winning the Lady of Belmont, a sort of tricky bed test: whoever successfully beds the lady wins the lady, but the suitors are intentionally tricked by being given a cup of drugged wine to induce sleep and hence failure. In terms of exciting drama, this plot is at least as theatrically charged, if not more so, than the test of a choice among three caskets. But while the bed-trick plot might provide titillating theatre, it yields no rich hoard of potential *meaning* with allegorical and analogical overtones. Instead, Shakespeare browsed elsewhere for his casket plot, which he would intertwine with his flesh-bond plot found in an Italian novella. He found the romance plot he wanted to adapt in a collection of allegorised, medieval tales, the *Gesta Romanorum*, using probably the revised translation of 1595. Although allegory has grown out of fashion now, Shakespeare pursues directions and sources that afford telling clues for the drama he ultimately creates.

The Merchant of Venice, however, is more than a romantic play because its subject of love includes the love of friendship as well as romance, the love of parent and child, and the love of master and servant. In his exploration of the elemental experience of human love in Shakespeare's plays, Arthur Kirsch, for example, uses the analogies afforded by Freudian psychology and Christian theology to stress the importance of the reservoir of medieval drama, particularly the morality and mystery plays, as a formative influence for 'the theatrical sensibility of Shakespeare and his audience'.[18] Love, in its many guises, is unquestionably an enduring staple throughout Shakespeare's plays. Part of the dramatic assault *The Merchant of Venice* makes on our sensibilities has to do essentially with the problem of loving and not loving or hating. Even more specifically, the play involves us, as it does its characters, in tough choices that are not often without real risks, and therein art mirrors nature. Loving wisely, not foolishly, in all aspects of life and human relationships may be the most difficult challenge of all, and Shakespeare's dramas continually explore and enact that challenge whether in *The Merchant of Venice* or *King Lear*. Bottom's old observation, 'And yet, to say truth, reason and love keep little company together now-a-days' (3.1.144), is probably just as generally true now-a-days. However, the old expectation that reason and love should be compatible has significantly eroded since nineteenth-century Romanticism and its distrust of human reason. But a medieval–Renaissance perspective on true human love is articulated by Milton's Raphael when he instructs Adam, the father of mankind, how to love rightly:

> In loving thou dost well, in passion not,
> Wherein true Love consists not; Love refines
> The thoughts, and heart enlarges, hath his seat
> In Reason, and is judicious, is the scale
> By which to heav'nly Love thou may'st ascend,
> Not sunk in carnal pleasure, for which cause
> Among the Beasts no Mate for thee was found.[19]

If God is love, as John asserts (1 Jn 4.8,16), and if humans are made in the image and likeness of God, as Genesis maintains (1.26–7), then the pervasive preoccupation in medieval–Renaissance literature with matters of love, both true and false choices, is not solely aesthetic but also profoundly ethical, psychological, philosophical, and theological as well as the stuff of life itself. We can realise our fullest human and humane potential through love, but to avert tragedy in life, as well as on stage, we must try to avoid Othello's self-indictment 'of one that lov'd not wisely but too well' (5.2.344).

The Merchant of Venice derives much of its powerful dramatic energy from the hard choices for or against wise love that its

characters confront and we experience empathetically. Shakespeare's
emphasis on wise love is probably the most significant addition
to the variety of literary sources he transformed for the invention
of his play. The educative bent of this play first reveals itself in
Antonio's indication of a learning process about to occur (1.1.5),
followed in the next scene by Nerissa's keynoting the human difficulty of happily finding moderation, the golden mean between
extremes (1.2.5–7), and Portia's confirmation of the human dilemma of knowing and doing what is good (1.2.11–17). Shakespeare allows different conceptions of love to jostle for supremacy
in the play. Those who choose love as primarily a motive and act
of gaining and getting what is desired and deserved lose. Those
who choose love as primarily a motive and act of giving and
hazarding all for the sake of the beloved win. Those who make
the symbolic leaden choice enjoy the play's blessings. Perhaps
the most efficient way for a modern reader to foreground an Elizabethan ethic regarding which choices should be blessed is to read
Chapters 5 through 7 of Matthew's gospel juxtaposed with Chapter
6 (vs 20–49) of Luke's gospel, as well as their attendant glosses
in the Geneva Bible, the version most accessible to Elizabethans.[20]
Why these chapters? These chapters record Matthew's and Luke's
versions of Christ's Sermon on the Mount, and this teaching explains who will be 'blessed' and why. As we shall discover, Shakespeare adapts specific ideas and imagery from these important
chapters. Essentially the blessed will be those who rightly love
God and all others as God has loved them. The conception that
ideal human love should be modelled on divine love is basic to
such teaching. Edmund Spenser's Easter sonnet to his bride-to-
be captures this idea in its concluding couplet: 'So let us love,
dear love, like as we ought: / Love is the lesson which the Lord
us taught' (*Amoretti*, Sonnet 68). This divine inspiration orients
the lessons of Matthew's and Luke's chapters where God's vision is contrasted with that of the world. In God's eyes the blessed
will include those the world rejects – the poor, the hungry, the
suffering, and the persecuted for God's sake. Those not to be blessed
will be those who look good in the eyes of the world, those worldly
ones who put their trust in riches and the pleasures of the flesh,
in vainglory, earthly pomp, and fame.

    The Merchant of Venice explicitly concerns itself with this im-
portant matter of 'blessing' in a variety of ways, as Morocco
suggests in his awareness that an important right choice will make

him 'blest', but a wrong choice will make him 'cursèd among men!' (2.1.46). Portia's father blesses her with his wealth and a test designed to ensure right love; Lancelot asks for his father's blessing after he reveals his comically intended deception (2.2.65,69–70); Shylock sees Jacob's thriving as 'blest' and as an analogy for his usury which he sees as thrifty 'blessing' (1.3.81–2); love rains its joyful 'blessing' on Portia when Bassanio chooses rightly (3.2.111–13); Jessica sees Bassanio as having the joys of heaven on earth because Portia as a wife is 'such a blessing' (3.5.63); 'the quality of mercy . . . droppeth as the gentle rain from heaven . . . [and] is twice blest' in blessing the giver and the receiver (4.1.180–3); Portia blesses Antonio with 'life and living' (5.1.286); and Lorenzo responds to the 'special deed of gift' for him and Jessica as if it were a heaven-sent blessing: 'Fair ladies, you drop manna in the way / Of starved people' (5.1.294–5). A brief summary of some of the lessons presented by Matthew and Luke serves to highlight significant ideas we will explore in more detail later: you have heard 'an eye for an eye and a tooth for a tooth', but you are called to endure double injury, rather than revenge yourselves; you have heard that you should love your neighbour and hate your enemy, but that is wrong; love your friends and love your enemies; give to everyone who asks of you; do unto others as you would have others do unto you; judge not, and you shall not be judged; cast out the beam in your own eye before trying to remove the speck in your brother's eye; be merciful, as your Father is merciful; forgive, and you shall be forgiven; give, and it shall be given unto you, measure for measure; whoever kills another, shall be culpable of judgement; whoever calls his brother 'fool' shall be punished; swear not at all because oaths tend to be superstitious; let your speech be simple and true, and you will not be so light and ready to swear; avoid the righteousness of the Scribes and Pharisees who misinterpret and falsely observe the Law; the gospel is not the destruction but the fulfilment of the Law; who teaches others to break the least of the ten commandments, shall be least in God's kingdom, unless pardoned.

The greatest challenge to the enjoyment of blessing, then and now, may be the radically new emphasis on loving all men, enemies as well as friends: 'For if ye love them, which love you, what reward shall you have? Do not the Publicans even the same?' (Mt 5.46; Lk 6.32). The powerful conclusion to this advocacy of divinely wise and selfless love reads: 'Wherefore love ye your enemies, and do good, and lend, looking for nothing again, and your reward shall be great, and ye shall be children of the Most High: for he is kind unto the unkind, & to the evil' (Lk 6.35; Mt 5.45,48). No wonder money and love are so intricately linked in our play. Giving and lending freely are ways of loving. In *The Merchant of Venice* individuals, regardless of their group identifications (Jew or Christian, man or woman, parent or child, master or servant) are judged according to how well they love God and one another. The law of charity tempers the strict law so that characters, and the audience, are challenged to know and to be ideally human. For Elizabethans, inner human harmony is established by the rational soul's right rule of one's animal or fleshly nature. Humans are all basically bound together by the bond of flesh, but unless they are also bound together in the spirit of love they can never be truly unbound, truly free.

Because Shakespeare is so talented in breathing life into his characters, we sometimes have to recollect that his characters are not historically 'real' but artifacts, the products of Shakespeare's conscious and ingenious artifice. It is ultimately misleading to try to interpret Shylock as a 'real' Jew or Antonio as a 'real' Christian. The paradox, of course, is that Shakespeare's created fictions become 'real people' when the actors 'become' the characters. John Russell Brown wisely reminds us: the play's 'characters are capable of many different interpretations. Their apparent reality encourages this; and so does the tendency to view them out of their dramatic context, in light of partisan predispositions. They are complex creations, and all critics have not seen the same aspects. At the risk of confusion, one must try to see them whole, and then relate them to the play as an entity of its own.'[21] One example may suffice to indicate the importance of keeping Shakespeare's artistry foremost in mind. Shylock is a fictional Jew, a fictional character created with a specific role for a particular play. Inconsistencies encountered in his character that make little sense when applying the criterion of 'reality' may not be inconsistencies when viewed within the context of the play's illusion. For example, Shylock is presented as a Venetian Jew, yet he seems surprisingly knowledgeable about the specific Gadarene miracle in the New Testament (Mk 5.1–13). As a Jew, Shylock would not be expected to know the New Testament but rather the Old Testament, from which all but several of his biblical allusions derive. Nor would it be predictably Jewish for him to prefer for

Jessica a husband from the tribe of Barabas, the name of the Jewish criminal in the New Testament who was released in place of Christ and whose name Marlowe chose for his Jew of Malta. What might be the artful purpose behind giving such New Testament allusions to a Jewish usurer like Shylock, one who does business with Christians but who confesses his hatred of them? How might Elizabethan audiences, more thoroughly familiar with the Bible than most modern audiences today, contextualise such allusions to further their understanding of a complex character like Shylock?

'MY FATHER JEW' (2.6.26)

Seldom is the impact of the Renaissance ignored for the refinement of native as well as imported literary forms in sixteenth-century England. But the pervasive importance of theology and philosophy in Elizabethan life and letters also should not be underestimated, especially in light of the revolution set in motion by the Reformation and its subsequent intense debate over matters of faith which influenced such various subjects as the individual, family, nation, law, and wealth. In his attack on atheism, Thomas Nashe, from whose works Shakespeare borrowed and vice versa, insists on the crowning importance of theology to all the 'Humaine Artes': 'No knowledge but is of God. . . . Logic, Rhetoric, History, Philosophy, Music, Poetry, all are the handmaids of Divinity' (2.125–6). In light of this belief, it should, therefore, not surprise us that even the popular dramatist, Thomas Middleton, wrote over a 3000-line poem on a theological subject, *The Wisdom of Solomon, Paraphrased* (1597). Given the much greater degree of secularisation in our modern age, we must resist the temptation to slight the theological underpinnings of sixteenth-century England, even though the age-old dilemma of harmonising theory with practice was as problematic then as now. Any scholar who has worked extensively on *The Merchant of Venice* has had to recognise the depth and the complexity of such influence in the play's sundry twists and turns. Part of this influence is frequently acknowledged by observing Shakespeare's close and creative use of the Bibles of his era, chiefly the Geneva Bible (1560), the Bishops' Bible (1568), and Lawrence Tomson's New Testament (1576) bound with the Geneva version of the Old Testament to make the Geneva–Tomson Bible (1587).[22]

Not only does *The Merchant of Venice* have the greatest number of biblical allusions in Shakespeare's canon, but also, the importance of knowing the Bible, and interpreting how Shakespeare used it, is stressed by M. M. Mahood's appendix devoted to this subject in her New Cambridge edition (pp. 184–8). Naseeb Shaheen also convincingly argues that 'Shakespeare's private reading of the Bible – not his home background, school exercises, or church attendance – was the *main* source of the comprehensive knowledge of the Bible that is evident in his plays.'[23] Barbara Lewalski thinks the play's patterns of biblical allusion and imagery are 'so precise and pervasive as to be patently deliberate'.[24] Frank McCombie demonstrates Shakespeare's interest in and use of the Bible's wisdom literature, especially *The Wisdom of Solomon*, *Ecclesiasticus*, and *Proverbs*, for *The Merchant of Venice*, and Shaheen concurs that among the biblical books most used by Shakespeare were its '"Wisdom Books"' (p. 212).[25] Indeed, the Geneva Bible is dedicated to Queen Elizabeth, and in the dedicatory epistle true wisdom is presented as the requisite virtue for a ruler to preserve political stability in the realm: 'it is manifest, that the quietness and peace of kingdoms standeth in the utter abolishing of idolatry and the advancing of true religion: ... Wherefore great wisdom, not worldly, but heavenly is here required, which your grace must earnestly crave of the Lord, as did Solomon, to whom God gave an understanding heart to judge his people aright, and to discern between good and bad' (sig. ii\^v). For the Elizabethans, political stability depends on moral stability.

What might all this have to do with the oft, and sometimes subtly, emphasised play on various manifestations of 'wisdom' and 'folly' in the range of choices and hazards *The Merchant of Venice* presents? Antonio bemoans the melancholy that makes 'a want-wit' (1.1.6) of him; Gratiano plays 'the Fool' to redress Antonio's supposed attempt at 'wisdom' (1.1.79–92); the clown Lancelot speaks more wisely than he knows when he comically asserts, 'It is a wise father that knows his own child' (2.2.63); Shylock praises Jacob's 'wise mother' (1.3.65) for the idea of stealing Jacob's blessing (1.3.65); Morocco discovers from the scroll in the golden casket that the winner of Portia needs to be 'as wise as bold' (2.8.70); Arragon wins 'a fool's head' (2.9.58); Portia concludes, 'O, these deliberate fools! / When they do choose / They have the wisdom by their wit to lose' (2.9.79–80); and Shylock extols the 'wise young judge' (4.1.220) before the peripateia when

Gratiano will mockingly take up this refrain. We are just beginning to glimpse Shakespeare's sophisticated range for enlivening the grasp of folly and the pursuit of wisdom when humans are faced with conundrums involving faith and love. Although this play is riddled with biblical allusion and theological reference, it cannot, of course, be reduced, like some medieval plays, to a dramatised sermon. That it cannot be so reduced testifies to Shakespeare's artistic control of his medium.

But some important preliminary historical knowledge, both of Shakespeare's century and of ours, is required before we can grapple with some possible answers to the play's essential questions. First, some questions about basic ideas and terminology frequently used in discussing this play ought to be aired. The fundamental problem for a twentieth-century audience's responses to *The Merchant of Venice* revolves precisely around the Jewish-Christian tension embodied in the opposition between Shylock and the Venetian Christians, especially his enemy, Antonio. Some have thought Shakespeare transcends his era and is the first to champion the plight of the Jews through his characterisation of Shylock, while others find this play objectionably anti-Semitic and racist. Is this play racially biased or anti-Semitic, or is it religiously biased or anti-Judaic, or both?[26] What were the Elizabethan perceptions of Jews? How are those perceptions similar to and different from modern views? Does Shakespeare both reflect and transcend the conceptions of his age, and if so, how?

Danson significantly observes what is all too seldom noted in the play's criticism, that the use of Jewish characters in Elizabethan–Jacobean drama is not only not 'culturally predetermined', as has been argued, but it is 'unusual', and we should note that Shakespeare's *choice* to write about Christians and Jews 'remains remarkable'.[27] Why did Shakespeare decide to create his most famous Jewish character at this point in his theatrical career for his only play that includes Jewish characters? Like Moors, Jews were unfamiliar and exotic figures in Elizabethan London, but Shakespeare used a Moor in three different plays, *Titus Andronicus*, *The Merchant of Venice* and *Othello*. Some of the reasons are more obvious than others, and it is likely we will never know all the reasons. Shakespeare is clearly responding to the challenge set by his brilliant contemporary, Christopher Marlowe, whose Barabas, as the Jew of Malta, is a darkly masterful comic villain. He is also probably responding to the recent heightened interest in an historically real and very visible Jewish convert in Elizabethan London, Dr Roderigo Lopez from Portugal. However, such an overwhelming amount of material has been written on Shylock and the Christian–Jewish conflict in the play that we need refresh our awareness regarding only the most salient information and concentrate on whatever new evidence appears.

What is some of the historical information that we need to recall? With several exceptions, there were probably no unconverted Jews living in London during Shakespeare's lifetime.[28] Jews had been expelled from England by King Edward I in 1290, and they were not legally readmitted until 1655 under Cromwell.[29] Therefore, Shakespeare's knowledge of Jews would be necessarily secondhand, gathered from hearsay, literary portrayals, and what he could observe of converted Jews living in London, such as Lopez and his family. Christian usurers, however, were plentiful in London, and their cruelty, greed, niggardliness, and deception were often satirically presented in Elizabethan dramatic and non-dramatic literature.[30] What scholars reveal that dominated Elizabethan thought about Jews was essentially a theological conception which, unlike some modern conceptions, is not racial or ethnographical. This theological tradition of *adversus Judaeos* has been admirably explained by G. K. Hunter in terms of moral *choice*: 'Jewishness [is] a moral condition, the climactic "Jewish choice" being that which rejected Christ and chose Barabbas, rejected the Savior and chose the robber, rejected the spirit and chose the flesh, rejected the treasure that is in heaven and chose the treasure that is on earth.'[31] Alan C. Dessen has also explored how the Elizabethan stage used the Jew to expose this moral condition of wrong choices, whether by Christians or by Jews, and Gratiano in our play has been analysed as a '"Jewish" Christian or a Christian Shylock'.[32]

This theological perspective is indigenous to Christian thought in medieval–Renaissance Europe. Indeed, this perspective informs Robert Wilson's otherwise surprising portrayal of a virtuous Jewish moneylender, who serves as a foil to a despicable Christian merchant, in his comedy, *The Three Ladies of London* (1584), and the play demonstrates how 'Jews seek to excel in Christianity, and Christians in Jewishness.'[33] Likewise, Jessica in our play, unlike her father, is not despised or mistreated by Christians prior to her elopement with Lorenzo, because she tells us that she is not related to Shylock in moral behaviour, despite her biological relationship to him (2.3.17–18). The difference in her behaviour is perceived by Lancelot, who weeps to leave her, and by Lorenzo, who praises her virtues, loves her, and marries her. Jessica freely chooses to convert to Christianity, as does Barabas's daughter Abigail in Marlowe's *The Jew of Malta*, and both daughters claim their fathers are bad examples to them. Although individual practitioners of the Christian faith are criticised in these plays, the Christian faith itself is not criticised. Meyer Jack Landa confuses this issue when he mistakenly asserts that the play is 'a scathing indictment of the Christianity of the day'.[34] Bad Christians do not make Christianity bad, any more than bad Jews would make Judaism bad. The Elizabethan age and stage uphold the primacy of the Christian faith. Abigail makes this point very clearly in her rationale for conversion: 'My sinful soul, alas, hath paced too long / The fatal labyrinth of misbelief, / Far from the Son who gives eternal life' (3.3.63–5). Likewise, following Paul's teaching (1 Cor 7.14), Jessica maintains: 'I shall be saved by my husband; he hath made me a Christian' (3.5.15).

This emphasis on a *theological* understanding of Jews should not be underestimated. As Heiko Oberman has demonstrated in his study of the Jewish question in the sixteenth century, 'strictly speaking, "anti-Semitism" did not exist prior to the race theory of the nineteenth century', but the 'roots' of anti-Semitism are much older so that for the Renaissance and Reformation the animosity against the Jews as the deniers of Christ 'was an inherited assumption' from the Middle Ages, an assumption which was reexamined in the Renaissance but also passed on 'with new strength'.[35] The Jews were not seen as a race but as a religion. That view itself was problematic. The Jews were seen by Christians as God's Chosen People from whom would come the promised Saviour so that the Old Law would be fulfilled, not destroyed, through Christ in the New Law. The ultimate reward of 'inheritance' (Gen 15.1; Eph 1.3–14) promised to God's chosen children was the Messiah and eternal life in heaven. The 'root' of the Christian faith in the faith of Israel is made visually obvious in the ancestral tree printed at the beginning of the Bishops' Bible (1568); this tree pictorially showed Christ's direct line of descent from the patriarchs through the tree of Jesse. Therefore, Christians honoured the role of Israel in biblical salvation history and claimed the ancient patriarchs and prophets as their own. When a patriarch, such as Abram/Abraham or Jacob/Israel, 'converted'

or turned to God, the Bible describes God's recognition of this
choice through His renaming of the patriarch. 'Conversion',
therefore, is a basic principle of the Judaeo-Christian tradition,
conversion(s) from man's rude will to His will.[36] According to
Christian belief, Christ, as the long awaited Messiah, was the human
Jew, as well as the Son of God, who fulfilled the Old Law in the
New Law and so opened the membership in God's chosen family to include all people, regardless of race or rank, who chose
Him as the way to the Father. The Jews who kept their covenant
with God *before* the coming of Christ are not hated but honoured
by Christians. The anti-Judaic attitudes of Elizabethans apply to
those Jews *after* Christ who do not choose to believe in Him.

The divisive 'conversion', then, for Jews and Christians is the
specific conversion to Christ, not to God the Father. Perception
here is a matter of perspective. Whose vision is being adopted
for 'seeing'? According to a Jewish or modern perspective, the
Christian insistence on the Messiah as Jesus Christ would be seen
as a disenfranchising of the Jewish view of their own identity
and choices.[37] According to a sixteenth-century Christian perspective, the insistence on embracing Christ as the promised Messiah
would be seen not as reductive but as liberating and redemptive,
the necessary faith for salvation. Although in theory the ideal
motive for religious conversion was a genuine change of heart,
in practice all too often personal, political, or economic motives
betrayed such theological idealism, depending significantly on
historical time, place, group, or individual. Whether Jews did or
did not convert to Christianity, rewards at the hands of their host
societies could be either weak or strong. In medieval England,
for example, the convert was financially penalised: the convert's
wealth could be confiscated with the remission of one-half of that
penalty.[38] In the Renaissance, for example, successful careers could
be enjoyed by historical Jews, converts like Roderigo Lopez in
London, and non-converts like Judah Abrabanel (alias Leone Ebreo)
in Naples and Venice, as well as fictional Jews like Robert Wilson's
Gerontus in Turkey. Depending on time and place, such as sixteenth-century Venice, late sixteenth- and seventeenth-century
Netherlands, or the Ottoman Empire, Jews might not be forced
to convert, as they were during the Spanish and Portuguese In-
quisitions, in order to avoid various penalties or to achieve the
status of success. However, the very idea of constrained conversion is a major stumbling block for modern audiences living in a

historical period of enlightened thought about religious tolerance and freedom. If it seems as if we and Renaissance Europeans inhabit different worlds of thought regarding the matter of religious conversion, it is because we do. Tolerance may have been a sixteenth-century ideal, but, as Oberman clarifies, as an ideal it had 'the character of a Christian restorative, not of a modern, pluralistic ideal'.[39]

In order to contextualise *The Merchant of Venice* within the historical ideas of religious intolerance and forced conversion we should remind ourselves that the ideal of religious freedom follows a tortuous path of evolution, particularly in some new directions after the Reformation. Renaissance tolerance of intolerance applies among Christians as well as between Christians and Jews; the phenomenon of constrained conversion – varying in degree of difficulty for a variety of religious persuasions – is no stranger to Renaissance Europe. In practice, for example, Charles V's Augsburg *Interim* (1548) for the Holy Roman Empire allows a measure of religious freedom to rulers that is denied to their subjects, that is *cuius regio, eius religio* (subjects must follow the faith of their ruler). Moreover, the extremely complex history of this problem demands careful attention to different national histories in Western countries. For example, the first official European declaration of religious tolerance, the Edict of Nantes (1598–1685), a royal decree which allowed freedom of worship and considerable rights to French Protestants (Huguenots) in Catholic France, had no parallel in Tudor and Stuart England. England's Erastian policy, and its unique *via media* between the Lutheran and Reformed traditions, admitted no religious liberty to its Catholic recusants but allowed them to coexist peacefully with England's Anglicans if they did not directly threaten national security. This *de facto* coexistence was qualified by various parliamentary laws, such as the Act of Uniformity (1559), which attempted to impose religious uniformity. As William Monter reminds us, 'At no time was the English political nation, gathered in Parliament, favourable to religious liberty – to expect that would be to make them different from all other early modern Europeans.'[40]

Despite discrimination of the ghetto, Jews received relatively better treatment in sixteenth-century Venice than elsewhere.[41] Although the Jewish–Christian rapprochement in Renaissance Italy broke down midway through the sixteenth century, primarily through the reactionary Grand Inquisitor, Cardinal Carafa (Pope Paul IV), Venice (which had ghettos) and Livorno (which had none) continued their tolerance of Jews even though the leadership over the diaspora of converted Jews in Christian Europe passed to Amsterdam and Hamburg after 1600. If Shakespeare knew about the ghetto, he, like Robert Wilson and Christopher Marlowe before him, did not use it in his play. He also gave to his Jew a Christian servant for his Venetian household. If Shakespeare knew about the remarkable acculturation of Sephardi Jews in Renaissance Italy, except for the use of a Christian servant, he had his Jew explicitly reject such social and cultural assimilation outside the world of commerce, behaviour surprisingly more like the Sephardi Jews of Amsterdam.[42] However, Shylock's disdainful rejection of assimilation, except for his expertise in Venetian commerce, seems to be rooted less in historical Jews (whether of Venice or Amsterdam), and more in Marlowe's portrayal of these specific traits in his Barabas. Herein, as we shall see, Barabas and Shylock radically contrast with an earlier Elizabethan literary Jew, Wilson's good Gerontus, who moves comfortably and graciously in his cosmopolitan milieu.

Some advances were made in the sixteeth and seventeenth centuries toward limited forms of religious tolerance among Christians, but anti-Semitism remained Europe's most socially acceptable form of intolerance. Monter aptly observes that 'the most significant victims of religious intolerance at all times in early modern Europe were the Jews', and only with the French Revolution did Pierre Bayle's visionary principle of *universal* religious toleration begin to be enacted.[43] The difficult development of religious tolerance and the cessation of religious persecution, in practice and in theory, depend chiefly on the evolving secularisation of Western societies, the increasing separation of Church and State so that religious affiliation could be safely relegated to the free domain of private life without fear of endangering the socio-political community. Aquinas argued against the use of constraint to convert pagans and infidels; he opted rather for preaching and example to encourage free conversion. However, the prevailing attitude, articulated well by Augustine to fight heresy, espoused that Christians should be intolerant of error; if the Christian faith was the true faith, it alone had the right to exist, and the toleration of false belief amounted to the error of indifferentism. Regarding our modern shock at such a double standard, a shock that becomes outrage over Antonio's conversion stipulation for Shylock, Elisabeth Labrousse judiciously offers some historical counsel: 'It would be an anachronism to denounce outrageously the unfairness of such a double standard.... For age after age it appeared dazzlingly evident that Truth, by definition, enjoys rights of its own – and that it would be ... criminal to even think of extending these rights to "errors". If we do not try to gain a sympathetic understanding of this ingenuous principle ... we are doomed to superficiality ... and ignore the slow and difficult awakening of the ideal of toleration.'[44]

Religious tolerance is most unfortunately not the viable perspective in the sixteenth century that it has become for our modern era. The modern emphasis falls more decisively on human goodness, defined in terms of basic morality regardless of one's profession of faith or lack of it.[45] Morality is also very important in the Elizabethan era, and the differing definition of what it means to be a 'good' man is the point of the first comic exchange between Bassanio and Shylock in our play (1.3.11–14). However, most Elizabethans would see any non-Christian as disadvantaged in terms of knowledge of truth; one must first know what is good and true in order to enact it. For the Elizabethans, right values depend primarily on true faith and adherence to what they see as true faith, Christianity, the faith believed necessary for salvation.[46] Therefore, a sixteenth-century Jew could be morally good and do good deeds (for example, Gerontus, Abigail, and Jessica), but in order to be saved, sixteenth-century Christians believed, one has to be justified by faith in Christ, their Messiah. After the Reformation the emphasis falls even more heavily on justification by faith; good deeds, the deeds of charity, however, are still necessary effects or consequences of the inner life caused by faith (Jas 2.14–27; Gal 5,6; Rom 10.9).

The nature of sixteenth-century Christian thought on Jews and the significance of Jewish history for Elizabethan Christians are more complex, therefore, than is usually granted when these subjects are addressed as pertinent background for *The Merchant of Venice*. We will consider here three Elizabethan examples that help to illustrate this complexity: Peter Morwyng's translation of Joseph ben Gorion's *History of the Jews' Common Weal* (1561), Thomas Nashe's opposite treatment of Jews in *Christ's Tears over Jerusalem* (1593) and *The Unfortunate Traveller* (1594), and the life-and-death history of Roderigo Lopez, a famous Jewish convert from Portugal, who lived in Elizabethan London for thirty-five years. Critics often remark the general xenophobia of Elizabethan London, but allowance for more enlightened thought on the part of some Elizabethans is privileged usually to members of the higher classes.[47] But as likely as this seems, it is not necessarily true, any more than it is true for people today. Privilege of birth and education should open one's eyes, but that choice ultimately depends on the individual. For example, in his *Light in August* William Faulkner purposefully presents one of his most refined racial bigots, Gavin Stevens, as a Harvard graduate, a Phi Beta Kappa, and the District Attorney. In the past as in the present, however, individuals can stand against stereotypical thought embedded in one's culture. The Oxford scholar, Peter Morwyng, singles out good Jewish leaders of the past to inspire his Elizabethan readership. Nashe, a Cambridge graduate, is capable of revealing both compassionate and vicious sentiments toward Jews. Different members of the same Elizabethan nobility could admire or despise the Jewish convert, Roderigo Lopez.

Critical emphasis on Elizabethan anti-Judaism is often so pronounced that one senses that there could have been no Elizabethan conception of a 'good' Jew. However, we must be aware of another historical–theological perspective, that Peter Morwyng clarifies for us in his sixteenth-century translation of the popular Hebrew text of Joseph ben Gorion, *A . . . History of the Jews' Common Weal*: the Jews who kept their covenant with God the Father are to be honoured and emulated by contemporary Christians.[48] Morwyng, a scholar of Magdalen College, Oxford,[49] apparently worked from both the Hebrew and Latin texts, and he reveals a scholarly interest in the Hebrew language and syntax, and even the use of Hebrew names.[50] Basic to Morwyng's purpose in providing an English translation that will render accurately the true meaning of the Jewish historiographer is his belief in the didactic function of literature, so unlike our modern theory. His readers are to apply the deeds of the Jews to their own 'manners' so that they 'should learn to know good from evil', using these recorded Jewish deeds as exemplary or admonitory to 'amend' their lives.[51]

Morwyng's epistle to his Christian audience is quite revealing in how a well-educated Englishman of the mid-sixteenth century might view the Jewish people and their commonwealth. Morwyng's attitude is very similar to that of the Jewish author he translates: there are good Jews and bad Jews, much as there are good Christians and bad Christians. The Jews, however, are 'the stock of faith', the true 'root', and Christians are the grafts into this stock.[52] Morwyng warns his Christian audience that calamities similar to those the Jews suffered could befall them too if they persist in sinful rebellion: 'thou seest the Jews here afflicted with divers kinds of misery, because they fell from God'.[53] Their 'own doggedness and intestive [sic] hatred' caused God to destroy Jerusalem and scatter His 'own children'.[54] Throughout his history Joseph praises the nobility, faithfulness, courage, and virtue of those Jews who keep their covenant with God.[55] Morwyng likewise suggests that the fame of the Jews, in the Bible and elsewhere, contributes to the readers' 'pleasure' and 'profit' in this Jewish history, and readers are expected to take delight in beholding 'pictures of ancient persons', the 'lively images of their minds which appear in their acts'.[56] But ungodly Jews are condemned for their criminal acts, which produce so much civil strife. In this text not the cruelty of their enemies but rather the self-destructiveness of the Jews accounts for God's ominous conversion from patience to wrath in the just punishment of His Chosen People. As Thomas Wilson puts it, 'whatsoever is done beside the word of god, and otherwise than he will have it done . . . is of all others the worst and most wicked'.[57] The cause for evaluating human good and evil is theological, not political or economic, and although the effects of such evaluation often had political and economic consequences, cause should not be confused with consequence.

Thomas Nashe provides a very interesting Elizabethan perspective on Jews because he can be sympathetic or cruel depending on his choice and the literary context. Described as able 'to reflect his age and its tastes in an arresting manner',[58] Nashe is a particularly valuable writer for his tonally opposite treatment of Jews in two of his works. Nashe's popular *Christ's Tears over Jerusalem*, based in part on Morwyng's translation of Joseph's book, is Nashe's attempt at theological sermonising, and as such it fits comfortably within a long tradition of history used for moral and didactic purposes in literature, such as Boccaccio's *De Casibus Virorum Illustrium*, *A Mirror for Magistrates*, and the play by Greene and Lodge, *A Looking Glass for London and England*.[59] Like Joseph and Morwyng, Nashe also honours the Jews as the Chosen People of God. But he adds to the history of the Jews' commonwealth his own fictional oration for Christ, wherein Christ prophesies and weeps over the future suffering and desolation of Jerusalem, in order to draw a direct application to sinful London and her timely need for repentance.[60] Although the 'hart' of Jerusalem is 'harder than stone' (2.23) and is confirmed in its sinful rebellion, finally deserving God's punishment, Nashe's pain-filled lamentation in the persona of Christ sincerely bewails such great suffering and so great a loss of 'the Daughter of [His] people' (2.21). Nashe's addition of this oration underscores the view of Jewish sinfulness that Hunter explained in 'the Jewish choice'. Unlike Joseph and Morwyng, who present Jewish rebellion against God the Father as the essence of sinfulness, Nashe deliberately shifts the focus from rebellion by God's 'adopted Sonnes' (2.18) against their Father to rebellion against the Father's 'natural Sonne' (2.18), Christ. Presumably Morwyng, as a Christian and Nashe's countryman, would have shared this view. But if he does, Morwyng does not articulate it.

Nashe envisions a specifically Christian view of the history of Jewish sinfulness because he links those Jews who stoned their own prophets with those who condemned Christ (2.17–27). Therefore, in Nashe's *Christ's Tears over Jerusalem* belief in Christ as the one, true way to the Father, not merely keeping faith directly with the Father, becomes the standard by which humans are judged. Nashe's shift in emphasis and focus is part of this larger artistic plan, one not shared by Joseph, who is writing a history of the Jews. Nashe is not really interested in that history per se; he is interested in the ends that history can serve in the larger drama of the history of human sinfulness among God's chosen peoples, Jews and Christians. For Nashe the cities of Jerusalem and London not only mirror each other, but also are familiarly related through faith in the Father, so that Jerusalem is London's 'great Grand-mother' (2.15). The devastating plague epidemic in London (1592–4) prompted Nashe to compare the suffering of his sin-ridden London with the suffering of the wayward Jews during the siege and destruction of Jerusalem.

Thus, although historical professing Jews were exotic non-entities in Shakespeare's London, the importance of 'Jewishness' as a theological concept and the importance of the Jewish people and their history was by no means far removed from the analogical thought processes of Elizabethan Londoners. Nashe's message is a contemporary one: Christian London is no less sinful than Jewish Jerusalem. If London does not repent and reform, she may suffer the same awful desolation that befell Jerusalem.[61] Nashe would have found the emphasis on didacticism in Morwyng's rationale for why England should study Jewish history. But Morwyng's general emphasis on learning good from bad through the study of history, and the revelation of moral condition through moral choice, is transformed by Nashe into a specific historical analogue: Nashe is warning London against the possible fate of her 'Jewish choices'. What is noteworthy here for *The Merchant of Venice* is Nashe's emphasis on a common brotherhood of sin; Christians cannot pretend to be morally superior to Jews in their deeds. This perception of the fleshly bond of human sinfulness is important because it unites all humanity. However, as Oberman argues, in the early modern period, Christians will increasingly divorce their wickedness from that of Jews,[62] and in this kind of spiritual *apartheid* the groundwork for a preferential hierarchy of sinfulness is laid which fosters the later developments in history of 'racial' prejudice against Jews.

Nashe, however, later gives us another view of Elizabethan prejudice against Jews that derives its graphic nature not from history but from popular stereotypes. His *Unfortunate Traveller* (1594), published in the year of Lopez's trial and execution, is nothing akin to the piety of his *Tears,* and the nastiness of his depictions of Jewish characters may have been inflamed by the Lopez episode. Here the fictional Jews, Zadoch and Zachary (a physician), dwelling in sixteenth-century Rome, are presented as vicious individuals, like Marlowe's Barabas, and such malevolent clichés as 'all Jews are covetous' (2.304) pervade this part of Nashe's text. Indeed, G. R. Hibbard suggests that these Jews interest Nashe because they 'can be used as a means of outdoing Marlowe' and his *Jew of Malta,* but Nashe's 'comic tone is broken' when he describes Zadoch's execution, a horror of ingeniously cruel tortures: 'it is hard to escape the conclusion that there is sadism here as well as savage anti-Semitism'.[63] We gain some perspective on Nashe's horrific description when we recall that public executions in England were designed to be real spectacles, and R. B. McKerrow observes that Nashe's tortures are little worse than those suffered in 1591 by Dr Fian, who was accused of witchcraft.[64] Lest the execution of a Roman Jew be considered too curiously, it should be noted that Nashe repeatedly culminates the jests and adventures of his hero, Jack Wilton, with episodes of punitive violence which involve Jack himself, military captains, a Jewish would-be murderer, and an Italian murderer named

Cutwolfe. Cutwolfe's execution was intended by Nashe to be the
tour de force to climax the book, but Nashe appears to have spent
his descriptive energies on Zadoch's execution. As Hibbard argues, Nashe's admiration of the executioner's art in the death of
Cutwolfe 'palliates some of the unpleasantness of the description
and makes it less nasty than the account of the execution of Zadoch,
where the emphasis is on physical horror throughout'.[65] One might
excuse Nashe's descriptive violence because he is writing fiction,
but so is Shakespeare. Nashe's gruesome description of this Christian execution of a Jew, who undergoes severe provocation and
is guilty of *attempted* murders, provides a literary backdrop worth
bearing in mind for the alternative consequences that might have
been Shylock's in the hands of an Elizabethan author other than
Shakespeare.

In English history the legal consequence for Roderigo Lopez,
also judged guilty of *attempted* murder, was to be hanged, drawn,
and quartered. But prior to his running afoul of the law, Roderigo
Lopez enjoyed considerable respect and success in London even
though he was a Portuguese Jewish convert. The story of Lopez's
life, as well as his trial and death, is instructive for how we can
understand individual, as opposed to general, evaluations of this
man, suggesting that for some Elizabethans the virtues and talents of a man like Lopez could far outweigh his Jewish and foreign
background. The once fashionable suggestion that Dr Roderigo
[Ruy] Lopez[66] could have influenced Shakespeare's creation of
Shylock seems to have run its course in popularity; Mahood, for
example, thinks Shylock 'bears very little resemblance to Lopez'
(p. 7), and Christopher Spencer concisely reviews the arguments
of earlier critics regarding Lopez, without advancing the case
further.[67]

However, there are other similarities, often overlooked, between
Lopez and Shylock that could have contributed to Shakespeare's
own imaginative response, which will be specifically explored in
later chapters. Both Lopez and Shylock had wives with Old Testament names (Sara and Leah) and had children who needed to
be financially provided for; both were intelligent; both were pro-
fessionals in their careers and had substantial means; both became converts from Judaism (one apparently willingly, the other
far more constrained); both were foreigners or aliens in their respective cities of London and Venice (Roderigo, as a Portuguese
convert, was alien by nationality but not by faith; Shylock, as a

Venetian Jew, was an alien by faith but not apparently by residence); both were personally involved with another man named
'Antonio' whom they were accused of intending to murder; and
finally, both stood trial for attempted murder. There are, of course,
many stark differences, the most obvious being their contrasting
occupations of physician and usurer as well as the final outcomes
of their respective trials, death versus life or 'tragic' versus 'comic'
endings. Moreover, the importance of 'living', not just 'life' itself,
may relate the two. The financial provision for Shylock and for
his daughter and son-in-law may be related in spirit to Elizabeth's financial kindness to Lopez's widow, and the Queen also
granted Lopez's son Anthony '"a parsonage of 30l. a year . . . for
his maintenance at school"'.[68] Perhaps the several hanging references in the play, Lancelot's initial wish for a halter for his master (2.2.86) and Gratiano's farewell wish for the gallows (rather
than a baptismal font) for Shylock (4.1.396), may even recall Lopez's
death by hanging.[69] Hanging, however, was a common execution
for criminal offences.

Moreover, the roughly thirty-five-year history of Roderigo Lopez
in London might serve as a touchstone example of the historical
possibilities for how Elizabethans regarded and treated Jewish
converts living in their midst. These possibilities shed light on
how Shakespeare complexly manipulates the range of his audience's views on Jewish characters, whether converts or no. Lopez
is more famous today for his trial and death, which probably
ignited anti-Judaic sentiment,[70] than for his life, which provides
insights into the variety of Elizabethan attitudes and the basic
importance of religion in shaping those attitudes. Despite being
a foreigner from Portugal as well as a convert from Judaism in a
country that expelled Jews some three hundred years earlier, Lopez
rose rapidly to the top of his medical profession to become, in
1586, chief physician to Queen Elizabeth and other members of
her court. But he was accused of attempted murder, that is, of
complicity in a Spanish plot to kill Antonio Pérez (an eminent
Spanish refugee) and to poison Queen Elizabeth. Lopez had received one very precious jewel and was supposed to receive 50,000
crowns for the murder. In his own defence Lopez explained that
he never intended harm to the Queen, but rather he intended to
deceive the Spaniard and 'cozen him of his money'.[71] If this was
Lopez's true intent, he ran a very perilous course to obtain such
wealth. Despite Lopez's foreign background and the gravity of

his offence, he was given a trial before a special commission at
the Guildhall on 28 February 1594. How fair was his trial remains
another matter. Thomas Nashe, who could be compassionate or
bigoted in his literary presentations of Jews, praises the high calibre
of English lawyers at the trial.[72] On the other hand, the Earl of
Essex, no friend to Lopez, presided over this trial, and the pros-
ecutor, Sir Edward Coke, Solicitor-General, revealed the extreme
of religious bias in his description of Lopez as '"a perjured and
murdering villain and Jewish doctor, worse than Judas himself".'[73]
This shocking comparison with Judas, the Jewish betrayer of his
Jewish master, Jesus, is all the more damning for being declared
'worse'. What could be 'worse' for a Christian jury than the ultimate betrayal of its acknowledged Saviour? This religious interpretation is echoed at the actual hanging of Lopez when William
Camden reports that on the scaffold Lopez professed that he loved
the Queen as well as he loved Christ Jesus, 'which being spoken
by a Jew, as it was, was but only laughed at by the people'.[74] But
Dr Gabriel Harvey, of Cambridge, specifically described Lopez
as a convert from Judaism to Christianity: 'Doctor Lopus, the
Queenes Physitian, is descended of Jewes: but himself A Christian, & Portugall.'[75]

It appears that as long as Lopez lived a life 'of a well-tried
honesty', as Camden calls it,[76] he could be seen as the convert he
was. As soon as Lopez fell from grace, however, it was easy for
some, but not all including apparently the Queen herself, to reveal their darker suspicions about the genuineness of Lopez's
conversion to Christianity.[77] Sir Francis Bacon wrote the govern-
ment's official declaration of Lopez's crime, and even though Lopez
was never one of Bacon's favourites, at an earlier date Bacon was
fair enough to describe Lopez as '"a man very observant and
officious and of a pleasing and pliable behaviour"'.[78] The darker
suspicion, always latent in some Elizabethans' thoughts, did not
apparently afflict all who knew Lopez. Individuals respond to
their common culture differently precisely because they are individuals. A converted Jewish foreigner, like Lopez, could clearly
inspire positive or negative evaluations of his character, depending on the eye of the beholder. For example, in the libellous 'Leicester's Commonwealth' (1584) Lopez is described as '"Lopez the
Jew"' and is believed to know poisoning and other such arts.[79]
But a friend of Leicester, who must have known Lopez firsthand
as the chief physician in Leicester's household, starting around

1576, gives quite a favourable description of Lopez as '"a very honest person and a zealous"'.[80]

The notoriety of Lopez's trial and death tends to obscure for us some astonishing facts about the success story of Lopez's life, astonishing given what we traditionally believe about the state of rampant xenophobia in Elizabethan culture. For a foreign Jewish convert, Lopez enjoys almost incredible success in his medical profession, rising to the highest places in London. Before 1569 Lopez had become a member of the College of Physicians because his colleagues asked him in that year to give the three-day lecture on anatomy at the college, but Lopez refused to perform this public duty.[81] A patient built and gave a house to Lopez, some of the greatest lords and ladies of the realm sought Lopez's expertise, and in 1589 Elizabeth granted him a monopoly for the importation of aniseed and sumach into England.[82] Then as now, individuals could stand against the prejudice of common thought and value a man on his own merits, despite blood and birth. For some in sixteenth-century London there is a 'largesse' in spirit, along with the ungracious religious bias and perhaps professional jealousy, that it not usually noted. Queen Elizabeth delayed for three months to sign Lopez's death warrant, and in, a rare exercise of her royal prerogative, she allowed Lopez's widow to retain much of her executed husband's property.[83]

This review of Morwyng's translation of Joseph's Jewish history, Nashe's different treatment of Jews, and the history of a Jewish convert in Elizabethan London enlightens us about the complex, although religiously biased, Elizabethan view of Jews and Jewishness. Elizabethans seem to judge Jews before Christ's coming as good in terms of how well they keep their covenant with God the Father. Jews after Christ could be seen as Jewish in name but Christian in deed if they practised the new law of love for all people, not just their own group, or Jewish in name and in deed if they made what Elizabethans would see as a morally and theologically wrong choice, a 'Jewish choice' as G. K. Hunter explains. Elizabethan Christians would honour the role of the Jews in salvation history, but they would also stress the primacy of justification by faith as the way to eternal salvation.

We need to be constantly aware of whose eyes we are seeing through in Shakespeare's play, whether those of a Gratiano or a Bassanio, because not all Christians are the same in their attitudes and actions any more than one would naively maintain that all Jews are the same. It may be precisely this illogic of 'all or nothing' that instigates Shakespeare's more complex portrayal of good and bad within all humans, so unlike Barabas's partial assertion in *The Jew of Malta*: 'Some Jews are wicked, as all Christians are' (1.2.113).[84] In what amounts to a reversal of Barabas's terms, Derek M. Cohen emphasises one aspect of Elizabethan thought, the equation of Jewishness with wickedness, and ignores the *complexity* of both the historical background and Shakespeare's creative use of it: *The Merchant of Venice* is *not*, as Cohen declares, 'a profoundly and crudely anti-Semitic play'.[85] Shakespeare attacks as well as praises both Jews and Christians, less as groups and more as individuals judged according to how truly they live their faith, how well they love God and each other. The name identity of 'Jew' or 'Christian' can be merely nominal unless the outward show of the name corresponds to the meaning that name signifies for Elizabethans.

'Jew' and 'Christian' can be emotionally charged words then and now. Shakespeare's 'What's in a name?' comes back to haunt us. No, a name is not the substance of the self, but as Shakespeare's fancy with 'naming' his characters reveals, especially in this play where he essentially 'creates' the names 'Shylock' and 'Jessica', more often than not the word has its own evocative power. The direction of that power can shift over time from a positive to a negative field as ideas and societies change. Given the extant evidence, however, this popular play was considered a 'comedy' until the modern era when some have wanted to reclassify it as a 'tragedy', stressing the tragic potential in Shylock dramatised, for example, in the nineteenth century by Henry Irving, who portrayed Shylock as a martyred patriarch, or in the twentieth century by Laurence Olivier, who portrayed Shylock as a nobly tragic figure in a production, directed by Jonathan Miller (National Theatre, 1970), that emphasised the tragic. Mahood notes that this play has been 'highly vulnerable to changing theatrical and social pressures' so that 'its stage history has been rich, but it has not always been happy'.[86] Why in modern times especially has a hue and outcry been raised against this play? What has 'happened' historically that might, at least in part, account for why this play, generically classified as a comedy, offends modern sensibilities?

Enlightened audiences of the twentieth century, aware of the ideas of religious tolerance and freedom, understandably find the

Jew-baiting and the conversion stipulation for Shylock in the trial scene particularly disturbing. Probably because of our fear of taint by chronological association, we of the twentieth century vigilantly try to distance ourselves as much as possible from Hitler's atrocities against the Jews, which were motivated by essentially 'racial', not 'religious', prejudice.[87] The horror of the Holocaust occurred, tragically, in our modern world, not in Shakespeare's world. Except for a few areas in the world today, we do not witness any more the once popular wars of religion. The folly of such wars based on religious difference was brilliantly satirised during the Enlightenment by Jonathan Swift in his *Gulliver's Travels*. But despite some chronological advances toward religious tolerance and freedom, Swift's friend, the poetic genius Alexander Pope, could not attend a university, vote, or hold public office solely because he was a Roman Catholic in Protestant eighteenth-century England. On the other hand, racial tolerance would take at least another hundred years to press for relief. Surely progressive for its time is Shakespeare's use of an interracial marriage between a white woman and a black man, which is prepared for in the possible match between Portia and a tawny Moor, the Prince of Morocco, and which is actually dramatised in the marriage between the Venetian Desdemona and the blackamoor, Othello. To know and to do, as Portia reminds herself and us (1.2.11–17), are different human activities. Modern civilised humanity is supposed to hold certain truths to be 'self-evident'. But how, when, and to whom and for whom such truths become 'self-evident' is quite another issue. To know that all religions and races should be treated fairly and equally is an intellectual achievement in itself, but to live by those truths is a challenge of a different magnitude.

'WAS THIS INSERTED TO MAKE INTEREST GOOD?' (1.3.86)

The subject of usury in *The Merchant of Venice*, unlike the Jewish question, has been far more neglected. Despite some recent interest, usury is arguably the most underestimated and misunderstood element in *The Merchant of Venice*. For example, Leonard Tennenhouse argues that Shylock is 'the very embodiment of mercantile logic'.[88] But Shylock, according to Elizabethan ideas, is the antithesis of mercantile logic, and he himself unequivocally stresses his own antipathy for merchantry because it is risky

business. For most Elizabethans usury could be defined as lending and contracting for gain, that is expecting or taking *anything*
beyond the principal lent, without risk or adventuring, and usury
technically violated the Elizabethan Act Against Usury of 1571.[89]
Next to the theologically based conception of Jewishness, the theologically based conception of usury is the most difficult concept
for a modern audience to recover. Although Walter Cohen appreciates the play's concern with the problem of usury, he treats
it as a solely economic issue, overlooking its theological context
in his discussion of the religious dimension of the play's action.[90]
Without this context, as Norman Jones has demonstrated, we cannot
adequately understand the problem of usury. Theologians condemned usurious lending because it violated God's commandment to love one's neighbour as oneself; it also violated dependence
on God by avoiding the risk inherent in natural enterprise, and it
violated nature because inanimate money could not breed, nor
was time, a common property to all, a saleable commodity.[91]

We still, however, appreciate a distinction between quantity and
quality of wealth – the mass of it does not excuse illicit means to
amass it. For example, the wealth of a shipping magnate merits
social approval, but the wealth of a Mafia boss does not. For the
majority of Elizabethans usurious wealth would be viewed as
devilishly ill-gotten gain. Today interest is a legally valid, socially
accepted economic concept and practice; interest rates drive national economies. The prevailing Elizabethan view of the whole
matter of interest could not be more radically different from ours.
However, the modern age has kept a vestige of their view by
tending to avoid the demand of interest on loans to family members and friends. Without a true conception of what usury meant
to Elizabethans, we cannot hope to appreciate Shakespeare's characterisation of Shylock as a Jewish usurer and Antonio as a Christian
merchant, and how these double identifications interrelate Venice with Belmont through the language and themes of money and
wealth, or wealth and 'love's wealth'.[92]

Too often scholars overlook the fact that usury is Shakespeare's
chosen *addition* to the flesh-bond plot he found in *Il Pecorone*.[93]
Critics are often divided regarding Shylock's identity; some emphasise his identity as a Jew, and others stress his identity as a
usurer.[94] Such division is misleading because it obscures for us
how purposefully Shakespeare unifies in Shylock both the religious and professional aspects of his identity and opposes those

traits in his adversary, Antonio. Faith and wealth, or what one believes and how that belief affects livelihood, share important common ground in the theological discourse of Shakespeare's age that needs to be understood in order to appreciate how and why Shakespeare interweaves dilemmas of faith and wealth to produce dramatic unity, another major issue over which critics have been divided. Shakespeare's uncommon choice of Jewish and Christian characters complements his equally arresting choice of usury. Usury is the main contention between Antonio and Shylock. Shylock tells us he hates Antonio because he is a Christian and even more because he lends money freely (1.3.37–40). Antonio hates Shylock because he practises usury and therefore violates human friendship (1.3.125–32) and makes victims moan. Miles Mosse articulates the concept for usury and Jews that is at the centre of *The Merchant of Venice*, calling usury 'this unchristian, this heathenish, this Jewish kind of practise', whereby usurious Christians become heathens or Jews in terms of their behaviour.[95] Unlike our typically modern divorce between issues of wealth and faith, the Elizabethans would see matters of money and faith as integrally interrelated. They would be inclined to argue that how one views and uses wealth depends on one's faith and whether or not one rightly understands that faith and enacts its principles or betrays them. Shakespeare's humane treatment of a Jewish usurer should prove an educational experience for an Elizabethan audience, many of whom might expect or even desire to see inhumane treatment.

Shakespeare's obvious interest in etymology and what's in a name reminds us to be sensitive to his use of the word 'usurer' and its variants because the term itself is being hotly debated and 'defined' and 'redefined' around the time Shakespeare writes *The Merchant of Venice*. This contemporary debate makes our play a very timely dramatic work for an Elizabethan audience in London, especially in its complex use of covert usury and mental usury.[96] Both Shakespeare's contemporaries, Thomas Nashe and Thomas Lodge, emphasise the actual problem of usury in late Elizabethan London. In arguing that ambition is the essence of sin (2.84), Nashe excoriates the proud citizens of London for their rampant avarice, for their sinful usury (2.92–108): 'O intolerable Usury! not the Jews (whose peculiar sin it is) have ever committed the like' (2.95). Thomas Lodge cites 1596, one year before the generally accepted date for composition of our play, as a disastrous

year of legal penalties for 'Master Usury' and other devils, engendered by Mammon, who plague England but who get their
deserved comeuppance because of a case in the Court of Star
Chamber.[97] As we shall see in Chapter 4, both Thomas Wilson
and Miles Mosse, in their major sixteenth-century Elizabethan
treatises on usury, emphasise the importance of the etymology
and terminology for defining 'usury', going so far as to claim
that usurers convict themselves of guilt in their consciences by
preferring to call their 'usury' by another name that smells sweeter,
such as 'usance', which is reserved in Shakespeare's canon only
for Shylock's vocabulary. Indeed, what we have come to think of
as popular terms, such as 'moneylender' and 'moneylending', do
not even appear to be used in England until the eighteenth and
nineteenth centuries, as the evidence in the *The Oxford English
Dictionary* indicates. We need to know Shakespeare's language;
for example, 'use' allows for financial, sexual and legal puns as
the less flexible word 'moneylending' does not.

We can see how Shakespeare's interest in the language and
idea of usury fits within his own canon of works by observing
several suggestive facts: (1) the explicit term 'usurer' and its variants
is somewhat common in Shakespeare's canon (about 25 instances),
with the number of references to usury expanding if synonymous
words like 'interest' are added to the list; Shakespeare uses the
plural form of usury but never the singular; (2) except for the
single reference to a usurer in the only history play in Shakespeare's canon to do so (*1H6* 3.1.17), Shakespeare's use of this
word and its variants tends to 'cluster' in works relatively early
(c.1596) and relatively late (1604–13) in his career.[98] The fact of
this early and late 'cluster' pattern in the chronology of his canon
may be significant. The early mid-1590s was a particularly controversial time for discussing the subject of usury, as is made
clear by Miles Mosse's prefatory reference to ongoing heated debate,
specifically in London, and his publication in 1595 of his six sermons (delivered 1592–3) on the controversial subject of usury.
The Merchant of Venice, which as a play has the most references
to the explicit language of usury if we include usurious 'interest',[99]
would dramatise an especially pertinent topic for London. The
late clustering is more difficult to theorise about other than to
note that the debate over usury in Parliament seems to get reignited
early in James I's reign. The subject was reintroduced in 1604
and again in 1606, 1614, and 1621, with the debate culminating

finally in 1624 with the revision of medieval usury law; the new law permitted lending at interest at 8 per cent.[100] Perhaps this political climate of debate about usury contributes to the performance of *The Merchant of Venice* at Court in February of 1605, and Brown notes that 'the King commanded a second performance on the following Tuesday'.[101]

But perhaps the single most important observation regarding Shakespeare's use of usury language is that only *Timon*, a tragedy, comes close to equalling *The Merchant of Venice* in its use of this language.[102] In his condemnation of usury, Nashe complains that charity is at its lowest ebb in England because the ambition to gain wealth has turned men into *Timonists* [misers], and 'it is now grown a Proverb *That there is no merchandize but Usury*'.[103] Why this connection between *The Merchant of Venice* and *Timon of Athens*? Some of the reasons will become clearer as we proceed, especially the ideological bond between the concept of usury and the concepts of love, friendship, and wealth, but one pivotal reason surfaces if we seek historical perspective on the subject of usury. Because the definition and evaluation of usury developed largely out of canon law, the concept and its definition were chiefly rooted in theological and legal discourse, which was embellished by the philosophical discourse of the ancients, especially Aristotle and Cato. The English authors of the sixteenth century are remarkably 'catholic' in their wide reading of works on usury, as Miles Mosse's long list of pagan, Catholic, and Protestant authors reveals. This rich and complex perspective, now so completely foreign to our modern, secularised view of money and loans, enmeshes the subject of usury with other closely related subjects, such as faith, love, and friendship in both their earthly and heavenly aspects.

How can a subject so apparently 'cold' as usury be interrelated with the likes of faith, love, and friendship, all of which affect the many bonds our play dramatises? For Elizabethan Christians lending freely is a way to show wise love (Lk 6.35), but lending at interest violates the love of friendship. The very complex subject of how usury evolves from being perceived as sinful by Catholics and Protestants alike to being not just 'tolerated' but lawfully 'allowed' by England's Parliament of 1624 merits the attention of historians.[104] Many factors contributed to this evolutionary process, not the least of which were changing social conditions, economic necessity, and religious beliefs. The chief problem was to

square God's law with human law and current human needs given
new socio-economic changes. The general consensus among Elizabethan leaders was that usury violates the word of God because
it violates the commandment of love – to love another and do
unto another as you would have done unto you. There were both
civil and ecclesiastical punishments for the practice of usury.
Therefore, Christians were not supposed to indulge in what was
perceived as a 'Jewish' practice.[105]

In the play's Venice Shylock's occupation of usury is lawful,
but he is probably not forced to practise it, and he does choose
to champion usury over merchantry as the better livelihood. Because Jews were not allowed participation in many professions
open only to citizens of Christian states, usury on the Continent
was one of the few economic livelihoods left open to Jews. However, contrary to popular opinion, usury was not the *only* profession open to Jews.[106] Jews, not only 'Marranos' or forced converts,
were leaders in medicine, and Renaissance monarchs especially
employed them as their personal physicians.[107] In 1552 Venice had
a population of about 160,000 inhabitants, 900 of whom were Jews,
and these Jews were mainly merchants, and a considerable number
had established partnerships with Christian merchants; by 1586
Venice had some 1700 Jews.[108] Sixteenth-century English records
occasionally mention foreign Jews as 'traders, diplomats, doctors,
or scholars', and one Bohemian Jew as a mining engineer in
Raleigh's Roanoke expedition.[109] After Jews were readmitted to
England in the seventeenth century, England attempted to make
some amends for her earlier ill treatment, especially economic
exploitation, of Jews during the Middle Ages, and they tended to
be better off in England than on the Continent.[110] During the
Renaissance, with the exception of England, there probably existed
a higher proportion of Jewish moneylenders, but this profession
did not exclusively belong to the Jews. However, as John T. Noonan
explains, theologians condemned both Christians and Jews alike
for practising usury because it was considered both 'immoral and
unnatural', but Jews themselves, of course, did not feel bound by
canon law and therefore could freely practise usury without much
open competition from Christians, except for the Lombards of
northern Italy who, as manifest and successful usurers, spread
throughout Europe.[111] In his historical study of a respected medieval Jewish usurer in Marseilles, Joseph Shatzmiller explains that
although Shylock the character may provoke sympathy, the play

itself is part of the long anti-usury tradition of Europe and shows no sympathy for usury.[112]

According to biblical law all usury is prohibited for Jews (Ex 22:25–7; Ez 18:7–8), except in their dealings with non-Jews (Dt 23:20–1); however, Jews could not take usury from alien residents dwelling in their midst (Lv 25:35). Although the Talmudic law relaxed the restriction on the latter issue, the jurists emphasised that this Deuteronomic exception should not be practised unless there were no other means of subsistence. Usurious loans by Jews to foreigners were looked upon with disapproval (Ps 15:5).[113] More than one critic has stressed that Shylock must reflect the Christian theological interpretation of 'the Jew', not a faithful Jew, because Shylock violates some of the particulars of his faith as well as the spirit of the Old Testament and the teachings of the Talmud, which emphasise Jews should incline toward mercy and charity in their lending and be moderate in usury taken of Gentiles.[114] Although the issue of usury is not explicitly addressed in the New Testament, except to illustrate parables (see Mt 25:14–30; Lk 19:11–27), the New Testament makes no distinction between Hebrew and Gentile, suggesting that loans should be essentially gratuitous (Lk 6:30; Mt 5:42).

The subject of usury encompasses the concerns of both justice and mercy, the letter and the spirit of the law, the Old and New Testaments, Jew and Christian, brother and alien, friend and foe – most of the central contrasts that have been so frequently re-marked upon in *The Merchant of Venice* but so seldomly linked to the specific context of usury. Christians often critically associated the unjust, illicit gain of usury with the Jews and the Old Law. Usury was thought to be forbidden by natural law because it was contrary to commutative justice; in demanding anything above his principal lent, the lender unjustly expects in return more than he actually lent and therefore that to which he is not entitled. Canon law assimilated usury to theft, and the view of usury as theft influences Shakespeare's motif of stealing.[115] Some held usury accountable as 'the very hell of evil' and 'the principal cause of all want and scarcity in any common weal'.[116] Hence, usury was often regarded as theft. More importantly, usury was held to be inimical to mercy because it overthrows the rule of charity and 'usury cutteth the throat of mercy'.[117] There were other consid-erations too. Risk was then believed to be a necessary factor in legitimate enterprise, and usury violated that condition because it was calculated, certain gain ensured by bonds and pawns. The philosophical objection to usury was grounded chiefly on the classical authors, Aristotle and Cato. Aristotle condemned usury as unnatural because it confused ends with means: money was a means of exchange and not an end in itself, and inanimate matter, strictly speaking, cannot 'breed' or reproduce itself. But by the last decade of the sixteenth century clever Puritan preachers, especially those at Cambridge, could argue against Aristotle and with William Perkins that although money itself cannot breed, it can be made to be fruitful by man.[118] Cato stressed the moral consequences: the usurer is like a thief because he takes more than his principal lent entitles him to, and the usurer is a murderer for consuming in his greed the means by which another lives.[119]

As usury evolves toward its current status of modern acceptance, important changes have to occur in how people think about usury, and the pertinent legal facts need to be recalled because modern critics of our play perpetuate the erroneous opinion that usury was 'legal' in Elizabethan England.[120] Norman Jones has demonstrated that only the Queen could legally borrow at interest, and although some minimal reconsideration is beginning to occur in the Parliamentary debates that produced the Act Against Usury of 1571, that statute is not overthrown until the 1624 Usury Act. This statute, in force at the time Shakespeare wrote *The Merchant of Venice*, was somewhat of a compromise between the most liberal English law on usury, which was Henry VIII's statute in 1545, and the most conservative statute of Edward VI in 1552, which totally prohibited usury. The Act Against Usury of 1571 was essentially conservative, intended not for regulating usury but for repressing it.[121] However, this statute had some liberalising effects. The statute nullified contracts made in excess of ten per cent and penalised them with treble forfeiture of the principal; loans at under ten per cent were punishable by forfeiture of the interest. Although this statute's *intent* was *against* usury, the statute's *effect* over time was to create a *de facto* acceptance of 10 per cent interest as normal, so that in the popular mind usury became eventually associated with exorbitant interest rates.[122] Given the extant information, it seems that 'reconsideration' continues in the 1580s and 90s chiefly by way of two arguments: (1) arguments that focused essentially on defining or redefining what was usury, and what was not, to limit the definition more precisely; and (2) arguments that focused on specific and exceptional conditions, such as providing for orphans, relieving necessity, lending to the rich, mutual sharing in the profits, sharing in the risk and adhering to moderation.[123] The rules of charity, good conscience, and gratitude were always to be followed in these matters.

By the sixteenth century multiple factors of new ideology, social necessity, and the enormous increase in trade and wealth contributed to the evolving view of money as not a 'barren' entity but as a commodity that could be bought and sold at a profit as could any good, especially in northern and central Europe. The demand for money created 'money markets', which in turn caused the founding of great banking houses, such as the Bank of Amsterdam, to serve these new markets. The ideological and practical paths began to be paved for the modern acceptance of interest. Rather than condemning all excess regardless of degree, an increasing distinction began to be made between moderate and acceptable versus exorbitant and unacceptable rates. In due course the sin and crime of usury began to be increasingly limited to the 'loan shark'. Moreover, as Max Weber and R. H. Tawney have argued, the socio-economic effects of the Reformation also contributed to the development of capitalism through certain aspects of the Protestant ethic, such as diligence in one's work or 'calling', general frugality and commitment to saving rather than consuming, and success in work as a sign of being one of the elect.[124] Eventually the complicated scholastic doctrine regarding usury self-destructs because of the inherent self-contradictions in reasoning, for example the sterility of money which, however, can be made to breed by men, and the increasing difficulties in drawing the line between licit and illicit loans.

In the course of about one generation in England, as might be seen, for example, in the contrast between a conservative father, Sir Nathaniel Bacon, and his more liberal son, Sir Francis Bacon, views on the so-called sin of usury have begun to modify as the gap between divine law and human law widens through reinterpretation of these laws. In a country that had no banks, syndicates of small lenders were later complemented by grand usurers in Jacobean London, like Thomas Sutton, who some think was the historical model for Ben Jonson's Volpone.[125] Despite an uneasy coexistence between old and new attitudes toward usury, the laity in the Parliament of 1624 succeeded in displacing the view of usury as sinful with the new view of moderate usury as beneficial for the nation's economy, reducing the rate to 8 per cent. However, the Archbishop of Canterbury challenged this bill, revealing how old ideas die hard, so that before it passed a peculiar proviso had to be added: '"That no Words in this Law contained shall be construed or expounded to allow the practise of Usury in point of Religion or Conscience"'.[126] The 1571 statute, the wide-ranging economic changes over the next fifty years, and the increasing emphasis in English moral theology on individual intent, free conscience, and the principle of equity gradually combine to foster a new rationale for economic expediency and self-aggrandisement as well as a shift in the responsibility for economic ethics from the domain of theology to that of the individual's conscience. But in the 1590s this impending divorce between secular and divine law regarding usury had not yet occurred; the seeds for change had been planted, but the harvest was yet to come. Thus, the timing of Shakespeare's dramatic incorporation of Elizabethan views for and against usury in *The Merchant of Venice* reflects the popular interest in the ongoing and difficult debate on usury towards the end of Elizabeth's reign.

Shakespeare's innovations for his protagonist and antagonist regarding the interrelated matters of religious faith and usury need to be appreciatively underscored. His play has become so popular that we tend to perceive it as somehow 'normative' for its time in presenting a Christian merchant as protagonist and a Jewish usurer as antagonist. Such a clash between the opposed forces of different faiths and of different professions would be rather an exciting novelty for Shakespeare's audience, a refreshing surprise to their expectations. How so? An Elizabethan would not be especially surprised to meet a Jewish usurer as an antagonist in a play because Christians typically associated Jews with the practice of usury, even calling usury 'this Jewish kind of practise',[127] so that 'Christians' were 'Jews' if they behaved like them in contracting usurious loans. But, particularly for an Elizabethan audience, a Christian *merchant* who opposed usury would upset typical expectations because the two largest groups of usurers in London were the 'Christian' merchants and goldsmiths. We must reassess the play in its literary and historical contexts to bring to light Shakespeare's careful innovations regarding his Jewish usurer and his Christian merchant.

Because in theory there were no unconverted Jews living in London at the time Shakespeare wrote *The Merchant of Venice*, Shakespeare's imaginative creation of Shylock does not depend on historical Jewish usurers for its impetus. Instead, Shakespeare recasts a variety of literary sources to create his Jewish usurer, and his originality herein must be emphasised. Excepting the undated *Ballad of Gernutus*, none of Shakespeare's accepted literary sources for his play depict the antagonist as clearly both Jew and usurer.[128] For example, Marlowe's Jew, Barabas, is hardly ever thought of or remembered as a usurer because usury was only one of his many sidelines which is fleetingly referred to in a handful of lines midway into the play (2.3.187–95). What is most memorable about Barabas's wealth is his panegyric celebration of it (1.1.1–47) which immediately introduces him as a fabulously wealthy Jewish *merchant* inquiring after his richly laden ships. In historical London the Elizabethan usurers who daily plied their trade were Christians (not Jews by profession of faith), and most were merchants by trade. One critic, Paul N. Siegel, has argued that Shakespeare's audience would have glimpsed contemporary Puritan usurers – Puritan individualism and its 'cash nexus' – in Shakespeare's characterisation of Shylock.[129] In Elizabethan dramatic literature the typical usurer–prodigal paradigm depicts the usurer as a merchant, and in Thomas Wilson's influential sixteenth-century treatise on usury the merchant Gromelgayner is a classic example of the usurious merchant who seeks the gain of gold and silver.

Shakespeare smartly truncates the expectations of his audience, inviting their rapt attention to his surprises – to what, how and why he has changed the conventions available to him. Not only does Shakespeare divorce his Christian merchant from usury, but he makes his protagonist violently opposed to usury, whether in lending or borrowing. Moreover, his presentation of Antonio as a royal merchant anticipates the merchant-prince figure who will increasingly gain dominance in Elizabethan popular literature by the turn of the century. Shakespeare combines the contemporary popular interest in Jews and Jewishness, historical as well as fictional, with the growing controversy over usury and merchantry, but he also newly recasts these interests to develop a dramatic texture of great subtlety and complexity that proves time and again to work theatrical magic on the stage. While we must familiarise ourselves with the issues the play raises, we must not lose sight of the intricate artistry of the whole drama, which incorporates these issues into its own staged world in order to hold 'the mirror up to nature: to show virtue her feature, scorn her image, and the very age and body of the time his form and pressure' (*Hamlet* 3.2.22–4).

2

'O me, the word "choose"': Structure and Language

In terms of dramatic structure *The Merchant of Venice* is undoubt-
edly a comedy. This matter is worth pausing over briefly. Since
the 1950s a growing number of critics and producers have emphasised the play's tragic potential – its limitation, darkness, or
ambiguity. *The Merchant of Venice*, however, follows the typical
upward trajectory of comedy (beginning complication to ending
resolution), so unlike the typical rise and fall trajectory of tragedy. Polonius's facetious description of drama's hyphenated genres (2.2.396–9) alerts us to be aware of the overlapping hybrid
character of genre in Elizabethan drama. Despite this drama's flexible and fluid nature, its virtually uninterrupted flow of action
on the open stage of the Elizabethan public theatre, several basic
structural elements help to determine the general classification of
comedy, which can be further defined into more specific subgenres,
such as romantic comedy, tragicomedy, problem play, and romance. Three of the most important of these elements are comedy's problematic opening, its 'happy' ending, and its absence of
literal death.

The opening of comedy is usually downbeat and its ending
upbeat. Act I introduces the play's main complication, but it also
sets the tone for comic expectation by establishing the upward
rhythm of comedy in each of its three scenes. Antonio's (1.1) and
Portia's (1.2) melancholy are momentarily alleviated by appropriate distraction and hope. Bassanio hopes to thrive; Antonio
hopes to help his friend (1.1); Portia will not have to worry about
being chosen by the suitors she has justly mocked (1.2); Bassanio
and Antonio get what they mistakenly but happily think is a
friendly loan; and Shylock mistakenly but happily thinks he has
hit upon a winning scenario (1.3). After the opening act has set
the rhythm and expectation of comedy, there is increasing fluc-

tuation between the raising and dashing of hopes as a result of the various characters' choices. Raised hopes and satisfaction, however, outweigh dashed hopes and dissatisfaction. Lancelot, Jessica, Lorenzo, Portia, Bassanio, Nerissa, Gratiano, and Antonio all escape the dangers they most feared and realise their aspirations. Morocco, Arragon, Shylock, and Antonio all suffer losses. However, Morocco and Arragon receive the strict justice of their penalty which they swore oaths to accept, but both Shylock and Antonio are spared death and half of their financial losses are recovered. Each of the subsequent four acts introduces an act of comic resolution which in turn (with the exception of the concluding act) instigates or abets some other complication. Act II happily resolves both Lancelot's and Jessica's dilemmas of choice. But in the eighth scene Salarino and Solanio forecast that Antonio 'shall pay for' (2.8.26) Shylock's grieved and enraged response to his loss of daughter and ducats. Act III happily resolves the casket test, and Bassanio and Portia win each other. But in the midst of their happiness arrives Antonio's letter, which disrupts the Belmontian celebration and sets in motion the rescue attempt. Act IV resolves the tragic potential of Shylock's flesh bond but then immediately introduces the dilemma of the rings episode. Act V is the true *lysis* or 'untying' that reveals what has been unknown and resolves all in the spirit of the play's central choice, the choice of the leaden casket.

After weathering trial and tribulation in good humour, comedy ends 'happily', that is, with an emphasis on discovery, reunion, love, and above all, a non-mortal resolution. For a comedy to end 'happily', not all its players need to be equally happy or fortunate. At the end of *A Midsummer Night's Dream* Egeus is probably not overjoyed that Theseus has overruled his patriarchal command for his daughter to marry the man of his choice; instead, Hermia gets Lysander, the man of her choice. Or we might note, for example, some others who end not so happily in Shakespeare's comedies, as Bianca's and the Widow's public embarrassment in *The Taming of the Shrew*, Thurio's exposed cowardice in *The Two Gentlemen of Verona*, Conrade's, Borachio's, and Don John's apprehensions in *Much Ado About Nothing*, Falstaff's discomfiture in *The Merry Wives of Windsor*, Malvolio's outrage in *Twelfth Night*, and Lucio's abhorrence at marrying his whore in *Measure for Measure*.

The inclusion of tragic tonality, whether in imagery or motive

(Shylock's 'Hath not a Jew eyes' speech), or tragic matter (the flesh bond which is offered apparently as a comic gesture but which is revealed by the third act as potentially life threatening), does not change the dramatic structure to tragedy. The presence of literal death(s) is the qualification most obviously basic to tragic drama. If Portia did not succeed in changing Shylock's determination to take his bond, the closure of *The Merchant of Venice* would not be perceived as comedy. Shakespeare explicitly avoids literal death in this play, whether Antonio's or Shylock's. Tragicomedy almost always embraces the danger without the death. On rare occasions, however, even death can be encompassed in a comedy if death does not strike in the final scene. In *The Winter's Tale*, for example, two innocents – the young prince, Mamillus, and a good Sicilian lord, Antigonus – die in the third act, but this romance's restorative ending confirms its accepted classification within the broad genre of comedy. Titles, such as *All's Well That Ends Well*, broadly hint that as long as all ends well, much can be taken in stride in comedy. *The Merchant of Venice* opens on the keynote of melancholy and closes with the ring of mirthful laughter. It opens with a closely knit nucleus of Venetian male friends trying to help each other, and it closes in Belmont with the enlargement of that male group through new friendships and the addition of three special women. It opens with an awareness of the human need for the prop that sustains the house and ends with the restoration of some of those props: the impoverished nobleman is no longer a debtor; the beggared merchant is no longer a beggar; and the poor gentleman will in time be given his father-in-law's wealth. The play opens with an emphasis on concern over people, not just things, and by the end of the play the business of living becomes fused with the business of loving.

In the last half of this century not only has there been increasing debate over the genre of this play and its placement in Shakespeare's canon, but also there continues to be critical division over the question of the play's unity.[1] Thomas Wheeler sums up the decade of criticism in the seventies: 'many critics have come to the conclusion that a satisfying interpretation is not possible', but despite the diversity of views, two schools of thought predominate – one tends to see the play as relatively simple and successful in the satisfaction it brings to audiences, despite the problem of Shylock, and the other tends to see the play as exceptionally complex, an 'ironic comedy', that is subtle, yet severe, in questioning its audience and its characters.[2] *The Merchant*, however, embraces aspects of both of these extreme positions. It is a comedy that celebrates wise love, which is no 'simple' concept, and it is very complex in its execution of this concept through the tough choices and questions presented as well as through the recurrent but controlled use of irony that enriches, without overwhelming, the comedy and its harmonious conclusion. To be satisfying, a comedy need not be essentially 'simple'; to be complex, it need not be chiefly 'ironic'. In the 1980s there has been less emphasis on thematic interpretation and concern about the play's integration of its diverse elements and more emphasis on new approaches to parts of the play that might illuminate current scholarly interests, especially regarding the relationship between the English stage and particular aspects of sixteenth-century cultural history, such as topics related to human sexuality, gender, and politics. Culling out parts of this play, such as its use of transvestite disguise, to shed light on these larger issues runs the risk of losing sight of the whole for the part. The more definitively partial and selective one's focus is, the less one is likely to see how that part fits into the whole world of the play.

Kenneth Muir, in his incisive repudiation of several current interpretations of the play, stresses not so much their wrongness as their inherent danger of being too selective and partial,[3] and we would do well to return to the fundamental challenge of trying to understand the play as a whole and to grapple with the problem of artistic unity. The argument in favour of some form of 'unity' seems to be growing in dominance, even if critics are reluctant to define that 'unity' in artistic or conceptual terms. Norman Rabkin, for example, sees the play as having the coherence of experience and process that is characteristic of life itself; the play is 'a constantly turbulent experience . . . a welter of emotions and ideas and perceptions and surprises and intuitions of underlying unity and coherence rivalled only by our experience in the real world', so that the play as 'a model of our experience' insists that 'the meaning is ultimately ineffable'.[4] Mahood's analysis of our experience of the play opts for trying to preserve the 'complexity of the theatrical experience' by resisting any definition of the play's essential 'unity', which she suggests is 'intuitive' because such understanding is 'the individual possession of each member of an audience' (p. 25). From a structural perspective, however, Mahood suggests the play can be ordered as 'naturally' comprising five movements that do not correspond to the Folio's division of the play into acts, except for the final movement limited solely to Act V.[5] Mahood's grouping of the play's scenes into five larger units is one helpful approach to the play's structural unity that is based primarily on a linear sense of the play's narrative progression and its alternation of scenes between Venice and Belmont that can be grouped according to themes associated with characters' actions (such as, 'elopement', 'debit and credit', 'the renewing of love'). But this linear approach does not take into account the play's thematic emphasis on the casket choice staged in the play's centre. Appreciating this central emphasis is important for understanding how Shakespeare unifies the apparently disparate elements of this play.

Perhaps the chief deterrent for seeing Shakespeare's overall unity in this play derives from a tendency to overemphasise the idea of opposition in the play, whether of plots, settings, ideological dilemmas, or the relationships of characters. The most frequently emphasised opposition by critics is the contrast between Venice and Belmont. In his edition of the play John Russell Brown tries to convey a sense of its whole by suggesting the play is about wealth, literally and figuratively, but he also finds the play dichotomised between the theme of appearance and reality in the casket scenes and the theme of justice and mercy in the trial scene.[6] There is, however, no real thematic dichotomy between Belmont and Venice because the theme of appearance and reality in Belmont also occurs in Venice (as in Shylock's feigning good will toward Antonio in his 'merry' bond, and Lancelot's and Jessica's adoption of disguise), and the themes of justice and mercy in Venice also occur in Belmont (for example, strict justice governs the penalties for loss in the casket test, with no mitigation, but mercy tempers the penalties for loss of the betrothal rings at the play's end).

Shakespeare designs and orders a series of contrasts in this play; these contrasts are not merely opposed but rather purposefully interrelated. For example, the apparently merry jest of Shylock's flesh bond with Antonio for Bassanio in Venice (1.3) is counterbalanced in Belmont by the truly merry jest of Portia's rings episode that results in Antonio's new soul bond with Portia for Bassanio (5.1). Moreover, these motifs of contrast in Venice and Belmont are conceptually subsumed under Shakespeare's governing dramatic idea of choices for and against wise love. Although many have written about love in this play, and only a few about wisdom, the proper marriage of wisdom and love to form the concept of wise love has been neglected. Wise love as the ideal union of knowing and doing well is symbolised by the choice of the leaden chest. The dominant dramatic symbol in the play is the casket test with its three chests of gold, silver, and lead. The particularised meaning of this symbol will be explored in the next chapter, but its general impact on the play's structural unity must be considered here.

Although Shakespeare's innovations are remarkable in this play, especially his sophisticated use of usury, biblical allusion, and the casket choice as theme and symbol, he arranges these new, unpredictable emphases in familiar, predictable patterns of comic structure. Trying to grasp a sense of Shakespeare's dramatic architecture for *The Merchant of Venice* is difficult business. None of the quartos of the play record scene or act divisions; the Folio introduces a division of the script into five acts, and Nicholas Rowe in the eighteenth century is the first editor to divide the acts into scenes. The lack of such 'literate' divisions on the Elizabethan page and stage reminds us of the oral and fluid nature of Shakespeare's drama in the public theatre. Plays flowed from beginning to end without any intermission; the only apparent 'breaks' in the continuity of the action occurred when the stage was cleared of actors or when a Chorus spoke, as in *Romeo and Juliet* or *Henry V*. In light of the ongoing critical debate over the importance of act division for Elizabethan drama, the 'scene' is probably the basic structural unit of the plays, but dramatists were familiar with five-act structure from the classics, however much or little they cared to use it in their own ordering of their material for a play.[7]

From the pragmatic viewpoint of theatrical success, Shakespeare knew he had a diverse audience to please, which included a cross-section of English society, quite literally representatives from every social class in the realm, who presumably would want to see something 'new', especially in the wake of the revival of Marlowe's *The Jew of Malta*. But in the Elizabethan public theatre this large audience, less ideologically than socially heterogeneous, probably would not want to see a play so radically different from, or defiant of, their *expectations* that the play might fail to please them. Shakespeare did not make the same mistake John Fletcher later did when he tried to present a new kind of pastoral tragicomedy in *The Faithful Shepherdess* but failed because he disappointed the *expectations* of his audience.

In *The Merchant of Venice* Shakespeare uses at least two structural methods familiar to his audience: (1) a linear development of scenic sequence that progresses by events from the beginning, to the middle, and then to the end of the dramatic narrative; and (2) a centralised thematic emphasis in a scenic centrepiece (3.2) to which and from which scenes progress with some conceptual correspondence to their counterparts in the other half of the play. He effects structural unity through a carefully interrelated linear sequence of scenes that operate like mirrors to one another through their analogical or even parodic comparisons.[8] Each scene in the play centres on some degree of conflict that arises from the problem of having to make a choice, some choices being more difficult than others. Shakespeare anchors this linear sequence of 'choice' scenes by giving the play a thematic centre (3.2), a structural feature that significantly contributes to the play's artistic unity. A dramaturgic emphasis on a climactic or conceptual centre in Shakespeare's plays has been well discussed in terms of Elizabethan ideas of form drawn from visual arts (such as painting) and oral narrative (such as epics and ballads) by critics like Madeleine Doran, Bernard Beckerman, Mark Rose, and Bruce Smith.[9] The conceptual centre of *The Merchant of Venice* is the leaden casket choice (3.2). This central scene resolves the casket plot, and it liberates the woman who will in turn resolve the flesh-bond plot that enabled the resolution of her dilemma. The play opens in Venice, but the story of Belmont is what activates and resolves the story of Venice. Shakespeare, therefore, conjoins linear and centralised methods of structuring his dramatic events and their meanings.

Compared to the rival flesh-bond plot, the casket plot has suffered for too long as the neglected stepsister among the play's critics. The hub of critical controversy over this play focuses on Shylock and the flesh bond, and it seems likely that Shakespeare probably began his idea for this play with the story of the flesh bond as presented in Ser Giovanni's *Il Pecorone*, 'a collection of tales . . . written in Italian at the end of the fourteenth century and . . . printed at Milan in 1558'.[10] However, Shakespeare's imaginative development of dramatic meaning for the whole of his play derives not from this story but from the far more critically neglected story of the caskets, found in the selection of stories from the medieval *Gesta Romanorum*, translated by Richard Robinson

and published in London in 1577 and, with revisions, in 1595.
This allegorised medieval story is Shakespeare's own meticulously
developed addition to the flesh-bond story. Both stories have in
common their derivation from *medieval* sources, a literary fact which
should signal to us the enduring attractiveness of medieval stories for Shakespeare and his contemporaries and which should
deter us from dismissing the importance of allegory which dominates the *Gesta Romanorum*. Through his many developments of
the source for his casket story, Shakespeare improves upon the
meaning of this specific choice of caskets as a test of true love.
By substituting the allegorical story of the triple-choice love test
for the wooing trick in *Il Pecorone* Shakespeare chooses to emphasise *choice* in this play.[11] Not only does this story in the *Gesta
Romanorum* emphasise 'choice' in its language and events, but it
also defines the nature of right choice in its motto for the leaden
vessel: 'Who so chooseth me, shall find that God hath disposed'.[12]
Choices that adhere to the will of God are essentially right, and
choices that go against the will of God are essentially wrong.

   If the action of this play revolves around choice, in both its
scenes and acts, we must clarify what is meant by significant 'choice'
for the Elizabethans and recognise that God, not man, is the measure
of all things, especially choices involving faith and morals. The
ultimate standard for judging what is good and true is the will
of God, not the will of the individual, who can err in choosing
what only appears to be good and true. Translating St John
Chrysostom's opinion, Thomas Wilson affirms: 'Of a truth that
which is done according to the will of God, although it seem to
be wicked, yet it is altogether pleasant and acceptable before God.
Contrariwise, whatsoever is done beside the word of God . . . though
it be esteemed as a thing acceptable to God, yet it is of all others
the worst and most wicked.'[13] For the Elizabethans 'choice' needs
to include a binary proposition – to choose or not to choose. For
example, Adam and Eve are free to choose to eat the forbidden
fruit or not to eat it, but any choice that violates God's will is, by
Elizabethan definition, a wrong choice and will entail negative
consequences. The growth of modern secularism increasingly attempts to separate God's law from human law. Once the theological standard for judging human choice is displaced, other
standards – personal, political, economic, cultural – can take its
place. A helpful example of this historical phenomenon, germane
to our play, concerns the English Parliament's evolving discus-

sion of usury from a theological perspective in 1571 to an economic evaluation in 1624, when Parliament finally chose to legal-
ise interest at the rate of 8 per cent.[14] Unlike notions more current
in our modern era, a choice, to be a choice on the Elizabethan
stage, need not involve a wide variety of options nor be ideal in
nature, lacking any negative consequences to the chooser.

Each of the play's scenes and acts, or what most have come to
accept as the play's scenes and acts, revolves around the action
of choosing, that in turn is guided by wise or unwise 'knowing'.
In other words, the problem of choice in this play relates fundamentally to the significance of the choices symbolised by the casket test. Does one choose selfish gain, based on one's own perceived
desires and deserts, which can be grounded on appearance, not
truth? Or does one choose the selfless giving and hazarding of
all for the love of another? Figure 1 (on pp. 50–1) illustrates some
of the conceptual correspondences among these scenes of choice
that Shakespeare symmetrically orders around the play's thematic
centre, the choice of the leaden casket (3.2). Unlike the rigorous
symmetrical arrangement of scenes that might be posited for other
plays,[15] there can be no exact scene-for-scene correlation between
both halves of this play on either side of its thematic centre because there are twice as many scenes leading up to the central
scene of choice (3.2) as there are scenes leading out from the centre to the conclusion.

These numerous scenes leading up to the play's conceptual centre
introduce the audience to all the various main characters (except
the Duke) and to a variety of ventures, in which all these characters (except the ladies of Belmont) determine the outcomes. Portia
and Nerissa get their opportunity for the active role of adventuring after Bassanio's right choice liberates them. These many scenes,
none of which comes within 100 lines of the length of the play's
three longest scenes (3.2, 4.1, 5.1), tend to escalate dramatic pac-
ing and to create for the audience the illusory sense of a faster
passage of time. This illusion accords well with the bustling activities of that extraordinary day in Venice that spans scenes one
(1.1) through eleven (2.8), just over half of all the play's scenes.
The play opens sometime in the morning because Bassanio promises
to meet Lorenzo and Gratiano at the midday meal, at 'dinner
time' (1.1.70). During the course of this day Bassanio seeks Antonio's
help; Antonio agrees to Shylock's bond; Bassanio prepares for
his festive 'supper', which is to be held no later than 5:00 p.m.

(2.2.94, 143); Lorenzo and friends plan to 'slink away' during this feast to prepare their reentry as masquers (2.4.1–3); Jessica notifies Lorenzo of her planned disguise to elope, and Lorenzo decides she will be his torchbearer for the masque (2.4.23); Lancelot leaves Shylock to serve Bassanio; Shylock attends Bassanio's supper; Lorenzo and Jessica elope; the masque is cancelled so that Bassanio and Gratiano can take advantage of the wind, and they set sail for Belmont immediately; Antonio says farewell to Bassanio; Shylock rouses the Duke to find Jessica but just misses the departing ship; and Antonio certifies that Jessica and Lorenzo were not on board Bassanio's ship. Meanwhile, in Belmont, on this same day Portia bids farewell to her present suitors and prepares to receive the Prince of Morocco that evening (1.2.104); 'after dinner' (2.1.44) the next day he makes his hazard, loses, and departs. Meanwhile, back in Venice, on the day of Morocco's erroneous choice in Belmont, Shylock cries in the streets for 'justice' regarding his daughter and ducats, according to Salarino's and Solanio's recounting of the events of the preceding evening (2.8).[16]

After the opening tumultuous first day and its aftermath, we are supposed to suspend incredulity and believe the time of almost three months elapses during which Antonio's ships miscarry; Shylock promises to better the instruction of revenge; Arragon chooses and loses; Bassanio and Gratiano court and win Portia and Nerissa; Salerio happens to meet Lorenzo and Jessica and persuades them to come to Belmont with him (3.2.227–9) where he delivers Antonio's letter moments after the success of Bassanio's choice. Shakespeare adroitly uses two successive scenes – Arragon's failure crowned by the announcement of a young Venetian lord's arrival (2.9) and Salarino's and Solanio's later taunting of Shylock about Jessica's flight juxtaposed with Tubal's reports about Jessica and Antonio (3.1) – 'to peize the time / To eche it, and to draw it out in length' (3.2.22), in order to suggest the passage of nearly three months. After the play's long central scene of the leaden casket choice (3.2) caps this temporal illusion, the play takes six scenes to conclude. We see two short scenes (3.3 and 4.2), two intermediate scenes (3.4 and 3.5), and two long scenes (4.1 and 5.1). Like the scenes with Morocco (2.1 and 2.7), the scenes with Shylock (3.1 and 3.3) framing Bassanio's scene establish temporal simultaneity between Venice and Belmont. While Bassanio is sailing, courting, and choosing for three months, Shylock is lamenting

L. and J. choose love's teasing and serious talk. Women choose to arraign men. Pardons sought and granted. A. chooses new soul bond for B.'s fidelity to P. P. and N. dispense rewards and reveal truth. G. chooses to reaffirm protection of N.'s ring. (BELMONT)

5.1 [1.1]
(A. lends twice for B. to have P.; symbolic leaden choice)

P. receives ring from G. N. chooses to get G.'s ring. Women choose to outface and outswear men as they direct the play to its end. (VENICE)

4.2 [1.2]
(in choice, women move from passive to active role

A. chooses to pay debt stoically. Court expects and argues for mercy. P. advises the need for mercy. S. chooses to refuse. P. interprets bond literally. S. chooses now to refuse bond. Venetian legal penalty for S.'s attempt to murder A. Duke and A. choose conditional pardons. S. accepts. B. insists on reward. P. chooses ring. B. refuses. A. persuades B. to give ring. (VENICE)

4.1 [1.3–2.1]
(deception, the apparent truth)

J. freely chooses conversion. L. G. quips; L. rebuts. L. and J. praise P. and tease as lovers. (BELMONT)

3.5 [2.2–2.5]
(secular and spiritual 'conversions')

L. praises P.'s selfless friendship. P. expects no tangible reward. (Transvestite disguise for love's sake.) (BELMONT)

3.4 [2.6–2.9]
(choices of self-love vs other-love; gains and losses)

A. chooses to beg S. S. chooses not to give mercy. (VENICE)

3.3 [3.1]
(hate/revenge chosen over love/mercy)

3.2 CONCEPTUAL CENTER: Paradoxical choice of Leaden Casket (wisdom, the essential truth; love, the gift and risk of self for beloved).
(BELMONT)   B. chooses rightly to give and to hazard. P. chooses to ratify his choice. L. and J. choose to follow Sal. to Belmont.
(BELMONT)   A. chooses to send for B. by Sal. P. and B. choose to respond generously to A.'s letter.

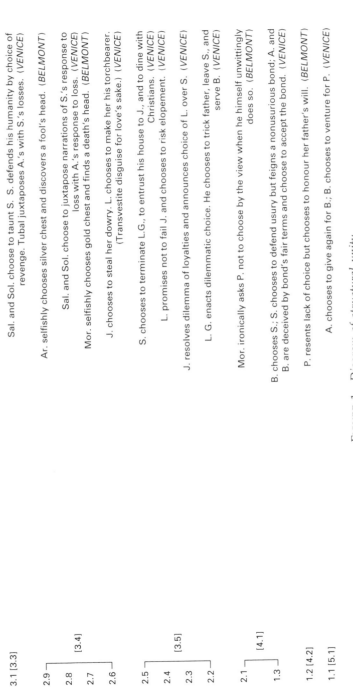

3.1 [3.3] Sal. and Sol. choose to taunt S. S. defends his humanity by choice of revenge. Tubal juxtaposes A.'s with S.'s losses. (*VENICE*)

2.9 Ar. selfishly chooses silver chest and discovers a fool's head. (*BELMONT*)

2.8 ⌐ [3.4] Sal. and Sol. choose to juxtapose narrations of S.'s response to loss with A.'s response to loss. (*VENICE*)

2.7 ⌐ Mor. selfishly chooses gold chest and finds a death's head. (*BELMONT*)

2.6 ⌐ J. chooses to steal her dowry. L. chooses to make her his torchbearer. (Transvestite disguise for love's sake.) (*VENICE*)

2.5 ⌐ S. chooses to terminate L.G., to entrust his house to J., and to dine with Christians. (*VENICE*)

2.4 ⌐ [3.5] L. promises not to fail J. and chooses to risk elopement. (*VENICE*)

2.3 ⌐ J. resolves dilemma of loyalties and announces choice of L. over S. (*VENICE*)

2.2 ⌐ L. G. enacts dilemmatic choice. He chooses to trick father, leave S., and serve B. (*VENICE*)

2.1 ⌐ [4.1] Mor. ironically asks P. not to choose by the view when he himself unwittingly does so. (*BELMONT*)

1.3 B. chooses S.; S. chooses to defend usury but feigns a nonusurious bond; A. and B. are deceived by bond's fair terms and choose to accept the bond. (*VENICE*)

1.2 [4.2] P. resents lack of choice but chooses to honour her father's will. (*BELMONT*)

1.1 [5.1] A. chooses to give again for B.; B. chooses to venture for P. (*VENICE*)

FIGURE 1 *Diagram of structural unity*

his losses and rejoicing in Antonio's losses, anticipating the for-feiture and taking a solemn oath in the synagogue to have his bond (3.1).

Now time begins to tighten its noose. In the scene immediately preceding Bassanio's determination to make his choice without further delay, Shylock asks Tubal to 'bespeak' an officer of the law 'a fortnight before' (3.1.100) the expiration of the bond. Im-mediately after Portia has sent Bassanio off to Venice, we see Antonio now under arrest, pleading with Shylock to no avail and announcing that 'tomorrow' (3.3.34) he will pay the forfeit. To-morrow finds Bassanio and Gratiano in Venice, and the disguised Portia and Nerissa arriving on their heels. There is no explicit indication of how much time passes until the play ends, but it seems likely that, because Bassanio and Portia left Belmont in haste after their marriage ceremony, they arrived in Venice early the next day for the trial. The trial is probably held in the morn-ing because the Duke entreats Balthazar to come to his home for 'dinner' (4.1.397), the main midday meal. Portia refuses because she is in haste to leave, and she later tells Nerissa that they will leave that night 'and be a day before our husbands home' (4.1.3). They arrive in Belmont about two hours before dawn (5.1.303). Bassanio, who had promised such a hasty return that he implied he would not sleep but travel at night (3.2.322–4), arrives mo-ments later.[17] If this temporal scheme is accepted, we discover a remarkable symmetry in the temporal correspondence of two days for the play's opening sequence (1.1–2.8) and two days for its closing sequence (3.2–5.1) with both two-day sequences counter-balanced on either side of the play's central illusion of three months (2.9–3.1).[18]

Shakespeare's control over his dramatic structure is also evi-denced by how effectively he employs scenic alternation between Venice and Belmont and scenic juxtaposition. There are only three junctures in the play where no scenic alternation occurs: 2.2–6 (five consecutive scenes in Venice), 3.4–5 (two consecutive scenes in Belmont), and 4.1–2 (two consecutive scenes in Venice). The dominant pattern of scenic alternation suggests that Shakespeare wants us to see connections between these two places, despite their apparent differences. Venice is a very public place, a bus-tling major city where the majority of scenes are undesignated as 'city' or 'street' scenes, where various lodgings are mentioned but only one house is entered and exited – Shylock's house. Belmont, on the other hand, is geographically removed from Venice. It is a private estate where virtue, beauty, nobility, and wealth reside and where only one house is entered and exited – Portia's house – and this house is shared, given to Bassanio and entrusted to Lorenzo and Jessica. In the course of the play Shylock's house is deserted by all but its patriarch, and by contrast, Portia's house swells with new life and joy.

Thematic interplay among the choices involved in the flesh-bond and casket plots and the subplot of Jessica and Lorenzo's marriage is structurally enforced through Shakespeare's exceptionally effective linear use of scenic juxtaposition that conceptually relates to the play's centrepiece (3.2) and its emphasis on choice as well as on the meaning of right choice. In the introductory exposition and complications of the first act, the explanation of the casket plot (1.2. 23–7) immediately precedes the formulation of the flesh bond (1.3). Shylock is unwittingly self-deceived in his judgement that revenge through deceptive entrapment is good. His desire and hope for gain through deliberate deception of Antonio and Bassanio with his merry bond (1.3) is immediately followed by Morocco's desire and hope to be 'blest' (2.1.46), but Morocco is frustrated by his own unwitting self-deception that he himself does not choose by externals. Portia, however, is not so deceived. Morocco's erring literalism and lack of self-knowledge is followed by Lancelot's comic literalism and self-knowledge. Before receiving his father's blessing and help in obtaining a new master, Lancelot confesses his deliberate but playful deception of his father through his true, although nominal, identification of himself (2.2). Jessica does not deceive herself, nor is she deceived by her father's values so she forgoes his blessing (2.3). Jessica's plan to use deception to escape from her father is joyfully received by Lorenzo, and Lancelot is their friendly go-between (2.4). On this day of 'departures' the play's action revolves around choices of secular and spiritual 'conversion' (turning away from something/someone old and turning toward something/someone new). These verbalised 'conversions' become visualised in action – Lancelot converts his service from a Jewish to a Christian master, Jessica converts her faith through her elopement (2.3, 2.6), Portia declares herself and her wealth to be 'converted' to Bassanio (3.2.167), and the women convert or 'turn to men' in their use of cross-dressing (3.4.78).

The transfers of personal loyalties result in a series of choreographed departures that entail 'loss' succeeded by 'gain' for those who choose wisely and loss only for those who choose unwisely. Lancelot leaves 'a rich Jew's service' for a poor gentleman who has 'the grace of God' (2.2.122–5), but he continues his friendship and service to the Jew's daughter and her Christian lover (2.2–2.5). For a hateful reason Shylock leaves his house to break his principle against dining with Christians (2.5), only to discover upon his return that his leavetaking from Jessica was not temporary. Lorenzo's friends help him steal Jessica while Jessica steals from her father to give to Lorenzo. Jessica uses deliberate deception and disguise to achieve love and a new life, literally and spiritually. Both Lorenzo and Jessica give and hazard for each other, risking the danger of elopement and giving up their home city of Venice in order to escape Shylock's reach. Jessica's and Lorenzo's choice of love (2.6) immediately precedes Morocco's erroneous golden choice (2.7). Jessica's tossing down a casket of gold to Lorenzo anticipates by contrast Morocco's desire to gain by his election of the golden casket. Shylock's anguished but confused lamentation over his loss of daughter and ducats is heard right after Morocco's loss, but it is contrasted with the description of Antonio's generous farewell in his loss of Bassanio that ends this scene (2.8). Arragon's erroneous assumption of desert (2.9) immediately follows Antonio's sacrifice and precedes Shylock's powerful but faulty explanation of the revenge he desires and deserves, despite Antonio's own losses (3.1). The indications of Shylock's and Antonio's losses (2.8, 3.1) are framed by the losing choices of Morocco (2.7) and Arragon (2.9). The fortunate choices of Lancelot, Jessica, and Lorenzo (2.2–2.6), on the other hand, scenically precede the misfortunes of Shylock and Antonio, which are temporally and spatially concurrent in the structure of scenes (2.8 and 3.1). Shylock's losses are Lancelot's, Jessica's, and Lorenzo's blessings, just as Antonio's losses become Shylock's expected gain.

Bassanio's selfless choice to give and hazard for love (3.2) follows Shylock's anticipation of revenge (3.1) and is in turn followed by Shylock's refusal to give up his legally promised gain of Antonio's flesh. With Shylock's behaviour and Antonio's deprivation still in our mind's eye, we next see Portia, whose generous giving, along with Antonio's and Bassanio's friendship, is praised (3.4.1–23) before Shakespeare adopts a lighter tone in unfolding Portia's plan to use male disguise and to consult cousin Bellario for a venture in Venice (3.4.45–4), thus giving the audience some necessary plot information before Balthazar and his clerk enter the courtroom. Striking visual and verbal parallels among these scenes of choices for and against wise love present themselves to the audience. The last scene in Act III looks back to how Lorenzo and Jessica have come to enjoy their new status as chosen master and mistress of the house, and we see their happy marriage, which Shylock explicitly repudiates in the trial (4.1.291–3) and which Antonio blesses through the 'gift' of Shylock's wealth (4.1.384, 390). This scene also prepares for Antonio's conversion condition in the subsequent trial scene by using Jessica's and Lancelot's comic quarrel about damnation to introduce the idea of salvation through conversion to Christianity (3.5). Lorenzo's comic conversation with the Fool (Lancelot) anticipates in a much lighter tone the idea of social justice because Lancelot will have to answer to the commonwealth for his impregnation of the Moor (3.5.30–2). The facetiously disputatious Lancelot, who claims to speak plainly (3.5.3) but who defies the matter (3.5.58) and who quips that whim should govern appetite (3.5.50–2), parodies the darker manifestation of these traits by Shylock in the dispute in court that follows. Lancelot's foolish use of 'dear discretion' (3.5.52), that is excessive discrimination between words and intended meaning, will be countered in the next scene by Portia's wise use of such linguistic discretion.

The trial that follows this pregnant scene opens with a disputation about why Shylock would '*choose* to have / A weight of carrion flesh', rather than ducats, and he retorts, 'I'll not answer that − / But say it is my *humour*' (4.1.40–3, my italics). The audience knows, however, that the answer to this 'present question in the court' (4.1.168) is that Antonio's flesh will feed Shylock's appetite for revenge (3.1.42–3). The trial scene resolves the problem of Shylock's choice of flesh while simultaneously giving occasion for counter choices of 'spirit' (4.1.364). Shakespeare's legal legerdemain has Shylock and Antonio reverse positions as plaintiff and defendant to discover the merits of justice and mercy: 'change places, and handy-dandy, which is the justice, which is the thief?' (*Lr* 4.6.153–4). Shylock is placed in the position of having to make the leaden choice, of giving and hazarding all, in light of what has just been demonstrated about the merits of literalism, strict justice and mercy. The trial ends by giving rise to new choices regarding gifts and oaths of faith (4.1.402–50) which the ladies of Belmont will now actively direct and redirect through their playful outfacing and outswearing the men (4.2). Portia's and Nerissa's anticipated lovers' 'quarrel' to come is prefaced by the mock lovers' 'quarrel' between Jessica and Lorenzo, whose bantering duet on love's tragic potential (5.1.1–23) moves to a shared meditation on heavenly music as well as the introduction of human music to welcome home Portia and Nerissa (5.1.54–88). The women continue to refine their role as choosers, not merely the chosen (1.2), adopted since their liberation through the right choices of the men (3.2). These husbands will be comically arraigned by their wives as 'judges', whose playful dispute over the rings is also a happy piece of comic instruction that results in reaffirmed choices of love and wiser understanding of them through new oaths and a new bond, a soul bond, that reunites Portia, Bassanio, and Antonio.

If the play's scenes revolve around choice, especially dilemmatic choice, it should not be too surprising to discover that the act division recorded in the Folio, also coheres, without any need to regroup scenes, to Shakespeare's dramatic logic of choice and its structuring. The play's choices are not merely haphazard but artistically orchestrated. From a structural perspective each act of the play revolves around the idea and the action of choosing. Act I introduces the essential choices of the main characters: Bassanio chooses to venture for Portia by seeking Antonio's aid; Antonio chooses to help Bassanio despite the cost; Portia chafes at her lack of choice in marriage but affirms her resolve to obey her father's will; and Shylock chooses to entrap Antonio. Act II presents the play's subplot as revolving around choices of secular and spiritual 'conversion' and literal and figurative 'departures'. Meanwhile, in the Belmontian main plot in Act II, the choices of the autonomous Princes of Morocco and Arragon involve secular 'conversion' and 'loss'. They choose to take the oath and turn away from their past right to marry and bear legitimate offspring should they lose their venture. But their venture involves no essential transfer of personal loyalty because they remain personally infatuated, narcissistically self-obsessed. They depart as 'losers' (2.7.77), incurring the strict justice of their penalty. In Act III the choices revolve around giving and hazarding selflessly, or refusing to do so by opting for choices of selfish gain based on one's own biased sense of desire and desert. Choices for the love of romance and friendship punctuate choices for the denial of love that in turn promote enmity. In Act IV choices concern literal and spiritual interpretation, opaque and wise perception of self and others, and the need for and the consequence of both justice and mercy. In Act V choosing focuses on the art of loving wisely and keeping faith through playful instruction and receptive learning.

Thus, Shakespeare achieves artistic unity by structurally, linguistically, and conceptually integrating his two main plots – the flesh-bond and the casket choice – and his three sub-plots – Lancelot's transfer of service from Shylock to Bassanio, Jessica's transfer of loyalty from Shylock to Lorenzo, and the final rings episode, which grows out of the resolutions of the casket plot (3.2) and the flesh-bond plot (4.1) in order to effect the final resolution of the play. He especially effects artistic unity through the thematic development of choices for and against wise love in a dramatic structure of scenes sequentially juxtaposed to comment on each other by their various reflections of the play's central choice. This structural interrelation of the play's two worlds of Belmont and Venice is further supported by a variety of interconnections involving the transference of characters, shared language and symbols, and repeated actions of choice that relate to the meaning of the central casket choice. Some characters move back and forth between Venice and Belmont (Bassanio, Gratiano, Portia, and Nerissa), but by the end of the play all the main characters, except Shylock, journey 'from Venice / As far as Belmont' (5.1.16–17). The two worlds of Venice and Belmont share important symbolic props, such as betrothal rings (Shylock's turquoise and Bassanio's and Gratiano's hoops of gold), caskets (Jessica's stolen casket tossed to Lorenzo and the three caskets of gold, silver, and lead), paper scrolls (Shylock's bond and the scrolls in each of the three caskets), keys (Shylock's to lock up his house and chests and Portia's to unlock each of the three chests), and two domestic domiciles (Shylock's house and Portia's house). Repeated actions of choosing dominate the play from beginning to end, often with the repetition of operative words and their meanings from the casket choice, whose three scenes of choosing are literally and thematically central to the play.

'PLAY UPON THE WORD' (3.5.36)

Language forges the subtlest linkages between Venice and Belmont through the repetition in Venice and in Belmont of some significant words and their variants (e.g., 'friend', 'judge/judgement', 'oath', 'blessing', 'teach', 'learn'), the same word used in both literal and figurative senses (e.g., 'see', 'bound', 'heart'), and related verbal contrasts (e.g.,'flesh' and/or 'blood' versus 'spirit'; 'eye' (sight) versus 'head' (insight); 'old' versus 'young'; 'foolish/fool' versus 'wise/wisdom').[19] Shared verbal repetition in dual settings invites comparative evaluation. Although the lexicon of the trial scene – 'justice', 'law', and 'mercy' – dominates primarily the world of Venice, the most frequently repeated words and their variants that conjoin both Venice and Belmont are significantly related to the concept and language of the casket test, especially the leaden choice. The words 'love', 'give', and 'choose' (and their variants) are the most reiterated words in both Venice and Belmont. The other operative words from the casket mottos – 'hazard', 'gain/get', 'desire' and 'deserve' – also recur in the settings of Venice and Belmont so that a refrain of this language haunts the audience's auditory memory. Accustomed to the expectation of gorgeous rhetoric in Shakespeare's plays, we might be surprised by the relatively common or plain words that make up this linguistic refrain, almost a 'leaden' vocabulary.

While there is plenty of Shakespeare's characteristic wordplay (for example, the puns on 'gentle/gentile') in *The Merchant of Venice*, there is also an awareness of the slipperiness of language that is significantly voiced in the scene preceding the trial. Lorenzo retorts to Lancelot: 'How every fool can play upon the word! I think the best grace of wit will shortly turn into silence, and discourse grow commendable in none only but parrots. . . . I pray thee understand a plain man in his plain meaning' (3.5.36–48). The problem of human communication, of aptly suiting words to matter or of using 'a tricksy word' to 'defy the matter' (3.5.53–8), pervades the play. The human use of language is so crucial to Shakespeare's drama of speech acts that it cannot be confined to a single chapter of inquiry. We will focus here on some particular aspects of Shakespeare's language in this play by exploring his creative use of names, especially for his Jewish characters, and by comparing the dramatic contexts for the two most famous speeches from the play, Shylock's 'Hath not a Jew eyes?' and Portia's 'The quality of mercy is not strained.' If we contextualise Shakespeare's set speeches within their immediate dramatic contexts, we see more clearly how Shakespeare uses these speech acts to scrutinise the merits of speaker and speech for their particular dramatic moment as well as for the whole play.

The specific context for Shylock's speech suits the scenic juxta-position for this scene, preceded by Arragon's mischoice and fol-lowed by Bassanio's right choice, just discussed. When Shylock enters, Solanio and Salarino disrupt their discussion of the news on the Rialto about Antonio's losses to ask Shylock what news he knows from the merchants. Shylock surprisingly does not an-swer their question but switches the discussion to what is brood-ing on his mind, Jessica's elopement, and by the end of this scene we discover that the time is about a fortnight shy of the expira-tion of the bond. Jessica's flight serves to enflame further Shylock's earlier announced hatred of Antonio (1.3.34). Despite Solanio's and Salarino's earlier announced awareness that Shylock would make Antonio a scapegoat for his misfortune (2.8.25–6), they fool-ishly and mercilessly taunt Shylock about his loss. When they ask again, this time explicitly about Antonio, Shylock lumps Antonio and Jessica together in the same category of a 'bad match' (3.1.35).

Now Shylock begins his refrain, never foreseeing how his own looking *to* the bond does not include the kind of looking *at* the bond that Portia will use against him: 'Let him look to his bond. He was wont to call me usurer; let him look to his bond. He was wont to lend money for a Christian courtesy; let him look to his bond' (3.1.37–9). Shylock explicitly reintroduces his resentment based on his difference of opinion with Antonio over the subject of usurious lending. Shylock passionately objects to Antonio's calling him a usurer, but Shylock is in fact a usurer, who de-fends usury and who repeats here his antipathy toward free lending. Why should Shylock be offended at the truth of being named that which he is – a usurer? This important matter will be ex-plored when we consider the scene in which the bond is trans-acted (1.3), but for now it is important to note that Shakespeare has not abandoned usury as the bone of contention between Shylock and Antonio but continues to develop it, once again through Shylock's initiation. Salarino, aware of Shylock's anger, still con-fidently believes in his rational but naive assumption: 'Why, I am sure if he forfeit thou wilt not take his flesh. What's that *good* for?' (3.1.140–1, my italics). Like the difference between Bassanio's and Shylock's definition of 'good' (1.3.11–12), Salarino assumes 'good' refers to the economic logic about human flesh that Shylock cleverly used to deceive Antonio and Bassanio about his true motive (1.3.155–60). After flippantly reducing the value of human flesh to fish-bait, Shylock frankly confesses his hidden motive, 'it will feed my *revenge*' (3.1.42–3, my italics). 'Revenge' is a pivotal word in Shylock's speech; he uses it four times here and once again later in this scene with Tubal (3.1.74). Shylock is the only character in the play to use the word 'revenge', and he repeats it five times, all within this scene. One of the premises underlying Shylock's riveting speech is that revenge is a 'good'.

Shylock's speech is remarkable primarily for how Shakespeare uses it for simultaneity of opposite dramatic effects. In this same speech Shakespeare simultaneously attracts us to Shylock emotionally and distances us from him intellectually. We share the emotional pain of another suffering human being who is intent on being seen as equally human to those tormenting him. But the quality of reasoning evinced in both the argument and its conclusion distances the audience, who is invited to see more than Shylock does about what it means to be human. The emotional content of the speech is wrenching, and Shakespeare probably wants his audience to empathise with Shylock's sense of his suffering humanity ('he hath disgraced me') and his sense of common humanity ('hath not a Jew hands, organs, dimensions, senses, affections, passions?'). This human being has suffered at the hands of Antonio, and the audience can believe that Shylock has a legitimate complaint because they have witnessed the unchristian behaviour of Antonio toward Shylock in the opening of their first scene together (1.3). It is not hard for us to imagine Antonio's past disgraces of Shylock, especially the financial thwartings that make up half of Shylock's list of Antonio's wrongs, and so we begin to nod in assent to Shylock's litany. But Shylock brings a thoughtful audience up short when he claims Antonio has done all his maltreatment for one 'reason': 'I am a Jew' (3.1.46). Is that true on the basis of what the audience has seen thus far? If it is true, how can we explain Antonio's positive change in attitude toward Shylock, who is still a Jew, that occurs solely on the grounds of Shylock's declaration that he will forgo usury in this bond (1.3.145–71)? If Antonio is as universally anti-Jewish as Shylock claims, why do we hear of no Jewish enemies in Venice other than Shylock?

Given Shylock's speech habits, his reiteration of the first person pronoun ironically reveals that the grudge between these two men is much more a personal than a national or an ethnic matter. Shylock emphasises here *his* need for 'revenge' against Antonio:

'he hath disgraced *me*, and hindred *me* half a million, laughed at *my* losses, mocked at *my* gains, scorned *my* nation, thwarted *my* bargains, cooled *my* friends, heated *mine* enemies . . .' (3.1.43–5; my italics). These lines develop the same personal emphasis in Shylock's first confession of hatred for Antonio:

> He hates our sacred nation, and he rails
> On *me*, *my* bargains, and *my* well-won thrift
> Which he calls interest. Cursed be *my* tribe
> If I forgive him!
>
> (1.3.40–4, my italics)

Shakespeare probably borrows from Marlowe this pronominal emphasis and rhythm of line; compare Barabas: 'So they spare *me*, *my* daughter, and *my* wealth' (1.1.151, my italics), or '*My* purse, *my* coffer, and *myself* is thine' (3.4.89, my italics).[20] Likewise, Shylock's language of revenge owes something to Barabas. Shylock's phrase, 'it shall go hard' (3.1.56), repeats Barabas's exact phrase, 'it shall go hard' (2.3.17, 93), used in his death plot against the Christian Lodowick, just as Barabas's threat to have the 'heart' of Lodowick foreruns Shylock's same threatening language for Antonio (3.1.100).

If Antonio does hate the 'sacred nation' of Jews, we never hear or see any evidence of it for other Venetian Jews, in particular Tubal and Jessica; we see his hatred for only one member of that nation, Shylock. Shylock's Jewish friend, Tubal, has no hostile relationship with Antonio. Therefore, Tubal may not be a usurer, or at least not an exorbitant one who leaves victims moaning for relief. Later in our scene of Shylock's intended 'revenge', the re-surfacing of the first person pronoun suggests again Shylock's commitment to himself rather than to his nation: 'The curse never fell upon our nation till now, *I* never felt it till now' (3.1.67–8, my italics). Therefore, he also laments his unshared experience of misery – 'no satisfaction, no revenge, nor no ill luck stirring but what lights o' *my* shoulders, no sighs but o' *my* breathing, no tears but o' *my* shedding!' (3.1.74–6, my italics). And his reason for wanting to rid the Rialto of Antonio has naught to do with his nation but with his own accumulation of wealth: '*I* will have the heart of him if he forfeit, for were he out of Venice *I* can make what merchandise *I* will' (3.1.100–2, my italics).

Like Shylock's distaste for the truth of being called a 'usurer', like his difference of opinion with Lancelot about the consumption of food, like his difference of opinion with Jessica about the atmosphere of his house, is Shylock's reasoning here another instance of his opinion, one that he may well believe to be true but which does not necessarily square with other evidence? When Shylock questions, 'Hath not a Jew eyes' (3.1.46), does his perception of 'reality' match up with the audience's vision? Or is Shylock's 'eye of reason . . . with rage yblent'?[21] Unlike Antonio, Solanio and Salarino definitely do fit the accusation Shylock is levelling. Unlike Antonio, they never emphasise Shylock's usury, only his Jewishness. Because Solanio and Salarino do fit Shylock's description of prejudice against him simply because he is a Jew, is Shylock confusing Antonio with them? If so, such unfortunate confusion may account for Shylock's illogical shift in focus from the specific to the general, from 'he', meaning Antonio, to 'you' (3.1.50), meaning Christians. Antonio should no more be equated with Solanio and Salarino, whether in his attitude toward his ventures at sea or toward Shylock, than Shylock should be equated with other Jews, like Tubal or Jessica. Gratiano is guilty of Jew-baiting, but his friend Bassanio never is. From Shylock's first scene we discover he hates Christians, and in particular he hates Antonio, whose personal humiliation of him has given Shylock cause for hatred.

Although Antonio is no more religiously enlightened about contemporary Jews than any of the other Christian characters, who all see the Christian faith as the faith necessary for salvation (nor can we expect them to see it otherwise in the sixteenth century), Antonio does not abuse Shylock for his Jewishness but for his *usury*, which Antonio sees as unkind and therefore, with the religious bias of the period, as not Christian, or 'Jewish'. Similarly, when Antonio interprets why Shylock hates him, he focuses not on the fact that he is a Christian but on his practice of free lending (3.3.21–4) which is, of course, traditionally believed at this time to be action that accords with the Christian faith. Shylock begins his speech by confirming Antonio's awareness of an enmity based primarily on professional difference over the morality of lending freely or at interest. However, Shylock does not continue to stress this, as Antonio would, or as Shylock did in his opening aside. Instead, Shylock drops the subject of usury and focuses on religious difference.

Is Shylock projecting his reasons for hating Antonio onto Antonio?

The complex subject of the enmity between Antonio and Shylock is the focus of another chapter, but for this speech by Shylock what needs to be noted is *Shylock's* interpretation of Antonio's hatred even though Antonio is no longer acting or speaking hatefully toward Shylock as he formerly did. Indeed, Antonio accepts the bond by affirming that he will now speak well of Shylock, saying 'there is much kindness in the Jew' (1.3.146). If Antonio has 'reformed' his behaviour toward Shylock during the past two and a half months, as Shylock himself indicates in Antonio's humbled presence on the Rialto and as Antonio's behaviour verifies (3.3), why does Shylock continue to present Antonio in the light of hatred? Is it because Shylock believes Antonio's reformation is feigned, as his own was in suggesting a loan on the basis of friendship? Is it because Shylock cannot truly 'see' Antonio's change because he himself wants to continue his hatred for Antonio?

Shylock knows the process for how to win a friend through lending (1.3.131–5), but he lacks the motive of good will to do it. In part this motivational deficit derives from a faulty or too limited definition of what it means to be human. Shylock's list of what makes Jews and Christians equally human is accurate in so far as it goes. The problem, more easily recognisable to an Elizabethan than to a modern audience, is that Shylock starts with a definition of man as an animal and never moves beyond it.[22] According to medieval–Renaissance philosophy, humans held a sensitive soul (the five outer senses and the five inward wits) and a physical body in common with animals. It is man's rational soul that raises him above the animals and makes him godlike.[23] All of Shylock's examples relate to traits humans share with the physical, fleshly animal level of creation. The one possible exception is, 'If you tickle us, do we not laugh?', but that appears in a list of parallel constructions that are based on involuntary reaction, on the lack of free will to choose – pricking must cause bloodshed, tickling laughter, poisoning death, and wronging revenge. The revenge response signals that it is in a separate category from the rest because the auxiliary verb changes from the involuntary nuance of 'do' to the voluntary nuance of 'shall'. One interpretation might be that Shylock knows that he is dressing up the case for revenge, and therefore he purposefully slips into a list of involuntary bodily reactions an action (revenge) that the audience knows humans can govern by choice. Given Shylock's verbal context, 'revenge' appears to be a necessity. While ani-

mals follow bestial nature and automatically revenge a wrong
done them, humans have a choice, a hard choice.

For humans the natural reaction to wrong received is revenge;
the gracious reaction is forgiveness. But does Shylock 'know' this?
Does Shylock 'believe' this? Because Shylock's understanding of
what it means to be human does not go beyond the sensitive
soul of animals to the rational soul of humans, he does not 'see'
revenge as a choice, but as a necessity, and therefore he does not
'see' the antidote to revenge, which is the choice of forgiveness.
Even though Shylock has already demonstrated his skill in the
use of deceptive rhetoric (1.3.130–70), in this speech he is probably not trying to deceive others so much as he is unwittingly
self-deceived, in the same way that Morocco and Arragon 'choose
amiss' (2.9.64) and convince themselves of the rightness of their
reasons to choose as they do. The erring ratiocination of Morocco
and Arragon, to be discussed in the analysis of their choices, sets
the stage for Shylock's similar faulty use of discursive reason or
'ratio'. Shylock similarly tried to reason the case for usury on the
basis of religion and Scripture (1.3.60–89). Like usury, revenge is
seen by Shylock as good, as legitimate. Like his ex-servant Lancelot,
Shylock is given to disputation and literalism, but in more serious degrees. In the course of the play Shylock uses the debater's
language of defence to argue the cases for usury (1.3), rejection
(2.5), revenge (3.1), obduracy (3.3), and the illegal use of a legal
bond (4.1). But to what purpose? One's own self-centred gain and
ill will.

'What I purpose' (4.1.35), as Shylock says later regarding his
intent for Antonio, is revealed to the audience during his private
conversation with Tubal: 'I thank God, I thank God . . . I am very
glad of it. I'll plague him, I'll torture him . . . I will have the heart
of him' (3.1.81–100). His purpose is not simple revenge or the
fair evening of a score, the lawful allowance in the Old Testament of *lex talionis* – 'an eye for an eye, a tooth for a tooth' –
which was intended to prevent excessive revenge, for example,
the taking of a life in return for the taking of an eye. As with the
taking of 'excess' in lending money, Shylock intends to take 'excess' in revenge: 'it shall go hard but I will *better* the instruction'
(3.1.56–7, my italics). In seeking to use human law to revenge
himself excessively on Antonio, Shylock disregards the strict balance of *lex talionis* (Lv 24.20) as well as Yahweh's claim to the
right of vengeance.[24] Shakespeare's audience would be aware of

the conceptual wrongness of Shylock's conclusion, his distortion and misuse of the Old Testament concept of *lex talionis*. An Elizabethan audience would also know that Matthew's version of Christ's Sermon on the Mount directly addresses the question that Shylock raises here: 'Ye have heard that it hath been said, An eye for an eye, & a tooth for a tooth' (Mt 5.38), and the gloss in the Geneva Bible explains, 'Albeit this was spoken for the judges, yet every man applied it to revenge his private quarrel.' Shylock plays 'judge' in his own cause and intends to execute *personal* and *excessive* revenge.

But an Elizabethan audience would also be forced by Shakespeare's language here to recognise the power of Shylock's most compelling argument. He argues that on the basis of Christian example he has been taught that revenge is what a Christian returns for injury suffered: 'If a Jew wrong a Christian, what is his humility? Revenge. If a Christian wrong a Jew, what should his sufferance be by Christian example? Why, revenge!' (3.1.53–6). 'Humility' and 'sufferance' are ironic here; humility is not the same idea as humiliation, and long-suffering is not merely the fact of suffering but the attitude taken toward such suffering. Christians are not called to inflict humiliation or pain but to endure their own sufferings in the proper spirit of true humility and patience (1 Cor 7; Rom 12.17). This is precisely the point that Christ addresses when He introduces in His Sermon on the Mount the concept of *lex talionis* in order to revise it in favour of forgiveness and endurance: 'But I say unto you, Resist not evil: but whosoever shall smite thee on thy right cheek, turn to him the other also' (Mt 5.39). Shylock has Salarino and Solanio rightly on the hip. As Christians they do not practise toward him what has been preached to them as their faith based on the law of love and the incarnation of love. Nor do they learn from this encounter to look within, but they continue to look outward and see only the speck in Shylock's eye and match him with Tubal as a devilish man (3.1.62).

Solanio and Salarino, however, are not the only examples of Christian behaviour Shylock knows. Bassanio treats him respectfully and avoids the Jew-baiting of Solanio and Salarino and later Gratiano. Although Bassanio sets no example of revenge toward Shylock, Shylock hopes to spite Bassanio by sending his former servant to 'help to waste / His borrowed purse' (2.5.48–9). If Shylock now believes that he has learned the example of revenge from Christian behaviour, he has forgotten his opening aside, in which he initiated the hope for revenge against Antonio's free lending, and erroneously implies that his religion will not favour forgiveness: 'Cursed be my tribe / If I forgive him!' (1.3.43–4). Is Shylock, like Antonio in *The Tempest*, responsible for making 'a sinner of his memory / To credit his own lie' so that he believes the 'truth' he creates 'by telling of it' (1.2.99–102)? Bad example can be imitated or rejected. For the instances in which Shylock's argument about 'learned' revenge are true, he speaks cogently to our basic instinct of mutual return, and his rationale is recapitulated in *Othello* by Emilia's revenge speech (4.3.86–103). There, however, Desdemona responds by delivering the correct perspective we do not get in our scene, '[God] me such uses send, / Not to pick bad from bad, but by bad mend' (4.3.104–5). 'To depart from evil is understanding' while 'fear of the Lord [faith] is wisdom' (Job 28.28).

Does Shylock have Antonio on the hip? Shylock does not give Antonio credit for his positive change toward 'kindness' – Antonio's figurative 'conversion' or turning away from his former stance of hateful retribution toward Shylock (1.3.145–71) – as in all fairness Shylock should. On the other hand, Antonio has not been fully tested as a Christian yet because he has returned verbal kindness for Shylock's apparent 'kindness' rendered at the end of the bond scene (1.3). What will Antonio choose to do when called upon to respond to a far greater challenge, to return kindness for injury? We are reminded by Shylock's emphasis on the pivotal instruction of Christian *example* that the Elizabethan stage Jew could be used to expose the discrepancy between Christian behaviour and Christian faith in order to make its Christian audience see themselves more clearly. Barabas also indicates this disjuncture between theory and practice in his view of Christians: 'For I can see no fruits in all their faith, / But malice, falsehood, and excessive pride, / Which methinks fits not their profession' (1.1.114–16). As Marlowe suggests, Christians may 'brag of faith' (1.1.121), but words are not deeds. Living example conveys the most persuasive instruction. Hence, Christ closes His discussion of *lex talionis* with the extraordinary new commandment that His followers love not only their friends and neighbours but also their enemies so that they might resemble their Father, in whose image and likeness they were created (Mt 5.43–8).

If Shylock reasons from the premise of man's animal nature,

Portia reasons from the premise of man's god-like nature. Instead of seeing with the flesh's eye as Shylock does, Portia sees with the eye of faith. Shylock's emphasis on the flesh is countered here by Portia's emphasis on the spirit.[25] 'Flesh' versus 'Spirit' are familiar Pauline terms for what is opposed to God (outward flesh) versus what is from God (inward spirit). Although Shakespeare inherits the word 'flesh' from his literary source, *Il Pecorone*, he expects his audience to hear in Shylock's use of the word and appetitive imagery the Pauline metaphorical meaning of 'flesh': 'If ye bite & devour one another, take heed lest ye be consumed one of another. Then I say, walk in the Spirit [in the man regenerate], and ye shall not fulfill the lusts of the flesh' (Gal 5.15–16). Portia's eloquent speech on mercy assumes that humans want to resemble God in their goodness. And how might one do that? By seasoning justice with mercy, the mitigation of human faults and failures through forgiveness.

As Shylock appeals to our sensitive nature, Portia appeals to our higher, rational nature, in particular to wisdom, the divine wisdom of mercy tempering justice in the affairs of fallible humanity. Critics have found at least several sources for the ideas and images in Portia's speech: Seneca's *De Clementia* (i.19) and the debate over the contradictory claims of mercy and justice; Ecclesiasticus's natural analogy of God's mercy in time of trouble 'like a cloud of rain, that cometh in the time of drought' (35.20); Epitia's plea for mercy that complements 'sacred Majesty' in Giraldi's *Hecatommithi* (II.429); the recognition in the Psalms that 'no flesh is righteous in [God's] sight' (Ps 143.2); the knowledge that the merciful will be 'blessed' (Mt 5.7); and the realisation that we must render mercy if we expect mercy (Ecclus 28.2; Mt 5.7), that we must forgive our debtors if we would be forgiven our debts (the Lord's Prayer).[26]

To this list should be added James's epistle (3.13–17) and the Judge's argument for mercy in Anthony Munday's *Zelauto* (1580). James distinguishes between 'the wisdom of the world' and 'the wisdom of God' (heading), that is, between the 'wisdom' that is 'earthly, sensual, and devilish' because people cherish in their 'hearts' the evil of 'bitter envying and strife' (3.13–16) and the wisdom that is heavenly in its unstrained and merciful nature: 'But the wisdom that is from above, is first pure, then peaceable, gentle, easy to be entreated, full of mercy and good fruits without judging, and without hypocrisy' (3.17). The gloss on this matter of 'judging' significantly explains, 'And examining things with extreme rigor as hypocrites, who only justify themselves, & condemn all others'. This doctrine is preceded by the ideas that all men are sinners and therefore should not be rigorous toward their brothers, and that although the tongue is a little member of the body, it is capable of 'a world of wickedness' (3.1–2, 5–6). The common flesh bond of sin and the hypocritical versus the honest use of speech in the trial will be explored more when we consider that scene. But James's juxtaposition of these ideas provides a nexus for Shakespeare's inclusion of the other emphases in Portia's speech – the blessing of mercy, the prayer for mercy, and the monarchal example of the earthly power of justice tempered by the heavenly power of mercy.

John Russell Brown has noted some parallels between Shakespeare's trial scene and the Judge's plea for mercy to the greedy, furious, and bloody Christian usurer, Signor Truculento, in Munday's narrative, *Zelauto*.[27] But Shakespeare also improves upon the message of *brotherly* love the Judge urges for these Christian adversaries by expanding this message to include the love of *enemies*, who are brothers in the flesh but not in the spirit because they do not share the same faith. From *Zelauto* Shakespeare seems to develop another overlooked idea, the notion of shared suffering to promote just judgement. The Judge articulates, but ultimately does not enforce, the idea that the plaintiff should experience the suffering of the defendant, namely that the unmerciful usurer should be a 'partaker' of his victim's 'pains' so that he shall know if he demands 'a reasonable request'.[28] Shakespeare enacts this idea through the role reversal of plaintiff and defendant in his trial when Shylock changes places with Antonio to face the legal threat of loss of life and goods. The role of the unmerciful usurer naturally underscores the plea and prayer for mercy, as Thomas Wilson indicates in sentiments that parallel some of Portia's (4.1.194–8): 'O lord, have mercy on us . . . if thou narrowly mark our naughtiness and wicked doings, who shall be able to stand before thee in judgement?' Therefore, God sets the example of '*free mercy*' that men should follow in being 'charitable' to each other.[29]

One reason Shylock does not see the wisdom of mercy when Portia advises him to 'consider this' (4.1.194) is his blindness to his own need for it. Otherwise, wisdom is 'easily seen' by those who 'love her, & found of such as seek her' (Wis 6.12). In the

Bible wisdom is an essential attribute of God (Job 28.12–27; 1 Cor 1.24; Ap 7.12), and in Proverbs divine wisdom is imaged as a woman (Prv 8.22–31). Portia as fictive androgyne is an appropriate figure on stage to voice such wisdom integrally associated now with mercy. Portia's natural image of rain for mercy originates above in the heavens, whereas Shylock's natural images originate below in the flesh.[30] 'In the course of justice, none of us / Should see salvation' (4.1.195–6), Portia counsels, and Shylock's answering insistence upon 'the law, / The penalty and forfeit of [his] bond' (4.1.202–3) recall the biblical economics of faith and love for an Elizabethan audience – the ultimate wisdom of mercy, the 'debt' and death of sin paid by the merciful cancellation of that just bond upon the cross. Paul challenges, 'Where is the disputer of this world? hath not God made the wisdom of this world foolishness'? (1 Cor 1.20). Shylock's revenge speech is disputatiously divisive: 'I/we' versus 'you'. Portia's mercy speech is universally inclusive – all men, Jew and Christian alike, need mercy, just as all men need rain. For Portia the heart is metaphorically the seat of love, wherein mercy is 'enthronèd' (4.1.190), but for Shylock the heart is literally the source of life blood, to be cut out because he will not choose to find mercy in his heart for his enemy.

'OVER-NAME THEM' (1.2.30)

In literature the significance of names has enjoyed a time-honoured tradition. Shakespeare is likewise interested in the problem of naming his characters, and 'what's in a name' has always been a critical fascination for his casting of characters. As William Faulkner suggests in *Light in August*, 'a man's name, which is supposed to be just the sound for who he is, can be somehow an augur of what he will do, if other men can only read the meaning in time'.[31] Sir Philip Sidney explains the importance of names in a similar fashion. In his praise of the educational value of comedy to 'open [one's] eyes', especially to one's faults, Sidney observes the functional and linguistic importance of names. The character's name, along with other significant characteristics, such as specific manners of speech and gesture, serves as the 'signifying badge'. Through a comedy 'we get as it were an experience what is to be looked for of a niggardly Demea, of a crafty Davus, of a flattering Gnatho, of a vainglorious Thraso; and not only to know what effects are to be expected, but to know who be such by the signifying badge given them by the comedian'.[32] For example, Gratiano is a functional name. In Florio's Italian dictionary 'Gratiano' is defined as 'a gull, a fool or clownish fellow in a play or comedy', most appropriate for Gratiano's self-defined role ('Let me play the Fool', 1.1.79), and in the *commedia dell'arte* Gratiano was the name of the comic doctor.[33] To recognise that characters' names are significant, however, is quite a different matter from trying to interpret what the significance might be. Shakespeare chooses or creates all the names for his characters in this play, despite the abundance of names which he could have simply borrowed from his several fictional sources.

The question of names in *The Merchant of Venice*, especially the biblical names, has proved particularly puzzling, and as Murray J. Levith notes, 'more has been written on Shylock's name than any other in Shakespeare, and many sources for it have been suggested'.[34] For naming a Jewish father and daughter Shakespeare probably follows Marlowe's lead and looks to the Bible for inspiration in naming. Some have been surprised that Marlowe would choose the name of a New Testament Jew for his Barabas when he gives his daughter Abigail an Old Testament name. Marlowe, however, takes two of the best biblical names for his purposes, and Shakespeare is hard pressed to match the choice. Marlowe's genius here is his awareness of the functional significance of his name choices. Barabas, for example, is introduced in a 'choice' scene in the New Testament that illustrates Hunter's illumination of the concept of the 'Jewish choice': will the people choose Barabas or Christ to be crucified? Barabas's name, moreover, is glossed in the Geneva–Tomson Bible as meaning 'sonne of confusion'. The name of his daughter Abigail is also biblical, the name of Jesse's daughter, a name meaning 'the father's joy', which suits Barabas until Abigail converts to Christianity, and then he kills her. Even Barabas's Turkish slave has a biblical name, 'Ithamore', meaning 'wo to the change' (Exod 6.23).

The use of such biblical names is an important point of dramatic originality. A Jewish character need not be given any proper name, as is the case in Shakespeare's source, *Il Pecorone*, or the name need not be biblical, as is the case in Wilson's play where the Jewish moneylender is Gerontus, and in the undated ballad where the Jewish usurer is Gernutus. Nor do usurers in English

Renaissance drama have biblical names, as Stonex's references to such usurers indicate: 'Gripe', 'Pisaro', 'Hog', 'Vermine', 'Littlegood', 'Lucre', 'Hoard', 'Quomodo', 'Tenterhooke', 'Morecraft', 'Earthworm', 'Whirlpit', 'Sir Giles Overreach', 'Bloodhound', 'Rufaldo', and 'Hornet'.[35]

More work continually needs to be done on this topic of naming, but for our purpose here of exploring the play's artistic unity, we will focus only on those names that have posed the greatest obstacle to understanding the logic and pattern of Shakespeare's choice of names, some of which he invents, such as Jessica, Nerissa, and Bassanio, or adapts, such as Shylock. For the biblical names the obvious starting point is the Bible, in the vernacular versions we can be reasonably certain Shakespeare knew, especially the Geneva Bible, the Bishops' Bible, and the Geneva–Tomson Bible. When the Geneva Bible was first published, in 1560, it included an appendix of two tables, the first being 'the interpretation of the proper names which are chiefly found in the Old Testament'.[36] The most thorough concordance for the meaning of these proper names, the listing of their various forms from different translations, and the sketching of biography for the bearers of major names (e.g., Jacob) is the one done by Robert F. Herrey (1578).[37] From 1580 to 1615 this concordance was bound with all the quarto Geneva Bibles, except for those with Tomson's version of the New Testament.

I suggest that some of the unique information in this concordance indicates that Shakespeare, as well as Marlowe, knew it and used it.[38] Before we begin to try to unravel the sense underlying Shakespeare's name choices, a word of caution regarding the matter of names is appropriate. Shakespeare often proves as complexly eclectic as he is in the multiple use of his literary sources for plot, so that a name can have several meanings or associations, not just one, and therein Shakespeare enriches the linguistic texture of his drama through wordplay. Different members of the audience, depending on knowledge and background, would catch the nuances most familiar to them.

The names for the Jewish characters – Shylock, Tubal, Chus, and Jessica – pose the most problems, and to a lesser extent, the allusions to the biblical names, Jacob, Laban, Leah, Hagar, Daniel, and Balthazar.[39] A recent critic makes much of the Hebrew derivation of these names. Given the vernacular biblical apparatus readily available to Shakespeare and his fellow Elizabethans regarding the significance of Hebrew nomenclature, we cannot conclude, as does Gary Goldstein, that *The Merchant of Venice* was written by Edward de Vere, the Earl of Oxford, because 'the names of the four Jewish characters, and in particular the name of Shylocke' derive from the Hebrew text of the Old Testament, and given de Vere's level of education, he, not Shakespeare, could probably read Hebrew.[40] If we grant that the Bible is the primary source (but not the only source in the case of Shylock) for all of these names, a very interesting pattern appears to govern why Shakespeare chose the specific names he did for his Jewish characters. This pattern derives from the importance of genealogy in the Bible regarding the role the Jews play in the salvation history of mankind. Shakespeare's use of biblical names looks simultaneously to the Old and to the New Testaments. I suggest that, like Shakespeare's choice of the name Gratiano, these names are more important for their functional significance than for their etymological significance, and this significance of a name for what a character is and does, not just what a name means per se, has been largely overlooked in the play's criticism.

Both the Old and New Testaments have important genealogical lists to illustrate the descent of mankind from Adam and Eve and to validate the genealogy of God's Chosen People, and the genealogy of the Messiah who was to come through the Chosen People. The Messiah's direct line of descent was to derive from Jacob and Leah through their son, Judah, and his tribe, that is, through the root of Jesse and the house of David. The Messiah was to be both the new Adam and the new David, and He was to be the spiritual 'inheritance' promised to Abraham and his seed, their ultimate 'blessing', in addition to God's physical blessings of land and progeny as gifts to His people. The Messiah was to be the fulfilment of the Law (the Mosaic Law regulating the civic and spiritual duties of Jews). As 'the Anointed One' or 'Christ' ('Messiah'), through divine love He would save God's people from the wages of sin and death, incurred through man's first choice of disobedience in the Garden of Eden. Already a constellation of related words and ideas begins to surface, recalling the play's similar interest in matters of family (parents and offspring), gift/blessing and inheritance (physical and spiritual), the law and the new law of love, promise/oath and covenant, choice and consequence, and loss and deliverance.

How does Shakespeare's choice of biblical names for his Jewish characters relate to the genealogical emphasis in the Bible that establishes the Judaeo-Christian line of descent for the salvation of humankind? The easiest way to grasp a picture of this emphasis is to examine the helpful 'tree' of the family of man, graphically depicted in the opening pages of the Bishops' Bible, to illustrate 'Christ's Line' from Adam and Eve.[41] (See adapted illustration, Figure 2.) Visual emphasis is accorded important names, such as Noah, who will repeople the world after the Deluge through his three sons: Sem (from whom the Hebrews will descend), Cham (from whom the Ethiopians and Egyptians will descend), and Japheth (from whom the Europeans will descend). Cham and Japheth father non-Jewish or Gentile nations, and therefore this biblical genealogy depicts the Judaeo-Christian direction of Sem's line. Especially strong visual emphasis is given to the important names of Jesse (Ishai or Isai) and David, from whom the Messiah will descend and repeople the kingdom of God (sig. 5^r).

Shakespeare's choice of the names Tubal and Chus for Jewish characters has always puzzled critics because these are not Jewish names, and Noble even suggests these are 'Scriptural mistakes' on Shakespeare's part.[42] They are not. It appears that Shakespeare appropriates these names from two of Noah's sons – Chus descends from Ham and Tubal from Japheth – to use as names for Shylock's 'countrymen' primarily because they are *not* in the Judaeo-Christian line of direct descent. Ham and Tubal represent the non-Jewish stock from which the rest of the world's population descends after God's wrathful justice for human sinfulness has been executed through the Flood. This global destruction is counterbalanced by God's mercy to Noah and his sons because this one good man, and his offspring, are delivered to start a new life in a renewed world in order to preserve the Church of God: 'Noah delivered the Church, and preserved it by his obedience' (Gn 5, 29, gloss).

The glosses in the Geneva Bible are particularly helpful here for understanding this. Ham (Cham), the father of Chanaan, does not receive Noah's blessing but is cursed because Ham saw his father's nakedness (Gn 9.26).[43] But Shem (Sem) and Japheth (Japhet) showed Noah decent respect; Shem, father of the Hebrews, is blessed and 'in his stock is the Church preserved' (Gn 10.21, gloss), and Japheth, father of the Gentiles, is also blessed because God promises that Japheth's stock will 'dwell in the tents of Shem'. This means that 'the Gentiles, which came of Japheth and which

74

'This Table setteth out to the eye the *genealogy of Adam, so passing by the Patriarchs, Judges, Kings,* Prophtees [sic], and Priests, and the fathers of their time, continuing *in lineal descent to Christ our Saviour.*'

[Illustration of their taking forbidden fruit in the Garden]

('Sem obtained Asia, Cham Africa, Japhet Europa . . . The generation of Sem shall be followed . . . for of the other two sprang the gentiles.)

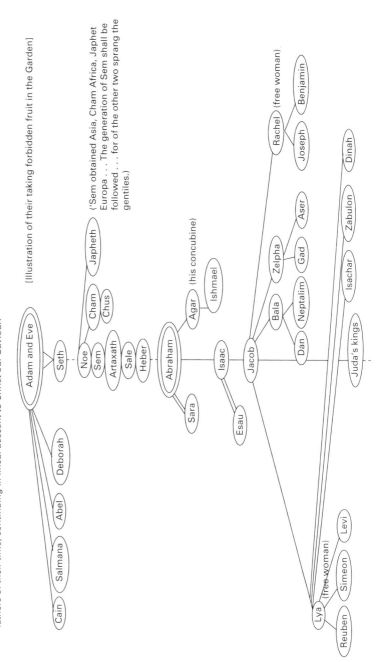

75

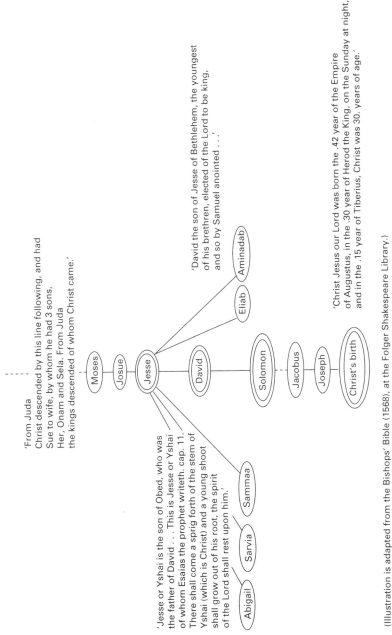

'From Juda
Christ descended by this line following, and had
Sue to wife, by whom he had 3 sons,
Her, Onam and Sela. From Juda
the kings descended of whom Christ came.'

'David the son of Jesse of Bethlehem, the youngest
of his brethren, elected of the Lord to be king,
and so by Samuel anointed . . .'

'Christ Jesus our Lord was born the .42 year of the Empire
of Augustus, in the .30 year of Herod the King, on the Sunday at night,
and in the .15 year of Tiberius, Christ was 30. years of age.'

Moses

Josue

Jesse

David

Solomon

Jacobus

Joseph

Christ's birth

Eliab

Aminadab

'Jesse or Yshai is the son of Obed, who was
the father of David . . . This is Jesse or Yshai
of whom Esaias the prophet writeth. cap. 11.
There shall come a sprig forth of the stem of
Yshai (which is Christ) and a young shoot
shall grow out of his root, the spirit
of the Lord shall rest upon him.'

Abigail

Sarvia

Sammaa

(Illustration is adapted from the Bishops' Bible (1568), at the Folger Shakespeare Library.)

FIGURE 2   *Diagram of biblical genealogy*

were separated from the Church, should be joined to the same by the persuasion of Gods spirit and preaching of the Gospel' (Gn 9.27 and gloss). In our play set in Italy, where so much word-play revolves around 'Jew/Hebrew' and 'Gentile', it is worth bearing in mind the definition of 'Gentiles' given in this Bible: 'The Jews so call all countries ['isles of the Gentiles'] which are separated from them by sea, as Greece, Italy, &c. which were given to the children of Japheth, of whom came the Gentiles' (Gn 10.5, gloss).

Herrey's concordance further reveals the significance of the names 'Tubal' and 'Chus'. Shakespeare's choice of 'Tubal' for a Venetian Jew is particularly apt because 'the Jewes called Italy by his name' (sig. E1^v). In prophesying the vocation of the Gentiles who by faith will be made the children of Abraham, Isaiah says that God 'will scatter the rest of the Jews, which escape destruction, into divers nations', and one of those nations is 'Tubal', glossed as 'Italy' (Isa 66.19, glosses). Although Tubal does not originate as a name for a Hebrew in the Bible, it can become the name for either a Gentile or a Hebrew in the course of human history. The meanings of the name 'Tubal' are *'borne*, or *brought*, or *worldly*, or *confusion*, or *slander*' (sig. E1^v). If Shakespeare cultivates any of these meanings, the most promising ones are 'worldly' and 'confusion'; indeed, 'Barabbas' is taken to mean 'son of confusion'. Like Shylock, Tubal is a very wealthy Hebrew, and his 'torturing' of Shylock with news of joy about Antonio's losses, that is counterpointed with news of sorrow about Jessica's losses, might be seen on one level as a 'confusion' of emotional extremes and a confusion of priorities, the focus being on loss of worldly wealth, whether Antonio's ships or Shylock's ducats. Solanio prepares us for such enacted 'confusion' when he describes Shylock's verbal confusion of ducats and daughter: 'I never heard a passion so confused, / So strange, so outrageous, and so variable' (2.8.12–3).

'Chus', the form of the name in the Bishops' Bible, is mentioned only once in the play, and the name means *'blacke*, or *Ethiopia*' (sig. B2^v). The gloss for 'Cush', the form of the name in the Geneva Bible, is fuller: *'blacknesse*, or *heate*. A country called now Ethiopia . . . so named of *Cush* the sonne of Ham'; Ethiopia in Hebrew is called *'Chus*, or *Chush*'; it is the 'country from the Indus next Egypt, between flood Nilus and the ocean sea' (sigs. B3^r, B6^r), and 'Chus' [sic] is so designated on the map in the Geneva Bible (fol. 2^r). A Moor, for example, would logically come from this area of Africa, and interestingly enough Shakespeare introduces into Belmont the Prince of Morocco as well as a Moorish woman for whose pregnancy Lorenzo will justly hold Lancelot account-able, despite 'how every fool can play upon the word!' (3.5.31–6). Built into this play is a cosmopolitan sense of the peoples and places of the world; Portia's suitors come from 'the four corners of the earth' (2.7.39) and Antonio's ships sail to six different far-flung ports. At the same time, the unworldly jostles the worldly when life and death, conscience and devil, heaven and earth are at stake.

Thus both names for Shylock's 'countrymen' are not originally Hebrew names, but their bearers represent Noah's other two sons who, together with Shem, father the nations of the world. They are eponymous names for their respective countries, Italy and Ethiopia, to which Jews migrated after the loss of their own na-tive land. These name choices are not really errors on Shakespeare's part, as has been thought. Rather they seem to suggest Shake-speare's thematic interest in the family of man that is bred on the literal bond of flesh, all being sons and daughters of Adam and Eve, but which can only be harmoniously united if based on the spiritual bond of the knowledge of God. The significance of Shake-speare's biblical name choices presents a major challenge to a twentieth-century production that endeavours to communicate some portion of this significance to its modern audience, an audience so much less familiar with this matter than its Elizabethan coun-terpart. One possible approach would be to use helpful programme notes, an interracial cast that would visually signal cosmopolitan Venice as well as the play's interest in 'the family of man', and something like the map of the world covering the stage floor that was used in some scenes of Terry Hands's Royal Shakespeare Theatre production of 1971.

'SHYLOCK IS MY NAME' (4.1.172)

How does Shylock's name fit in this possible schema of biblical salvation-history for mankind? Two biblical names have been suggested as the basis for Shylock's name, and it has not been observed that both names are in the line of Shem, that is, the family of Hebrews, as well as in the direct line of Christ, as are the names of Shylock's immediate family, his wife Leah and his

daughter Jessica. The two names are 'Shelah' (Gn 10.24, 11.12; 1
Chr 1.18, 24) and 'Shiloh' (Gn 49.10). Because spelling and pronunciation are not standardised in the sixteenth century, we will
confine our consideration of this matter to the biblical sources
we can be reasonably certain Shakespeare knew. Shakespeare would
not know the Hebrew but rather the current English translitera-
tions of the Hebrew and the English definitions of Hebrew names.
For example, the most accurate transliteration of the Hebrew for
'Shelah' is 'Shalach'.[44] This is much more similar in sound than
sight to 'Shylock', but to what extent Elizabethans *heard* that pronunciation when the Bible was read in church is difficult to determine on the basis of the variant spellings ('Selah' in the Bishops'
Bible and 'Sala' in the Lucan genealogy in the Geneva Bible, Lk
3.35), all of which suggest a softer 'ah' pronunciation than the
normalisation to 'ach' which begins in the seventeenth century.
Yet this very problem seems to be understood, and even casually
treated, by Morwyng in his translation of Joseph's Jewish history, because he renders one Babylonian Jewish name with inter-
changeable spellings, 'Shiloch' and 'Shiloh'.[45] We will return later
to the importance of this name in Joseph's history.

Shelah is the grandson of Shem, Noah's firstborn son. As Karl
Elze, followed by Jacob L. Cardozo and Christopher Spencer, points
out, that name appears in the same Chapter 10 of Genesis as do
the names Tubal and Chus, and Elze also notes that Shelah's name
reappears in the next chapter (11.12–15), followed by the name
Iscah (11.29) that Elze thinks might serve as the basis for Shakespeare's Jessica (rendered as 'Jesca' in earlier English Bibles and
'Ischa', 'Jese', or 'Jescha' in Italian Bibles).[46] This cluster of names,
drawn from two successive chapters in Genesis, seems quite suggestive. Moreover, when Shelah is first introduced he is significantly identified as the father of Eber, from whom the Hebrews
take their name.[47] But the biblical glosses provide an even fuller
interpretation of how Elizabethans might interpret the importance
of the genealogical line of Shem (Shelah – Eber – Abraham – Isaac
– Jacob – Jesse – David – Christ) as the stock through which the
Church of God was to be preserved. Shelah's name appears four
times because the focus is on highlighting the importance of this
genealogy. A fifth and sixth appearance of the same name, but
not the same person, has not been noticed; another 'Shelah', the
youngest son of Judah and a Canaanite woman, is referred to
once in Genesis (38.5), in the genealogy of Judah, because 'the

Messiah should come of him' (38.1, gloss). Again, in the First Book of Chronicles, where Judah's sons are listed, the gloss explains that although Judah was not Jacob's eldest son, yet the genealogy for the sons of Israel begins here because the author 'would come to the genealogy of David, of whom came Christ' (2.3, gloss).[48]

Given the signposting of these glosses, it is quite possible that in his reading Shakespeare noted the reappearance of the same name, 'Shelah', within these two important, related genealogical contexts, the first establishing the stock of the Hebrews and the second establishing within that stock the direct line of Christ through Judah. If so, Shakespeare could find in the name 'Shelah'/ 'Shelach' doubly rich associations, a name that anticipates the fathering of the Hebrews in general and the fathering of Christ in particular. For example, when the name of 'Shelah' is reintroduced in 1 Chronicles, the focal emphasis on genealogy also reappears in both the argument to the first book and its text and glosses – 'This first book containeth a brief rehearsal of the children of Adam unto Abraham, Isaac, Jacob, and the twelve Patriarchs, chiefly of Judah and of the reign of David, because Christ came of him according to the flesh' ('The Argument') – and there are specific references to Shem, Arpachshad, and Shelah because from them would come the stock of Abraham, the Hebrews 'which were afterwarde called Israelites of Israel, which was Jacob: and Jews of Judah, because of the excellency of that tribe' (1.18,24 and glosses).

According to Herrey's concordance of names, 'Shelah' means *sending or spoyling* (sig. D7ʳ). If Shakespeare refers to these meanings, what does 'sending' indicate? Elze takes the meaning as 'shot', as in a missile or weapon,[49] which accords well with the related sense of 'spoiling' as robbery, pillage, destruction. Perhaps it is no coincidence that one of the most common criticisms levelled against usurers in Elizabethan anti-usury literature is that they are spoilers of others in a trade that is equivalent to theft and murder. Bishop John Jewel, commenting on how David complained about the land where he was persecuted (Ps 54), maintains: '*Usury and deceipt departeth not from their streets*, one seeketh to spoil and eat up another.' Jewel consistently links the 'unmerciful spoiling' of usury with deception, theft, and murder, popular associations at the time: usury is 'theft, it is the murthering of our brethren.'[50] And in the undated *Ballad of Gernutus* the cruelty of its Jewish

usurer is described as the spoiling of his victim: 'he [the mer-
chant] must spoiled be' and 'the bloody Jew' is ready 'to spoil
the blood of Innocent, / by forfeit of his Bond'.[51] This emphasis
on the usurer as a spoiler underlies the debate over usury between Shylock and Antonio (1.3), as an Elizabethan, but not a
modern, audience would understand the ideas and language of
that debate. Shylock is, of course, proud to be a usurer because
by making money 'breed' he becomes very prosperous, as was
his favourite patriarch, Jacob. But how one gets wealth and how
one views wealth are issues in the play that relate all its characters. Is Shylock a 'spoiler' of the commonwealth if he leaves
moaning victims in his path (3.3)? Does Shylock have a spoiling
mind if he can be crafty and subtle (1.3)? Does he rejoice in another's misfortune (3.1, 4.1)? When does 'thrift' become 'theft' and
no true 'blessing' (1.3.82)?

   The other biblical name suggested as closest in form to Shylock
is 'Shiloh' (Gn 49.10).[52] 'Shelah' and 'Shiloh' are similar enough
in appearance, and both have negative etymological meanings but
positive functional associations with the biblical themes of blessing and salvation for God's chosen people. Like the negative
meaning of 'Shelah', 'Shiloh' can mean in Syrian 'mocked, or
deceiving' (sig. D7^v), as noted only in Herrey's concordance,[53] and
these meanings are appropriate for Shylock. The name of Shylock's
favourite patriarch, Jacob, similarly means *'a supplanter, a deceiver'*
(sig. C1^v), and Jacob supplants his older brother Esau through
buying his birthright (Gn 25.31) and stealing Isaac's blessing (Gn
27.18). In the Geneva Bible and the Bishops' Bible the gloss for
'Shiloh' in Genesis (49.10) significantly refers to Christ the Messiah, a meaning that at first appears incongruous for Shylock.
But let us reconsider the context for the appearance of 'Shiloh' in
Genesis, which not surprisingly complements the genealogical motif
associated with the name 'Shelah'. When Jacob prepares for death,
as a father he blesses his twelve sons, who will father the twelve
tribes of Israel, and he closes his blessing of Judah with these
words: 'The scepter shall not depart from Judah, nor a lawgiver
from between his feet, until Shiloh come, and the people *shall be*
gathered unto him'. 'Shiloh' is glossed in the Geneva Bible: 'which
is Christ the Messiah, the giver of all prosperity: who shall call
the Gentiles to salvation'. Although Shylock is no 'Messiah', an
Elizabethan audience could link the wordplay on his name to his
requested conversion, which would be seen as a turning toward

their Messiah in the gathering together of God's people.

The Genevan gloss on 'Shiloh' significantly emphasises the calling of the Gentiles to salvation, and this calling enlarges the definition of God's elect. It is understandably a definition Shylock resents and resists until the trial. The old emphasis on salvation through flesh-and-blood descent within the favoured nation of Israel becomes now the new emphasis on rebirth in the spirit that enables all people, regardless of race or rank, to be part of God's kingdom. Hence, Shakespeare's comic use of the Gobbos (a blind father blessing his hairy son) to parody Jacob's obtainment of his father's blessing is not merely clever allusion or local colour but another episode in the play that points to its subtext of the divine comedy of salvation. Isaac's blessing is no ordinary prayer. His 'worldly blessings' given to Jacob embrace God's 'heavenly promises' and convey the inheritance of His promise and the 'lawful authority whereby the grace of God's election was testified'.[54] As Danson keenly observes, Jacob's subtle stealing of his father's blessing from his older brother Esau was interpreted as prefiguring God's election of the Gentiles.[55] God's choice of Jacob over Esau was thought to confirm this idea of God's unquestionable election of His own, and this idea contradicts Shylock's recalcitrant view of Lancelot as the fleshly outsider, as 'Ishmael' (see Rom 9.8, gloss) or 'Hagar's offspring' (2.5.42), which will be considered later. Likewise, Esau's selling of his birthright to Jacob for food is glossed: 'Esau's earthy mind careth but for to satisfy his carnal desire' (Bishops' Bible, Gn 25.33, gloss). How Shakespeare might use Jessica's selling of her father's and mother's betrothal ring, a possible symbol of her physical birthright, to parody this biblical event will be considered in the next chapter. But at least we should observe here that Jessica's and Lancelot's parodies of the Esau-to-Jacob transferrals of birthright and blessing are probably associated with our characters' mutual departures from 'Shylock' (whose name can recall the Judaeo-Christian line of 'Shelah' and 'Shiloh'). Shakespeare thereby unifies this material in light of the Christian scheme of biblical salvation-history so dear to his own audience.

'Shiloh', as a place name, has another meaning in the Old Testament which ironically suits Shakespeare's dramatic emphasis on Shylock's 'house'. 'Shiloh' is the ancient site where the Israelites set up the Tabernacle, the House of God in which was kept the Ark of the Covenant (Jos 18.1; Jgs 18, 31; 1 Sam 1.24).[56] 'Shiloh' in this sense also relates to the aforementioned ideas and to Jacob's blessing of his son Judah, through whose tribe 'Shiloh' would come. Because the Israelites fell to 'graven images', God forsook 'the habitation at Shiló, even the Tabernacle where he dwelt among men' (Ps 78.60) and delivered the Ark and His people to the enemy. When the Ark was returned, God 'refused the tabernacle of Joseph . . . the tribe of Ephraim' and chose 'the tribe of Judah & mount Zion which he loved'; thus, David brought the Ark to Jerusalem, where eventually it was placed in the Tabernacle of Solomon's Temple (see Ps 78.55–72 and glosses). Shakespeare's Shylock may have a 'sober house' (2.5.35), but it does not appear to be a godly house by either Judaic or Christian standards, according to Jessica and Lancelot. In his affection for earthly treasure Shylock uses his house as a symbolic tabernacle for his locked up gold and silver coins bearing their own graven images. It is from this symbolic house that Jessica steals with her father's 'idols' secured in a small wooden ark, a 'casket . . . worth the pains' (2.6.34), tossed to Lorenzo. To play upon a name and its associations appeals to Shakespeare's fertile imagination. The potential for connections between 'Shelah' and 'Shiloh', to create the adapted name 'Shylock', is not hard to see when placed within the larger context surrounding these biblical names, the context of fatherly begetting and blessing of offspring, fleshly birth and spiritual rebirth, earthly and heavenly rewards, and God's grand scheme of salvation for all the peoples of the world.

   Shylock has become such a famous character that we have to remind ourselves that we do not know his name until Shakespeare wants us to know it. Forty-three and a half lines of speech are uttered by Shylock and Bassanio before we hear the name of the man from whom Bassanio seeks a financial loan. 'Shylock, do you hear?', and we hear Shylock's name for the first time. The name is well placed. Bassanio's half-line interrupts what appears to be Shylock's self-debate over his available resources (really Shylock's self-revelation to the audience) and completes the metre of Shylock's half-line to us, 'If I forgive him!' (1.3.44). This scene's opening dialogue is filled with clues suggesting what kind of a name the audience might expect to hear. Probably the various members of an Elizabethan audience, depending on their individual knowledge, would hear in his name several different but related meanings. One overlooked clue that Shylock actually repeats is the pride he takes in his particular tribe, never specifically identified in the play, as well as his 'sacred nation': 'Cursed be my tribe / If I forgive him!' These are his words that immediately precede Bassanio's utterance of his name. Within the next five lines Shylock introduces the name of his friend, 'Tubal, a wealthy Hebrew *of my tribe*' (1.3.43–9, my italics). As we know now, Tubal is not a Hebrew name in the Bible, but it is glossed in the sixteenth century as associated with Italy and therefore can be an appropriate name for an Italian Jew after the loss of Jerusalem.

What tends to confirm the general argument for the importance of biblical genealogy is the names Shakespeare chooses for Shylock's immediate family and Shylock's desired identification with the patriarch Jacob.[57] If Shylock wishes to be like Jacob, then the choice of Leah for a wife links him more to Laban, who deceived Jacob by substituting Leah for Rachel. The wife Jacob chose and preferred was Rachel. But if Shylock is to be associated with Jacob and the tribe of Judah and their specific role in salvation-history, then his wife's name must be Leah. Moreover, like Jacob and Leah, Shylock and Leah have only one daughter, but unlike Jacob's Dinah ('judgement') who 'went out to see' the Gentiles and gets raped (Gn 34.1–31), Shylock's Jessica clambers up to her father's casements 'to gaze on' her Gentile husband-to-be, and honourable marriage, not rape, is her blessing. The story of Jacob's only daughter provides an interesting contrast to what Shakespeare will do with Shylock's only daughter and the related motifs of marriage with strangers, dowry, deceit, and revenge. When we discuss Jessica's name, as a probable feminisation of Jesse, we will see again the important emphasis on the Messianic line.

Other non-biblical suggestions have been offered for Shylock's name which raise possible puns. Norman Nathan suggests 'shullock', used as a term of contempt meaning to idle about, to slouch, and Christopher Spencer posits two puns in a '"semi-morality" combination *Shy* and *Lock*, suggesting apartness, secrecy, and hoarding – all characteristics approriate for [the] usurer'.[58] Some in Shakespeare's audience might respond to the name only at this basic level, as they would to the names of some other usurers in the drama, 'Morecraft' and 'Littlegood'. But to Spencer's good suggestion should be added the stronger Elizabethan sense of 'shy' that signifies not merely timid apartness but rather distrust and suspicion, cautious reservation, wariness in speech and deed, and even averseness to a specified person or thing.[59]

Indeed, this sense of 'shy' informs Barabas's Latin motto, which translated means, 'I am always closest to myself', just as Shakespeare's second syllable, 'lock', captures Barabas's line preceding his motto: 'Warily guarding that which I ha' got' (1.1.186–7). Despite volumes of criticism on Marlowe and Shakespeare, we still have much to learn about how Shakespeare responded to the dramatic challenges Marlowe set.[60] Some critics have also noted that 'Shylock' might possibly be derived from a British surname.[61]

The most important non-biblical source for Shylock's name is Morwyng's translation of Joseph's *History of the Jews' Common Weal*. Sir Israel Gollancz was the first to suggest that Shakespeare's Shylock might have been derived from Ben Joseph's Babylonian Jew, 'Schiloch'.[62] It seems quite likely that Shakespeare was aware of this Jewish name, especially because it is juxtaposed with the name of his enemy in arms, Antonius, the conquering Roman captain's name. If Nashe could read and use Joseph's history, as he did for his *Christ's Tears over Jerusalem* (1593), so could Shakespeare. If Shakespeare does borrow these two names for his characters and adapts them as 'Shylock' and 'Antonio', he also adds to these nominal references other layers of meaning for these names, or their approximate forms, found elsewhere, particularly 'Shelah' and 'Shiloh' in the Bible. Shakespeare could rely on most of his audience's recognition of biblical wordplay in names, but an awareness of these two names in Joseph's history would speak to a select audience and would be 'caviary to the general' (*Ham*, 2.2.437).

However, the close association of these two specific names in Joseph ('Schiloch' or 'Schiloh' and 'Antonius' or 'Antony') is intriguing for how closely the forms of these names parallel Shakespeare's 'Shylock' and 'Antonio'. Although these two men play a small role in Joseph's history, does their moment have any elements, other than the names, that might have caught Shakespeare's interest? There are a few possibilities worth mentioning. The crux of the story revolves around life-and-death battle between Hebrews and Romans. Antonius is described as 'a valiant man and a good warrior' who is defending the town of Askalon against a siege by the Hebrews, including 'Schiloch the Babylonian' (sig. L5ʳ). In the battle waged the Hebrews 'took a good heart unto them, & stood manfully in their stations . . . trusting in the Lord God of Israel', resolved that it is better to die in battle 'than to fly from our enemies' (sig. L5ᵛ). 'Antony' slew many, including

'Schiloh the Babylonian' (sig. L5ᵛ). This story's slaughter is the stuff of tragedy, but Shakespeare's comedy features no literal battle but rather a battle of wits that ends with no deaths. This, however, may seem a rather tenuous connection. If Shakespeare responds to the context for these names, the references to 'Babylonian' and to 'Roman' honour might also have caught his attention. Schiloch is a Babylonian Jew, and in the trial scene Portia will use Daniel's Babylonian name (Balthazar) to identify her disguised self as a lawyer-judge. Shakespeare's Antonio is praised as 'one in whom / The ancient Roman honour appears / Than any that draws breath in Italy' (3.2.294). Although the concept of Roman honour is commonplace, Joseph is surprisingly openminded about giving praise to the enemy when merited. [63]

'GENTLE JESSICA' (2.4.19)

Shakespeare's 'invention' of the name Jessica for Shylock's daughter is pivotal for illuminating how Shakespeare uses the biblical names, their genealogical and etymological significance, for Jewish–Christian conflict and resolution in the play. Marlowe once again suggests a direction which Shakespeare will develop further. Marlowe names Barabas's daughter 'Abigail', which means 'the father's joy', and Barabas says as much, and much more, when he hugs his bags of gold retrieved for him by Abigail: 'O girl! O gold! O beauty! O my bliss! / Farewell, *my joy*, and by my fingers take / A kiss from him that sends it from his soul' (2.254–9, my italics). But the audience would also know that Abigail was the daughter of Jesse, from whose root comes Christ, the Messiah promised to Abraham and his stock, according to Christian theology (1 Sm 16:11–13; Mt 1, 5; Lk 3.32). Marlowe's *quadruple* use of literal conversion to Christianity (whether feigned or real) challenges Shakespeare to develop his own *double* use of it, which we will examine later. But for the understanding of naming here, we need to observe that Abigail's fake conversion to retrieve her father's gold makes her his 'joy'. But when Barabas proves his villainy by murdering Abigail's beloved, who never offended Barabas (3.3.41), Abigail leaves her 'hard-hearted' and 'unkind' father (3.3.36) to convert sincerely to Christianity. For this 'false and unkind' conversion and for her desire that he repent, Barabas claims she has 'lost' him (3.4.2), and he kills her now that he no longer per-

ceives her as his joy, refusing to repent his murders. Jessica, however, is granted a happy ending, and like many of Shakespeare's
comic heroines she, not her father, is in control of their parting;
Shakespeare rewrites Barabas's fatal lines about being 'lost' for
Jessica's comic ending: 'I have a father, you a daughter, lost' (2.5.55).

What is of special interest here is the shared allusion to Jesse
in the names of Abigail and Jessica, both of whom willingly convert to Christianity. The most likely explanation, thus far, of how
Shakespeare got the name Jessica is that Jessica is a feminisation
of Jesse, and Shakespeare may also intend wordplay on the name
'Iscah' or 'Jesca' as it is rendered in some earlier English Bibles.[64]
The first theory has received much less comment than it deserves.
Jesse had two daughters, Abigail and Zeruiah (1 Chron 2.16). It
might be argued that if Shakespeare wanted a female name related to Jesse, he had one ready made in Zeruiah. But he could
not expect many in his audience to recognise that name. Jesse, on
the other hand, is a very familiar name with associations that are
meaningful for the Judaeo-Christian lineage of the Church of God
mentioned repeatedly in the Geneva Bible's glosses and illustrated
prominently in the Bishops' Bible. If one was illiterate, one would
know the name Jesse from having heard it at church and possibly from seeing it depicted in cathedral art, especially 'Jesse win-
dows'.[65]

Isaiah's well-known prophecy about the 'root of Ishai [Jesse]'
(11.1; 11.10) is explained by Paul as Christ who reigns over the
Gentiles, and the striking gloss on that passage further demonstrates why 'gentle Jessica' (2.4.19) is so aptly named: 'Then seeing [Christ] took both the Jews and the Gentiles to his Fathers
glorie, they ought by his example to love together' (Rom 15.12).
Jessica, a Venetian Jewess, and Lorenzo, a Venetian Christian, do
just that. And so would Marlowe's Abigail and Don Mathias were
it not for Barabas's genealogical discrimination against all Christians as 'heretics' (2.3.309) because they are 'not of the seed of
Abraham' (2.3.227). The idea for an alliance of love between a
female Jewess and a male Christian originates in Marlowe's play,
but there is a notable difference. Unlike Jessica, who intends to
convert to Christianity by her marriage to Lorenzo, Abigail's love
for Don Mathias does not include any mention of a desire to convert. Not until it is tragically too late for Abigail and Don Mathias
does Abigail realise her father's perfidy and how he has sacrificed her in obtaining his 'extreme revenge' (3.3.42). Barabas's own

description of his 'one sole daughter, whom [he] hold[s] as dear
/ As Agamemnon did his Iphigen' (1.1.135–6) is a 'dear' description indeed because he will 'sacrifice her on a pile of wood' before he will let a Christian have her (2.3.52). Shakespeare's Jessica,
on the other hand, is prematurely 'wise' (2.6.54), and although it
troubles her deeply to be ashamed to be her father's daughter,
she recognises her father's unkindness before it would cost her
marriage, or perhaps even her life, as happens in Abigail's case
(2.3.15–20).

Shakespeare's decision to use the 'root' name of 'Jesse' for his
'Jessica' has etymological, in addition to functional, significance
that may also owe something to the idea of 'sacrifice' or 'oblation' that Marlowe develops for his Abigail. What does 'Jesse'
(frequently spelled 'Ishai') mean? The Geneva Bible glosses the
name as meaning 'a gift or oblation'. Herrey's concordance elaborates on this fundamental significance: *'a gift or an oblation*, or a
debitour, or *being'*, and it explains Jesse's importance: 'Christ promised all to come of his stock. Isa. 11.1' (sig. C5ᵛ). Modern attempts
to define the meaning of 'Jesse' tend to focus on 'being', rendering the meaning as 'Jehovah exists' or 'the Lord is'.[66] But that is
not the primary sense Elizabethans would have found in their
Bibles. The idea of 'gift' complements the elaborate variations of
the theme of 'giving', as opposed to the expectation of gaining
and getting, articulated in the meaning of the casket choices. Jessica's
first action in the play is an action of giving as she gives a ducat
to Lancelot, and this action distinguishes her from her father, who
dislikes giving in general, and in particular to Lancelot. Lancelot,
himself a 'merry devil', is leaving their house of 'hell' because
his master, whom he sees as 'the very devil incarnation' (2.220–
21), has not *given* to him: 'Give him a present? Give him a halter!
I am famished in his service' (2.2.86–7). But his new master is
introduced as a giver: 'give me your present to one Master Bassanio,
who indeed gives rare new liveries' (2.2.89).

But the idea of 'gift' for Jessica also applies to her very self as
well. She, as Shylock's and Leah's offspring, is God's gift to them;
God's promise of carnal blessings to Abraham and his seed includes the gift of progeny, as well as land (wealth, prosperity).
To be barren in the Old Testament means to be miserable or cursed,
and this idea of the gravity of barrenness explains the penalty of
barrenness (the forfeit of lawful propagation) which errant choosers
in the casket test must incur, a risk many suitors lack the courage

to undertake (1.2.101–2). This barrenness appropriately foils the joyful, jesting wagers on offspring in which the lovers indulge just as Lorenzo and Jessica enter Belmont (3.2.314–17). The sense of 'oblation' in the meaning of 'Jesse' further develops the basic meaning of 'gift' by designating the gift or sacrifice as one intended for God. This nuance could inform Jessica's conversion through marriage by which she hopes to 'be saved' (3.5.15).[67] Like Portia, it can be argued that Jessica 'stand[s] for sacrifice' (3.2.57).

But the addition of 'debitor' for 'Jesse' in Herrey's concordance is most intriguing because creditors and debtors abound in this play about loving and lending versus hating and lending, as they do not in Marlowe's play. Did the additional nuance of indebtedness catch Shakespeare's imagination for the daughter of a usurer (a creditor) whose approximate biblical name (as 'Shelah') meant a spoiler? Jessica is indebted to her father for her 'flesh and blood', but she claims not for her 'manners' (2.3.17–18). However, she seems to have learned his manners for how to deceive and steal effectively, but her intent is to give what she steals, not to gain and get solely for herself. Eloping with two jewels and two sealed bags of ducats, she will be further indebted to her father when she steals from him (just as he steals from others, given the common depiction of the usurer as a thief), a sufficient dowry to give to Lorenzo. For the name of a runaway Venetian daughter, Shakespeare, who knew Italian, might also take an oral hint from the Renaissance Italian verb, 'Iesse' used for 'Gisse', meaning 'should goe'.[68]

If we might digress briefly, an overlooked rationale that supports the argument that Jessica is a feminisation of Jesse rests on Shakespeare's similar formation of the names of the three female characters in the play. Jessica, Portia, and Nerissa all have names that are feminine conversions of masculine names so that all three women 'turn to men' (3.4.78) in names as well as cross-gendered disguise. The strongest clue for Portia's name is the evaluation of her as 'nothing undervalued / To Cato's daughter, Brutus' Portia' (1.2.165), who was renowned for her courage and wisdom, two qualities needed to thrive in the casket test. Being fathered and husbanded by such noble Romans, the historical Portia, whom Shakespeare will praise in *Julius Caesar*, serves as a model for the ideal woman and wife, and like her, Shakespeare's Portia flexes the stereotypical gender roles of their eras to resolve the hard choices they face.[69] Portia (Porcia in Latin) bears a feminine version of one of her father's names, Marcus Porcius Cato Uticensis, which derives from their most famous ancestor, Marcus Porcius Cato Censorius. From this illustrious ancestry Shakespeare garners some traits for his Portia: Cato Major strongly upheld traditional morality and had great legal ability (he wrote an encyclopedia that included a treatise on jurisprudence), and Cato Minor enjoyed a reputation for fairness and great moderation. Cato Major, the great-great-grandfather of Portia, also wrote that usurers were murderers because they destroyed the means by which one lived, and he expelled them from Sardinia.[70]

Some suggestions offered by others involve wordplay on Portia's name, even in conjunction with Nerissa's name. Norman Nathan thinks that Portia's name is 'witty' because Shylock is defeated by someone whose name means 'pig'.[71] Nathan argues, however, that Portia's name is meant to suggest 'port' because the unnamed Lady of Belmont rules over a port, and Shakespeare's Portia figuratively functions as a safe port or 'harbor for most of the characters in the play'.[72] Perhaps the wordplay that yields the most meaning is the Latin 'portio' for 'portion' (pronounced similarly to 'Portia') in the biblical sense of physical inheritance (Dt 21.17) as well as spiritual inheritance – 'The Lord is the portion of mine inheritance' (Ps 16.5).[73] Portia is a wealthy heiress, but her father, unlike Shylock, wisely realises that his daughter, not his ducats, is his real treasure, his real gift. Conjoining the possible seaworthy meaning of Portia's name with that of her maid, Nerissa, Nathan finds that Shakespeare derives Nerissa from the 'Latin *Nereis*, the name of a sea nymph and daughter of Nereus'.[74] The plural form of her name, 'Nereids', is used for all fifty daughters of Nereus, and hence a class of nymphae whose name derives from their father. The sea god 'Nereus', an old man of the sea, was believed to have great wisdom.[75] If Shakespeare is inventing Nerissa's name from 'Nereis', derived from Nereus, then Nerissa tries to emulate her paternal namesake's wisdom as well, just as Portia does the reputed wisdom of her paternal namesake and her own father, who, Nerissa tell us, 'was ever virtuous' (1.2.23). Nerissa's first appearance on stage presents her as a voice of wise counsel ('good sentences') for Portia's dilemma of not being free to choose or refuse a husband.

In addition to the feminisation of 'Jesse', a less obvious, but possible, suggestion for another biblical source for Jessica's name is 'Iscah', which is glossed in the Geneva Bible: 'Some think that this Iscah was Sarai' [Abrams wife] (Gn 11.29).[76] As we have noted, 'Iscah' is spelled 'Jesca' in earlier English Bibles, and the appearance of the name has the advantage of occurring in the chapter following the introduction of the names, Tubal, Chus, and Shelah. But the name Iscah is disyllabic, and Jessica is trisyllabic. Is the '-ca' ending of Jessica not only Shakespeare's feminine and Hebrew sounding suffix but also derived from the ending of 'Iscah'? Could Jessica be primarily a feminisation of Jesse and secondarily a play on 'Iscah'? There are pros and cons, but perhaps the former outweigh the latter. The argument against 'Iscah' rests on the general unfamiliarity of the name. It does not appear in the original Genevan table of names, but it does in Herrey's concordance, where 'Iscah' ('Iescha') is interpreted to mean: *'anoynting, covering, or shadowing,* or in the Syrian, *espying.* daughter of Haran' (sig. C5ᵛ). The name 'Iscah' appears on the same leaf as 'Ishai' (Jesse), separated by only one name entry, so perhaps the name caught Shakespeare's attention in this way, and he decided to couple meanings from two different names as he may have done with Shelah and Shiloh for Shylock.

The etymological meanings of 'Iscah' are suggestive for the character of Jessica Shakespeare creates, but not as helpful as the functional significance. For example, the idea of 'shadowing' could be allegorically interpreted as it appears in the Geneva Bible (Gal 4, heading) and as Andrew Willet uses the word: *'the lawe had a shadowe of good things to come'.*[77] Jessica functions typologically in her fulfilment of the Old Law in the New. The idea of 'espying' also fits Jessica's use of the window to espy a Christian 'worth a Jewès eye' (2.5.41). But this espying motif might also derive from Masuccio's *Il Novellino,* thought to be a source for the Jessica-Lorenzo plot, because the lover espies his damsel at a window. Then again, Marlowe also uses this window/look-out motif (2.3.259–62). How much the motif owes to the physical nature of the public playhouse is another matter because the window-stage at the balcony level invited such dramatic imagery, the balcony scene in *Romeo and Juliet* being the most famous example. However, if Shakespeare does associate Jessica with Iscah, he may suggest a thematic contrast between mother Leah and daughter Jessica through eye imagery. Leah (meaning *'painful,* or *wearied',* sig. C7ᵛ) appears to suffer from weak eyes, being described as 'blear-eyed' or 'tender-eyed' (Gn 29.17), but Sara was reputed for her holy faith which believes in 'things which are not seen' (Heb 11.1).

Jessica too has eyes of faith, 'a Jewès eye' being proverbial for
something of great value,[78] because she seeks God's grace.

The functional significance of linking Jessica's name to Iscah/
Sara concerns two points, Sara's virtuous reputation and Paul's
typological explanation of Sara, Leah, and Hagar that enriches
why Shakespeare chose Leah for Shylock's wife and why Shylock
chooses to see Lancelot as 'Hagar's offspring' (2.5.42).[79] Sara is
presented in the New Testament as the ideal wife (1 Pt 3.6) and
as a model of faith (Heb 11.11). The beautiful and faithful mother
of Israel (Is 51.2) is a model of virtue for the gentle Jessica, praised
by Lancelot as 'most sweet Jew' (2.3.11) and judged by her husband as having proved herself wise, fair, and true (2.6.53–8).
Lancelot's direction to Jessica to 'look out at window' to see a
Christian worthy of her 'Jewès eye' immediately precedes Shylock's
demand: 'What says that fool of Hagar's offspring, ha?' (2.5.42).
The 'triple relevance' of this biblical allusion from Shylock's perspective has already been explained.[80] But Shakespeare's line also
enriches greatly a hint found in Marlowe, when Barabas calls
Lodowick 'this offspring of Cain' (2.3.298).

What has gone unnoticed is the irony for Shylock, and as another of Shylock's biblical allusions that can be interpreted ironically it fits the comic pattern Shakespeare has devised for Shylock's
biblical allusions. 'Hagar' (Sara's Egyptian servant) means 'stranger',
and like Barabas (2.3.309), Shylock sees all Christians as heretics,
as estranged from the blood-and-flesh line of Abraham and Sara.
Shylock is a religious stranger in Christian Venice, but he also
takes pride in that fact, as does Barabas, seeing himself as superior to those not so descended, the offspring of Hagar. Hagar
was Pharoah's daughter, given as a slave to Sara, but God commanded Abraham to cast out Hagar and her son by Abraham
(Ishmael). Just as Hagar is the national mother of the twelve tribes
of Ishmael (Gn 25.11–6), so Leah and Rachel, the wives of Jacob,
become the mothers of the twelve tribes of Israel. For an Elizabethan audience aware of Paul's epistle to the Galatians, Shylock's
allusion boomerangs, and ironically links him with Hagar and
Ishmael while Lancelot, as a Christian, becomes the offspring of
Sara, born of God's promise. St Paul (Gal 4.21–31) surprisingly
uses the story of Sara and Hagar as an allegory to illustrate the
relationship between the Old Covenant of Mount Sinai (identified as Hagar) and the New Covenant of Christ (identified with
Sara). He bases his allegory on important associations of slavery/

flesh with the law, as opposed to liberty/God's promise with the spirit. Paul concludes that just as God commanded Abraham to cast out the slave woman and her son, so Christians should rid themselves of the enslaving doctrine of the Judaisers; salvation does not consist in the observance of the letter of the law, but salvation is God's free gift to those who live in the liberty of His holy spirit – 'the son of the servant shall not be heir with the son of the free woman' (Gal 4.29–30). Christians are born not after the manner of the flesh, but after the manner of the spirit, that is, 'after the *manner* of Isaac, children of the promise' (my italics). Jessica adapts Paul's language in her crucial conclusion about the bond, and the lack of it, between her and her father: 'But though I am daughter to his blood / I am not to his manners' (2.3.17–18).

The glosses in the Geneva Bible are most revealing for how an Elizabethan audience might be expected to hear the complexity of Shylock's line that indicates for them his mistaken view of salvation-history: 'Agar, and Sina represent the Law: Sara and Jerusalem the Gospel: Ishmael the Jewish Synagogue and Isaac the Church of Christ.' Paul claims Christians are born of the free woman [Sara], not the servant [Hagar]: 'we are in the Church of Christ, which is our mother, & out of the Synagogue which is a servant under the Law'. Thus, Shakespeare's audience would see Jessica's physical mother as Leah and her spiritual mother as Sara. As a namesake of Iscah, Jessica is allegorically a type of the free woman, Sara, although Shylock treats Jessica much as he treats Lancelot, as a servant, ordering her about to do his will, no tenderness in his language (2.5.3–49). This night she becomes a free woman literally and spiritually. Having been locked up in Shylock's 'sober house' (2.5.35), this night she has her father's keys and sets herself free from the house she calls 'hell' (2.3.2). Jessica becomes the heir or 'possessor' of God's promise to Abram, to which Shylock refers in his defence of a different kind of 'breeding', the breeding of gold and silver (1.3.63–88). But it is the lesser half of that divine promise, the promise of physical prosperity to God's chosen people, that Shylock the father proudly desires and thinks he deserves. Jessica the child intends to embrace the better half of the promise, the promise of spiritual prosperity, the inheritance of God Himself (Gn 15.1; Ps 16.5). According to Paul's allegory, an Elizabethan audience would also see Lancelot Gobbo, the literal servant in the play, as free-born in the spirit, and Shylock, the literal master, as enslaved to the Law. Shylock, not Lancelot,

would be seen as Hagar's offspring. These ideas and their imagery embedded in Shylock's view of Lancelot as 'Hagar's offspring' clarify Lancelot's hard choice, to run or not to run (2.2),
and his pregnant utterance, as he, like Jessica, exchanges one master
for another: ' . . . to bid my old master the Jew to sup tonight
with my new master the Christian' (2.4.17–18).

'GOOD LANCELOT GOBBO' (2.2.4)

The various meanings of the name, Lancelot Gobbo (spelled 'Jobbe'
in the first quarto), have been well analysed.[81] This clown appropriately bears a mixed name that looks toward the Old Testament, with 'Gobbo' being taken for 'Job', and toward the New
Testament, with Lancelot being a Christian name.[82] If 'Gobbo' is
intended as a nominal reference to the biblical Job, then Lancelot's
nominal linkage with God's long-suffering servant Job is comically parodic. Lancelot is in some ways almost an anti-Job figure.
Job courageously withstood the devil's testing of him, insisted
on his innocent conscience, resisted the 'friendly counsel' (2.2.23)
of his misguided friends, and humbly sought God's pardon for
himself and his friends for questioning God's will; therefore, the
exemplary 'patience of Job' (Jas 5.11) was blessed by God. Lancelot,
on the other hand, weakly avoids the choice offered by 'hard
conscience' (2.2.22) – to serve in good conscience his 'froward'
master and 'suffer wrong . . . patiently' – the choice that is biblically suggested as the way 'a servant' may follow Christ's example (2 Pet 18–23). Instead, our merry devil Lancelot, who has run
out of patience, will follow the friendly counsel of the fiend himself to run away from his master, whom he sees as 'a kind of
devil' (2.2.18), deserving no present or pardon but a halter. With
'rare fortune' (2.2.90) Lancelot runs into the man he wants for his
new master, one who will give him the good comforts of this
earth, which Lancelot receives proudly (2.2.131–40). But for all
his interest in the flesh, Lancelot does astutely observe and value
the difference in spirit between his two masters: 'The old proverb is very well parted between my master Shylock and you, sir:
you have the grace of God, sir, and he hath enough' (2.2.124–6).
   Shakespeare's choice of the name 'Gobbo' to play on 'Job' might
also be in part a clever response to Marlowe's own ironic use of
Job for Barabas. In the present adversity Barabas's countrymen

counsel him to 'remember Job', the exemplar of patience, but Barabas distorts this well-meant counsel by preferring physical comforts over spiritual ones (1.2.181–92), as his successor, Shylock, is also prone to do. If the impatient Lancelot and his preferment-seeking father do tend to act in anti-Job fashion by emphasising their own earthly prosperity, at least they acknowledge in Job-like fashion the primacy of the life of the spirit, the importance of having God's 'grace'. Their mutual choice to abandon the rich man to serve the poor gentleman is only an apparently foolish choice. The Gobbos may often be comic fools in their use of language and reasoning, but they are essentially well-grounded in their recognition of God's grace. This fundamental trait of right belief enhances Shakespeare's comic use of his servant named Gobbo, unlike Marlowe's tragic use of his servant, Ithamore, the Turkish slave whose intents and actions illustrate the baleful meaning of his name through the woeful changes he helps effect.

 Shakespeare rises to the challenge set by Marlowe's use of biblical names and transcends it through richer complexity of meaningful associations as he develops the idea of the family of man and God's chosen and blessed people. Shakespeare's probable adaptation of the biblical names 'Shelah' and 'Shiloh' for Shylock and 'Jesse' and 'Iscah' for Jessica are like 'two-headed Janus' (1.1.50), the god of beginnings and endings, because the names simultaneously look back to the Old Testament and forward to the New Testament. Such nominal direction is an augur, as Faulkner would say, and a signifying badge, as Sidney would say, of what the characters will do. It is up to the audience to read the meanings of their names in time. Ironic reversals in verbal imagery, as well as dramatic imagery, pervade the whole of this play and contribute greatly to the complex texture of its meanings that depend on the perspective adopted and how the quality of that vision develops.

3

'Give and hazard': Friends and Lovers

Therefore the lottery that he hath devised in these three chests of gold, silver, and lead, whereof he who chooses his meaning chooses you, will no doubt never be chosen by any rightly but one who you shall rightly love.

(1.2.24–7)

In these three chests lies the heart of the play's dramatic meaning, its exploration of the definition and difference between wise love and foolish desire which ideologically unites the seemingly disparate elements of this richly textured play. Indeed, one of Shakespeare's significant verbal changes is to substitute the word 'chest' or 'casket' for his source's 'vessel'. The very word 'chest' or 'casket' signifies the outer housing for inner contents, either of which may be valueless or valuable. In terms of the animate body the 'chest' houses the 'heart', and Antonio's heart is the flesh Shylock desires and thinks he deserves. Inanimate chests or caskets are containers for earthly treasures (gold, silver, precious stones) as well as for fleshly bodies committed to earth when buried.[1] Shakespeare chooses to develop the truth of noncorrespondence between the outer view and inner worth for the choice of lead and the falsity of correspondence between the outer view and inner worth in the choices of gold and silver. The 'romantic fairy world of Belmont' is not incompatible with 'the historical reality of money-making Venice', although W. H. Auden suggests it is.[2]

To understand the meaning Portia's father intends for this 'choice' test of wise love we need to appreciate how Shakespeare carefully uses and adapts the marriage test and its allegorisation found in his literary source, the *Gesta Romanorum*.[3] As we have noted, Shakespeare's choice of this test constitutes a major artistic de-

95

parture from the superficial wooing test found in *Il Pecorone*, which
he rejects. Far from being the 'flimsy' affair or 'pretty hollow-
ness' Harley Granville-Barker calls it,[4] the choice of chests is vital
to the play. The literal and symbolic dimensions of the casket
test serve as a dramatic modus operandi through which Shakespeare interconnects the play's various claimants and their claims
regarding their hard choices. Shakespeare uses the chests as a
test of wise love, the would-be lover having to discern and choose
what is really good over what only seems good. In the play, wisdom is spiritual understanding that prompts the emulation of divine
love, the ability to perceive the spirit behind the letter so that
one can rightly discriminate between truth and falsehood and can
choose rightly in loving not 'too well' but 'wisely' (*Oth.* 5.2.418):

> O love, be moderate, allay thy ecstasy,
> In measure rain thy joy, scant this excess!
> I feel too much thy blessing: make it less
> For fear I surfeit.
>
> > (3.2.111–14)

Shakespeare maintains the essential meaning of the marriage
test in the *Gesta Romanorum* at both the literal and allegorical levels of meaning. He changes many details, however, to make his
version of the test more challenging to interpret and more suitable for his own dramatic imagery, themes, and characters. The
fundamental purpose of this 'love test' is to prove the inner worthiness of a spouse in a choice between 'good and evil', spiritual
'life and death'.[5] The meaning of the test is to define right love
and to enact that definition through the right choice. In both the
source and the play the rightness of human love is modelled on
the ultimately right example, divine love. In the allegorisation of
the story the wisely providential father is God, and the literal
marriage between woman and man betokens the soul's espousal
to God when she, safely anchored in 'the ship of charity' by the
virtues of 'faith and hope', sails through hazardous 'worldly tem-
pests' overcoming 'the temptation of the flesh' and renewing 'the
virtues that the soul receiveth in Baptism' for eternal salvation.[6]
The gold and silver vessels generally symbolise worldliness or
the flesh, the false glister of pompous shows and the false glister
of worldly 'wisdom', which appear to 'shine' but which contain
carrion death, the price of sin.[7] The lead vessel represents the

virtuous life of humility and obedience that God's 'chosen' will 'choose', and therefore it contains the 'precious stones' of 'faith and her fruitful works'.[8] Shakespeare develops the idea of Portia's 'virtuous' and 'holy' father (1.2.23) as a god-like father who wisely knows his own child and who provides for her financially and emotionally after his death.[9] Their relationship serves as the standard by which the other two, less wise, parent–child relationships in the play will be measured, those of Shylock and Jessica and the Gobbos.

Shakespeare heightens the element of risk or uncertainty in the source's test by adding 'injunctions' (2.9.16) to which the suitors must swear before attempting the test. These injunctions help to ensure the validity of the test and reveal what's at risk – legitimate family, spouse and heirs. Losing suitors must never reveal their choice, must leave Belmont immediately, and must suffer the penalty to sacrifice forever their right to marry (2.9.9–15). This severe penalty of barrenness emphasises matters of the heart not the pocketbook, making the consequences dangerously personal. This test demands courage. Men of noble rank come from the four corners of the world to sue for Portia, but not all have the courage to risk the test. Six suitors leave, lacking the courage to try, just as Morocco arrives. Morocco, Arragon, and Bassanio are all bound by courage, but to be 'bold' (2.7.70), as Morocco discovers, is not sufficient by itself.

Shakespeare keeps the metals for the chests, but he changes the mottos in several ways. He changes the main verb from 'find' to 'gain' and 'get' on the gold and silver chests and to 'give and hazard' on the leaden chest; the revised verbs clearly separate the 'takers' from the 'givers'. He distinguishes between the general ('many men') and the individual ('he'), and he most changes the appearance of the leaden motto from the obviously attractive clue that the chooser 'shall find that God hath disposed for him' to the threatening clue that the chooser 'must give and hazard all he hath'. The conception of love as the gift or hazard of oneself is, of course, the cornerstone of the mystery of God's love for man, and in the *Gesta Romanorum* that mystery is set forth as God's gift of His only Son through the Incarnation and Baptism.[10] The spirit of hazarding, as opposed to the spirit of calculation, is allied with Providence. Shakespeare also improves on the contents of the vessels. He adds a scroll to each which provides a literal interpretation of the meaning of each choice. He changes the symbolic contents from a dead man's bones, earth and worms, and precious stones to three 'heads' – a death's head, a fool's head, and a picture of Portia's head. These stage props symbolically illustrate the same emphasis on wisdom that the scrolls make literally clear. By substituting Portia's picture for the leaden vessel's gems, Shakespeare changes the definition of what is truly 'profitable' in the source from physical wealth to personal wealth.[11] Portia's suitors are told to choose the casket containing her picture and thus to find the gem richer than all others, Portia herself. Finally, Shakespeare adds the variety of suitors and creates the characters of Morocco and Arragon as important dramatic foils for Bassanio and as analogues for Shylock.

Like Antonio, Portia appears on stage suffering from a weary melancholy, but in her case she knows the cause of discomfort, the difficulty of obeying a dead father's good will when she chafes under such curbing of her own vibrant will in the matter of choosing a husband: 'Is it not hard, Nerissa, that I cannot choose one, nor refuse none'? (1.2.21–2). Hard indeed! Especially for a woman of Portia's calibre. She herself inherits her father's wisdom, and he might well have left the young heiress to choose according to her own good judgement. In her comic evaluation of her suitors Portia demonstrates that she judges not by what the 'fond eye doth teach' (2.9.26). As Nerissa overnames the suitors, Portia, with much more incisive reasoning than is displayed in a similar scene in *Two Gentlemen of Verona* (1.2.1–50), effectively 'reads' the hearts and minds behind the noble titles and fancy doublets. This early in the play Portia reveals her wisely judicial temperament which is complemented by her pedagogic bent in desiring to learn and to teach the right following of 'good sentences' (1.2.9–10, 13–15). Apologising for her goodnatured mocking (1.2.47), Portia holds a higher definition of what it means to be a man than the sorry 'dumbshow[s]', 'beast[s]', and 'sponge[s]' courting her and who pass for men because God made them (1.2.39–81). Her incisive sporting with the definition of manhood anticipates Shylock's less incisive but more seriously expressed definition of humanity (3.1.46–53). Yet, despite her no-nonsense insights for others, Portia is wise enough to admit her own potential limitation; she knows how hard it is to know and to do what is right: 'the brain may devise laws for the blood, but a hot temper leaps o'er a cold decree' (1.2.15–16). Both Portia and Nerissa reveal they are young women uncommonly wise and witty.[12] One aspect of their wisdom is the friendship, grounded on mutual respect, that they share despite apparent inequity in the social rank of birthright, as is also the case for the friendship between the nobleman Bassanio and the merchant Antonio as well as the friendship between the master's daughter (Jessica) and his servant (Lancelot). Portia is the wisest character in the play, and her wisdom shines more brightly with each new act because her wisdom is not hoarded but shared in courageous, loving deeds.

But despite Nerissa's good counsel, Portia's understandable fear of the risks she runs prompts her to think about contrivances to avoid the worst, such as setting a tempting glass of wine on the wrong casket for the German sponge (1.2.78–81). The law-abiding Nerissa doesn't object to Portia's ingenious contrivances as long as Portia does 'perform [her] father's will' (1.2.76). Portia does agree, moreover, with Nerissa's praise of her father's test, and reining in her frustration, she repeatedly confirms her *choice* to obey his wise will: 'If I live to be as old as Sibylla, I will die as chaste as Diana unless I be obtained by the manner of my father's will' (1.2.87–8). Not even for the bold and wise soldier-scholar 'best deserving a fair lady' (1.2.97) will she break faith with her father: 'I could teach you / How to choose right, but then I am forsworn. / So will I never be . . . / Let Fortune go to hell for it, not I' (3.2.10–21). Nerissa warned Portia not to doubt her father's plan, but it has taken the proof of Morocco's and Arragon's mischoosing to bring Portia to the profound belief in the rightness of her father's will: 'If you do love me, you will find me out' (3.2.41). Bassanio's moment of choice puts them both on the rack, but as much as she rightly loves Bassanio, she is resolved to obey her father, and therein she recognises that if Bassanio fails, it will be because he does not rightly love her.

What then are we to make of the clues in Portia's language that refer to the choice of the leaden casket? Critics have much debated the significance of the song sung during Bassanio's choice, but we must observe that linguistic clues precede the choices of Morocco and Arragon as well as Bassanio.[13] Why? First of all, any clues that might be found in Portia's language do not invalidate the test. As any teacher or student knows, as any television gameshow host or contestant knows, as anyone who has played charades knows, a clue is but a clue. A clue is not an answer. The success of the communication of the clue depends on the nature of the recipient. A bucket will hold water, but a sieve will not. Many can hear the same riddle, but only a few will unravel it. Nerissa does not criticise Portia's flexible contrivances as long as the Lord of Belmont's will is not violated: Portia must marry whoever chooses the leaden casket. Portia would not want to give Morocco and Arragon helpful clues to the leaden chest just as she wanted to give the German suitor a contrary clue.

How then do we explain the clues for the leaden chest in her speeches to Morocco and Arragon? To Morocco she says, 'In terms of *choice* I am not solely *led* / By nice direction of a maiden's *eyes*' (2.1.13–14, my italics), and 'First forward to the temple, after dinner / Your *hazard* shall be made' (2.1.43–4, my italics). To Arragon she says, 'To these injunctions everyone doth swear / That comes to *hazard* for my *worthless* self' (2.9.16–17, my italics). From Portia's perspective she does not intend these to be clues. She has no contrary 'clues' for the gold and silver chests, which would better suit her intent if she was interested in helping Morocco and Arragon to lose. The subliminal bias for the language of the leaden casket in her speech reveals how central that choice is to her own life, not just because the choice is momentous but because the values inherent in that choice are her values – humility, hazard, and self-sacrifice.

But the clues for the leaden casket choice are intentional on Shakespeare's part. Shakespeare's clues operate at a subliminal level for the audience to involve it subconsciously in the choice by planting clues that are mentally received but not understood until later, and sometimes understood only at an intuitive rather than a cognitive level. For example, the impact of Portia's interpretation of Shylock's bond in the trial scene is heightened by the submerged back-to-back clues for exact weight and bloodshed (4.1.251–4). Portia's speech to Morocco precedes the audience's knowledge of the caskets' mottos and the verb 'hazard', which is Shakespeare's addition to the source some members of his audience would have known, so that we recognise 'hazard' as a clue only retrospectively. Nor are we astute enough to catch the puns on 'led/lead' and 'eyes' except by way of hindsight or some level of subconscious recognition. Shakespeare's art of preparatory verbal clues helps to account for why his climactic moments have such impact. He tills the soil of the imagination so that the fruit it bears is deep-rooted and nurtured even if we don't cognitively understand that process at the time it is happening in the theatre or in a first reading of the text. By the time we hear Portia's clue to Arragon we may be more perceptive although we still don't know for certain whether the silver or lead casket holds Portia's picture. No test designed by the human mind is foolproof, but this one is exceptionally good, as any teacher knows from student discussions of what they would have chosen and why.

By the time Bassanio chooses, the audience knows, at least by process of elimination, what the right choice is. Now Portia's speech is filled with a host of subtle and not so subtle verbal hints, both for Bassanio on her part and for the audience on Shakespeare's part, especially when he has Portia shift to the third person and discuss Bassanio's choice for our convenient overhearing (3.2.43–60). Portia thrice uses the verbs or their synonyms that appear on the leaden casket – 'hazard' (3.2.2), 'venture' (3.2.10), and 'sacrifice' (3.2.57) – and in her modest admission to Bassanio that he already has won her affection appears the phrase 'beshrew your eyes' (3.2.14), a warning about the quintessential problem of eyes and the nature of perception, the very idea that appears again later in the song (3.2.67). She scolds 'these naughty [worthless] times' (3.2.18), wishes 'to peize the time' (as with the lead weights of a clock) (3.2.22), and her battle cry is 'Go, Hercules!' (3.2.60), which puts us in mind of the greatest adventurer from classical mythology. Through Portia's self-identification – 'I stand for sacrifice' (3.2.57) – she not only figuratively embodies the idea of sacrifice, but she also analogises herself with Hesione as a sacrificial victim, pointing out, however, that her rescuer is motivated by love, unlike Hercules, who was motivated by reward (3.2.53–7).[14] And the entire lovers' banter that precedes the moment of truth is a tissue of meanings playfully related to the choice of lead: the emphasis on giving all one has to the other (3.2.16–18), the emphasis on the endurance of pain necessary to a sacrificial definition of love (3.2.24–6, 37), and the emphasis on trust, truth, and fidelity, not treasonous seeming truth (3.2.26–36).

Their teasing playfulness, easing the tension of the moment, appropriately turns on the teaching and learning of true love. In their wordplay Portia does not violate her father's will. When Bassanio exults that she teaches him 'answers for deliverance' (3.2.38), he addresses the immediate context of their exchange over the torture of what they both are experiencing. Although Bassanio already knows that his life rests on his love for Portia, both of them suffer some 'mistrust' and 'fear' (3.2.28–9, 61) that they will not win each other. The best clue Portia gives is her last one, her articulation of her father's intention: 'If you do love me, you will find me out' (3.2.41). Bassanio already knows that he loves her, but whether he loves her rightly is what the test will determine. If Bassanio hears any of these many clues, he responds to them only at a subliminal level, as we shall see when we examine the structure and content of his soliloquy, which reflects his own character and wisdom before his journey to Belmont.

'O, THESE DELIBERATE FOOLS!' (2.9.79)

Portia incisively sums up why Morocco and Arragon lose: 'O, these deliberate fools! When they do choose / They have the wisdom by their wit to lose' (2.9.79–80). The rational delibera-tions of the worldly wise prove the foolish nature of their seem-ingly wise wit, their abuse of the letter by their blindness to the spirit. Shakespeare's addition of these two princely suitors re-fines our perception of worldliness in the play and heightens our appreciation of Bassanio's wisely loving choice. In his first ap-pearance on stage Morocco pleads not to be judged solely on the basis of appearances, namely by his dark skin as a tawny Moor, which would be foreign to the European preference for their own fair skin. Portia is not Desdemona, but to Portia's credit her ob-jections to Morocco's 'complexion' are not simply skin-deep. The Elizabethan meaning of 'complexion' includes the sense of one's 'temperament' or 'habit of mind', and 'complexion', as Morocco uses it, meaning the natural appearance of the skin, was orig-inally thought to show one's temperament.[15] After Morocco chooses and reveals his inner self, Portia pronounces her judgement: 'A gentle riddance! . . . Let all of his complexion choose me so' (2.8.78–9). Here she uses 'complexion' in its older sense of 'disposition', as it is similarly used in a later reference to Jessica's 'complexion' (3.1.25). Portia does so not solely because she typically uses the outer habits of her suitors as semiotics – signs by which to read their inner characters – but because Morocco's choosing has dem-onstrated his superficially 'golden mind' (2.7.20).

   In her first use of 'complexion', however, when the Prince of Morocco is but an announced name to her, Portia welcomes his arrival. But she also lets the audience know her personal prefer-ence for a husband when she uses 'complexion' this time strictly in its sense of skin colour: 'If he have the condition of a saint, and the complexion of a devil, I had rather he should shrive me than wive me' (1.2.107–8). She does not reject him outright but rather would prefer him as a spiritual companion, a confessor, than as a marital companion. Judged by today's standards this remark would be seen as arguably racist. Yet Portia's remark is obviously not intended to be intellectually demeaning but rather physically preferential. If beauty is in the eye of the beholder, Portia is letting us know that she finds the less familiar less attractive, the opposite of Desdemona's taste regarding the choice of a husband. For Portia's two princely suitors Shakespeare has chosen foreign character types whose temperaments are well known on the English stage, the Moor as boldly brave and the Spaniard as falsely proud. Of those who take the test, Bassanio is the only Italian, the only suitor from her own nation, and he, not surprisingly, carries the day. But Shakespeare probably decided to use together the princely names of Morocco and Arragon on the basis of 'The Thirty-Fifth Novel' in his much used William Painter's *The Palace of Pleasure*. The story's presentation of 'past Princes' provides a standard by which Shakespeare's princes may be judged as less than princely because it focuses on the King of Morocco and introduces the King of Arragon as princely models of courtesy and humility, not merely proud princes of puissance.[16]

Moreover, it is Morocco, not Portia, who cherishes outward show. His well-sounding plea, not to be judged by the colour of his skin, is ironic because he himself reverts to judgement of himself by colour when he boasts that his blood is as red as that of any fair-skinned creature (2.1.1–12). Should Morocco choose rightly, he would prove himself to be truly fair in matters of the heart. But his vanity regarding his own physical worthiness is clear from his celebration of his own courageous exploits. Strength of mind, not arms, will be needed to win this psychomachia, and Morocco continues to reveal his weakness there when he misreads the test as a game of chance and not merit. The consequence of his choice is foreshadowed by his reliance on 'blind fortune' (2.1.36). His exaggerated claim that the consequence of losing might make him 'die with grieving' (2.1.38) relates to the pattern of 'bragging jacks' (3.4.77) that the women expose in the male tendency to egoistic exaggeration. Bassanio will also be proved false to his bold oath that he will die when Portia's ring parts from his finger (3.2.185). Shylock too will forfeit his oath to have his bond when he is faced with a tough choice involving personal risk. Ironically the brave Morocco, who can tangle with lions and bears, avoids the leaden chest because it 'threatens' (2.7.18).[17]

Morocco will not hazard for lead because he reads the motto literally, as if lead were the object of his hazard, and he sees lead literally as a dross metal, devoid of any symbolic value. He is caught by the appearance of lead as he is by gold when he claims, 'A golden mind stoops not to shows of dross, / I'll then nor give nor hazard aught for lead' (2.7.20–1). He is blind to the truth of his own statement, 'men that hazard all / Do it in hope of fair advantage' (2.7.18–19); indeed, the fair advantage is Portia, not the lead itself. He argues that Portia's 'heavenly picture' (2.7.48) ill consorts with a leaden casket since 'never so rich a gem / Was set in worse than gold' (2.7.54–5), signalling his bias for gold and revealing his own ignorance that a gem is a gem regardless of its setting. Morocco, having been fooled by the glister of gold, finds a death's head, the appropriate reward for what the scroll, stuck through the 'empty eye' of that skull, proclaims to be Morocco's lack of wisdom. Morocco's own vocabulary of death also prefigures the deadly contents he will unlock – 'incision' (2.1.6), 'slew' (2.1.25), 'die' (2.1.38), 'shrine', 'mortal' (2.7.40), 'cerecloth', 'obscure grave', and 'immured' (2.7.51–2).[18] Morocco's discovery of 'a carrion death' (2.7.66) provides a subtle but palpable verbal and visual symbolic link between the character of his choice and Shylock's, because Shylock is harshly called an 'old carrion' (3.1.29), and he defends his own desire in the trial for 'a weight of carrion flesh' (4.1.41).

Morocco's choice of what 'many men' desire looks outward to common consensus; Arragon's preoccupation with what 'he deserves' looks inward to self-estimation. Morocco was preoccupied with the outer beauty of Portia, whom many men admire; Arragon is so self-absorbed he barely acknowledges Portia's presence. Like Morocco he too errs in assuming that he has a golden mind when he says of 'base lead': 'You shall look fairer ere I give or hazard' (2.9.22). He unwittingly contradicts himself when he observes that the fool chooses by 'the fond eye' (2.9.26), which is what he has just done when he rejected lead on the basis of its unfair appearance. He therefore falsely distinguishes between himself and 'the fool multitude' (2.9.25). Shylock likewise sees Antonio as a 'fool' for free lending (3.3.2), but he pries not to his own interior. Claiming to choose not by 'show' (2.9.25), Arragon none the less contra-

dicts himself again and chooses more by the 'show' of the motto
than by the show of the metal as Morocco had done. His, like
Morocco's, is a literal, not a spiritual, interpretation. Although he
sounds clever, his arrogance hoodwinks any true self-knowledge.
Each important insight he pronounces, such as, none 'should pre-
sume / To wear an undeservèd dignity' (2.9.39), is contradicted
by his action: 'I will assume desert' (2.9.50). Like Arragon, Antonio
will assume desert over Portia's commandment to Bassanio regarding the ring (4.1.445–67). Arragon's selfish pride disqualifies
him from loving rightly; he is so in love with himself that he
could not possibly love another. Like Morocco's scroll, Arragon's
emphasises the foolishness of the chooser who kisses shadows
and therefore deserves 'a shadow's bliss' (2.9.67) and the fool's
head which he finds. For one who strove to stand aloof from the
'many', he now has one too many heads. Even if he does complain, at least Arragon has learned enough to admit he is a fool
(2.9.74–75). Like Morocco's speech, Arragon's language foreshadows
the prize he finds – 'fool', 'fond' (2.9.25–6), 'common' (2.9.31),
and 'cozen' (2.9.37). Moreover, like the verbal-visual symbolic link
between Morocco's carrion death and Shylock's association with
the same, Arragon's discovery of a fool's head links the character
of his choice with Shylock's. Shylock, like Arragon, proudly sees
others as 'fools', whether Lancelot (2.5.42) or Antonio (1.3.35; 3.3.2),
remaining blind to the speck in his own eye: 'I'll not be made a
soft and dull-eyed fool, / To shake the head, relent, sigh, and
yield' (3.3.15).

Thus, both Morocco and Arragon fail because they are worldly
men who literally interpret the metals and mottos of the caskets
they select.[19] Morocco focuses more on the literal significance of
the showy metal, and this corresponds to the source's allegorisation
of golden choosers as given to the 'riches and pomps of this world'
which 'outwardly shine'.[20] Arragon focuses more on the literal
significance of the motto, and this corresponds to the allegorisation
of silver choosers as 'Justices & wise men of this world which
shine in fair speech' but are spiritually dead within.[21] Shakespeare's
careful revision of his source's mottos and contents for the gold
and silver chests suggests that he creates these choosers to be
basically similar in their worldly orientation but slightly different in how they express it.[22] Morocco and Arragon earn their death's
head and fool's head by their wrongheaded judgements. Morocco
is fooled by his false outward gaze, while Arragon is fooled by

his false inward gaze. As they 'see', so do they 'choose'. The challenge, as Kent puts it to Lear, is to 'see better' (*Lr* 1.1.158).

The gold and silver choices of Morocco and Arragon serve as dramatic analogues for Shylock's own choices of what he desires and thinks he deserves: his gold and silver gain of usury and his assumption of deserving fleshly revenge according to the rigour of the law. Like Morocco and Arragon, who literally reject the leaden chest, Shylock symbolically rejects it because he considers the true wisdom of giving and hazarding mere foolishness, insisting rather on personal gain, whether of earthly treasure or flesh. Both Morocco and Arragon ironically err exactly where they think they excel, just as Shylock does when he is undone by the letter and strict justice. Like Morocco and Arragon, self-preoccupation blinds Shylock to his own presumptive egotism. These mischoosers defeat themselves. Morocco, Arragon, and Shylock are not excluded simply because they are 'alien (and Marlovian)', as James Shapiro suggests.[23] Jessica is also Marlovian in her reflection of Marlowe's good Jewish daughter, Abigail, and she is not excluded, either prior to or after her marriage to Lorenzo.

The contest between the values of Morocco, Arragon, and Shylock against those the play celebrates is clarified in Castiglione's *The Book of the Courtier*. Here virtue is defined as 'a wisdom and an understanding to choose the good' while vice is 'a lack of foresight and an ignorance that leadeth to judge falsely'.[24] As we have seen with Morocco and Arragon and will see with Shylock, wisdom which 'consisteth in a certain judgment to choose well' is crucial for men 'because men never choose the ill with opinion that it is ill, but they are deceived through a certain likeness of good'.[25] Shakespeare cultivates our sympathy for all who choose amiss in the play because in each instance the chooser passionately believes he is doing what is right, although afterwards he will be proved wrong in his own eyes as well as the eyes of others. Morocco's, Arragon's, and Shylock's choices are effective foils to Bassanio's choice of lead, the choice of wise love.

'CHOOSE NOT BY THE VIEW' (3.2.131)

Bassanio, true to his generous nature, arrives in Belmont as the only suitor who is announced as bringing 'gifts of rich value' (2.9.90). Portia will complete the circle of gift-giving, initiated by

Bassanio, when she gives him the tangible gift of the ring, a sign of her faithful love. To a modern audience Bassanio's interest in 'a lady richly left' (1.1.160), whose inherited wealth could help him repay his debts, suspiciously suggests that Bassanio might be more interested in what Portia has than what Portia is. However, Shakespeare has taken measures, such as even the small indication of Bassanio's nature as a bringer of gifts, to reassure his audience that Bassanio's attitude toward Portia's wealth is kept in its proper perspective. Part of this propriety concerns the Elizabethan acceptance of the idea that marriage among members of the higher classes should uphold economic and social considerations, the equitable or advantageous joining in matrimony of persons who are reasonably alike in nobility of family and estate. Parents, therefore, were entrusted with the responsibility of arranging suitable matches for their heirs, who, left to their own devices, might otherwise err in their youthfulness by choosing appearance (a pretty face) over substance (honourable name and substantial wealth). Portia's father fulfils his parental role through the 'good inspiration' (1.2.24) of his lottery, but Shakespeare does not give Bassanio a living father to voice his opinion.

Consequently, the nobles' expectation of wealth through marriage is not seen in the Renaissance as a perversion of marriage but rather as a most reasonable condition of marriage. Ann Jennalie Cook explains that 'Claudio, Fenton, Bassanio, and Petruccio have all been denounced as fortune hunters even though their behavior was standard practice among non-fictional gentlemen of similar rank and in similar circumstances.'[26] Granting this historical perspective on marriage customs, we must also observe that Shakespeare emphasises the quality of love, not economic or social propriety, as the primary reason Bassanio and Portia deserve each other. Although Bassanio is seeking his fortune through a love quest, that venture does not reduce Bassanio to a heartless fortune hunter, as seems to be a pervasive opinion in criticism.[27] To refute the condemnation of Bassanio as mercenary, we need to recognise just how honourably Bassanio behaves during his suit. When Bassanio wins the test, he proves he is no predatory fortune hunter because he refuses to claim his prize until Portia herself chooses to ratify his triumph (3.2.139–48). Bassanio has also been forthright with Portia about how financially poor a gentleman he is because he has no wealth except his bloodline (3.2.251–4). Portia loves Bassanio despite his lack of gold and silver. The fact that

Bassanio passes the Lord of Belmont's test reveals that Portia's
father was not chiefly interested in finding for his daughter a
husband suitable in name and land, but rather, suitable in heart
and soul, one who 'shall rightly love' (1.2.27). Therefore, how
can we agree with Leonard Tennenhouse that the casket test lo-
cates power in the female aristocrat and challenges the suitors to
value Portia primarily for her aristocratic blood, a challenge
Bassanio meets?[28]

Bassanio, the giver and hazarder, will not make the same mistakes as Morocco and Arragon. By not having him read the mottos aloud, Shakespeare spares the audience unnecessary repetition
but, more importantly, presents Bassanio's silent contemplation
of the caskets as evidence of thinking before speaking. The added
theatrical advantage is that the song can be sung, as Portia commands, 'Let music sound *while* he doth make his choice' (3.2.43,
my italics) and as Shakespeare specifically directs, *'the whilst Bassanio
comments on the caskets to himself'* (3.2.62 SD). The backdrop of
music sets the mood for the harmonious resolution of the casket
test. In addition to recognising the song's obvious rhymes with
'lead', the audience, who, unlike Bassanio, now knows for sure
that the lead chest is the right one, enjoys a simpler musical variation on the meaning of the Lord of Belmont's test, a meaning
that Bassanio will present far more philosophically and eloquently
in the poetry of his choice. Paradox characterises the song's simple idea and imagery: the birth of fancy is its death because eye-
engendered affection does not live forever, as does true love in
the heart or head. At best we can suggest that the song's clues
may subliminally inspire Bassanio. That the song itself does not
give Bassanio the answer is clear from the very different idea
and imagery in Bassanio's soliloquy.[29] Where is there any concern with fancy? Romantic love? Instead we find Bassanio concerned with tainted legal pleas, cloaked religious error, bearded
cowards, cosmetic beauty, skulls in sepulchres, and treacherous
shores. It is as if Bassanio was too absorbed in his own thoughts
to pay any close attention to the song.

Portia's understandable but unwarranted fear is laid to rest with
Bassanio's opening couplet: 'So may the outward shows be least
themselves: / The world is still deceived with ornament', and
later 'Thus ornament is but the guilèd shore / To a most dangerous sea' (3.2.73–4, 97–8). The world? Deceived? Ornament?
Bassanio's deductive 'so' introduces a conclusion that could only

come from a thoughtful examination of the caskets and their mottos. His entire speech is a philosophical elaboration of the idea of noncorrespondence, that things may not be what they seem, that 'seeming truth' may 'entrap the wisest' (3.2.100–1), in this danger- ous, fallen world in which we live. Did he learn this in Belmont? No. The Bassanio who speaks these lines and sagely observes, 'There is no vice so simple but assumes / Some mark of virtue on his outward parts' (3.2.81–2), is the same alert Bassanio who warns Antonio, 'I like not fair terms and a villain's mind' (1.3.172). We know that in seeking Portia, Bassanio has not been a victim of show since his initial paean of Portia celebrates her 'wondrous virtues' more than her beauty and extols her as 'nothing under- valued to Cato's daughter, Brutus' Portia' (1.1.162, 164–5). Simi- larly, after he makes the right choice, he properly identifies Portia's picture as her 'counterfeit' (3.2.115), and although he almost gets entrapped by the glory of her beauty that the painter has captured, he regains his balance in the end: 'Yet look how far / The substance of my praise doth wrong this shadow / In underprizing it, so far this shadow / Doth limp behind the substance' (3.2.126–9).

Motivated by true love that seeks to give and risk, not gain and get, that is bred in the heart or head, Bassanio avoids the straits of 'eye' and 'I' that proved such guilèd shores for Mo- rocco and Arragon. The character of the 'I' governs how the 'eye of reason' is used. Seldom noticed is how free Bassanio's lines are of the laboured reasoning that characterises Morocco's and Arragon's speeches.[30] Shakespeare may present here in these two different modes of reasoning the distinction between man's lower faculty of 'ratio' (discursive reason) and his higher faculty of 'intellectus' (intuitive reason).[31] Morocco and Arragon exemplify the mental calculation of ratio and its liability to error, but Bassanio begins his soliloquy as if in a state of immediate intuition of the truth. His soliloquy does not proceed step-by-step to deduce his choice, but rather his opening truth is the crucial principle upon which his choice depends, and his soliloquy merely illustrates that truth through a variety of examples. In their ratiocinations, Morocco and Arragon demonstrate reason confounding itself, wit superseding wisdom, 'ratio' triumphing over 'intellectus'. They misuse the lower rational faculty, which is closely related to the senses and whose function is *scientia* or the knowledge of things visible. Bassanio's spiritual understanding is properly based on the higher rational faculty, whose function is *sapientia* or wisdom.

Given the caskets' various rewards of different 'heads', we should recall Milton's explanation that wisdom will not desert us if we avoid 'attributing overmuch to things / Less excellent' because 'true Love' is 'judicious', has its 'seat / In Reason', not 'carnal pleasure'.[32]

Wisdom cannot be purchased for gold or silver (Jb 28.15). God has 'chosen' the 'vile things of the world', that which in 'man's judgement' is 'almost nothing', in order 'to bring to naught things that are' valued by the world so that 'no flesh' should be arrogant (1 Cor 1.28–9, glosses). Bassanio's generosity of spirit parallels his generosity of mind, and therefore he is capable of the true lover's judgement by the mind's eye, not the flesh's eye. It is not that Bassanio does not use his eyes but rather that he uses them rightly. The 'view' of the lead chest and motto move him because he 'sees' the 'meaning' that Portia's father intended. Only the wise who understand and act on that meaning can 'rightly love'. Shakespeare's casket test represents a test of wise love, proving the internal worthiness of the suitor by a choice whose very nature reveals inner character and the way in which the chooser perceives reality, whether literally or spiritually. The casket test illustrates that as a man perceives, so he is; each suitor's choice is a projection of his moral character. In so far as a person can regard the heart of another, he emulates divine inward vision: 'For *God seeth* not as man seeth. For man looketh on the outward appearance, but the Lord beholdeth the heart' (1 Sm 7).

Bassanio's auspicious name suggests that the more informed members of an Elizabethan audience would see him as the 'touchstone' true lover. Shakespeare invents the name 'Bassanio' for the true lover who will choose rightly. One theory is that 'Bassanio' derives from the Greek 'basanos' for touchstone.[33] This theory holds more weight than appears at first glance because in this play Shakespeare's specific use of minerals from the bowels of the earth – the precious metals (gold and silver), the precious stones (diamond and turquoise), and the base metal and stone (lead and touchstone) – fits a pattern of rich symbolism that would probably be more readily perceived by Elizabethan than modern audiences. A touchstone is a dark-coloured stone (basanite or Lydian stone) used for testing the quality of gold and silver, which left a telltale streak upon a touchstone when rubbed on it. Shakespeare seems to be interested in the touchstone. He gives the name of Touchstone to the clown in *As You Like It*, and in *Pericles* he refers to the touchstone in a context that resembles that of our play and its interest in the testing of inner truth against outward show for proving the worth of a man and his love. In the tournament's test of knightly mettle in *Pericles*, the well-attired fifth knight's device bears a 'hand environed with clouds, / Holding out gold that's by the touchstone tried', and the motto reads, '*Sic spectanda fides* [So should faith be tested]' (2.2.36–8) because tried gold is a symbol of fidelity. Pericles, the sixth knight, immediately follows, and his shabby 'outward show' conceals his inner worth, much like the symbolism of the base, dull leaden casket in the *Merchant*, where it, like Pericles, appears to be outfaced by its more lustrous peers. In *Pericles*, as in our play, some misjudge by the outer view, but one does not: 'Opinion's a fool, that makes us scan / The outward habit by the inward man' (2.2.56–7), and Pericles, like Bassanio, becomes a winner, in this case a winner of both the tourney's test and the love of a good king's daughter.

In our play the inward man, Bassanio, is aptly named because he is metaphorically presented as the human touchstone for testing the quality of love, and lead may be seen as a dramatic correlative for the literal touchstone. The lack-lustre grey colour of lead is a visual reminder on stage of what the touchstone can look like. Basanite is fairly dark grey in colour, although the colour can range from grey to black, and one place where this type of extrusive igneous rock can be found is Italy.[34] Not only can 'touchstone' refer to a specific type of stone, but the term can also be applied to stones of similar colour and texture.[35] As a mineral, lead is technically not used as a touchstone, but its unattractive (dull) appearance and its specifically grey coloration can resemble the touchstone (basanite) in appearance. When Bassanio chooses lead, he unmasks the gold and silver for what they symbolise in a test of love, where the object of choice is not gold, silver, or lead but Portia herself.

When Bassanio chooses, he symbolises the function of the touchstone because he rejects what is falsely ornamental, the 'gaudy gold' and the silver, that 'pale and common drudge 'tween man and man' (3.2.101–4). Silver is described here as 'pale' because it is lighter in colour than gold, with which it is directly compared, and because it is whitish in hue.[36] Morocco clarifies this when he describes the silver as having a 'virgin hue' (2.7.22). Bassanio concludes his choice with a play upon the word 'paleness' that further distinguishes his 'leaden' touchstone from the figuratively false metals of gold and silver: '*Thy* paleness moves me more than eloquence' (3.2.106, my italics). The contrast between 'pale lead' as 'colourless' (lacking in vibrant hue) and the 'colours' of rhetoric ('eloquence') has long been appreciated.[37] But lead's 'paleness' has a visual, as well as this verbal, dimension that is indicated by Bassanio's emphasis on lead's particular 'paleness' as opposed to the 'pale' of silver. Lead is not white in hue, nor is it lighter than gold or silver in colour, but rather, darker than both. Lead is not literally colourless, but rather, a greyish colour somewhat like basanite, the touchstone. Morocco indicates this specific coloration of lead when he refuses to choose it because the lead chest resembles an 'obscure [dark] grave' (2.7.51). Because lead resists corrosion, it was used to line coffins, so as a metal its property, as well as its darker, lifeless colour, associates it with death. Unlike Morocco and Arragon, Bassanio chooses the lead chest precisely because it so 'threaten'st' rather than 'dost promise aught' (3.2.105).

The true lover has to be selfless, to die to his selfish nature so that he can be willing to give and hazard all, including life itself, for the beloved. 'Fancy's knell' (3.2.70) is a literal dead-end because simple fancy is not true love; true love paradoxically dies to selfishness to live selflessly. Overlooking this specific aspect of Shakespeare's conception of love, as well as the coherence of Shakespeare's artistic choices for the casket test, Freud and psychoanalytic critics suggest the caskets really represent three women, and they encounter their greatest interest and difficulty in trying to account for how death fits symbolically in this choice. Because Freudian critics see the third casket as a *pretended* 'choice' of literal death that involves merely an *awareness* of death – not a willed *choice* of spiritual death to one's selfish self – their view of the third casket as man's replacement of the mythical Goddess of Death with the Goddess of Love, 'the fairest and most desirable' of women, must necessarily involve the process of substitution and wish-fulfilment.[38] Aside from its dark, lacklustre appearance, two other properties of lead also contribute to Bassanio's choice of the leaden casket, and he indicates their merits in his soliloquy. Lead is the heaviest of metals, and Bassanio criticises the falsity of 'lightness': 'Look on beauty, / And you shall see 'tis purchased by the weight, / Which therein works a miracle in nature, / Making them lightest that wear most of it' (3.2.88–91). The poverty of lead, compared with the preciousness of gold and silver, prompts Morocco to reject lead as 'dross' (2.7.20) and Arragon to dismiss lead as 'base' (2.9.19). In his choice of poor or 'meagre lead' (3.1.104), Bassanio demonstrates that he, like Portia, humbly stands for sacrifice. Catherine Belsey, however, reads the casket test in Lacanian terms as 'a riddle about the nature of desire', but Bassanio is not 'motivated by desire' nor is the leaden chest 'the appropriate emblem of desire'.[39] Lead becomes the symbolic touchstone for testing the quality of the gold and silver choosers, their desires and their deserts.

Thus, it is not the superficial appearance of lead, gold, or silver that inspires Bassanio, but rather the *meaning* of these metals, and their mottos, as devised by Portia's father. Because Bassanio aids physical vision with spiritual vision, the flesh's eye abetted by the mind's eye, he becomes the only suitor to act on the crucial clue for thriving that Nerissa gives us – only Bassanio chooses according to the '*meaning*' of these three chests (1.2.26, my italics). Shakespeare's invention of Bassanio's name appropriately foreshadows what he will do and why he is drawn to the leaden chest, why it speaks to him and moves him. The whole of the casket test comprises the single most important verbal and dramatic symbol in the play, and we will need to return to it repeatedly to explore its many layers of significance that resonate throughout the whole play. Through Bassanio's wise choice Shakespeare celebrates spiritual comprehension that does not overlook but rather transcends the letter, just as mercy does not replace but rather tempers justice.

Gain may be, paradoxically, the reward of giving and hazarding; as a consequence of Bassanio's right choice, he wins Portia. But the mystery underlying the test is that only in giving and risking for another freely, not motivated *primarily* by the expectation or intent of personal gain, does one find true rewards. If we view Bassanio's choice within the context of the play and of Shakespeare's change of his source through the addition of Morocco and Arragon as foils to Bassanio, we cannot conclude, with Terry Eagleton's materialist reading, that Bassanio is reducible to a 'self-loving parasite' who 'elevates love over riches in the very act of purchasing a woman'.[40] Unlike Morocco, Bassanio recognises this test is no game of chance: only one who chooses truly can 'chance as fair' (3.2.132).[41] It is only after reading the 'gentle scroll' that the courteous Bassanio 'come[s] by note to give, and to receive' (3.2.139–40). Although Bassanio had told Antonio that he intuited 'such thrift' for this venture (1.1.174), Bassanio, even with scroll and picture in hand, can barely believe he has won, can barely trust his senses, so unlike both Morocco and Arragon, who assumed they should win. Bassanio's humility and courtesy are particularly impressive here. As the winning Jason, he does not seize his prize. He refrains from believing as true what he 'sees' until all is 'confirmed, signed, ratified' by Portia's own choice. Even though he has fulfilled his oath and met the Lord of Belmont's test, Bassanio hazards it all for Portia's confirmation.

This beautiful love scene reaches a crescendo with Portia's remarkably plain and true, and therefore remarkably eloquent, confirmation of love, a speech which leaves Bassanio almost speechless. With correspondent humility Portia wishes, not for herself but for him, that she might 'exceed account' (3.2.157), and if the best student makes the best teacher, she, like Prince Hal, masters 'a double spirit / Of teaching and learning instantly' (*1H4* 5.2.63–4). Portia demonstrates her true mastery over her mansion, servants, and above all herself, when she gives all she has to Bassanio. This personal and financial 'conversion' (3.2.166), appropriate for an Elizabethan concept of marriage, is one of several in the play, and the legal and economic wordplay here continues to bond the gifts of heart and treasure chest. Portia ratifies it with the gift of a ring to Bassanio, which she wisely recognises is a hazard on her part: 'when you part from, lose, or give away [the ring], / Let it presage the ruin of your love, / And be my vantage to exclaim on you' (3.2.172–4). This ring is a symbol of loving fidelity. But it is given upon a condition, resembling herein the many instances of conditional gifts or favours in this play. In accord with this romantic play's emphasis on realistic constraints, Bassanio's acceptance of this gift means that he *should* honour Portia's request and *not* do whatever he pleases with the ring. Portia, however, does not ask Bassanio to swear an oath; Bassanio, in what we see throughout the play as all too common a male habit, chooses to swear an extravagant oath (even though he has just said he could barely find words to express his joy): 'But when this ring / Parts from this finger... / O then be bold to say Bassanio's dead!' (3.2.183–5).

Gratiano, whose 'eyes... can look as swift' as Bassanio's, 'beheld the maid' and won Nerissa, swearing his own oaths of love until his mouth was dry (3.2.195–208). Both Gratiano and Nerissa risked their marriage on Bassanio's choice of the right casket.

Coming on the heels of Jessica's and Lorenzo's successful elopement, the three marital unions triple the comedic blessings of young, true love. Shakespeare's artistic confidence in his revisionary work with Marlowe's *Jew of Malta* reveals itself in matters major – such as his reversal of Marlowe's early placement and tragic function of the conversion stipulation regarding both faith and wealth (to be examined in Chapter 5) – as well as in matters minor, his comedic reversal of Marlowe's satiric use of the myth of Jason and the golden fleece as a metaphor for romantic adventuring. Marlowe reserves his use of this metaphor for the end of his play and a satirically humorous context of illicit romance between a courtesan (Bellamira) and a slave (Ithamore), who later die by Barabas's poisoned posy. Marlowe parodies his own pastoral lyric, 'The Passionate Shepherd', through Ithamore's unwitting inversions (Adonis does not love but forsakes Venus; Dis reigns below, not above) in his foolish appropriation of this seduction poem: 'I'll [Ithamore] be thy Jason, thou [Bellamira] my golden fleece' (4.4.86). But Shakespeare deliberately avoids the darker satire of Marlowe's metaphor and opts for a lighter, happier version that accords well with Bassanio's figurative equation of Portia's 'sunny locks' and the 'golden fleece' (1.1.169–71). Unlike Marlowe, Shakespeare introduces the mythic metaphor at the beginning of his play in order to climax its licit realisation at the play's midpoint through the hazardous but ultimately happy winning of wives. With the joyful exultation, 'We are the Jasons, we have won the fleece' (3.2.240), Shakespeare's precise metaphorical expression hearkens back to Bassanio's private discourse with Antonio, in which the adventure for Portia is analogised with the most famous Greek mythic quest. Unlike Marlowe's use, Shakespeare's allusive use of this myth, as a trope of adventuring for love, figures positively at the beginning and midpoint of his play and relates by way of pun to the merchant-adventurer's 'fleece' (fleets) that finances the lover's quest.

As the newly affianced couples in Belmont bawdily wager for an heir, Lorenzo, Jessica, and Salerio arrive from Venice to convert the merrymaking to melancholy with the news of Antonio's forfeit of his bond to Shylock. The lovers' winning of 'the fleece' is countered by the friend's loss of 'the fleece' (3.2.141). Emphasis falls here on the hazardous nature of adventure, whether romantic adventures, mercantile adventures, or this particular romance venturing, financed by a merchant's love through the

means of a usurer's feigned venture of love that is in fact a calculated bond for the return of revenge. Portia, with her deep love
of amity, intuits that no letter could so rob Bassanio of his sanguine
self unless it bore news of 'some dear friend dead' (3.2.244). In
sharing with Portia his sorrow and fear, Bassanio once again
demonstrates his honesty and humility by reconfirming his financial
poverty (3.2.251–9) and by faulting himself 'to feed [his] means'
(3.2.262) through his friend's bond to his enemy. Although she
does not know Antonio, Portia immediately understands how dear
a friend he is, a 'true friend' (3.2.307), and she generously offers
twice the bond's value, then twice that sum followed by treble
that amount, in order to save Antonio. Bassanio has been 'dear
bought' (3.2.312) in terms of the emotional strain – the 'dismay'
of doubt, despair, fear and jealousy – Portia has endured to have
him win her by her father's will (3.2.61, 108–10).[42] But Portia continues her standing for 'sacrifice' when she also chooses to sacrifice her wedding night to relieve her husband's friend.

With faster speed than the men can race toward Venice, Portia's
lightning-quick mind has already determined a plan that will enable
her and Nerissa to be present in person to aid the dear friend of
their new spouses. Portia, aware of the gravity of the situation,
marries Bassanio and immediately sends him to Venice, but her
effervescent sense of humour allows her to find what comedy
might be found in this case. In private with Nerissa she explains
her plan to disguise themselves as lawyers to litigate in the trial
without their husbands knowing who their godsends are. This is
the feisty daughter the Lord of Belmont curbed to ensure that
such a wondrous daughter would obtain none other than a wise
lover for a husband. Portia now revels in her freedom to do as
she likes. She will be no moth of peace left at home. The delight-
ful humour in her new venture corresponds to the same humour
of exposure that she evinced in the judgement of her suitors. To
imitate men, and not abominably, Portia and Nerissa will need
to swagger, brag, tell 'quaint lies', and practise 'a thousand raw
tricks' (3.4.68–77) like the macho youths of their day. The arch
failing of the men in this play is their tendency to false pride,
their sense of maintaining worldly honour at all costs, often
exhibited in their braggadochio oaths. Such male conception
of worldly honour reaps tragic consequences in the duel scenes
of *Romeo and Juliet*. But here the duel will be comedically one
of wits as the women dress down in order to raise up the hopes

of the men. Their adoption of disguise or personal ambiguity, like that of Lancelot and Jessica, is another comic variation on the play's thematic discrimination between well-motivated, as opposed to ill-motivated, deception.

Portia's wise response to Lorenzo's praise of her noble appreciation of 'god-like amity' demonstrates the ideal standard by which deeds of loving friendship should be performed. Disguise may be Portia's necessary method, but love, for both Bassanio and Antonio, is her motive.[43] Lorenzo claims that if Portia actually knew how 'true a gentleman' Antonio was she 'would be prouder' of the relief she sends than her 'customary bounty' allows (3.4.6–9). Portia plainly admits, 'I never did repent for doing good, / Nor shall not now' (3.4.10–11). She voices her understanding of true friendship, the binding of two friends by an equally shared spiritual love – 'whose souls do bear an equal yoke of love' (3.4.13) – so that they proportionately resemble each other in appearance, morals, and spirit (3.4.15). With magnanimous empathy Portia sees Antonio as 'the bosom lover' of Bassanio and therefore 'like [her] lord' and 'the semblance of [her] soul' (3.4.12–20). In reality, Antonio has nothing to cause him anxiety about his relationship with Bassanio now that Bassanio has another love in his life, and this truth Antonio will need to discover for himself. Without the slightest trace of jealousy or competitive rivalry Portia proclaims how 'little is the cost' (3.4.19) to her to save Antonio from 'hellish cruelty' (3.4.21): 'This comes too near the praising of myself, / Therefore no more of it' (3.4.22–3). No points are given for self-aggrandisement in her ledger. Portia's proper self-confidence is based not on false pride, but on true self-knowledge; as Raphael counsels Adam: 'Oft-times nothing profits more / Than self-esteem, grounded on just and right / Well manag'd'.[44] She fulfils here the biblical exhortation to show 'brotherly love and modesty' (Gal 6, heading) and to eschew the rewards and praises of men (Mt 6.1–4).

Portia exemplifies the art of knowing and doing good, with wisdom deeply rooted in humility to bear the fruit of true self-knowledge. In his medieval treatise on friendship, Aelred of Rievaulx astutely suggests that a good marriage must be founded on friendship.[45] Paul counsels husbands to love their wives as they do themselves (Eph 5.28–31) and thereby introduces an idea of genderless discrimination that precludes husbands from treating wives as objects or possessions because no man loves his own

self that way. With love spacious enough to embrace her husband's friends, Portia graciously places the newly arrived Lorenzo
and Jessica in charge of her estate. The heartfelt good wishes Portia,
Lorenzo, and Jessica exchange aptly convey their shared gentility
(3.4.35–44).

'PLACÈD IN MY CONSTANT SOUL' (2.6.58)

Like Bassanio, Lorenzo also prophetically fulfils his name and
wears 'the laurel' of victory in his Venetian venture.[46] In the description of Jessica as 'wise, fair, and true' (2.6.57), Shakespeare
significantly substitutes 'wise' for the word 'kind' that appears
in the conventional phrasing – 'fair, kind, and true'.[47] Jessica, like
her other female counterparts in the play, Portia and Nerissa, is
young and wise. Her wisdom in discerning her father's nature,
before it is too late for her beloved, spares Jessica the tragic ending that befalls Barabas's Abigail. As Lancelot comically strug-
gles to resolve his conflict over domestic duty, Jessica is tormented
by inner strife in her conflict over filial duty. It deeply disturbs
her to be ashamed of her father's morals when she owes her life,
her 'blood' (2.3.17), to him. But Lorenzo's 'promise' to Jessica
(2.3.19), which he does faithfully keep, enables her to transfer
her allegiance to a husband whose morality of love she is happy
to adopt: 'Beshrew me but I love her heartily' (2.6.53). Although
Lancelot is but a servant, both Jessica and Lorenzo treat him kindly
as a 'friend' (2.3.9), and Lancelot returns their affection. Not so
for Shylock.

Lancelot's departure from his master parodies comedically
Jessica's much more difficult decision, and as parody it helps explain
why Jessica leaves what they both see as Shylock's house of 'hell'
(2.3.2). According to Lancelot, Shylock abuses him as a servant
by denying him sufficient food: 'I am famished in his service'
(2.2.86). According to Shylock, Lancelot must leave because he is
'a huge feeder' and is 'snail-slow in profit', so Shylock is un-
kindly preferring him to Bassanio in order that Lancelot might
'help to waste / His borrowed purse' (2.6.44–9). Two such opposed perspectives would be irresolvable as to legitimacy were it
not for other evidence in the play. Hardly can Lancelot 'rend apparel
out', as Shylock claims, if he is a drone that does naught but
sleep all day (2.5.4, 45–6). But Shylock is not intentionally perverting

the truth, or he would not send Lancelot to waste Bassanio as he *believes* Lancelot has wasted him. Shylock is, rather, self-deceived as was Arragon when he reasoned his way to his silver choice on the basis of his own merit. Aside from the provocative motif that Shylock's viewpoint rarely concurs with that of another – including his daughter, his servant, and to a lesser extent his friend Tubal – what is of interest here is Shylock's priorities for people. Shylock admits that Lancelot 'is kind enough' (2.5.44), but he eats too much. The appetitive factor of food consumption outweighs the spirit of kindness. In Shylock's view, as in Morocco's (2.1.1–7), the physical criterion of outward show takes precedence.

As Jessica rightly realises, 'manners' or morals should have a higher value in human relationships than 'blood' (2.3.17–18). Father Shylock's lesser identification of his child by flesh and blood – 'My own flesh and blood to rebel! . . . I say my daughter is my flesh and my blood' (3.1.28, 30) – echoes father Gobbo's similar identification of his child – 'I'll be sworn if thou be Lancelot thou art mine own flesh and blood' (2.2.70–95). Such identifications are superficial, nominal at best, as the Gobbo comedy reveals when the 'proof' of familial flesh-and-blood identity turns on the *name* of the wife and mother: 'her name is Margery indeed' (2.2.75). The fatherly confusion of sand-blind Old Gobbo parodies the biblical story of another blind father's confusion, Isaac's mistaken recognition and blessing of Jacob.[48] Paul's interpretation of this biblical event (Rom 9 and glosses) suits Shakespeare's concern in the play with choices according to the flesh versus those according to the spirit, in this case, according to 'the promise' of God that His children will not be defined merely by the flesh (by kindred) but by His free grace. Thus, the Father's chosen own to receive His blessing are identified not just by fleshly generation but by regeneration through the spirit of His grace, whether a Lancelot or a Jessica.

The higher value of the spirit permits Jessica and Lorenzo to transcend through intermarriage the boundaries of flesh (tribe and nation), whereas Shylock would insist on those boundaries, preferring for Jessica's husband a native son ('any of the stock of Barabbas', 4.1.292) over a loving alien like Lorenzo. Unlike the figuratively blind Shylock, the literally blind Gobbo kindly sees his child, not his tangible possessions (be they ever so few), as the 'staff' or 'prop' of his old age (2.2.54–5). Unlike her old father and unlike Lancelot's old father, the young and wise Jessica is not deceived even momentarily by familial definitions based merely on 'flesh and blood', nor like Morocco does she base definition of one's self on flesh and blood criteria (2.1.1–7). Shakespeare's juxtaposition of parent-child relationships explores *both sides* of the difficult truth of Lancelot's comic claim: 'It is a wise father that knows his own child' (2.2.63).

For Shylock, the flesh tends to outweigh the heart in his hierarchy of values, revealed in how he treats others. He treats Jessica as a servant, not a daughter. In his only domestic scene Shylock uses many more imperatives in his dialogue with Jessica than he even does with Lancelot: 'Do as I bid you' (2.6.51). There is no gentle calling for his daughter ('What, Jessica!'), and when he does speak to her his language is abrupt, commanding, devoid of tender expression, except for the possible intonation of 'Jessica my girl', which tends to be undercut by his subsequent order, 'Look to my house' (2.5.15–16). How differently Portia entrusts her house to Jessica and Lorenzo! In this brief scene Shylock the patriarch shows how little he shares with Jessica, because there is no room in his vocabulary for 'our': 'my keys', 'my girl', 'my doors', 'my house's ears', 'my casements', and 'my sober house' (2.5.12–35). Even Marlowe's Barabas kindly greets his daughter when she first enters, 'But whither wends my beauteous Abigail?' (1.2.225), and he is concerned about her sorrow, 'O, what has made my lovely daughter sad?' (1.2.226), and attempts to console her over their loss of wealth, 'Thy father has enough in store for thee' (1.2.229). Before his deadly rejection of Abigail for her conversion, Barabas confides in soliloquy that his wealth is for her: 'all I have is hers' (1.1.137).

If Shylock loves Jessica more than his material wealth, he does not seem to have communicated that to her. Unlike Portia's father, who locks up a picture of his daughter in a casket so that he can give her away to the man with the right key, who unlocks their future, Shylock hoards his daughter herself in his house, under lock and key, as the keeper of his earthly treasure: 'There are my keys ... / Fast bind, fast find' (2.6.52). Shylock gives no indication of being interested in finding Jessica a husband, let alone a worthy husband, and in his societal role as a father he markedly contrasts with other more responsible Shakespearian fathers, such as Prospero. If she was 'fledged', as Solanio asserts (3.1.24), Shylock neglects what Elizabethans perceived as his patriarchal duty, namely to find a suitable husband, as Portia's father, despite his imminent death, did for her. The image of Jessica as incarcerated in her rich father's house anticipates her father's distraught wish, once she disappoints him, that he have her hearsed at his foot with his ducats in her coffin (3.1.70–1). Some of Shakespeare's patriarchs – Capulet, Shylock, Leonato, Lear – tend to turn vicious when their daughters cross, or appear to cross, their wills: 'Better thou / Hadst not been born than not t'have pleas'd me better' (*Lr* 1.1.233–4).

To marry, a man and woman must leave their parents and cleave unto one another so that 'they twain shall be one flesh' (Eph 5.31). Jessica's departure in itself is not so disturbing as is the manner of her departure, her deceptive, rebellious elopement and her stealing from her father's treasure two sealed bags of ducats and two precious stones. For this some critics would seem to agree with Shylock's interpretation: 'She is damned for it' (3.1.26). Some literary and historical perspectives help us put the nature of Jessica's flight in a broader Elizabethan context of rough justice rendered to the unkind father, who is both usurer and miser. Similar imagery of theft bonds the family of Shylock, Jessica, and Lorenzo. Even Lancelot is so described: 'thou a merry devil / Didst *rob* [Shylock's house] of some taste of tediousness' (2.3.2–3, my italics). For conservative Elizabethans usury is considered theft, not 'thrift' (1.3.82), and therefore the usurer is seen as a thief in taking 'excess' on a loan. This 'excess' is believed to be a violation of social justice, brotherly love, and natural process.

Turnabout is often considered fair play in Elizabethan comedy: therefore, Lorenzo plays the thief in order to get his wife (2.6.24), and Jessica steals some of her father's wealth as a dowry to give to her husband. The usurer now has the theft done unto him that he has done unto others. Shylock sees 'theft' as 'thrift' when it serves his advantage, for example, Rebecca's 'wise' deception (1.3.65) that results in Jacob's theft of his father's blessing for his heirs. But when deception and theft are practised against Shylock, his perspective shifts, and he sees them as a 'curse' (3.1.67). Shylock's return is a twofold penalty, the loss of inanimate (gold and jewels) and animate (daughter) wealth, which parallels the Elizabethan view of the avaricious usurer as essentially a barren man.[49] Shylock's gold and silver may breed, but his offspring appears sterile and 'dead' to him. Shylock's symbolic barrenness parallels the penalty of barrenness to which the wrong choices of Morocco and Arragon are subjected. Shylock's thievery for self-love's gain contrasts with Jessica's and Lorenzo's thefts for love of another; their liberal natures counterpoint Shylock's niggardliness: 'In such a night / Did Jessica steal from the wealthy Jew, / And with an unthrift love did run from Venice / As far as Belmont' (5.1.14–17).

Elopement is a stock convention in comedic literature, and the likely Italian source for some aspects of Jessica's elopement is the fourteenth tale in Masuccio Salernitano's fifteenth-century *Il Novellino*. In this story the young daughter of a miser flies from the clutches of her old, avaricious father to the arms of her lover, confiscating fifteen hundred of her father's ducats. This incident is presented as an occasion for joy. In an appended note Masuccio predicts that his readers will praise the girl's foresight because she managed 'to obtain out of the hoard of her miserly old father a greater sum of money than would have been given to her as a dower'.[50] We have no idea how many ducats Jessica takes, although the number must exceed the fourscore she spends in Genoa. At least she limits herself to two bags plus whatever she can gild herself withal.[51] Masuccio's tale ends with the reconciliation of the family; Shakespeare may also hint the same for his family through a 'conversion' of the children's rebellion to a possible future reconciliation by means of Antonio's attempted interbonding of them through a shared inheritance of wealth and faith. As with Celia's father in *As You Like It*, it takes more than a daughter's desertion to precipitate a reformation of a wayward father.

Jessica's elopement, then, is a Venetian dramatic correlative of the Belmontian casket test. Shakespeare specifically links Jessica's choice to that of the caskets in Belmont when she throws down a 'casket' of wealth (2.6.34) to her beloved.[52] That Jessica takes both gold and jewels recalls the very contents of the leaden casket in Shakespeare's source, the *Gesta Romanorum*.[53] Like Portia, Jessica marries an 'unthrift lover' (5.1.16) whose vows of love are true. As a dowry for her husband, the gift of the disinherited Jessica's *stolen* wealth parodically precedes the gift of Portia's *legally inherited* wealth to her husband. However, Portia's gendered 'conversion' through male disguise follows Jessica's earlier one, suggesting deliberate interconnections between these two greater and lesser heroines and the trope of 'conversion'. Both women also relate their different financial 'conversions' of stolen versus legal wealth to a freely willed, larger 'conversion' of self through marriage, whether of personal fidelity (Portia) or religious faith

(Jessica). Portia's interrelated conversion of personal fidelity and wealth to her husband – 'Myself, and what is mine, to you and yours / Is now converted' (3.2.166–7) – immediately precedes her turning over of her new lord's estate (in his absence and her intended absence) to the temporary manage of Jessica and her husband. And the teasing banter over Jessica's voluntary *spiritual* conversion through marriage (3.5) immediately follows the scenes of Portia's multiple conversions (3.2; 3.4). Linking all these various conversions is the element of risk in the human venturing for love. For example, all the emphasis on the need for secrecy regarding the intended elopement of Jessica and Lorenzo underscores the hazard of being caught. Such risk, with severe penalty, is not avoided in *The Two Gentlemen of Verona* (3.1), and in Masuccio's story the worry over such danger constantly intrudes itself upon the lovers' plans.[54] But, as the old proverb puts it, 'Nothing venture, nothing win'.[55]

The Venetian boys' bawdy and unmerciful mockery of Shylock's lamentation – 'Crying his stones, his daughter, and his ducats' (2.8.23–4) – puns on Shylock's two stones in the sense of testicles.[56] Jessica, the product of Shylock's organ of generation, has figuratively castrated him by deserting him and stealing his 'two stones, two rich and precious stones' (2.8.20). This might account for the introduction here of the number symbolism of 'two' in a play that features 'three' as the dominant number. Jessica also takes only 'two sealèd bags of ducats, / Of double ducats' (2.8.18–21). That the bags are 'sealèd' suits Shylock's penchant for safeguarding his riches. But why only two bags, two stones, and 'double ducats'? The emphasis on 'two' here may accomplish two ends: (1) two is the number of testicles and suggests 'breeding' potential, indicated by Shylock's propagation of his daughter, and (2) two is also a number used in the marriage mystery of 'two-in-one' ('they twain shall be one flesh', Eph 5.31). If so intended here, the taking of 'two' of everything looks forward to the nuptial celebration when the twoness of man and woman become the oneness of husband and wife.[57] Jessica sells one stone, but appears to keep the other one. As an only child Jessica is technically Shylock's firstborn (cf. Za 12.10; Lk 2.7). Part of the primogeniture rights of firstborn sons includes a 'double portion' (Dt 21.17) of the father's wealth. As an only child, a firstborn, and a daughter, Jessica could be entitled to inherit all her father's wealth. But perhaps her 'double-dealing' here relates to the 'double portion' rule applicable to the firstborn. Shylock, who formerly saw himself as 'blest' (1.3.81), now feels cursed (3.1.67) once Jessica leaves as she does, because the idea of 'blessing' (1.3.82) can apply to all a man's possessions, and Shylock has lost his only child as well as a double portion of wealth.

We expect a rich man like Shylock to have a store of precious stones, but why does Shakespeare select the particular gems he does, the diamond and the turquoise? Do the specific stones convey symbolic meaning the way the 'pearl' does in *Othello*? As a gem, the diamond appears to be significant for its association with what is heavenly or celestial. For example, in Spenser's *The Faerie Queene* Arthur's shield is made of no 'earthly mettals', but it is 'all of Diamond perfect pure and clean', and in Phineas Fletcher's *The Purple Island* Fido carries a shield of '"one pure diamond, celestial fair"'.[58] Shakespeare is also probably influenced by Marlowe's figurative use of the diamond as the recurrent metaphor for Abigail, who is Barabas's most treasured gem. Through Ludowick's suit to have Abigail, Marlowe puns on Barabas's diamonds (his wealth) – 'Tush man, we talked of diamonds, not of Abigail' (2.3.150) – and his diamond (Abigail) – 'This [Abigail] is thy diamond; tell me, shall I have it?' (2.3.289).[59] When Barabas feigns he will give Ludowick much wealth for the match because he says the son of the Christian governor 'would disdain / To marry with the daughter of a Jew', Ludowick responds, ''Tis not thy wealth, but her that I esteem' (2.3.291–5). Like Abigail, Jessica is the richest gem her father has, although he does not realise it.

The other gem Jessica steals is Shylock's turquoise. This stone is in a ring, and Shylock's reaction to its loss hints of nobler possibilities in his character. Unlike Shylock's reaction to the loss of his Frankfurt diamond, he values the turquoise not for its price but for its meaning. In two poignant lines Shakespeare embodies Shylock's young manhood as a bachelor and his ability to prioritise on the basis of humane bonds, not cold cash contracts: 'it was my turquoise, I had it of Leah when I was a bachelor. I would not have given it for a wilderness of monkeys' (3.1.95–7). Is it likely that Jessica knows the personal meaning of this ring to Shylock? It does not seem so because he shares so little with her, whether tangible or intangible, and because Shylock no longer wears this ring on a regular basis, suggesting to the uninitiated that it has no more particular value for him than his other jewels. It is stashed among his other precious stones from which Jessica helps herself on the eve of her elopement. And Jessica has to steal quickly because Shylock's parting words threatened that he might change his mind and 'return immediately' (2.5.50).

If Jessica knows the meaning of this ring and parts with it so casually, her action would be heartless, especially in light of the distinctions between monetary value and emotional value made again in the later rings episode. But in that episode the men know full well the meanings of their rings, and Shakespeare has made certain we know they know by staging their reception of these first gifts. There is nothing of the like for Jessica's situation. Moreover, Jessica has not been presented as an unfeeling rebel, out to spite her father, but as a feeling daughter deeply troubled by her filial disaffection. As we have seen, Shakespeare juxtaposes Jessica's *selling* of her father's betrothal ring, a token of fidelity, as a parodic precursor to Portia's *giving* of her ring to Bassanio in the next scene (3.2.171). The significance of this ring episode in the play relates complexly the meanings of its precious stone to the ring's specific associations: (1) Leah gave it to Shylock, probably as a betrothal ring; (2) Shylock wishes to identify himself with Jacob; and (3) Jessica steals this ring as part of her self-appointed dowry but sells it for a monkey in Genoa.

The turquoise, as Jackson Campbell Boswell ably explains, has both positive and negative as well as Eastern and European associations. It was associated with the wealth and health of its wearer and was a favourite engagement ring in Germany until this century, but it was also believed to cause sterility in women who owned it.[60] The fact that Shylock bought his diamond in Frankfurt may suggest German influence on the choice of the turquoise for a betrothal ring. Boswell suggests that Jessica parts with the ring because of the European superstition about sterility and that she shows 'her contempt for a Hebraic talisman by trading it for a monkey'.[61] But if Jessica knew possession of this stone caused sterility, she probably would not have taken it in the first place. Moreover, at the time of Robert Wilson's *The Three Ladies of London* (1584) the turquoise ('Turkasir') is one of the precious stones that English gentlewomen want to have imported.[62] The turquoise, derived chiefly from Persia and Turkestan, has no particular Hebraic associations and does not appear in the Bible. Jessica, therefore, probably takes this stone for its well-known quality to monitor and preserve the well-being of its wearer.[63] Once safe in Genoa with Lorenzo, Jessica, having not been crossed by Shylock's reach, may feel she no longer needs such a talisman for personal protection. In joyous relief she rids herself of such superstition by selling it for a monkey, an inanimate stone for an animate pet. Monkeys were popular pets, especially among noblemen, kept for the laughter they provoked by their mimicry and giddy behaviour.[64] A monkey could be seen as the animal version of the human fool, whom noblemen also kept for their entertainment.[65]

Jessica, having lost her former fool or 'merry devil' Lancelot, has just escaped the confines of Shylock's 'sober house' and should be in the mood to celebrate with laughter and freespending. In her first experience of the carnival masquerade atmosphere of *Venezia-città-galante*, amid evening music and festive hopes, Jessica, the torchbearer, lights the lovers' way to Genoa, where she spends four-score ducats in one night and buys a pet, later journeying onward to Belmont. Jessica's freewheeling caper is not meanspirited. Herman Melville's assessment of the highjinks of sailors who come ashore after confinement on duty might apply to Jessica, who has just escaped her domestic duties: their excessive behaviour partakes not of 'crookedness of heart . . . [but] exuberance of vitality after long constraint'.[66] In her strong defence of Jessica against the negative attitude many critics have adopted, Camille Slights suggests we need 'not accept Tubal's biased and secondhand account about her honeymoon extravagance'.[67] But if we believe Tubal's reports about Antonio's argosies, then we must grant him equal credibilty for his news about Jessica. Moreover, Tubal tells Shylock he saw the ring Jessica gave in exchange for the monkey (3.1.93–4).

The allegorical significance of Shylock's betrothal ring concerns not the precious stone but the purpose of the ring and the name identities of those involved with it. Shylock wishes to resemble the rich Jacob, but as we have seen, his choice of Leah allies him more with Laban, who deceived Jacob by substituting the elder Leah for the younger Rachel whom Jacob chose. When Jacob takes advantage of Laban's temporary absence to leave his father-in-law, taking with him his wives and goods, Rachel steals her father's household gods or idols (Gn 31.19,30).[68] Thus, Laban's loss is twice metaphorically expressed as having his 'heart' stolen (Gn 31.20, 26). Laban, unlike Jacob, was an idolater (Gn 31.29, gloss). For his practice of usury, Shylock can be seen as an idolater like Laban and like Morocco; as Thomas Wilson explains, usurers are 'wise worldly rich men' who, like idolaters, make 'the world their god'.[69]

Rachel, not unlike Masuccio's heroine and Jessica, might have stolen her father's household gods because her father gave no dowry, as Elizabethan commentator Andrew Willet suggests.[70] Therefore, Jessica's stealing of her father's idols, gold and gems, comically parodies Rachel's graver theft from her father, graver because the Bishops' Bible twice criticises Rachel's 'superstitious' confiscation of her father's idols: 'It was not godliness, but superstition that moved Rachel to this theft' (Gn 31.19, 32, glosses).

Jessica, on the other hand, avoids the superstitiousness of her father's reliance on mundane signs (2.5.18, 22–6) and demonstrates her non-superstitious nature by being able to part with her father's idols. Moreover, Jessica's *selling* of an unrecognised *symbol* of her fleshly ancestry in order to obtain the merriment of a hairy pet monkey may also parody the action, but not the knowing intent, of the hairy Esau's *selling* of his actual birthright *privilege* to his brother Jacob for a bowl of lentil pottage to feed his flesh (Gn 25.27–34; cf. Heb. 12.17). In the Geneva Bible Esau's action is glossed: 'Thus the wicked prefer their worldly commodities to God's spiritual graces: but the children of god do the contrary' (Gn 25.33, gloss). Many of the biblically astute in an Elizabethan audience would probably see Jessica's action as 'contrary' in spirit to Esau's because she has left her earthly father and his 'idols' to seek her heavenly father's spiritual graces and salvation. From their Christian perspective the contents of the gold and silver caskets (a death's head and a fool's head) would be appropriate rewards for a man who considers his daughter dead to him when in fact he has been foolishly dead to her. Shylock's loss of Jessica heightens his pathos for the audience, but his reduction of her to his 'Christian ducats' (2.8.16) simultaneously undercuts this appeal. If Shylock would make the symbolic leaden choice, he would find his daughter and she him.

Within the context of the play the parallel matters of marriage and money link Jessica to Portia chiefly as a foil figure in her filial rebellion, disobedience, and theft. These paralleled contrasts, however, do not so much detract from the 'wise, fair, and true' Jessica, but rather make her unwise and unkind father look bad by comparison with Portia's noble father. As Masuccio contends concerning his eloping heroine, the vices of the miserly old father are 'the real causes of the flout that was put upon him'.[71] Like Portia, Jessica proves no hoarder of wealth, but gives it to her husband. She also freely spends wealth, although for less noble ends than our chief heroine. Like Portia and Nerissa, Jessica intentionally deceives the eyes of others for love's sake. Unlike her father, who uses verbal deceit for hateful revenge, Jessica's visual deceit serves the liberation of young love, although her actions will cause her father much distress over his losses.

The parallel usage of male disguise for all three women in the play complements the pattern of their feminine names, all derived from their patriarchal names, as we have seen. But there is a telling difference in attitude between Portia's and Nerissa's playful attitude toward their adopted costumes of lawyerly disguise, and Jessica's evident shame for having to don boy's attire and to hold a candle to her shame as a torchbearer. Jessica's shame properly reflects her Jewish upbringing because the Old Testament forbade women to dress in male attire (Dt 22.5).[72] But another perspective obtains here that should elicit more sympathy for Jessica. Having a torch to illuminate what she sees as shameful attire also bespeaks what that attire signifies in this instance (her own stealthy rebellion) and recalls her earlier expression of sadness over the sin she felt in having to be ashamed of her father's morals. In keeping with the choice of 'base lead', Jessica sacrifices her shame and humbly goes forward to give and hazard all she has for the love of Lorenzo.

'GOD-LIKE AMITY' (3.4.3)

Lorenzo's deistic description of true friendship as 'god-like amity' is not merely highflown poetry. The love of true friends is god-like. In John's gospel the love between God and man is explicitly defined in terms of friendship: 'Ye are my friends, if ye do whatsoever I command you. Henceforth, call I you not servants . . . but I have called you friends' (Jn 15.14–15). In Boethius' *Consolation of Philosophy* Lady Philosophy exhorts, 'But forsothe freendes schulde nat ben rekned among the goodes of fortune, but of vertu, for it is a ful hooly maner thyng'.[73] Friendship, as a good of virtue, is unlike the goods of fortune, which are desired for either the power or pleasure they afford. True friendship, moreover, pursues no temporal gain, no worldly advantage, nothing outside of itself because it is its own fruit, its own reward. In this play the concepts of friendship and romance are necessarily interrelated because both friendship and romance have to be rooted in wise love if they are to be true. This play is entitled for Antonio, who is the merchant of Venice and the central figure of friendship as the 'dearest friend' (3.2.291), the 'true friend' (3.2.307). In some respects Antonio is the most difficult character to analyse in the play. He is never given a lengthy aside, like Shylock, or a soliloquy, which would make his innermost thoughts more accessible to the audience.

Antonio is arguably the most important character in the play, especially in terms of plot progression; however, Shylock, as the antagonist, creates the most dramatic tension; Portia, as the lodestar, guides the other characters; and Bassanio, as the suitor, wins the heroic exploit of true love. But Antonio causes both main actions of the play, the casket plot and the flesh-bond plot, to be activated by his generous financing of Bassanio's venture through the flesh bond with Shylock. The resolutions of these plots fall to Bassanio in his casket scene and to Portia in the trial scene. In the final act all three principals play various related roles in the instigation and resolution of the ring episode, but it is Antonio who causes Bassanio's actual giving away of his ring, and Antonio is also the reason Jessica and Lorenzo receive Shylock's deed of gift which Portia delivers to them. Roles of causation and resolution obviously overlap in this play because friends help lovers and lovers help friends. Antonio is also the character who confronts the opportunities for the most serious moral growth in the play – the challenges of loving friend and foe wisely. Antonio's reputation for being 'the best conditioned and unwearied spirit / In doing courtesies' (3.2.292–3) in Venice would seem to 'complete the role of the good man', as described by Seneca in one of his moral essays, as one who selflessly and freely bestows benefits: 'Help one man with money, another with influence, another with advice, another with sound precepts'.[74] But in his opening speech Antonio announces the play's interest in what might be the learning aptitude of a man who now has 'much ado to know [himself]' (1.1.5). Flannery O'Connor's modern concern with what it means to be 'a good man' surfaces in Bassanio's and Shylock's discussion of that idea for Antonio, and in the audience's varying assessment of Antonio's goodness regarding his friends as opposed to his enemy, Shylock.[75]

For his theme of friendship, Shakespeare appropriately introduces Antonio in the midst of some of his many Venetian friends who, like Benvolio to Romeo, are trying to alleviate their friend's new and mysterious melancholy by discovering its cause. This friendly circle is not what one might expect to see in the opening scene of a play billed as *The Merchant of Venice*. Where is the Venetian merchant busily absorbed by his business? Business risks are far-flung from Antonio's mind, which is not 'tossing on the ocean' (1.1.8). Rather, the friends of this 'royal merchant' (4.1.29) set the expected mercantile atmosphere by their detailed descriptions of his wealthy ventures and seaworthy hazards. Salarino and Solanio would be melancholy through their fear of the potential loss of mercantile wealth: 'I know Antonio / Is sad to think upon his merchandise' (1.1.40). As William Faulkner reminds us, 'Man knows so little about his fellows. In his eyes all men or women act upon what he believes would motivate him if he were mad enough to do what the other man or woman is doing'.[76]

Antonio patiently explains that he is grateful for his good fortune, and his astute business strategy helps to assuage such worrying: 'My ventures are not in one bottom trusted, / Nor to one place; nor is my whole estate / Upon the fortune of this present year" (1.1.42–4). Later Antonio will confide to Bassanio that he really has not been quite so astute because 'all his fortunes are at sea' (1.1.176). This apparent contradiction can probably be attributed not to Antonio's lying but to Shakespeare's change of mind or false start. Antonio's prudence accounts for his worldly success in handling his wealth, unlike the prodigality of both Bassanio and Lorenzo, who are seriously in need of money. But Shakespeare also has to put his prudent merchant in a position of need so that borrowing will be necessary, as it is for the merchant in *Il Pecorone*.[77] Shakespeare has another false start when he introduces Bassanio as Antonio's 'noble kinsman' (1.1.57), following the emphasis on kinship in *Il Pecorone*.[78] Shakespeare, however, drops that association in favour of the emphasis on friendship, again his important change of *Il Pecorone*. Although Antonio seems older than his friends because he is prudent, and seems even fatherly because he is financially providential, it is his role as *friend* that Shakespeare chooses to emphasise.

After Antonio refutes the proposed financial cause, Solanio concludes that romantic love must be the cause of Antonio's strange melancholy. But Antonio decisively refutes that motive too. Salarino and Solanio are left as mystified as Antonio, but they none the less attempt to 'make [him] merry' (1.1.60) through their well-meant but feeble humour: 'Then let us say you are sad / Because you are not merry' (1.3.47–8). Realising their failure to alleviate Antonio's mood, they excuse themselves to make room for Antonio's 'worthier friends' (1.1.61), Gratiano and Bassanio, especially the latter, of whom Solanio later hypothesises: 'I think he [Antonio] only loves the world for him' (2.8.51). Antonio none the less graciously confirms Salarino's and Solanio's worth in his regard and offers them the polite excuse of 'business calls' (1.1.63) for their departure. Venice is indeed a world of 'business' – the business of wealth and the 'business' of love. Even Lorenzo arrives tardy for his tryst with Jessica because business – 'his affairs' (2.6.23) – are to blame. In such an environment of expected hustle and bustle on the Rialto, Antonio's preoccupation with friendship is most praiseworthy. Friendship as a possible cause for Antonio's melancholy surprisingly seems not to occur to Salarino and Solanio, until we recollect that no one but Antonio thus far knows about Bassanio's intended pilgrimage to Belmont.

The most obvious reason for Antonio's melancholy concerns the subject of friendship and the feared loss of one well loved. Critics surprisingly take little notice of the emphasis on melancholy in *Il Pecorone* as the natural response to the absence of someone loved. Financial losses are inconsequential compared with the absence of a loved one.[79] In this source both the merchant (Ansaldo) and the suitor (Giannetto) become understandably melancholic when separated from another loved one. Shakespeare limits melancholy to his merchant and contrasts his subdued mood with the joyful mood of the suitor, Bassanio. Shakespeare, however, resounds the melancholic note for Portia's entrance into the play, and here he unmistakably links her melancholy to the absence of a lover and to her negligible choice in the matter of obtaining a husband.

Once Bassanio enters and the two friends are left alone to discuss Bassanio's intended 'secret pilgrimage' (1.1.119) to Portia, we discover that Antonio already knew that his dearest friend was hoping to go on a journey of love that would put literal as well as at least some emotional distance between these two friends. That Bassanio shared his secret with his best friend may partially reveal why Antonio could not articulate to Salarino and Solanio at least this predictable reason for his newly found melancholy. 'Today' (1.1.120) is the day on which Bassanio has promised to share all his news with Antonio. Just how new and how strange this melancholy is for Antonio should be underscored in relation to the only event of new occurrence in his life that we hear about, namely, Bassanio's pilgrimage. Like the melancholy of two other young protagonists, Romeo and Hamlet, the melancholy of Antonio is introduced as a recent and marked change of natural temperament. If we are to judge by Antonio's friends, he is normally far more disposed to conviviality. So recent is Antonio's mood swing that even Bassanio seems to be ignorant about it when he approaches and merrily demands of Salarino and Solanio: 'Good signors both, when shall we laugh? Say, when?' (1.1.66). Bassanio immediately senses their reserve and desists, but before he can attend to Antonio, Lorenzo absorbs his attention about his elopement plan. The garrulous Gratiano is left to observe how 'marvellously changed' (1.1.76) their friend has become, and like Salarino and Solanio, he too falsely concludes that Antonio buys 'the world' (1.1.74) with too much care about it. Not one to appreciate the sounds of silence when a man has warm blood in him, Gratiano says that his 'love' for Antonio urges him to declare his disapproving view of men who use 'a wilful stillness' to cultivate a reputation for wisdom: 'But fish not with this melancholy bait / For this fool gudgeon, this opinion' (1.1.101–2).[80]

Bassanio dismisses Gratiano's 'reasons' as 'an infinite deal of nothing' (1.1.114–15), but as the play progresses, Antonio, who already enjoys a stellar reputation for honour (3.2.291–5), grows increasingly interested in the subject of his 'reputation', a reputation for extraordinary love of Bassanio that will need some tempering wisdom taught by Portia. Shakespeare also invests Antonio's opening lines with a genuine sense of bewilderment – 'how I caught it, found it, or came by it, / . . . I am to learn' (1.1.3–5) – which enshrouds his use of this melancholy motif with a much greater sense of mystery than the same motif in the source, because Shakespeare's merchant is grappling for self-knowledge. In addition to the normal reason for Antonio's melancholy just discussed, at least two other more mystifying reasons could be adduced for Antonio's 'mysterious' melancholy. An Elizabethan audience could find such black humour premonitory of some impending sorrow, and they would not be disappointed in such an expectation when Antonio later describes his 'griefs' (3.3.32), as the depth of his melancholy intensifies with the increase of his troubles. Danson also convincingly suggests that Antonio's melancholy can be seen spiritually, as symptomatic of his moral illness of malice toward Shylock.[81]

This opening scene revolves around the interrelation of lucre and love: Antonio's mercantile wealth – his loving use of it as well as his non-obsession with it – and Bassanio's loss of wealth and his need for it in order to travel to win Portia, who is herself a wealthy heiress. We discover later that as a financial friend to Venice, Antonio's generosity steads many Venetians in distress (3.3). Free lending is Antonio's way of befriending those in need. Antonio's habit is not idiosyncratic but based on the Bible: 'a good man is merciful and lendeth', and the gloss reads, 'he showeth what is the fruit of mercy: to lend freely & not for gain . . . that he may be able to help where need requireth, and not to bestow all on himself' (Ps 112.5). Free lending, without hope or exaction of profit on the loan, is the prescribed way of Christian love (see Lk 6.30, 34–5). Therefore, lending freely is loving rightly, and the play emphasises the spirit of giving even more than it does actual gifts. Because Antonio is so generous and non-demanding in his lending, it is easy to mistake his loans as outright 'gifts', as some critics have done who analyse the import of the play's theme of giving.[82] But the concept of a 'loan' is different from the concept of a 'gift' because it is reasonable to expect the return of the principal of a loan, whereas there is no expectation of return of the gift.[83]

Shakespeare and Venice allow for the social justice of properly repaid debts because Bassanio's intention to repay his debts is not contradicted by Antonio (1.1.131–3) but accepted by him (3.2.316–17), and in the trial the Duke hopes that Shylock will 'forgive a moiety of the principal' owed (4.1.26). Antonio's wealth helps others in the form of free loans, but the manner and attitude of Antonio's non-insistent, openhanded lending emulates the spirit of giving. In terms of his giving and hazarding for friends, Antonio figuratively passes the casket test. The most valuable riches are spiritual, and wise love is the greatest 'wealth' one can possess: 'Lay not up treasures for your selves upon the earth . . . / But lay up treasures for your selves in heaven . . . / For where your treasure is, there will your heart be also' (Mat 6.19–20). The play explores various values through 'loves', and 'heart' becomes an important symbol: what one loves is what one really treasures.

The play's problematic issue of worldly wealth concerns not only the possession of wealth but even more importantly the proper attitude toward wealth, which is crucially tested in both Venice and Belmont. Thomas Moisan, for example, describes the ambivalence in Shakespeare's culture toward wealth in two opposing views, one favouring the compatibility between godliness and wealth and the other challenging such linkage. Moisan, however, focuses on the possession of wealth but not the more important issue of the possessor's interior motive.[84] Regardless if one is wealthy or poor in pocket, the rich man or the poor man must always be poor in *spirit* if he is to be godly. The Bible suggests that it is theoretically much more difficult for those who enjoy Lady Lucre's favours to achieve such purity of heart. Antonio's free lending directly opposes Shylock's usurious lending, indicating Antonio's healthier attitude toward the possession and use of wealth.

Later in the play Solanio describes Antonio: 'the good Antonio, the honest Antonio – O that I had a title good enough to keep his name company! – ' (3.1.10–12). Although a fair amount of criticism has been devoted to the name of Antonio,[85] one important possiblity has been overlooked for why Shakespeare might have chosen the name 'Antonio' for an Italian, Christian character who is profoundly opposed to the giving and taking of usury. 'Antonio' is the name of St Antonino (1389–1459), a great moral theologian, Dominican reformer, and Archbishop of Florence (the banking capital of Europe) during the fifteenth century. He enjoyed a reputation for a great spirit of charity, and his most famous work is the *Summa theologica* (also known as the *Summa moralis*), in which he takes a stongly conservative stand against usury. Raymond De Roover explains that the name of this prolific writer is Antonio, which is the name he used in his signatures, but Antonino, a diminutive of Antonio, was given to him because of his small stature; the nickname stuck, even in the calendar of saints.[86]

St Antonino's work was known and respected by some of the more influential authors of the anti-usury literature in Renaissance England, because they refer favourably to him; he is cited in the major sixteenth-century treatises by Wilson and Mosse, which Shakespeare probably knew.[87] Noonan observes that the important work of Antoninus was 'frequently consulted in practice in the next 150 years': 'As the late seventeenth century is to draw all departures from the usury prohibition together in a final, all-inclusive departure, so Antoninus draws together all the strict rules of the early usury teaching into a tight set of rules. No later writer of note will be as severe, as uncompromising, as true to the logic of the earlier conceptions, as he.'[88] Antonino was even surprisingly strict regarding the *depositi a discrezione* (bankers' 'free gifts' to depositors) because of the concept of mental usury which condemns the *expectation* of gain on a loan,[89] and it is to this important concept we will return when we consider how Shakespeare's Antonio eventually becomes a mental usurer in his relationship to Bassanio. According to De Roover, 'Sant' Antonino' is one of the few scholastics to specify usury as 'a kind of *turpe lucrum*' (ill-gotten gain, such as that derived from prostitution, gambling, simony, etc.), and as such, usurious gain had to be restored directly to the injured party or his heir.[90] Noonan explains, 'the enormity and viciousness of usury are particularly impressed on St Antoninus . . . by his daily contact with a highly commercial society', and Antoninus claims that 'not only open usurers, but all cooperators in usury, are "worthy of eternal death"'.[91] We would be hard pressed to find a better historical candidate as an intended namesake for Shakespeare's Antonio, who often delivers from a usurer's forfeitures 'many that have at times made moan to [him]' (3.3.23).

Opposed to the sinful gain of usury, which negates both love and hazard by insisting on taking 'excess' on a loan, Antonio expresses love to his fellow Venetians through his free lending to those in need. Antonio's commitment to human friendship, free lending, and to relative unworldliness would particularly impress Elizabethan audiences because such traits would be seen as striking contrasts to those typically associated with merchants, whether on the Elizabethan stage or in London's mercantile community. As a benevolent merchant, generous with his wealth to his friends, Antonio would be a very intriguing character to Elizabethans precisely because Shakespeare truncates expectations regarding the typically perceived role of the merchant. Antonio's non-obsessive concern for his physical wealth would be even more praiseworthy, however, were it not sullied by a streak of excessive pride, overconfidence in his mercantile wisdom. Although Antonio's prudence in managing his wealth is a virtue that some of his friends could learn to emulate, his self-reliant pride in his prudence is not a virtue. Antonio will discover within three months' time how fragile is his pride in outwitting the seas' hazards, when he becomes 'beggared by the strumpet wind' (2.6.20).

Bassanio is the Venetian who has most benefited from Antonio's generous nature. As a gentleman and a nobleman, Bassanio is embarrassed by the extent of his indebtedness to his friend: 'To you, Antonio, / I owe the most in money and love' (1.1.129–30). Antonio has already established his generous love on previous occasions and has just asserted he will stead Bassanio again, using language that anticipates the locked and unlocked caskets of Bassanio's Belmontian hazard: ' . . . be assured / My purse, my person, my extremest means / Lie all *unlocked* to your occasions' (1.1.138, my italics). Antonio's 'unlocking' of all he has for Bassanio serves as an analogue in the way of friendship to Portia's conversion of all she has to Bassanio in the way of marriage (3.2.166–7). Such gestures of personal divestiture sharply contrast with Shylock's characteristic gesture of 'locking up', of fast binding (2.5.51–3). But Bassanio's embarrassment over borrowing and losing what he borrows probably inspires his puerile circumlocution on archery in order to recover a loss. Instead of establishing either the honour or the wisdom of the plan, Bassanio's indirectness offends Antonio's sense of his own genuine generosity more than if Bassanio 'had made waste of all' Antonio has (1.1.156). All Bassanio has to do is state directly what Antonio should do for him. Antonio is 'prest unto it' (1.1.160); his credit 'shall be racked even to the uttermost' (1.1.180) to help his friend. Although Antonio probably intends only the common meanings of 'prest' and 'racked', Shakespeare's use of these words may figuratively anticipate the psychosomatic torture that the unsuspecting Antonio will undergo for Bassanio.

Antonio, however, has already revealed his characteristic strain of prudence. His liberal offer has been prudently prefaced by the condition of honour: Bassanio's plan, like Bassanio himself, must 'stand . . . within the eye of honour' (1.1.135–6). Several scenes later Bassanio's own impetuous indiscretion contrasts with his friend's prudence in the granting of favours. Gratiano says he has a suit to Bassanio, and Bassanio responds without reflection or conditions, 'You have obtained it' (2.2.149). After Bassanio hears Gratiano's request, then Bassanio finds it necessary to place conditions on his too quick acquiescence. The 'too wild' Gratiano gains his friend's trust with a promise to play in Belmont a role ironically similar to the one he criticised earlier to Antonio – the sober, silent, civil man of 'sad ostent' (2.2.160–8). And Gratiano apparently keeps that promise, or at least keeps it enough to win Nerissa's love and not to darken Bassanio's hopes.

With comic ironies piling up, Bassanio must in his turn caution Gratiano about a weakness in the direction of excess – one that is relative to his own weakness because he notes that Gratiano's vociferousness might impress those who do not know Gratiano as 'something too liberal' (2.2.156). In his own suit to Antonio,

Bassanio describes his fault as being 'something too prodigal'; he has disabled his own estate 'by something showing a more swelling port / Than [his] faint means would grant continuance' (1.1.122–9). Bassanio's conspicuous consumption and prodigal ways as a young gentleman would not be foreign news to an Elizabethan audience. Thomas Wilson explains that 'unnecessary liberality, more used in England than elswhere' frequently reduces a man to poverty.[92] Thomas Lodge warns young men against prodigality and lavish spending on 'brave attire' that will make them impoverished victims of usurious loans.[93] Recognising his tendency to prodigality, Bassanio loses his inherited and borrowed wealth because of his excessive liberality, as instantiated, for example, in his reputation for giving new liveries (2.2.89) and in his order for the newly hired Lancelot to receive 'a livery / More guarded than' those of his fellow servants (2.2.129–30). Bassanio and Gratiano are comparable friends in their excessive liberality, manifested in different ways: Bassanio is too extravagant with wealth and words; Gratiano is too wild with behaviour and words.

Although both Antonio and Bassanio are exceptionally generous friends, they are not the twin prodigals that Shylock mistakenly sees them to be (1.3.18; 2.5.15, 49). Antonio's business hazards are legitimate risks native to the natural enterprise of merchantry. Antonio prudently manages his wealth as Bassanio does not; Antonio's 'argosies with portly sail' (1.1.9) have enabled his estate, while Bassanio's too 'swelling port' (1.1.123) has disabled his. These two bosom friends, who share each other's strong suit for love, also counterbalance each other's weaknesses. Bassanio has erred in the direction of imprudence regarding his funds – the physical wealth of inheritance, loans, or gifts. As we shall discover, Antonio will err in the direction of imprudence regarding his friend – the emotional wealth of friendship. Bassanio's human failing concerns prodigality; Antonio's concerns pride. While Bassanio could learn from Antonio's financial prudence, Antonio could learn from Bassanio's insightful humility. Bassanio forthrightly acknowledges his great indebtedness to Antonio, and his accurate admission of his weakness for prodigality reveals self-knowledge: 'I owe you much, and like a willful youth / That which I owe is lost' (1.1.45–6).[94] Antonio will need to learn to be more humble and self-knowing. Pride, the arch enemy of humility, makes Antonio and Shylock comparable enemies in their blindness to their faults and helps to fuel their mutual malice.

Of Antonio the friend, however, Salarino declares, 'A kinder
gentleman treads not the earth' (2.8.36). His praise seems accurate enough regarding Antonio's goodness to his friends, especially
Bassanio. Antonio's melancholy manifests itself most markedly
in his tears on the occasion of his farewell to Bassanio – the only
time he cries in the play. However, not to dampen Bassanio's
spirits, Antonio kindly turns aside his face so that Bassanio will
not see the tears he sheds at their leavetaking (2.8.47–50). Although
Solanio concludes from this description that Antonio 'only loves
the world for [Bassanio]', both Solanio and Salarino so love Antonio
that they, as in the opening scene, determine to try to cheer Antonio
'with some delight or other' (2.8.53–5). However, when Antonio
requests Bassanio's return to see him at his death, he concludes
his letter: 'Notwithstanding, use your pleasure; if your love do
not persuade you to come, let not my letter' (3.2.318–19). Antonio
now, not unlike Bassanio's earlier circumlocution about shooting
arrows, does Bassanio 'more wrong / In making question of [his]
uttermost' (1.1.154–5). After reading Antonio's letter, Bassanio
reveals once again his humility and indicts himself for being 'a
braggart' when he, 'rating [himself] at nothing', told Portia 'all
the wealth [he] had / Ran in [his] veins' (3.2.252–7). He condemns
himself further:

> . . . When I told you
> My state was nothing, I should then have told you
> That I was worse than nothing; for indeed
> I have engaged myself to a dear friend,
> Engaged my friend to his mere enemy,
> To feed my means.
>
> (3.2.257–62)

This nearly ideal friendship has its human problems.

The idea embodied by Antonio, that one should lend freely to
friends, also informs Shylock's expectation that his Jewish friend
Tubal will furnish him with 3000 ducats to loan because Shylock
says he does not have that amount handy at the moment (1.3.45–
50). As Benjamin Nelson suggests, the taking of interest on a loan
can be seen as a financial expression of enmity,[95] and we will
consider the importance of these ideas about lending when we
discuss in our next chapter how and why the bond is formulated
as it is. For our present concern, it should be noted that Shake-

speare adapts Marlowe's lead in giving his Jew a friend. Unlike Marlowe, however, Shakespeare concentrates the several unnamed Jewish friends of Barabas into one Jewish friend, who bears a significant name and who is given a larger and slightly different role to play because Shakespeare is deeply interested in developing the theme of friendship, as Marlowe is not. In *The Jew of Malta* Marlowe presents Barabas's Jewish friends as essentially good friends who do not embrace Barabas's Machiavellianism. They too have suffered by having half their wealth unfairly confiscated by the hypocritical Christian rulers of Malta in order to pay the Turkish tribute. Yet they seek to comfort Barabas in his lamentation over his lost wealth by advising him to 'be patient, gentle' and to 'remember Job' (1.2.170–81). Even though we will discover later that the clever Barabas has already hidden much of his vast wealth so that he might not suffer as much financial loss as his friends, Barabas is far more ireful than they. He perverts their spiritual counsel by claiming that he has far greater wealth than Job ever had so he, not Job, deserves to curse (1.2.181–99).

Shakespeare's use of Tubal is more complex because there are both negative and positive functions to his role, just as there is opposition, as explained earlier, between the negative meaning of the name 'Tubal' ('worldly', 'confusion') and the potentially positive significance assigned to that name ('Tubal' as 'Italy') in the Geneva–Tomson Bible. Shakespeare's Tubal does not compare favourably with Barabas's fellow Jews because he does not offer spiritual counsel to his distressed friend. Instead, in accordance with the meaning of his name, he offers a worldly perspective, focusing only on the loss of physical wealth. He also confuses Shylock emotionally with his alternate news, that brings tears of grief juxtaposed with tears of joy. Lancelot Gobbo's trying of 'confusions' with his sand-blind father (2.2.29) is a laughable anticipation of Tubal's more sophisticated 'confusion' of Shylock.[96] Moreover, Barabas's friends are patient despite their suffering, but Tubal's calm lacks such merit because he has suffered no financial loss. The language of Barabas's friends even conveys more empathy: 'Good Barabas, be patient . . . 'tis a misery / To see a man in such affliction' (1.2.200–13).

On the other hand, Tubal, as a worldly man, appears in a better light than Shylock because he does try to keep some sense of balanced perspective. He reminds Shylock that 'other men have ill luck too' (3.1.77), even though he focuses only on secular mishap.

Tubal does not goad Shylock into a frenzied state of anger against
Antonio; Shylock's desire to 'torture' Antonio is counterbalanced
by Tubal's information about Jessica, which 'tortures' Shylock
(3.1.91–5). This language of 'torture' reappears in the beginning
of the next scene but with a totally different purpose, not emotional entrapment but liberation. Like Shylock, Bassanio is on a
roller coaster of emotions, caught between the fear and joy of
choosing. Having to wait to make his choice is like living upon
the rack (3.2.25). But Portia is a far kinder friend, and a better
counsellor, than Tubal because she orients herself and others toward
love, and therefore, toward life, not toward hate and death. As
Bassanio exclaims: 'O happy torment, when my torturer / Doth
teach me answers for deliverance!' (3.2.37–8).

Tubal, therefore, can be played as a well-intended, calm friend
who counterbalances Shylock's grief with ecstasy, in pendulum
fashion, but Tubal is himself confused because he lacks the wisdom and the love to comfort Shylock. To Tubal's credit, he does
help Shylock by actively searching for the runaway Jessica. But
unlike the discourse of Barabas's friends, Tubal's language does
not transcend what is worldly, nor does it convey any apparent
warmth for Shylock. How different is the friendly counsel Nerissa
provides for Portia's moral edification when Portia is bemoaning
her loss of choice (1.2.3–29). How different is the language of
love that characterises the conversation of such friends as Antonio
and Bassanio, as well as the descriptions of Antonio by his other
friends – Salarino, Solanio, and Lorenzo.

Joy and pain attend the hazards for love in *The Merchant of
Venice*. The choices made in the name of friendship or romance
are related to each other by being choices either for or against
wise love. Choices for wise love, symbolised on stage by the leaden
casket, are also necessarily choices against worldliness, symbolised by the golden and silver caskets. Lorenzo's praise of 'god-
like amity' recalls this fundamental meaning of the opposition
between true and false love: 'Know ye not that the amity of the
world is the enmity of God? Whosoever therefore will be a friend
of the world, maketh himself the enemy of God . . . God resisteth
the proud, and giveth grace to the humble' (Jas 4.4,6). True friendship roots itself in an esteem for virtue. One wishes for the friend's
own good, not to gain by the goods of the friend. Antonio's friends
do not desert him when he loses all his worldly wealth because
his past good deeds have earned for him a lasting wealth of friends.

To varying degrees in this play all true friends and lovers stand for self-sacrifice, for the wisdom of the leaden choice. From a classical perspective the recurrent imaging of the quest for Portia as the quest for the Golden Fleece encompasses more than the oft noted sense of risk and venture associated with the young Argonauts.[97] The Golden Fleece itself symbolises the idea of selfless sacrifice, as well as human sacrifice in particular, epitomised in Portia's message, 'I stand for sacrifice'. The myth of the Golden Fleece begins as a story about the consequences of the betrayal of love. Like Jason, who later betrays Medea's love, a Greek king named Athamus tires of his wife and marries another, who tries to kill the firstborn prince, Phrixus. In answer to the mother's prayers, Hermes sends a wondrous ram with golden fleece who snatches the boy from the altar of sacrifice and takes him to King AEetes of Colchis, on the Black Sea. Later, in gratitude for his rescue, Phrixus sacrifices to Zeus the ram who saved him and gives the fleece of pure gold to the king who befriended him. Jason, the cousin of Phrixus, is later assigned the great adventure of bringing back the Golden Fleece from 'Colchos' strand' (1.1.170) if he wishes to regain the rightful rule of his country, which has been usurped by his evil cousin Pelias.

In classical myth the sacrificial significance of the ram with the precious golden fleece anticipates the Christian idea of human redemption through self-sacrifice: 'Knowing that ye were not re-deemed with corruptible things, as silver and gold ... But with the precious blood of Christ, as of a Lamb undefiled, & without spot' (1 Pt 1.18–19). Shakespeare's contextualised allusions to this classical myth (1.1.168; 3.2.240–1) encode the precious value of standing for sacrifice through the venturing of self. Choosing the leaden casket over gold and silver ranks as much as a heroic venture as that of Jason questing after the Golden Fleece or that of Alcides rescuing the virgin Hesione from deadly sacrifice. In this play, however, the heroic deed must be matched by an equally heroic integrity of intent. Friends and spouses alike will confront challenges, especially in the play's final two acts, to keep their deeds of love as beneficial for the other and as free from self-interest as possible. The difficulty for mortals to achieve the fullness of charity through friendship informs the play's conclusion as friends and lovers strive through their fallibility – their 'muddy vesture of decay' (5.1.64) – to achieve the ideal of loving wisely.

4

'Pardon this fault': Antonio and Shylock

The relationship between Antonio and Shylock is complicated, and the audience is clearly meant to compare and contrast these two through Shakespeare's elaborate juxtaposition of scenes and groupings of characters. But unlike Antonio, who gives the play its title, Shylock is noticeably absent from the opening and closing scenes of the play, as if Shakespeare intended to circumscribe his energies. In placing Antonio and Shylock within their different settings, where they appear without the other, we have considered how and why Shakespeare created for Antonio his friendship with Bassanio that is tested by a seeming paradox: the *renunciation* of the exclusivity of that friendship in enabling Bassanio to woo Portia and the *validation* of that friendship in Antonio's potential sacrifice of life and living for Bassanio. We have also considered how and why Shakespeare has developed a variety of personal relationships for Shylock – a friend to Tubal, an 'old' master to Lancelot Gobbo, a husband to Leah, and a father to Jessica. This focus has directed our attention to the more private life of these characters, but now we must shift to the more public side of Antonio and Shylock in their professional roles as Christian merchant and Jewish usurer.

The three scenes in which Antonio and Shylock appear together testify to the interplay of their personal and professional relationships. These three scenes are structurally positioned near the beginning, middle, and end of the play. The trial scene Shakespeare inherits from his literary source, *Il Pecorone*, but two of these scenes are wholly Shakespeare's invention, the powerful confrontations between Antonio and Shylock in the bond scene (1.3) and in the jailer scene following their reversal of fortunes (3.3). Consequently, these scenic additions reveal much about Shakespeare's artistry in crafting this complex play that generates so much bipolar criticism of pros and cons for Antonio and Shylock. When critics group themselves so decidedly in 'either/or' camps of interpretation, one can suspect that both camps have some truth to offer. But how, when, and where to bring these truths to bear requires a willingness to trust the text of the play and remain sensitively open to its many twists and turns.

Antonio and Shylock, like many paired characters, such as Hal and Falstaff, are foils to each other, meant to be compared regarding their situations, motives, words, and deeds. Both men can be unenlightened about themselves as well as others, and both err in the direction of proud self-righteousness. When they err, both should know better, given the essential doctrines of their respective faiths. But Portia has already prepared us to expect human dilemmas regarding the knowing and doing of good. Given the intelligence of both men, who will prove 'not bred so dull but [he] can learn' (3.2.162)? Although both men begin by openly and angrily conveying their grievances against the other, a major shift occurs midway through the scene when Shylock chooses to dissemble his real desire by feigning a conversion of kindness toward Antonio in the so-called 'kind' bond. The 'honest Antonio' (3.1.11) chooses to accept what he and Bassanio believe are the bond's 'fair terms' (1.3.172); Antonio trusts Shylock's apparent change of heart and overtrusts his own strategical merchantry. Although both men share the motive of hate for each other, both differ in their motives for breaking their customs. This one time Shylock claims he will forgo his customary usury to buy Antonio's favour, but he reveals his true motive in his opening aside and later in his rationale for why he will break his custom to dine with the prodigal Christian, namely to feed on him in hate (2.5.14–15). This one time, for the sake of love, Antonio will break his custom against usury in order to help his friend pursue another love.

Part of Shakespeare's success in portraying these two men derives from the tension between love and hate he arouses in the characters as well as in the audience, who can respond with divided feelings of love and hate for the very same character, either Antonio or Shylock. For example, until this scene the audience has seen Antonio as a very generous, loving friend, and if the actor plays him warmheartedly, the audience will join Antonio's friends in lamenting the strange melancholy that robs him of good cheer. But in this scene we learn about another side to Antonio.

We hear Shylock's moving complaint against Antonio for hatefully treating him not as a man, but as a dog, and Antonio verifies this. What ideas, attitudes, and feelings might the members of an Elizabethan audience bring to bear on this charged conflict between two such men as Antonio, a Christian merchant, and Shylock, a Jewish usurer?

Perhaps the starting point for inquiry is to observe that unlike *Il Pecorone*, where there is no prior personal connection between the merchant and Jew figures, Shakespeare significantly chose to establish a personal relationship of antagonism between Antonio and Shylock before they contract the bond. This emphasis on personal enmity is very important because our protagonist and antagonist are already 'bound' by murderous hatred, especially regarding the subject of usury, before they confront each other in this scene. In his adaptation of his sources Shakespeare often heightens dramatic tension by personalising relationships; for example, Mercutio's personal antagonism for Tybalt as an affected duellist is established before the fatal confrontation in the opening scene of the third act. And the enmity here runs deep on both sides. However, Shylock and Antonio, like the mis-choosers Morocco and Arragon, deserve our sympathy because they, like us, often choose wrongly when they are passionately convinced that they choose rightly. Shylock believes he is right to practise usury as he does and to hate Antonio for his opposition. Antonio just as strongly believes he is right to hate and ridicule Shylock for the same practice. It is one thing to hate a deed and quite another to hate the doer of the deed. Each man will be weighed in the balance and found wanting; disagreement should not degenerate to persecution.

Antonio and Shylock know each other, and they hate each other. Why? What are some of the possible reasons to which the text directs our attention, and how do these matters relate to the rest of the play? The bond scene opens not with Antonio and Shylock, but with Bassanio and Shylock, and therefore we recall why this is appropriate from the ending of the play's first scene. Bassanio *appears* to be doing what Antonio directed him to do, but in reality he is not. Unlike the merchant in *Il Pecorone*, who alone knowingly contacts the Jew for money,[1] Antonio enlists his friend's aid, hoping to obtain a loan on his credit as a merchant ('of my trust') or for the sake of friendship (1.1.185). Antonio never intended Bassanio to obtain money at usury or from a usurer. As a young lord, Bassanio has apparently all but beggared his own inheritance, perhaps through excessive prodigality. He has become increasingly dependent on his friend's generosity, revealing an understandable ignorance of commercial transactions in Venice. Shakespeare has Bassanio, with almost tragic irony and surprising ignorance, seek out the one person with whom Antonio would prefer not to do business, apparently unaware that Shylock is his best friend's worst enemy. The opening exchanges of this scene give the audience its first impressions of Shylock and reconfirm Bassanio's naiveté about high finance on the Rialto. Shakespeare's creation of this scene is a masterfully executed piece of drama that is, I think, the most innovative and timely example of covert usury in Elizabethan drama. This very problematic scene well merits close attention.

'WHEN DID FRIENDSHIP TAKE / A BREED FOR BARREN METAL OF HIS FRIEND'? (1.3.125–6)

In Shakespearian drama *how* a character speaks is as important as *what* is spoken, but given the minimal clues afforded by the printed page there is much more difficulty in recovering the variables of *how* than of *what*. Shylock's first line is stunningly brief, opening and closing with monosyllabic words, 'Three thousand ducats, well'. Shylock's 'well', which is repeated three times in the first five lines, is a common word for someone to utter when buying time to 'bethink' (1.3.25). Shylock's repetitive verbal echoing of Bassanio emphasises how much he needs to think about this loan and be assured he may take it, suggesting that this loan will not be easily or freely given. But 'well' will also be reiterated in Shylock's final speech in the play when he requests to depart from the court because he is 'not well' (4.1.392), so that 'well' (as interjection and as adjective) verbally frames Shylock's entrance and departure. Thus far the only other male character in the play presented as 'not well' is Antonio, who suffers from a mystifying melancholy and who will later be physically 'bated' through anxiety, thus inviting the audience to compare the relative 'well-being' of these two men by the play's end. Although this sense of 'well' is not operative yet for Shylock in this scene, the repetition of 'well' may raise the question in the audience's mind of whether all's well indeed. Shylock's opening exchange with Bassanio is characterised by a repetitive tick as he repeats words, phrases, and syntactical patterns. The repetitive manner subsides once Antonio enters, but it reappears throughout the rest of the play, most notably in his insistence on his bond. What might this speech habit signify? An obsessive quality? A concern with being understood? Perhaps more criticism needs to be devoted to Shylock's distinctive manner of speech.[2]

Although costuming could visually help to identify Shylock as a Jew to an Elizabethan audience, it is not until his rejection of Bassanio's dinner invitation to discuss the loan, offered in response to Shylock's request to speak with Antonio (1.3.25–31), that Shylock says anything that identifies him as a Jew: 'Yes, to smell pork, to eat of the habitation which your prophet the Nazarite conjured the devil into' (27–8). The language of Shylock's rejection makes it clear that he chooses to do business with Christians, but he does not choose to socialise with them – not eat, drink, or pray with them (28–30) – implying that for him Christians are business commodities. This is Shylock's first biblical allusion.[3] Shylock's allusion, revealing specific knowledge of the Gadarene miracle in the New Testament, is surprising for a Jew, and as a surprise it calls attention to Shakespeare's artful use of Shylock's scriptural allusions throughout the play to characterise Shylock as an intelligent literalist, quite similar to Morocco and Arragon, who also choose and rationalise cleverly but not wisely. The general method underlying Shakespeare's choice of Shylock's scriptural allusions is irony. The allusions reflect Shylock's literal understanding and lack of spiritual insight, according to Protestant interpretations of these allusions in biblical glosses likely to be known to many members of Shakespeare's audience. Shylock's repudiation of pork as unclean, here devil-possessed food, is legitimately Jewish as is his view that Christ, 'the Nazarite', is only a 'prophet'. Shylock, however, further denigrates 'the Nazarite' as a mere conjuror, not a true miracle-worker. He also reveals his contempt for Christians who are foolish enough to eat pork, the animal into whom the Christians' own prophet 'conjured' the devil. The choice of the word 'Nazarite' is probably intended to be a cutting epithet.[4] The Jews believed their Messiah would come from the house of David, from the tribe of Juda, the land of Judea (southern part of Palestine), and the town of Bethlehem (Mi 5.1 ff.). From a Jewish perspective, Jesus, identified in the New Testament some dozen times as 'Jesus of Nazareth', is from Galilee (northernmost region of Palestine) and the insignificant Jewish town of Nazareth (despite his reputed birth in Bethlehem), and hence no Messiah.

But of all the miracles in the New Testament that Shakespeare could have chosen for Shylock's allusion, why this particular one? The significance of this choice derives from its possible ironic inferences. Shakespeare's audience, not Shylock, would contextualise this scriptural text as they knew it from their vernacular bibles, and for them, that context would boomerang back against Shylock. In the Geneva Bible, for example, the Gadarene swineherds, dismayed over the loss of their swine, beg Jesus to 'depart from their coasts' (Mk 5.17), and the gloss reads: 'Mark how love of riches and worldly respects hinder men to receive Christ.' Shylock's usurious breeding of inanimate gold and silver brands him in the popular view as a lover of worldly gain. Shylock, moreover, uses this allusion to label Christ as a 'prophet', as one might expect him to do. But the point of this miracle was to indicate Christ's divinity, which even the devil himself declared: 'What have I to do with thee, Jesus, the Son of the most high God?' The gloss here reads: 'The devil is constrained to confess Jesus Christ, and yet ceaseth not to resist him.' Again, a playgoing audience, profoundly aware of Scripture, would hear ironies and perceive layers of significance that would be less accessible to a modern audience far less familiar with such allusions. Shylock's scriptural allusions need not be 'historically' Jewish, what one would expect to hear from 'a real Jew', as Gerald Friedlander remarks.[5] Shakespeare, not Shylock, chooses and crafts these allusions to develop complex dramatic meaning for his play that engages his audience's discernment.

As a Venetian Jew, Shylock is both an 'insider', on grounds of his Venetian residence, and an 'outsider', a religious alien in the Christian society of Venice. Despite his Venetian status, Shylock might also be considered a political 'outsider' whose friends are described as his 'countrymen' (3.2.284) and whose ancestral home of Jerusalem was conquered and destroyed by the Romans in 70 AD. Given the traditional Elizabethan view that Jerusalem was destroyed for her sins, it is perhaps ironic that Shylock lives in Italy, the land of the conquerors of his ancestors, and that his chief enemy enjoys a reputation as 'one in whom / The ancient Roman honour more appears / Than any that draws breath in Italy' (3.2.295). Although Shylock may be alienated, he also alienates; unlike his daughter, he chooses to keep his social distance and scorns Christians as fools.

Shakespeare significantly chooses to present Shylock's first words as words about money. Shakespeare continues to develop from the play's first scene the double interest in money and love because, as we know, how one uses and views wealth indicates how one does or does not love others. But active hate becomes here the new ingredient added to the love-and-money theme, and by its inclusion we will better understand love, according to Sidney's argument for epistemological comparison in drama. But before we discover this hate as Antonio enters, we learn much about Shylock prior to Antonio's entrance. Shylock appears a consummate business man, his repetition creating a verbal contract of clear and knowing agreement on the terms, 'Three thousand ducats for three months and Antonio bound'.[6] It is not until Bassanio and Shylock differ over the interpretation of so basic yet so meaningful a word as 'good' that we glimpse how the different values of these two men affect their perception of others and their ability to communicate. For Bassanio the description of Antonio as 'a good man' (1.3) is an ethical definition. Shylock's 'Ho' (1.3.13) laughingly prefaces his quadruple repetition of 'no' to correct Bassanio's misperception of his meaning; he intended 'good' as an economic, not ethical, definition: 'my meaning in saying he is a good man is to have you understand me that he is sufficient' (14–15).

As Shylock assesses the risk of Antonio's ventures at sea to conclude that such risk still leaves Antonio economically sufficient, he reveals another speech habit, glossing of metaphors and puns to make plain his 'meaning': 'land rats, and water rats' are glossed as 'water thieves, and land thieves (I mean pirates)' (1.3.20–2), and later he explains to his own daughter Jessica, 'stop my house's ears – I mean my casements – ' (2.4.33).[7] No doubt these are meant to be comic lines for the audience's laughter, in keeping with the traditional convention of the Vice character in Elizabethan drama as both dangerous and funny. But Shakespeare's investing Shylock with an opening pun on piracy also generates humour for an Elizabethan audience, who could absorb the usury context for Shylock's wordplay that escapes modern audiences as well as most critics of this play. Thomas Wilson, author of the influential and longest English treatise against usury in the sixteenth century, *A Discourse upon Usury* (1572), indicts usury as 'a gainful *piracy*, contrary to nature'; any man who thinks usury is not a sin and therefore lends for gain is 'an heretic', and any man who thinks usury is a sin yet practises it, 'then he is straight ways a *land pirate*'.[8] Shakespeare thus counterbalances the seafaring pirates who bedevil mercantile shipping with the usurious land pirates who plunder ashore. Shylock's glossing of figurative expressions may also reveal a tendency to literalism that would invite comparison with other literalists in the play, like the Princes of Morocco and Arragon, whose visionary capacity, as we have seen, comprehends primarily the letter and not the spirit of 'meaning' and who also suffer defeat by not gaining what they desire most and think they deserve. However, of the play's comic literalists, the most humorously laughable are the Gobbo father and son comedy team.

Shylock insists on financial assurance, and his recitation of Antonio's ventures at sea reveals he knows more about those business affairs than does the best friend Bassanio. The audience, however, has had no verbal clues as to Shylock's professional identity, except that he must have a reputation for wealth, or Bassanio would not approach him for a loan. But his wealth, unlike Antonio's, must not come from merchantry because he disapproves of how Antonio puts his means in supposition, in 'ventures . . . squandered abroad' (1.3.18). Risk or hazard, an important theme in the play, is a natural element in merchantry, but not in usury, and in the play's opening scene Solanio and Salarino graphically portray the merchant's hazards that Shylock finds so foolish (1.1.15–40). We do not discover that Shylock's wealth comes from usury until he tells us so in his opening aside, which is occasioned by Antonio's unexpected entrance upon the scene. This aside is crucially important for the audience's awareness of Shylock's true intentions. Until this aside we have been given only intriguing hints about Shylock. Now he reveals himself to us and explains why a bond with Antonio is more than just another business deal. In this aside the word 'hate' enters the play for the first time, and in characteristic fashion Shylock repeats it (1.3.34, 40) to underscore that the passion is mutual between him and Antonio.

We discover Shylock looks down on Antonio as 'a fawning publican' (33). This line has occasioned some commentary.[9] As an indicator of Shakespeare's art it is important in both thematic and dramatic terms, revealing Shylock's sense of superiority to Antonio, which is countered by the audience's ironic awareness of Shylock's biblical allusion. 'Publican' is a cant term of abuse for a sinner, and Shylock's 'fawning publican' appears to be a biblical allusion to the contrast established between the humble publican who fawns on God, seeing himself as a sinner, and the self-righteous Pharisee who arrogantly sees himself as far superior to the publican because he keeps the letter of the law (Lk 18.9–14). The purpose of this parable was to show men how to pray, humbly and not proudly, and Shylock has just emphasised his preferred separation from Christians in the matter of prayer: 'every man that exalteth himself, shall be brought low, & he that humbleth himself, shall be exalted' (Lk 18.14).

In this allusion Shylock proudly identifies himself with the Pharisee, but for an Elizabethan audience such an association would align Shylock with those who sought to deaden the life-giving spirit of religion, those who redirected the Old Testament's emphasis on God's love for man to an extreme emphasis on God's justice and man's own meritorious right to salvation through adherence to the Law.[10] The New Testament depicts the Pharisee as 'a goodly apple rotten at the heart' (1.3.93), as the spiritual opposite to the earlier Old Testament patriarchs, like Abraham and Jacob, who are praised as models of faith. Consequently, to be a Pharisee was to be a hypocrite, a man outwardly but not inwardly religious, a petty interpreter and practitioner of the Law, and a self-righteous judge of the poor and ignorant. Matthew's concise description of the Pharisees' vain worship parallels the meaning of the proud Pharisee/humble publican parable: 'O hypocrites, Esias prophesied well of you, saying, "This people draweth near unto me with their mouth, and honoureth me with the lips, but their heart is far from me"', and the glossator clarifies this message, '"God . . . detesteth all good intentions, which are not grounded on his word"' (Mt 15.7–8). Although Shylock pharisaically views Antonio as a 'fawning publican', he will later accept the Christian's dinner invitation out of hate, and therein his motive and action parody Christ's motive of love for dining with publicans and sinners, for which the Pharisees rebuked Him (Lk 5.30–32). The theme of false pride versus true humility, explored in the casket plot, ominously reappears in the flesh-bond plot. Who is humble? Proud? Who will be exalted? Brought low?

How else might Shylock's allusion promote revealing irony? Shylock's earlier recitation to Bassanio regarding what he will not do with Christians curiously mixes the appetitive and the spiritual: 'I will not eat with you, drink with you, nor pray with you' (1.3.30). Why should eating and drinking go hand-in-hand with praying? For a sixteenth-century audience this association would seem quite natural given the religious sense of 'feast' in the Bible and in ecclesiastical calendars as well as in the central recurring 'feast' in Christian worship, the commemoration of the Last Supper through the sacrament of Holy Communion. In Shylock's concealed motive for attending Bassanio's banquet 'feasting' will degenerate to 'feeding' (2.5.14–15). But Shylock's insistence on not praying with Christians should surprise us as well as Elizabethans because it is so obvious. That a Jew would not choose to pray with Christians should not even need mentioning because no one would expect it. The essential difference between Jews and Christians in the sixteenth century was perceived as being a *religious* difference, not economic or racial, as has already been explained.

Therefore, Shakespeare's inclusion of difference in praying anticipates Shylock's fawning publican line, its biblical definition of true prayer as apposite, occurring more readily to an Elizabethan audience than to a modern one, as is the case with so many of the biblical allusions in this play. The irony is that Shylock misses the true 'meaning' of this allusion, just as he will the true 'meaning' of his most important biblical allusion, the Jacob–Laban story that he introduces in defence of usury. Shylock's scorn of humility and insistence on pride here links him unwittingly to the unjustified Pharisee. Richmond Noble suggests that Shylock intends to criticise Antonio as a 'creature of the ruling class' of Gentiles, who oppressed the Jews just as the tax gathers or publicans had done in the time of Christ.[11] But 'fawning' then makes little sense unless Shylock indicates by it that he *expects* Antonio to fawn or beg for the intended loan. If so, Shylock's expectations will be truncated when Antonio instead proudly confronts Shylock and 'storms' (130) at him, just as Antonio's expectations for a 'merry bond' (167) will be truncated later. Ironic inversions of characters' expectations, such as those of Morocco and Arragon, pervade this play, linking both plots in yet another way.

But Shylock remains ironically opaque to how 'publican' as a term of contempt could apply to himself, not Antonio, in a way that is intimately linked to his own profession of usury. In one of the most influential sources Shakespeare used for developing his usury motif in this play, Miles Mosse's *The Arraignment and Conviction of Usury* (1595), there appears an historical description of usurers as publicans based on a statement by Plutarch: 'the Publican

was a most infamous person . . . the usurers play the Publicans. . . .
For the Publicans were such as gathered tolls or customs. . . . And
the usurers will have their custom penny . . . their ravenousness . . .
did suck up, & soak dry the poor people . . . no marvel . . . he be
of bad report among men.'[12] Shylock's own awareness of 'bad
report' is reflected in his self-conscious use of more socially acceptable words ('usance') and euphemisms ('thrift') to avoid the
opprobrium of the word 'usury'.[13] Shakespeare's crafting of this
one line is extraordinary, and the small pieces of the play's mosaic illuminate the whole. Although Shylock intends the derisive
meaning of publican as infamous sinner to describe only Antonio,
Shakespeare allows the biblical and usury contexts for that word
to boomerang back on Shylock. But Shakespeare also does not
leave Antonio unscathed. Shylock is right to call Antonio a publican given the specific use of this term in Matthew's forceful
reminder that Christians are called to love their enemies, and
Antonio fails therein with Shylock: 'For if ye love them, which
love you, what reward shall you have? Do not the publicans even
the same?' (Mt 5.46). Perhaps 'fawning' refers to Shylock's view
of how Antonio appears to love his friend Bassanio, whom he
probably confers with privately during Shylock's aside to us. Thus
Shylock's opening line appropriately introduces the substance of
the powerful aside that follows.

Shylock's aside reveals very clearly that he hates Antonio for
two reasons: (1) because he is a Christian, and this reason coheres with his just pronounced social antipathy for Christians;
(2) he hates Antonio even more for professional reasons because
Antonio 'lends out money gratis, and brings down / The rate of
usance here with us in Venice' (36–7). We learn that Shylock thinks
money lent freely, that is without taking any interest or anything
above the principal lent, is 'low' (humble or even base) foolishness, just as he had also seen Antonio's merchantry as a squandering affair. The purpose of this aside is to alert us to Shylock's
true feelings toward Antonio and the reasons for these feelings
as well as his motivation to wrestle Antonio to defeat: 'If I can
catch him once upon the hip, / I will feed fat the ancient grudge
I bear him' (38–9). Norman Nathan suggests the wrestling phrase,
'upon the hip', might be Shakespeare's recollection of Jacob's
wrestling with the angel in Genesis 32, which comes two chapters after Shylock's allusion to the wand device in the Jacob–Laban
story (Genesis 30).[14] When Jacob wrestles with the angel, God

rewards his endurance by renaming Jacob ('supplanter') as 'Israel' ('contender with God'). Because Israel had power with God, God would enable Israel to prevail with men. But the overlooked gloss in the Geneva Bible clarifies the significance of God's wounding Jacob's thigh in this match in a way that is directly appropriate for Shylock and the fawning publican problem he raises: in overcoming their temptations the faithful should continue to feel the smart of battle and be humble, not proud (see Genesis 32.25–32).

Both the Geneva and Bishops' Bibles, however, use the word 'thigh', not 'hip'. Equally likely is the possible Elizabethan conception of Laban, not just Jacob, as a cunning wrestler who seeks to catch his opponent, Jacob, 'on the hip': 'yet is he [Laban] glad to have *Jacob* on the hip for a bad bargain as he hoped, and thinking thereby to gain *Jacobs* service for little or nothing, *would* God saith he, this bargain might stand'.[15] If so, an ironic reversal begins to build here which will reach fruition in the debate over how to interpret the Jacob–Laban story. The possible reversal is that Shylock is not as similar to the patriarch of his choice, 'the very rich Jew' as the Bishops' Bible calls Jacob, but is more like the cunning wrestler Laban, who seeks a bad bargain.

Shylock, however, is not the only one guilty of unkindness, and he is less blameworthy than his Christian adversary in this respect. This scene's testimony to Antonio's unkind treatment of his enemy should literally shock a 'Christian' audience into an awareness of precisely how Antonio fails as a Christian: by Antonio's example he wrongly teaches Shylock to counter injury with injury, at least up to this point in the play. As a Christian, Antonio is supposed to repudiate carnal hatred for his enemy and embrace love for all; 'Ye have heard that it hath been said, love thy neighbour, and hate thine enemy. But I say unto you, Love your enemies: bless them that curse you: do good to them that hate you, and pray for them which hurt you, and persecute you' (Mt 5.43–4). Antonio should uphold the New Testament's calling to a new definition of love of neighbour. The law of love for God and for neighbour is also basic to the Old Testament (Dt 6.5; Lv 19.18; Tb 4.15). But in the New Testament there occurs a radical shift in definition of 'neighbour' and the extent to which love is commanded. Unlike the Old Testament, where 'neighbour' usually means 'fellow Jew' or 'countryman' (someone closely connected with the Jews, e.g., a resident alien or a proselyte), the New Testament expands the definition of 'neighbour' to include *all* men, and hence the point of the parable about the Good Samaritan (Lk 10.29–37).

Antonio demonstrates here he has 'much ado to know himself' (1.1.7) in more ways than one; he needs to recognise his own spiritual malaise in failing to love his enemy Shylock. Love of neighbour is based on love of God (Mt 5.45) who is perfect love (1 Jn 3.14–22). If one does not love one's neighbour, one does not love God. Love must prove itself in deeds. Christ sums up all the commandments of the Old Testament in the two commandments of love for God and love for one's neighbour (Mt 22.34–49; Lk 10.25–28). Antonio's hatred of usury as a violation of neighbourly love prevents him from seeing Shylock as his neighbour in need of love.

Why does Antonio hate Shylock? Shylock has already explained his religious and, more important to him, at least, professional reasons for hating Antonio. Before Antonio can speak, Bassanio interrupts Shylock's self-musing, and Shylock cleverly cloaks what he has just told us by pretending he has been calculating his available money. Since he says he cannot immediately raise 3000 ducats, Tubal, 'a wealthy Hebrew of [his] tribe' (49), will 'furnish' him. Mahood rightly notes that Shylock's expectation of Tubal's help follows the injunction of Deuteronomy 23.20, namely that Jews must lend freely to each other and can take interest only from Gentiles (1.3.49 n.). However, like many members of a modern audience, Bassanio will also overlook Shylock's equivocation about his need to borrow money from Tubal. At the end of this tense scene Shylock confidently disposes of any such need for Tubal and decisively announces he will go to his 'house', and he will 'purse the ducats straight' (1.3.167–8). Shylock's parting announcement about his true fiscal fluidity recapitulates for this scene his public dissonance between word and deed versus his private consonance in his practice of deception.

Shakespeare's audience, unlike a modern audience, would know the classic Deuteronomic defence for usury, but Shakespeare does not have Shylock articulate it. Instead, this very passage seems to underlie Shylock's treatment of others as enemies when he exacts usury.[16] The chief problem concerns the definition of neighbourly love in relation to lending. As we know from the play's first scene, lending is an act of loving. But for the true Christian, usury is bad faith. Lending freely is a biblically prescribed way of loving your neighbour rightly: 'Wherefore love ye your enemies, and do good, and lend looking for nothing again, and your reward shall be great, and ye shall be the children of the most High: for he is kind unto the unkind, & to the evil' (Lk 6.35). The idealistic gloss on this passage emphasises the spirit of sacrifice, which will be rewarded spiritually by God: 'not only not hoping for profit, but to lose the stock & principal forasmuch as Christ bindeth himself to repay the whole with a most liberal interest'.[17]

Before we examine Antonio's speech, we must observe how awkward this situation is for him. When Antonio enters the scene, he must be at the very least surprised to find his best friend conversing with his worst enemy, especially because he never instructed Bassanio to seek a usurious loan, but rather, one based on his own credit or friendship. What a dramatic on-stage pause Shakespeare allows for Antonio before he actually speaks! What should he do for his friend? Presumably, during Shylock's aside, Antonio could take Bassanio aside, who has already probably crossed the stage to greet his friend, and explain the compromising nature of this situation. They could then go on to seek the kind of loan Antonio originally intended. But for the purposes of the play Antonio must, of course, contract with Shylock, and *why* he chooses to do so is important. He announces his decision as curtly as possible:

> Shylock, albeit I neither lend nor borrow
> By taking nor by giving of excess,
> Yet to supply the ripe wants of my friend
> I'll break a custom.
>
>   (1.3.53–6)

Antonio abruptly breaks off his address to Shylock and asks Bassanio: 'Is he yet possessed / How much ye would?' The dynamics of dialogue catch us here. Before Bassanio can respond to Antonio's question, Shylock interrupts and wrests the dialogue with Antonio back to himself. Bassanio will be excluded from their intense exchange for the next seventy-eight lines. In Antonio's response we discover one reason for Antonio's antagonism toward Shylock. Antonio personally abhors the practice of usury because he neither lends to others nor borrows for himself by taking or by giving any 'excess' above the principal lent or borrowed. Antonio's professional antagonism perfectly balances Shylock's toward him.

We need to recall here what was mentioned earlier about the importance of usury in this play. The entire theme of usury is Shakespeare's addition to *Il Pecorone,* and the novelty of Shakespeare's decision to present 'a royal *merchant*' (4.1.29, my italics) who disapproves of usury is not usually appreciated in the play's criticism.[18] The common pattern in both Elizabethan literature and Elizabethan society itself was to depict merchants as usurers or at least heavily implicated in usury.[19] Shakespeare's departure from this typical connection would have caught his audience's attention and probably caused it to focus on the contrast he was establishing between different ways of regarding and handling wealth. Indeed, just as Shakespeare innovatively adapts the concept of mental usury for his merchant, so also Shakespeare is almost *avant garde* in abandoning the old, despicable usurer–merchant figure in drama for the new, heroic merchant-prince figure that begins to gain dominance in popular literature in the 1590s.[20] In this respect both Gratiano's (3.2.238) and the Duke's (4.1.29) description of Antonio as a praiseworthy principal citizen, as a '*royal* merchant' (my italics), is doubly important for its twofold connotations of 'substantial' and 'princely' – royal in treasure and trust – and helps to account for the fact that Antonio appears to be the only merchant in Venice that Shylock deeply resents. Yet despite Antonio's anti-usury position, he says he will violate his principles 'to supply the ripe wants of [his] friend' (55). This sounds very noble. But is it?

Although Antonio intends a great sacrifice to do business with his enemy to help his friend, he remains blind to how his extremes of love for Bassanio and hatred for Shylock reflect inauspiciously on his own professed practice of Christianity: should one do evil to do good?[21] Bassanio also erringly champions such a logic in the trial when he begs the law to be wrested on Antonio's behalf: 'To do a great right, do a little wrong' (4.1.212). But complicating this principle is another current, qualifying principle which Mosse records from scholastic theology: 'It is a lawful thing to use another man's sin, to good end and purpose.'[22] The tension between such opposing principles may underlie this scene in order to make a wise judgement of Antonio's dilemma all the more intriguing for an audience. In using love for a friend to excuse the violation of a principle, a rationale Antonio repeats in the ring episode, Antonio will *use* the very man he hates and condemns precisley for that which he condemns him. If one errs, it is better to err in the direction of love than its opposite (Prv 10.12; 1 Pt 4.8). But Antonio also fans the flame by urging Shylock to lend not in friendship, but in enmity, so that he 'mayst with better face / Exact the penalty' (128–9). All that glisters is not gold. Shylock catches Antonio – 'Methoughts you said you neither lend nor borrow / Upon advantage' (61–2) – in order to debate the bone of their contention. Antonio's sarcastic confirmation, 'I do never *use* it' (63, my italics), sets up Shylock's opportunity to defend the profession of use or usury that he sees as infinitely superior, or 'well-won', compared with risky mercantile squandering of wealth.

What follows is the remarkable debate between Shylock and Antonio on scriptural justification for usury. Remarkable for at least two reasons: (1) of all the many passages in Scripture that relate to usury Shylock surprisingly chooses one that is not directly concerned with usury, the Jacob–Laban story (Gn 30–1) about how God rewarded Jacob with wealth for his service to Laban, who had tried to defraud Jacob of his wages, so that Jacob could now leave Laban and provide for his own family; (2) the novelty of this choice is all the more noteworthy because until very recently it was thought that the use of this biblical story never appeared in any English sixteenth-century literature on usury.[23] We now know that the second most important treatise on usury in Elizabethan England, Miles Mosse's *The Arraignment and Conviction of Usury* (1595), did use the Jacob–Laban relationship in order to condemn the practice of sinful usury and to illustrate that the unlawful financial gains of the usurer would be taken away from the usurer just as 'God took the goods of covetous *Laban*, and gave them to holy *Jacob*: so he will take the riches which they have unlawfully gathered, from them, and from their house, and from their children: and will bestow them upon others, who shall show themselves better employers and disposers of his blessings.'[24] In his concluding exhortation to the usurer to repent and be spared damnation, Mosse uses this specific analogy to support the scriptural thesis which governs all six of his sermons: '*He that increaseth his riches by usury and interest, gathereth them for him that will be merciful to the poor*' (Prv 28.8).[25] The point here turns on the means of gaining wealth and what the attitude toward wealth should be. Thus Mosse uses Solomon's proverbial Old Testament wisdom to motivate the usurer to reform: 'the nature of *worldly men* is such, that the *loss of their goods* will rende their hearts in pieces, when the fear of the loss of heaven will not stir their affections'.[26] This basic idea of 'worldly men', who are the choosers of the gold and silver caskets, also significantly appears in the allegorisation of the casket story in Shakespeare's source for it, the *Gesta Romanorum*. In this world gold and silver are the desired metals of monetary exchange, as the base metal lead is not.

Shylock sees his version of the scriptural story of Jacob and Laban as not 'directly interest' (1.3.72), but usury is usury, regardless of its method of obtainment, whether direct or indirect.[27] In order to defend his usury as a 'way to thrive', Shylock proudly introduces his lineage, identifying for Antonio his references:

> This Jacob from our holy Abram was
> (As his wise mother wrought in his behalf)
> The third possessor; ay, he was the third –
>
> (63–6)

Already Antonio loses patience with Shylock's interpretation of Scripture and interrupts him, 'And what of him, did he take interest?' (67). Why is this lineage information included when it clearly interrupts the flow of Shylock's story? A director of this play might be tempted to streamline this material by simply omitting Shylock's three lines on lineage, but such an omission would damage the interlocking themes of inheritance, blessing, physical and spiritual wealth – how obtained and how passed on. Shylock's opinion of Rebecca as 'wise' contradicts the Geneva Bible's interpretation of her false 'subtlety' as well as Jacob's co-operation in her lying; by using deception to steal Isaac's blessing both of them sought to overrule God's timing for the deliverance of this blessing, which had been assured to Jacob, the younger son, and not to Esau (Gn 27.9–19, glosses).

As we have noted, the English Bible is obviously an important source for this play, and the significance of Shylock's rehearsal of Jacob as the third possessor of God's promise to 'holy Abram' would not be lost on an Elizabethan audience for whom Shylock's language would recall the issue of inheritance, Abraham being the original possessor of God's promise (Gn 15), with Jacob, after Isaac, being the third inheritor.[28] Basic to our play is the issue of inheritance and conveyance of patriarchal blessing, whether through a casket test designed by a 'holy' (1.2.23) father or a clever deception designed by a 'wise mother' (1.3.65). Shylock again invokes 'father Abram' (1.3.153) to counter the Christians' suspicions about his bond, but this invocation produces an ironic effect. In the Old and New Testaments Abram is presented as a just man and the exemplar of faith in God (Gn 15.6; Ps 31.1; Rom 4.6,20). Abram's reliance on God through faith contrasts with Shylock's reliance on himself through cunning, especially regarding how to thrive in this world. Moreover, as an exemplary father figure, Abram will contrast with the father Shylock, whose house will be described as 'hell' (2.3.2), because fathers 'ought both to know God's judgments & to declare them to their children' (Gn 18.19, gloss). Is Shylock, to adapt Jessica's line, a son to Abram by blood but not by manners? Like Barabas in Marlowe's *The Jew of Malta*, Shylock mentions his descent from Jacob with 'pride and satisfaction', as Brown notes.[29] But also like Barabas, he focuses carnally on the blessings of this earth that God promised Abram: 'I am the Lord, that brought thee out of Ur of the Caldees, to give thee this land to inherit it' (Gn 15.7). Both Shylock and Barabas are similarly obsessed with the physical, not the spiritual, wealth of a patriarch.[30] The chief blessing, however, which was to be the Israelites' inheritance is spiritual, namely God Himself: 'Fear not, Abram, I am thy buckler, *and* thine exceeding great reward' (Gn 15.1).

Shylock concludes his scriptural justification of usury: 'This was a way to thrive, and he was blest; / And thrift is blessing if men steal it not' (82–3). His conclusion clarifies how he interprets the biblical story that transformed Jacob from a poor servant of Laban's to a 'very rich' man, according to the Bishops' Bible (Gn 30, chapter heading for vs 43). 'Thrift' is Shylock's euphemism for what he considers 'well-won' gain (42), just as later, 'justice' will be his euphemism for personal 'revenge'. But his conclusion is riddled with unwitting ironic nuances. One of the commonest sixteenth-century criticisms of usury as unlawful gain is that it is theft, the stealing of an excess above the principal lent, and more than one writer on the subject points out how usurers adopt various euphemisms or more socially acceptable terms to cloak their enterprise, one of which is 'thrift'.[31] The anonymous author of *The Death of Usury* (1594) argues that the usurer lends to the rich to augment his own gains, 'such thrift is a branch of theft . . . and all his money will but turn to his own misery'.[32] Shylock's use of 'steal', which might otherwise seem out-of-place, is very apropos. Shylock seems to recall that Jacob explicitly repudiates 'theft' in his 'righteousness' – his taking only the spotted animals from Laban – to which God will testify by 'rewarding' Jacob's 'labours' (Gn 30.33 and gloss). But from an Elizabethan perspective, Shylock contradicts Jacob's righteousness on several counts: he does not see Jacob's labour as a 'venture' with 'all increase of our labor . . . to be looked for at God's hand' (Bishops' Bible, Gn 30.30, gloss); he uses fraud to repay injury; and his usury is theft, the taking of that which is not his own.

Although others might see Shylock as a thief because he is a usurer, Shylock does not. It is important to recall here that usury is not the only possible profession for a sixteenth-century Jew. The wealthy Jew in *Il Pecorone* is never identified as a usurer. Tubal, although presented by Shylock as wealthy enough to lend 3000 ducats, is probably not a usurer because Antonio bears him no professional hatred. Marlowe's Barabas is not a usurer by profession nor are Nashe's Zadoch and Zachary. Nor is moneylending merely a means of survival for Shylock. He champions his profession, justifying it by scriptural analogy with how patriarch Jacob grazed his uncle Laban's sheep. His rejoinder to Antonio's criticism reveals he is proud of how fast he can make his wealth breed. The nature of Shylock's self-perception is very important. Unlike other antagonists in Shakespeare's plays, who do wrong knowingly and gleefully, such as Richard III and Iago, Shylock believes himself to be right in his views of the merits of usury and revenge. He may in fact be wrong, but much of Shylock's stature as a character that elicits our sympathy for him stems from our awareness that he does not do wrong because he thinks it wrong but because he thinks it right.

Thomas Wilson, however, provides an Elizabethan perspective on this crucial issue of intent when he defines intent as 'good' not on the basis of an individual's unenlightened perception but only on the basis of accordance with God's law: 'Yea, usury is a manifest and voluntary known theft which men do use knowingly and wittingly, for either they think they do evil, and forbear it never a whit, or (that which is worse of all) they think they do well, and so, by oft using of this filthiness, do lull themselves in sin without any sense or feeling of their most wretched wickedness and horrible dealing . . . for intents imagined without gods warrant are deeds accursed, although in appearance they seem most godly. For god saith: thou shalt not do that which is good in thine own eyes, but do thou that only which I command thee.'[33] As with other characters in this play, notably Antonio, this tendency to individualism is not limited to Shylock. Antonio thinks himself right in treating a usurer as a dog, and similarly Lancelot Gobbo justifies his desertion of Shylock in a comic parody of this very human problem. Like Shylock, Antonio too must be educated. Hence, the play dramatically enacts the need 'to learn' (1.1.5), the need for wisdom – to know what's right and to have the courage to do what's right: to be 'as wise as bold' (2.8.70).

Antonio immediately contradicts Shylock's vested interpretation of Jacob's thriving:

> This was a venture, sir, that Jacob served for,
> A thing not in his power to bring to pass,
> But swayed and fashioned by the hand of heaven.
>
> (83–5)

Antonio describes Jacob's strategy as both a laborious service as well as a 'venture', subject to God's providence, unlike the ventureless and toilless gain of usury, which relies not on God but on human cunning. Jacob's wand strategy was not his own idea, but Jacob was so inspired by God through a dream (Gn 31.9–12), whereas Shylock's only dream in the play parodies that of his patriarch for he dreams not of God nor of heaven ('Jacob's ladder', Gn 24.12), but superstitiously of money-bags: 'There is some ill a-brewing towards my rest, / For I did dream of money bags tonight' (2.5.18). Antonio objects that Shylock is trying to justify 'interest', and his sarcastic rebuttal, 'Or is your gold and silver ewes and rams?' (87), is grounded on the Aristotelian idea that the breeding of inanimate money is unnatural, unlike the natural breeding of animate matter.[34] As Mahood explains, Antonio's later phrase, 'a breed of barren metal' (126), derives from 'Aristotle's play upon the Greek word for "interest" which means "offspring"'.[35] Midpoint in the play Shylock's usurious offspring of gold and silver mocks the double loss of his familial offspring, Jessica, and her financial thievery from the usurer–thief himself. Shylock's symbolic sterility recalls the penalty of barrenness which results from the mistaken choices of the worldly Morocco and Arragon. It is probably no coincidence that Jessica enters Belmont precisely when Gratiano suggests a wager for who will produce the first male heir (3.2.216–17). Shylock's ill-bred wealth, conjoined with Antonio's surety, for which he takes no breed of barren metal, provides the means whereby the quest was financed; upon its successful completion, the marital breeding of human flesh can be happily anticipated. The interesting point here is the financial 'wager' of 1000 ducats. This natural use of money and flesh, or proper use of a thing ('usury') as Mosse would say, provides a subtle contrast to Shylock's unnatural usury, in which his 'offspring' at this point in the play has effectively become only his money.[36]

The classical notion that money is sterile by nature informs the frequent depiction of usurers as avaricious in vain. Thus, Edmund Spenser allegorises Avarice in *The Faerie Queene* to criticise Avarice's trade of 'accursed usury' and his barrenness – 'yet child nor kinsman living had he [Avarice] none / To leave them [his bags of money] to'.[37] The very identification of Shylock as a usurer brands him for most Elizabethans as a worldly man, a lover of barren metal. Wilson summarises for his age the negative view of the usurer articulated by the ancients: Cato calls the usurer a murderer, Cicero says usurers are liars, Aristotle thinks bawds and usurers are similar because they both gain by filthy means, and Plutarch compares usurers to ravenous Harpies.[38] And as we noted earlier, Shakespeare's contemporaries, Thomas Nashe and Thomas Lodge, also condemn the current mammonism, the avaricious usury in London.[39] Indeed, when Nashe defends the plays on the English stage for their moral edification and their power to give a man's name immortality on earth, he argues that usurers oppose these plays because they do not get a good name in them, they see all 'Arts' as 'vanity', and they are interested in only what they can 'get' by something (1.212–13).

Although the notion that Jews misread Scripture was commonplace in Shakespeare's era, Antonio takes pains to instruct Bassanio that even 'the devil can cite Scripture for his purpose' (90) so that, as the messages on the scrolls in the caskets admonish, one has to discriminate between inner and outer realities, to beware the 'goodly outside falsehood hath' (94). Mosse seems to be original in contending that the very worst usurers are the ones who misuse Scripture by citing it in their defence.[40] Hence, Shylock's vested use of Scripture could be seen as devilish. Usury, moreover, was believed to be 'the only invention of the devil to destroy all charity, that in right should be used betwixt man and man!'[41] Therefore, usurers were often called devils, and Wilson's treatise repeatedly makes this association: usurers 'do not live in any

vocation, but being the devil's known apprentices in earth, and
bound to do as he would have them, seek when they are dead to
serve him in hell', and therefore one should not 'harken to the
devils sophistry' because 'they that will neither give nor lend freely
are the very members of the devil'.[42] Indeed, Wilson argues that
one of the chief reasons 'Jews are so universally hated wheresoever
they come' is usury, through which 'they rob all men that deal
with them, and undo them in the end'; Wilson claims the Jews
were banished from England 'for their usury'.[43] Shylock, however, is not sidetracked by Antonio's schooling of Bassanio but
begins to calculate the rate of interest on the intended loan when
Antonio, his patience wearing thin, peremptorily demands, 'Well,
Shylock, shall we be beholding to you?' (97). The opportunity is
ripe for Shylock to impress upon Antonio the difference between
his past ridicule and his present need of the usurer.

Shylock's speech is one of the most powerful in the play, revealing how genuine are his grievances. His stark honesty here
serves as an effective dramatic foil for the deception to come in
the formulation of the bond. Antonio's treatment of Shylock –
his rating, spitting, spurning, and name-calling, all of which he
does not deny but affirms he will repeat – starkly reveals this
Christian merchant's failure to love his enemy. Antonio's misperception of Shylock needs the corrective vision of a properly
perceived flesh bond. Antonio must learn that all men are brothers
in the flesh and are bound by fleshly frailty to one another, en-
suring the need for forgiveness. Shylock complains that Antonio does
not treat him as a fellow human being but as a dog: 'What should
I say to you? Should I not say / "Hath a dog money? Is it possible
/ A cur can lend three thousand ducats?"' (112–14). The derogatory
use of 'dog', however, has a wider biblical context for Christian as
well as Jewish traditions because the historical and figurative appearances of dogs in the Bible are almost always opprobrious. Unlike the cherished pets of today, dogs in biblical times were commonly
seen as scavangers feeding on offal. Indeed, these wild, dangerous,
unclean animals were among the most despised. To call oneself a
dog could, therefore, be a sign of deep humility, but to be called a
dog by another, such as Antonio calls Shylock, is a great insult.
This insult can also be specifically applied to those who do not
know the law, and so Paul calls the Judaisers or false teachers 'dogs'
(Phil 3.2). Antonio probably intends this as well because he sees
Shylock as violating God's law in the unkind practice of usury.[44]

But the full appropriateness of 'dog' imagery for a *usurer*, whether Jewish or Christian, has been overlooked. Shylock's complaint here clarifies that Antonio treats him as a dog because he practises usury: 'And all for *use* of that which is *mine own*' (105, my italics). Shakespeare's pun on 'use' here is complemented by the phrase 'mine own', which alludes to one of the commonplace criticisms of the usurer's *false* complaint – 'I may be defeated of *mine own*' – because the usurer in fact 'demandeth consideration for that which is none of the usurer's own'.[45] The image of a dog would be a familiar, not exotic, one for the usurer who daily plagued London. The image of the usurer as a biting dog derives etymologically from the meaning of usury as 'biting' according to the Hebrew word 'Naeshaech', which 'signifieth properly *Morsus*, a biting or gnawing of a thing', as in 'the gnawing . . . of a dog upon a bone'.[46] The English anti-usury writers of the 1590s criticised the opinion of one pro-usury position that 'unless usury be *Naeshaech*, biting, unless by it a man . . . prey upon him as a dog upon a carrion: some hold opinion that it is not forbidden in the word of God'.[47] But many condemned all sinful usury as biting – 'usury hath the name of biting: for it doth secretly bite, gnaw, and consume a man'.[48] Although Shakespeare does not use the specific term 'biting' for his dog imagery in this play, he does employ this idea in Shylock's threat – 'since I am a dog beware my fangs' (3.3.7), in Shylock's motif of 'feeding',[49] and in the image of Antonio's being 'bated' or having little flesh to spare.[50] Wilson's text gives the fullest articulation of the 'cur dog' image for the usurer as well as the 'biting' and 'gnawing' of the 'unmerciful and cutting usurer', who is in the habit of 'devouring noble men and gentlemen even to the very hard bones, till their goods and lands be quite and clean made away': the usurer lives idly, 'making money of money, an evil dish of meat for him to feed upon that is an hungered, and yet surely a thing most mete for usurers to eat upon' because the 'meat' or 'food' of gold is fatal.[51] Antonio's description of Shylock as a 'cut-throat dog' (103) probably derives from the English anti-usury literature of Thomas Wilson and Miles Mosse, where Wilson seems to be original in his repeated use of 'cut-throat' to describe the usurer, and Mosse adapts both this language and idea when he contends usury overthrows the rule of charity because '*usury cutteth the throat of mercy*'.[52]

Shylock's self-portrayal of his patient sufferance of Antonio's dehumanising treatment seems strikingly original, but Nashe and

Marlowe preempt Shakespeare's cluster of details for a 'currish' description of a 'Jewish' figure and therefore shed light on how an Elizabethan audience might receive Shylock's speech. An overlooked passage in Nashe's satiric *Have with You to Saffron-Walden* (1596) parallels Shylock's self-description when Nashe criticises the use of the word 'Intelligencer' as a negative epithet for a man, explaining just how opprobrious the term is by metaphorically applying it to a Jew-like person, or, as G. K. Hunter would say, to anyone who makes a 'Jewish choice': 'A Jew he is, that but for the spoil loves no man; a cur, that flatters & fawns upon every one, low crouching by the ground like a tumbler [a kind of greyhound], till he may spy an advantage, and pluck out his throat.'[53] Nashe's emphasis on the 'Jewish' love of 'spoil' here relates to the possible meaning of Shylock's name discussed earlier. The meaning of 'spoil' as a noun ('valuable goods') is probably played upon by Nashe here with the meanings of 'spoil' as a verb 'to steal or plunder' and 'to destroy or injure'.[54] Even though Nashe is using 'Jew' in a figurative sense, whereas Shakespeare's use is literal, the parallels are striking in their emphasis on dog/cur imagery, the imagery of false appeal (flattering and fawning), the false humble pose (crouching near the ground), and the clever but dire intent (the purpose of feigning in order to take advantage of another as would a cut-throat). In Shylock's attack upon Antonio's mistreatment of him these same associations for a Jew are brought into play. Shylock complains that Antonio has treated him as a 'cut-throat dog' (103), 'a stranger cur' (110), who should not be expected to have 'money' (113) to lend. In Shylock's repudiation of Antonio's treatment of him he mocks a possible response that rests on feigned flattery and humility, on ironically bending 'low' and feigning 'humbleness' to repay Antonio's outrageous 'courtesies' by lending money (115–21). Perhaps it is Marlowe who first establishes this particular cluster of associations when he has Barabas in *The Jew of Malta* explain how he can never forget an injury but pursues revenge through dissembling:

> We Jews can fawn like spaniels when we please,
> And when we grin, we bite; yet are our looks
> As innocent and harmless as a lamb's.
> I learned in Florence how to kiss my hand,
> Heave up my shoulders when they call me dog,
> And duck as low as any barefoot friar.[55]

But neither Nashe nor Marlowe specifically employ usury or lending for gain in their contexts, and herein Shakespeare's imagistic borrowing from either Nashe or Marlowe or from both is enhanced by his own development of this imagery within his context of usurious lending.

Antonio confirms Shylock's perception of the professional basis for their enmity when he threatens to mistreat Shylock again:

> If thou wilt lend this money, lend it not
> As to thy friends, for when did friendship take
> A breed for barren metal of his friend?
> $\qquad$ (124–6)

The fact that Shylock himself discriminates between friend and foe in how he lends money supports Antonio's thesis that friends do not charge interest on loans to friends. Shylock would expect his friend Tubal to furnish his financial needs without exacting interest, in accord with the Deuteronomic injunction, an injunction that is based, as we have seen, on discriminating between insiders and outsiders. Even today, despite our modern capitalistic acceptance of interest, people tend not to want to charge interest on financial loans to their family and friends. As we know now, the medieval–Renaissance bias against usury, like its bias against Jews, was rooted in theological doctrine. Because usury was thought to violate the commandment of brotherly love, to violate 'mutual friendship' as Wilson would emphasise,[56] the emphasis on *friendship* is particularly strong in this debate between Antonio and Shylock.

Antonio's juxtaposition of friendship and enmity may clue Shylock to shift his tactics from an aggressive to a conciliatory approach because his immediate about-face is the stunningly brilliant strategy of his 'kind' offer. Herein Shylock counterbalances Antonio's willingness to break his principle (against usury) for 'love' with his own apparent willingness to break his principle (for usury) for 'love':

> Why look you how you storm!
> I would be *friends* with you, and have your *love*,
> Forget the shames that you have stained me with,
> Supply your present wants, and *take no doit*
> *Of usance* for my monies . . .
> $\qquad$ (130–4, my italics)

Bassanio, speaking for the first time since Antonio and Shylock began their dialogue, interjects, 'This were kindness' (135). 'Kind', in both senses of 'natural' and 'benevolent', governs the word-play on this term because taking no usury would be seen as the natural as well as the considerate action. Brown notes that Shylock's short line, 'This is kind I offer', and Bassanio's interjection, 'This were kindness', suggest that 'Antonio hesitates – so Shylock pro-ceeds.'[57] Antonio probably hesitates out of sheer surprise at Shylock's atypical offer.

The next surprise belongs to the audience. *After* Shylock adds his pound of flesh condition in 'merry sport' (1.3.141), then Antonio accepts the bond, genuinely affirming that the bond shows 'much kindness in the Jew' (1.3.146), and this is significantly Antonio's first reference to Shylock as 'the Jew'. The audience, having the advantage of Shylock's aside, is not deceived about the nature of Shylock's true intentions. How can 'a royal merchant' (4.1.29) be so deceived? We might argue that Antonio's remark about Shylock's kindness is ironic, were it not for Bassanio's taking that remark at face value, because now Bassanio attempts to dissuade Antonio from believing the Jew 'grows kind' (171): 'You shall not seal to such a bond for me; / I'll rather dwell in my necessity' (147–8).[58]

Why does Antonio accept this bond, despite Bassanio's warn-ing? This matter is rather complicated so we must look at Antonio's misperception and foibles here as well as at the sheer genius of Shylock's formulation of the contract. To do so necessitates an awareness of some of the most basic as well as most innovative opinion regarding what constitutes usurious contracts in London of the 1590s. In the first place Antonio is overly confident in re-lying on his own business strategy of scattering his ventures in different ships to different places (1.1.41–5). Herein Antonio fails to bridge the gap between knowing the good and doing it when he ironically ignores the spirit of God-reliance governing his ear-lier interpretation of why Jacob's 'venture' was 'blest'. Antonio's excessively confident self-reliance falsely persuades him that he faces no risk:

Why, fear not, man, I will not forfeit it.
Within these two months, that's a month before
This bond expires, I do expect return
Of thrice three times the value of this bond.
                                        (149–51)

Risk, however, is an integral aspect of natural enterprise, and one of the reasons usury was condemned as *unnatural* enterprise is because it involved no risk and no concomitant trust in God's providence.[59] Although all men had no choice but to risk their goods in essence because no man has omnipotent control, the usurer guaranteed himself *certain, riskless* gain, through the *means* he used to ensure gain, through bonds and pawns, for example, lending only upon sufficient security.[60] In violating this fundamental principle of risk in accepting Shylock's bond, Antonio unwittingly adopts the usurer's stance, ironically counterbalancing Shylock's feigned adoption of the Christian stance with his 'kind offer' (135). Such overweening self-reliance, by merchant or usurer, could be seen by Elizabethans as akin to Pharisaical infidelity because faith and hope should rest primarily in God, not in man. Just as Antonio errs here in accepting a bond he sees as riskless, so also Shylock, overly confident in his abilities and his understanding of 'justice' and the 'law', enters the courtroom expecting no risk. Both men, overconfident about their 'deserts', will be educated through painful reversals.

But all this does not go far in explaining Antonio's initial response to Shylock's explanation of his 'single bond' as the 'merry sport' of requiring for the forfeit 'an equal pound of [Antonio's] fair flesh, to be cut off and taken / In what part of [Antonio's] body pleaseth [Shylock]' (141–4). Why does Antonio affirm, '*Content*, in faith! . . . there is much *kindness* in the Jew' (145–6, my italics)? Antonio's true contentment here and appreciation of the Jew's *kindness* indicate that he sees this bond as both natural and benevolent. How? His perception of benevolence probably stems from Shylock's insistence on not taking any monetary interest and his announced intention of no harm but only 'merry sport'. But how can Antonio view this bond as 'kind' or 'natural', that is, non-usurious?

Clues are provided in Shylock's artful palliation of all suspicions, and he spells out for the merchant's gentleman friend what has probably already occurred to the merchant:

> . . . Pray you tell me this:
> If he should break his day what should I *gain*
> By the exaction of the forfeiture?
> A pound of man's flesh, taken from a man,
> Is not so *estimable, profitable* neither . . .

As flesh of muttons, beefs, or goats. I say
To *buy* his *favour*, I extend this *friendship*.
If he will take it, so; if not, adieu,
And for my *love*, I pray you wrong me not.
                                    (155–63, my italics)

A man's pound of flesh constitutes no true gain because, unlike
the marketable flesh of animals, a pound of man's flesh is not
worth money, 'not so estimable, profitable' (159). Antonio is particularly susceptible to this reasoning because he has viewed Shylock
for so long as a 'cut-throat dog' (103). For too long Antonio has
viewed Shylock as a base creature motivated solely by monetary
greed, so that it does not even occur to him how a pound of his
flesh might be very 'estimable, profitable' in feeding a man's
appetite for revenge. Both Antonio and Bassanio fall for Shylock's
brilliantly deceptive 'fair terms' (172) and overtrust Antonio's
mercantile sagacity. Both men, however, also share the responsibility for accepting this bond. Antonio did not have to continue
Bassanio's initial negotiation with Shylock, and Bassanio could
have persisted in trying to dissuade Antonio.

But there is more at stake here given the usury literature of
Elizabethan England. Traditionalists held that gain in usury was
anything taken above the principal, not necessarily money.[61] Wilson
makes this point by quoting a passage from St Ambrose which is
particularly haunting in view of Shylock's pound of flesh, albeit
a man's flesh: 'Thou shalt not take usury of meats, nor yet of *any
other thing whatsoever*, for *flesh* is usury, apparel is usury, and
whatsoever is taken above the principal is usury, *whatsoever name
you give unto it.*'[62] However, a more modern definition of gain
had just recently been articulated by Miles Mosse in his influential work, printed in 1595, about a year before the composition of
Shakespeare's play. Mosse prefers to follow the lead of the late-
medieval theologian Gabriel Biel, because he tends to limit the
concept of usurious gain to money or 'that which can be measured or valued by money'.[63] Does Shylock's pound of flesh constitute usurious gain? According to the traditional definition it
clearly does. According to Mosse's definition it looks as if it technically does not, or at least so it might appear in this light to
Antonio. Shylock has said he will take no *money* for *money* lent
(133–4), and hence Antonio could credit Shylock with 'kindness'
for forgoing the typical usurious expectation of financial gain.

However, it was thought that the *expectation* or *hope* of gain by itself made a man a usurer.[64] The audience, but not Antonio or Bassanio, already knows that Shylock expects or hopes to gain by feeding his ancient grudge if he can catch Antonio at a disadvantage. Intention determines the good or evil nature of a man's outward deeds, and Mosse lectures the usurious on the ultimate futility of hypocrisy because, no matter how the usurer's deeds might deceive others or appear to conform to man's laws, God sees 'the wills, purposes, and intents' of men,[65] or 'mens laws can only restrain the outward deeds . . . but the laws of God restrain the evil thoughts . . . of the heart'.[66] Regarding the issue of intent, Shylock's best defence becomes offence: 'O father Abram, what these Christians are, / Whose own hard dealings teaches them suspect / The *thoughts* of others!' (153–5). Distinguishing between what Shylock is and what he does, Mahood claims that 'his social role as usurer' is something 'of which we have seen nothing in the play'.[67] To the contrary, Shylock's verbal defence of usury is complemented by his clever enactment of it in this scene.

Shakespeare's formulation of the flesh bond is his own striking adaptation of what Mosse describes as covert usury, adapting the latest strategies in theory and practice, especially the lenders' elaboration of contracts to *appear* non-usurious in order to avoid the legal repercussions of the Act Against Usury of 1571.[68] Covert usury is one type of usury by compact, which in turn is a branch of outward and actual usury. Usury by compact occurs 'when he that lendeth covenanteth with the borrower to receive again not only his own, and his principal, but also increase and advantage', and covert usury is that usury by compact that is not 'clear, and manifest: but . . . is cloaked or covered with the title of honesty'.[69] Covert usury is a particularly dangerous kind of usury because it lends for gain 'under the colour of some lawful contract',[70] using a variety of hypocritical pretences, such as pretending to befriend the borrower or to lend freely to him.[71] Shylock is clearly compacting because he instructs Antonio: 'Go with me to a notary, seal me there / Your single bond' (137–8). By 1595 Christian usurers in London are so skilful at trying to evade the anti-usury intent of the Act Against Usury of 1571 that Mosse writes his treatise to educate specifically a London audience; he bewails the almost unknowable variety of Protean disguises that 'exceeding subtle and crafty' usurers adopt to ensnare their victims.[72]

Mosse's specific description of 'covert and cloaked usurie . . . and how it seazeth upon lawful contracts'[73] directly illuminates Shylock's formulation of a lawful bond that is *apparently* non-usurious but in fact is usurious.

Although one strategic move of usurers is to feign friendliness to their would-be debtors, the precise language in Shylock's ingenious appeal recalls the explicit diction of Mosse's unique emphasis on the non-usurious lender's legitimate expectation of the borrower's love and good will because that is justly merited and does not constitute a monetary gain: '*I* may also add . . . the lender may lawfully expect the *love* and good will of the borrower. For that he hath justly deserved by his *kindness*: and besides *love is not a thing which can be valued for money*: and therefore he that expecteth love cannot be said to gain from *lending*.'[74] Therefore, according to Mosse, if a lender expects only 'the procuring of the *favour*, and *friendship* of the borrower',[75] he may rightly 'lend to *purchase* the *love* and liking of another'[76] or 'to *purchase* their *favour*'.[77] The verbal parallels between Mosse and Shakespeare are obvious. Shylock cleverly cloaks his ulterior motive by affirming that he extends 'this *friendship*' (161) in '*kindness*' (136) in order to 'have [Antonio's] *love*' (131) and 'to *buy* his *favour*' (161), without any expectation of financial '*gain*' (156).

Shakespeare's crafting of Shylock's language and logic in response to the usury debate of his era is exceptionally apt in the shrewdly deceptive formulation of a 'kind' bond. Because Shylock pretends to be lending in order to gain nothing illegitimate, like monetary excess, but only the legitimate love and favour of the borrower, he does not appear to be usurious. He thus cleverly tailors his argument to suit Antonio's belief in friendship and to counter Antonio's earlier espousal of enmity (127). Now we can understand why even Bassanio concludes that the 'terms' of this bond are 'fair', though he remains suspicious about the true intent of 'a villain's mind' (172). Although Bassanio exits falsely persuaded of 'fair terms', at least he intuitively distrusts Shylock's mind. Not so the overly confident Antonio, who feels no 'dismay' because his 'ships come home a month before the day' (173–4) on which his bond would be forfeited.

In light of Shylock's deceptive use of *avant garde* arguments regarding usurious bonds, one possible historical interpretation, presented by Walter Cohen, requires reconsideration. How can we see Shylock the usurer as the embodiment of decaying feudalism, 'an old man with obsolete values trying to arrest the course of history'?[78] Despite Shylock's roots in a medieval Italian source, Shylock as usurer is not reducible to a feudal figure. Shakespeare has modernised Shylock's case for usury by giving him some of the latest arguments and language current in Elizabethan debates about usury. Because Elizabethan England has no banks, unlike more economically progressive countries on the Continent, individual 'Christian' usurers in England (many of whom were merchants) tend to be seen as contemporary, not feudal, operators who have become increasingly sophisticated about how to ply their trade in a country in which usury is still technically illegal and in which no unconverted Jews are admitted to practise this occupation. Shylock, as a 'money-man', seems modernly capitalistic regarding his trade of moneylending, but, unlike Antonio, he seems old-fashioned in his repudiation of the too risky overseas trade of goods which constitutes legitimate commerce in the contemporary Elizabethan view. Therefore, as Cohen suggests, Antonio may be more modern 'as the embodiment of progressive forces' because as a merchant-financier he represents rising mercantile capital.[79] However, Antonio's brand of mercantile capitalism is traditionally conservative because he vehemently opposes usury, and this stance renders him atypical for many Elizabethan merchants in Shakespeare's audience. By the time usury is legalised in England in 1624, and while attitudes toward usury as legitimate lending continue to evolve, Antonio will seem even more fiscally conservative.

However, Shylock's pound of flesh does constitute usurious 'gain' from both traditional and progressive viewpoints: (1) usurious gain is traditionally defined as *anything* taken above the principal; (2) gain, from the more modern perspective, is money or money's worth. Despite Shylock's clever denial of usurious intent as well as financial profit, the pound of flesh does have financial worth. For Shylock, the monetary worth of Antonio's flesh has considerable economic reality: if he can rid Venice of Antonio, he can make whatever merchandise he will (3.1.100–2). In the trial the worth of Antonio's flesh exceeds an almost unimaginable sum (4.1.85–6) until Shylock decides to forgo the pound of flesh and gain instead *thrice* his original bond (4.1.314–15), a 'profitable, estimable' threefold increase on his principal.[80] Shylock, therefore, stands to gain whether or not Antonio keeps his day. Should Antonio repay the loan in time, Shylock will have succeeded at

least in purchasing Antonio's good will and consequently perhaps a kinder relationship with him on the Rialto. If Antonio
forfeits, as he does, the pound of flesh is Shylock's 'gain'. Recognising the true nature of Shylock's flesh bond with Antonio cor-
rects the prevalent misperception that Shylock lends without taking
any interest, a fundamentally mistaken view that fosters similar
views, for example, the opinion that Shylock's offer reveals the
true nature of his 'submerged' self, how 'humane, kindly, and
patient' Shylock really is.[81]

In light of his biblical defence, Shylock's deceptiveness in the
formulation of the bond distances him from his preferred patriarch, Jacob, and ironically links him with the 'covetous Laban',
who respects only 'his own gain'.[82] Laban himself was guilty of
fraud in depriving Jacob of his wages (Gn 31.7). Christian David
Ginsburg notes the importance of the gloss in the Bishops' Bible
(1568) for Shylock's reference to the Jacob–Laban story: 'It is not
lawful by fraud to seek recompense of injury: therefore Moses
sheweth afterward [Gn 31.9] that God thus instructed Jacob.'[83]
Shylock, however, uses fraud to recompense the injuries he has
received formerly from Antonio. God, however, took Laban's wealth
from him and gave it to Jacob (Gn 31.1–2). But Shylock, in defending and practising the deceitful theft of usury, remains blind
to these scriptural lessons by ignoring the fate of the covetous
who use fraud, and the fate of the usurious, whom Solomon describes as awaiting the same loss of illicit wealth (Prv 28.8). Shakespeare establishes a partial parallel between the unhappy relationship of Antonio and Shylock and that of Jacob and Laban, wherein
personal injury festers, but which is eventually resolved peacefully (Gn 32.44–55).[84] Jacob also differs from Shylock in taking an
anti-revenge position, unlike his deceitful and vengeful sons, when
his only daughter, Dinah, is raped by a Gentile (Gn 34.5–31).[85]
But Shylock, perhaps unlike some members of Shakespeare's audience, is not mindful of his patriarch's denial of revenge. Likewise, Shylock's expletive, 'by Jacob's staff' (2.5.36), reveals a similar
opacity to this symbol, which was a sign of Jacob's initial poverty before God enriched him with the increase of Laban's flocks,
and therefore Jacob humbly extols God, not himself, as the cause
of his thriving (Gn 32.10, gloss).

Thus, Shakespeare's use of Jacob for Shylock is richly double-
edged. Shylock's identification with Jacob is apparently appropriate because Jacob is an Old Testament patriarch; Jacob is renamed

Israel, from whom came the twelve tribes and Shylock's lineal descent and identity as a Jew; Jacob is married to Leah, whose son Judah fathers the tribe from whom Shiloh will come; Jacob ('supplanter', 'deceiver') uses deception to gain his father's earthly blessing; and Jacob thrives, becomes very rich. On the other hand, Shylock's identification with Jacob is also ironic because the external similarities are not matched by the internal life of faith for which Jacob is honoured in the Old and New Testaments. Shylock dreams of money-bags, not Jacob's ladder. Shylock embraces revenge and not the reconciliation Jacob seeks with Esau, Laban, and the Shechemites. Shylock wrestles with men to gain gold and silver (not with God to prove his inner worth). Shylock becomes very rich by relying not on God but on his own cunning, which includes the use of fraud and theft that Jacob eschews in his dealings with Laban; Shylock herein resembles Laban more than Jacob. Like Laban, Shylock bemoans the loss of his 'household idols' which his daughter steals – as Rachel did from Laban – but which Jacob refuses to honour (Gn 35.2).

Thus Shylock's bond fulfils all the criteria for being sinful usury because it involves lending for gain, compacting for gain, and not risking or 'adventuring' the principal.[86] We must admire Shylock's ingenuity for he has succeeded masterfully in adapting anti-usury arguments to his own ends in creating a bond that *appears* to be not usurious. This bond thus contributes to the play's enactment of the problem of wise choices, of discerning between appearances and realities. Without an awareness of the complexity of sixteenth-century thought on usury and its theological underpinnings, many 'economic' issues in the play will confound our modern assumptions. For example, W. H. Auden believes Shylock, as a usurer, acts unprofessionally because 'he refuses to charge Antonio interest'.[87] Marc Shell argues that Shylock's pound of flesh is not 'use' but only 'a conditional security'.[88] René Girard sees Shylock as demanding 'no interest for his money, no positive guarantees in case of default'.[89] David Bady also misses how Shylock's bond with Antonio is indeed usurious, constituting not 'an equivalent value' but rather 'excess'.[90] Lars Engle sees Shylock's merry bond 'as unbusinesslike a proposition as one could find', and he lauds Shylock as a Jacob figure who '"blesses"' the Christians' financial ventures, erroneously maintaining that Scene 3 of the play depicts 'the diabolism forced on Shylock by Antonio's near-hysterical resistance' to usurious exchange.[91] Walter Cohen claims that Shakespeare deviates from the anti-usury tracts and that Shylock genuinely refuses to take usury but instead takes legitimate interest.[92] Unfortunately, Cohen misunderstands what constitutes legitimate interest and misreads Mosse's careful definition of it.[93]

'Interest' could be used negatively as a synonym for usury. Antonio's use of 'interest' in this sense (1.3.43, 67–9, 86) particularly offends Shylock, who himself prefers the term 'usance' (1.3.37, 100, 134), 'usance' being one of the better terms that Wilson and Mosse say usurers adopt to salve their guilty consciences.[94] Mosse explains that 'usurers are convicted in their own consciences' because they 'dare not call a spade a spade, nor usury, usury', but they 'say in somewhat a finer phrase, he taketh usance . . . as being indeed ashamed of the direct name of usury'.[95] Indeed, 'usance' is unique in Shakespeare's canon, used only in *The Merchant of Venice* and only by Shylock in this bond-formulation scene (40, 137, 103). 'Interest' could also refer not to usury but positively to the concept of just compensation for damages suffered by the lender, specified as due only 'from the appointed day of payment forward', a usage which, for whatever reasons, Shakespeare does not employ in this play.[96] 'Interest' in this latter sense cannot be applied to Shylock's pound of flesh because Shylock's stipulation satisfies a sixteenth-century definition of usury, as has been explained, and violates the principles governing legitimate interest: he has suffered no fiscal damage through this bond nor has any gain been hindered by this bond (Bassanio offers far more in return than Shylock's principal), and the pound of flesh was stipulated in the bond on the day of borrowing and not added afterwards as a compensation on the due date of the bond.

If we wish to find Shylock's 'thrift' as 'blessing' the financial market by making loans at interest available to the Christian community, then it is curious that Shakespeare presents no evidence in the play that supports this kind of interpretation, evidence of societal appreciation for a good Jewish moneylender, such as, for example, the historian Joseph Shatzmiller establishes for the Jewish moneylender, Bondavid, in medieval Marseilles.[97] Nor does Shakespeare present evidence of 'good will' for Shylock, such as is evinced by the honest Jewish moneylender in Robert Wilson's Elizabethan comedy, *The Three Ladies of London* (1584).[98] Instead, Shakespeare presents evidence to the contrary: Shylock's own daughter proclaims her house is hell and flees it, Shylock's own servant leaves him for a more generous master, and Antonio says Shylock's clients make moan to him for relief (3.3.23). The recent studies on usury by two historians concur about the negative presentation of usury in Shakespeare's play. Norman Jones maintains that 'Shylock was the usurer in the flesh, to many English people, both educated and uneducated.'[99] Joseph Shatzmiller explains that although Shylock the character might evoke sympathy, 'it is difficult to find any sympathy in the play for the profession of moneylending' because the play 'fits comfortably within a long European anti-usury tradition'.[100] Both Wilson and Mosse, writing over twenty years apart, one before and one after the Act Against Usury of 1571, catalogue the list of evils that create an economic crisis in the commonwealth when usury 'causeth destruction and confusion universally',[101] and they try to counter the new opposing trend that seeks to redefine usury so that it might be tolerated under certain circumstances which might still accord with the rule of charity.

But at the end of this scene what does Antonio's newfound praise of Shylock reveal: 'Hie thee, gentle Jew. / The Hebrew will turn Christian, he grows kind' (1.3.170–1)? Antonio's anti-usury position is not divorced from religious belief, but rather, grounded in it. In this play the issues of faith and profession are not bifurcated but fused; hence, Shylock tries to justify his profession of usury by appealing to Scripture, and Antonio attempts to refute Shylock's interpretation of the Old Testament. From Antonio's perspective, Shylock's Jewish faith is an integral part of his usury, his beliefs dictating his practices. Shylock's line, 'You call me *misbeliever, cut-throat dog*' (103, my italics) emphasises this point. Solely on the grounds of offering an apparently non-usurious bond, Shylock has 'converted' Antonio's negative opinion of him so that Antonio sees Shylock as being Christian or 'kind' in his behaviour now. To the audience's eyes, however, Shylock has proved himself a master of appearances in this scene. Antonio's eyes cannot read Shylock's heart. We cannot fully agree with Hazlitt's well-expressed sympathy for Shylock, 'He is honest in his vices', or Girard's similar sentiment: 'the "honesty" of his vices makes him almost a refreshing figure compared to the sanctimonious ferocity of the other Venetians'.[102]

Shylock's feigned change of heart toward Antonio is counterbalanced by Antonio's genuinely changed opinion of Shylock. Instead of cursing Shylock, he now praises him. Antonio honours Bassanio's earlier dinner invitation to Shylock, not for the original business intended, now accomplished, but probably for social conviviality. Shylock thinks he has been invited out of flattery and so he goes in hate (2.5.13–15), but Shylock probably misperceives, just as he miscalculated that Antonio would fawn or flatter in seeking the loan. This is a special feast to which Shylock has been invited because it includes Bassanio's 'best esteemed acquaintance' (2.2.144). After this feast Antonio will assist the Duke, whom Shylock has roused, in trying to ascertain Jessica's whereabouts (2.8.4–11). Three months later, when misfortune afflicts Antonio, the merchant will appeal to Shylock as if he expects it is possible for Shylock to be kind to him: 'Hear me yet, good Shylock – ' and 'I pray thee hear me speak – ' (3.3.3, 11). Shylock now repels Antonio, and Antonio reflects that Shylock hates him because he actively opposed Shylock's usury (3.3.20–4). By the time of the trial Antonio will be convinced of the hardness of Shylock's heart toward him, and instead of addressing Shylock by his proper name, Antonio will revert to seeing him once again not as a man but as a type of hardheartedness, 'the Jew' (4.1.70–83). Thus, the striking peripateia that occurs midway in this bond-formulation scene provides a crucial clue for understanding the basis of Antonio's hatred of Shylock on the grounds of usury and for understanding the deadly deception behind Shylock's merry sport. Many have argued that Antonio hates Shylock solely because he is a Jew, and Shylock himself states this to Solanio and Salarino (3.1.46). But the ending of the play's third scene tends to refute this opinion. Shylock is still a Jew, but Antonio has changed his negative attitude to a positive one because Shylock appears to be forgoing usury on this loan, and therefore, Shylock redeems himself in Antonio's eyes.

This important confrontation scene, with all its twists and turns, reveals how fundamentally opposed to actual usury Antonio is and how fundamentally in favour of it Shylock is. Shakespeare's general audience, of course, did not know the Talmud and the emphasis in Jewish law on charity in lending. They traditionally associated Jews with the practice of usury. Mosse, publishing his work in 1595 to educate a Christian audience in London about usury, makes this point by calling sinful usury 'this unchristian, this heathenish, this Jewish kind of practice'.[103] The moral debate over usury was very topical for Shakespeare's audience; Christians who practised usury could be seen as 'Jewish' in their behaviour. Wilson, writing in 1569, had complained that England was the worst country in Christendom for the practice of usury, even worse than Italy, and the English 'Christian' usurers were 'no better than Jews. Nay, shall I saye: they are worse then Jews.'[104] The theological idea of the 'Jewish choice', in conjunction with one dramatic convention for the stage Jew, promoted this perspective by sometimes serving as the litmus test for whether a 'Christian' character was truly behaving like a Christian or whether he was a nominal Christian, more 'Jewish' in behaviour and intention.[105] Thus, the 'Christian' merchant appears radically deficient in his unkind treatment of his enemy, Shylock. Although Antonio's announced intention of breaking his custom against usury seems noble, love for a friend overcoming hate for an enemy, such a choice is also fraught with irony. By the end of the scene Antonio is more kindly inclined toward the 'gentle Jew' (170), and his expectation that Shylock 'will turn Christian' is perhaps Shakespeare's first hint of the conversion stipulation to come in the trial scene. But by the second time the audience sees the Christian merchant and the Jewish usurer together, the former's hopeful expectations will prove false, while the latter's hopes will seem ascendant. When we next see Antonio and Shylock on stage together, usury surfaces again as the bedrock for personal hatred.

'THEREFORE HE HATES ME' (3.3.24)

Although only a brief thirty-six lines long, this short scene, Act II, Scene 3, is far more important than the small amount of critical commentary devoted to it suggests. Mahood rightly observes that the use of 'Jew' in the stage direction and in the speech headings of the quarto and folio texts is significant because 'Shylock appears only as the moneylender, not the father' (3.3.0 n.). Much more confronts us here:

> Jailer, look to him. Tell not *me* of mercy.
> This is the *fool* that lent out money gratis. . . .
> The Duke shall grant me *justice*.
>> (3.3.1–8, my italics)

Shylock's attitudes toward money and mercy are related. Generosity with physical wealth, lending money 'freely', is as *foolish* as

generosity of spirit, showing mercy instead of strict justice. Earlier Shylock had condemned Antonio to Solanio and Salarino
because Antonio lent money out of Christian charity: 'He was
wont to call me usurer; let him look to his bond. He was wont to
lend money for a Christian courtesy; let him look to his bond'
(3.1.37–9). Usury is intimately associated with the subject of mercy.
The recurrent criticism of usury was its violation of charity; no
degree of faith could excuse the absence of charity, and the usurer was consistently regarded as an unmerciful man whose 'biting and cutting exchange' effected 'unmerciful dealings'.[106] For
Shylock wisdom is all justice and no mercy, and he now is in a
position of power to interrupt Antonio at will and to refuse to
hear him speak:

> I'll not be made a soft and dull-eyed fool,
> To shake the head, relent, and sigh, and yield
> To Christian intercessors.
>
> (14–16)

Perhaps Shylock would be more tolerant of Jewish intercessors,
but his own harsh reaction to his daughter's betrayal of him suggests leniency is not his typical response, because there he hun-
gers for 'satisfaction', for 'revenge' (3.1.74) against Jessica. He even
regrets the amount of money he has had to spend in searching
for his own flesh and blood: 'And I know not what's spent in the
search . . . the thief gone with so much, and so much to find the
thief' (72–4). In this scene he reaffirms his hatred for Christians
that he made clear in his earlier scene with Antonio and in his
reason for going to the Christian feast, that is, 'in hate, to feed
upon / The prodigal Christian' (2.5.15–16).

For Shylock, to relent or yield is to be a 'dull-eyed fool'. The
imagistic emphasis here on 'dull-eyed' as 'easily deceived' recalls
the imagery in the casket test that contrasts ways of seeing, with
the eyes or with the mind, as well as the basic emphasis on wise
versus foolish 'perception' and the problem of genuinely discerning
between appearances and realities for understanding the truths
therein. Shylock clearly does not value mercy as a legitimate response to human fallibility, whether it be Gobbo's supposed feeding
at his expense, Jessica's elopement, his client's 'forfeitures' (22),
or his enemy's 'prayers' (20). He perceives mercy as mere folly.
Wilson consistently develops the antithesis between wisdom and

folly in his criticism of usurers as 'wise worldly rich men' whose 'certain cunning' based on 'carnal reason' falls far short of true wisdom, that must be rooted in godliness: 'the wisdom of this world is foolishness in-deed before god'.[107] This scene, then, not only recalls the thematic contrast between wisdom and folly in the casket choice's test of false and true love, but also anticipates the contrast between wisdom and folly in matters of hate, which will be tried in the courtroom in the next staged confrontation between Antonio and Shylock.

Shylock's verbal repetitions pound home his obsession with his bond, that will allow him to feed his ancient grudge against Antonio according to 'the course of law' (26). His insistent repetition checks any possible misunderstanding of his purpose, so seriously embraced that he has 'sworn an oath' (5) to have his bond. From a Jewish viewpoint Shylock's deceptive bond, masked as 'merry sport' but intended to rob Antonio of life, would be branded as wicked. When Oliver Cromwell's plan to resettle the Jews in England was being debated, Rabbi Menasseh ben Israel (1604–57), the spokesman on behalf of the Jews, offered an explanation of the Deuteronomic text that allows Jews to take usury of aliens. In this explanation he clarifies what constitutes a 'wicked' Jew according to their own law, namely that the usury must be moderate and 'not biting and exorbitant': 'In our Law it is a greater sin to rob or defraud a stranger, than if I did it to one of my own profession: because a Jew is bound to show his charity to all men.'[108] As a Jewish moneylender, Shylock compares unfavourably with the virtuous Gerontus in Wilson's *The Three Ladies of London* and the kind Bondavid in medieval Marseilles.

Moreover, Shylock clarifies once again that he passionately champions his practice of usury, because he criticises Antonio as having called him 'dog' *before* Antonio 'hadst a cause' (5). Shylock, however, should know usury is the very 'cause' that Antonio explained in their debate, and once again Shylock's interpretation radically differs from another's, whether it be Antonio's, Lancelot's, or Jessica's. Shylock's insistence here that Antonio had no 'cause' reveals how entrenched he is in his belief that usury is not cursed but blessed and how deaf he is to Antonio's lessons about the basic dehumanisation of biting usury because it depends on the using but not the loving of others. Solanio now confirms the 'most impenetrable cur' image that Shylock says he will embody henceforth: 'beware my fangs' (18). Now the seemingly powerless Antonio finds he has to be concerned about the reason why Shylock 'seeks [his] life' (21):

> I oft delivered from his forfeitures
> Many that at times made moan to me;
> Therefore he hates me.

His reasoning confirms Shylock's ambition, shared with Tubal, that if Shylock can only get rid of Antonio, he can do whatever business he likes in Venice (3.1.100–3). In the preceding scene Bassanio has described Antonio to Portia as not only his 'dearest friend' but also 'the kindest man, / The best conditioned and unwearied spirit / In doing courtesies', his unflagging performance of kind deeds making him an exemplar of 'ancient Roman honour' in Italy (3.2.291–5). Antonio's courtesies include being financially merciful to Shylock's moaning victims.

Antonio's appearance here shocks and moves the audience. Shylock claims Antonio 'used to come so smug upon the mart' (3.1.36–7), but now the bankrupt Antonio is but a beggar. By deleting the rescue attempt in *Il Pecorone*, where 'many merchants joined together to pay the money',[109] and by dramatising the metamorphosis wrought by Antonio's suffering in this scene, Shakespeare underscores Antonio's experience of deprivation. The 'royal merchant' (4.1.29) has been humbled by adversity, his over-confidence undermined by his losses at sea and his realisation of the bond's danger. The audience sees not the formerly haughty, peremptory 'petitioner' but now the prayerful petitioner who must address his creditor as 'good Shylock' (3), requesting not a loan but life itself. Antonio, being legally bound to Shylock, is now also physically bound, and the presence of the jailer on stage high-lights Antonio's restriction of freedom. Antonio must be rather pathetically following at Shylock's heels so that Shylock commands, 'Follow not!' (16).

What a complete reversal in roles and positions of power Shake-speare enacts here! Antonio's mental anguish has already begun to manifest physical symptoms in the loss of so much weight that he will hardly be able to spare a pound of flesh to his 'bloody creditor' (34). The fears expressed in general terms by Solanio and Salarino (3.1) receive much more concrete articulation in the next scene in Belmont. Salerio describes Shylock's plying the Duke morn-ing and night for his bond as malicious inhumanity (3.2.271–82), but he simultaneously recognises the stranglehold of Venetian law because the 'twenty merchants, / The Duke himself, and the magnificoes / Of greatest port' (278–80), who try to persuade Shylock to change his mind, are also bound by the laws of the state. And in confirming this fear, Jessica lays to rest much critical debate that argues that her flight causes or exacerbates Shylock's murderous resolve toward Antonio.[110] She explains that when she was still with her father she heard him swear to his countrymen, Tubal and Chus, 'that he would rather have Antonio's flesh / Than twenty times the value of the sum / That he did owe him' (3.2.285–7), and 'if law, authority, and power deny not' (3.2.288) Shylock's bond, Antonio will pay.

Antonio's rational recognition of his dilemma echoes the threat of law and justice that Salerio and Jessica have prepared us for (3.2.270–89) and that Shylock asserts when he declares the Duke shall grant him 'justice' (3.3.8):

> The Duke cannot deny the course of law;
> For the commodity that strangers have
> With us in Venice, if it be denied,
> Will much impeach the justice of the state,
> Since the trade and profit of the city
> Consisteth of all nations.
>
> (26–31)

Antonio's and Shylock's fundamental opposition over usury is revealed to be part of their larger ideological opposition over the value of wise love, in particular its manifestation as 'mercy', which will be further explored in the trial scene.

5

'A Daniel come to judgement': The Trial

Prayer does indeed seem 'bootless' (3.3.20) as the peril for Antonio mounts: 'These griefs and losses have so *bated* me / That I shall hardly spare a pound of flesh' (3.3.32–4). Shakespeare probably intends a pun on 'bated', recalling Shylock's earlier response that Antonio's flesh was good 'to bait fish withal; if it will feed nothing else, it will feed [his] revenge' (3.1.42–3). Shakespeare powerfully coalesces the idea of the inner consumption of Antonio's flesh and life, due to biting usury, with the idea of literally cutting off the same flesh and life, due to sharp-edged revenge. The problems of usury and free lending, enemy and friend, hate and love, folly and wisdom, appearance and reality, safety and risk, keeping the law and violating the law (man's as well as God's law), giving and forgiving, justice and mercy are all 'bound up' in the formulation of the flesh bond and its resolution in the trial.

The trial scene is more linguistically and thematically 'bound' to the earlier scenes involving Antonio and Shylock, as well as the casket choice scenes, than has usually been thought to be the case. The flesh bond in Venice, like the casket test in Belmont, is both literally and symbolically meaningful. As the casket test is the literal means by which Portia gains a true husband, the flesh bond is the literal means by which Shylock can revenge himself on Antonio and by which Antonio can demonstrate his love for Bassanio so that Bassanio can sue to love Portia. As the casket test symbolically separates gold- and silver-choosers, as foolish lovers, from the lead-chooser, as wise lover, the taking of the flesh bond separates those who gain and get through hate from those who give and hazard through love. The choice of the leaden casket represents wise love just as the choice to take the bond represents foolish hate.

The bond scene anticipates the trial scene because usury and murder are conceptually associated in sixteenth-century thought and are carefully linked together through Shylock's flesh bond. Shylock will ultimately be held accountable to Venetian law for attempted murder, not for usury, which is lawful in Venice, as it is not in England. Shylock, however, thinks he has enabled himself to attempt murder, with no legal risk to himself, because he has a legal bond. Shylock attempts the paradox of a 'legal murder', not unlike the paradoxical idea of usury as 'legal theft'. Shylock's bond of covert usury, which he offered with deliberate deceit, is the lawful means by which he has caught Antonio 'on the hip' in order to have his 'heart'. As Shylock earlier confided to Tubal, 'I will have the heart of him if he forfeit, for were he out of Venice I can make what merchandise I will' (3.1.100–2). Shylock's language comes full circle in the trial scene when Gratiano vindictively underscores for the audience Shylock's original intent, which has now backfired: 'Now, infidel, I have you on the hip' (4.1.330). Both usury and revenge interrelate through their opposition to mercy and justice. In the trial Shakespeare continues to develop the Elizabethan concept of usury specifically through Cato's condemnation of the usurer as a murderer. It is Cato who declares that the usurer kills a man by destroying the means by which he lives. Cato is significantly Portia's nominal ancestor, as we have seen, and following Cato's moral insight, Portia will be the one in the trial to *prove* Shylock's attempted murder of Antonio.

Shylock has, however, already bettered Cato's instruction because he seeks not the prop that sustains Antonio's house, now lost at sea, but the very organ that sustains the life of Antonio's body: 'For if the Jew do cut but deep enough / I'll pay it instantly with all my heart' (4.1.276–7). Thomas Wilson clarifies the interrelation of the usurer and the taking of his victim's heart: 'God lendeth life and living for love, the usurer gaineth all that he may for loan, yea he taketh men's hearts (as I might say) out of their bodies', and Wilson observes that the borrower is 'stabbed at the very hart' by the usurer, whose own heart lacks charity since he is a 'cutthroat'.[1] At the time of notarisation Shylock must have specified in his written bond from what specific part of Antonio's body the pound of flesh was to be cut, but Shakespeare, despite several clues, significantly chooses to withhold that explicit information from the audience until the trial scene. 'A pound of flesh, to be cut off / Nearest the merchant's heart', and Shylock confirms the bond's language, '"Nearest his heart": those are the very words' (4.1.228–9, 250). Shylock literally desires Antonio's heart and thinks he deserves it. When confronted with legal risk to himself, Shylock literally forgoes Antonio's fleshly heart, but does Shylock figuratively gain Antonio's spiritual heart when he is placed in the position of giving and hazarding all? Shakespeare's literal and symbolic use of 'heart' in this scene will prove complexly educative.

The trial is the dramatic climax of the conflict in the play between Antonio and Shylock. It presents and resolves two different conflicts: (1) the conflict between good (love) and evil (hate), and (2) the conflict between a good (justice or the law) and a greater good (mercy or the law of love). The choice of 'either/or' pertains to the more obvious choice between good and evil. The choice of 'both/but' pertains to the more complex choice of a lesser and greater good. Nevill Coghill observes that the play presents 'the theme of justice and mercy, the Old Law and the New', recognising that both principles are '*inherently right*, and they are only in conflict because, whereas God is absolutely just as He is absolutely merciful, mortal and finite man can only be relatively so, and must arrive at a compromise'.[2] Both goods – justice and mercy – will be demonstrated as necessary but in what priority is the issue of choice. Man needs and seeks justice, but given human frailty, mercy shines brighter. The trial scene anticipates the rhythm of completion, fulfilment, or 'seasoning' that Portia announces in the final act and which characterises the play's ending: 'How many things by season seasoned are / To their right praise and true perfection' (5.1.107–8).

The play's educative bent regarding the choice of wise love continues to be shaped even more artfully in this scene. Who teaches? Who is willing to learn? What is learned? At the end of the bond-formulation scene Antonio showed he could change his unchristian treatment of Shylock, whereas Shylock's professed 'change' of friendship toward Antonio was hypocritical. But Antonio's befriending of Shylock is still not the moral perfection to which Antonio is called as a Christian by the new law of love. Antonio treated Shylock kindly because Shylock apparently met him on his terms for friendship, namely the friendship of free lending. Now Antonio knows Shylock is his sworn enemy, and Shylock will reveal the full measure of his hatred in this scene. Will Antonio be able to rise to love Shylock not as a supposed friend but as a known enemy? Shylock will be proved literally guilty of attempting to murder Antonio, but, as a Christian, Antonio will be spiritually guilty of murder if he returns Shylock's hate: 'Whosoever hateth his brother, is a manslayer' (1 Jn 3.15). The extent to which Antonio can renounce his hatred and practise the new law to 'love one another', not only 'in word' but 'in deed & in truth' (1 Jn 3.11,18), will be 'the special fruit of [his] faith and a certain sign of [his] regeneration' (1 Jn 3.14, gloss). In the manner of Sidney's prescription for comedic epistemology this scene continues to explore in profound ways the many paired opposites, such as letter and spirit, that pervade this play.

'I STAND FOR JUDGEMENT' (4.1.103)

The trial opens not with what the audience might expect, a confrontation between Antonio and Shylock or one between Shylock and Portia, but with the Duke's compassion for Antonio. The Duke seems surprised to see Antonio appear in court even before his 'stony adversary' (4.1.4) arrives: 'What, is Antonio here?' (1). Antonio's honesty and courage impress us. He rightly recognises that 'no lawful means' (9) can remove him from Shylock's reach. He does not try to avoid the penalty but stoically opposes Shylock's 'fury' with his 'patience', his 'quietness of spirit' (11–12). The trial's prelude, before Portia arrives disguised as Balthazar, turns on judgement as reason. Man's 'reason' is often termed his 'judgement', and the reasons given for the various judgements of self and others in the opening of the trial further reveal the minds and hearts of the characters. The Duke reasons with Shylock and expects 'a gentle answer' (16–34). Shylock's 'answer' explodes that expectation; he has sworn an oath by his nation's 'holy Sabaoth' to have his bond (35–9). Shylock now dominates the discussion by posing questions for the court and answering them as he pleases: 'You'll ask me why I rather *choose* to have / A weight of carrion flesh than to receive / Three thousand ducats' (40–2, my italics). Perhaps Shylock recalls Salarino's earlier question, 'Why, I am sure if he forfeit thou wilt not take his flesh. What's that good for?' (3.1.41). If he does, he does not now fully disclose his reason. Shylock was far more open with Solanio and Salarino when he explained why Antonio's flesh would feed his revenge.

Now Shylock will 'not answer that', other than to dismiss it as

his 'humour' (42–3) and to provide a series of irrational, instinc-
tual examples of human behaviour that are animalistic in their
lack of free choice concerning what they 'cannot abide' (44–58).
Shylock, empowered by the law, arrogantly holds the court almost 'in contempt' when he intentionally provides an 'answer'
that is 'no answer' (63), reasoning that as 'there is no firm reason
to be rendered' for such examples, 'so can [he] give no reason,
nor [he] will not, / More than a lodged hate and a certain loath-
ing' he bears Antonio (53–61). As in the formulation of the bond,
Shylock appears honest but is not. As in his response to Salarino's
question earlier, Shylock's definition of what it means to be human does not go beyond the level of the sensitive soul that man
has in common with animals. As the audience knows, Shylock
can give reasons for his hatred of Antonio, but he will not in this
court. Why not? Is it because hate is not a prosecutable offence
in courts of law unless that harboured hate is translated into a
word or deed that violates some statutory law?

Shylock's answers may not please the court, but they are lawful. He seems to recognise that it is important to keep his answers
technically lawful. He tells the court not the whole truth but only
part of the truth as to why he insists on his bond. Shylock's partial revelation allows him to vent his spleen without apparently
endangering himself, and Shylock's evasiveness recalls the evasiveness of Silvayn's Jew in *The Orator* (1596), who refuses to explain
fully why he pursues such a 'strange' suit.[3] The implication is
that both creditors have something to hide, but in Shylock's case
the self-hiding is darker and more devious because the audience
– but not yet the court – knows he intends murder, whereas
Silvayn's court knows the Jew intends mutilation but no murder.
Silvayn's inclusion of the idea of punitive legal consequences for
the execution of a lawful bond that results in murder, not just
mutilation, probably influences Shakespeare's innovative creation
of the punitive Venetian law he introduces after the resolution of
Shylock's bond (4.1.342–59).[4] Shakespeare's court may suspect
Shylock and fear Antonio's death, as Antonio himself does (3.2.316),
but it will be Balthazar's task to *prove* in court that Shylock attempts to murder Antonio. Balthazar's proof will not be useful
in judging the bond itself but in subsequently judging the author
of the bond and his purpose. With dramatic irony the disguised
Portia must undisguise Shylock, who desires to use a bond (legal
by one law) to commit an act (illegal by another law) without

any legal risk to himself. Shylock desists, however, as soon as he discovers such risk.

Bassanio tries his voice at reasoning in a tense stichomythia with Shylock, who twice gets the last word. At this point Antonio momentarily loses his hard-earned 'quietness of spirit' and counters the court's reasoning with his own, that it is useless to try to 'soften' the hardhearted Jew; Antonio is resolved to suffer his judgement. Shylock mockingly refuses Bassanio's offer of twice the bond's sum (84), as well as his later prayerful appeal (127), and the Duke rationally challenges Shylock, 'How shalt thou hope for mercy, rendering none?' (88). Shylock confidently returns, 'What judgement shall I dread, doing no wrong?' (89). The Duke's line recalls James's admonition that those who show no mercy should expect none in return, but Shylock's rejoinder also reveals his ignorance of this idea's corollary, that only those who are merciful need never fear judgement (Jas 2.13).

Shylock's falsely self-righteous retort highlights his own vulnerability at the same time as it introduces his most powerful defence of his bond, his 'tu quoque' speech on the Christian use of slaves (90–100). Shylock analogises the 'rightness' of his bond with the Christian ownership of human flesh in the form of slaves. His reply indicts the Christians' failure to live according to their creed. Although slavery might be legal according to man's law, it is not 'legal' if judged by God's law. This is one of the many instances in the trial scene when the interplay between the laws of man and God serves to underscore the necessity, but also the inherent injustice, of fallible man's law, and the perfect justice of God's law. But Shylock's 'justification' of human flesh as purchasable commodity becomes double-edged and undercuts his rationale in light of its biblical resonance. As we shall see when we discuss the Duke's judgement of Shylock (364), the New Testament opposition of 'flesh' and 'spirit', articulated by Paul, would call to mind for Elizabethans that Shylock's worldly wisdom works only for this world, this earthly city of Venice. In his defence of taking and owning flesh Shylock represents the man who ironically is a slave to himself, 'enslaved' to the 'flesh' because he refuses to live in the 'spirit' (Gal 5.13–18; Rom 7.14–23).

Shylock's spiritual blindness, his self-righteous arrogance, his hypocritical reverence for literal legalism, and his contempt for mercy continue to build Shakespeare's characterisation of Shylock, begun in Shylock's first scene (1.3), as a false Pharisaical Jew, not a true patriarchal Jew as Shylock would like to see himself. The values for which Shylock stands in the trial are all associated with the New Testament's condemnation of the 'ambition, covetousness, and hypocrisy' of the Pharisees, who are presented as the moral opposites of the Old Testament prophets: 'Woe be unto you, Scribes and Pharisees, hypocrites: for ye build the tombs of the Prophets. . . . If we had been in the days of our fathers, we would not have been partners with them in the blood of the Prophets' (Mt 23.29–30; cf. vs 1–39). According to Graham Midgley, Shylock is 'strict in his religion'.[5] But this view needs considerable qualification. Shylock has been shown to be strict about ritual defilement, such as the eating of pork, but he also violates several important commandments of the Mosaic Law. He violates the sixth of the Ten Commandments by seeking Antonio's life (Ex 20.13); once Antonio is impoverished, he violates the Old Testament injunction against the taking of usury from the poor (Dt 15.4); and he pays no heed to God's will, 'Vengeance and recompense are mine' (Dt 32.35; cf. Rom 12.19). When Shylock tells Tubal to meet him at the synagogue, after promising to torture Antonio, we can only assume that he will pray as the proud Pharisee does, bent on God's recognition of his deserts. Given Shylock's transgressions of the Mosaic Law such assumption of desert is unwarranted. 'Examining things with extreme rigor as hypocrites, who only justify themselves, & condemn all others', Shylock embodies the choice of 'worldly wisdom' against the choice of heavenly 'wisdom' that is 'full of mercy . . . and without judging, and without hypocrisy' (Jas 3.15–17, gloss).

Sir Henry Irving, who played Shylock nobly as a martyred patriarch, is reported to have said: '"Shylock is a bloody-minded monster, – but you mustn't play him so, if you wish to succeed; you must get some sympathy with him."'[6] Shylock is not a 'monster'. He is a man who is capable of doing monstrous deeds, like all men, but who differentiates himself by actualising his potential through his attempts. As we have seen, Shylock does receive sympathetic treatment by Shakespeare, but how he gets that sympathy is quite a complex matter. Shakespeare's choices here are better appreciated if we attempt to place Shylock in his contemporary dramatic context. As a Jewish antagonist in an Elizabethan comedy, Shylock finds a middle ground between Marlowe's Barabas and Wilson's Gerontus: Shylock is not nearly so dark a man as Barabas nor nearly so good a man as Gerontus. Like Barabas,

Shylock is deceptive in dealing with Christians, for, as Barabas explains: 'It is no sin to deceive a Christian' because 'faith is not to be held with heretics', and 'all are heretics that are not Jews' (2.3.306–9). Marlowe probably influences Shakespeare's use of Machiavellian deceit and egoism for a Jewish antagonist, because in *Il Pecorone* there is no element of deceit in the Jew's bond and his murderous intent is not implicit but explicit: 'the Jew . . . wished to commit this homicide in order to be able to say that he had put to death the greatest of the Christian merchants'.[7] If so, Shakespeare once again imaginatively transforms that influence by adapting the Machiavellian motive and method to enhance Shylock's humanity as an antagonist. In *The Jew of Malta*, Machiavel presents the prologue and introduces the play as 'the tragedy of a Jew / Who smiles to see how full his bags are crammed, / Which money was not got without my means' (ll. 30–2), revealing his brotherhood with Barabas. The popular distortion of Machiavelli as a devil figure who embodied fraud and dissimulation for egoistic and usually deadly ends hovers in the background of Shylock's Machiavellian deceit in formulating the vengeful flesh bond and in cloaking his intent to murder Antonio in the trial. Shylock's verbal skill resembles that of Barabas and Richard III, Shakespeare's earlier Machiavellian master of deceit.

But Shylock is given much more humanity because Shakespeare elaborates on the understandable motives for his deceit. Shakespeare also creates much more sympathy for Shylock by not indulging the Machiavellian spirit to its extreme manifestation; he curtails the range and actualisation of villainy as well as the motive and the method. Shakespeare replaces the delight in the motive of villainy, characteristic of Barabas, with the righteous belief in the motive of lawfulness, characteristic of Shylock. Moreover, Shylock's method of operation is far more dignified than that of the Machiavellian Barabas because he pursues his vengeful bond in the open marketplace and ultimately the Venetian courtroom. The typical Machiavellian method of secretly hatched deep plots, using underhanded means, such as poison and hired assassins, does not contaminate Shylock's apparently lawful method. On the other hand, this very openness of execution heightens the horror because the characters and the audience must anticipate watching a vivisection.

The tolerant and forgiving nature of the Jewish moneylender Gerontus, however, makes Shylock's implacable hardheartedness appear all the more inhumane. Gerontus's opponent is a dishon-est and cowardly Christian merchant (Mercadore) who is two years late in repaying his legitimate debt because he fled Turkey in order to avoid paying it. When Mercadore finally returns, Gerontus expects to have his principal and interest, but Mercadore begs for more time and Gerontus kindly grants him several time ex-tensions until it is clear to Gerontus that Mercadore is a liar and a cheat. In Turkey converts to Mohammedanism are forgiven all their debts, so at the trial Mercadore pretends that he will con-vert to Mohammedanism solely to avoid paying Gerontus the debt he owes. Even though Mercadore verbally abused Gerontus for his arrest, calling him a 'sitten scald drunken Jew', Gerontus rises above all the mistreatment he has suffered at Mercadore's hands and attempts to bargain for just the payment of the principal, then one-half of the principal, and finally forgives Mercadore the whole debt because Gerontus 'would be loth to hear the people say, it was long of me / Thou forsakest thy faith'.[8] The lesson Gerontus hopes Mercadore learns is to pay his debts when they are due so that he will have 'a good name' among men.[9]

The contrast between Mercadore and Antonio, like the contrast between Gerontus and Shylock, could not be greater. Antonio honestly and bravely faces up to his bond; he avoids all cheap tricks like running away or fake conversions.[10] Although Shylock's cool control and juridical mentality are impressive, making him a formidable opponent in the courtroom, his proud self-com-placency blinds him to his own hypocrisy, and his ironically im-perfect knowledge of the letter of his bond and the laws of Venice entrap him. For Antonio and Shylock we must recall here the Elizabethan perspective for judging the goodness of an individu-al's choice on the basis of God's law, not on the individual's rewriting of that law according to his own will: 'For god saith: thou shalt not do that which is good in thine own eyes, but do thou that only which I command thee.'[11]

In the spirit of the leaden casket, the willingness of Bassanio and Antonio during the trial to give all for the other, to die for each other (111–16), morally opposes Shylock's willingness to take all, according to his desire and desert. The human generosity of these two friends evokes, as Sir Israel Gollancz first noted, the greatest sign of love in opposition to Shylock's hate: 'Greater love than this hath no man, when any man bestoweth his life for his friends' (Jn 15.13).[12] Antonio consoles his friend by his humble readiness for death: 'I am a tainted wether of the flock, / Meetest for death; the weakest kind of fruit / Drops earliest to the ground, and so let me' (114–16). This significant speech, which is not to be found in any of Shakespeare's literary sources, importantly indicates some growth in humility on Antonio's part and as such contrasts with Shylock's overweening pride. 'Tainted wether' is a curious self-description. For Antonio, 'tainted' (diseased) certainly refers to his being financially discredited, and therefore 'of the flock' he is the weakest, the least well and most fit for death.

But the imagery in Antonio's speech may also suggest moral taint, an awareness of sinfulness appropriate for a Christian who is 'well prepar'd' (260) for death. Perhaps, after Bassanio's offer of life, Antonio feels apologetic for his letter's hint of doubt about the strength of Bassanio's love for him (3.2.318–19); if so, Antonio's counter-offer here is somewhat sullied by his own desire to have Bassanio live in order to immortalise him in an epitaph (117–18). Perhaps Shylock's 'tu quoque' speech stirs in Antonio some awareness of how he failed earlier in treating Shylock the usurer as less than a slave, indeed, as less than human – a 'dog' as Shylock proclaims (1.3.107–14). Antonio may now begin to grasp a more profoundly human understanding of why Shylock hates him. It is difficult to ascertain precisely what Antonio now sees as 'tainted' about himself, although the audience's larger vision perceives more keenly Antonio's taint in his failure to love his enemy as his enemy. However, he has taken a step in the right direction of truthful self-knowledge which nurtures moral growth.

Antonio's pastoral analogies for himself as 'a tainted wether' and 'the weakest kind of fruit' convey a sense of humility as well as acceptance that signals a departure from his self-righteous pride in his initial confrontation with Shylock (1.3.122–9). The ground is at least fertile for the growth of mercy. During the remainder of the trial, while Portia litigates and delivers her moving speech on the quality of mercy, Antonio – despite the almost unbearable tension for him – maintains a remarkable reticence, recalling his characterisation in the play's first scene, as a man given to silence and therefore 'reputed wise' (1.1.95–110). What wisdom might be truly Antonio's will be put to the test when it is his turn in the trial to choose either the 'earthly wisdom' of revenge or the 'heavenly wisdom' of mercy (see Jas 3.13–18). Except for Antonio's two brief affirmations and his important farewell speech to Bassanio, we can only read between the lines what Antonio is thinking and feeling and how that is clarified when he finally participates in the judgement of Shylock. We are denied the explication of a soliloquy.

With the court at a stalemate, the disguised Nerissa and Portia enter as clerk and civil doctor 'informèd *thoroughly* of the cause' (169, my italics), courtesy of the learned Bellario. Quick-witted Portia, like her father, has wisely left little to mere chance. Before she left Belmont, she sent her 'honest-true' servant, Balthazar, with a letter, ahead of her to her male cousin Bellario, a doctor of law in Padua, and smartly told Balthazar to bring back with him 'what notes and garments' Bellario gives (3.4.45–5). She and Nerissa will then meet Balthazar at 'the common ferry / Which trades to Venice' (3.4.53–4). There Portia and Nerissa presumably debrief Balthazar of Bellario's gifts, his legal expertise and garments, and Portia even assumes her servant's name for her new legal identity. Bellario's letter to the court allows Portia flexibility in the trial, and her eloquent speech on mercy is probably her own, her bettering of the legal opinion with which Bellario has furnished her (155–6). Bellario is wholly Shakespeare's creation and his realistic addition to his literary source, *Il Pecorone*. Shakespeare lets his Elizabethan audience know that Portia's legal expertise comes in borrowed robes.

Bellario's letter introduces Balthazar by name and advises the court to expect a paradox, a wise but young judge: 'I never knew so young a body with so old a head' (160). The wedding of youth and wisdom is comedically developed for the play's celebration of wise love. As the scroll in the golden casket reveals, Morocco needed to be 'as wise as bold, / Young in limbs, in judgement old' (2.8.70–1) in order to choose rightly. As Danson observes, Portia is presented here in terms of the Renaissance moral commonplace and the classical topos of the *puer senex*, the individual who combines in one person the best of youth and the best of age.[13] Viewed within a biblical context, moreover, Portia as wise youth will be aptly named Balthazar/Daniel because Daniel was also a wise young judge, and 'Daniel' means 'judgement of God', as glossed in the Geneva Bible's Table of Names. Confronting Portia's reconciliation of the best opposites stands 'old Shylock' (171), who is neither young nor wise. It is not coincidental that Shylock is referred to as an 'old' man six times in the play, because from an Elizabethan perspective he allegorically represents the 'old man' as interpreted by Paul.[14]

Shylock would probably not be pleased to hear the name of his announced judge. In the New Testament Balthasar is the name of one of the three wise men who followed the star to Bethlehem in order to bring gifts of homage to the child in the manger. In the Old Testament that name, rendered in various forms such as Belshazzar, Belshatsar, or Baltasar, is the name of the idolatrous Babylonian king, whose father Nabuchodonosor had destroyed Jerusalem and brought most of the Jews into Babylonian captivity.[15] Among those Jews was young Daniel, who was given the new Babylonian name of 'Belteshazar' (Dn 1.7) so that he might forget his religion. This name is a close variant on the name of King Belshazzar, which is glossed as meaning 'without treasure, or searcher of treasure'.[16] The glossator calls attention to this importance of names and renaming: 'for the Jews gave their children names, which might put them in remembrance of some point of religion: therefore this [pagan renaming] was a great . . . sign of servitude which they [the Jews] were not able to resist' (Dn 1.7, gloss).

For Shylock, then, Balthazar is the name of the enemy. That is why Shylock joyfully renames Balthazar as Daniel once the wise young judge desists from advocating mercy and tells Shylock what he wants to hear, that his bond is legal and that he may prepare to take it. The richness of Shakespeare's dramatic use of Daniel, from both the Book of Daniel and the apocryphal Book of Susanna, would not have been lost on an Elizabethan audience, who would have recognised in the refrain used by Shylock and Gratiano – 'a Daniel come to judgement' – various levels of meaning for Portia's role as teacher and judge in the trial and Shylock's misperception of that role. Portia's assumed title as a 'doctor' (152) of civil law conjoins the ideas of 'teacher' and lawyer.[17]

Let us begin with the Book of Daniel, where the pertinent allusion for the trial scene concerns the service of interpretation that Daniel is called upon to perform for King Belshazzar (Dn 5.1–31). Despite his Babylonian captivity, Daniel, a great Hebrew prophet, remains true to his faith, and his reputation for 'wisdom' in expounding 'hard sentences' is known to the Queen, who advises her husband to request Daniel's help (Dn 5.11–12). The reason the King needs Daniel's wisdom is important. The idolatrous King, who has 'praised the gods of gold and silver' (Dn 5.4, 23) in the midst of a Bacchanalian feast, orders the holy vessels of gold and silver which his father had taken from the Temple of

Jerusalem to be filled with wine so that his guests might drink
from them. 'At the same hour' appeared the fingers of a man's
hand, which wrote a message on the wall that greatly troubled
the King but which none of his wise men could interpret (Dn
5.5–9). Before Daniel reads the handwriting on the wall, he delivers an important homily on the fatal sin of pride and man's
refusal to learn from God's lessons staring him in the face. As
God deposed and punished the king's father for a heart 'puffed
up' and 'a mind hardened in pride', so will He punish the father's
son, who has not 'humbled [his] heart, though [he] knewest all
these things' (Dn 5.18–24). Daniel, as the judgement of God, interprets the written words to show that God's just anger will end
the life and rule of Belshazzar: 'thou art weighed in the balance,
and art found too light' (Dn 5.27).

In the Venetian courtroom stands a man with balance in hand
to weigh the flesh of another, but who will be weighed himself
and found wanting. Might not an audience see some of the parallels between Shakespeare's trial and the story of Belteshazzar/
Daniel? Does Balthazar's interpretation of the bond relate to Daniel's
wise interpretation of that which is written, especially 'hard sentences', in order to pass God's judgement on an idolater of gold
and silver who has heard the needed lesson but will not learn it
because his mind and heart are hardened with pride? Where indeed has one laid up one's treasure? Who is without treasure or
in search of it? And what will be God's judgement of him? Like
the proud king, but unlike the prophet Daniel, Shylock cannot
read the handwriting on the wall, as we would say proverbially
today. Nor can Shylock interpret rightly the written word of his
bond. Although he does not see much beyond the nominal letter
of his allusion, Shylock speaks more wisely than he knows when
he hails Portia as a Daniel come to judgement. Daniel recites the
history of King Belshazzar 'to show God's judgements against
the wicked' (Dn 5.1, gloss).

The Book of Susanna in the Apocrypha provides another rel-
evant context for understanding Portia's role in the judgement of
Shylock. In honouring Balthazar as a 'wise young judge' (220),
Shylock seems not to penetrate once again the merely literal re-
semblances of his comparison. Daniel is indeed described as 'a
young child' (Sus v. 45) who has the wisdom of an Elder, not
unlike the youthful Portia disguised as Balthazar. What Shylock
overlooks, however, is that Daniel's wisdom lay in saving the

life of an innocent by entrapping with their own words those who sought false judgement, significantly convicting them 'by their own mouth' (v. 61), much as Portia does when she uses Shylock's own demands for justice against him (311–12). When Shylock cries out, 'My deeds upon my head! I crave the law, / The penalty and forfeit of my bond' (202–3), little does he expect his deeds to exact his own penalty. Shylock's two props in the courtroom, the scales and the knife, would also strike Elizabethans as iconographically incongruous. As a symbol of justice the companion attribute to the scales is the sword, not the knife, which more frequently symbolises wrath, as in Spenser's depiction of 'rancour's rusty knife', which is fit for 'unmanly murder'.[18]

The 'biter bit' motif recurs throughout Elizabethan drama, but Shakespeare's use of it here has particular poignancy because of the biblical contexts in both the Old and New Testaments: 'He that diggeth a pit, shall fall into it' (Eccl 10.8); 'his mischief shall return upon his own head, and his cruelty shall fall upon his own pate' (Ps 7.16); and 'he [God] catcheth the wise in their own craftiness . . . when they themselves are entangled in the same snares, which they laid for others' (1 Cor 3.19, gloss). Once Shylock's deeds come home to roost, Gratiano parrots Shylock's Daniel refrain in his own inimitable foolery. Gratiano's mockery of Shylock rubs salt in the wound and makes Portia's task of trying to teach Shylock about the rigour of justice and the human need for mercy all the more difficult, to say nothing of increasing the danger for Antonio should Gratiano's barbs enrage Shylock enough to take his bond and suffer the consequences. Gratiano's misbehaviour here reveals the difficulty of learning. Gratiano, the comic fool that he is, indicts his own ignorance when he thanks Shylock for teaching him 'that word', Daniel (4.1.337). In her literal capacity as 'civil doctor' Portia serves the law of man, the strict laws of Venice. In her allegorical capacity she can be seen as a female Daniel, the judgement of God in the trial.

'THIS STRICT COURT OF VENICE' (4.1.200)

Shakespeare inherits from *Il Pecorone* the cities of Venice and Belmont for his settings. In that source the reputation Venice enjoys for being 'a place of strict justice' is a very important factor for understanding why the Jew's bond is legal, according to Venetian law, and how Shakespeare uses literary law for his literalistic legalism in the trial.[19] From a historical perspective we should also be aware that in the sixteenth and seventeenth centuries Venice's reputation as a city was so powerful that aspects of the city's reputation, such as its wealth, its pleasure, its wisdom, and its justice, might be taken together to constitute what scholars now refer to as 'the myth of Venice'. David McPherson explains that 'England . . . was the country in northern Europe in which the myth had its most profound effects.'[20] Despite discrimination, Jews enjoyed relatively favourable treatment in Venice.[21] The image of wealthy Venice as the pleasure capital of Europe, hinted at in the feasts, masques, and carnival atmosphere of the night when Jessica elopes, has been steadily left behind as Shakespeare advances the ideas of 'Venice the Just' and 'Venice the Wise', to borrow McPherson's epithets, for the legal crisis in Venice to be resolved by trial. In her ideological study of the city in Shakespeare's city comedies, Gail Kern Paster finds that the city is confronted with a crisis of law enforcement that entails inhumane consequences, requiring the city either to enforce or to refuse to enforce 'a monstrous law'. The resolution of the city's [Venice's] crisis 'is always to reconstitute the city for a greater inclusiveness largely achieved by means of redefinition and conversion'.[22]

The challenge here lies in accepting and trying to understand Shakespeare's use of literary or stage law for his trial. The influence of real law, English and Venetian, on the play intrigues a number of critics, and we will consider such ideas where pertinent.[23] Given the litigious atmosphere of Elizabethan England and the presence of members from the Inns of Court in the audience, Shakespeare could rightly expect a keen interest in the law on stage. But what we must constantly remember is that it is law *on the stage* and hence essentially fictive. Stage law is used more for dramatic purpose than legal theory, although Shakespeare's cultivation of a good measure of verisimilitude would enable the audience to suspend their disbelief even more avidly. Therefore, we have to grant Shakespeare his artistic freedom to make the 'legal' choices he does, even if they violate our best sense of what might be legally 'right'.

Nowhere is this more essential than when we must grant, as the text and Shakespeare's literary sources do, the *legality* of the creditor's bond, regardless of how it was offered or what its in-

tent is. With a sense of practical fairness, we demand, how can a
bond offered with intentional deceit as a jest but meant to be
executed with the intent of deadly mutilation be judged 'legal'?
Alice N. Benston, for example, expresses the frustration of many
readers when she argues that Shylock's murderous intent makes
his bond 'a sham' or 'a fraudulent contract' that the court can
declare null and void.[24] The Venetian court, however, has no power
to tear up Shylock's bond because the bond is recognised by
Venetian statutory law as legal. In Shakespeare's chief source, *Il
Pecorone*, the Jew clearly wants to murder the merchant, and although every one thinks 'the Jew was in the wrong' because he
refuses the money offered, yet because 'the Jew's case was legal
and formally made out, nobody dared to deny him, but only to
plead with him'.[25] What is judged 'legal' varies, of course, according to culture and historical period. The Elizabethan Doctor
of Laws, Thomas Wilson, presents a telling example from Roman
history of the lawful exaction of the debtor's flesh and life as
penalty for debts owed: '*Septimus Florens* reporteth if one man
were a debtor to many, his body was given unto them, to be
equally cut in pieces, and whereas he had not to pay in his purse,
his quartered body should pay for all, to give a terror to others
how to break with their creditors; and as this was amongst the
Romans so the Grecians used the same.'[26] Now no longer legal,
the then legal buying and selling of human flesh (slavery) constitutes Shylock's powerful defence of the legitimacy of his bond
(89–100).

Herein Shakespeare's possible literary sources for a flesh bond
– *Il Pecorone*, *The Ballad of Gernutus*, *Zelauto*, and *The Orator* – are
particularly helpful for revealing the shared literary conventions
for a legal flesh bond: (1) the courts accept the legality of the
bonds as written and signed; (2) attempted mutilation or murder
do not invalidate the bond; (3) the principle of literalistic legalism governs the interpretation and execution of the bond, and
the letter of the bond is binding for both debtor and creditor;
and (4) the power to refuse the bond lies only in the will of its
author. In other words, the creditor can take his pound of flesh,
without incurring any legal risk to himself, *if* he does not violate
the letter of the written agreement in the process. If the creditor
violates the letter of his bond in executing it, he is subject to grave
legal penalty. That penalty usually emulates the spirit of *lex talionis*,
a life for a life (*Il Pecorone* and *Gernutus*) or a right eye for a right

eye (*Zelauto*). But no creditor in these sources is held accountable to another law for having attempted mutilation or murder; they leave the courtroom emptyhanded, but they go with impunity.

To the judgement of flesh bonds in literature, Shakespeare significantly adds another condition: the creditor may freely leave the court after taking his bond according to its letter, or after refusing to take his bond, *if* he does not violate another law in the process. Shakespeare's addition of the Venetian law against attempted murder renders Portia's judgement of Shylock compound and complex. She first passes judgement on the interpretation of the bond (302–40), and then she uses another law to pass judgement on the author of that bond and the illegal use to which he would have put his bond (342–59). In Shakespeare's fiction, attempted murder via a legal bond is brought to justice by law, as it is not in the medieval *Il Pecorone* or the Renaissance *The Ballad of Gernutus*. Given Shakespeare's version of Venetian law for his play, it is conceivable that if Shylock had written his bond in such a way as to have been able to take a pound of flesh according to the letter of his contract, and if he had not attempted murder, but rather, non-lethal mutilation (a shallow chest wound, with surgeon present to treat the wound), he could have taken a pound of Antonio's flesh with impunity. Shakespeare uses the literary conventions concerning flesh bonds that his audience could know from a variety of sources, but he also improves upon them through his additions and his cultivation of the themes of literalism, justice, mercy, and education.

Shakespeare makes the legality of Shylock's bond unmistakably clear. When Portia first enters the court, she proclaims to Shylock: 'Of a strange nature is the suit you follow, / Yet in such rule that the Venetian law / Cannot impugn you as you do proceed' (173–5). Again, when Portia examines the bond, she declares: 'Why, this bond is forfeit, / And *lawfully* by this the Jew may claim / A pound of flesh, to be cut off / Nearest the merchant's heart' (226–9, my italics). Later Portia reasserts that Shylock's bond is legally valid, 'The court awards it, and the law doth give it' (296). Without exception, everyone in the court recognises that Antonio 'stand[s] within [Shylock's] danger' (176) because the bond is lawful. As much as Bassanio and other Venetians would like to wrest the law to save Antonio's life, it cannot be done without impeaching 'the justice of the state' (3.3.29) that legally guarantees the benefits foreigners enjoy in Venice: 'there is no power in

Venice / Can alter a decree establishèd' (212–15). Where then resides the power for the defeat of Shylock's bond? In Shylock and only in Shylock. Therein lurks the terror of the trial and the essential danger to Antonio. Shylock alone has the legal right to choose, either to take or to refuse his bond. Therefore, before the trial scene begins, Antonio, 'twenty merchants, / The duke himself, and the magnificoes / Of greatest port' (3.2.278–80) have been begging Shylock to show mercy, and in the trial the Duke, Bassanio, Gratiano, and Portia all repeatedly voice appeals to Shylock to 'be merciful' (229). If Shylock cannot be persuaded either to be merciful to Antonio or to forgo his bond for some other reason, it will go hard for Antonio.[27]

In terms of psychic pain it does. As the trial escalates in tension, Antonio begs Portia to resolve his agony of anticipation: 'Most heartily I do beseech the court / To give the judgement' (239–40). Why does Portia take so much time? Portia is sometimes criticised for her dilatory tactics and for preaching mercy to Shylock, but not practising it.[28] Such criticism overlooks the complex interplay of her pedagogic and judicial functions in the trial. Shakespeare ingeniously exploits Paul's metaphor for the Law as a 'Schoolmaster' to 'bring us' to Christ (Gal 3.24) in his characterisation of Portia as a law judge who also plays the role of a schoolmistress in her exposition of justice and mercy in order to bring us out of the court of strict justice and into the court of God-like mercy.[29] Portia believes and practises mercy, or she would not be helping Antonio as she is, nor would she keynote the call for 'mercy' when she presents Shylock to the Duke and Antonio for judgement (359, 374). Shakespeare, keenly aware of the pedagogic power of role-playing, has Portia adopt the role of devil's advocate in her sentence of 'all justice' (317) to teach Shylock, and us, the need for the seasoning grace of mercy. Like the Duke in *Measure for Measure*, who has all the answers but who also draws out the trial, Portia gives Shylock, as the Duke gives Angelo, every chance to do what is right and in the process educates all the onlookers too. However, Shylock, like Angelo, remains obdurate until the tables are turned on him. Portia similarly delays revelation in the mock trial of Act V in order to effect a more harmonious lesson. Teaching, however, is but teaching; the student has the last word: 'Good sentences, and well pronounced. / They would be better if well followed' (1.2.9–10).

Shylock's important and carefully chosen words in the bond,

'"nearest his heart"' (250), are not revealed to the audience until Portia refers to them (226), but they receive climactic emphasis when Antonio is directed to lay bare his bosom: 'For if the Jew do cut but *deep enough*, / I'll pay it instantly with all my *heart*' (276–7, my italics). Antonio's ironic statement, symbolising his offering of both love and life for Bassanio, renders shockingly clear that Shylock wants to murder Antonio. Shylock does not contradict this: 'We trifle time; I pray thee pursue sentence' (4.1.294). Prior to the trial scene the only clue that Shylock wants Antonio's heart is Shylock's promise to Tubal, 'I will have the heart of him if he forfeit' (3.1.100–1). The amputation of a pound of flesh certainly need not cost a life, an issue explicitly addressed in *The Ballad of Gernutus* and *The Orator*. But Shylock's 'very words' (250) specified in the written bond, as they were not in his oral offer, indicate that he desires to take the flesh from a life-threatening place. Since the heart is the seat of love, as well as life, Shylock's specific wording about the heart, at the time the bond was signed, could have been jestingly presented as appropriate, especially given his stated desire to buy Antonio's 'favour' (1.3.161) with this bond, which Shylock punningly suggests Antonio should not refuse: 'And for my *love* I pray you wrong me not' (1.3.166, my italics). It would hardly do to write the word 'murder' in a 'merry bond'.

Thus, Portia has proved in open court that Shylock indirectly attempts to murder Antonio because Shylock cares not if the mutilation causes Antonio to bleed to death (253–8) and that he directly attempts to carve flesh nearest the heart until her 'tarry a little' pauses his knife in mid air. However, despite this evidence of criminal intent and attempt, Portia has no more legal right to deny the taking of a lawful bond than did the judges in *Il Pecorone* and *The Ballad of Gernutus*. Whatever 'Venetian law' governs the legality of bonds of this nature, it guarantees the creditor's right to take his bond, as long as he takes it according to its letter. At this point in the trial Shylock's bond has the procedural priority of legal resolution, over other matters that might relate to this bond. Therefore, Portia does not introduce here the subsequent Venetian legal penalty (343) even though she already has all the evidence she needs to enforce that law. Not only would this legal action appear to be procedurally out of order but also this punitive law, unlike the literalistic law governing bonds, would not deter Shylock from taking his bond because he might as well take it if he is going to suffer a legal penalty either way. Nor

would this action teach Shylock much about the danger of legalistic literalism. The taking or not taking of Shylock's bond first
must be definitively resolved and resolved by Shylock's choice.

'Tarry a little' indeed. What has Shylock not seen? What has
Shylock assumed in 'this strict court of Venice' (200), which is
intolerant of assumptions, let alone equity? To what extent does
Shylock contribute to the cause of his own defeat? Shakespeare's
artistic brilliance in the trial's first reversal, Shylock's negation of
his bond, has too often been unfairly dismissed by critics as a
cheap triumph – a mere 'quibble', the 'merest technicality', or a
'trick'.[30] To the contrary. Portia's reversal works legally in this
strict court precisely because it is strict construction. Literalistic
legalism is what is at stake in a *strict* court where law is not
assumed to have 'spirit'. Instead, Shakespeare deliberately contrasts the letter of the *law* with the spirit of *men*. The letter of the
law allows only for justice and judgement. If either Antonio or
Shylock are to receive any mercy, it will not come from the law
but from the hearts of men. Therefore, Portia's literal interpretation involves no wordplay and no trickery. If Portia's interpretation
did stoop to such means, it would make a mockery of the law of
strict justice, and Shylock would have the right to complain of
being cheated and not legitimately defeated. In *Il Pecorone* the
Jew articulates the desire for literalistic legalism: 'I tell you frankly;
if you offered me more ducats than this city is worth, I would
not be satisfied, and take them. I wish to act according to the
letter of the agreement.'[31] Because Shylock's bond is legal according to the letter of Venetian law, the letter of the bond itself – not
the letter of the law – is what is left open to interpretation.[32] Shylock
therefore denies his bond once he discovers he has not been literal enough in the wording of it and that there are legal consequences for taking the bond in violation of its 'tenour'. Through
careful interrelation of imagery, idea, and characterisation, Shakespeare measures up to the task of avoiding the interpretation's
potential reduction to mere quibble or technical trick.

How, then, does Portia's interpretation legitimately work within
the stage law of the play? As we have seen, Shylock is a literalist
who glosses his figures of speech. With exquisite irony there is
one figure of speech he does not gloss, and it is his most important, 'a pound of flesh'. This irony is intensified by Shylock's failing to hear the clues Portia gives him, just as Morocco and Arragon
missed the verbal clues in the casket choice. Selfish literalists hear

and understand only what they want to hear and see. Portia has just given Shylock the essential linguistic clues when she asks Shylock if he has 'the balance' ready 'to *weigh* the flesh' (251, my italics), and if he should have a surgeon ready to prevent Antonio from too much loss of *blood* (254). Shylock has the balance ready, but he cannot admit the surgeon: 'Is it so nominated in the bond? / ... I cannot find it, 'tis not in the bond' (255, 258). The precise literal meaning of the words, 'a pound of flesh', means just that – a pound (neither more nor less) of flesh (flesh per se, not blood, hair, or bone that could accompany the flesh). It is Shylock, not Portia, who desires a figurative interpretation of 'a pound of flesh' to mean an approximate pound of flesh inclusive of whatever pertains to the particular pound taken. Because Shylock insists on the letter of his bond, however, he should have been more literal, more specific in his written expression in order to gain what he intends.

Shylock *assumes*, as does everyone in the court, except Portia, that the taking of a pound of flesh will entail the loss of blood. Shakespeare's preparatory use of blood imagery before and during the trial also lulls us into this assumption: Bassanio imagines every word in Antonio's letter 'a gaping wound / Issuing life-blood' (3.2.264–5); Antonio refers to Shylock as his 'bloody creditor' (3.3.34); Gratiano denounces Shylock's desires as 'bloody' (4.1.138); and Bassanio asserts that the Jew shall have his 'flesh, blood, bones and all' before Antonio will lose 'one drop of blood' on his account (4.1.112–13). Literalism is usually derided as a defect in the trial scene, but Portia's interpretation of the bond reveals how literalism can be a legal virtue, not a vice, when used by a wise judge, not a vengeful plaintiff. Just as the Duke and Portia err in assuming Shylock will be merciful, so also Shylock errs in assuming the intended meaning of his bond is inscribed in his literal wording.

Why does Shylock, careful literalist that he is, fail to gloss his phrase even though he himself has repeatedly voiced his insistence on a literal interpretation of his bond in a strict court that must uphold such literalism? Shylock is not ignorant about this specific example of literalism because earlier in the play he used the explicit phrase 'flesh and blood' to describe his relationship to Jessica (3.1.30). He could just as easily have described her as the daughter of his flesh, or as Jessica does, 'a daughter to his blood' (2.3.17). He would have communicated the same intended meaning but in different *words*. Shylock's use of the words 'flesh and blood' to signify related but different entities is underscored in the play by Salarino's rejoinder: 'There is more difference between thy *flesh* and hers than between jet and ivory; more between your *bloods* than there is between red wine and Rhenish' (3.1.31–3, my italics). As we have seen, the linguistic nuances of 'blood' and 'flesh' differ in their inner versus outer orientation; 'blood' signifies more the inner vital life principle whereas 'flesh' signifies more the outer physical frame.[33]

'The letter' and 'the spirit' interplay in both Venice and Belmont, but with different emphases. Belmont emphasises more the 'spirit'; interpreting the 'meaning' of the letter's 'spirit', as intended by its author, is essential. Venice emphasises more 'the letter'; interpreting the 'meaning' of the letter itself, regardless of the 'spirit' of its author, is essential. But the letter of the law is not overlooked in Belmont any more than the 'spirit' of humans is ignored in Venice. We should recall here that the literal interpretation of the bond, and consequent legal penalty for the plaintiff if he should be less than literally exact in executing the bond, is precisely the convention inherited by Shakespeare from all his possible literary sources that use a flesh bond.

Unlike these sources, however, Shakespeare develops the theme of literalism throughout his whole work and improves on the artistic function of the 'no jot of blood' legacy. Given Shakespeare's development of biblical allusion for Shylock's characterisation, there may be another reason why some members in an audience would see Shylock's 'oversight' as properly 'Jewish'. Shylock has been presented as strict in his avoidance of ritual defilement: for example, he won't eat pork or contaminate himself by socio-cultural association with Christians. Aside from helping to betray the 'sportive' nature of the bond as feigned, should 'blood' be specifically included, Shylock's avoidance of the word 'blood' in this context of 'sacrifice' *apparently* keeps the letter of the Mosaic Law, just as earlier Shylock *apparently* offered a non-usurious bond. According to the Mosaic Law, Hebrews regard the blood of all living beings, humans and animals, as the sacred life principle over which God has sole rights. Therefore, Hebrews were forbidden to partake of the blood of animals or to shed the blood of their fellow men: 'Likewise whosoever he be of the house of Israel . . . that eateth any blood, I will set my face against that person that eateth blood . . . *For the life of the flesh is in the blood*, & I have given it unto you to offer upon the altar, to make atonement for your souls' (Lv 17.10–11, my italics).

The motif of Shylock's figurative cannibalism, which is another of Shakespeare's additions to *Il Pecorone*, glances darkly at this injunction. An allegorical dimension of this blood and flesh imagery pertains to its sacrilegious, as opposed to its sacramental, association with 'feeding'. Shylock's figuratively cannibalistic appetite for Antonio's flesh to 'feed fat' (1.3.39) his hate may be seen as a black parody of an opposite feeding, the loving sacrifice of flesh and blood in the Christian sacrament of Holy Communion. English Protestants symbolically receive Christ's body and blood with the bread and wine in order to nourish spiritual life and to prevent the death of sin (Jn 6.54–8). The play's linguistic emphasis on flesh and blood might have some religious relevance for Elizabethans because in 1559, at the accession of Elizabeth I, a third Act of Uniformity was passed, and the Book of Common Prayer was modified to make it more widely acceptable, one revision being the addition of references to the body and blood of Christ. 'Hunger' that satisfies the 'flesh' versus hunger that satisfies the 'spirit' is a motif that links Lancelot and Shylock in contrast to Jessica.

In the Old Testament, as Shylock should know, God punishes those who unjustly shed the blood of their fellow men (Ps 5.6, 26.9; Prv 29.10). Shylock fails to observe the letter of His Law. He mockingly reduces the value of human flesh to less than that of animal flesh (1.3.158–60), and his bloody intent and method contaminate the sacrificial offering he would make of Antonio. With an oath in heaven sworn to take Antonio's flesh, Shylock rationalises his sacrifice of Antonio on behalf of his 'sacred nation' and the repayment of Christian revenge. His attempted slaughter, however, is really an oblation to satisfy his own blood vengeance, not God's justice. Slaughtered animals had to be presented first as offerings to the Lord; their blood had to be poured out on the altar of the Lord, or one would be guilty of bloodshed (Lv 17.3). God allowed His people to use animals for food, but they were forbidden to eat any flesh from which the blood had not been drained (Gn 9.4; cf. Lv 3.17). Thus, from a Jewish perspective the shedding of the flesh's blood, whether for food or sacrificial offering, is bad form and bad faith.

There is also another allegorical dimension to the sacrificial language of blood and flesh that dominates the trial scene. In the

Old Testament the covenant between God and His people was ratified in the blood of the animals which Moses directed the people to sacrifice (Ex 24.5–8). In the New Testament the covenant is ratified in the blood of Christ on the cross. The use of a sheep metaphor to describe Antonio ('a tainted wether of the flock') evokes Antonio as a type of sacrificial lamb to Shylock's hatred, and as Lewalski argues, the plot situation and language in the trial scene suggest the crucifixion scene, 'a typical killing of Christ by the Jew'.[34] If so, the burden of analogy weighs heavily on Antonio's shoulders because the Sacrificial Lamb set the example of forgiving those who killed Him: 'Father, forgive them: for they know not what they do' (Lk 23.34). In many ways Antonio physically embodies in the trial scene Portia's motto, 'I stand for sacrifice' (3.2.57), which counters Shylock's motto, 'I stand for judgement'.

When Shylock proclaims, 'My deeds upon my head' (202), he echoes the sentiment of the Jews when they chose Barabas over Christ, and the phrasing signifies the willing acceptance of total responsibility for what one does and what happens to one consequently (cf. 2 Sm 1.16). But the clear biblical echo here is also telling because Shylock once again avoids the specific mention of the loaded word 'blood' which is the word in Matthew: 'His blood be on us, and on our children' (Mt 27.25). Shylock's preference of Barabas over any Christian is one version of what G. K. Hunter explains as 'the Jewish choice', the choice of Barabas over Christ, and as such, this choice also constitutes a symbolic rejection of the leaden chest, the choice of wise love. Because Christ is associated with 'Wisdom', one of His divine attributes and one of His titles as the second person of the Trinity, Shylock's choice of Barabas symbolises a rejection of such wisdom.[35] Man's knowledge of spiritual things comes from the Spirit of God and not from the spirit of the world, 'which teacheth things wherewith the world is delighted, and which men understand by nature' (1 Cor 2.12, gloss). Paul claims that the natural man, 'whose knowledge and judgement is not cleared by God's Spirit' considers spiritual things foolish because without spiritual discernment he cannot know them (1 Cor 2.14, gloss). Shylock's misguided literalism understands the letter of the law in terms of his own blind self-righteousness. According to Paul, however, the choice of Christ, not Barabas, would free Shylock from such self-defeating self-dependence through self-fulfilling dependence on God by means of faith and grace (Gal 3; Rom 10.3–4). Thus, the spirit of the New Law as expressed through Christ and as implicitly signified by the meaning of the leaden choice, designed to temper the letter with the spirit, self-reliance with God-reliance, is rejected by Shylock overtly in his words and deeds and implicitly in his attitude of literalism. Shylock does not begin to shift his stance from rejection to acceptance until he confronts successively his own legal risk and liability, his own dire need prompting him to see differently.

Continuing his pervasive patterns of 'threes', Shakespeare structures Portia's judgement of Shylock in three parts. The first two pertain to Portia's literal interpretation of the bond; the third pertains to the legal consequences of Shylock's attempt to murder Antonio. The literal form and progressive order of these three parts enlighten our understanding of what Shakespeare wants Portia to accomplish. In the two parts of her interpretation of the language of the bond, Portia gives Shylock his desired principle (literalism), used now, however, with good intent and for a good end, and she reads the bond, as he insisted, according to 'the tenour' (231). 'This bond doth *give* thee here no *jot* of *blood*' (302, my italics) comprises Portia's first part of her interpretation of what 'a pound of flesh' 'expressly' (303) means. As we have seen, there are two ways to read the words literally; one can deconstruct 'flesh' or 'pound'. Shakespeare chooses to present the flesh/blood dilemma before the exact measure of weight, a pointed reversal of the order in *Il Pecorone*. Most importantly, Shylock tacitly acknowledges the legitimacy of Portia's interpretation because he voices no objections to it. Shylock does, however, indicate his surprise at the legal penalty he faces if he transgresses this interpretation in the taking of his bond.

Enter 'Hazard'. Now Portia introduces the principle of risk native to the casket choice and foreign to usury. Shylock may still take his bond. But if he violates the letter of it by shedding even one drop of 'Christian blood' (306), his 'lands and goods are by the laws of Venice confiscate / Unto the state of Venice' (307–8). The personal hazard of financial wealth is the significant turning point at which Shylock begins to back away from his bond. Of the various possible literary sources for this reversal, Shakespeare stands alone in adding the risk of wealth. The sources use only the death penalty as the factor of risk that defeats the plaintiff's desire to take his pound of flesh.[36] In Portia's first pronouncement she makes no mention of loss of life but rather *only* loss of wealth. The

importance of wealth in motivating Shylock to abandon his bond
is reinforced moments later when he protests the wealth penalty
after the Duke mercifully grants him his life. The hazard of wealth
is enough to bring Shylock up short: 'Is that the law?' (310). His
shocked surprise at this potential loss of his wealth parallels
Morocco's initial shock upon discovering his golden error: 'O hell!
What have we here?' (2.7.62). In response to Shylock, Portia affirms the 'quid pro quo' of her argument, 'Thyself shall see the
Act. / For as thou urgest justice, be assured / Thou shalt have
justice more than thou *desirest*' (310–12, my italics). Shylock now
declares he is willing to settle for the lucrative offer of thrice his
bond, but, because he has refused legal tender 'in the open court'
(334), he cannot now reclaim either the triple offer or his principal. For Shylock to have 'all justice' he must receive 'nothing but
the penalty' (317–18).

   Now Portia will 'raise the waters' (2.2.39) and offer the other
possible literal interpretation and its consequent legal penalty: 'If
thou tak'st more / Or less than a just pound . . . / Thou diest,
and all thy goods are confiscate' (322–8). For the first time Portia
announces the only penalty, the death penalty, that knowledgeable members of an Elizabethan audience would have been expecting to hear. But unlike his sources, Shakespeare continues to
include the financial penalty which would enlist their attention
and should ours. Now Shylock's speechless pause ('Why doth
the Jew pause?') recalls that of Arragon, who also falsely 'assume[d]
desert' (2.9.50): 'Too long a pause for that which you find there'
(2.9.52). Why the need for this second gloss and its double jeopardy when Shylock has clearly begun to lose interest in his bond
after Portia's first pronouncement? There are several possible reasons, but they all interrelate through the lesson Portia is trying
to teach Shylock by making him experience it: the danger of 'all
justice' and the wisdom of mercy. Portia also raises the stakes to
help ensure that Shylock will no longer desire to take his bond.

   What we must not lose sight of is Shylock's sole power of choice
over the refusal of his bond. Portia underscores this by repeatedly telling Shylock that he may still 'take [his] forfeiture' (331,
339). In other words, Portia's literal interpretation of the bond
and the consequent legal penalties attendant on this interpretation do not nullify Shylock's bond. At any moment Shylock can
still turn and carve his pound of flesh ('the law allows it'), but
now he can do so only at his own 'peril' (340), at his own haz-

ard. Not until Shylock himself completely denies his bond in open court (341–2) is Antonio legally free from danger. When Shylock angrily retorts, 'Why then the devil give him good of it!' (341), we might recall Arragon's chagrin over his losing suit, and Portia's rational rejoinder: 'To offend and judge are distinct offices, / And of opposèd natures' (2.9.60–1).

Why do we now hear no more about Shylock's 'oath in heaven' (224)? Oaths and promises bond the plots of both Venice and Belmont, as we have seen and will continue to see in the final act. Shylock has asserted he would not 'lay perjury upon [his] soul', not 'for Venice' (225–6), but he will choose to break his oath to save himself. That Shylock is deterred here by consequences risky only to himself reveals once again Shylock's commitment to himself. The audience, however, must momentarily rejoice in Shylock's essentially comedic choice because his decision allows both Antonio and Shylock to live. But Shylock's reasoning here, like his reasoning in so many other instances, reveals his need for enlightenment. It is not wrong to break an evil oath. This right logic does not occur to Shylock probably because he does not see his oath as evil, yet he should.

This need for continual enlightenment and the opportunity to do good ushers in another of Shakespeare's major additions to his sources, the Venetian legal penalty for attempted murder of a Venetian citizen by an alien.[37] Simple defeat is the goal of the literary sources in which the flesh-bond story appears, and the Jew leaves the court in a rage of anger or of grief, but he suffers no legal penalty for attempted murder.[38] After the plaintiff refuses to take his bond, Shakespeare alone transforms the plaintiff into a defendant now held accountable to another Venetian law, a law that punishes attempted murder. Once again Portia similarly begins another reversal for Shylock, 'Tarry, Jew: / The law hath yet another hold on you' (341–2), based on Shylock's 'direct or indirect attempts' (346, 355) against Antonio's life. Portia's legal language recalls similar language in England's Act Against Usury of 1571, which legislates against usury taken 'directly or indirectly'.[39] This legal language of methodology subtly links Shylock's directly intended usury and attempted murder to the indirectness of some of his methods. Shylock's bond is usury obtained indirectly or covertly. This usurious bond is the legal means by which he illegally seeks Antonio's life through attempts in the courtroom demonstrated as both indirect and direct. By judicious indirections

Shylock finds directions out. According to 'the laws of Venice' Shylock's indirect attempt (to let Antonio bleed to death if he does not cut deep enough) and his direct attempt (sharpened and poised knife to cut the flesh nearest the heart) to murder Antonio are liable to the legal penalty of loss of life, which only the Duke can pardon, and loss of all wealth, half going to the state and half to the person against whom the offender contrived. Once again Venetian law puts Shylock in peril of losing his life and wealth, but this time half of his loss would be Antonio's gain.

The interrelation of 'life' and 'living' throughout the play reaches a climax in the trial scene's several different reversals, which we cannot fully appreciate until we understand Shakespeare's exploration of the nature of that interrelation. In the eyes of the law, the erstwhile plaintiff has just become the defendant, and the defendant is now in the position of the plaintiff. Shakespeare's invented reversal is not concerned with simple defeat but with moral education through the hard school of experience. The interpretation of Shylock's bond provides a lesson in the operation of strict law whereas the use of the Venetian legal penalty provides a lesson in the human need for mercy given the universal nature of human fallibility and the course of justice in which 'none of us / Should see salvation' (4.1.195–6).

'THOU SHALT SEE THE DIFFERENCE OF OUR SPIRIT'
(4.1.364)

Shylock receives the strict justice he craves until, at Portia's instigation, the Duke's intentionally educative line inaugurates the trial's second peripeteia to demonstrate difference in spirit. Shylock and the audience wait to hear what judgement will be passed on Shylock now that it has been proved in open court that Shylock has violated Venetian law in seeking the life of a citizen and consequently is subject to the penalty of the law, the loss of life and wealth. Mahood argues that a modern audience has trouble with the judgement passed on Shylock in the trial because 'the conditions imply that Shylock is being judged not so much on what he has done as on what he is: his very being as a Jew, and his social role as usurer of which we have seen nothing in the play'.[40] This sounds appealing, especially to a modern audience, but Shakespeare's judgement is much more complex and fairer than this. The verdict definitely is based on what Shylock has done (attempted murder by means of a legal bond of covert usury). Like Angelo, Shylock is condemned by the law to die, not for what he is, but for what he does. Like Angelo, Shylock is saved from the death penalty through the intercession of his judges.

Will Shylock receive justice? Mercy? Both? Neither? In his characteristic mode of self-interest, Shylock craved the civil law as long as it was on his side. Shylock myopically never saw the law from Antonio's side, just as he has not been accustomed to seeing anything from another's perspective, whether Lancelot's hunger or Jessica's misery. But seeing is believing for Shylock. The Duke's instructive line about seeing the difference between how Shylock has behaved and how he will behave ironically echoes Shylock's erroneously triumphant parting prediction to Lancelot: 'Well, thou shalt see, thy eyes shall be thy judge, / The difference of old Shylock and Bassanio' (2.5.1–2). With the usurer's mental calculation of no risk to himself, Shylock had banked on a no-lose situation for himself only to discover the personal risk, 'the danger' (358), inherent in dependence on the letter of the law as well as in violation of the law. By his own reiterated choices Shylock himself is brought to judgement under the law, and he stands now in peril of losing his life and his wealth, half of which would go to the state and the other half to Antonio. As Alexander Pope reminds us, 'To Err is *Human*; to Forgive, *Divine*'.[41] Balthazar commands, 'Down, therefore, and beg mercy of the Duke' (359), and Gratiano characteristically interrupts with the countering voice of vindictiveness: 'Beg that thou mayst have leave to hang thyself' (360). Balthazar's injunction underscores for us that the law allows only for strict justice. What mercy Shylock can therefore receive depends not on the law but on the hearts of those entitled to administer the law's penalty.

Taking the initiative to speak first, the Duke prevents Shylock from having to beg, as Shylock did not do for Antonio (3.3). The Duke pardons Shylock's life as Shylock refused to do earlier in the trial for Antonio: 'That thou shalt see the difference of our spirit, / I pardon thee thy life before thou ask it.' He also generously offers to reduce the legal penalty of half Shylock's wealth to a fine if Shylock is humble (364–9). The Duke's language, '*difference* of our *spirit*', is appropriately chosen to contrast with Shylock's earlier insistence on 'flesh'. An Elizabethan audience would take 'spirit' in its common sense, as we do, but would also hear significant verbal allusion to Paul's use of this specific word and its distinction from 'flesh' when he describes 'the battle betwixt the spirit and the flesh' (Gal 5, heading). In Galatians Paul contrasts the enslavement of the natural man to the 'flesh' (sin) with the freedom of the regenerate man who lives according to the 'spirit' (grace). Shylock earlier claims his right to Antonio's flesh by analogy with the idea of slavery (purchased flesh), not realising, of course, how his analogy reflects on his own enslavement to the 'works of the flesh', such as 'hatred' and 'murders' (Gal 5.19–21).

The other dimension of Shakespeare's wordplay here involves the interrelation of the concepts of 'the Law' and the new law of love. To be led not by the flesh but by the spirit means to fulfil the Law through its full summation in the new law: 'Thou shalt love thy neighbor as thyself' (Gal 5.14). In an imagistic description of what it means to live according to the flesh, Paul uses language that informs Shylock's metaphors of fleshly feeding: 'If ye bite & devour one another, take heed lest ye be consumed one of another' (Gal 5.15). As we have seen, Shylock's definition of what it means to be a man is based only on the earthly or natural part of the human being; the Duke is now calling attention to the spiritual or supernatural part of the human being because he intends to show love to Shylock, to temper the law's strict justice with the spirit of mercy.

Mahood claims: 'Like Angelo in *Measure for Measure*, Shylock has willed more evil than he performed. Because our sense of right decrees he ought not to die, the equivalent of equity, the mercy of the Duke, in the end overrules statutory law' (p. 18). There are several important confusions here that blur what Shakespeare emphasises through the Duke's judgement. First, for the same cause of *attempted* murder, Roderigo Lopez was executed. 'Our sense of right' is not quite operative for Elizabethan or Venetian law. *Attempted* murder is sufficient cause for the death penalty in the laws of Venice and England, as George W. Keeton reveals.[42] Second, the Duke does not show mercy 'because our sense of right decrees' that Shylock deserves life. The Duke's speech is based on the contrary belief. Although Shylock has done nothing to deserve clemency, the Duke is resolved to show mercy to Shylock so that he might see and learn from the 'difference' between them. Third, the concept of equity should not be confused with the concept of mercy. Equity is a species of justice, but mercy relates to justice by opposition, not similarity.[43] Hence, if a judgement transcends the strict letter of the law, it may be equitable or merciful, depending on the desert of the offender. Equity is reasonable justice due; it credits the offender with fair desert to some degree. Mercy is a free gift; it qualifies justice and rewards where there is no merit of desert. To suggest the Duke's pardon of life is an example of equity diminishes the Duke's idea and degree of free giving (mercy) and overcredits the offender with merit. Portia's imagistic portrayal of mercy as free-dropping heavenly rain makes this important distinction clear. Portia responds to the Duke, keeping the legal proprieties of the financial judgement in due order by reminding the court that this specific judgement on Shylock's wealth applies 'for the state, not for Antonio' (366).

The resilient Shylock, however, objects, and the desire upon which he grounds his objection is pivotal for understanding all that follows:

> Nay, take my life and all, pardon not that:
> You take my house when you do take the prop
> That doth sustain my house; you take my life
> When you do take the means whereby I live.
>   (370–3)

Shylock desires wealth more than life without wealth. If he is to be granted life, it must be on his terms. In abstract logic the gift of life is always more important than the gift of wealth. As the Nurse in *Romeo and Juliet* bemoans, 'Death's the end of all' (3.3.93), and in this sense Lancelot's 'joke' about his death ultimately proves 'comic' for his old father only when its falsehood is revealed (2.2.52–78). Wealth is the means for life, not the end. As with his defence of usury, Shylock tends to misprioritise the means above the end. But in practical logic Shylock raises a legitimate objection to which the play has been sensitive, namely the practical need for wealth to enable the living of one's life, whether it is Bassanio's need for 3000 ducats or Jessica's and Lorenzo's need for Shylock's deed of gift.

With his characteristic habit of not seeing 'reality' but rather what he wants to see as 'reality', Shylock overreacts to the Duke's judgement. Shylock is not facing destitute poverty because the Duke has not categorically claimed the state's full half of the financial penalty. If Shylock reforms his false pride exhibited in the courtroom, the Duke's consequent reduction of the penalty to a fine means that Shylock will receive a portion of his wealth or a part of his 'prop'. Nothing comes of nothing, but something can be made of something. However, to Shylock the degree of financial loss must feel like absolute poverty. Herein we also see that Shylock's objection rests upon a very important assumption, namely that he believes the other half of his wealth is completely lost to him because the law assigns it to his enemy Antonio. But no one in the court has a more feeling knowledge of the fear Shylock is now experiencing than Antonio. Antonio was, just moments earlier, in Shylock's predicament of poverty, and he comforted Bassanio by reasoning that quick death under Shylock's knife was a more merciful ending than penurious old age (260–8). As Shylock was defeated on his own stated terms, so he will find some mercy on his own stated terms.

Portia now significantly turns to Antonio and asks, 'What mercy can you render him, Antonio?' (374). The language of the request is crucial. Shakespeare could just as easily have substituted the word 'justice' for 'mercy' to suit the metre of his line. But the idea, not the metrics, is what's at stake here, and intonation also significantly affects how the audience will respond to the intended meaning of this request. Earnest empathy will provoke a very different response than ironic sarcasm. But the very choice of the word 'mercy' should be a clue to Antonio to bend in this direction and away from the strict justice that is repeatedly emphasised as the purpose of Venetian law. This line ushers in Shakespeare's second critical alteration of the trial scene in *Il Pecorone*. He transforms the former defendant into a judge of the former plaintiff; in the source only the judge renders judgement. This is Shakespeare's 'stage law' at its finest. Procedural questions of real law reveal this trial to be 'unusual' and 'casual' as E. F. J. Tucker has noted, especially since Portia, like the enforced Angelo in *Measure for Measure*, directly defies the legal principle 'that no person may officiate as judge in his own cause (iudex in propria causa)'.[44] What Tucker does not mention is the even more blatant legal travesty of allowing the defendant Antonio to participate in the judgement of the plaintiff Shylock.

Shakespeare must have found merit in putting the shoe on the foot which would feel the pinch the most because he does this again in *Measure for Measure* when Isabella is asked to plead for Angelo, and she, like Antonio, responds generously. But like the actress playing Isabella, the actor playing Antonio should pause for a long, even uncomfortably long, time before replying. What is being asked of Isabella and Antonio is excruciatingly hard to do – to counter a desire for fleshly revenge with a gesture of generous spirit toward a known enemy. The Duke in *Measure for Measure* underscores this difficulty: 'Against all sense you do importune her' (5.1.433). Before Antonio can respond, Gratiano, whose jeering mockeries of Shylock punctuate each successful move that Balthazar makes in bringing Shylock to judgement, cries out, 'A halter gratis, nothing else for God's sake!' (375). Shakespeare uses Gratiano to embody in one figure during the trial the Christian example of revenge. Gratiano exemplifies the 'Jewish choice' (the moral condition based on the rejection of Christ), explained by G. K. Hunter, and Alan Dessen rightly describes Gratiano as a '"Jewish" Christian or a Christian Shylock'.[45] Gratiano's function in the trial is twofold. First, Gratiano's voice of vengeance serves as an effective foil for Antonio's voice of mercy. Second, the theme of the educative value of suffering is dramatised through the contrast between Gratiano and Antonio. As Kent in *King Lear* exclaims, 'Nothing almost sees miracles / But misery' (2.2.168–9). Gratiano has suffered nothing and learned nothing. Antonio, however, has suffered and learns. Shakespeare's innovative additions to his literary sources allow us to witness Antonio's moral growth even if we are denied the confessional explanation a soliloquy could provide.

Portia's appeal to Antonio appears to be ironic but is not. Antonio is precisely the character on stage who has the most cause for revenge, but he is also the character who has the most opportunity for growth. Now that the tables are turned on Shylock, the audience waits breathlessly to behold what measure of mercy the Christian merchant – who formerly called Shylock a dog, spat on him, and spurned him – will show the Jewish usurer whose now fully revealed, murderous hatred of Antonio should have added fuel to the fire. But we observe none of Antonio's former vindictiveness. Antonio, who earlier was in exactly Shylock's position, having lost all his wealth and in peril of losing his life, can now empathise with Shylock's horror of poverty. Antonio, 'by the art of known and feeling sorrows / [Is] pregnant to good pity' (*Lr*, 4.6.225–6). Antonio mercifully responds now not to an animal but to a man who has financial needs, perhaps recalling Shylock's 'Hath a dog money'?

Antonio delivers a tripartite judgement that structurally recalls Portia's tripartite judgement on Shylock's bond, but with the intentional difference of rendering not strict justice, but rather, mercy seasoning strict justice. The first part of his judgement is his kind request that the court 'quit' the fine and allow Shylock to keep fully one half of his wealth (376–7). The second part of Antonio's decision is more complex and concerns his legal half of Shylock's wealth.[46] With that half Antonio gives, rather than gets, because he requests his half 'in use' (379) or in trust, and he cannot touch the principal, which he judiciously conserves to give to Shylock's natural family.[47] The terms of the trust are not absolutely clear. Brown and Mahood suggest Antonio probably administers his half of Shylock's estate productively, rendering it to Lorenzo and Jessica upon Shylock's death, and Brown thinks Antonio gives 'the legitimate profits to Shylock' during his life.[48] Richard Posner argues that 'if Shylock is the beneficiary of the trust during his life, then the *whole* forfeiture has been remitted subject only to Jessica's rights on Shylock's death', but 'if the income of the trust is to accumulate for Jessica only *half* of the forfeiture has been remitted'.[49] Changes in the law resulted in confusion about the subject of uses or trusts in Shakespeare's day, and from the play we cannot determine with certainty whether half or all of Shylock's legally forfeited wealth is remitted.

Although much critical puzzlement exists over the precise meaning of this part of Antonio's judgement, some clarification may be gained if we consider several questions. Why isn't Shylock rendered all his wealth with no qualifying conditions? To return unconditionally all of Shylock's wealth, after having granted him his life, would reestablish the status quo, granting all mercy and no justice. Shylock, after all, did attempt murder. Why does Antonio want to set up a trust for Shylock and give this wealth to Lorenzo and Jessica after Shylock dies? Antonio's trust achieves some measure of just penalty because Shylock at least loses the freedom to administer this half of his wealth. Antonio's trust, however, is still very merciful if Shylock receives the profits of this wealth during his lifetime. Moreover, Antonio wisely provides for the welfare of Shylock's children so that under his administration there will be at least half of Shylock's current wealth still in existence for inheritance. Presumably Shylock could either lose or give away the other half of his wealth before he died so that Jessica and Lorenzo would receive nothing.

In the articulation of the trust idea Shakespeare purposefully
has Antonio use the language of thievery to describe how Lorenzo
obtained Jessica – 'the gentleman / That lately *stole* his daughter'
(380–81). As we have seen, the imagery of thievery bonds this
family for Shakespeare's development of the usury theme, contrasting the merits of the loves for which one steals. Antonio's
explicit use of 'stole' recalls here that the usurer's wealth was
judged stolen gain, and his holding of his half of Shylock's wealth
in trust is a kinder version of the historical precedent for the confiscation of a converted usurer's wealth. As Lewalski and Danson
point out, there is historical precedence in Europe and in England for the confiscation of a convert's wealth because it was
obtained through sinful usury, and for the customary remission
of usually one-half of that wealth.[50] Herein Shylock's ending counterbalances Antonio's gain of life and the return of half of Antonio's
living in Act V, a parallel that derives at least some of its meaning from ideas about usury, as we shall see.

From the perspective of the court and the audience, the poverty-
stricken Antonio appears all the more generous for his dispensation of Shylock's wealth. With his half of Shylock's wealth, Antonio
is 'kind' in the sense of 'natural' as well as 'merciful' because he
ministers to the usurer's physical needs and conserves the body
of wealth to restore it ultimately to Shylock's immediate family.
Given Shakespeare's concern with the Christian attitude toward
usury, one can view Antonio's role in the disposition of Shylock's
'stolen' wealth as the dramatic enactment of a biblical proverb.
Proverb 28.8 reads: 'He that increaseth his riches by usury and
interest, gathereth them for him that will be merciful unto the
poor.' Miles Mosse's book against usury published in 1595, which
I have argued elsewhere is an important new source for usury in
The Merchant of Venice, uses this very proverb for the texts of his
six sermons against sinful usury, designed to put usury on trial
for a London audience so that it might be arraigned and convicted in the consciences of Elizabethans. His various interpretations of this proverb illuminate the quality of Antonio's mercy
shown to a usurer. Mosse treats the usurer as a wretched creature whose wealth God will take not only from him but also from
his family and will give it to 'one that will be merciful to the
poor'. Although Mosse himself tends to be kindhearted and forgives his enemies, his animosity toward sinful usury is so strong
that he desires to see the natural course of inheritance defeated

by God when the usurer's wealth is taken away from him and his family.[51] 'Balthazar' ('without treasure') as Shylock's 'Daniel' ('the judgement of God') enables the enactment of the proverb Mosse explicates. Mosse, however, serves to highlight the extraordinary generosity of Shakespeare's first two parts of the judgement Antonio passes on Shylock.

As guardian and minister of half of Shylock's wealth, Antonio uses it to minister to the needs of a poor usurer and his heirs, not to defeat them as Mosse would hope. Yet some critics, such as Norman Rabkin, see Antonio's 'fiscal' settlement as lacking 'any suggestion of kindness'.[52] Although Shakespeare intends to restore Antonio's wealth in Act V, obviating any real need for Shylock's wealth, why might he want to emphasise *giving* here, not gain? Shakespeare intends Antonio's anagnorisis to teach Shylock by right Christian example the value of mercy and giving. Shylock, who knows what it means to adhere to the letter, would probably be the first to acknowledge that Antonio, the very man who has the most 'reason' to seek counter-revenge, does respond to what he himself defines as 'mercy' in this situation, not life itself but life with 'living'. How Antonio plans to dispose of that 'living' after Shylock's death, when he has no further need for it, would probably give Shylock more pause. But there is one clue that Shylock's anger against Jessica is beginning to abate. In the trial Shylock no longer wishes Jessica were dead, hearsed at his feet with his ducats in her coffin; he now contemplates her alive and marriageable, although his preferred choice of a husband for her is very harsh.

On the basis of Antonio's response here, does Antonio hate Shylock simply because he is a Jew? Shylock got an answer to the contrary at the end of the play's third scene, but he did not really hear it. Antonio's disposition of Shylock's wealth, however, would tend to prove to Shylock that his former simplistic view of Antonio is invalid. If Antonio hated Jews simply because they are Jews, he would not provide for the daughter of a Jew, nor would he alleviate a Jew's financial distress as he now does, especially when he knows that this is precisely what the Jew himself says he wants. It cannot be argued that Antonio is merely trying to befriend his Christian friend, Lorenzo, because Antonio does not limit his language to Lorenzo but includes Jessica by name and by role, specifically her role as 'daughter', not so much as 'wife', and stresses the 'familial' consequences of his judgement. According to Mosaic Law, a daughter was entitled to inherit a father's possessions if he had no son (Nm 27.1–8). However, such a daughter had to marry within her father's tribe to prevent the paternal inheritance from passing to another tribe (Nm 36). From a Jewish perspective Jessica violates this rule, but from a Pauline perspective the rule is overruled through her conversion to Christ in whose Mystical Body all are made one. For the Elizabethans, the possibility of human unity is generally conceived in religious terms, but today we generally conceive of the possibility of human unity in political terms.

However, it is not likely that Antonio provides for Jessica simply because she intends to convert to Christianity through her marriage to Lorenzo. There is no evidence that either Antonio or Shylock knows Jessica's intention because not even her confidant Lancelot seems aware of it. Jessica's scene with Lancelot in Belmont (3.5) opens with Lancelot's continuation of his old theory that Jessica's best hope for Christian salvation lies in the off chance that one of her parents could have been a Christian. It is she who informs him that her hope lies not in the flesh of her parents but the spirit of her husband. Even Gratiano, who helps Lorenzo steal Jessica, greets her in Belmont as Lorenzo's 'infidel' (3.2.317), an example of Gratiano's crude but also ignorant humour. One could always suspect or assume that Jessica would convert because she marries a Christian.[53] But suspicion is not knowledge, and Shylock does not have any lines of suspicion about Jessica's conversion, only lines lamenting the knowledge of her flight with a Christian and his belief in her damnation for that. Herein Shylock's lack of knowledge starkly contrasts with Barabas's explicit knowledge about Abigail's conversion in Marlowe's play.[54] Thus, Shakespeare's development of Antonio's role thus far in his judgement of Shylock is exceptionally generous. Not even Elizabethan men of the cloth like Mosse, whose job it is to be merciful, can match Shakespeare in his kindness to a usurer, let alone a Jewish usurer, and his family.

The third part of Antonio's judgement is the most controversial today, namely Antonio's request that in return for the kindness he has just shown Shylock, Shylock will convert to Christianity and sign a deed of gift making Jessica and Lorenzo the heirs of all the wealth he possesses at the time of his death (382–6). Antonio's conversion request for Shylock understandably shocks and offends a modern audience well-versed in the enlightened ideas of religious toleration and freedom. We find it revolting. Today we, unlike the Elizabethans, see any conversion stipulation, no matter what the circumstances or how well presented, as a violation of the individual's basic human rights. But our evolved ideas did not exist as viable concepts for Shakespeare's generation any more than their theological and hierarchical conceptualisation of the universe and man dominates modern thought today. As discussed in Chapter 1, Renaissance Europe tolerated the political legitimacy of constrained conversion for Christians as well as for Jews, depending on the will of the local ruler.

There is no issue in the play, however, more sensitive today than the treatment of the Jew and especially the conversion to Christianity asked of him. In the 1988 Folger Shakespeare Theatre production of this play, directed by Michael Kahn, Antonio's lines for the conversion stipulation were simply cut. However, if we disembody the conversion request from its dramatic and historical contexts and if we ignore its union with Antonio's deed of gift request, we do aesthetic violence to the body of the play. We overlook that the conversion and deed of gift requests are Shakespeare's *additions* to his literary source, *Il Pecorone*, and we misjudge Shakespeare's purpose for these additions by judging them according to only our own modern ideas. We cannot unfairly expect the Elizabethans to have the foresight that has now become our hindsight. Just as we would not want to assume their approach of 'theological judgement' for our era, we should not assume they should share our modern 'political' or 'cultural' approach, based on twentieth-century values. We approach choice of religion in terms of personal rights that are guaranteed in part by separation of Church and State. The Elizabethans approached choice of religion in terms of theological 'rightness' manifested in part by union of Church and State. We know what the modern perspective is. The challenge lies in trying to know and to understand the Elizabethan perspective and how Shakespeare adapts that perspective to his own artistic vision for his play.

It is very difficult for a modern audience to recover a full Elizabethan sense of Antonio's lines even though enough historical scholarship has now established that the conversion stipulation, appreciated from the Elizabethan perspective, is an *attempt*, not a guarantee, to save Shylock from himself, to save his soul. Baptism is not a guarantee for salvation because the individual has a free will to choose whether or not to *live* the gift of faith; a non-embraced faith is a dead faith (see Jas 2.14, gloss). Shylock could be baptised publicly, but never embrace that baptism in his heart, as was the case for converts called 'Marranos'. Unlike 'Conversos', who internally embraced conversion, 'Marranos' were so called because they were believed to be converts in name only, who had undergone formal conversion to avoid other penalties, such as death or loss of wealth.[55] Or 'Marranos' might convert not just to avoid penalties but to be able to thrive. Patrick Stewart's very original acting choices for Shylock's responses to his judgement seem to align with this perspective. As Mahood aptly observes about the Royal Shakespeare Company's production of 1978 (directed by John Barton), Stewart drops his tin of cigarette stubs (his idiosyncratic prop) in response to the final judgement, but Portia picks it up for him – 'tobacco he would live to smoke another day' (p. 53). In response to Gratiano's unkind joke in which death by halter is advocated over life by font, Stewart laughs as he exits, suggesting not only that he who laughs last, laughs best, but also that Shylock is irrepressibly a survivor, who will continue to use his intelligence to survive, nay even thrive, in Venice.

We can travel some significant distance toward understanding Shakespeare's inclusion of the conversion stipulation if we recall the different positions of Elizabethan England and medieval or sixteenth-century Venice regarding the toleration of Jews. Shakespeare does not alter his medieval source's depiction of Venice, where Jews are not required to convert in order to enjoy economic wealth and legal protection. This is a different world from Shakespeare's Elizabethan England, where Jews must convert to Christianity (whether feigned or true conversion) in order to enjoy similar benefits. Shakespeare, however, *adds* Antonio's conversion condition to his source, just as he adds the idea of usury and interrelates both additions. From a historical perspective Shakespeare seems to mute the negative potential of forced conversion as it generally operated in his era. Shakespeare both adapts and distances his conversion trope from the Marrano phenomenon of Renaissance Europe by individualising or personalising it; the specific conversion condition for Shylock is the *exception* and not the general rule. Not the State of Venice but rather a particular Venetian citizen formulates the conditions for the conversion and the deed of gift. In seconding that individual's voice the Duke brings his authority to bear even more decisively by also threatening a revocation of his earlier pardon if Shylock refuses. Not all Jews in Venice but only this particular one is confronted with these conditions. Shylock is in this position not simply because he is a Jew, but because he, unlike Tubal, violated the laws of Venice through attempted murder and thereby placed himself in a position of legal jeopardy.

Although, as a Jew, Shylock is not a Venetian citizen but rather an alien, until now he has been relatively free to pursue his choices in matters of faith and wealth. He has been given chances to follow alternate routes than the one he insisted on travelling. On the other hand, Shylock gives Antonio no choice at all when he insists on having his bond according to strict law. But Antonio and the Duke do give Shylock a choice between two options: (1) the verdict of strict law attendant upon his proven murder attempt, or (2) their joint verdict relieving that law's rigorous penalties. Rarer in sixteenth-century England was the opinion that forced conversion should not be practised, as a minority group member, the Catholic Robert Parsons, argued surprisingly on behalf of Jews in his defence of English Catholics against the imposition of religious conformity: 'Surely, as I am now minded I would not for ten thousand worlds, compel a Jew to swear that there were a blessed Trinity. For albeit the thing be never so true, yet should he be damned for swearing against his conscience, and I, for compelling him to commit so heinous and grievous a sin.'[56]

It is the question of Shylock's 'conscience' that Shakespeare addresses throughout the play, particularly at the end of the trial in the interrelation of faith and wealth to adapt the idea of constrained conversion for one individual. Moreover, in Shakespeare's Venetian setting his isolation of constrained conversion as lawful in a particular legal judgement against a particular criminal distinguishes this condition from the general application of the contemporary historical phenomenon of forced conversion which was applied to all Jews simply because they were Jews, not because they had been proved in court to have attempted a criminal violation of the law against a native citizen. Shakespeare shows his back above the elements in his play's kinder version of what Elizabethans generally would think a *usurer* such as Shylock deserves but does not get at the end of the trial. It would be comforting to believe that Shakespeare the private man shared Parsons's tolerant perspective regarding the forced conversion of Jews. But what Shakespeare the private man believed is probably unknowable.

On the other hand, what Shakespeare the public dramatist intends to effect in a particular comedy is relatively knowable. As a maker of plays designed 'to please' large, heterogeneous audiences encompassing every class in Elizabethan society, Shakespeare knew he could challenge his audiences, but not to the point of diminishing economic returns for his commercial theatre. Success at the 'box office', then and now, remains an important issue.

Moreover, Shylock can say 'no' to Antonio's request just as Barabas in Marlowe's play refuses to convert when he is presented with the hard choice between loss of wealth or conversion. But a refusal to accept Antonio's conditions will return Shylock to the position he was in before the Duke decided to show mercy, the position of being subject to strict justice, the loss of both life and wealth. The Duke more than supports Antonio's judgement by insisting, 'He shall do this, or else I do recant / The pardon that I late pronouncèd here' (388–9). Shylock's choice to refuse would be a choice for death. History is full of examples of martyrs for their faith, and the Second Book of Maccabees (7.1–42) offers biblical examples of such Jewish heroism. But Shylock does not choose literal death. Nor do we expect him to choose to die rather than to convert because Shylock, despite his tenacity, has revealed throughout the play a greater commitment to himself than to Judaism through his telling reiteration of the first person pronoun whenever this subject arises.[57] Given the comedic genre and structure of this play it is appropriate that Shylock does choose life because the opposite choice of death would contribute to the direction of tragedy. Over martyrdom Shylock chooses a return of at least half of his 'living' and consequently life, as he defines it, worth living.

Shakespeare challenges his Elizabethan audience's compassion on two fronts: how to pass judgement on Shylock as a Jew and as a usurer. In critical discourse on the play the judgement of Shylock as a Jew has long overshadowed the judgement of Shylock as a usurer. Yet the financial penalties for penitent converts pale in contrast to the temporal penalties some Elizabethans advocated for unrepentant usurers, regardless of their religious allegiance. Thomas Wilson wishes a death penalty was mandated for usurers 'to hang on the gallows' (290) because the usurer is 'the greatest thief and ravener that can be in a commonweal (285), 'the worst man that liveth' for destroying far more people than typical thieves and murderers.[58] In his translation of The Market or Fayre of Usurers (1550) William Harrys claims that usurers have worthily deserved

'at the hands of the temporall magistrates the punishment of losing both honor[,] body and goods with other corrections'.[59] In
Elizabethan England, however, the penalties for usury were primarily financial but sometimes included imprisonment. Regarding usury's 'stolen' gain, 'conversion' is judged the appropriate
response. Financially speaking, Christian and Jewish usurers should
convert their illicit gain through restoration. Religiously speaking, Christian usurers should figuratively convert and Jewish
usurers should literally convert, repenting the sin of usury and
reforming their lives accordingly. Therefore, the very idea of conversion – financial, moral, and religious – is central to the problem of usury and consequently to the vital interrelation of faith
and wealth issues in our play. 'Conversion' of opinion is the whole
point of Wilson's treatise against usury: 'Now, blessed be the lord
god of Israel ... I am heartily glad to see such a *conversion* of
you, my dear brethren' is what Preacher Ockerfoe exclaims in
his concluding joy over having reclaimed those who tried to rationalise the legitimacy of usury.[60] Against this backdrop of punitive
judgement for sinful usurers, financial penalties for Jewish converts because of their usury, severe penalties for attempted murder, the reputation for strict justice of the city in which the play
is set, and the emphasis on the idea of 'conversion' (literal and
symbolic), we can better gauge what Shakespeare does for Shylock
and how his resolution both reflects and transcends his era.

How can we better understand Antonio's intention behind his
conditions and Shylock's acceptance of them?

> Two things provided more: that for this favour
> He presently become a Christian;
> The other, that he do record a gift,
> Here in this court, of all he dies possessed
> Unto his son Lorenzo and his daughter.
>
> (382–86)

It might be argued that Antonio is intentionally vindictive in
his judgement, repaying Shylock measure for measure, but such
an interpretation distorts what actually happens in the play and
fails to account for the important foil function of Gratiano in this
scene.[61] Because no one expected Antonio to win in court, let alone
to be placed in a position to judge Shylock, the fact and the terms
of Antonio's judgement come as a surprise to all. Herein the BBC/

Time-Life television version (1981), directed by Jack Gold and produced by Jonathan Miller, scores an unforgettable moment of stagecraft at the expense of violating the logic of surprise and the lines of the play. In an emotionally wrenching response to Antonio's judgement a weeping Shylock is cruelly thrown to his knees as a crucifix, in the form of a necklace, is hung around his neck, and he is made to kiss the cross. Forcing Shylock to his knees tends to contradict the Duke's earlier language of prevention that counters Portia's request that Shylock kneel to beg for his life (4.1.364–5). More importantly, the production's misuse of Christian symbolism defies two dramatic issues: (1) the element of surprise, and (2) the propriety of the prop used. The very presence of such a prop demonstrates that the Venetians came prepared to enact Antonio's conversion condition. But no one, except perhaps Portia, knows what the outcome of the trial is going to be. Indeed, the Venetians expect Shylock will win until Portia begins the process of reversal. And not even Portia herself knows what Antonio's response to Shylock will be until he renders it. Moreover, this specific prop hardly suits either a Venetian courtroom or the font of baptism.

For the Gratianos, onstage and in the audience, Antonio's surprise request is an unpleasant one because it is seen as too kind. Before Shylock leaves the stage, we are reminded once again of the difference between mercy and strict justice vengefully voiced, between Antonio and Gratiano: 'Had I been judge, thou shouldst have had ten more, / To bring thee to the gallows, not to the font' (4.1.395–6). Like Lancelot earlier, who thought his old master should be given nothing but 'a halter' (2.2.86) in return for his niggardly treatment, the literalists in this play find the call to seeing and showing a different 'spirit' to one's enemies too difficult a commandment of love to follow.[62]

We might begin the challenge of analysing the intent and function of the final part of Antonio's tripartite judgement by noting that Antonio, seconded by the Duke, distinctly perceives the first and second parts of his judgement on his legal right to half of Shylock's wealth (376–81) as a 'favour' (362), that is, an act of graciousness or kindness that transcends what strict legal justice requires, the complete loss of half of Shylock's wealth to Antonio. We have already seen how Antonio's trust, set up with his half of Shylock's wealth, is a generous act, especially in the present circumstances, that enacts Proverbs 28.8. In the first part of

Antonio's judgement he does Shylock a favour by speaking on his behalf for the remission of even the fine the Duke contemplates taking in lieu of the State's half of Shylock's wealth. But Antonio's 'favour' is a conditional one, and it is crucial to understand how and why Antonio has interrelated the two conditions he specifies, the spiritual stipulation of the *conversion* and the financial stipulation of the *deed of gift* for Shylock's heirs. These two intertwined conditions present Shylock with another example of the play's hard choices. In return for Antonio's favourable financial response, the return of wealth constituting what Shylock himself specified as what he sees as true mercy, Shylock is being asked to *give*, to give 'all he hath' in the spirit of the leaden casket motto – give all his wealth upon his death to his children and give up that which keeps him from giving properly, adherence to the letter of the law without its spirit, adherence to a Pharisaical view of the Law without its fulfilment in the New Law.

Shakespeare's addition of the conversion and deed of gift stipulations should not be dismissed as merely gratuitous additions to his literary sources, any more than one would so dismiss his entire addition of the Venetian legal penalty for Shylock. The conversion trope is integral to the whole play, and as such it is intimately linked to deeds of giving. Shakespeare has carefully prepared his Elizabethan audience for this conversion request through numerous clues. As we have seen, one way Shakespeare anticipates conversion is through the names he chooses for Jessica and Shylock, their biblical meanings and suggestive associations. He perhaps first subtly plants the seed for the idea of Shylock's literal conversion by foreshadowing it when Antonio proclaims Shylock's figurative conversion – 'The Hebrew will turn Christian, he grows kind' (1.3.171) – solely because Shylock says he will forgo interest and lend freely to Antonio to win his friendship. The Christian clown Lancelot presents a 'symbolic' conversion when he chooses to leave his 'old master the Jew' for his 'new master the Christian' (2.4.17–18), but he also parodies the reverse conversion in his rationale for departure: 'for I am a Jew if I serve the Jew any longer' (2.2.91).[63] Although Lancelot's conversion remains figurative whereas Jessica's is literal, their similar choice of departure from Shylock as an act of conversion may be distinguished in terms of purity of motive. The clown's motives smack of the flesh's tug – liveries, food, and females (2.2.86–136) – whereas Jessica more wisely elevates the claims of spirit over flesh and blood.

In her first appearance on stage Jessica informs the audience that she intends to end her personal strife over blood alliance versus moral non-alliance with her father by becoming Lorenzo's 'loving wife' and 'a Christian' (2.3.15–20). In her comic debate with Lancelot preceding the trial scene, Jessica reveals both her conversion by marriage and her reason for it: 'I shall be saved by my husband; he hath made me a Christian' (3.5.15). The literalistic Lancelot continues his earlier hypothesis of faith by birthright first expressed in his departure scene, 'Most beautiful pagan, most sweet Jew, if a Christian do not play the knave and get thee, I am much deceived' (2.3.10–12). Now Lancelot expostulates on Jessica's damnation because 'the sins of the father are to be laid upon the children', according to the Second Commandment as it stands in the Catechism of the Book of Common Prayer. But Lorenzo's earlier optimistic line, that grants that Shylock could come to heaven for his daughter's sake (2.4.33–4), accords well with Jessica's Pauline version of salvation by marriage and comedically opposes Lancelot's darker view of humans as agents of damnation. As agents cooperating in God's salvific plan, children can help save their parents, much as the child Pearl functions in Nathaniel Hawthorne's *The Scarlet Letter*. Lancelot's argument takes a decidedly laughable turn when he explains his 'bastard hope' for Jessica (3.5.5–10). Lancelot's funny line about 'bastard hope' may be a touch of outrageous historical humour. According to Salo Baron, prejudice against Jews could be so perverse that 'adulterous Christian parentage could be considered more honorable than legitimate descent from a Jewish parent', as was the case as late as the eighteenth century concerning some English descendants from a Jewish Portuguese convert, Sir Edward Brampton (?1440–1508).[64] If Shakespeare and some members of his audience were familiar with this specific kind of bias, Shakespeare renders it laughable through Jessica's and Lorenzo's spirited rejoinders to Lancelot's carnal joke.

Literalism fuels the humour of Lancelot's lines, and this is most apparent when Lancelot playfully blames Lorenzo for Jessica's conversion because 'this making of Christians will raise the price of hogs' (3.5.18). Herein Lancelot further reduces the literalism of Shylock's first reference to the significance of pork in his allusion to the Gadarene miracle. Like the Gadarene literalists, Lancelot esteems hogs more than Christ (Mt 8.30). Through his literalism Lancelot perverts the value of conversion because he reduces the spiritual to the physical. Walter Cohen suggests that Lancelot's comedy here helps to 'demystify the serious religious issues of the plot'.[65] Beyond such clarification this comic scene also includes prioritisation for both Lancelot and Shylock. Lancelot's comic values, vis-à-vis Jessica's and Lorenzo's remarks, clarify Shylock's values, and the shared misprioritisation of former master and servant is indicted as folly differing not in kind but in degree of gravity. For Lancelot damnation, like salvation, is a matter merely of regeneration by the flesh, as it is in Shylock's literal view when he declares Jessica 'is damned' for rebelling against her 'own flesh and blood' (3.1.26–8). But as Paul explains, regeneration by the spirit is more significant than regeneration by the flesh; salvation is not a matter of physical birthright but of spiritual birthright so that the way to salvation lies open to all peoples in the world, regardless of parentage, if they live according to true faith: 'For there is no difference between the Jew and the Grecian: for he that is Lord over all, is rich unto all, that call on him. / for whosoever shall call upon the Name of the Lord, shall be saved' (Rom 10.12–13). This important scene comically parodies the salvation question raised earlier and in so doing sets the stage for the terms in which Antonio's conversion request for Shylock might be best understood. Lancelot's fooling by literally playing 'upon the word' (3.5.36) anticipates the literalism that will occur in the trial scene on a much more serious level of discerning folly from wisdom.

What might be Antonio's intent for asking Shylock to convert and for linking that request with the deed of gift condition? The legal language itself, 'a deed of gift' (thrice mentioned in Acts IV–V), accentuates the value of giving so vital to the theme of the leaden casket choice. The terms of a deed of gift, unlike a will, cannot be changed. This final part of Antonio's judgement is not a mere redundancy of his preceding trust provision for Shylock, which will go to Lorenzo and Jessica after Shylock's decease. In that determination *Antonio* is the administrator of Shylock's wealth as a trust, and giving the profits to Shylock, he provides for Shylock during his life and for Shylock's children after his death. In the deed of gift request Antonio is constraining *Shylock* to do the giving and the providing for his family as a father should naturally do.[66] Some might object that, left to his own devices, Shylock would not be likely to sign a deed of gift for Jessica and Lorenzo, and therefore Antonio is taking a subtle kind of revenge on Shylock. But Shylock has not been inclined toward 'giving' to anyone, and a miser left to his own devices is not likely to change. Far from taking revenge, Antonio sets a Christian example of mercy for Shylock by practising in his trust fund what he preaches to Shylock through the deed of gift. Despite his present situation of lamented poverty, Antonio selflessly creates a trust that will stead Shylock during his lifetime and his offspring after his death. Shylock would recognise, given the age's obsession with patriarchy and inheritance, that Antonio assumes a generous fatherly role in providing for the offspring of his would-be murderer, an act of providential fatherhood that Shylock would not have extended to his enemy. Antonio sees that the sins of the father are not laid upon the children.

Antonio's request for a deed of gift invites Shylock to assume his natural and just role as a father and participate in this providential giving. Antonio's language warmly stresses the familial consequences of his judgement, for upon Shylock's death his ducats should naturally go to 'his *son* Lorenzo and his *daughter'* (4.1.386, my italics), to his family. Although Shylock uses Jacob's inspired wand device to justify his usury, Shylock seems to have forgotten why Jacob wanted to collect his wages from Laban in the first place. Through his role as financial provider Antonio recalls for us that the very biblical story Shylock used to defend his usury (1.3.66–85) originates with Jacob's desire to 'travel' for his 'own house' because 'the order of nature requireth that every one provide for his own family' (Gn 30.30 and gloss). That Shylock does not demur (even in an aside) regarding this disposition of his wealth speaks well for him and his prospects for moral change. As Bishop Gervase Babington declares in his commentary on Jacob's desire to provide for his own family, 'For *he that provideth not for his family* (saith the Apostle) [gloss refers to 1 Tm 5] *hath denied the faith, and is worse than an infidel.'*[67] Consequently, Antonio invites Shylock to give his wealth, upon his death when he no longer needs it, to his children to revivify familial bonds. Shylock's new son-in-law responds to the tenor of Shylock's *'special* deed of gift' when he voices his appreciation in Old Testament diction for heavenly mercy: 'you drop *manna* in the way / Of starvèd people' (5.1.292–5, my italics). The conversion of Jessica's rebellion to a possible reconciliation with her father, whose requested conversion in the trial scene is intended to effect a change in 'manners', is hinted by Antonio's interbonding of Jessica and Lorenzo with Shylock through shared wealth and faith. The merchant at-

tempts to rescue the usurer from himself by converting his wealth
from the unnatural, barren breeding of usury to natural, profitable breeding. Antonio weds Shylock's wealth to the natural cy-
cle by linking prosperity with posterity as Portia's father did in
settling his wealth on her.

Antonio's request for Shylock's deed of gift is integrally related to his probable intent and purpose for the conversion request because both requests directly relate to Shylock's attitude
toward wealth and his defence of usury. We recall that from
Antonio's perspective usury is the black fruit of hateful human
enmity, the insufferable denial of loving friendship among humans. On a literal level, Shylock's conversion should technically
prevent his practice of sinful usury or at least drive it under-
ground, with Shylock continuing to thrive as a usurer until caught
by the authorities. But Shylock himself might not be so eager any
longer to amass gold and silver through usury now that he expe-
rientially has glimpsed what it is like to be reduced to poverty as
he has done in the past to his moaning victims. As Thomas Wilson
reminds us, two ways to know a faithful Christian from an infidel should be by the deeds of alms giving and free lending, 'the
fruits of charity'.[68] Despite his own present poverty, Antonio's
use of wealth to help others sets that example. Mariana's plea of
forgiveness for Angelo might also be adapted for Shylock now:
'They say best men are moulded out of faults' (5.1.439).

On a moral level, Antonio probably hopes Shylock's conversion will accomplish much more for Shylock, namely change his
attitude toward wealth and its purpose. Antonio rightly recognises that wealth is a good thing if it is properly valued and used.
Hence, Shylock's plea for 'living' is granted. But Shylock has
heretofore seen gold and silver in the usurer's terms of covetous
idolatry, wealth as a good solely in and of itself, to be enjoyed
and loved for its own sake and not simply to be used as a means
for obtaining what is necessary or worthy of one's love.[69] Wise
love is the standard that should guide one's use of earthly treasure. Shylock should recall Ecclesiastes' wisdom about the deceptive 'vanity of vanities' of this world (1.2). And the question put
to Christ regarding the demand for one's physical inheritance
receives this answer: 'Take heed, and beware of covetousness;
for though a man have abundance, yet his life standeth not in his
riches', and the gloss reads: 'Christ condemneth the arrogancy of
the rich worldlings, who as though they had God locked up in

their coffers . . . set their whole felicity in their goods, not considering that God gave them life and also can take it away when
he will' (Lk 12.15). And of such a 'fool', God rhetorically asks to
whom will those hoarded riches then go? (Lk 12.20). Within this
context Antonio's conversion stipulation might be seen not just
as an attempt to save the soul of a *Jew* but also the soul of a *usurer*.

Antonio's two conditional requests are purposefully conjoined:
Shylock's signing of the deed of gift is his first enactment of the
meaning of the conversion request because it constitutes his first
deed of giving to others. From a sixteenth-century Christian perspective what would be considered the consequence if Antonio
had not stipulated the conversion request? According to such an
Elizabethan perspective, if Shylock does not reform and forgo his
practice of sinful usury, he should be damned for it.[70] As a result
of his experience in the trial, Shylock might become a better man
in humanistic terms, but according to sixteenth-century Christian
doctrine, even if he did, he could not be saved eternally because
salvation depends on faith in Christ. Thus, the provisions of the
combined judgements of the Duke and Antonio seek to help save
Shylock's body, goods, family, and soul.

Thus, the flawed Antonio, 'a tainted wether of the flock', educated through his own suffering, becomes a better Christian and
tries to love his enemy by converting him into a friend. Antonio
intends to achieve what Shylock had pretended to do in their
bond-formulation scene, gain the other's love and favour through
kindness. The bond has come full circle. Whether Shylock will
respond genuinely and favourably is something only he has the
power to determine and which we will discuss later. Antonio transforms his flesh bond with Shylock by recognising their brotherhood in the flesh and by befriending Shylock and his heirs
financially in a new soul bond. Portia's words on mercy bear fruit
in Antonio's deeds. Her tripartite judgement of *strict* justice is
counterbalanced structurally and thematically by Antonio's tripartite judgement of *merciful* justice. Shakespeare realises that the
most effective form of education is living example. Instead of the
Christian example of revenge that Shylock protested earlier, he
witnesses the Christian example of mercy seasoning, but not denying, justice. Thus, Shylock is brought out of the safe world of
usurious profits, self-righteousness, and dependence on the letter
without the spirit, into the world of giving and hazarding. He is
consequently subsumed into the play's rhythm of rewarding those

who give. The worldly chooser of gold and silver thus has his desires and deserts placed within a more salutary perspective. His earthly treasure is put to benevolent use and his flesh bond is defeated by the well-intended use of the literalistic principle on which it rested.

Shakespeare's purpose for interlinking the physical, financial, and spiritual parts of the final judgement passed on Shylock by Antonio and the Duke has an even broader allegorical significance for the play. The Duke grants Shylock his physical life, which Antonio supports with 'living' and, from his perspective, new spiritual life. The allegorical significance of Shylock's conversion in terms of the law and Judaeo-Christian salvation-history has been admirably interpreted by Lewalski and Danson. Lewalski argues that when Shylock's '"forced conversion"' is viewed within the context of the trial scene's symbolic action, it 'is not antisemitic revenge; it simply compels Shylock to avow what his own experience in the trial scene has fully "demonstrated" – that the Law leads only to death and destruction, that faith in Christ must supplant human righteousness'.[71] Lewalski rightly denounces Shylock's false claim of legal righteousness, fearing no judgement because doing no wrong. But she overstates the opposition between the Old Law and the New Law in this play, concluding that the trial scene 'culminates in the final defeat of the Old Law' and that through the use of 'the laws of Venice as symbol' we see how 'the Law leads only to death and destruction'.[72]

Such an interpretation is too extreme, too strictly Pauline in its polemical emphasis and overlooks how Shakespeare respects the Old Law and the law in his play. Shakespeare would find in the Geneva Bible's glosses on Paul's epistles a reverent emphasis on the punitive nature of the law as constructively correctional and therefore necessary for fallible man: 'Not that the doctrine of the Law is abolished, but that the condemnation thereof is taken away by faith' (Gal 3.25, gloss). Scholars have found sufficient evidence of Pauline influence, but that is not the only New Testament influence the play reflects. For example, Matthew presents Christ's position on the Law in terms that clearly complement Shakespeare's rhythm of 'seasoning' in the play: 'Think not that I am come to destroy the Law, or the Prophets. I am not come to destroy but to fulfil them' (Mt 5.17), and the glossator explains, 'The Gospel is the stablishing & accomplishing of the Law.' The New Law is not meant to be the destruction but rather the perfect completion of the Old Law: 'Til heaven and earth perish, one jot, or one title of the Law shall not scape, til all things be fulfilled' because 'the doctrine of the Law containeth nothing unprofitable or superfluous' (Mt 5.18, gloss). In the courtroom Portia similarly upholds the necessity of observing the law, in this case the Venetian law, because Bassanio asks 'Balthazar' to use his authority to wrest the law in order to save Antonio – 'To do a great right, do a little wrong' (212) – but the wise young judge refuses to do evil in order to do good.

It is not so much the Old Law and law that the play criticises but rather the abuse or misinterpretation of both. The Elizabethans value the role of the Old Law in salvation-history, and the patriarchs and prophets of the Old Law – Abram, Jacob, and Daniel – are honoured in this play as men of faith, wisdom, courage, and love. Christ clarifies this reverence for the law when He condemns the Pharisees immediately after He validates the Old Law: 'For I say unto you, except your righteousness exceed the righteousness of the Scribes and Pharisees, ye shall not enter into the kingdom of heaven', and the glossator observes that neither the Scribes nor the Pharisees 'expound the Law truly, nor observe it well' (Mt 5.10). Shylock's Pharisaical posture regarding his legalistic self-righteousness has been weighed in his own scales and found wanting.[73] Not the spirit of mercy, but rather, literalistic legalism saves Antonio's pound of flesh; however, this literalism is used with good intent, not Shylock's foul intent for strict construction that overlooks how it can be used against him.

Danson persuasively interprets Shakespeare's allegorical purpose for Shylock's conversion within the biblical context of Paul's teaching in Romans about the 'fortunate fall' role of the Jews in the history of Christian salvation. Paul elaborates on Isaiah's prophecy, 'The remnant shall return, *even* the remnant of Jacob unto the mighty God' (10.21), to interpret the role of the Jews in salvation-history. That is, God's calling of the Gentiles does not entail the rejection of the Jews but their temporary blindness to the Gospel will ultimately prove a 'fortunate fall', preparing the way for 'the return of that saving remnant – the conversion of the Jews – [which] must occur before all things can be accomplished and God's Kingdom be established'.[74] Paul (and the Geneva Bible's glossator) warns the Gentiles that they are the ingrafted branches upon the holy root of Abraham and the Church of the Israelites, and therefore they are not to be boastful of God's calling them, reminding them

that 'all Israel shall be saved'.[75] Regarding the complex relationship between contemporary Jews and Christians, Paul explains:
'As concerning the Gospel, they are enemies for your sakes: but
as touching the election, they are beloved for the fathers sakes'
(Rom 11.28). Danson argues, 'Bringing destruction upon himself
through a vain self-righteousness, and failing to hear the Gospel
message of mercy freely granted, Shylock at his trial plays out
the role of the Jew as it appears in the New Testament version of
salvation-history.'[76] Summarising the allegorical dimension of the
conversion condition, Danson concludes:

> Thus salvation was made possible for the believing Gentiles
> through the unbelief of Israel; and now Israel's unbelief will
> allow God to show his free mercy to the Jews when in time
> their unbelief shall pass away. As Adam's disobedience was
> made the occasion for God's mercy to Adam's descendants, so
> the Jews, when they have acknowledged the insufficiency of
> their 'blinde zeale' to the law, will discover the mystery of grace.[77]

With the fortunate falls of Gentiles and Jews 'shut up all in
unbelief, that [God] might have mercy on all', Paul's version of
salvation-history celebrates the glorious 'mercy' of God and the
'unsearchable' wisdom of His 'judgements' (Rom 11.32–3) in his
transformation of good out of evil, the very divine qualities that
humans are called to emulate in Shakespeare's trial scene. To
develop further Danson's argument we should remind ourselves
of the play's use of Hebrew names that look simultaneously to
the Old and New Testaments in relation to the recurrent theme of
physical and spiritual inheritance. In Paul's use of Isaiah's prophecy about the remnant of Jacob for his view of Jewish history, the
name of 'Jacob' or the name 'Israel', which God gives to Jacob, is
most prominent. In addition to the other factors already considered,
the use of Jacob's name in Paul's context for the conversion of the
Jews may well be another reason Shakespeare selects Jacob for
Shylock's preferred patriarch. Elizabethan Christians believe the real
treasure promised to the family of Abraham is the spiritual blessing
of the Messiah. Shylock's promise to convert enables him, from the
Elizabethan perspective, to identify truly with his favourite patriarch Jacob and to inherit rightly the blessings promised to Abraham.[78]
   The language of economics – treasure, debt, purchase, bond,
redeem, inheritance – serves as linguistic currency for the bibli-

cal doctrine of spiritual salvation from 'sin' ('debt') or 'death' (which Elizabethans pronounced like 'debt'): 'And forgive us our debts, as we forgive our debtors' (Mt 6.12). In Judaism the personal note of indebtedness or 'the bond' is also a common metaphor for sin.[79] Thus, Paul images the redemption of that bond on the Cross: 'And putting out the hand writing of ordinances that was against us . . . [God] even took . . . & fastened it upon the cross' (Col 2.14). The language of the glosses on this passage in the Geneva Bible and the Geneva–Tomson Bible underscores the appropriateness of such biblical metaphors for illuminating the allegorical emphasis in Shakespeare's trial on overcoming the 'handwriting' (glossed as the rites and ceremonies of the Law) of our 'testimonies of our guiltiness whereby we manifestly witnessed as it were by our own handwritings, that we deserved damnation' (Geneva–Tomson Bible). This message concludes that Christ's death paid in full our debt so that such handwritten laws of old are now fulfilled in Him and His victory on the cross over man's arch enemies (Satan and death). Although Shylock's bond is tried in a civil court and the 'rites' judged according to Venetian statutes are commercial bonds (not religious ordinances), none the less, Shylock's handwritten bond for a debt could be allegorically seen by an Elizabethan audience as a testimony of his own guilt whereby he becomes liable to the debt of death in this strict court. The irony of a man's being condemned by his own handwriting balances the condemnation of the guilty by God's handwriting on the wall, symbolically represented for the audience by the person of a lawyer-judge named 'Balthazar'. According to the gloss in the Geneva–Tomson Bible, 'Christ is *the only bond* of the Jews and Gentiles, whereby they be reconciled to God' (Eph 2.13, my italics).

The allegorical use of Paul's biblical language of difference between 'flesh' (faith in worldly or outward things) and 'spirit' (faith in Christ) also informs the Duke's educative line to Shylock about seeing such a difference. Paul emphasises that 'by the *blood* of Christ' and 'through his *flesh*' 'the partition wall' ('the Law of commandments which standeth in ordinances') between Jews and Gentiles is overcome for their new unity in peace (Eph 2.13–15, my italics). Basic to Paul's preaching is the Old Testament idea of God as the spiritual 'inheritance' for the Jews, an idea which Paul argues is fulfilled in the redemptive role of Christ for those Jews who embrace the Gospel and preach it to the Gentiles (Eph 1.13–14).[80] Paul tells the story of his life and his conversion from

the Pharisees (the strictest Jewish sect) as a hortatory exemplum
to those Christian persecutors who are of Shylock's mind, whose
zeal for literalistic legalism blinds them to the true 'spirit' of 'faith'
(Phlm 3.4–12).[81] With an awareness sensitive to this metaphorical
richness Shakespeare interweaves throughout his play the common concerns of physical and spiritual rewards that bond together
his two *apparently* opposite plots of love and hate, freedom and
debt, spirit and flesh, life and death.

The interweaving of the conversion trope with money matters
places *The Merchant of Venice* comfortably within the known Elizabethan dramatic context, where the plays by Wilson and Marlowe
precede Shakespeare in this regard. Shakespeare's play, however,
is less normative and more unique in its complex texture of artistic unity. Neither Wilson's nor Marlowe's plays articulate the theme
of money and debt in the rich imagery of Shakespeare's blessing
and inheritance tropes, nor can either play begin to match Shakespeare's myriad-minded use of the conjunction between love and
wisdom for effecting the play's artistic unity. In Wilson's play
the dishonest Christian merchant pretends that he will convert to
Mohammedanism solely to escape the payment of a legitimate
debt, 3000 ducats plus interest, to the kindhearted Jewish moneylender Gerontus. Here religious conversion is reduced to merely
a cheap trick, but the merchant later clarifies that his trick was
done 'for the greediness of the money' because he never really
intended to convert: 'not for all da good in da world, me forsake
a my Christ'.[82]

It is Marlowe's play, with its quadruple use of conversion, that
most inspires Shakespeare's own innovative response. Jessica's
conversion parallels Abigail's second and true conversion, with
some remarkable differences. And Barabas's two encounters with
the conversion possibility contrast starkly with Shylock's. At her
father's request Abigail feigns conversion to get into the former
house of Barabas, which has been 'convert [ed]' to a 'nunnery'
(1.2.130), in order to recover for him the bags of wealth he hid
there. Abigail's vigil at the window to toss down money-bags to
her father (not to her Christian beloved) is obviously parodied
and changed in Shakespeare's scene of Jessica's elopement. Abigail
is a wonderfully devoted daughter, but Marlowe makes her learn
the hard way that her father is not a man of good faith. When
Barabas cruelly murders her beloved, whom Abigail notes had
never offended her father, Abigail genuinely resolves on conver-

sion to Christianity and uses powerful language to correct the
pretence of her earlier feigned conversion:

> Then were my thoughts so frail and unconfirmed,
> And I was chained to follies of the world,
> But now experience, purchasèd with grief,
> Has made me *see the difference of things.*
> My sinful soul, alas, hath paced too long
> The fatal labyrinth of misbelief,
> Far from the Son who gives eternal life.
>
> (3.3.59–64, my italics)

Abigail is fully cognisant of the discrepancy between what some
Christians in Malta do and what their faith prescribes for them
to do (1.2.229–36), but her conversion is so genuine that with her
dying breath (a death caused by her father because she converted)
she begs Friar Barnardine, after her confession of sin, 'Convert
my father that he may be saved, / And witness that I die a Christian' (3.6.38–9).[83] In the scene immediately following Abigail's
deathwish, Barabas imitates Mercadore's cheap conversion trick
and pretends to convert to Christianity in order to avoid legal
prosecution by the friars, who now know his murderous role in
the deaths of the Governor of Malta's son and Abigail's beloved,
Don Mathias.

How and why might Marlowe's inclusion of Abigail's well-
intentioned but extraordinary conversion request for Barabas influence Shakespeare's own imaginative response in his addition
of Antonio's similar request for Shylock? Critics have probably
overlooked the possible influence of Abigail's conversion request
because of Friar Barnardine's satiric rejoinder to Abigail's innocent reminder that she dies a Christian: 'Ay, and a virgin, too –
that grieves me most' (3.6.40). Neither Abigail nor Antonio could
reasonably expect either Barabas or Shylock to be desirous of
conversion to Christianity, yet both Marlowe and Shakespeare allow
their characters' requests to register the Elizabethan concern about
salvation. Portia reminds the audience 'that in the course of justice, none of us / Should see salvation' (4.1.195–6). Abigail seeks
to protect her father's physical life from the danger of the law,
despite her knowledge of his contrived murder of her beloved
(3.3.73–5; 3.6.30–6). Antonio likewise seeks to protect Shylock's
physical life from the danger of the law by granting his request

for wealth, despite his knowledge of Shylock's criminal attempt. Both Abigail and Antonio as well-meaning benefactors seek to go beyond physical to spiritual 'saving' of their respective malefactors. But in terms of the challenge to personal graciousness Antonio's conversion request for the potential saving of a fellow-sinner is even more amazing than Abigail's. Abigail does not know that she and the rest of the nuns die because of her father's 'alms' gift of a pot of poisoned porridge (3.4.46–86). Shakespeare, however, grants full knowledge to Antonio about Shylock's murderous attempt against him, and within the same hour and place of trial subjects Antonio to the hard choice between revenge or mercy. Despite these heightened circumstances, Antonio, like Abigail, requests what most Elizabethans would see as a potentially salvific conversion.

But it is the Maltese Christians' *tragic* use of 'conversion' as a 'threat' in order to *gain* Jewish wealth that most captures Shakespeare's interest for his *opposite* use of the conversion trope to suit his *comedic* intent and dramatic structure. When Barabas is summoned before the Christian Governor of Malta to pay the Turkish tribute, the unfair terms decree that each Jew must pay half his wealth or 'straight become a Christian' (1.2.73–4). If any Jew resists, then he shall lose all his wealth. Unlike his fellow Jews in Malta, Barabas chooses to resist both conditions and loses all. The Christian example of villainy sets in motion *The Tragedy of the Jew of Malta*. These corrupt Christians disregard the spiritual status of the Jews and value only their financial status. Unlike Shylock, Barabas chooses not to become a Christian; the conversion threat is readily dismissed, and most of the remaining confrontation focuses on Barabas's objections to his wealth's confiscation. Shakespeare probably had in mind Marlowe's corrupt version when he envisioned its opposite, his own salvific version. Not only does Shylock mention the name 'Barabbas' (292), although his primary reference here is probably to the New Testament Barabas as the antithesis of Christ, but also his speech protesting the loss of wealth as the loss of life mirrors Barabbas's speech in *The Jew of Malta* (1.2.147–52). No doubt there were people in Shakespeare's London audience who had seen Marlowe's play and were waiting to remark what Shakespeare would do differently in his treatment of the theatrical convention of Jew versus Christian. Marlowe's Jew is selfish and avaricious, but as yet the audience has not detected any villainous behaviour to merit the unjust, hypocritical treatment he receives from the Christians, who literally steal his wealth and give none of it back despite his desperate pleas and despite the Christians' later change in policy from payment of the tribute to martial defiance of the Turks, that now negates their original rationalisation for confiscating the wealth of Maltese Jews (2.2.1–56).

Shakespeare's scene differs strikingly. The audience appreciates Shylock as a man with genuine grievances, but none the less one who villainously wants to murder another man and thereby dominate the usury market in Venice. For his attempted crime the court can legally claim his life and wealth. The Venetian Christians are humanly flawed, some more than others, but not all are despicably corrupt. They do grant Shylock his 'life and living' (5.1.286) when the law denies it, and from their religious perspective even attempt to grant him new life through Christ. Antonio had requested that Shylock presently sign the deed of gift 'here in the court' (385), but the Duke kindly hearkens to Shylock's request to leave immediately, firmly insisting that Shylock sign the deed sent after him. Although Girard believes 'everyone agrees that Shylock is a scapegoat', his own analysis of 'the scapegoat' as both structure and theme in *The Merchant of Venice* ignores the biblical context for this significant term that would refute its applicability to Shylock from the perspective of an Elizabethan audience.[84] The term 'scapegoat', apparently invented by Tindale (1530), signifies the goat, chosen by lot, upon whom the sins of the people would be symbolically laid before the goat was sent out into the wilderness on the Day of Atonement.[85] Shylock, unlike the biblical scapegoat, is not innocent; he is responsible for his own sins. Not chance or lot but rather choice influences why Shylock finds himself in the position he now does. For Elizabethans the scapegoat of Leviticus 'is a true figure of Jesus Christ, who beareth the sins of the people', the innocent one who stands for sacrifice to atone for the sins of all.[86] Therefore, Shakespeare's audience would probably tend to see Shylock not as a scapegoat but as a human sinner, like all others, sent not into the wilderness but sent instead to the perfect 'Scapegoat' who could save Shylock from the wilderness.

Will Shylock choose to be a 'Converso' or a 'Marrano' in Venice? We cannot know what happens after Shylock leaves the court, although an actor's choice of exit will often prompt our imaginations, for example, Sir Laurence Olivier's offstage howl (National

Theatre production of 1970) or Patrick Stewart's resilient laughter at Gratiano's unforgiving joke (Royal Shakespeare Company's production of 1978). But Shakespeare provides some clues for the direction Shylock may pursue once he has had the time to reflect on all that has happened. Lewalski suggests that Shylock 'recognizes the logic which demands his conversion': 'His incredulous question "Is that the law" (IV.i.309) when he finds the law invoked against him shows a new and overwhelming consciousness of the defects of legalism.'[87] It is not 'the defects' so much as the punitive nature of the law that Shylock discovers here, the law that Shylock had heretofore seen, from his perspective only, as rewarding in nature because he thought the law was on his side. But the law is inanimate and theoretically impartial; it does not 'choose' sides. Choice, along with partiality, is the prerogative of human beings. Shylock has to grant the legitimacy, not the defect, of Balthazar's 'legal' interpretation because it is based on the very principle he upheld, the letter of his bond and the letter of the law.

Why does Shylock accept the judgement passed on him? Portia solicits Shylock's response by specifically inquiring: 'Art thou contented, Jew? What dost thou say?' (4.1.389). If Shylock refused, the consequences would be deadly (loss of life and wealth) given the Duke's threat to recant his recent pardon. Although Shylock is greatly constrained in his choice, the threat of death does not force him to accept his judgement. He has just explained to the court that he welcomes death if he has not wealth. Therefore, the Duke and Antonio respond to Shylock's legitimate need and grant him half his wealth freely and the other half in trust. In so doing, they grant Shylock what he proclaims he desires most. Given Shylock's own testimony, he has specified no other basis for which he would complain against the court's judgement. As has been observed, choice, to be choice, does not have to equate with ultimate personal preference. More often than not, human choices involve varying degrees of constraint. For example, Shylock would probably prefer not to have half his wealth in trust to be administered by Antonio, nor to have to convert and sign a deed of gift for his rebellious daughter and her Christian husband in order to receive half his wealth without any fine and the profits from the other half held in trust.

But all the play's characters have been, or will be, in Shylock's position of having to make hard choices, hard because these choices involve constraint. Were it not for being bound by the injunctions, Morocco and Arragon would rather not have to give up their right to legitimate marriage and offspring because they lost at the casket lottery. Portia chooses to obey her father, but she chafes under that constraint, lamenting her lack of choice in the selection of her husband. Antonio would rather not have to beg Shylock for mercy nor to endure the legal loss of his flesh to Shylock's knife. Bassanio would rather not be placed in the position of having to choose between giving away Portia's ring or dishonourable ingratitude. Shylock, like Angelo in *Measure for Measure*, is severely constrained but not completely forced to obey an ultimatum from a judge who is also a duke. Like Shylock, Angelo could refuse and suffer whatever penalty the Duke might give. But like Shylock's acceptance of conversion, Angelo's acceptance of marriage will be nominal if he does not reform his former coldness and embrace his wife with love. The personal difficulty of shifting from rejection to acceptance has been eased somewhat for both Shylock and Angelo because both men have just witnessed the pleading on their behalf by persons whom they have grievously wronged.

Shylock's ultimate preference might not blind him now to the Christian example of kindness in the judgement passed on his request for wealth. Why not? Shylock is beginning to 'see' the 'difference' through the *contrast* between what he attempted to do to Antonio and what the Duke and Antonio do to him and for him in return. Shylock, however, would probably not readily see the conversion request, like its related deed of gift, as the paradox it is, the apparent penalty but real blessing it is meant to be from an Elizabethan perspective. He would probably receive it as a penalty, at least at this traumatic moment in time, but it is a penalty that he chooses to live with. However, he might not see it as vindictively motivated. Why not? If Shakespeare wanted to have Shylock condemn the judgement passed on him, he need only write such an objection as an aside to the audience. The absence of any such voiced complaint indicates that Shakespeare does not want Shylock to complain but to accept. Today we, unlike most Elizabethans, would complain that if Shylock has not lived as a good Jew should, why not let him keep the inspirational Jewish faith and reform within it? But our modern ideal of religious tolerance evolved historically after Shakespeare.

Shylock, however, does accept the terms of his judgement, and how Shylock expresses his acceptance reveals a sign of positive growth. When he decided earlier not to risk the taking of his flesh bond, he cursed before getting ready to leave: 'Why then, the devil give him good of it / I'll stay no longer question' (341–2). The tone and content of Shylock's final lines are markedly different. To borrow Paul's metaphor, has 'the Law' been an effective 'schoolmaster' in bringing Shylock to new knowledge (Gal 3.24–5)? Earlier Shylock proudly asserted he feared no judgement because he believed he was not guilty of doing anything wrong. In terms of objective fact, attempted murder is wrong, and given the Old Law Shylock should know this, just as Antonio should know that hating one's enemy is wrong according to the New Law. By indulging their own subjective truths and rude wills, both men blind themselves to the objective truths of the Old and New Law. Both undergo the adversity of deprivation to strip away their blinders.

Within the eschatological framework of the trial the relationship between law, mercy, and conversion is helpfully illuminated by the Epistle of James to converted Jews dispersed throughout the world. Shylock rationalises that he follows the law, but he follows some laws and breaks others. James clarifies that whosoever breaks one 'point' of 'the whole Law' violates all of it (Jas 2.10–11). Who then can stand? Paralleling Portia's reasoning in her mercy speech, James explains that one should speak and act so as to be judged 'by the Law of liberty', which is glossed as 'the mercy of God which delivereth us from the curse of the Law' (Jas 2.12, gloss; cf. Mt 5.18–19). James outlines the logic of Portia's speech on mercy: since we all need mercy, we should render the deeds of mercy. The cause of salvation is true faith, and the consequences of true faith are good deeds (Jas 2.14, gloss). Portia's general emphasis on knowing and doing what is good receives articulation in the trial through the explicit interrelation of faith and merciful deeds. Given James's message, Antonio's deeds of mercy would be the effect of true faith, and his request for Shylock's conversion might recall for Elizabethans the conclusion of James's Epistle: 'Brethren, if any of you hath erred from the truth, and some man hath converted him, / Let him know that he which hath converted the sinner . . . shall save a soul from death, and shall hide a multitude of sins' (Jas 5.19–20).

Both Antonio and Shylock experience painful reversals, humbled by the educative power of suffering so that they might learn to see feelingly. For the first time in the play Shylock now utters a line of genuinely admitted deficiency that resembles Antonio's earlier admission of deficiency ('a tainted wether of the flock' and 'the weakest kind of fruit'): 'I am not well' (392). Shylock's physical distress is a literal sign of the recent trauma's impact and a figurative sign of his past spiritual sickness, just as Antonio's melancholy can be interpreted similarly on literal and figurative levels of significance. Shylock's agreement, 'I am content', precisely echoes Antonio's same line moments earlier (378) when he stood for mercy seasoning justice. There are, of course, a variety of tones an actor could choose from to deliver Shylock's line – bitter, sarcastic, sly, tearful, resigned, to name a few. I believe Shylock's line suggests an embattled acknowledgement of the insufficiency of the letter of the law, of strict justice, without 'the gentle rain' of mercy (181). This recognition is indeed psychologically and spiritually traumatic for Shylock. Shylock wilfully and blindly had believed he was doing no wrong, but therein he was proved wrong. The intelligent Shylock, however, had earlier revealed some potential for proper perspective when we discovered he valued Leah's turquoise ring for its meaning and not its price. It is to his credit that now he seems more open to learning, and the quiet manner of his agreement to the terms of his judgement suggests this. Barabas, for example, goes to his death never having learned anything not taught in the school of Machiavel.

Given Shylock's old beliefs about the Christian example of revenge (3.1.52–6), what would he probably *expect* to see the court do to him? 'Hates any man the thing he would not kill?' (67); 'What, wouldst thou have a serpent sting thee twice?' (69). Shylock believed he would witness in Christians the ethic of revenge that he himself practised and that he believed they practised. Although Gratiano does not disprove him, Antonio truncates his expectations. For Shylock, Antonio's merciful justice probably constitutes the biggest surprise of a very surprising turn of events. No longer should Shylock feel so inclined to dismiss Antonio as the Christian fool he thought he was, whose free lending and giving means 'low simplicity'.

With the darkness of his desires and the vanity of his deserts unveiled, Shylock is beginning to feel a new appreciation for giving, for generosity of wealth and spirit, now that he has discovered such needs for himself. As Chaucer clearly reminds us, knowing what one lacks is the beginning of humility, and humility is the root of self-knowledge.[88] Shylock parallels Morocco and

Arragon, who also mischoose and lose their suits but who also learn through loss what they lacked – wise love. In some ways Shylock's bond is the written equivalent of the judgemental scrolls read in the casket plot; the judgements inscribed suit the suitors. Shylock does not get what he desires, the pound of flesh or thrice his loan; he does not get what he deserves, the bare principal; he is put in the position of giving and hazarding all he hath – this very sentence constituting his opportunity for salvation in terms of the values celebrated by the play.

Shakespeare's art of parallel reversals for Shylock and Antonio acts as a sign to indicate the comedic direction of his play, just as he used parallel reversals in *Romeo and Juliet* to indicate the tragic direction of that play (e.g., the two contrasting balcony scenes). In their first scene together Antonio accepts Shylock's conditions; in their last scene together Shylock accepts Antonio's conditions. Shylock knew his condition was full of 'hate' when he feigned the purchase of Antonio's 'favour' (1.3.161); Antonio believes his is merciful in granting 'favour' (4.1.382). In the trial Shylock's flesh bond with Antonio is exchanged for a new soul 'bond' as they become united in one faith. Throughout the play spiritual faith is supposed to lead one to the right attitude toward physical wealth. Honouring Shylock's legitimate need for such wealth, Shakespeare reverses this typical order and has Antonio use financial wealth, in his judgement passed on Shylock, to lead Shylock back to spiritual faith. Not back to the faith of the hypocritical Pharisees but back to the true faith of Shylock's and Antonio's patriarchs, Abram and Jacob, their faith as fulfilled in God's promise of the Messiah to Abram's seed. In his opposition to the factionalism of humankind, Paul's imagery of familial unity for the 'sons of God by faith' bespeaks the human concord that the trial scene attempts to emulate for an Elizabethan audience: 'For all ye that are baptized into Christ, have put on Christ. / There is neither bond nor free: there is neither male nor female: for ye are all one in Christ Jesus. / And if ye be Christ's, then are ye Abrahams seed, and heirs by promise' (Gal 3.24–9).

Shakespeare has Shylock fade quietly from the stage, with no further speech. Morocco exits in grief and Arragon in anger, but neither of their mischoices receive any mercy, only just deserts. Shylock's very silence recalls the proverbial idea in the play's opening scene that wise men are given to silence and foolish men are given to talk (1.1.88–103). Differing in degree of wisdom and contentment, Shylock's final silence none the less is related to Antonio's final silence, his loss of words ('I am dumb', 5.1.279) when it becomes his turn for the 'providential' restoration of his ventured wealth. Therefore, it is significantly Gratiano, the aptly named fool, who continues to speak as Shylock leaves, reminding us once again of the *difference* between the wisdom of mercy and the folly of vengeance, between Antonio's 'favour' to Shylock and Gratiano's gallows wish for Shylock (395–6). If, within the context of the play itself, the financial settlement for Shylock is vindicated as merciful, so also then must be the religious settlement because the two issues of faith and wealth are so closely interrelated throughout the play. Moreover, Shakespeare deliberately creates for Antonio's joint condition a union of complementary judgements on Shylock's wealth (the deed of gift) and faith (the conversion) so that Shylock, and we the audience, do not mistake where the intended emphasis falls in this judgement – on mercy seasoning justice.

The endings of Shakespearian comedies do not reward vindictive villains, and by the end of this play Antonio will be twice blessed for having given and received mercy. Shylock has been vindictive, but he is not rewarded for his criminal attempts; rather he is subjected to legal penalty for them. Just like Angelo's judgement in *Measure for Measure*, Shylock's attempted criminality will find the hearts of his judges inclined to season justice with mercy in order to teach an invaluable lesson to us all: the human need for mercy in the face of vain self-righteousness, selfish literalism, and hardhearted revenge. The greater the need for the lesson, the more traumatic is the learning process, as Shylock's and Angelo's experiences evince. In both Shakespeare's comedies and tragedies the value of the insight gained theoretically outweighs the often extraordinarily traumatic price paid for the learning of it.

6

'Joy be the consequence': Union and Reunion

Given the Sidneyan emphasis on comedy as a genre of enjoyable learning through the comic offsetting of human virtues and vices, the mock trial of Act V appropriately follows the legal trial of Act IV. This time Antonio and Bassanio are 'on trial', and Portia once again is the arbiter who demonstrates she 'can learn' (3.2.162) by practising the mercy she earlier preached to Shylock, this time in a less serious situation. As we have seen, Antonio and Bassanio resemble each other in their virtues of generosity and honesty and counterbalance each other in their faults of excess: Antonio errs in the direction of emotional excess and Bassanio in the direction of financial excess. The symbolic reenactment of the casket choices in the trial is complemented by a similar reiteration, in a lighter key, of the casket mottos in the mock trial of the comic dénouement. The rings episode of Act V further unifies the play structurally and thematically through its verbal echoing of the casket mottos – desiring, deserving, and hazarding.

The ideology of the casket choice once again provides the unifying resolution, which is achieved through the thematic emphasis on interpretation – literal and spiritual – and the proper perspective of loving wisely. Antonio, Bassanio, and Portia are further enlightened and refined through the concluding rings episode and the new bonds of understanding that it fosters. As Nerissa wisely warned at the play's beginning: 'they are as sick that surfeit with too much as they that starve with nothing' (1.2.5–6). Portia, too, pays tribute to the Greek wisdom of moderation when she wisely begs for moderation in her love as Bassanio chooses rightly the leaden casket:

O love, be moderate, allay thy ecstasy,
In measure rain thy joy, scant this excess!

246

I feel too much thy blessing: make it less
For fear I surfeit.

$$(3.2.111-14)$$

Herein Portia and Nerissa, as near paragons of virtue, lead the way and inspire the men to be the best they can be – 'by season seasoned . . . / To their right praise and true perfection' (5.1.107–8).

After Antonio attempts to remedy his defective relationship with Shylock in the trial, he is confronted with moderating what has now become an excessive relationship with Bassanio. Antonio must learn not to overvalue with pride his love for Bassanio and to cause Bassanio to break faith with Portia. Before the forfeiture of the bond becomes a probability in Act II, Antonio tries not to ask for any dividends on his love investment in Bassanio. His magnanimity reveals itself especially in his parting with Bassanio, who takes Antonio at his word once he leaves for Belmont:

And for the Jew's bond which he hath of me,
Let it not enter in your mind of love.
Be merry, and employ your chiefest thoughts
To courtship, and such fair ostents of love
As shall conveniently become you there.

$$(2.8.42-6)$$

The first hint that Antonio may expect something in return from Bassanio appears after Antonio is pinched by adversity, the painful educator. After Antonio discovers that what he confidently thought was a riskless bond has become in fact a life-threatening reality, then he betrays a desire to reap returns, even though he lovingly and courageously bears the penalty for Bassanio. In Antonio's letter to Bassanio he declares that all debts are cleared between Bassanio and him: '*if* I might but see you at my death' (3.2.317, my italics). This is an understandable but none the less restrictive condition. Shakespeare's change of *Il Pecorone* is an important indicator of the direction he will pursue with Antonio. In the source the merchant *unconditionally* asks his godson, 'If misfortune comes to you, that you be pleased to return [from Belmonte], so that I may see you before I die – then I will depart contented'; after this request he practically disappears from the rest of the story.[1] Shakespeare, however, significantly enlarges Antonio's role throughout his dramatic narrative. By the next scene

Antonio's expectation of Bassanio will have shifted slightly in a more ominous direction. Whereas Antonio's letter requests merely to see Bassanio at his death, now he desires to have Bassanio *see him pay* his debt: 'Pray God Bassanio come / To see me pay his debt, and then I care not' (3.3.35–6).

The Renaissance ideal of giving, whether of physical or spiritual gifts, stresses giving without a primary motive of gainful return. The paradox of the leaden casket choice is that only in primarily selfless giving will the giver then receive a return. Seneca, for example, defines the good man as the bestower of benefits, even on the ungrateful and despite the discovery of deception; Seneca's definition recalls Antonio's attempt in the trial to do what he thinks is good in response to Shylock's stated, and unstated, needs, despite Shylock's deception of him through a 'merry' bond.[2] Seneca also accents what should be the selfless nature of such giving: 'To seek, not the fruit of benefits, but the mere doing of them . . . [to make] the gift for the sake of giving'.[3] This emphasis on no expectation of return is precisely the emphasis prescribed by Luke's strict definition of 'lending' as 'giving' (Lk 6.35). Portia, as we have seen, embodies this ideal in the play, except when she plays a role in this mock trial to guide Bassanio to a higher level of knowing and doing good. Portia eschews pride, praise, and reward for her deeds of wise love; she keeps no bank account. Even at the end of the trial Portia upholds this ideal in front of Bassanio and Antonio when she refuses any reward other than the self-satisfaction of knowing she has done a good deed (4.1.411–14). The doing of good is its own reward, and like the candle that throws its beam into the darkness, so the good deed enlightens the 'naughty world' (5.1.91).[4] By expecting no praise or return, Portia sets an example for how to do good and how to love wisely, an example that proves instructive for Antonio in the rings episode.

However, as the tension mounts for Antonio in the trial scene, so do his expectations grow ever greater for how Bassanio should repay his love. We must recall here that Shakespeare's presentation of his merchant's stance against usury explodes his audience's expectations of the typical dramatic paradigm of the merchant as a greedy usurer, and that his portrayal instead anticipates the evolving ideal of the merchant-prince, a noble citizen. Antonio's personal purity regarding the practice of actual usury is very admirable.[5] But perhaps even more innovative is Shakespeare's choice to taint Antonio with another kind of usury, the 'serpent in the bosom' that is mental usury.[6] Mental usury is one of the kinds of usury being debated in London at the time Shakespeare writes his play. In sixteenth-century English literature Mosse provides the most thorough discussion of what mental usury is, and why it is sinful, like actual usury, when he publishes in 1595 six of his sermons in order to arraign and convict sinful usury in the consciences of his London audience. Mental usury, a concept that derives from scholastic theology, is a kind of usury committed in the mind of the lender, no actual contract with the borrower being made; it is simply the *expectation* (intent or hope) of *gain* on a loan.[7] Gain, as we have seen, may be traditionally defined as *anything* taken over the principal lent – money or goods or even good words and deeds, including, for example, 'some thankful recompence', 'a good word' spoken or 'a certain pleasure' done on one's behalf.[8] Judged according to this traditionally broad definition of 'gain', Antonio gradually becomes a mental usurer in his expectation of ever-increasing recompenses of Bassanio's love as a result of his now forfeited loan for his friend.

The problem of how Antonio is a mental usurer turns on the definition of 'gain', and herein Shakespeare provides another challenge to his audience for their comparative evaluation of the Christian Antonio and the Jewish Shylock in terms of their responses to sinful usury. Shylock is a wilful practitioner of actual usury who becomes enlightened about its dangers. Antonio becomes a mental usurer who needs to be more enlightened about its dangers. Shakespeare, we recall, adapts the more limited and progressive definition of gain that is found in Mosse's book for Shylock's deceptive defence of his bond as not constituting any monetary gain (1.3.155–63). Antonio seems to understand this particular definition, and he accepts it. Now Shakespeare will revisit the Mossian definition of 'gain' in order to criticise Antonio's fall into the snare of mental usury regarding his escalating expectations of emotional satisfaction from Bassanio. We remember that Mosse, following the medieval nominalist Gabriel Biel, supports the argument that usurious gain should be defined only in terms of money or money's worth. If one accepts this definition, then the lender's expectation of love, friendship, or gratitude from the borrower constitutes no 'gain' and therefore no mental usury because love is not something that can be valued for money.[9] According to this opinion, Antonio would not be judged a mental usurer if he expected Bassanio to repay his loan in words or deeds of love.

But even in Mosse's presentation of this newer perspective the emphasis falls on the lender's legitimate use of a loan to procure or 'purchase' the love and favour of another, not to ensure or overbind pre-existing love from the debtor.[10] Because Antonio already has Bassanio's love as his dearest friend, Antonio is not in this position of 'buying' Bassanio's good will through his loan and thereby legitimately expecting Bassanio's love in return. Antonio's generosity reasonably deserves Bassanio's loving gratitude, but Antonio's 'expectation' of dividends on Bassanio's love strains too far in desiring that his deserts be so rewarded. During the trial Antonio displays a dangerously growing expectation of repayment that will ultimately culminate in his ring request:

> You cannot better be employed, Bassanio,
> Than to live still and write mine epitaph.
>   (4.1.117–18)

> Commend me to your honourable wife,
> Tell her the process of Antonio's end,
> Say how I lov'd you, speak me fair in death:
> And when the tale is told, bid her be *judge*
> Whether Bassanio had not once a love:
> *Repent* but you that you shall lose your friend
> And he *repents* not that he pays your debt.
>   (4.1.269–75)

Speaking more wisely than he knows, Antonio will find Portia his judge in the rings episode to follow, and repentance shall be his.

Is Antonio's melancholy, his extreme love for Bassanio, or his lack of a wife meant to signify homosexuality? It is one thing to see Antonio's love for Bassanio as extreme in degree, and quite another thing to identify Antonio's love as homoerotic in nature. But in some modern criticism and stage productions Antonio's homosexual desire has become a recurrent feature.[11] There is no evidence in the play that Antonio is actively homosexual, and there is some evidence to suggest the contrary, namely that his love for Bassanio, although extreme in degree, does not incline toward sexual expression. In the first place, Antonio freely overextends himself to help Bassanio to a new relationship that he knows will include sexual intimacy. There is no sign that he is resentful or possessive of Bassanio from a sexual perspective. Antonio is naturally melancholic to have distance put between him and his best friend. As we have seen, in Shakespeare's literary source melancholy is presented as a normal reaction to the absence of someone loved, and there are no hints of homoerotic attraction in that context.

But did Shakespeare add such an attraction? Antonio's friend Solanio may err in guessing that a lady love is the cause of Antonio's melancholy, but his guess also indicates what he sees as his friend's possible interests. Nor does this same Solanio indicate any specifically sexual orientation on Antonio's part when he observes Antonio's great love for Bassanio at their leavetaking. Regarding the cause of his mysterious melancholy, Antonio decisively denies his friends' proffered interpretations of romance or ventured wealth. However, the audience increasingly discovers that love melancholy is an issue for Antonio, not the love of a lady but the love of a friend. If Shakespeare intends for Antonio's love to be homoerotic, why doesn't he provide more explicit linguistic or gestural signs as he does in Thersites' reference to Patroclus as Achilles' 'masculine whore' (*Tro* 5.1.17), or as Marlowe does in his portrayal of Edward II? In response to Bassanio's good offer to make haste to return from Belmont, Antonio selflessly urges: 'Slubber not business for my sake, Bassanio, / But stay the very riping of the time' (2.8.40–41). Such language hardly suggests sexual possessiveness, nor does Antonio's farewell gesture, which is not a kiss or an embrace but a mere wringing of Bassanio's hand (2.8.50). However, Antonio's tears on this occasion, Salarino's observation that Antonio acted 'with affection wondrous sensible', and Solanio's conclusion that Antonio 'only loves the world for [Bassanio]' (2.8.47–51) do indicate that Antonio's affection for Bassanio is very great indeed.

The argument that Antonio is latently homosexual might appear to find safer footing, but this argument is very difficult to prove from textual evidence. Graham Midgley maintains: 'Antonio is an outsider because he is an unconscious homosexual in a predominantly, and indeed blatantly, heterosexual society.'[12] If 'unconscious', how can we be so certain of our consciousness of it? What evidence can be adduced to establish a homoerotic 'preference' when this 'preference', according to the terms of this argument, has not been consciously preferred and has therefore never knowingly been expressed? Midgley's argument is based on an assumption, the assumption that Antonio is an outsider in his society. Far from being an outsider, Antonio has been the hub of the wheel of male camaraderie. He is still the centre of attention when the play opens, but now he is so because he is not his normal self; his friends are trying to cheer him. John D. Hurrell thinks Antonio's relationship with Bassanio suggests 'an incipient homosexual relationship'.[13] If 'incipient', what evidence confirms such incipience? How meaningful is the supposition of such 'incipience' if a homoerotic relationship is never realised, as the terms of this argument suggest? The extreme degree of Antonio's love for Bassanio might signal homoeroticism were it not for the qualifying historical perspective that male friendship in the Renaissance could be expressed extravagantly and yet convey no sexual intent.[14] Arguments favouring an interpretation of Antonio as either consciously or unconsciously homosexual often tend to be asserted and lack the critical context and acknowledgement of the 'implicit' or 'potential' nature of the subject that Bruce R. Smith is careful to provide in his treatment of the topic.[15]

Antonio's apparent lack of interest in romance and marriage could be interpreted as indicative of homosexual preference. But Salarino and Solanio also show no such interest. Indeed, the group of Venetian male friends in the play appear to have just arrived at a marriageable age because they are just beginning to show an interest in finding wives. Lorenzo promises to help his friends when their turn comes to steal wives. Gratiano reveals no interest in marriage until he sees Nerissa. And although Bassanio and Portia, on an earlier occasion when Portia's father was still alive (1.2.92), saw each other and exchanged lovers' glances (1.1.162–3), only now is he ready to begin a marriage quest for her. Aside from such practical considerations of chronological timing within the play or even the question of availability of a fourth boy to play another female role in the final act, might there be a thematic reason why Antonio remains unwived?

The most plausible answer involves the very nature of the relationship between Antonio and Bassanio. One of Shakespeare's significant changes of *Il Pecorone* is his transformation of the spiritual relationship of godfather and godson into a spiritual relationship of friendship between two 'companions' or peers 'whose *souls* do bear an *egal* yoke of love' (3.4.11–13, my italics) and whose friendship makes them resemble each other in 'a like proportion / Of lineaments, of manners, and of spirit' (3.4.14–15). This emphasis on 'equality' between friends like Antonio and Bassanio contradicts the assumption that Antonio is an old father figure to young Bassanio and therefore presents 'a recognizable pattern of homosexual attachment'.[16] Moreover, true friendship includes mutual assistance as a manifestation of love, which could be emblematically presented as personified Cupids helping each other.[17] By not giving Antonio a wife, Shakespeare continues to dramatise the claims of love in friendship as well as romance, even until the final moments of his festive conclusion.

If we can conclude anything about Antonio's sexual preferences, it might be that he tends to be removed from sexual concerns, whether male or female. Shakespeare keeps Antonio in the role of the 'dear' and 'true friend' (3.2.290, 307) – Bassanio's and now Portia's as well. We might object that Portia and Bassanio, however, get the best of two worlds, romance with each other and friendship with Antonio, whereas he gets 'only' friendship. The 'only' would be a typially modern evaluation because from a Renaissance perspective sexual activity could be seen as lessening the purity of a human relationship; male friendship, based on equality and virtue, is not supposed to include sex, as is common in the relationships between men and women.[18] According to the classical ideal, as expressed, for example, in Cicero's *De amicitia*, the friendship between men is considered the noblest of all possible human relationships and is ranked hierarchically higher than the relationship between men and women.[19] In the trial Antonio describes himself as 'a tainted wether of the flock' (4.1.114). Because 'wether' can signify a castrated ram or eunuch, this description has been used by Leo Rockas to suggest that Antonio is impotent or homosexual and by Ralph Berry to indicate a metaphorical sense of Antonio's sterility.[20] But homosexuals are definitely not impotents or eunuchs, and it seems most unlikely that Antonio would publicly declare either impotency or homosexuality in front of the court, the place nor the time being appropriate. Figurative eunuchism might seem a more likely interpretation because Antonio, like Don Pedro in *Much Ado About Nothing*, has no offspring and does not appear interested in marriage for himself. However, in metaphorical terms, Antonio is rich in affection and fruitful in good deeds so that he is neither emotionally nor spiritually sterile, and by the end of the play he is no longer financially sterile.

'Wether', however, can also simply mean a male sheep or ram, and it is so used in Wyclif's English translation of the Bible to identify the breeding rams ('the wethers') that Jacob separates from Laban's flock for his own wealth (Gn 30.35), the very story to which Shylock alludes in his confrontation over usury with Antonio.[21] Shakespeare uses 'wether' in this same sense in *As You Like It* (3.2.80–81) and *The Merry Wives of Windsor* (3.5.109–10), and so does Milton in his *Samson Agonistes*: 'a deceitful Concubine who shore me / Like a tame Wether, all my precious fleece' (ll. 537–8). Therefore, Shakespeare's figurative use of 'wether' for Antonio probably does not include its other possible meaning of sterility. The context for Antonio's utterance does not suggest a sense of castration because his self-description features two parallel constructions, the second of which conveys no nuance of sterility: 'a tainted wether of the flock' is paralleled by 'the weakest kind of fruit / Drops earliest to the ground, and so let me' (4.1.115–16).

On one hand, Antonio's emphasis on 'tainted' (diseased) and 'weakest' (unhealthy) is meant to comfort Bassanio and dissuade him from offering up himself in Antonio's place because within his community ('of the flock') Antonio sees himself as its most appropriate member for death. Similarly, in Antonio's second farewell, like his first leavetaking from Bassanio, he thinks of Bassanio's needs and repeats his former gesture of a manly handshake: 'Give me your hand, Bassanio. Fare you well. / Grieve not that I am fall'n to this for you' (4.1.261–2). Antonio once again seeks to comfort, not to upbraid, Bassanio by emphasising the appropriateness of his death, and in this respect, he proves a far kinder friend than Mercutio does to Romeo (3.1.90–108). On the other hand, as we have seen, Antonio's excessive preoccupation with Bassanio's remembrance of him unwisely neglects the new importance of Portia in Bassanio's life: 'You cannot better be employed, Bassanio, / Than to live still and write mine epitaph' (4.1.117–18). Although Antonio later rightly remembers Portia ('commend me to your honourable wife'), he undercuts that remembrance by competitive emotional rivalry with Portia for Bassanio's appraisal of the loves in his life: 'bid her be judge / Whether Bassanio had not once a love' (4.1.272–3).

Shakespeare structurally counterbalances Antonio's three requests for commemoration in the trial scene (4.1.117, 272, 446) with Bassanio's three sacrificial offers to save Antonio. The first of these offers (4.1.112–13) is uttered before Portia enters the courtroom so the theme of ideal friendship is pursued for its own sake, not just for the potential conflict of loyalties when one has to choose between the requests of friend and wife: 'The Jew shall have my flesh, blood, bones, and all, / Ere thou shalt lose for me one drop of blood' (4.1.112–13). Bassanio's second offer, like his first, focuses exclusively on self-sacrifice: 'I will be bound to pay it ten times o'er / On forfeit of my hands, my head, my heart' (4.1.207–9). It is Bassanio's third offer that has attracted the most critical attention, but it must be kept within the perspective of the other two offers. In response to the rising tension of the trial, the failure of his offers to deter Shylock from seeking Antonio's life, and Antonio's farewell and own testimony to how well he has loved Bassanio, Bassanio explodes with an offer that overreaches itself:

> Antonio, I am married to a wife
> Which is as dear to me as life itself;
> But life itself, my wife, and all the world,
> Are not with me esteemed above thy life.
> I would lose all, ay, sacrifice them all
> Here to this devil, to deliver you.
>   (4.1.278–83)

Portia, disguised as Balthazar, smartly remarks: 'Your wife would give you little thanks for that / If she were by to hear you make the offer' (4.1.284–8). Gratiano now chimes in to offer his wife on behalf of his friend, Antonio: 'I have a wife who I protest I love; / I would she were in heaven, so she could / Entreat some power to change this currish Jew' (4.1.286–8). Nerissa, disguised as Balthazar's clerk, retorts, ''Tis well you offer it behind her back; / The wish would make else an unquiet house' (4.1.289–90). Gratiano's offer comically parodies Bassanio's generosity because Gratiano does not offer himself but only his wife.

The men have a right to offer themselves, but in this moment of high-pitched emotion, they overreach themselves in offering the lives of their wives. The audience, knowing the real identity of the lawyer and the clerk, relishes the humour of their truthful rejoinders. Shylock's response parallels those of the wives in the letter of disapproval but not in the spirit of wry humour. After all, Portia and Nerissa are enacting the spirit of giving on behalf of Antonio through their disguised roles in this trial. Inimical to the spirit of giving, Shylock caustically condemns these Christian husbands as inferior to 'the stock of Barabbas' (4.1.292) because he does not rightly understand their well-meant, if exaggerated, intentions. The too liberal nature of these offers by Bassanio and Gratiano should not surprise us because Shakespeare has already linked these two friends through that shared foible. Were their offers to be literally executed on the spot, neither Bassanio nor Gratiano could probably live up to their words and tolerate the sacrifice of their wives. The discrepancy between what men vow to do and what they actually do is a realistic human problem of which Portia and Nerissa, as well as Shakespeare's audience, are quite well aware. The earlier *Love's Labour's Lost* opens with just such a conundrum, a well-meant oath shared by four young men that upcoming experience unbinds. Similarly, Bassanio and Gratiano intend well by their offers, but their verbal hyperbole would not withstand the test of action. Overwhelmed as they are by the trauma of this situation, they mis-speak and all too humanly promise more than they can or should deliver.

'A QUARREL HO, ALREADY!' (5.1.146)

The foundation for the rings episode of Act V is laid immediately after Bassanio hazards rightly for the leaden casket, and Portia herself hazards all she is and has, the gift of her complete love symbolised by the gift of the ring (3.2.170–1). But why does Portia add her conditional proviso? Portia cautions that if Bassanio loses or gives away this ring, its absence from his finger will 'presage the ruin of [his] love', which Portia reasonably predicts will then serve as her 'vantage to exclaim on [him]' (3.2.172–4). Does Portia's gift of her ring and the aftermath of its exchanges, as Karen Newman argues, mock 'the Elizabethan sex/gender system of exchange' so that 'Portia evokes the ideal of a proper Renaissance lady and then transgresses it; she becomes an unruly woman'?[22] Does Portia *become* unruly, or does she *feign* unruliness, later threatening sexual reprisals but not intending to enact them? If Portia becomes truly an unruly woman, why does her dominance of the masculine world of law derive from her prudently self-directed indebtedness to the masculine source for her legal knowledge, cousin Doctor Bellario? Portia's apparent unruliness seems to be less a self-serving strategy for personal ambition and more a playfully adventurous strategy for doing what is essentially good, equitable, and even kind, for others as well as herself.

Portia's conditional gift of her ring may be a subtly subversive manoeuvre of power, but it is not designed to overrule the humble offer of herself to her new lord. The dramatic exigency of a well made plot suggests that Shakespeare needs to set up the rings episode (a quarrel raised and resolved) with which he plans to conclude his play. Unlike his source, *Il Pecorone*, he does not spring the rings episode at the last moment without any prior preparation. But he also uses Portia's caveat to embellish further her wise awareness of general human frailty and particularly the fragility of male oaths. Her self-proclaimed empowerment here also limits itself to verbal power only – to scolding, exclaiming, 'lessoning' Bassanio for what would be his mistake. She threatens now no active consequences, no divorce in wealth or love, although her actual protest in Act V will adopt an appropriate sexual rhetoric of feigned consequences. The fact that Portia's initial gift of the ring is a conditional one, however, links it to other conditional gifts and favours in the play: e.g., Antonio's lending to Bassanio upon the condition of honour; Portia's, Nerissa's, and the suitors' acceptance of the Lord of Belmont's conditions for the casket test; Antonio's conditional judgement of Shylock in the trial, seconded by the Duke; and Portia's conditional re-presentation of the ring to Antonio to give to Bassanio. Interestingly, Shylock's conditional merry bond is one instance of *feigned* favour. Shakespeare's motif of conditionality heightens the potential for comic conflict because a condition can be met or violated. Conditional gifts and favours mirror real life and thereby enhance the degree of verisimilitude achieved in this romantic comedy.

Bassanio, moreover, fully recognises the symbolic value of Portia's ring, and with his characteristic hyperbolic exuberance, he makes too bold a promise: 'But when this ring / Parts from this finger, then parts life from hence: / O then be bold to say Bassanio's dead!' (3.2.183–5). Bassanio, of course, does not die when he gives away this ring, and Portia proves no 'mad woman' (4.1.441) to denounce him as she does. Portia and Nerissa earlier specified that one weakness of 'young men' is their tendency to be 'bragging jacks' (3.4.63, 77) and to swear what is not true or more than is wise to vow, to indulge in 'vehement oaths' (5.1.155). Before they leave Venice, they jestingly prophesy what sport they will have with this male weakness: 'We shall have old swearing / That they did give the rings away to men; / But we'll outface them, and outswear them too' (4.1.15–17). The Nerissa–Gratiano action provides comic duplication in a lighter, earthier vein, further enhancing the audience's perspective on the quarrel over fidelity between Portia and Bassanio.

Shakespeare ingeniously balances the positions of Bassanio and Portia in this lover's quarrel by pitting verbal fidelity against physical fidelity as the terms of their quarrel. A breach of faith is what is at stake in this argument. Bassanio has literally broken his pledge of faith to Portia regarding the ring. Portia repays Bassanio's verbal unfaithfulness by threatening bodily unfaithfulness.[23] Portia's and Nerissa's threatening of female physical infidelity appropriately suits male infidelity regarding those physical signs of marital fidelity, the betrothal rings. The ladies' specific threats also prepare for Gratiano's concluding pun in which he develops the bawdy meaning of 'ring' (5.1.307). Bassanio does not know, as does the audience, just how appropriate this feigned repayment is because Portia really limits her 'infidelity' to language itself, unaccompanied by correspondent deeds. In the Renaissance a man's honour depended essentially on his honesty; therefore, maintaining his honour was equivalent to keeping his word. A woman's honour depended essentially on her chastity; therefore, maintaining her honour was equivalent to keeping her chastity or physical 'honesty', that is, her abstinence from unlawful or immoral sexual activity.[24]

Portia aptly gives Bassanio a taste of what it feels like to experience a 'false heart of truth' (5.1.189) by articulating conjugal penalties in three worsening versions:

By heaven, I will ne'er come in your bed
Until I see the ring.

(5.1.190–1)

I'll not deny [the doctor] anything I have,
No, not my body, nor my husband's bed.

(5.1.227–8)

. . . pardon me, Bassanio,
For by this ring the doctor lay with me.

(5.1.258–9)

Shakespeare structurally balances Portia's three asseverations of justice with three ever more serious requests for pardon by Bassanio (5.1.219; 5.1.240; 5.1.247). The fallible nature of men's oaths receives added stress when Bassanio offers to swear now by Portia's fair eyes wherein he sees himself, and Portia wittily exposes the duplicity of such swearing: 'Swear by your double self, / And there's an oath of credit!' (5.1.245–6). Similarly, Gratiano's earlier attempt to swear 'by yonder moon' (5.1.142) would evoke the audience's laughter. Oaths were commonly sworn 'by' something of value, and so Juliet, in a reversal of this moment in our play, rebukes Romeo's attempt to swear his true love 'by' the inconstant moon; she asks him not to swear at all or, if he must, to swear by his 'gracious self' (2.2.107–16).

The bond of one's word is the verbal contract that parallels the written contract of the flesh bond in the play. Needing more consideration is precisely how this subject of oaths further unifies the plots of Venice and Belmont. Shakespeare enriches the motif of keeping one's personal faith with others by adding the motif of keeping one's religious faith with God. In Shakespeare's subtle use of biblical allusion the ideal for faithfulness is suggested by how God keeps faith with his people – the promise to Abram and his offspring, the blessing of Jacob, the rain of manna and the rain of mercy, the gift of love and redemption. As with the claims of justice and mercy, man must seek to emulate God's pattern of fidelity. Man, being human, often falls short. In addition to Bassanio's and Gratiano's verbal oaths, the other such significant oath in the play is Shylock's: 'And by our holy Sabaoth have I sworn / To have the due and forfeit of my bond' (4.1.36–7), and, 'An oath, an oath. I have an oath in heaven! / Shall I lay perjury upon my soul?' (4.1.224–5). Some judge Portia in the trial scene as guilty of insensitivity to Shylock's oath and the problem of perjury.[25] But that viewpoint ignores the larger context in which human oaths are placed in the trial, as well as overlooks the fact that Shylock's oath violates the Mosaic Law because he has sworn to murder another man; oaths that violate God's law are not obligatory, and therefore perjury does not apply. Serious oaths were often taken in a holy place; Morocco, Arragon, and Bassanio seem to take their oaths in 'the temple' (2.1.44; 2.9.2–3), and Shylock may go to his holy synagogue to swear an unholy oath (3.1.99–103). In the Old Testament Jews often swear lawfully by Yahweh's name (see Dt 6.13, gloss). In later Judaism, to prevent profaning

the name of Yahweh, other holy things are substituted in the for-
mula for an oath, such as to swear by heaven, by the temple, or
by the altar.

Oaths have their place in society, but they can be abused if
taken lightly or unnecessarily. The abuse of language signifies an
abuse of reason; wrong speaking and wrong thinking often go
hand-in-hand. It is precisely this problem of unnecessary oath-
taking and its relationship to human honesty that prompts the
New Testament message against the hypocritical Pharisees' hair-
splitting codification of formulaic oaths, for example, that it is
lawful to swear by the altar but not by the sacrifice on the altar.[26]
The advocacy of plain, honest speech and the avoidance of 'all
superstitious oaths' (Mt 5.34, gloss) are explicitly addressed in
Matthew's gospel – 'Swear not at all . . . by heaven, for it is the
throne of God' (5.34–7) – and in James's epistle –'swear not, neither by heaven, nor by earth, nor by any other oath: but let your
yea, be yea, and your nay, nay, lest ye fall into condemnation'
(5.12). The gloss on James's passage is most helpful for gaining
some perspective on the legitimacy of oaths by proper authority
versus illegitimate oaths of personal use: 'That which must be
affirmed, affirm it simply and without oath: likewise that which
must be denied: by this he taketh not from the magistrate his
authority who may require an oath for the maintenance of justice, judgement, and truth.' That Shylock swears 'by our holy
Sabaoth' recalls the formulaic language of the Pharisees criticised
in Matthew's gospel. 'Sabaoth' as the operative word, for Shylock's
oath 'in heaven' emphasises for the audience the irony of his oath
so unworthy of heaven; the Jews' holy Sabbath is a day of rest
from all labour, to say nothing of the unholy labour of cutting
bloody flesh in an act of murder.[27] Bassanio, Gratiano, and Shylock
all misuse the language of oaths in varying degrees of severity.
The proper use and the abuse of language serve as moral baro-
meters for evaluation of character.

The rings episode serves as a mock trial to allow Portia to practise
what she preached in Act IV and to heighten the self-knowledge
of Bassanio, Gratiano, and Antonio, educating Bassanio and
Gratiano about their unwise, excessive liberality and Antonio about
his unwise, excessive emotional expectation. The teasing discrepancy between knowing and doing enunciated by Portia early in
the play (1.2.11–18) surfaces again as Bassanio and Antonio are
prompted to act on the principle they know to be good, the principle

of giving and hazarding all. In the rings episode Bassanio and Gratiano are placed in the position of having to act symbolically on the liberal verbal offers they made to save Antonio by being asked to give the rings, symbols of all they have, to the lawyer and clerk who rescued Antonio. Portia is sometimes seen as responsible for contriving this test.[28] However, true to her humble nature, Portia needs no reward other than the satisfaction of having done a good deed: 'My mind was never more mercenary' (4.1.414).

It is Bassanio's insistence that sets in motion the dilemma over the rings. The Duke instructs Antonio to gratify the civil doctor, but Bassanio jumps in to offer as financial compensation the 'three thousand ducats due unto the Jew' (4.1.407) before Antonio can express how forever indebted 'in love and service' they are (4.1.409–10). After Portia's gracious refusal of reward, Bassanio persists that the lawyer take 'some remembrance' as 'a tribute / Not as a fee', begging that he not be denied and that he be pardoned (4.1.418–20). Portia's response reflects the nature of Bassanio's importunity: 'You press me far, and therefore I will yield' (4.1.421). She asks for Antonio's gloves, which she will wear for his sake, and for Bassanio's 'love' she asks to have his ring. Bassanio's embarrassed reluctance, physically indicated by his immediate withdrawal of his hand (4.1.423), first voices itself in a lie; 'Alas, it is a trifle; / I will not shame myself to give you this' (4.1.426–7), as he shames himself with equivocation. Bassanio proves uncharacteristically hesitant here because the requested gift of love bears the consequence of violated faith.

The discussion in the rings episode reiterates the mottos of the casket choices. Now Portia *desires* the ring ('now methinks I have a mind to it') and then claims she *deserves* the ring ('And know well I have deserv'd this ring') (4.1.429, 442). Although Bassanio does promise to buy in its stead 'the dearest ring in Venice', he is judged guilty of being 'liberal in offers' (4.1.430–6). Bassanio finally explains the true meaning of the ring. Portia cleverly responds that even if this is not just another of Bassanio's excuses, no woman would be mad enough to remain angry at her husband if she knew the circumstances under which the ring was given. But Portia does not ask for the ring again; she desists and leaves. Despite such shameful humiliation Bassanio does not give the ring; he chooses not to break faith with Portia. Only at Antonio's potent request does Bassanio finally give away his ring, and it is

Bassanio's *action* that prompts Portia to stage her mock trial, not his earlier verbal offer of all he has to save Antonio.[29] Antonio's involvement in the rings episode is precisely Shakespeare's crucial change of his source where the merchant is excluded and the husband acts on his own initiative. The importance of the ring stems from its meaning, the occasion upon which it is given, and the fact that it is a 'first gift' (5.1.167). Antonio now knows the importance of this sacred thing or 'ceremony' (5.1.206) to the wife who generously sent her new spouse with a surplus of gold to save his friend. None the less, Antonio urges Bassanio to break his vow to this very wife; 'Let him have the ring, / Let *his deservings* and *my love* withal / Be valued 'gainst your wife's *commandement'* (4.1.446–7, my italics).

Bassanio's dilemma here is not unlike Antonio's earlier one caused by the important bond of friendship. What should he do for friendship's sake? Just as Antonio found himself in a dilemma of choosing between loving his friend and violating a principle to achieve that act of love (1.3), so now Bassanio has to choose between an act of love and the violation of an oath to achieve that act. Bassanio repeats the leaden choice, this time, however, for his friend Antonio and this time in violation, not obedience, to an oath. The critical difference between these two tough choices is that Antonio resolves his with a greater rein of freedom, whereas Bassanio's choice is far more constrained. Herein both Bassanio and Shylock in the same scene find themselves constrained by Antonio to choose the difficult option of giving and hazarding that he himself has endured after discovering the full consequences of this choice in his bond with Shylock for Bassanio.

However, Antonio's constraining request for Bassanio *contrasts* with his request for Shylock because now Antonio practises mental usury and is deliberately self-serving in his demand. The essential difference for Antonio between these juxtaposed moments of influential constraint concerns his own degree of selfishness. When Portia appeals to Antonio to season justice with mercy, Antonio thinks he responds unselfishly by doing Shylock a favour, a conditional favour for which Shylock must give in return. Other than administering Shylock's trust, the supposedly destitute Antonio gains little for himself. When Bassanio and Antonio return to Belmont, Bassanio's description of his friend as one 'to whom [he is] so infinitely bound' (5.1.135) provokes Portia's clever rejoinder: 'You should in all sense be much bound to him, / For as

I hear he was much bound for you' (5.1.136–7). Portia, however, does not lose sight of how infinitely bound she is to Antonio for giving Bassanio to her by financing his venture. The manner of her imminent ring ceremony will testify to this as the language and action of bonding continues to resonate in the play's conclusion.

During Portia's witty arraignment of Bassanio, he bears his discomfort without directly indicting Antonio, so unlike Gratiano's 'telltale' (5.1.123) report on Bassanio: 'My lord Bassanio gave his ring away / Unto the judge that *begged* it, and indeed / *Deserved* it too' (5.1.179–81, my italics). Bassanio also graciously shoulders his friend's blame by declaring that his own 'honour' – 'beset with shame and courtesy' – could not suffer such 'ingratitude' to 'besmear it'; therefore, he 'was enforced' to give away the ring (5.1.216–19). Bassanio's proud sense of his male honour parallels Antonio's similar sense of honour in requesting Bassanio to give up the ring as a necessary gift of gratitude to reward the doctor. Although Portia left before she could hear Antonio's ring request, she might well surmise his role on the basis of what she already knows and Gratiano's hint when he hands her the ring: 'My lord Bassanio *upon more advice* / Hath sent you here this ring' (4.2.6–7, my italics). Portia ingeniously repeats her original argument against unreasonableness regarding the gift of the ring, only she changes the gender of who is being unreasonable to suit each scene. The 'wife', who would be 'mad' to remain opposed to such a gift (4.1.441–4), now becomes the unreasonable 'man' to ask that such a gift be given: 'What man is there so much unreasonable . . . / To urge the thing held as a ceremony?' (5.1.204–6).

Portia's 'man' refers ostensibly to the lawyer, but her reference is comically double-edged because what man there is who would – and did – so urge such a gift stands quite uncomfortably before her. Much of the humour in this scene stems from the audience's knowing discernment of the characters' different levels of awareness, here with Antonio and later with Bassanio, who earnestly pleads to Portia: 'Had you been there I think you would have begged / The ring of me to give the worthy doctor' (5.1.221–2). The extent to which Bassanio has felt pressured to break his oath manifests itself in his use of 'enforced' twice within eight lines of speech (5.1.216, 240). The first instance applies to his own enforcing honour, but the second reflects implicitly the enforcing influence of Antonio. Antonio steps forward and voluntarily indicts himself, 'I am th'unhappy subject of these quarrels' (5.1.238).

After Antonio's admission of his involvement, Bassanio begs, 'Portia, forgive me this enforcèd wrong' (5.1.240).

Choices involving a stiff measure of constraint or enforcement pervade this play, giving its comic conundrums substance and depth. Could Bassanio honourably refuse Antonio's request?[30] In making a request that necessitates a violation of fidelity, Antonio ironically violates for himself his own caveat about honour when he initially tells Bassanio that he will grant his request upon the grounds of honour (1.1.134–8). Now Antonio witnesses the consequences of his interference; he recognises that he has overstepped his bounds in succumbing to a faulty logic similar to Bassanio's in the trial – 'To do a great right, do a little wrong' (4.1.212). Antonio misconstrues his request for Bassanio to do a wrong (violate Portia's commandment) as doing a greater right (rewarding the deserts of the lawyer and himself). This same logic tainted Antonio's earlier intentions in the play 'to break a custom' (1.3.56) against usury in order to help Bassanio. In both these instances Antonio's intentions appear good but are morally suspect. Antonio's pride in his love for Bassanio and Bassanio's pride in his love for Antonio prompt them to violate principles in order to demonstrate that love or have it rewarded. In Chaucer's discussion of humility as the virtue that remedies pride and enables true self-knowledge, his fourth aspect of the virtue – a man cares not that other men 'holde hym nought worth' – is the aspect of humility that proves a stumbling block for both Antonio and Bassanio in their relationship.[31]

'AND DO YOU ... MEAN GOOD FAITH?' (3.2.210)

The resolution of the dilemma of the rings repeats the spirit of the casket choice, and Shakespeare's purposeful repetition of that choice suggests that it is a perennial choice: the choice of the leaden casket must be repeatedly reaffirmed in the course of true living and loving. During Portia's mock inquisition, Bassanio's three pleas to defend his giving of the ring (5.1.186–222) recall his earlier three pleas to defend himself from having to give the ring (4.1.426–39). He would lie if he could (as he did earlier in dismissing the ring as a trifle), but his naked finger betrays him (5.1.186–8). His second and third defences stress the *desire* ('naught would be accepted but the ring') and the *desert* ('he that held up the very

life / Of my dear friend') of the civil doctor (5.1.197, 214–15).
Portia counters by emphasising her desire and desert (5.1.199–
206) and by recalling for us Bassanio's own awareness of his weakness as being 'something too prodigal' (1.1.128): 'I will become
as *liberal* as you' (5.1.226, my italics). In a play that appreciates
the proper place of wealth in life, Bassanio's excessive prodigality needs taming. As a self-designated 'wilful youth' (1.1.145)
Bassanio has nearly beggared his inheritance through his lack of
prudence and must not do likewise to Portia's wealth that is now
his.[32]

Three different times Bassanio asks for Portia to forgive him
(5.1.220, 240, 247). In the confrontation over the ring bond, like
the interpretation of the flesh bond, Portia stands against the
falsification of the letter of a bond. Bassanio has indeed literally
broken his pledge never to part with the ring. His giving of it,
however, does not 'presage the ruin of [his] love', as Portia thought
it might (3.2.173). Shakespeare presents Portia wisely aware of
the potential for error in the man she loves, aware that lovers are
more eager 'to seal love's bonds new made than . . . / To keep
obligèd faith unforfeited' (2.6.7–8). Because she understands how
things 'are with more spirit chasèd than enjoyed' (2.6.13–14), she
wisely resolves on exclamation, not repudiation. Portia's ring, like
Othello's handkerchief, is very important as a lover's 'first gift'
(5.1.167); unlike Othello and his tragic situation, however, Portia
will forgive her beloved's 'loss' of the first gift given. Like
Desdemona, Portia knows that 'we must think men are not gods'
(*Oth.* 3.4.148). Despite Bassanio's literal failure 'to keep obligèd
faith unforfeited', the love between Bassanio and Portia remains
intact. That love is the spiritual reality that the physical ring merely
symbolises. However, Bassanio, possessing greater knowledge of
himself and his bonds with Portia and Antonio, truly desires and
deserves Portia's forgiveness. This time he vows his fidelity not
on his physical life but on his spiritual life: 'Pardon this fault,
and by my soul I swear / I nevermore will break an oath with
thee' (5.1.247–8).

Although Antonio is still ignorant about how infinitely bound
he is to Portia, he repentantly seeks forgiveness for himself (5.1.238)
and now for Bassanio (5.1.249–53), adhering to Bassanio's spiritual
orientation. Antonio dares to be bound again, this time with greater
humility and knowledge of himself and his friendship with
Bassanio. He vows to be Bassanio's 'surety' (5.1.254) in a soul

bond with Portia for Bassanio's fidelity to her: 'My soul upon the forfeit, that your lord / Will nevermore break faith advisedly' (5.1.252–3). The final adverb means 'intentionally' and may also pun on Antonio's role as a friendly advisor to Bassanio. Given human frailty, Antonio and Bassanio knowingly risk more in this soul bond than they knowingly did in their flesh bond with Shylock. Recalling the casket mottos and pride of Morocco and Arragon, Antonio's and Bassanio's love for one another has been gradually revealed through the rings episode as unwisely demanding too much of 'desire' – the mutual recognition and return of that love – and of 'desert' – a too exquisite sense of one's honour and the opinion of others. The soul bond offered to Portia by Antonio and Bassanio resolves the former imbalances. Both men once again give and hazard, this time their souls, that neither desire nor desert will overmatch Bassanio's keeping faith with Portia. Portia wisely triumphs in this scene, but she is not tying 'to break the last remaining bond that holds her husband to a former love'.[33] It is not so much that friendship must be 'subordinate' to marriage, as Anne Barton maintains, but that friendship should not be placed above marriage.[34] It is not so much that Antonio must acknowledge 'the exclusivity and primacy of the marital relationship' and 'the priority of Portia's claim', as Jan Lawson Hinely argues, but that one love should not serve to excuse the violation of another.[35]

Portia's response demonstrates that she never intended to threaten male friendship in any way. She does not rebuke Antonio but becomes 'a good divine that follows [her] own instructions' (1.2.12–13) because she forgives both Antonio and Bassanio with the return of the ring. By schooling the men through merry scolding, the women enact playful justice, counter-exchanging female *threats* of physical infidelity for male *acts* of verbal infidelity. This mock trial more humorously recapitulates the preceding trial's emphasis on mercy seasoning justice. Portia reenacts the gift of the original ring to Bassanio, this time by intentionally including Antonio. Before the ring is returned, Bassanio and Antonio initiate their own conditions for keeping faith with Portia. Portia responds to their conditions of a new soul bond with her important gesture and admonition, 'Then you [Antonio] shall be his surety. Give him this, / And bid him keep it better than the other' (5.1.254–5). Portia herself values her own willingness and ability to learn (3.2.16–62), and like Antonio and Bassanio, Portia also faces opportunities for personal development. She is so wondrous to begin with that her growth takes more the form of refinement and revelation of potential than dramatic change. While uttering her approval of Antonio's suretyship, she could have handed the ring herself directly to Bassanio, bypassing Antonio. Shakespeare chooses rather to emphasise a new triadic bond by her significant physical gesture.

Portia harmoniously *includes* Antonio in her relationship with Bassanio by handing Antonio the ring to give to Bassanio. Earlier Portia revealed her remarkable understanding of 'god-like amity' in how she described the nature of the friendship between Bassanio and Antonio. There Portia expanded the love of their friendship to include herself in their bond. Because Bassanio and she love each other and because Antonio is 'the bosom lover of [her] lord' (3.4.17), she can see Antonio as 'the semblance of [her] soul' (3.4.20). Through Portia's inclusive vision of male–female friendship, Shakespeare innovatively advances for his era the potential for loving unity between the sexes outside of marriage. As Eugene Waith demonstrates, the classical ideal of male friendship as the noblest of human relationships was often offset in Elizabethan literature by the supposedly inferior relationship between men and women: 'The love of men to women is a thing common and of course: the friendship of man to man infinite and immortal.'[36]

Shakespeare ennobles Portia's character by making her capable of knowing and acting upon the classical ideal of friendship usually reserved unto men alone. The idea that a woman can be a man's dear friend finds specific expression in Aelred of Rievaulx's medieval philosophy of friendship, which suggests a wife and husband should be good friends and guide their marital love by the spiritual love of friendship.[37] In the seventeenth century Jeremy Taylor considers some of the biases against men having women as friends. In his discourse on friendship Taylor specifically refutes the view that women cannot keep secrets by citing the story of Porcia's self-inflicted wound to prove her trustworthiness to Brutus, a story that Shakespeare retells in his *Julius Caesar*. This evidence supports Taylor's view that 'some wives have been the best friends in the world'.[38] But despite his tendency to open-mindedness, Taylor also limits the extent to which a woman can befriend a man: 'a man is the best friend in trouble, but a woman may be equal to him in the days of joy: a woman can as well increase our comforts, but cannot so well lessen our sorrows: and therefore we do not carry women with us when we go to fight: but, in peaceful cities and times, virtuous women are the beauties of society and the prettinesses of friendship'.[39] Shakespeare's Portia has more in common with the fighting spirit of Spenser's Una. Her battles are psychomachias, and where men fail, she proves herself a source of strength and solace in a difficult trial of life-and-death hazards.

Shakespeare gives to a woman the explicit Ciceronian defini-tion that male friendship is dependent upon equality and virtue (3.4.11–18); he thereby honours Portia as a woman equal to the noblest of men in the understanding and practice of true friend-ship. If anything, Portia spiritualises the idea of friendship by constantly emphasising the union of souls between friends. As with the true friendship between Hamlet and Horatio, Shakespeare elevates spiritual equality over the mundane concerns of economic or social equality. Although not equal in gender to Bassanio and Antonio, Portia proves to be their spiritual equal in the bonding of souls. Her wisdom regarding the fallibility of hot blood overleaping cold decrees informs her acceptance and forgiveness of failings in her friends. Taylor advises friends: 'But however, do not think thou didst contract alliance with an angel, when thou didst take thy friend into thy bosom; he may be weak as well as thou art, and thou mayst need pardon as well as he . . . the love of friends . . . must be allowed its share of both [the human and the divine]: it is human in giving pardon and fair construc-tion, and openness and ingenuity, and keeping secrets; it hath something that is divine, because it is beneficent; but much be-cause it is eternal.'[40] The initial admiration of the men for the women deepens in respect because Portia and Nerissa earn that respect by proving through their deed of rescue that love can lead fortune. The trial scene and the final rings episode allows the women to equal the men in the active mode as adventurers and choosers, not just the ventured for or chosen. In the trial scene the women literally give and hazard, and in the final scene they join the men in symbolically enacting the leaden choice.

Although Portia masterminds this reckoning of Bassanio and Antonio, her forgiveness is genuine. No matter what she knows and surmises about the circumstances regarding Bassanio's gift of her ring, the fact remains that Bassanio did break his deeply sworn oath. Therefore, Portia playfully carries her instruction a step further when she pardons Bassanio by re-giving him her ring through Antonio's hand and simultaneously asks Bassanio to pardon her for laying with that civil doctor. Fortunately, the speechless Bassanio seems not to be of Leontes' mind, but Gratiano forcefully objects that they have neither desired nor deserved this (5.1.263–5). Despite its comic ending, this 'trial', like its predecessor, has been painful for all the men concerned. For a split second Bassanio and Gratiano are in the position of having to be forgiving of their 'wayward' wives. But Portia once again comes quickly to the rescue and dispels their amazement through her truthful explanation, only to increase their wonder through seemingly miraculous tangible rewards for Antonio and Lorenzo and Jessica. Stephen Orgel suggests that English Renaissance literature reveals 'a generalized misogyny . . . even in its idealization of chaste and beautiful women who are also cold and untouchable'.[41] Shakespeare's non-misogynistic depiction of Portia and Nerissa contradicts this and may contribute to why audiences, past and present, would find Portia and Nerissa so attractive. In puzzling over why 'Portia's and Nerissa's ring trick' might appeal to Elizabethan women, Orgel suggests that this ending 'plays on both the male fears and the female fantasies of a patriarchal society' so from a female perspective the ending might be seen as 'a declaration of independence'.[42] But the re-giving of the ring is a re-declaration of male and female interdependence or mutual bonding, grounded on pledged marital fidelity. Portia and Nerissa neither intend cuckoldry nor desire 'independence'. This ring episode is not generated by the faults of wives but by the faults of husbands that wives try to amend lovingly and with a full measure of good humour.

In Belmont, as in Venice, the comedic spirit prevails with mercy seasoning justice. In having both given and received mercy, Antonio becomes 'twice blest' (4.1.182). Antonio does not lose an old friend but gains a new friend in Portia, who rewards him with the return of half his former wealth. Like Shylock, Antonio is granted 'life' in the trial, but 'living' is not awarded until after Antonio has bound himself anew in his soul bond with Portia. Now Portia addresses Antonio by name (5.1.286), rather than 'Sir' (5.1.139, 239). Acting upon her initial hint that Antonio's welcome would appear in more than 'breathing courtesy' (5.1.141), Portia gives him the uplifting letter about his argosies. Portia is now Antonio's 'sweet lady' (5.1.286). Shakespeare significantly restores half of Antonio's wealth, unlike *Il Pecorone*, in which the merchant does not recover any of his lost wealth, but instead marries the Lady of Belmont's maid. It is through Antonio's intercession that Shylock mercifully receives again the entire half of his wealth awarded to the State; it is through Portia that Antonio miraculously receives again half of his original wealth. Antonio and Portia parallel each other in the kind dispensation of wealth. The return of three of Antonio's ships, not all six originally ventured forth (4.1.314–18), probably relates not only to the idea of hazard inherent in merchantry but also to the idea of a virtuous kind of usury, namely spiritual usury. Spiritual usury is defined as 'liberality towards the poor and needy', that God will reward with 'a most liberal increase, as it were a *threefold* usury'.[43] Antonio's consistent financial liberality to the needy earns him a threefold increase, whereas Shylock is denied a threefold increase on his principal when he is finally willing to accept that offer (4.1.314–18).

In response to Portia's joyfully providential news about his argosies, Antonio exclaims, 'I am dumb!' (5.1.279), meaning, of course, that he is so overwhelmed that he is at a loss for words. For Antonio joyful silence replaces the melancholic stillness that Gratiano found so distasteful in the opening scene. The play comes full circle with the leitmotif of the 'dumb wise man' (1.1.86–106). Antonio may be seen as the true dumb wise man now, treasuring anew his wealth and his love's wealth. What appears to be a tragic beginning for Antonio is converted to a comic conclusion. After Antonio reads the letter, he confirms the certainty of its contents and finds the words to thank Portia: 'Sweet lady, you have *given* me life and living' (5.1.286, my italics). As in John Lyly's *Endimion*, both friendship and romance end up being winners. Just as Portia included Antonio in the manner of her ring ceremony, so also she probably includes him in the manner of the final 'exeunt'. As the couples pace off the stage, one couple has become a threesome, a circle of friends. A fitting exit for this triad of friends would be an arm-in-arm exit with Portia as the new link between Bassanio and Antonio. The advantage of visualising the number three for the last time, and in this way, relates to the meaning of that number which has been so prevalent, in various ways, throughout the play. This triad of friends now symbolises both love and harmony. Dante uses the number three to symbolise love, and as Alastair Fowler explains, 'With the triad, according to Pythagorean number theory, comes reversion to the limitation of oddness: unity and diversity are restored to harmony.'[44]

Punctuating closure of the final scene are the husbands' amazed and grateful questions as they discover their comic dimension of ignorance while the wives and the audience delight in that process of happy discovery: 'Were you the doctor . . . Were you the clerk?' (5.1.280–1). The women playfully reassume their legal identities as doctor and clerk as soon as the men recognise them. Staying in role, Portia informs Lorenzo that her 'clerk' has 'good comforts' for him too, which Nerissa jestingly proclaims she will 'give . . . without a fee' (5.1.290). This celebratory emphasis on 'giving' also incorporates the final mention of 'the rich Jew' (5.1.292). Shylock's presence is recalled symbolically through his 'special deed of gift' to his daughter and son-in-law (5.1.291–3, my italics). Lorenzo's appreciation of the 'fair ladies' who dispense such a life-sustaining gift also embraces his 'father Jew' (2.6.26), because he figuratively sees Shylock's gift as 'manna' for the starving. Lorenzo's metaphor likens the seemingly miraculous nature of Shylock's fatherly provision to God's fatherly care of his needy children by dropping manna from heaven (5.1.294–5). Although Portia and Nerissa are the agents who deliver Shylock's gift, Lorenzo's biblically providential metaphor recalls for the audience the biblically providential role (Prv 28.8) Antonio plays as the originator of this gift that mercifully orders what could be called 'the two usuries' (moneylending and propagation).[45] Shylock's financial 'breeding' will be given to 'feed' the needs of human breeding, including his own offspring.

With the day about to dawn, Portia promises 'to give light, but . . . not be light' (5.1.129) for she and Nerissa will answer 'faithfully' all 'inter'gatories' (5.1.295–9). Portia's and Nerissa's witty return to legal posturing allows Gratiano to exit as he began, playing the eponymous role of the fool. Now that the women are to be sworn under oath to tell the truth, the only truth Gratiano sportively cares about is Nerissa's choice of 'couching' time. Throughout this concluding act Gratiano's recurrent bawdry provides an engaging counterpoint to the ladies' politely expressed sexual threats and to the more honourable diction of Bassanio and Antonio. Because Gratiano is the only one of the troupe who explicitly enunciates his interest in bawdy body parts (5.1.144, 237, 265, 307), the final pun on Nerissa's 'ring' aptly suits Gratiano's indecorous decorum. But the audience's culminating laughter, like so many highpoints in the play, derives much of its pleasure from Shakespeare's mixed methods, in this case the simultaneous operation of expectation and surprise. We are not surprised that Gratiano would close on a bawdy note, and therefore our expectations are gratified. But we are surprised to have a new meaning introduced for an old word in the play, the bawdy meaning of 'ring' as pudend, and therefore we experience the pleasure of surprise.

But that surprise does not mean that 'the sexual subordination of women (these women) . . . closes the play'.[46] The wife's re-giving of the ring and the husband's reaffirmation to keep safe the ring are gestures of *mutual* fidelity ('Love me, and leave me not', 5.1.150) that reiterate on a lighter note the re-giving and re-bonding of Portia, Bassanio, and Antonio. This time around, however, Gratiano's respectful rejoinder to Nerissa's pretence of cuckoldry invests Nerissa's hoop of gold with its fleshly meaning, matching his verbal and sexual fidelity to hers:

> *Gra.* Were you the clerk that is to make me cuckold?
> *Ner.* Ay, but the clerk that never means to do it.
>
> (5.1.281–2)

The play ends with a double ring ceremony and a double play on 'ring'. As an object that is a circle, the ring can represent different meanings: it can signify spiritual perfection (that which has no beginning or end) as well as the physical fertility of female sexuality. As an object made of precious material it can signify wealth. As a gift between lovers it signifies their love and fidelity to one another. The ring as 'a hoop of gold' has proved not 'paltry' but most fruitful as a symbolic prop (5.1.147).

The audience might now borrow Nerissa's line, 'it is now our time, / That have stood by and seen our wishes prosper, / To cry "good joy"' (3.2.186–8).[47] Joy accompanies faithfulness, as Edmund Spenser indicates by specifically naming one of the enemies against faith 'Sansjoy'.[48] C. L. Barber concludes that no other Shakespearian comedy, 'until the late romances, ends with so full an expression of harmony as that which we get in the opening of the final scene of *The Merchant of Venice*'.[49] The opening of this final scene effects not only an admirable tonal modulation between Act IV and Act V but also a remarkable anticipation of what is to come, pointing the way to how the play's final lines bring the play full circle. The scene opens with the heavenly harmony of Jessica's and Lorenzo's duet on the moonlit splendour of this lovers' night. The scene ends with Gratiano's earthy harmony that wishes for naught but night's cloak (dawn being two hours nigh) so that he and Nerissa might consummate their marriage. The movement of the scene is not a descent but an encircling, an inclusion of differences – heaven and earth, comic and tragic, darkness and light, male and female, anxiety and joy, division and union – so that, as Portia exclaims in her comparative appreciation of greater and lesser entities, 'Nothing is good, I see, without respect' (5.1.99). Cyclic imagery – moon, patens, rings, voyagers' returns, night and day – and imagery of light-in-darkness dominate this final scene and its playful movement from love's teasing to love's comedic teaching and harmonious re-bonding.

Jessica's and Lorenzo's tribute to the love-inspiring beauty of this night singles out classical allusions to lovers who had tragic endings; through this tragic 'foil' they offset all the more the comic ending of their flight on such a night as this. The 'letter' of their lyrical exchange is the infidelity of lovers and its tragic consequences, but the 'spirit' is the fidelity of lovers who tease one another with false 'slander' (5.1.22) only to summon forth a fuller profession of love. So did Portia tease Bassanio earlier about 'treason' mingled with his love (3.2.26–33), and so will she tease him again when she judges his treason regarding her first gift to him. Teasing, romantic and unromantic, is fundamentally productive of comic speech and action in this play. The challenge for the comedian is to keep the teasing laughably in-bounds, as in Portia's mockery of her suitors, so that teasing does not cross the line into outright cruelty, as Solanio's and Salarino's teasing of Shylock about Jessica's flight tends to do. Solanio's and Salarino's antagonistic humour is somewhat like that of Antonio and Sebastian, who also expend their wit in mockery to irritate others, including another grieving father figure, Alonso (*Tmp.* 2.1.140). In Shakespeare's audience surely some laughed *with* such insensitive mockers but others probably laughed *at* them as well. On the other hand, Lancelot's teasing of his blind father about his death loses such emotional poignancy because Lancelot is only joking and so confesses as soon as he sees his blind father's painful reaction to his joke.

The Jessica-Lorenzo interlude smoothly picks up their teasing conversation almost where we last left them. In their previous private moment on stage, they had begun discussing the merits of lovers, of wives and husbands. Jessica concludes, in response to Lorenzo's request for her view of Portia, that Bassanio 'finds the joys of heaven here on earth', and therefore Bassanio should live 'an upright life' to merit 'such a blessing' as Portia is, or he shall never come to heaven (3.5.61–71). Lorenzo quickly finishes

her final half line with his teasing self-praise: 'Even such a husband / Has thou of me, as she is for a wife' (3.5.71–2). Lorenzo's
'good sweet' (3.5.59) is equally quick to banter in return, 'Nay, but
ask my opinion too of that' (3.5.73). The parley of puns that follows
shows how comfortable Lorenzo and Jessica are in each other's love.

With this same witty manner Jessica tempts Lorenzo to protest
his love for her when she playfully accuses him of 'stealing her
soul with many vows of faith, / And ne'er a true one' (5.1.19–
20). That Lorenzo loves her well has been truly proved by his
keeping faith with her and by sharing his faith with her. Taking
the bait of false accusation by his 'pretty Jessica', who 'slanders'
him 'like a little shrew', Lorenzo '*forgave* it her' (5.1.21–2, my italics). This lighter comic context for forgiveness of breaches in faith
modulates the preceding trial's more serious treatment of love,
forgiveness, and faith and simultaneously anticipates these very
issues in the mock trial to follow. Literally and figuratively their
loving banter on love's tragic potential emphasises their own contentment by contrast to such tragic love and also foreshadows
the impending 'quarrel' among the newlyweds over vows not
faithfully kept. Both sets of lovers' 'quarrels' result in fuller professions of love. As music pours forth into the air, Lorenzo's discourse on music's 'sweet harmony' (5.1.57) uses the occasion of
instrumental music to relate to Jessica the essential concord of
the universe – the heavenly match between the music of the spheres
and its harmony in immortal souls. Although the angelic music
is inaudible to fleshly ears, 'the sweet power of [mortal] music'
is transformative in making 'attentive' the faculties of man and
animal (5.1.69–82). Lorenzo ends with a warning against 'the man
who hath no music in himself' and who therefore cannot 'be trusted'
(5.1.83–8). If Jessica relates this musical interpretation to her father,
as some members of the audience will by recalling Shylock's
antipathy for drum and fife music (2.5.28–9), it will not be her,
or our, last remembrance of him. On a far more comedic note
Shylock's absence from Belmont is commemorated through his
presence in the form of his 'special' deed of gift.

'EXCEED ACCOUNT' (3.2.157)

Anyone who has ever attempted to interpret the whole of this
play must be struck by Shakespeare's sophisticated articulation

of diverse ideas and feelings through complexly interrelated language patterns, actions, and characterisations. The sheer interconnectedness of the whole play daunts anyone who tries to analyse how the pieces of this mosaic fit together so intricately. The best way to appreciate the play's unity, of course, is to read it, to perform it, and to see it performed many times. The combined contributions of scholarly critics can answer many questions as well as raise more questions that need to be addressed. But no matter how responsibly scholars try to illuminate this play, the whole of it will always be greater than the mere sum of its parts. This play can never be 'fixed' in theatrical performance or in scholarly criticism. Trends for staging the play will continue to come and go, such as the nineteenth century's deletion of the fifth act or the twentieth century's presentation of Antonio's homoeroticism. But the living art of theatre is eternally mutable. In the hands of imaginative directors and actors the same speech or action can vary in import and in impact depending on seemingly small but significant choices of expression, such as a longer than expected pause, a cocked eyebrow, a shift in posture, or a change in vocal inflection. In the theatre the play enjoys a more flexibly fluid state of realisation that is denied to the critic, who is in the unenviable position of having to commit ideas to print that remain 'fixed' until the next go-round.

However, a close study of this play reminds us once again how much we need to uncover and recover in order to appreciate older and somewhat 'foreign' literary works. For example, we might refrain from labelling some aspect of this play as subversive until we understand, as best we can, the historical and literary context for that aspect. After such understanding, imperfect as it may be, we then confront the subsequent task of trying to determine how Shakespeare is using that aspect, whether modifying, endorsing, or criticising it. The concept of usury in late sixteenth-century England is a classic case in point, and as such it points to the inherent difficulty of the archeological task of ideological retrieval. For the modern age the giving and taking of interest has become accepted financial wisdom. Despite new progressive arguments in the debate over usury, for Shakespeare's society usury is still officially regarded as a sin and a crime, a violation of God's law and man's law, even though the growing popular 'toleration' of the rate of ten per cent is one of the unintended effects of the Act Against Usury of 1571. For the twentieth century the intent and action of lending in business has nothing to do with loving one another and everything to do with making a profit. How foreign to our ears sounds the old theory that 'God ordained lending for maintenance of amity, and declaration of love, betwixt man and man' and therefore condemned lending 'used for private benefit and oppression . . . [so that] no charity is used at all'.[50]

There are also, of course, some radical differences between modern and sixteenth-century perceptions of ideas we consider 'familiar'. Shakespeare challenges some of our assumptions about what is legal, what is good, and what is desirable because these notions can vary with culture and period, just as he confronted divorces between theories and practices in his own time. We, theoretically at least, have less condemnation for 'rebellion', for a disobedient daughter, especially if she's not our own child, than Elizabethan society would. Likewise, Elizabethans would greet the request for conversion to Christianity as potentially salvific, whereas we find any such request a violation of personal religious freedom. As Tyrone Guthrie notes, Antonio is pivotal to the plot of *The Merchant of Venice*, but it is difficult for a modern director to bring out Antonio's importance in a production.[51] One reason it would be easier for an Elizabethan audience to see Antonio's central importance in the play is their greater familiarity with the play's ideological context – ideas about usury, merchantry, love, law – and the various use of these ideas in Elizabethan literature that we must now 'recover' in order to 'see' as they could 'see'. Experiencing a play like *The Merchant of Venice*, whether in performance or study, especially excites us because there is always something new to discover.

Shakespeare's consummate creation of artistic unity out of so many contrarieties that make up *The Merchant of Venice* contributes significantly to why this play continues to haunt us as it does. So close-knit a dramatic texture depends much on subtle, refined discernments, on repeated acts of fair discrimination. Wise generosity should not be confused with foolish prodigality, nor should lawful justice be confused with unlawful revenge. Nor should 'love' be delimited to 'desire', as Morocco does in his choice to '*gain* what many men *desire*' (2.9.23, my italics) and as do several recent critics.[52] Both concepts of 'love' and 'desire' appear in the play and are carefully discriminated in the casket test. Lacanian psychoanalysis may be used to illuminate the concept of 'desire', but Shakespeare's play contains its concept of 'desire' within its own judicious perspective.[53] Desire is one element in love, but it must be properly oriented and ordered so that it serves, not swamps, love. Desire is not dangerous because it is hazardous but because it is primarily selfish; love is primarily self-giving. Perhaps there is no history in Western literature of 'happy love', as Denis de Rougemont claims, because 'happy love' is not the same idea as 'wise love'.[54] Wise love expects no primrose path of happiness without unhappiness along the way; wise love chooses to endure pain, sorrow, difficulty, change, hazard, and even death, yet 'bears it out even to the edge of doom' (Sonnet 116).

In her exploration of how *The Merchant of Venice* might illuminate its own as well as 'our own cultural moment', Catherine Belsey tentatively, but rightly, questions the conclusion that 'since Freud we have learned that all intense emotion is "really" sexual . . . and since *The Merchant of Venice* we have known that marriage, which includes every imaginable adult relationship, ought to be enough for anyone'.[55] Not 'marriage', however, but *friendship* seems to be the dominant and most inclusive adult relationship that Shakespeare celebrates in his remarkable treatment of love and its governing spiritual direction in this play. Husbands and wives should also be true friends, not just lovers, if marriages are to have comedic consequences. During the development of the modern period definitions of such fundamental ideas as 'wealth' and 'love' have increasingly narrowed down to a physical and secular meaning and have moved away from the older medieval–Renaissance emphasis on a spiritual dimension that elevates the physical. The wealth of true love is therefore primarily an 'expense of spirit' that is not wasted in shame (Sonnet 129). Although *The Merchant of Venice* can teach us much about ourselves, we can at best only approximate a recovery of some of its artistic wealth, given the degree of difficulty for reconstructing what is now 'lost' to us from the sixteenth century.

One reason why *The Merchant of Venice* is such a complex play is the variety and difficulty of its ideational discriminations. The play engages its audience, then and now, in felt discriminations between counterpoised concepts of crucial importance. What is false? True? What is appearance? Reality? What is folly? Wisdom? What is weakness? Strength? What is love? Lust? How do we know? And if we know, how do we choose? And how should we choose? Shakespeare's Friar Lawrence suggests a more complex interrelation of virtue and vice than simple opposition usually warrants: 'Virtue itself turns vice, being misapplied, / And vice sometime by action dignified' (*Rom.* 2.3.21–2). Antonio's virtue of love for Bassanio turns inside-out when he is initially willing to apply that love through hateful usury and by using the man he hates. Bassanio's vice of breaking a serious oath is dignified by his action of gratitude in rewarding deserving persons. The play celebrates not the virtue of power but rather the power of virtue. An emphasis on power as independent self-assertion that breaks ties that bind is seasoned by an emphasis on power as dependent self-sacrifice that fosters ties that bind. The secular power of the whiphand is countered by the spiritual power of the merciful heart. As Isabella reminds us, 'Why, all the souls that were were forfeit once, / And He that might the vantage best have took / Found out the remedy' (*MM* 2.2.73–5). Critics often see a conflict between law and love in this play, a conflict that often does exist between human law and love. But there is no such conflict for divine law and love, which Elizabethans believed humans were called to emulate. Paul equates law and love because the fulfilment of the entire law is accomplished through the law of love, love of God and neighbour (Rom 13.8–10). Shakespeare counterbalances the conflict between human law and love in the trial with the ideal resolution of such conflict through Portia's call to the imitation of the divine law of love. Both giving and forgiving are vital ideas that foreground the play's dramatic conflicts and resolutions.

Shakespeare further complicates his honed nuances of ideas by fleshing them out in a character's speech or action that can *attract and alienate* simultaneously our own thoughts and feelings. Often we are invited to feel for or with a character at the same time that we are challenged to evaluate the merits of that character's speech or action. Thus Shakespeare cultivates a fused tension bewteen imaginative empathy and aesthetic distance. If 'we' may be used loosely to indicate some (not all), we empathise with Antonio's desire to help his dear friend, but we cannot condone his inhumane treatment of Shylock for his usury. We feel for Shylock's raw anger at Antonio's mockery of his usurious gains, but we cannot approve his choice of bloody revenge. We empathise with Portia's feisty frustration over her tightly circumscribed freedom, but we would not readily condone a flouting of her 'holy' (1.2.23) father's deathbed inspiration. We sympathise with

Jessica's incarceration by an unwise, cold father, but we, knowing the true value of Shylock's turquoise ring (as Jessica probably does not) cannot rejoice over her stealing and casual selling of it. We can understand Antonio's need to have his friend Bassanio appreciate his sacrifice and to have proof of the equal return of Bassanio's love for him, but we might also think Antonio presses Bassanio too far. We understand how torn Bassanio is when he has to decide whether or not to give away Portia's ring, but even though the recipient is Portia herself in transvestite disguise, we also know that Bassanio has a habit of getting himself into compromising situations or ones conducive to his prodigal bent.

A close examination of the play-text increases our appreciation of Shakespeare's frequently daring use of *reversal* as a strategy for dramatic irony to engage and to manipulate the audience's and / or the characters' *expectations*. A master of verbal and dramatic paradox, this poet-dramatist uses disguise to unmask disguise, sacrifice to find fulfilment, and disharmony to know harmony. The play pervasively emphasises a counterbalance within rightly conceived hierarchy that complements Portia's idea of 'seasoning'. In twentieth-century productions Shylock's dramatic energy often overshadows the rest of the cast and the play itself. But Shakespeare's scenic architecture and linguistic cross-links suggest that a production might do better to 'season' the dramatic energies of the principal players – Portia, Bassanio, Antonio, and Shylock – by counterweighting their interplay and resisting the temptation to write more stage business for Shylock than the text implies.

If Shakespeare's comedy takes the pleasurably educative curve through the comparative perspective that Sidney advocates, at the end of the play we smile appreciatively at all that has been learned and felt through experiencing the stage as our imaginary world. Sidney's theory of comedy, that human folly is best exposed through foils, reverberates in Portia's awareness that human perception is refined through the principle of 'seasoning' (5.1.92–100). Such a principle engenders in Shakespeare's art true delight in the comparative use of multiple contrasts. As we have seen, some of these contrasts appear in his literary sources, but he adds many others. For example, the contrast between justice and mercy that so many critics find to be the backbone of the play is Shakespeare's addition to *Il Pecorone*, in which the disguised Lady of Belmonte delivers no speech on mercy nor even mentions mercy, and the

Jew receives no mercy, only strict justice. The concept and ideal of human friendship, without and within the state of marriage, is another such addition by Shakespeare, as is the contrast between free and usurious lending, as well as the theme of giving and hazarding that contrasts with the gain-and-get theme of desiring and deserving. Like Spenser, Shakespeare revels in syncretic vision, and in Shakespeare's play the two largest sources for allusive reference that he attempts to synthesise are the classical and biblical worlds.

For his Elizabethan audience Shakespeare gets the best of both worlds, the foreign and the familiar. Shakespeare heightens the theatrical entertainment value of his source's exotic settings, Italy's Venice and Belmont. But he also creates a local habitation for his Jewish usurer and Christian merchant by interrelating Elizabethan ideas (old and new) about usury with Elizabethan figurative, not just literal, definitions of 'Jew' and 'Christian'. 'Conversions' in various forms – name, crossdressing, wealth, and faith – pervade the play, and figurative, as well as literal, conversions occur in Shakespeare's fusion of the economies of finance and faith. The play's interplay of faith and wealth turns on the trope of conversion. For example, Christians figuratively become Jews if they practise usury (Antonio's mental usury of Acts III–IV), and Jews figuratively become Christians if they do not practise usury (Shylock's feigned and figurative conversion of Act I, Scene 3). The *Elizabethan* idea of the figurative conversion from Christian to Jew through wrong choices (e.g., Antonio's hatred, or Gratiano's vengeful attitude) promotes the spirit of tragedy. But from an Elizabethan perspective the figurative conversion of Christian from Jewish to Christian service (e.g., Lancelot's exchange of masters), or the literal conversion of Jew to Christianity (Jessica and Shylock) is used to defeat the spirit of tragedy – death and destitution – and to promote the comic spirit of ongoing life and living. Within the play the literal conversion of Jew to Christian is not counterbalanced by its exact reversal. Thus, in the play Christianity – not simply its practitioners, who vary in degree of fallibility – is prejudicially regarded as the true faith for salvation. This should come as no surprise given the religious bias of Elizabethan England. But in Shakespeare's play no group – Jew or Christian, male or female, rich or poor – has a monopoly on the problems of human ignorance and sinfulness or on the blessings of wisdom and love. The admirably attractive Portia is the play's lodestar, but although she may be presented as ideally human, human she is in her impatience, hopes, doubts, fears, playfulness, and humour. Within the Elizabethan plays of Wilson, Marlowe, and Shakespeare, both Christians and Jews fall as well as rise to the doctrines of their native faiths.

Shakespeare's originality in handling his literary source material involves not only the creation of new matter and the deletion of old matter but also the deft rearticulation and rearrangement of what is borrowed. In redesigning his sources Shakespeare 're-envisions' them: he disciplines their teeming multiplicity by establishing an interlocking sequence of scenes and by forging a network of interconnections among characters, words, deeds, ideas props, and costumes. These interconnections also repeat their patterns in varying degrees of levity or of gravity. For example, Portia's forgiveness in the rings episode is not nearly as weighty as the challenge to Antonio and Shylock to exchange forgiveness. On the other hand, Lancelot's verbal witticism with Shylock (2.5) is not as boisterously laughable as his facetious tricking of his father, in which he overplays his hand, or the father's and son's garbled suit to Bassanio (2.2), or even Lancelot's defying the matter with 'a tricksy word' (3.5.57) in his witsnapping with Lorenzo. Contextualising the play inside Shakespeare's canon as well as outside it, within contexts to which the play explicitly refers, such as usury debates or the Bible, contributes to identifying larger patterns of meaning that help to make sense of small linguistic details, such as Shakespeare's wordplay on pirates or publican. Even something as seemingly minor as a character's name can be charged with more significance, both etymological and functional, than we usually grant. Unlike the names in *Romeo and Juliet*, most of which derive from Shakespeare's main literary source, all the characters' names in *The Merchant of Venice* comprise deliberate artistic choices by Shakespeare, despite the nomenclature available to him in his literary sources.

If we take the basic critical concern with Shakespeare's attempt to integrate two apparently different plots from medieval sources and explore that 'union' within a wide range of possibilities afforded by history and literature, we find that Shakespeare not only interrelates the plots linguistically, structurally, and thematically, but also he counterbalances aspects of their dramatic functions. The casket plot provides a conceptual centre, and the flesh-bond plot provides a suspenseful climax. The identification of possible new sources for the play, such as Wilson's and Mosse's treatises on usury and Herrey's concordance of biblical names, will necessarily continue. But we also need to remain alert to seeing new ways in which he used the old, and generally recognised, sources. For this play Shakespeare's apparent range in reading and his retentive memory are almost as impressive as his imaginative employment of what he reads and recalls. Shakespeare's deletions are usually suggestive, but his additions are usually even more revealing. For example, to *Il Pecorone* he adds the medieval casket choice; the history of personal enmity between merchant and Jew; the issues of usury, friendship, and mercy; the development of stage law for the trial; the advantages and disadvantages of legal literalism, depending on how well used and for what end; the legal risk of wealth attendant upon a strict interpretation of the bond; the legal penalty for life and wealth attendant upon the proved violation of Venetian law; the roles and judgements of the Duke and Antonio in the trial; the merchant's role in the rings episode; the duplication of actions and relationships (Gratiano/Nerissa, Jessica/Lorenzo, the Gobbos), to say nothing of his more sensitive and sophisticated development of all the main characters, and his addition of other minor characters, such as Tubal, Solanio, Salarino, and Salerio. To the casket story and its allegorisation Shakespeare adds the will of a dead father; the oaths and injunctions; two suitors and their speeches and actions; and he changes the gender of suitor from female to male, significantly develops all the speech acts, and uses the caskets as symbolic props for the whole play, including his added distinction between giving and getting.

The process of 'seeing' in *The Merchant of Venice* is developmental, that is, a learning process attained, if it is, not without some effort, 'lest too light winning / Make the prize light' (*Tmp.* 1.2.452–3). Portia, for example, holds the answers (the interpretations that resolve the crises) to the play's three main tests or trials – the casket test, the Venetian trial, and the Belmontian mock trial. But like a good teacher, she offers clues but withholds the answers until others undergo for themselves the process of discovery. Much of this process entails some degree of discomfort and indicates the positive potential of suffering that fosters growth, not destruction. As Kent in *King Lear* expresses it, 'Nothing almost sees miracles / But misery' (2.2.165–6). Antonio's keen distress, Shylock's unexpected defeat, Portia's rigid confinement,

Jessica's familial deprivation, and Bassanio's guilty embarrassment all contribute to I/eye-opening opportunities. Whether in thematic or practical terms, recognitions of 'identity' and conquests of heart and mind are usually prefaced by some purgative period – a period of loss, exile, and searching that is common to both Shakespeare's comedies and tragedies. Antonio bemoans, 'Such a want-wit sadness makes of me, / That I have much ado to know myself' (1.1.6–7), and Gloucester bewails, 'I stumbled when I saw' (*Lr* 4.1.19). But how very difficult it is in our own lives to look at our misery philosophically. Shakespeare voices this perspective too. Romeo lashes back at Friar Lawrence's patient counsel, 'Hang up philosophy! / . . . Thou canst not speak of that thou dost not feel' (3.3.57–64). And Benedick astutely observes: 'Well, every one / Can master a grief but he that has it' (3.2.28).

In many of Shakespeare's plays, no matter how major or minor the suffering appears to be, the characters bear testimony to the spirit of human endurance. Even in a play as wrenchingly painful as *King Lear*, the cherishing of life persists in the voice of Edgar, who explains how he survived the pursuit of death:

(O, our lives' sweetness!
That we the pain of death would hourly die
Rather than die at once!), taught me to shift
Into a madman's rags, t'assume a semblance
That very dogs disdained.
                                        (5.3.185–8)

Literal death is avoided in *The Merchant of Venice*, as it is not in *The Tragedy of the Jew of Malta*. Shakespeare experiments with much more than the containment of Marlowe. Shakespeare seems to find Marlowe's voice less a source of threatening influence than an important catalyst for his own revisionist approach, which features his remarkable reversals of Marlowe's generic expectations and his characters' final fates. None the less, Shakespeare remains specifically indebted to his predecessor's play in matters large and small, such as voluntary/involuntary as well as true/feigned conversion, the Jew's good daughter, the source for Hebrew names, and even some speech patterns, images, and character traits. But in Shakespeare's comedy, with its temporary restraint of Time's sickle, all the characters enjoy the gift of more time for life and another chance for better living. And as 'sweet' as may be the gift of life itself, the 'sweetness' of love is perhaps greater. As Desdemona so movingly avows about Othello: 'Unkindness may do much, / And his unkindness may defeat my life, / But never taint my love' (4.2.159–61). But Shakespeare also enacts the destructive power of suffering when it is viciously inflicted or not well endured. Antonio's past history of unchristian, cruel, personal ridicule of Shylock for his practice of biting usury festers in Shylock's heart to breed his own repayment of personal hate and 'hellish cruelty' (3.4.21). When the cunning of malice dazzles before our eyes, we must ask with King Lear, 'Is there any cause in nature that make these hard hearts?' (3.6.77–8). Realistically enough, Shakespeare's dramatic worlds include such unrepentants as Don John, Barnardine, Iago, Goneril, and Regan. Suffering, however, has an educative value when it contributes to making humans more fully human in fostering their mutual understanding of empathy and love.

Although the theatre pleasurably affords its audience wish fulfilment and escape into fantasy, the characters on stage actively confront the play's conflicts on our behalf. The literary – not literal – escapism prompted by Shakespeare's plays may be seen not so much as an escape 'from' reality but rather as an escape 'into' the reality of his art. Shakespeare's imaginative innovations and his transmutative refashioning of a wide variety of materials for *The Merchant of Venice* are most impressive for the degree of artistic integrity Shakespeare achieves through his multifaceted embodiment on stage of a unifying poetic conception of wise love. In *The Merchant of Venice* the rhythm of Dantean divine comedy blesses the trials and tribulations, the hard choices, of the play's characters to the degree that they, and we, arrive at a greater heartfelt understanding of 'the love that moves the sun and all the stars'.[56]

Notes

Notes to the Preface

1. James C. Bulman (ed.), *The Merchant of Venice*, Shakespeare in Performance (Manchester and New York: Manchester University Press, 1991) p. 1. An excellent edition that came too late to my attention to be used in my text is *The Merchant of Venice* (Shakespeare's Globe Acting Edition), edited by Patrick Tucker and Michael Holden (London: M. H. Publications, 1991). For a helpful overview of stage history and major professional productions (1940–79), see Thomas Wheeler (ed.), *The Merchant of Venice: An Annotated Bibliography* (New York & London: Garland Publishing, 1985) pp. 257–30. Cf. Orson Welles and Roger Hill (eds), *The Merchant of Venice*, The Mercury Shakespeare (ed. for reading and arr. for staging) (New York and London: Harper & Brothers, 1939); Toby Lelyveld, *Shylock on the Stage* (1960; rpt. London: Routledge & Kegan Paul, 1961); John Russell Brown (ed.), *The Merchant of Venice* (New Arden Shakespeare) (1955; rpt. London: Methuen, 1969) pp. xxxii–xxxvi; John Russell Brown, 'The Realization of Shylock: A Theatrical Criticism', in *Early Shakespeare*, eds John Russell Brown and Bernard Harris (London: Edward Arnold, 1961) pp. 186–209; M. M. Mahood (ed.), *The Merchant of Venice*, New Cambridge Shakespeare (Cambridge: Cambridge University Press, 1987) pp. 42–53.
2. On 6 October 1986 at Georgetown University I was fortunate to attend Patrick Stewart's 'Shylock and Other Strangers', a spellbinding one-man, 90-minute 'lecture/performance', in which Stewart emphasised the thematic cash nexus of the play and the motivation of money, but he did not focus on the idea of usurious wealth or Shylock's profession of usury.
3. See D. W. Robertson, Jr, *A Preface to Chaucer: Studies in Medieval Perspectives* (Princeton: Princeton University Press, 1962) pp. 340–2, 352, 355, 365.
4. See T. Hawkes, *Meaning by Shakespeare* (London and New York: Routledge, 1992) p. 3. Subsequent quotations are from p. 3.
5. Richard M. Restak, M.D., *The Mind* (New York: Bantam Books, 1988) p. 205; subsequent quotations are from pp. 261–2.
6. W. Cohen, 'The Merchant of Venice and the Possibilities of Historical Criticism', *ELH*, **49** (1982) pp. 765–89; quotation is from p. 766.
7. Ibid., pp. 768, 773.
8. See Norman Jones, *God and the Moneylenders: Usury and Law in Early Modern England* (Oxford and Cambridge, MA: Basil Blackwell, 1989) pp. 199–205.
9. Cohen, pp. 772–3.

10. See Thomas Wilson, *A Discourse upon Usury* [1572], ed. R. H. Tawney (New York: Harcourt Brace, 1925) p. 231; cf. p. 258.
11. Cohen, p. 774.
12. Ibid., p. 776.
13. Ibid., p. 775.
14. For a list of such attempts, see Richard A. Gray, 'Case Studies in Censorship: Censoring *The Merchant of Venice*', *RSR: Reference Services Rev.*, **19**, iii (1991) pp. 55–69.
15. See T. Cartelli, *Marlowe, Shakespeare, and the Economy of Theatrical Experience* (Philadelphia: University of Pennsylvania Press, 1991). I am grateful to Bruce Smith for bringing this book to my attention.
16. See, e.g., Margreta de Grazia, *Shakespeare 'Verbatim': The Reproduction of Authenticity and the 1790 Apparatus* (Oxford: Oxford University Press, 1990).
17. See Chapter 1, n. 15.
18. See, e.g., Stephen Greenblatt, *Renaissance Self-Fashioning: From More to Shakespeare* (Chicago: University of Chicago Press, 1980); Paul Yachnin, 'The Powerless Theater', *ELR*, **21** (1991) pp. 49–74.

Notes to Chapter 1

1. C. S. Lewis, *The Discarded Image: An Introduction to Medieval and Renaissance Literature* (Cambridge: Cambridge University Press, 1970) p. 222. I am grateful to Father James P. Walsh, S.J., for reading an early draft of this chapter.
2. C. W. R. D. Moseley, *Shakespeare's History Plays: Richard II to Henry V*, Penguin Critical Studies, ed. Bryan Loughrey (London: Penguin, 1988) p. 5.
3. For Renaissance critical theory, see William Rossky, 'Imagination in the English Renaissance: Psychology and Poetic', *Studies in the Renaissance*, **5** (1958) pp. 49–73, esp. 58–9. Cf. John Milton, *Paradise Lost*, ed. Merritt Y. Hughes (New York: Odyssey Press, 1962) Book V, ll. 100–9.
4. O. B. Hardison, 'Shakespearean Tragedy: The Mind in Search of the World', *UC*, **6** (1986) p. 80.
5. Madeleine Doran, *Endeavors of Art: A Study of Form in Elizabethan Drama* (Madison: University of Wisconsin Press, 1954) pp. 3–6, 370–6.
6. Ibid., p. 6.
7. Wölfflin, *Principles of Art History*, cited in Doran, ibid., p. 6.
8. Doran, ibid., p. 372.
9. M. M. Mahood (ed.), *The Merchant of Venice*, New Cambridge Shakespeare (Cambridge: Cambridge University Press, 1987) p. 8. All quotations are from this edition and will be cited parenthetically in the text.
10. Lawrence Danson, *The Harmonies of 'The Merchant of Venice'* (New Haven and London: Yale University Press, 1978) p. 2.

11. Horace, *Ars Poetica*, in *Satires, Epistles, and Ars Poetica*, trans. H. Rushton Fairclough (1926; rev. & rpt. London: William Heinemann, 1929) pp. 478–9, ll. 333–4, 343–4: '*omne tulit punctum qui miscuit utile dulci, / Lectorem delectando pariterque monendo*'.

12. See Sir Philip Sidney, *An Apology for Poetry*, ed. Forrest G. Robinson (Indianapolis: Bobbs-Merill, 1970) pp. 23–4; 22, 38, 46. See Spenser, 'A Letter ... to ... Sir Walter Raleigh', in *The Faerie Queene*, ed. Thomas P. Roche, Jr (Harmondsworth: Penguin, 1978) p. 15.

13. Milton, *Areopagitica*, in *John Milton: Prose Selections*, ed. Merritt Y. Hughes, Odyssey Series in Literature (New York: Odyssey Press, 1947) pp. 224–5.

14. Nashe, *Pierce Penilesse* (1592), in *The Works of Thomas Nashe*, ed. Ronald B. McKerrow, 5 vols (1904–10; rpt. Oxford: Basil Blackwell, 1958) vol. 1, pp. 213–14. All references to Nashe's works are to this edition; volume and page will be cited parenthetically in the text.

15. Sidney, p. 44.

16. Arthur Sherbo (ed.), *Johnson on Shakespeare: The Yale Edition of the Works of Samuel Johnson* (New Haven: Yale University Press, 1958–90) vol. 7 (1968) p. 62.

17. A. Kirsch, *Shakespeare and the Experience of Love* (Cambridge: Cambridge University Press, 1981) p. 4. See also Marion Trousdale's astute analysis of a sixteenth-century view of language and literature in *Shakespeare and the Rhetoricians* (Chapel Hill: University of North Carolina Press, 1982) esp. pp. 114–18, 125–33, 146–51, 160–72.

18. Kirsch, p. 8. Cf. Barbara Lewalski, 'Biblical Allusion and Allegory in *The Merchant of Venice*', *SQ*, **13** (1962) pp. 327–8.

19. John Milton, *Paradise Lost*, ed. Merritt Y. Hughes (New York: Odyssey Press, 1962) ll. 589–94, pp. 199–200.

20. Unless specified otherwise, all quotations from the Bible are to the Geneva version (1560) and will be documented parenthetically in the text. See *The Geneva Bible* (a facsimile of the 1560 edition), intro. by Lloyd E. Berry (Madison: University of Wisconsin Press, 1969).

21. J. R. Brown (ed.), *The Merchant of Venice* (New Arden Shakespeare) (1955; rpt. London: Methuen, 1969) p. xxxvii.

22. See Richmond Noble, *Shakespeare's Biblical Knowledge and Use of the Book of Common Prayer* (1935; rpt. New York: Octagon Books, 1970) pp. 6–12, 58–9. Cf. Naseeb Shaheen, *Biblical References in Shakespeare's Tragedies* (Newark: University of Delaware Press; London and Toronto: Associated University Presses, 1987) pp. 27–8.

23. See Noble, pp. 96, 161; Mahood, pp. 184–8; Frank McCombie, 'Wisdom as Touchstone in *The Merchant of Venice*', *New Blackfriars*, **64** (1982) n. 13; Naseeb Shaheen, 'Shakespeare's Knowledge of the Bible – How Acquired', *ShakS*, **20** (1988) p. 212.

24. Lewalski, p. 327.

25. McCombie, p. 123; Shaheen, 'Shakespeare's Knowledge', p. 212. McCombie argues that Shakespeare used the Bible even more closely

than Noble suggests (p. 123), and elsewhere I have presented evidence suggesting even closer use for this particular play. See my essay 'Miles Mosse's *The Arraignment and Conviction of Vsurie* (1595): A New Source for *The Merchant of Venice*', *ShakS*, **21** (1993) pp. 11–54. This essay argues that Mosse's text is an important new source for understanding Shakespeare's use of usury in his play.

26. The term anti-Judaic conveys the sense of religious bias, the term anti-Semitic conveys more of a sense of racial bias, as well as religious bias, and anti-Zionist conveys the sense of political or national bias.

27. Danson, p. 59. In the extant vernacular drama of the Elizabethan period, there appear to be only four plays that feature Jewish characters: Wilson's *The Three Ladies of London* (1584), Marlowe's *The Jew of Malta* (1588; revival 1594), Greene's *Selimus* (1594), and Shakespeare's *The Merchant of Venice* (1597).

28. For information about several Jews in Elizabethan England, two 'known' (Joachim Ganz and Nathaniel Judah) and one secret (Ferdinand Alvares), see Salo W. Baron, *A Social and Religious History of the Jews*, 2nd edn, 16 vols (New York: Columbia University Press, 1952–76) vol. 15, pp. 126–7; cf. also, vol. 13, pp. 125–9. Richard Popkin has recently discovered that there was an actual Jewish merchant from Venice in England from 1596 to 1600. Alonso Nuñez de Herrera, in the employ of the Sultan of Morocco, was in Cadiz at the time of the Earl of Essex's raid and thus became one of the forty hostages transported to England for ransom. Popkin wonders if Herrera could have been 'a model for Shylock'. We need more information about Herrera to answer that question, but on the basis of what is known, Herrera, a most learned expositor of the Lurianic Cabbala and a successful *merchant*, does not at all resemble Shylock. Popkin suggests 'the phrase "The Merchant of Venice" could well have been associated with an actual merchant of Venice in London', Herrera. The play's title probably does not recall this actual Jewish merchant from Venice because Shakespeare's Jew is a usurer who thinks merchantry as a way to thrive is too risky. Shakespeare's merchant is a Christian, and Shakespeare derived his Venetian setting as well as the idea of a rich Christian merchant of Venice from his literary source, *Il Pecorone*. See R. Popkin, 'A Jewish Merchant of Venice', *SQ*, **40** (1989) pp. 329–31.

29. See Lucien Wolf, 'Jews in Elizabethan England', *Transactions of the Jewish Historical Society of England*, **11** (1924–7) pp. 8–9; C. J. Sisson, 'A Colony of Jews in Shakespeare's London', *E&S*, **23** (1937) pp. 38–51; Mahood, p. 19; *Encyclopedia Judaica*, 16 vols (Jerusalem: Encyclopedia Judaica, 1972) vol. 6, pp. 752–3.

30. See, e.g., Arthur B. Stonex, 'The Usurer in Elizabethan Drama', *PMLA*, **31** (1916) pp. 190–210; Arthur B. Stonex, 'Money Lending and Money-Lenders in England During the 16th and 17th Centuries', in *Schelling Anniversary Papers* (New York: Russell & Russell, 1923) pp. 263–85; Celeste Turner Wright, 'Some Conventions Regarding the Usurer in Elizabethan Literature', *SP*, **35** (1934) pp.

176–97; Celeste Turner Wright, 'The Usurer's Sin in Elizabethan Literature', *SP*, **35** (1938) pp. 178–94; J. W. Draper, 'Usury in *The Merchant of Venice*', *MP*, **33** (1935) pp. 37–47; E. C. Pettet, '*The Merchant of Venice* and the Problem of Usury', *E&S*, **31** (1945) pp. 19–33; Laura Caroline Stevenson, *Praise and Paradox: Merchants and Craftsmen in Elizabethan Popular Literature* (Cambridge: Cambridge University Press, 1984) pp. 92–106; and Norman Jones, *God and the Moneylenders: Usury and Law in Early Modern England* (Oxford and Cambridge, MA: Basil Blackwell, 1989) pp. 29, 172–3.

31. G. K. Hunter, 'The Theology of Marlowe's *The Jew of Malta*', *Journal of the Warburg and Courtauld Institute*, **17** (1964) p. 214.
32. Alan C. Dessen, 'The Elizabethan Stage Jew and Christian Example: Gerontus, Barabas, and Shylock', *MLQ*, **35** (1974) pp. 231–45, esp. 243.
33. See Geoffrey Bullough (ed.), *Narrative and Dramatic Sources of Shakespeare*, 8 vols (1957; 5th imp. London and Henley: Routledge and Kegan Paul and New York: Columbia University Press, 1977) vol. 1, pp. 450–1, 476–82. For an interesting but uneven argument that Wilson's work is a source for Shakespeare's *The Merchant of Venice*, see G. W. Cameron, *Robert Wilson and the Plays of Shakespeare* (Riverton, New Zealand: G. W. Cameron, 1982) pp. 68–72. The case for Wilson is not generally accepted, but Cameron does overlook the major point of comparison, the subject of usury and the contrast between Jewish and Christian behaviour to the detriment of the 'Christian'. There are two other possible minor points: (1) the tripling of marriages is unusual and is found in this play; and (2) only in this comedy do the same terms of Shylock's loan appear (3000 ducats for three months), albeit formulated in a different manner – initially 2000 ducats for three months but an additional 1000 was obtained through 'flatterie'. See Bullough, vol. 1, p. 478.
34. M. J. Landa, *The Jew in Drama*, intro. Murray Roston (1924; New York: Ktav Publishing House, 1969) p. 78. Cf. Barbara Tovey, 'The Golden Casket: An Interpretation of *The Merchant of Venice*', in *Shakespeare as Political Thinker*, eds John Alvis and Thomas G. West (Durham: Carolina Academic Press, 1981) pp. 233–4: 'the play also contains a veiled criticism of Christianity . . . what Shakespeare takes to be a corresponding flaw in the principles of Christianity'. Cf. Walter Cohen, who suggests that although the Christians in the play 'have fairly settled accounts with Shylock . . . the trouble is that Christianity has not', see Walter Cohen, '*The Merchant of Venice* and the Possibilities of Historical Criticism', *ELH*, **49** (1982) p. 773.
35. Heiko Augustinus Oberman, *Wurzein des anti-Semitismus* (*The Roots of Anti-Semitism in the Age of Renaissance and Reformation*), tr. James I. Porter (Philadelphia: Fortress Press, 1984) p. xi, *et passim*, esp. Ch. 18, 'The Jew and "We Wicked Christians"', pp. 123–4, and 'Epilogue: The Stony Path to Coexistence', pp. 138–43. The technical definition of 'race' in the anthropological sense can differ from popular use and misuse of the term. See Stanley M. Garn, *Human*

Races (Springfield, Ill.: Charles C. Thomas, 1961) pp. 3–9; cf. 127–32. For the complicated modern identification of Jews, see John R. Baker, *Race* (New York and London: Oxford University Press, 1974) pp. 232–47. Although religious bias can shade into racial bias, scholars, such as Heiko Oberman and G. K. Hunter, argue that the Elizabethan bias against Jews stems primarily from spiritual, not physical, characteristics. For example, Salarino's cruel taunt emphasises a spiritually qualitative difference between Shylock's and Jessica's literally shared flesh and blood (3.1.31–3); Jessica also values moral over physical lineage (2.3.17–18).

36. Nashe, e.g., uses 'converted' in this general sense to describe Jews who need 'to repent and be converted', again in God their Father. See Nashe, vol. 2, p. 19.

37. See Michael Ragussis, 'Representation, Conversion, and Literary Form: *Harrington* and the Novel of Jewish Identity', *Critical Inquiry*, **16** (1989) pp. 113–43.

38. See Danson, pp. 164–9. This historical penalty for Christian conversion compares very unfavourably with Robert Wilson's fictional version of the reward for conversion to Mohammedanism, namely the forgiveness of all debts, in his play *The Three Ladies of London*. See Bullough, vol. 1, pp. 480–1. For the entire play, see H. S. D. Mithdal (ed.), *An Edition of Robert Wilson's 'Three Ladies of London' and Three Lords and Three Ladies of London'*, in The Renaissance Imagination, vol. 36 (New York: Garland, 1988). Likewise, before the Counter-Reformation in Italy, Jews could avoid punishment for crimes by converting to Christianity. See William Monter, *Ritual, Myth and Magic in Early Modern Europe* (Athens, Ohio: Ohio University Press, 1984) p. 156.

39. Oberman, p. 13.

40. Monter, p. 37. The United Netherlands, despite its penal laws against Roman Catholics, probably enjoyed one of the best records among European governments regarding *de facto* religious toleration; Jews settled peacefully in this northern asylum some fifty years before Cromwell invited their return to England.

41. See David C. McPherson, *Shakespeare, Jonson, and the Myth of Venice* (Newark: University of Delaware Press; London and Toronto: Associated University Presses, 1990) pp. 61–7.

42. For information about assimilation of the Iberian Sephardim, as well as the German Ashkenazim, see Monter, pp. 155–64. Cf. also, Salo W. Baron, Arcadius Kahan *et al., Economic History of the Jews*, ed. Nachum Gross (New York: Schocken Books, 1975) pp. 56–7.

43. See Monter, pp. 170, 172. Regarding the history of religious toleration, see also Joseph Lecler, S.J., *Toleration and the Reformation* (London: Association Press, 1960); Henry Kamen, *The Rise of Toleration* (New York: Weidenfeld and Nicolson, 1967); Elisabeth Labrousse, *Pierre Bayle*, 2 vols (The Hague, 1963–4).

44. Elizabeth Labrousse, 'Religious Toleration', in *Dictionary of the History of Ideas: Studies of Selected Pivotal Ideas*, 4 vols (New York: Charles Scribner's Sons, 1968–73) vol. 4, p. 114; cf. pp. 112–20.

45. For a modern literary portrayal of this matter, see the short story 'The Lame Shall Enter First', by Flannery O'Connor, in *The Complete Stories* (1946; rpt. New York: Farrar, Straus and Giroux, 1974) pp. 445–82: 'I don't care if he's good or not. He aint *right!*' (p. 454).
46. Edmund Spenser's Una (Oneness) in Book I of his *Faerie Queene* exemplifies the necessary ideological union of truth and faith without which the Redcross Knight (Holiness) cannot be holy.
47. See, e.g., Mahood, p. 19.
48. See Joseph ben Gorion, *A Compendious . . . History of the Latter Times of the Jews' Common Weal*, trans. Peter Morwyng (London: Richard Jugge, 1561). (The standard name for the author is Joseph ben Gorion, ha-Kohen, but he is also referred to as Josippon or Yosippon.) All references will be to this edition. Cf. McKerrow (ed.), *The Works of Thomas Nashe*, vol. 4, pp. 212–23.
49. See *DNB*, vol. 13, pp. 1067–8.
50. Morwyng (trans.), sig. 3^{r-v}.
51. Ibid., sig. 5^{r-v}.
52. Ibid., sig. 5^v.
53. Ibid., sig. 5^v.
54. Ibid., sig. 6^v.
55. See ibid., sigs $Ee2^{r-v}$, et passim.
56. Ibid., sig. 5^v.
57. See T. Wilson, *A Discourse upon Usury* [1572], ed. R. H. Tawney (New York: Harcourt Brace, 1925) p. 363.
58. G. R. Hibbard, *Thomas Nashe: A Critical Introduction* (Cambridge: Harvard University Press) p. 253.
59. Ibid., p. 124.
60. Nashe probably directly derives the specific idea of Christ's lamentation from John Stockwood's sermon on the destruction of Jerusalem (1584). See McKerrow, vol. 4, p. 213. But Nashe may also derive some hints from the lamentation voiced by the sole surviving Jewish leader of the seditionists, Eleazar, at the end of Joseph's text. (See sigs $Kk2^v$–$Kk6^v$.) If so, Nashe further adapts Jewish history to serve his own needs for his Christian audience.
61. Nashe reminds his audience that some of the same signs – pestilence, famine, and earthquake – prophesied in the book of Daniel for the destruction of Jerusalem have already appeared for London, although they have not been heeded. See Nashe, vol. 2, pp. 172–3.
62. Oberman, pp. 123–34.
63. See Hibbard, p. 173.
64. See McKerrow, vol. 4, p. 292. McKerrow suspects that Nashe had seen this tract. Although the tortures inflicted on Dr Fian [alias John Cunningham] are designed not simply to punish him, as in Zadoch's case, but to extort the truth about his pact with the devil, these tortures are somewhat similar to those Nashe describes, and indeed, embellishes: the fingernails are removed by pincers and under every nail two needles are thrust wholly in, his legs, from

ankle to knee, are crushed in the cruel torment of the boots, and eventually he is strangled and burned. See Robert Pitcairn's *Criminal Trials in Scotland . . .*, vol. 1, pt 2 (1569–1593) (Edinburgh: William Tail and London: Longman, Rees, Orme, Brown, Green, & Longman, 1833) pp. 222–3.

65. Hibbard, p. 174.
66. Ruy is the technically correct name; see Mahood, p. 7, n. 1. But I will use the more familiar name 'Roderigo', as did Shakespeare's contemporaries, like Sir Francis Bacon.
67. C. Spencer, *The Genesis of Shakespeare's 'The Merchant of Venice'*, Studies in British Literature, vol. 3 (Lampeter, Dyfed, Wales: Edwin Mellen Press, 1988) pp. 79–80.
68. *DNB*, vol. 12, p. 134.
69. See Sidney Lee for other possible references, including a pun on wolf and Lopez/Lopus, cited in C. Spencer, pp. 79–80.
70. Margaret Hotine argues that the revival of Marlowe's *The Jew of Malta* at the time of Lopez's trial and execution in 1594 suggests that it 'could have been used to help create anti-Semitic prejudice', but Shakespeare's play appears to be 'a counterblast to recent anti-Semitism'. See Margaret Hotine, 'The Politics of Anti-Semitism: *The Jew of Malta* and *The Merchant of Venice*', *N&Q*, **38** (March 1991) pp. 35, 38.
71. See William Camden, *Annales – Tomus Alter, & Idem: or The History of the Life and Reign of . . . Elizabeth*, trans. Thomas Browne (London: Thomas Harper, 1629) p. 105. Cf. Arthur Dimock, 'The Conspiracy of Dr. Lopez', *English Historical Review*, **9** (1894) pp. 440–72.
72. See Nashe, vol. 3, pp. 215–16. Nashe appears to reflect the general view of those who attended Lopez's trial, but the Queen herself seems to remain unconvinced.
73. *DNB*, vol. 12, p. 134.
74. Camden, p. 105.
75. See Frank Marcham (ed.), *The Prototype of Shylock: Lopez the Jew . . . An Opinion by Gabriel Harvey* (London: Waterlow & Sons, 1927) p. 11.
76. Camden, p. 104.
77. Elizabeth reputedly scolded Essex when he obtained permission to examine Lopez's papers and found nothing, calling Essex a '"rash and temerarious youth to enter into a matter against the poor man which he could not prove"'. See J. E. Neale, *Queen Elizabeth I* (1934; rpt. Harmondsworth: Pelican Books, 1971) p. 340.
78. See *DNB*, vol. 12, p. 133.
79. Ibid., p. 133.
80. Ibid., p. 133. Regarding Lopez's downfall, see also Baron, *Social and Religious History*, vol. 15, pp. 128–9; cf. also vol. 18, pp. 141, 144.
81. See Marcham, p. 2.
82. *DNB*, vol. 12, pp. 133–4.
83. Ibid., p. 134.
84. See Irving Ribner (ed.), *The Complete Plays of Christopher Marlowe* (New York: Odyssey Press, 1963). All references to Marlowe's plays

will be to this edition and will be cited parenthetically in the text.

85. D. M. Cohen, 'The Jew and Shylock', *SQ*, **31** (1980) pp. 53–63.
86. Mahood, p. 42. For a concise review of the stage history, see pp. 42–53.
87. For a good, brief sketch of the evolution of religious tolerance for Jews, see Oberman, pp. 138–43.
88. Leonard Tennenhouse, *Power on Display: The Politics of Shakespeare's Genres* (New York and London: Methuen, 1986) p. 56.
89. See Jones, pp. 4, 64, 202. See Miles Mosse, *The Arraignment and Conviction of Usury. That is, The iniquity and unlawfulness of usury, displayed in six Sermons, preached at Saint Edmunds Burie in Suffolke, upon Proverb 28.8* (London: Widow Orwin, 1595) pp. 30–2. Mosse's first sermon (delivered in March 1592) is a helpful compendium of ancient and modern writers' definitions of usury, both broad and narrow. Mosse's differentiation between definitions of what does and does not constitute sinful usury helps to illuminate the changes for the idea of usury and the importance of this matter of definition for the future course of this concept in England.
90. See Cohen, pp. 769, 775, 778.
91. According to the scholastics, who followed Aristotle regarding the sterility of money, actual usury applied only to a contracted *loan* (a *mutuum*) involving fungible, as opposed to non-fungible, goods. A fungible good refers to a commodity whose use cannot be separated from its substance, that is, the commodity lent is consumed in the use of it. Fungible goods were goods that could be numbered (money), weighed (grain), or measured (wine). Money was classified as a fungible good because the lender did not expect to receive again the very coins lent but rather an equal quantity of the same species (e.g., a return of the same amount of money lent). A non-fungible good, such as a house, on the other hand, could be freely lent or rented and returned intact. According to the scholastics a lease or a rental differed as a contract from a loan; usury could occur in only one type of contract, a loan. For a clear and concise summary, see Raymond De Roover, *San Bernardino of Siena and Sant'Antonino of Florence: The Two Great Economic Thinkers of the Middle Ages*, in *The Kress Library of Business and Economics*, ed. James P. Baughman, no. 19 (Cambridge: Harvard University Press Printing Office, 1967) pp. 28–33.
92. For the development of the idea of 'love's wealth', see John Russell Brown, *Shakespeare and His Comedies*, 2nd edn (London: Methuen, 1962) pp. 61–75; Brown (ed.), pp. liii–lviii.
93. See Danson, p. 61, for the 'usurious Jew' in *Il Pecorone*. Cf. also Cameron, p. 68; Thomas Moisan, '"Which is the merchant here? and which the Jew?": Subversion and Recuperation in *The Merchant of Venice*', in *Shakespeare Reproduced: the Text in History and Ideology*, eds Jean E. Howard and Marion F. O'Connor (New York and London: Methuen, 1987) p. 192.
94. See C. Spencer, who summarised this division, pp. 78–88. Spencer sides with the emphasis on the Jew and downplays the emphasis

on the usurer because he finds so few explicit uses of the term
and its cognates compared with the use of 'Jew'.

95. Miles Mosse, sigs. B2^{r-v}.

96. In *Romeo and Juliet* Shakespeare similarly presents a topic of great
contemporary concern (violent duelling) which, like usury, is ra-
tionalised and practised, despite its technical illegality. For further consideration of this problem, see my '"Draw, if you be men":
Saviolo's Significance for *Romeo and Juliet*', *SQ*, **45** (1994) pp. 163–
89. Interestingly, *Romeo* has a negative reference to the usurer's
misuse of what he has (3.3.123–5).

97. Thomas Lodge, *Wit's Misery and the World's Madness: Discovering
the Devils Incarnate of This Age* (1596), in *The Works of Thomas Lodge*,
ed. Edmund W. Gosse, 4 vols (1883; rpt. New York: Russell &
Russell, 1963) vol. 4, pp. 37–8.

98. The early works are *Romeo and Juliet*, *The Merchant of Venice*, the
Sonnets, and *Much Ado About Nothing*. The later works are *Meas-
ure for Measure*, *King Lear*, *Timon of Athens*, *Coriolanus*, *Cymbeline*,
The Winter's Tale, and *Two Noble Kinsmen*.

99. There are eight references, four to 'usurer' and its variants and
four to 'interest'.

100. See Jones, p. 1; see esp. chs 1 and 7 and pp. 197–8, 202, 204.

101. See Brown (ed.) p. xxxii.

102. *Timon* has seven explicit references to usury.

103. Nashe, vol. 2, p. 93, cf. pp. 160–3; see McKerrow, vol. 4, p. 229 n.

104. See Jones, pp. 1, 6–46, 175–205; Carl F. Taeusch, 'The Concept of
"Usury"', *JHI*, **3** (1942) pp. 291–318.

105. See T. Wilson, p. 378: 'For the Jews had license from the King
[Henry III] to take two pence in the pound . . . a devilish usury. . . .
These Jews are gone. Would god the Christians remaining and
our country men this time did not use their fashions.'

106. See, e.g., Gerald Friedlander's assertion, 'the Church and Christian Society left one trade only at the disposal of the Jews – that
of money-lending'. Gerald Friedlander, *Shakespeare and the Jew* (London: George Routledge & Sons; New York: E. P. Dutton, 1921)
p. 5. Mahood notes that the transalpine Jews were the only authorised Jewish moneylenders in Venice (p. 15, n. 6).

107. See *Encyclopedia Judaica*, vol. 11, p. 1191; Cecil Roth, *A Short History of the Jewish People*, rev. and enl. edn (London: East and West
Library, 1969) p. 215. Before the expulsion of Jews from Spain and
Sicily in 1492/3, due to Arragonese intolerance, the Jews were particularly active in crafts, such as dyeing and silk-weaving; in Spain,
near Valencia, the manufacture of paper was a Jewish monopoly
for a long time. See Roth, p. 216; but cf. pp. 257–8. Cf. Baron *et al.*,
Economic History, pp. 55–73, esp. pp. 69–70; Baron, *Social and Religious History*, vol. 14, pp. 100–5.

108. See *Encyclopedia Judaica*, vol. 16, p. 98; Baron, *Social and Religious
History*, vol. 14, p. 101. Another Venetian estimate, around 1560,
reveals a marked increase in both populations, 190,714 inhabitants, of whom 1,157 were said to be Jews. See David McPherson,

'Lewkenor's Venice and Its Sources', *RenQ*, **41** (1988) p. 463 n. 23.

109. See Popkin, pp. 329–30.

110. See *Encyclopedia Judaica*, vol. 6, p. 753.

111. See John T. Noonan, *The Scholastic Analysis of Usury* (Cambridge, MA: Harvard University Press, 1957) p. 35. For an implicit reference to this lombard association with usurious avarice, see Chaucer, *The Merchant's Tale*, ll. 1245–7, p. 115. All references to Chaucer's works will be to *The Works of Geoffrey Chaucer*, ed. F. N. Robinson (Cambridge: Riverside Press, 1961).

112. J. Shatzmiller, *Shylock Reconsidered: Jews, Moneylending, and Medieval Society* (Berkeley: University of California Press, 1990) p. 71.

113. See 'Usury', *Encyclopedia Judaica*, vol. 16, pp. 27–32.

114. See, e.g., Friedlander, pp. 24–5; Hermann Sinsheimer, *Shylock: The History of a Character* (1947; rpt. New York: Citadel, 1964) p. 131; Benjamin Nelson, *The Idea of Usury: From Tribal Brotherhood to Universal Otherhood*, 2nd edn (Chicago: University of Chicago Press, 1969) pp. 99–100.

115. See De Roover, p. 32. Cf. T. Wilson, pp. 348, 351.

116. See T. Wilson, pp. 366, 379.

117. See Mosse, p. 83.

118. See W. Perkins, *A Golden Chain*, trans. R. H., 2nd edn (Cambridge: John Legatt, 1592) sigs N8ʳ–0. (Formerly STC 19659, now STC 19661.5. This translation enlarges the original Latin version, *Armilla Auera*, printed by John Legatt in 1590.) Perkins by no means holds a singular position on usury, as Laura Stevenson suggests (p. 95), but he does seem to belong to a group of less conservative thinkers – men like Fulke, Gibbon, Rogers, and Ames – because he allows for some usury and the fruitful use of money.

119. See, e.g., T. Wilson, p. 331.

120. See, e.g., Moisan, p. 196; John Lyon, *The Merchant of Venice*, Harvester New Critical Introductions to Shakespeare (Hertfordshire: Harvester Wheatsheaf, 1988) p. 27.

121. See Jones, p. 64.

122. Ibid., pp. 52, 63–5, 202.

123. See, e.g., Richard Greaves, *Society and Religion in Elizabethan England* (Minneapolis, University of Minnesota Press, 1981) pp. 599–608; I. P. Ellis, 'The Archbishop and the Usurers', *Journal of Ecclesiastical History*, **21** (1970) pp. 33–42; Jones, pp. 111–12, 148–9, 153, 157–8, 166.

124. See Max Weber, *The Protestant Ethic and the Spirit of Capitalism*, trans. Talcott Parsons, 2nd imp. (1930; London: G. Allen & Unwin, 1948). R. H. Tawney, *Religion and the Rise of Capitalism* (1926; rpt. New York: Penguin Books, 1947).

125. See R. C. Evans, 'Shakespeare, Sutton, and Theatrical Satire: An Unreported Allusion to Falstaff', *SQ*, vol. **40** (1989) p. 493.

126. See Jones, p. 197.

127. Mosse, sig. B2ᵛ.

128. Robert Wilson's *The Three Ladies of London* (1584) is not generally accepted as a source for our play, but in it a Jewish moneylender

in Turkey is opposed by a despicable Christian merchant from
Italy. Bullough rightly identifies Wilson's Gerontus as 'an entirely
virtuous moneylender' (p. 450). Mahood sees Gerontus as only a
'creditor' who does not do business with Lady Lucre's servant,
Usury, 'who hails from Venice' (p. 20). Gerontus is technically a
usurer because he expects payment of interest as well as principal, and he justifies his expectation by Christian example: 'And
yet the interest is allowed amongst you Christians, as well as in
Turkey.' See Bullough, vol. 1, pp. 479, 481. But Gerontus follows
the rule of charity in his moneylending, and so he resembles not
Shylock, but Shatzmiller's historical Jewish moneylender, Bondavid.
Although the contract for the flesh bond in *Il Pecorone* would be
judged as usurious by traditional standards, as we shall see in
Chapter 4, the Jew himself in *Il Pecorone* is never specifically identified as a usurer by profession, nor is the subject of usury raised.
129. P. N. Siegel, 'Shylock and the Puritan Usurers', in *Studies in Shakespeare*, ed. Arthur D. Matthews and Clark M. Emery (Coral Gables: University of Miami Press, 1953) pp. 129–38. Siegel notes
Elizabethans frequently charged Puritans with Judaism because of
their emphasis on Old Testament law, and he finds Shylock similar to a Pharisaical Puritan – intolerant of others and attributing
his own spiritual defect to others. Thus, the final act is an important triumph of love and friendship.

Notes to Chapter 2

1. For some representative views favouring unity, see C. L. Barber,
*Shakespeare's Festive Comedy: A Study of Dramatic Form and its Rela-
tion to Social Custom* (Princeton: Princeton University Press, 1959)
pp. 170, 191; Barbara Lewalski, 'Biblical Allusion and Allegory *in
The Merchant of Venice*', *SQ*, **13** (1962) pp. 327–8; Thomas H. Fujimura,
'Mode and Structure in *The Merchant of Venice*', *PMLA*, **81** (1966)
pp. 499–500, 511; Herbert S. Donow, 'Shakespeare's Caskets: Unity
in *The Merchant of Venice*', *ShakS*, **4** (1968) pp. 86–7; Allan Holaday,
'Antonio and the Allegory of Salvation', *ShakS*, **4** (1968) pp. 109–31;
Christopher Parry (ed.), *The Merchant of Venice*, The Macmillan Shake-
speare (Basingstoke: Macmillan, 1976) p. 2; Joan Ozark Holmer,
'Loving Wisely and the Casket Test: Symbolic and Structural Unity
in *The Merchant of Venice*', *ShakS*, **11** (1978) pp. 53, 72; M. M. Mahood,
'Golden Lads and Girls', *AJES*, **4** (1979) pp. 108–23; Walter Cohen,
'*The Merchant of Venice* and the Possibilities of Historical Criticism',
ELH, **49** (1982) pp. 779–81; David N. Beauregard, 'Sidney, Aristotle,
and *The Merchant of Venice*: Shakespeare's Triadic Images of Liberality and Justice', *ShakS*, **20** (1988) pp. 33–4, 48–9. For some dissents, see Sir Arthur Quiller-Couch and John Dover Wilson (eds.),
The Merchant of Venice (Cambridge: Cambridge University Press, 1926)

p. xi; John Middleton Murray, *Shakespeare* (London: Jonathan Cape, 1936) p. 192; W. H. Auden, 'Brothers and Others', *The Dyer's Hand and Other Essays* (New York: Random House, 1962) p. 221; Harley Granville-Barker, '*The Merchant of Venice*', in *Prefaces to Shakespeare* (Princeton: Princeton University Press, 1963) vol. 4, pp. 89, 91; Peter Phialas, *Shakespeare's Romantic Comedies* (Chapel Hill: University of North Carolina Press, 1966) pp. 161–71; John Lyon, *The Merchant of Venice*, Harvester New Critical Introductions to Shakespeare (Hertfordshire: Harvester Wheatsheaf, 1988) pp. 96–7; Karl F. Thompson, *Modesty and Cunning: Shakespeare's Use of Literary Tradition* (Ann Arbor: University of Michigan Press, 1971) pp. 76–82; Alan Hobson, 'With Undiscording Voice', in *Full Circle: Shakespeare and Moral Development* (London: Chatto and Windus, 1972) pp. 198–226; John W. Sider, 'The Serious Elements of Shakespeare's Comedies', *SQ*, **24** (1973) pp. 1–11; Alexander Leggatt, *Shakespeare's Comedy of Love* (New York: Harper & Row, 1974) pp. 145–50.
2. See Thomas Wheeler, *The Merchant of Venice: An Annotated Bibliography* (New York & London: Garland, 1985) pp. xvii–xviii.
3. Kenneth Muir, '*The Merchant of Venice*', in *Shakespeare's Comic Sequence* (New York: Barnes & Noble, 1979) p. 67.
4. Norman Rabkin, 'Meaning and "*The Merchant of Venice*"', *Shakespeare and the Problem of Meaning* (Chicago: University of Chicago Press, 1981) pp. 30–1.
5. See Mahood, pp. 25–42.
6. See J. R. Brown (ed.), *The Merchant of Venice* (New Arden Shakespeare)(1955; rpt. London: Methuen, 1969) p. lii; J. R. Brown, 'Love's Wealth and the Judgment of *The Merchant of Venice*', in *Shakespeare and His Comedies*, 2nd edn (London: Methuen, 1962) pp. 61–2.
7. *The Merchant of Venice* presents little difficulty for critically accepted division into scenes. Given James E. Hirsh's definition of 'scene' (the continuous occupation of the stage which can be broken only when the stage is cleared of all living characters), his scenic division of *The Merchant of Venice* accords well with the twenty scenes usually designated by editors for this play. See James E. Hirsh, *The Structure of Shakespearean Scenes* (New Haven and London: Yale University Press, 1981) p. 221. For the formulaic organisation of various types of scenes, see pp. 12, 53 n., 98–9, 132–4, 210–11. For the argument favouring the five-act theory of structure, see T. W. Baldwin, *On Act and Scene Division in the Shakespeare First Folio* (Carbondale: Southern Illinois University Press, 1965) esp. pp. ix, 7; T. W. Baldwin, *William Shakespeare's Five-Act Structure* (Urbana: University of Illinois Press, 1974).
8. For an analysis of Shakespeare's analogical use of scene, see Joan Hartwig, *Shakespeare's Analogical Scene* (Lincoln and London: University of Nebraska Press, 1983) esp. pp. 191–3.
9. For Doran's use of Wölfflin's concept of 'multiple unity', see Chapter 1. For the idea of the climactic plateau in Shakespearian dramaturgy, see Bernard Beckerman, *Shakespeare at the Globe 1599–1609* (New York: Macmillan, 1962) pp. 24–62. For triptych design within

scenes and plays with symmetrical scenic arrangement around a
centre, see Mark Rose, *Shakespearean Design* (Belknap Press of Harvard
University Press, 1972) pp. 1–26, esp. pp. 3, 95–125, 173–4. For the
influence of oral narrative on Shakespeare's thematic centres, see
Bruce R. Smith, 'Parolles's Recitations: Oral and Literate Structures
in Shakespeare's Plays', in *Renaissance Papers 1989*, eds Dale B. J.
Randall and Joseph A. Porter (Durham, NC: The Southeastern Renaissance Conference, 1989) pp. 75–88. Smith argues persuasively for
the immediate influence of 'the traditional structure of oral narrative' on the centralised design of Shakespeare's plays: 'We arrive at
the *final* truth only by working our way into and out of the *central*
truth' (p. 81). He advises modern readers and viewers to be attentive to the 'dynamic interplay' of both kinds of structure – the literate structures of linear narrative progression and the oral structures
of thematic centres (p. 88).

10. Regarding the versions of the sources Shakespeare used, see Brown
    (ed.), pp. xxvii–xxxii. Cf. M. M. Mahood (ed.), *The Merchant of Ven-
    ice*, New Cambridge Shakespeare (Cambridge: Cambridge Univer-
    sity Press, 1987) pp. 2–4.
11. My manuscript was completed when William Godshalk's fine in-
    terpretation of unity in *The Merchant of Venice* came to my atten-
    tion. Although we develop our emphasis quite differently, we agree
    that 'the element of choice is emphasised far beyond the point needed
    to maintain the requisite tension' (p. 95), and the elements of choice
    and bondage help to unify the casket and bond plots. See William
    Godshalk, *Patterning in Shakespearean Drama* (The Hague: Mouton,
    1973) pp. 87–100.
12. *Gesta Romanorum*, trans. and rev. Richard Robinson, ed. John Weld
    (1595; rpt. Delmar, NY: Scholar's Facsimiles & Reprints, 1973)
    p. 208. All references to this version of the casket story (History 32)
    are to this edition of the *Gesta Romanorum* (pp. 198–215).
13. Thomas Wilson, *A Discourse upon Usury* [1572], ed. R. H. Tawney
    (New York: Harcourt Brace, 1925) p. 363.
14. As Norman Jones has demonstrated, the discussion of usury in 1571
    revolved around the interpretation of God's law and how to square
    God's law with man's law, but by 1624 the divorce process was
    complete when the debate in Parliament avoided religious argu-
    ments in favour of economic ones. See Norman Jones, *God and the
    Moneylenders: Usury and Law in Early Modern England* (Oxford and
    Cambridge, MA: Basil Blackwell, 1989) esp. pp. 193–8.
15. See B. R. Smith, 'Parolles's Recitations', pp. 83–6.
16. The time for Salarino's and Solanio's scene (2.8) is not specified,
    but the past tense ('I saw Bassanio set sail') coupled with the switch
    to present immediacy ('With him is Gratiano gone along; / And in
    their ship I am sure Lorenzo is not') as well as the description of
    boys who 'follow' Shylock, presumably in the daytime when boys
    would be in the streets, indicate the next day's rehearsal of the
    preceding night's events. At the end of their discussion Salarino
    and Solanio determine to cheer Antonio 'with some delight or other'

which would be an appropriate activity for Antonio's first day without Bassanio in Venice. Moreover, Salarino mentions he heard 'yesterday' (2.8.28) about the wreck of a Venetian vessel and worried about Antonio.

17. Shakespeare, however, has Bassanio exit the trial, proclaiming they will 'fly' to Belmont the next morning (4.1.451–3). Perhaps Shakespeare does this because Portia's lines in the next scene (4.2.1–4), that immediately follow Bassanio's, indicate her departure for Belmont that night because she is so eager to return home *before* her husband. The audience rests assured, knowing that Portia gets a headstart. But the fact that Bassanio arrives moments after her suggests a change in travel plans, perhaps due to Gratiano's inability to persuade the civil doctor to come to dinner at Antonio's house (4.1.449–50; 4.2.8). In any event, the men must make a same-day departure, shortly after Portia's, in order to arrive in Belmont when they do. Shakespeare's seemingly inconsistent lines about the men's departure are not noticed in the theatre, where consistency of dramatic effect for the audience's concern outweighs attention to such detail.

18. For interpretations of time schemes that differ from my own, see H. H. Furness (ed.), *The Merchant of Venice*, The Variorum Shakespeare, 23 vols (Philadelphia: J. B. Lippincott, 1888), vol. 7, pp. 332–45. Although 'not real time but dramatic time' is what matters in Shakespeare, we cannot conclude from our play, as is sometimes thought, that the clock time in one world is 'wildly different' from the clock time in the other. See, e.g., William G. Leary, *Shakespeare Plain: The Making and Performing of Shakespeare's Plays* (New York: McGraw-Hill, 1977) pp. 73–4.

19. For frequency of words and their variants in the play, see Oxford Shakespeare Concordances, *The Merchant of Venice: A Concordance to the Text of the First Quarto of 1600* (Oxford: Clarendon Press, 1969).

20. Critics have overlooked Shakespeare's indebtedness to Marlowe's crafting of the same type of line in terms of syntax, stress, and idea of self-centredness which is essential to Barabas's motivation (1.1.171) and motto (1.1.187). More work needs to be done on this score. For essays stressing the differences between Marlowe's *The Jew of Malta* and Shakespeare's *The Merchant of Venice*, see S. C. Sen Gupta, 'Tragedy and Comedy: Barabas and Shylock', in *A Shakespeare Manual* (Calcutta: Oxford University Press, 1977) pp. 85–105; Stephen J. Greenblatt, 'Marlowe, Marx, and Anti-Semitism', *CI*, **5** (1978) pp. 291–307; Arthur Humphreys, '*The Jew of Malta* and *The Merchant of Venice*', *HLQ*, **50** (1987) pp. 279–93; and Thomas Cartelli, 'Shakespeare's *Merchant*, Marlowe's *Jew*: The Problem of Cultural Difference', *ShakS*, **20** (1988) pp. 255–60.

21. See Edmund Spenser, *The Faerie Queene*, ed. Thomas P. Roche, Jr (Harmondsworth: Penguin, 1978) I.ii.5.7, p. 56.

22. For Shylock's self-definition in physical, animalistic terms, see Fujimura, p. 506; John R. Cooper, 'Shylock's Humanity', *SQ*, **21** (1970) pp. 122–3.

23. See C. S. Lewis, *The Discarded Image: An Introduction to Medieval and*

Renaissance Literature (Cambridge: Cambridge University Press, 1970) pp. 152–65.

24. See Dt 32.35: 'Vengeance and recompense are mine [God's].' In the New Testament the use of the magistrate or the law to settle disputes among brethren must conform to good conscience and never be sought for the purpose of 'hatred, grudges, & desires of revengeance' (1 Cor 6.8, gloss).

25. In John's first epistle the 'world' is the inclusive, negative term that embraces the lust of the flesh, the lust of the eyes, and the pride of life that oppose the will of God (1 Jn 2.15–17), and in Paul's epistles that negative term is most often the 'flesh' but the general intended meaning is the same. Given the common allegorical equation of the world, the flesh, and the devil as the ideological triumvirate against godliness, it is not surprising that the medieval–Renaissance ideas of worldliness and bloodiness are seen as complementary in the literary portrayal of a usurer, whether he be Christian (Truculento in Munday's *Zelauto*) or Jewish (the Jew in the lost play of that name referred to by Stephen Gosson in *The School of Abuse*). Hence, Gosson's reference to *The Jew*, that played at the Red Bull Theatre, emphasises its representation of ideas that are theologically linked and especially linked to usurers – 'the greediness of worldly choosers, and bloody minds of usurers'. See Stephen Gosson, *The School of Abuse*, in The English Experience (no. 523) (1579); facsimile rpt. Amsterdam: Da Capo Press, 1972) sig. C6^v.

26. See Brown (ed.), pp. 111–12 (notes); Mahood (ed.), pp. 142–3 (notes); Leo Salingar, *Shakespeare and the Traditions of Comedy* (London: Cambridge University Press, 1974) p. 317.

27. See Brown (ed.), p. 165. For other verbal parallels with the trial, see pp. 162 and 168. See pp. 167–8 for another possible parallel in the repeated use of the word 'content' and 'contented'; cf. Shakespeare, 4.1.378, 388–90. The diction of 'desire' and 'desert' (pp. 163–65), appropriate to a judicial context, also recurs throughout the trial scene in *Zelauto* and may have encouraged Shakespeare to develop these ideas from his gold and silver caskets for his trial scene. Shakespeare is unique, however, in his emphasis on 'giving', native to the leaden casket.

28. See Munday's *Zelauto*, in Brown (ed.), p. 165.

29. See Wilson, pp. 232–3, 279, my italics.

30. Barabas ironically mentions God's providential wisdom – 'heaven rained manna for the Jews' (2.3.245) – in the same breath that concludes his deadly stratagem for the two Christian gentlemen in love with his daughter.

31. William Faulkner, *Light in August* (the corrected text) (New York: Vintage, 1990) p. 33.

32. Sir Philip Sidney, *An Apology for Poetry*, ed. F. G. Robinson (Indianapolis: Bobbs Merrill Educational, 1970) p. 45 and n. 225.

33. M. J. Levith, *What's in Shakespeare's Names* (Hamden, CT: The Shoe String Press, 1978) p. 79.

34. Ibid., p. 81.

35. See A. B. Stonex, 'The Usurer in Elizabethan Drama', *PMLA*, **31** (1916) pp. 196–205.

36. See Geneva Bible (1560) ed. L. E. Berry p. 11, for praise of the Hebrew scholarship of this Bible's English translators, who restored the literal meaning of the Hebrew text obscured in earlier vernacular versions. The table of Hebrew names is appended to the Geneva Bible 'for the increase of knowledge and furtherance of God's glory' (sig. iiii^v).

37. I have used R. F. Herrey's concordance (STC 13228b.12) bound in a 1594 Geneva Bible (STC 2163) (black letter quarto) printed in London by the Deputies of Christopher Barker. Herrey explains that he has presented 'all the strange names and words . . . throughout the whole Bible . . . written in the *Hebrew, Caldean, Syrian, Greek*, or *Latin* languages [following the Geneva translation with marginalia listing other translations]: to the end [the reader] mayst by that means, learn to be conduced unto so much of the interpretation . . . of them' as the reader 'shalt think needful' (sig. A2^r). My quotations for biblical names refer to this edition and are documented parenthetically in the text.

38. For example, the information about Tubal's association with Italy does not appear in the other concordance for the Geneva and Geneva–Tomson Bibles. The name 'Iscah' (a possible source for Jessica) and Marlowe's names for Barabas's two Jewish friends ('Zaareth' and 'Temainte', 1.1.175) are found only in Herrey's concordance. Herrey furnishes more information and biblical cross-references, and his biographical summations for many figures (such as Sarah, Hagar, Job, Jacob, Laban, Leah, Rachel, Daniel, Balthazar, Jesse, and Barrabas) are very helpfully designed to give the reader, at a glance, a sense of lives and their significance, with the pertinent biblical passages referenced for further reading. The other concordance lacks such biographies and is limited to etymological meaning.

39. Daniel and the Babylonian name given to him, Balthazar, will be reserved for discussion of the trial scene, where these names appear with charged meanings.

40. G. Goldstein, 'Edward De Vere's Hebrew', *ShOSN*, **26**, i (Winter 1990) pp. 6–11; quotation is from p. 6. Despite some good research on Hebrew phonology and transliteration, Goldstein erroneously assumes the necessity of knowing the Hebrew language in order to use biblical Hebrew names.

41. See *The Holy Bible* (Bishops' version) (London: Richard Jugge, 1568) sigs 3^r–7^r. All references to the Bishops' Bible are to this version. This diagrammed genealogy is accompanied by helpful commentary that places it within the largest possible historical context. For example, the history of mankind is seen in 'eight ages', which are determined not by years but by important acts that begin each age. For the first age ('Adam to Noe') the world was created; for the second ('Noe to Abraham') the world was purged by the flood; for the third ('Abraham to David') 'circumcision was given against original sin'; for the fourth ('David to the transmigration to Babylon')

the kings of Israel are anointed; for the fifth ('from thence to Christ') 'the transmigration of God's people into Babylon'; for the sixth (from Christ to the end of the world) 'the incarnation of the son of God'; for the seventh (for the dead from Christ's passion to the day of judgement') 'in the beginning of the seventh were the gates of heaven opened'; and for the eighth (from the day of judgement through eternity) 'in the beginning of the eight shall be the resurrection of the bodies, the reward of good and evil' (sig. 3ʳ). The Judaeo-Christian belief in the common descent of all humans from Adam and Eve is theoretically an anti-racist conception.

42. See Richmond Noble, *Shakespeare's Biblical Knowledge and Use of the Book of Common Prayer* (1935; rpt. New York: Octagon Books, 1970) p. 205.

43. This curse – 'a servant of servants shall he be unto his brethren' (Gn 9.26) – does not relate to the African negroes but serves as a divine sanction for Israel's enslavement of the Canaanites.

44. I am indebted to Jason Rosenblatt for this information. Cf. W. Gesenius's *A Hebrew and English Lexicon of the Old Testament*, trans. Edward Robinson, eds. Francis Brown, S. R. Driver, and C. A. Briggs (1907; rpt. Oxford: Clarendon, 1968). I wish to express my gratitude to Professor Rosenblatt and to Dean Robert B. Lawton, S.J. for discussing Hebrew names and meanings with me.

45. See P. Morwyng (trans.) Joseph ben Gorion, *A Compendious History of the Latter Times of the Jews' Common Weal* (London: Richard Jugge, 1561) sig. L5ʳ⁻ᵛ.

46. See Karl Elze, *Essays on Shakespeare*, trans. L. Dora Schmitz (London: Macmillan, 1874) pp. 282–3. Cf. Jacob L. Cardozo, *The Contemporary Jew in the Elizabethan Drama* (Amsterdam: H.J. Paris, 1925), pp. 219–24; Christopher Spencer, *The Genesis of Shakespeare's 'The Merchant of Venice'*, Studies in British Literature, vol. 3 (Lampeter, Dyfed, Wales: Edwin Mellen Press, 1988) pp. 95–6.

47. See Cardozo, p. 219; C. Spencer, p. 96.

48. In this instance 'Shelah' curiously has a different meaning from the 'Shelah' of Genesis 10 and 11, and is supposed to mean '*dissolving*' (sig. D7ʳ).

49. Elze, p. 282.

50. See John Jewel, *An Exposition upon the two Epistles of the Apostle Saint Paul to the Thessalonians* (London: R. Newberie, 1583) pp. 114, 116–17, 121. Cf., e.g., a description of the usurious rich man who is 'a most pestilent spolyer of his commonwealth', who has 'a warlike and spoyling mind, though it lie subtilly hidden, & be not in open wrath & anger', and whose 'hate' makes him 'pleased and glad' in the 'losse and hurt of the other'. See Richard Porder, *A Sermon of God's Fearful Threatenings for Idolatry . . .: with a Treatise against Usury* (London: Henry Denham, 1570) fol. 72ʳ⁻ᵛ. Cf. Wolfgang Musculus, *Commonplaces of Christian Religion . . . Of Usury*, trans. John Man (London: Henry Bynneman, 1578) p. 30: 'the unsatiable covetousness of the Usurer to spoil'.

51. See *The Ballad of Gernutus*, cited in Brown (ed.), p. 155. Critics disagree over whether this ballad predates or postdates Shakespeare's

play. A better case can be made for its predating and influencing Shakespeare's play, but that is a matter for another essay.

52. See Brown (ed.), p. 3; Mahood (ed.), 1.3.0 SD.

53. M. A. Lower (1850) seems to be the first to suggest that Shylock's name might be a form of 'Shiloh' (Gn 49.10) and notes Herrey's gloss. See citation in Brown (ed.), p. 3.

54. See the Bishops' Bible, Gn 27, heading and glosses on Gn 27.28. Hence, Esau weeps because Jacob has 'the spiritual blessing' while he must settle for only 'a temporal blessing' from Isaac (Gn 27.39, gloss).

55. L. Danson, *The Harmonies of 'The Merchant of Venice'* (New Haven and London: Yale University Press, 1978) pp. 73–6. Cf. also Dorothy C . Hockey, 'The Patch is Kind Enough', *SQ*, **10** (1959) pp. 448–550; René E. Fortin, 'Launcelot Gobbo and the Uses of Allegory in *The Merchant of Venice'*, *SEL*, **14** (1974) pp. 265–8.

56. The Bishops' Bible (large folio) and the Geneva Bible afford excellent illustrations, especially in Exodus. See esp. the Tabernacle and the Ark, surrounded by the twelve tribes of Israel, in the Bishops' Bible, fol. 53^r.

57. To which of the twelve tribes might Shylock and Tubal belong? For Shylock the best argument can be made for the tribe of Judah, chiefly on the basis of the name evidence just considered that 'Shelah' and 'Shiloh'. Shylock wishes to identify with Jacob, and Judah is the son of Jacob and Leah, from whose tribe Christ descends. In *The Jew of Malta* Barabas does not identify his tribe other than to claim he does not belong to the tribe of Levi because he cannot easily forget injuries (2.3.18–19).

58. See Norman Nathan, cited in Brown (ed.), p. 3; C. Spencer, p. 96.

59. See *OED*, 'shy', a., 1.; 4.

60. For a recent, significant contribution to this area of inquiry, see James Shapiro, *Rival Playwrights: Marlowe, Jonson, Shakespeare* (New York: Columbia University Press, 1991) esp. pp. 81–2, 104–12. Shapiro, however, does not consider many of the specific comparisons I analyse throughout this book, nor do we arrive at the same conclusion about the nature of Shakespeare's response to Marlowe's *Jew*.

61. For a 'Richard Shylok', see M. A. Lower, cited in Brown (ed.), p. 3; for a 'Richard Shacklock', see Robert F. Fleissner, 'A Key to the Name of Shylock', *ANQ*, **5** (Dec. 1966) pp. 52–4.

62. See Gollancz, cited in Brown (ed.), p. 3; Cf. Mahood (ed.), 1.3.0 SD.

63. Although some of the Roman soldiers behave despicably, Joseph praises Antonius and Titus, especially Titus who treats magnanimously the Jews who escape from their seditious brethren (sigs Ee3^v–Ee4^r).

64. See Elze, pp. 282–3; Noble, p. 162; Brown (ed.), p. 3; Mahood (ed.), 2.3.0 SD; Levith, pp. 81–2; Norman Nathan, 'Portia, Nerissa and Jessica – Their Names', *Names: Journal of the American Name Society*, **34** (Dec. 1986) pp. 425–9. Nathan specifies the feminising of Jesse to Jessica as 'a Venetianizing', the name having 'a Hebrew beginning and a Venetian ending, like the character herself'. But the ending '-ca' is not typically Venetian, neither Latinate nor Italianate which

would be '-a', as in Portia and Nerissa. The '-ca' ending seems to be rather Shakespeare's formation of a clearly feminine ending that also sounds Hebrew, as in Rebecca.

65. See Charles Sears Baldwin, *Three Medieval Centuries of Literature in England, 1100–1400* (New York: Phaeton Press, 1968) p. 175. In emphasising how medieval symbolism made the Old Testament part of the New Testament, Baldwin quotes from Cook's *Literary Middle English Reader* a passage on 'gentil jesse' that anticipates, without the pun, Shakespeare's introduction of 'gentle Jessica' (2.4.19). For manuscript illumination of the Tree of Jesse, see Lilian M. C. Randall, 'An Elephant in the Litany; Further Thoughts on an English Book of Hours in the Walters Art Gallery (W. 102)', in *Beasts and Birds of the Middle Ages*, eds Willene B. Clark and Meredith T. McMunn, pp. 107–8.

66. See E. G. Withycombe, *The Oxford Dictionary of English Christian Names*, 2nd edn (Oxford University Press, 1959) p. 167; Nathan, p. 429.

67. Marlowe is even more obvious regarding wordplay on sacrificed daughters when Abigail explains why she will convert to 'the Son that gives eternal life' (see 3.3.46–9, 59–65).

68. John Florio, *Queen Anna's New World of Words* (1611; rpt. Menston: Scolar Press, 1968) p. 232.

69. Shakespeare's interest in Portia may be influenced by Robert Garnier's play *Porcie* (1568), which Thomas Kyd had promised to translate after he did Garnier's *Cornelie* (1594), although he never did. Garnier, the foremost sixteenth-century French dramatist, was popular in the Countess of Pembroke's circle dating from about 1592. See F. P. Wilson, *The English Drama 1485–1585*, ed. G. K. Hunter, Oxford History of English Literature (Oxford: Clarendon Press, 1969) pp. 141–2; Rolf Soellner, 'Shakespeare's *Lucrece* and the Garnier–Pembroke Connection', *ShakS*, **15** (1982) p. 3.

70. See G. H. Hammond and H. H. Scullard (eds), *The Oxford Classical Dictionary*, 2nd edn (Oxford: Clarendon Press, 1970) pp. 214–16.

71. See Nathan, p. 428. But her name in the trial is not Portia, but Balthazar or Daniel. Moreover, the play's several references to eating pork, a distinction between Hebrews and Christians, never involve Portia but rather develop the significance of the Gadarene miracle referred to by Shylock (1.3.27–8). 'Porcus' does mean pig. I am indebted, however, to Joseph F. O'Connor for the information that many Latin names derive from livestock, and the hard 'c' in pronunciation changes to a soft 'c' around AD 400.

72. Nathan, p. 427. But 'portus' means port, harbour; 'porta' means gate, and we do not 'hear' the word 'port' in 'Portia' so much as see it in reading. The educated in Shakespeare's audience might respond to this on the basis of visual recollection of the printed name.

73. Cf. Levith, p. 81.

74. Nathan, p. 427.

75. See Hammond and Scullard (eds), p. 729.

76. In the Bishops' Bible no gloss appears for 'Iscah', but the gloss on

Abram does relate to the question of marriages with strangers: 'The godly shunned the marriages of strangers.'

77. Andrew Willet, *Hexapla Genesin . . . A Sixfold Commentary upon Genesis* (London: Thomas Creede, 1608) p. 172.

78. See Willet, p. 310, for a commentary on the biblical description of Leah's eyes.

79. For another related, but different, typological explanation of Leah and Rachel, cf. John S. Coolidge, 'Law and Love in *The Merchant of Venice*', *SQ*, **27** (1976) p. 250, n. 16.

80. See Mahood (ed.), 2.5.42 n.

81. See Levith, p. 80; Mahood (ed.), p. 82.

82. See Withycombe, 'Job', p. 169. Withycombe notes that Job's story was popular in medieval plays, but aside from the appearance of 'Job' in English surnames, the biblical name comes into use after the Reformation. See 'Lancelot', pp. 181–2.

Notes to Chapter 3

1. See *OED*, 'chest', 1., 3., 9. Although 'chest' is used in the Renaissance to mean 'coffin', the word 'casket' does not get so used until around the nineteenth century in the United States. See *OED*, 'casket', 3. Shakespeare does use 'casket' figuratively to describe the human body: 'They found him dead and cast into the streets, / An empty casket, where the jewel of life / By some damn'd hand was robb'd and ta'en away' (*Jn* 5.1.39–41).

2. See W. H. Auden, 'Brothers and Others', in *The Dyer's Hand and Other Essays* (New York: Random House, 1962) p. 221.

3. For specific source analysis, see Joan Ozark Holmer, 'Loving Wisely and the Casket Test: Symbolic and Structural Unity in *The Merchant of Venice*', *ShakS*, **11** (1978) pp. 54–60.

4. H. Granville-Barker, '*The Merchant of Venice*', in *Prefaces to Shakespeare* (Princeton: Princeton University Press, 1963) vol. 4, pp. 89, 91. Cf. also Hazelton Spencer's view that the casket test is only 'romantic stuff, . . . an irrational test . . . [with] Morocco's argument as sound as Bassanio's'. H. Spencer, *The Art and Life of Shakespeare* (New York: Harcourt Brace, 1940) p. 243.

5. R. Robinson (trans.), *Gesta Romanorum* (1591) (Delmar, New York: Scholars' Facsimiles & Reprints, 1973) p. 213.

6. See ibid., pp. 211–13, 198.

7. Ibid., p. 214.

8. Ibid., p. 215.

9. For an alternative Freudian and archetypal interpretation that sees the Lord of Belmont as an ogre-father figure, like Shylock, see Leslie Fiedler, 'The Jew as Stranger: or "These be the Christian husbands"', in *The Stranger in Shakespeare* (New York: Stein and Day, 1972) pp. 85–136.

10. See Robinson (trans.), pp. 198, 211.
11. See ibid., p. 207.
12. Frank McCombie presents Portia as the embodiment of wisdom, in his 'Wisdom as Touchstone in *The Merchant of Venice*', *New Blackfriars*, **64** (1982) p. 122.
13. For an examination of these clues and their function, in particular the song sung *during* the process of Bassanio's choice, see Holmer, 'Loving Wisely', pp. 57–60 and n. 10. Cf. the direction in the 'Platt' for III.2 ('Heere Musicke and a Song, whilst Bassanio comments on the Caskets to himselfe') in *The Merchant of Venice* (The Shakespeare's Globe Acting Edition), eds Patrick Tucker and Michael Holden, (London: M. H. Publications, 1991). In the *Gesta Romanorum* the clues are much more obvious. The would-be bride is advised to choose what is of 'profit' to her and to others; the silver vessel has the 'nature' clue in its motto, and the maiden reasons that her nature desires 'the lust of the flesh'; and the leaden vessel has the giveaway clue of what 'God' has disposed in its motto. The vessel with the least clues is the gold one, and the maiden does not choose it because she suspects such a precious exterior. See Robinson (trans.), pp. 207–8.
14. For several readings of Portia's line, see Harry Berger, 'Marriage and Mercifixion in *The Merchant of Venice*: The Casket Scene Revisited', *SQ*, **32** (1981) pp. 155–62.
15. See *OED*, 'complexion', 1., 3., 4. Cf. J. R. Brown (ed.), *The Merchant of Venice* (New Arden Shakespeare) (1955; rpt. London: Methuen, 1969) p. 61.
16. See William Painter (trans.), *The Palace of Pleasure*, ed. Joseph Jacobs (1980); rpt. New York: Dover Publications, 1966) vol. III, pp. 416–17. To the best of my knowledge this has not been heretofore observed. The good nature of the just and kind King of Morocco is the central point of the story, which teaches that mighty princes are mightier for their clemency than for their cruelty in their dealings with others, especially with their lowliest subjects (pp. 417–19, 430).
17. Catherine Belsey argues that 'Western literature presents desire as . . . hazardous' and that 'desire is perilous because it annihilates the speaking, knowing, mastering subject, the choosing, commanding self so precious to the Free West'. See C. Belsey, 'Love in Venice', *ShS*, **44** (1992) p. 43. But this is not the concept of desire that Shakespeare's play presents because 'desire' is a key word in the golden motto, that motto's insistence on 'gain' is opposed to the leaden casket's insistence on 'give and hazard', and Morocco's 'desire' does not annihilate the fact that he is in command of his speech, thought, and choice.
18. Morocco's exclamation, 'O hell! What have we here?' (2.7.62), recalls the allegorisation of the story in the *Gesta Romanorum*: 'Therefore if any man choose such life he shall have that he deserveth, that is to say, hell.' See Robinson (trans.) p. 214.
19. Sigurd Burckhardt argues that they fail only 'because they try to interpret the lines inscribed on the caskets rather than the substance'.

See S. Burckhardt, '*The Merchant of Venice*: The Gentle Bond', *ELH*, **29** (1962) p. 247. Cary B. Graham maintains that 'Morocco fails because he wrongly values the caskets; Arragon, because he wrongly values himself.' See C. B. Graham, 'Standards of Value in *The Merchant of Venice*', *SQ*, **4** (1953) p. 148. Charles Read Baskervill rightly sees Bassanio as an ideal lover in terms of Renaissance Neoplatonism, but he finds only Morocco a victim of 'sense' with Arragon being a cut above his competitor because he demonstrates 'reason'. See C. R. Baskervill 'Bassanio as an Ideal Lover', in *The Manly Anniversary Studies in Language and Literature* (Chicago: University of Chicago Press, 1923) p. 102. Lewalski notes but does not develop the similarity between the meanings of the gold and silver caskets in the source's moral and their choosers, seeing Morocco as 'a fit type of worldliness' and Arragon 'the very embodiment of Pride', B. Lewalski, 'Biblical Allusion and Allegory in *The Merchant of Venice*', *SQ*, **13** (1962) p. 337 and n. 27. J. Leeds Barroll finds transcendentalist implications and character differentiation in the casket scenes. See J. L. Barroll, *Artificial Persons: The Formation of Character in the Tragedies of Shakespeare* (Columbia: University of South Carolina Press, 1974) pp. 117–28. Danson finds Morocco to be 'a worldly chooser' and an idolator and Arragon to be 'the epitome of worldly wisdom'. See L. Danson, *The Harmonies of 'The Merchant of Venice'* (New Haven and London: Yale University Press, 1978) pp. 100–3. But Morocco's assumption of self-worth is not 'admirable', as Danson claims (p. 100), any more than Arragon's similar assumption is, because Morocco bases his definition of self-worth on the wrong premise (outward show). Although Arragon has the right premise (inner merit), he errs in assuming this general truth applies specifically to himself; therefore, Arragon's own proud assumption of desert contradicts his spoken wisdom. None of these interesting interpretations base their analysis on how Shakespeare significantly adapts his source.

20. See Robinson (trans.), p. 214.
21. See ibid., p. 214.
22. Some have thought that Morocco and Arragon are not particularly greedy or worldly. See, e.g., E. A. J. Honigmann, 'Shakespeare's "Lost Source-Plays"', *MLR* **49** (1954) pp. 297–8. However, the biblically related concepts of 'the world', 'the flesh', and 'outward things' reveal that they are. Others have thought Stephen Gosson's brief description of *The Jew* might indicate that this lost play first combined the casket plot of choosers with the usury plot of a bloody bond and therefore served as the immediate source for Shakespeare's play. For refutation of this theory, see Honigmann, pp. 293–307; Brown (ed.), pp. xxix–xxx; Mahood (ed.), p. 5.
23. See J. Shapiro, *Rival Playwrights: Marlowe, Jonson, Shakespeare* (New York: Columbia University Press, 1991) p. 108. Another point that qualifies Shapiro's emphasis on foreign alienation is that a Moorish woman must be *included* in Portia's Belmontian household to attract Lancelot's illegitimate intercourse for which Lancelot will be held accountable, according to Lorenzo (3.5.30–5).

24. Baldassare Castiglione, *The Book of The Courtier*, trans. Sir Thomas Hoby, ed. Walter Raleigh (London: David Nutt, 1900) Book IV, p. 305.

25. Ibid., p. 310.

26. See Ann Jennalie Cook, *Making a Match: Courtship in Shakespeare and His Society* (Princeton: Princeton University Press, 1991) p. 134; cf. also pp. 54, 56–8, 135n., 176–7n.

27. For some who see Bassanio as primarily mercenary in his motives, see Arthur Quiller-Couch and J. D. Wilson (eds), *The Merchant of Venice* (Cambridge: Cambridge University Press, 1926) pp. vii–xxxii; H. B. Charlton, 'Shakespeare's Jew', *Shakespearian Comedy* (London: Methuen, 1938) pp. 123–60; Mordecai Gorelik, 'This Side Idolatry', *Educational Theatre Journal*, **3** (1951) pp. 187–91; Max Huhner, *Shakespearean Studies and Other Essays* (New York: Farrar, Strauss and Young, 1952) pp. 71–9; John Russell Brown, 'Love's Wealth and the Judgment of *The Merchant of Venice*', in *Shakespeare and His Comedies*, 2nd edn (London: Methuen, 1962) p. 72 (Brown sees Bassanio's commercial justification as 'ill-judged', but he does not dismiss Bassanio as financially predatory); Norman Carrington, *Shakespeare: 'The Merchant of Venice'* (Bath: Brodie, 1967); Phyllis Rackin, 'Androgyny, Mimesis, and the Marriage of the Boy Heroine on the English Stage', *PMLA*, **102** (1987) p. 31.

28. See L. Tennenhouse, *Power on Display: The Politics of Shakespeare's Genres* (New York and London: Methuen, 1986) p. 56.

29. Eric Rasmussen argues that the appearance of two words in Bassanio's soliloquy that rhyme with 'lead', namely 'head' and 'bred' (3.2.95–6), indicate that 'consciously or unconsciously . . . Bassanio has, indeed, heard Portia's song and the important clues which it provides'. See Eric Rasmussen, 'Shakespeare's *The Merchant of Venice* III.ii.63–8, *Expli* **44** (Winter 1986) pp. 12–13. We cannot arrive at this conclusion on the basis of this evidence because Morocco's soliloquy also contains two words that rhyme with 'lead', namely 'head' and 'bed' (2.7.44, 58), yet Morocco has heard no such song. For a recent interpretation that differs from mine regarding Bassanio's choice and the song, see David Lucking, 'Standing for Sacrifice: The Casket and Trial Scenes in *The Merchant of Venice*', *UTQ*, **58** (1989) pp. 363–9.

30. Sylvan Barnet notes that there has been little attention paid to Bassanio's lack of 'reasoning' about the mottos, but he attributes Bassanio's correct choice not to 'intellectus' or wisdom but to his prodigal spirit, his 'acting on the right impulse'. See S. Barnet, 'Prodigality and Time in *The Merchant of Venice*', *PMLA*, **87** (1972) pp. 27–8. Cf. Lucking, p. 369. The issue is not so much that Bassanio's intuition 'eludes the machinery of reason . . . in the denial of reasons', but rather that Bassanio's intuition as 'intellectus' is a higher mode of reasoning than 'ratio'.

31. C. S. Lewis explains the medieval–Renaissance understanding of reason as 'the organ of morality'. Medieval philosophers technically define the Rational Soul as having a higher and a lower fac-

ulty. *Intellectus*, or understanding, is the higher faculty of the two because it is the immediate, simple grasping of self-evident truths (the faculty in man nearest to angelic *intelligentia*) whereas *Ratio* is reasoning, the proceeding 'step by step to prove a truth which is not self-evident'. See C. S. Lewis, *The Discarded Image: An Introduction to Medieval and Renaissance Literature* (Cambridge: Cambridge University Press, 1970) pp. 156–8. Cf. also Theodore Spencer, who cites Castiglione and Milton on this issue in *Shakespeare and the Nature of Man*, 2nd edn (New York: Macmillan, 1949) pp. 12–13. See also D. W. Robertson, Jr, *A Preface to Chaucer: Studies in Medieval Perspectives* (Princeton: Princeton University Press, 1962) pp. 74–5, where he cites Augustine's explanation of the functions of the lower and higher reason.

32. See John Milton, *Paradise Lost*, ed. M. Y. Hughes (New York: Odyssey, 1962) Book 8, ll. 563–93, pp. 199–200.

33. See M. J. Levith, *What's in Shakespeare's Names* (Hamden, CT: Shoe String Press, 1978) pp. 79, 89. Cf. also Hugh Mclean, 'Bassanio's Name and Nature', *Names*, **25** (1977) pp. 55–62; Norman Nathan, 'Bassanio's Name', *AN&Q*, **24** (1986) pp. 1–3. Mclean and Nathan suggest Bassanio's name may refer to the Bassano family of musicians.

34. See Annibale Mottana, Rodolfo Crespi, and Giuseppe Liborio, *Simon and Schuster's Guide to Rocks and Minerals*, ed. M. Prinz, G. Harlow, and J. Peters, The American Museum of Natural History (New York: Simon and Schuster, 1978) no. 309. Cf. 'Basanite', *Britannica*, vol. 1, p. 931. Some dictionaries misleadingly limit the colour of basanite to black.

35. See 'Touchstone', *OED*, 2.

36. For these meanings, see *OED*, 'Pale', a., 1.b., 1.d.

37. See Brown (ed.), pp. 82–3; Mahood (ed.) p. 117.

38. See Sigmund Freud, 'The Theme of the Three Caskets' (1913), in *Collected Papers*, 5th imp., 4 vols (London: Hogarth Press and Institute of Psycho-Analysis, 1949) vol. 4, pp. 244–56, esp. pp. 253–4. Nor is the lead casket 'dumb' (silent and therefore death-like), as Freud hypothesises, because lead's qualities speak to Bassanio. Cf. also, Sarah Kofman's recent response to Freud's thesis in which she sees the play as 'a drama of conversion in all its forms' (p. 162), the theme of ambivalence serving desire for love and awareness of death. See S. Kofman, 'Conversions: *The Merchant of Venice* Under the Sign of Saturn', trans. Shaun Whiteside, in *Literary Theory Today*, eds Peter Collier and Helga Geyer-Ryan (Cambridge: Polity Press, 1990) pp. 142–66.

39. See Belsey, pp. 44–5.

40. See Terry Eagleton, *William Shakespeare* (Oxford and New York: Basil Blackwell, 1986) p. 45.

41. Morocco's allusion to a game of dice (2.1.31–5) as his metaphor for the casket test underscores how blind he is to the true nature of the test, and appropriately 'blind Fortune' (2.1.36) leads him. The choice of Hercules to portray the consequence of being beaten by

one's own 'rage' ('wild folly') at a game of chance foreshadows Morocco's own foolish self-defeat in a test which proves who 'is the better man' (2.1.33).

42. Cf. Mahood (ed.), *The Merchant of Venice*, New Cambridge Shakespeare (Cambridge: Cambridge University Press, 1987) 3.2.312 n. There is no need to worry about 'the indelicacy of Portia telling Bassanio that he is costing her a lot of money' (p. 125) because anyone who can spontaneously offer 36,000 ducats to cancel 3000 ducats is not worried about the cost to the purse but the cost to the heart.

43. Phyllis Rackin argues that 'Portia's masculine disguise enables her to save Antonio, but her female reality, which enables her to love and marry Bassanio, is what motivates her to do it in the first place.' See Rackin, p. 31. However, in this case, to argue that 'her female reality' is the enabling cause of her love is too reductive a position because it delimits the reality of human love to gender, whereas Shakespeare is deliberately expansionist here by depicting Portia as motivated by love for both Bassanio and Antonio, just as Bassanio returns to Venice motivated by love for Antonio and Portia.

44. See Milton, *Paradise Lost*, ed. Hughes, Book VIII, ll. 571–3, p. 199.

45. See Aelred de Rievaulx, *L'Amitié Spirituelle*, ed. J. Dubois (Bruges: Editions C. Beyaert, 1948) p. 667 B–D.

46. Levith suggests Lorenzo's name comes from the Latin *laureos* for '"laurel-crowned one"', and this presents him as 'a successful lover and a poet'. See Levith, p. 80. Catherine Belsey finds, however, that 'love in Venice generally has a poor record' (p. 41). See Belsey, pp. 41–53.

47. For examples of this conventional figure, see Mahood (ed.), 2.6.53–8 n.

48. There are differences between Lancelot's and Jacob's trickery and receipt of paternal blessing; Shakespeare cultivates these to heighten his comic effect, making Lancelot less culpable and much funnier than Jacob. Lancelot's deceptive gag is his own idea, his motive is goodnatured humour, he steals no blessing from a firstborn brother, and he confesses his joke and true identity *before* he gets his father's blessing.

49. See, e.g., Edmund Spenser, *The Faerie Queene*, ed. T. P. Roche, Jr (Harmondsworth: Penguin, 1978) I.iv.27–8, pp. 85–6.

50. See G. Bullough (ed.), *Narrative and Dramatic Sources of Shakespeare*, 8 vols (1957); 5th imp. (London and Henley: Routledge & Kegan Paul and New York: Columbia University Press, 1977) vol. 1, pp. 503–5. Shakespeare cleans up Masuccio's version by having Jessica and Lorenzo be chaste lovers, wedding before bedding. And in his afterword Masuccio advises young ladies to follow the course of virtuous marriage before indulging in 'the secret sport of Venus' (p. 504). Masuccio's tale ends with the lovers' reconciliation to the father, that 'foolish old man' whose 'inordinate suspicion' and 'senile avarice' caused the 'flout' he received and his 'heavy loss' in the first place (pp. 504–5). Cf. also, Brown (ed.), p. xli. From the

perspective of social historians, Jessica's theft can be interpreted as the stealing of her dowry. See Margaret Loftus Ranald, *Shakespeare and His Social Context* (New York: AMS Press, 1987) pp. 69–70; Cook, pp. 136–7.

51. The dizzying sense of wealth in this play suggests that if Shylock can refuse 36,000 ducats from Bassanio in order to take his bond, then Jessica can not have left her father destitute, as some seem to imply in their criticism of Jessica's theft. Moreover, sums of wealth for dowry could be vast. Vincentio Saviolo records an instance of 'a hundred thousand crowns'. See *Vincentio Saviolo: His Practise* (1595), ed. James L. Jackson, in *Three Elizabethan Fencing Manuals* (Delmar, New York: Scholars' Facsimiles & Reprints, 1972) pp. 471–2. For some actual dowry figures in Elizabethan England, see Cook, pp. 128–32.

52. Herbert S. Donow points out this verbal parallel of 'casket' between the two plots. See H. S. Donow, 'Shakespeare's Caskets: Unity in the Merchant of Venice', *ShakS*, **4** (1968) p. 91.

53. See Robinson (trans.), p. 215.

54. See Bullough, vol. 1, pp. 502–3.

55. See Morris Palmer Tilley, *A Dictionary of Proverbs in England in the Sixteenth and Seventeenth Centuries* (Ann Arbor: University of Michigan Press, 1950) N320, p. 507; cf. N319.

56. See *OED*, 'Stone', 11; cf. Mahood (ed.), 2.8.23–4 n. for the same meaning, see *Rom.* 1.3.53, *Wiv.* 1.4.111–12, and *Tim.* 2.2.111.

57. For the significance of 'two-in-one', see Alastair Fowler, *Triumphal Forms: Structural Patterns in Elizabethan Poetry* (Cambridge: Cambridge University Press, 1970) pp. 72–3, 153, 159.

58. See Spenser, *The Faerie Queene*, ed. Roche, I.7.33, p. 127 and p. 1096 (notes).

59. For other references to this same imagery in *The Jew of Malta*, see 2.3.35, 48–68, 90, 134.

60. See J. C. Boswell, 'Shylock's Turquoise Ring', *SQ*, **14** (1963) pp. 481–3.

61. Ibid., p. 483.

62. See R. Wilson, *The Three Ladies of London*, in *Narrative and Dramatic Sources, of Shakespeare*, ed. Bullough, vol. 1, p. 479.

63. See Steevens's commentary, quoted in *The Merchant of Venice*, ed. H. H. Furness, The Variorum Shakespeare (Philadelphia: J. B. Lippincott, 1888) p. 132. Cf. also, Maurice Charney, 'Jessica's Turquoise Ring and Abigail's Poisoned Porridge: Shakespeare and Marlowe as Rivals and Imitators', *RenD*, **10** (1979) p. 40.

64. See *The Works of Thomas Nashe*, ed. R. B. McKerrow (1904–10; rpt. Oxford: Basil Blackwell, 1958) vol. 2, p. 269. Cf. Horst Noldemar Janson, *Apes and Ape Lore in the Middle Ages and the Renaissance* (London: The Warburg Institute, University of London, 1952) esp. ch. 7, pp. 199–237.

65. Ibid. Cf. the Italian emphasis on foolishness in derivatives ('sciminésco', 'scimionàte') of the word for monkey or ape, 'scímia'. See John Florio, *Queen Anna's New World of Words* (1611; rpt. Menston:

Scolar Press, 1968) p. 477. For a different and very negative view of
the monkey as associated with lechery or human derogation, see
Charney, p. 39.

66. See Herman Melville, *Billy Budd, Sailor*, eds Harrison Hayford and
Merton M. Sealts, Jr (Chicago and London: University of Chicago
Press, 1962) p. 52.

67. See Camille Slights, 'In Defense of Jessica: The Runaway Daughter
in 'The Merchant of Venice', *SQ*, **31** (1980) p. 361.

68. E. E. Stoll seems to have been the first to have noted this biblical
parallel. See Stoll, 'Shylock', in *Shakespeare Studies: Historical and Comparative in Method* (New York: Macmillan, 1927) cited in R. Noble,
Shakespeare's Biblical Knowledge and Use of the Book of Common Prayer
(1935; rpt. New York, Octagon Books, 1970) p. 97. An excellent modern
example of the idolatry theme may be found in James Joyce's short
story, 'The Sisters'. See J. Joyce, *Dubliners*, eds Robert Scholes and
A. Walton Litz (New York: Viking, 1969), p. 18.

69. See T. Wilson, *A Discourse upon Usury* [1572], ed. R. H. Tawney (New
York: Harcourt Brace, 1925) pp. 361–2. Cf. Ecclus 10.9: 'There is nothing
worse than a covetous man: [. . . there is not a more wicked thing
than to love money:] for such one would even sell his soul.'

70. See Andrew Willet, *Hexapla in Genesin . . . A Sixfold Commentary upon
Genesis* (London: Thomas Creede, 1608) p. 326. Willet sees Rachel's
taking of her father's household gods as a compensatory act for
Laban's improvident neglect of dowry because he exchanged (or
sold) his daughters in return for Jacob's years of labour.

71. See Bullough, vol. 1, p. 505.

72. Boswell, *op. cit.*, thinks Jessica herein 'flouted the Jewish tradition'
(p. 483), but Jessica's obvious sense of shame tempers her violation of
tradition. The glossator of the Geneva Bible explains that gendered cross-
dressing 'alter[s] the order of nature' and therefore 'despite[s] God'.

73. See Chaucer (trans.), *De Consolatione Philosophiae*, in *The Works of
Geoffrey Chaucer*, ed. F. N. Robinson (Cambridge: Riverside Press)
vol. III, 2, p. 342.

74. See Seneca, *De Beneficiis*, in *The Moral Essays*, trans. John W. Basore,
Loeb Library edn, 3 vols (London: W. Heinemann; Cambridge, MA:
Harvard University Press, 1935) vol. 3, p. 11.

75. See F. O'Connor's short story, 'A Good Man Is Hard to Find', in
The Complete Stories (1946; rpt. New York: Farrar, Straus and Giroux,
1974) pp. 117–33.

76. See W. Faulkner, *Light in August* (the corrected text) (New York:
Vintage, 1990) pp. 47–8.

77. See Bullough, vol. 1, p. 469.

78. In *Il Pecorone* the merchant is the 'godfather' to the young lover.
See Bullough, vol. 1, p. 463. Such a false start, e.g., also appears in
Othello, in which Cassio is given 'a wife' (1.1.21). Shakespeare is
probably following his source here (Cinthio), but he deletes this
idea for the rest of *Othello*.

79. The suitor suffers melancholy after each of his two failures to obtain the Lady of Belmonte. The merchant becomes 'very melancholy'

after he thinks he has lost his godson – 'so great is the love [he] bear[s] him'. The merchant counsels his godson against giving himself 'over to melancholy': 'since I [Ansaldo] have found you [Giannetto] again, I am satisfied'. See Bullough, vol. 1, pp. 144, 145–6, 143, 145.

80. For an interesting earlier juxtaposition of the ideas of the foolish gudgeon and the melancholic young gentleman who gets hooked by the usurer (a merchant degenerated from his true vocation), see Thomas Lodge, *An Alarum against Usurers* (1584), sigs B1^v–B2^r, in *The Works of Thomas Lodge* (New York: Russell & Russell, 1963).

81. See Danson, p. 32.

82. See, e.g., Ronald A. Sharp, 'Gift Exchange and the Economics of Spirit in *The Merchant of Venice*', *MP* **83** (1986) pp. 250–1, 261. Sharp's good essay on gifts does not note that the unusual equation of lending and giving is based on a specific passage in the Bible (Lk 6.35) that could be interpreted as a precept to set an ideal of spiritual perfection. The glossator of the Geneva Bible, for example, favours such an idealistic interpretation of lending: 'Not only not hoping for profit, but to lose the stock & principal forasmuch as Christ bindeth him self to repay the whole with a most liberal increase' (Lk 6.35, gloss). Considerable debate over the interpretation of this biblical passage pervades discussion of the concept of usury. See e.g., J. T. Noonan, *The Scholastic Analysis of Usury* (Cambridge, MA: Harvard University Press, 1957) pp. 232, 275, 306, 390, 393; B. Nelson, *The Idea of Usury: From Tribal Brotherhood to Universal Otherhood*, 2nd edn (Chicago: University of Chicago Press, 1969) pp. 51, 117–18.

83. For differentiation between lending and giving and for the lender's right to expect the exact (nothing in excess) repayment of the loan, see T. Wilson, pp. 276–7; Miles Mosse, *The Arraignment and Conviction of Usury . . .* (London: Widow Orwin, 1595) pp. 28–9, 33–5, 74.

84. See T. Moisan, '"Which is the merchant here? and which the Jew?": Subversion and Recuperation in *The Merchant of Venice*', in *Shakespeare Reproduced: The Text in History and Ideology*, eds. J. E. Howard and M. F. O'Connor (New York & London: Methuen, 1987) pp. 188–206, esp. pp. 191–7.

85. See, e.g., Cynthia Lewis, '"Wise Men, Folly-Fall'n": Characters Named Antonio in English Renaissance Drama', *RenD*, n.s. **20** (Evanston: Northwestern University Press, 1990) pp. 197–236. See esp. n. 25; we differ regarding the facts about Antoninus's influence and stance against usury. Cf. also Levith, pp. 78–9.

86. R. De Roover, *San Bernardino of Siena and Sant'Antonino of Florence: The Two Great Economic Thinkers of the Middle Ages*, in *The Kress Library of Business and Economics*, ed. James P. Baughman, no. 19 (Cambridge: Harvard University Printing Office, 1967) p. 5. For a brief and lucid explanation of scholastic thought on usury in light of evolving social pressures, see pp. 27–33.

87. See T. Wilson, p. 331; cf. p. 197; Mosse, sig. B5^r, pp. 59, 153; John Blaxton (ed.), *The English Usurer: or, Usury Condemned, By the Most Learned . . . Divines of the Church of England . . .* (London: John Norton, 1634) p. 36.

88. Noonan, p. 77. De Roover, however, notes that Antonino was more lenient than most in granting qualified approval, especially to *merchants*, for the title *lucrum cessans* (the lender's right to claim the same return he might have obtained if he had not deprived himself of the capital lent, that is, a kind of compensation for potential profit forgone because of the loan). Aquinas, and most scholastics, rejected this title.

89. See De Roover, p. 31.

90. Ibid., p. 32.

91. Noonan, p. 78.

92. See T. Wilson, p. 227. Wilson adds that no fault so impoverishes a man as borrowing at usury does.

93. See T. Lodge, *An Alarum against Usurers*, sig. C1^r.

94. Milton's Satan, e.g., indicts himself after his fall for never having truly understood the virtue of gratitude because of his 'Pride and worse Ambition': 'And understood not that a grateful mind / By owing owes not, but still pays, at once / Indebted and discharg'd'. See Milton, *Paradise Lost*, ed. Hughes, p. 85, Book IV, ll. 40–57.

95. See Nelson, pp. 85–9.

96. Regarding Lancelot's use of 'confusions' for 'conclusions', see Brown (ed.), 2.2.35 n.; Mahood (ed.), 2.2.29 n. Shakespeare's comic use of this word also involves the plain meaning of 'confusion' ('the confused condition of anything') and the use of its plural. See *OED*, 'confusion', 5.c.,d.; cf. also entry no. 3. and the example cited from Heywood. In addition to 'experimenting' ('trying conclusions') with 'riddles' ('conclusions'), Lancelot is purposefully using a 'tricksy word' to 'defy the matter' (3.5.57–8), that is, to *confuse* his father for humour's sake, whether in his directions given to Shylock's house, his assumption of the title 'Master', or his attempt at 'scholarly' amplification (2.2.32–53). Confusion is disorder, and in this instance, comic disorder.

97. Cf. Mahood (ed.), p. 10: 'Despite talk of Jason and Hercules, Bassanio's venture has more in common with the Grail story than with the pursuit of the Golden Fleece.' Although Lucking concentrates on the theme of sacrifice in the plot, he overlooks the mythological meaning of the Golden Fleece. See Lucking, pp. 363–4, 366.

Notes to Chapter 4

1. G. Bullough (ed.), *Narrative and Dramatic Sources of Shakespeare*, 8 vols (1957); 5th imp. (London and Henley: R&KP and New York: Columbia University Press, 1977) vol. I, p. 469. The Jew in *Il Pecorone* is never specifically identified as a usurer, but his flesh bond with Ansaldo would be seen by Elizabethans as a usurious contract for reasons similar to the ones explained herein for Shylock's flesh bond.

2. See, e.g., Milton Crane, *Shakespeare's Prose*, 2nd imp. (Chicago: Uni-

versity of Chicago Press, 1952) pp. 80–3; Brian Vickers, *The Artistry of Shakespeare's Prose* (London: Methuen, 1968) pp. 82–8. Vickers argues that Shakespeare's 'prose reaches maturity with *The Merchant of Venice*, and of all his varied tools Shakespeare seems to make the most original application of the symmetries of syntax' (p. 88) with Shylock's 'miserliness with words' (p. 83) complementing 'the brief symmetries' of rhetorical structures that 'consistently characterise Shylock' (p. 87). Cf. also, John Leslie Palmer, 'Shylock', in *Comic Characters of Shakespeare* (London: Macmillan, 1946) pp. 53–91; Virgil K. Whitaker, 'The Romantic Comedies', in *Shakespeare's Use of Learning* (San Marino: The Huntington Library, 1953) pp. 178–93; B. Ifor Evans, *The Language of Shakespeare's Plays* (London: Methuen, 1959) pp. 101–8; H. N. L. Sastri, 'Shylock's Language', *IJES*, **3** (1962) pp. 121–31.

3. For the *Merchant*, Noble argues that Shakespeare used both the Geneva Bible and the Bishops' Bible with the emphasis falling on the latter (see R. Noble, *Shakespeare's Biblical Knowledge and Use of the Book of Common Prayer* (1935; rpt. New York: Octagon Books, 1970) p. 61). An overlooked example of just how closely Shakespeare is using the Bible, in this case the Genevan version, appears in Shylock's designation of the time of year ('In the end of autumn', 1.3.73) for the generation of Jacob's sheep. This information corresponds to the gloss in the Geneva Bible – 'As they which took the ram about September, & brought forth about March' (Gn 30.41) – and such specific information about the time of year does not appear in the Bishops' Bible. Mahood rightly sees Shakespeare's use of New Testament passages in Shylock's mouth for dramatic irony at Shylock's expense, but she overlooks similar irony in the Genesis allusions, suggesting instead that the effect of those passages is different and does not depend on immediate audience recognition (M. M. Mahood (ed.), p. 186).

4. The Geneva Bible, however, favourably glosses the term as a typological fulfilment of those holy men in the Old Testament who took the 'Nazarite' vow. See Mt 2.23, gloss. Cf. M. M. Mahood (ed.), *The Merchant of Venice*, New Cambridge Shakespeare (Cambridge: Cambridge University Press, 1987) 1.3.28 n.

5. Gerald Friedlander, *Shakespeare and the Jews* (London: George Routledge & Sons; New York: E. P. Dutton, 1921) p. 24.

6. Lars Engle suggests that Antonio, a merchant, must be bound because Bassanio is a lord, and a lord in Elizabethan England could not be imprisoned for debt. See Lars Engle, '"Thrift is Blessing": Exchange and Explanation in *The Merchant of Venice*', *SQ*, **37** (1986) p. 27. However, Arthur B. Stonex argues that 'under the Statute 13 Eliz. c. 7' merchants, unlike gentlemen, could not be imprisoned for debt if they pleaded bankruptcy, and this loophole probably fostered much of the gentleman's hatred for the usurious merchant. See Arthur B. Stonex, 'Money Lending and Money-Lenders in England During the 16th and 17th Centuries', in *Schelling Anniversary Papers* (New York: Russell & Russell, 1923) p. 278. Until

further evidence is forthcoming, it appears that according to English standards neither Bassanio nor Antonio could be imprisoned, and interestingly enough Elizabethan references to actual imprisonment for usury are few indeed. See N. Jones, *God and the Moneylenders: Usury and Law in Early Modern England* (Oxford and Cambridge, MA: Basil Blackwell, 1984) pp. 98, 111; Richard Greaves, *Society and Religion in Elizabethan England* (Minneapolis: University of Minnesota Press, 1981) pp. 598, 600–1. Whatever may be the historical case for sixteenth-century England, Shakespeare follows his literary source, *Il Pecorone*, by having Antonio imprisoned, despite apparent bankruptcy. See Bullough, vol. I, p. 471: 'the Jew had Ansaldo arrested'. But Shakespeare also significantly develops the bare statement in his source by devoting a scene to the pleas of the no longer free Antonio, now on stage with his jailer (3.3), thus heightening the anxiety for Antonio.

7. See Mahood's explanation of the menacing meaning of 'pirate', and her disapproval of a chiming pronunciation of the term in her edition (1.3.20 n.). But Vickers explores how Shakespeare adapts rhetorical symmetries for different ends (comic as well as serious) so that by 3.1 Shylock is 'both a figure of fun and a figure of fear'. See Vickers, p. 88. Shylock's pronunciation of 'pi-rats' is an intended echo of his 'land rats and water rats', and the humour here need not detract from the sense of menace. Indeed, the dramatic tradition of the Vice character from medieval drama depends on the *fusion* of homour and danger.

8. See T. Wilson, *A Discourse upon Usury* [1572], ed. R. H. Tawney (New York: Harcourt Brace, 1925) pp. 326–7. I suspect that Wilson's text may be a likely source for some particulars in Shakespeare's play and is important as a general influence in its repeated emphases, especially its sustained development of the importance of charity and mercy as antidotes to usury, and perhaps even more significantly, the historical and moral interrelation of Jews and usury, which receives the fullest treatment I know of in sixteenth-century English literature on the subject of usury. The possible particular parallels between Wilson and Shakespeare will be presented throughout this chapter, but in brief summary, they include Wilson's euphemistic use of 'usance', his 'land pirate' cited from Baldus, his repeated use of 'cut throat', the recurrent imagistic use of 'dog/ cur' and 'devil' imagery for usurers as well as the 'biting/feeding' motif and what appears to be his unique emphasis on the 'heart' and the usurer's taking of hearts from his victims' bodies. (Wilson's possible relation to Portia's mercy speech has been considered.)

9. John Russell Brown summarises some of the commentary on this line. See J. R. Brown (ed.), *The Merchant of Venice* (New Arden Shakespeare) (1955; rpt. London: Methuen, 1969) pp. 23–4, n. 36. Cf. Mahood (ed.), 1.3.33 n.

10. The name 'Pharisees' means '"those who separate themselves" from the ignorant "people of the land"' who incur ritual defilement when they transgress the Law. The historical Pharisees were the Jewish

religious party who came together in the second century BC for practising the Mosaic Law as exactly as possible. They were lay-men, not priests, they zealously embraced the Law and the tradi-tions of the fathers which added new regulations to the Mosaic Law, and they, as a group, are the immediate ancestors to mod-ern Judaism. The Pharisees deserve credit for having preserved Judaism from total destruction after the Romans destroyed Jerusalem and its temple. St Paul (Saul) was a Pharisee before he converted to Christianity, and this fact helps to explain some of the polemi-cal language and tone he adopts in writing against Pharisaism, especially regarding the subjects of justice, justification, and the Law. See Louis F. Hartman (trans. and ed.), *Encyclopedic Diction-ary of the Bible*, 2nd rev. edn (New York: McGraw-Hill, 1963) pp. 1827–9.

11. Noble, p. 164.
12. See Miles Mosse, *The Arraignment and Conviction of Usury . . .* (London: Widow Orwin, 1595) pp. 148–9.
13. For 'usance', see Mahood (ed.), 1.3.37 n. Mahood cites Wilson here, and there is another appearance of this euphemism in Wilson's text when the 'unlearned' lawyer (p. 193) argues in favour of usury or 'moderate usance' (p. 244). 'Usance', however, does not have to be used euphemistically. Cf. Wilson, pp. 308, 312, 332. Cf. Richard Porder, *A Sermon of gods fearful threatenings for Idolatry . . . with a Treatise against Usury* (London: Henry Denham, 1570) fols 84^v, 101^v.
14. See N. Nathan, '"On the Hip"', *N&Q*, **197** (1952) p. 74. But it should be noted that in Jacob's history there is an earlier appearance of wrestling imagery applied to Rachel (Gn 30.8).
15. Bishop Gervase Babington, *Certain Plain, Brief, and Comfortable Notes upon every Chapter of Genesis* (London: A. Jeffes and P. Short, 1592) sig. R. Bishop Babington contrasts the greed, deceit, and foolish-ness of 'a subtle worldling' (sig. 07^v) like Laban with the 'faith and truth' of a good servant like Jacob (sig. R1^v) and thereby de-velops the glosses in both the Geneva and Bishops' Bibles.
16. Complicating this perspective is the Christian interpretation of the Deuteronomic passage as a temporary exemption for the Jews toward strangers, but one that was not meant to be directed against Chris-tians. See the glosses on Deut 23.20 in both the Geneva and Bish-ops' Bibles. See Mosse's arguments that sinful usury violates moral law applicable to all people and nations, but that God can make exceptions to His laws for His own reasons, so that usury accom-modated the hardhearted and was to be exercised only against pagan Gentiles dwelling in the Israelites' midst (pp. 122–6). Mosse cites Wolfius for the view that the usury exemption was tolerated so that the Jews could take usury of strangers in order to take care of their own poor and the strangers' poor as well as converts (p. 128). Cf. Wilson, who stresses that on the basis of Exodus the Jews might 'lawfully' practise usury upon strangers only '*before* Christs coming' (p. 283, my italics).
17. For the concept of spiritual usury as a virtuous kind of usury, see

Mosse, p. 13. Cf. Justinus's description of Christian 'duties of humanity', cited in Mosse, p. 45. It should be noted, however, that sixteenth-century writers on usury are usually be noted, however, that sixteenth-century writers on usury are usually not so idealistic as Luke's verse and its gloss because many of them are careful to distinguish between 'lend' (expect the principal returned) and 'give' (expect nothing returned). See T. Wilson, p. 359.

18. The importance of how carefully Shakespeare develops the anti-usury position for his merchant Antonio is underscored by the absence of any usury motif in the newly discovered, fourteenth-century French analogue, *Le Miracle de un marchant et un juif*. See J. Madison Davis and Sylvie L. F. Richards, 'The Merchant and the Jew: A Fourteenth-Century French Analogue to *The Merchant of Venice*', *SQ*, **36** (1985) pp. 60–2. In Shakespeare's possible literary sources for his play, usury appears in the undated *Ballad of Gernutus*, where Gernutus is a Jewish usurer, and in Anthony Munday's *Zelauto or The Fountain of Fame* (1580), where Truculento is a Christian usurer. Barabas in Marlowe's *The Jew of Malta* (c.1588–92) is presented as a Machiavellian merchant/miser (Prologue and 1.1.1–48), although in his various past professions, including physician and engineer, he has been 'a great usurer' (4.1.39) whose 'extorting, cozening, forfeiting / And tricks' of usury filled jails with bankrouts and hospitals with orphans (2.3.187–97). The godly man's strict avoidance of borrowing or lending at usury receives special emphasis in Mosse's treatise (sigs A4–A4^v, B3^v).

19. See L. C. Stevenson, *Praise and Paradox: Merchants and Craftsmen in Elizabethan Popular Literature* (Cambridge: Cambridge University Press, 1984) pp. 92–106. Cf. also, Stonex, pp. 265–9, 275–9; Arthur B. Stonex, 'The Usurer in Elizabethan Drama', *PMLA*, **31** (1916) pp. 190–210. The usurer in Wilson's *A Discourse upon Usury* (1572) is a merchant significantly named 'Gromel gainer' (pp. 192, 249, 251), and Wilson's use of the name 'Gromel' to signify a miser interested in only his own gain antedates the evidence cited in the *OED* for 'Gromel (l)' as an obsolete form of 'Gromwell'.

20. See Stevenson, p. 108, n. 2.

21. See Romans 3.8. Mosse stresses this scriptural passage, and the idea that Christians should not do evil to do good, in his attack on usury which purports to serve a good cause, such as relieving orphans or redeeming Christians from the Turks. Cf. Wilson, p. 262.

22. Mosse, sigs B3^v–B4^r. Mosse cites this idea from 'the great Schoolmen'.

23. See H. H. Furness (ed.), *The Merchant of Venice*, The Variorum Shakespeare (Philadelphia: J. B. Lippincott, 1888) p. 44, where Ambrose Eccles puzzles over this Jacob–Laban allusion, finding 'little appositeness or ingenuity'. While John Russell Brown presents various interpretations of Shylock's argument, he represents past scholarly opinion in maintaining that the Jacob–Laban story is not associated with usury in any Renaissance treatment of the subject and therefore must originate with Shakespeare: 'The Laban story

has not been found in any sixteenth-century book on usury.' See Brown (ed.), p. 26, n. on ll. 72–85.

24. Mosse, pp. 167–8. Mosse's marginal gloss refers the reader to Genesis 31.9 for an explanation of God's taking away Laban's goods.

25. Frank McCombie traces the play's echoes of the Wisdom literature of the Old Testament and suggests Shakespeare may have connected his memory of Proverbs 28.8 with Proverbs 26.19 to develop Shylock's phrase 'merry sport' as well as Antonio's ultimate control of Shylock's wealth as a result of such 'sport'. See F. McCombie, 'Wisdom as Touchstone in *The Merchant of Venice*', *New Blackfriars*, **64** (1982) pp. 117–18. Cf. my analysis of Shakespeare's dramatic use of Proverbs 28.8, which is given unique prominence in English usury literature in Mosse's text: J. O. Holmer, 'The Education of the Merchant of Venice', *SEL*, **25** (1985) pp. 311–24; 'A New Source for *The Merchant of Venice*', *ShakS*, **21** (1993) pp. 11–54.

26. Mosse, p. 167; my italics.

27. See Brown (ed.), 1.3.72 n. It is noteworthy that in the written clarification of the 1571 statute, 'direct or indirect' attempts at usury are deemed unlawful. See Jones, p. 64. For some of these attempts at getting interest *indirectly* see Jones, pp. 118–44. The composition of Wilson's text (1569) just antedates this statute, but none the less Wilson also stresses that usurious gain should be taken 'neither directly nor indirectly' (p. 334). Cf. the confusion of this issue in Leah Wood Wilkins's argument that Shylock's equation of flesh and money is an attempt 'to collect interest without taking interest', in L. W. Wilkins, 'Shylock's Pound of Flesh and Laban's Sheep', *MLN*, **62** (1947) pp. 28–30. Many Elizabethans, especially after the Act Against Usury of 1571, developed a great variety of ruses to evade the law by various subterfuges to take some advantage beyond the principal without risk, such as through 'gifts'.

28. For the meaning of Abram's name, see Naseeb Shaheen, 'Shylock's "Abram" in *The Merchant of Venice*', *N&Q*, **38** (1991) pp. 56–7.

29. See Brown (ed.), 1.3.67–9 n.

30. Just as Shylock is fascinated by Jacob's 'thriving', so Barabas recalls only Job's wealth when his fellow Jews attempt to inspire him with Job's patience in the midst of adversity (1.2.181). For an emphasis on spiritual (not just carnal) generation from Abram, see Babington, sig. H8ʳ; A. Willet, *Hexapla in Genesis . . . A Sixfold Commentary upon Genesis* (London: Thomas Creede, 1608) p. 172.

31. See Mosse, p. 143. See also, Wilson, pp. 183, 265, 276, 285, 325, 356, 379; Bishop John Jewel, *An Exposition upon the two Epistles of the Apostle St Paul to the Thessalonians* (London: R. Newberie, 1583) pp. 114, 177–19; Phillip Stubbes, *The Anatomy of Abuses: Containing A Discovery . . . of such Notable Vices . . . in a very famous Island called Aligna . . .* (London: Richard Jones, 1583) sig. K8ᵛ; Benjamin Nelson, *The Idea of Usury: From Tribal Brotherhood to Universal Otherhood*, 2nd edn (Chicago: University of Chicago Press, 1969) pp. 9–10; and Brown (ed.), 1.3.85 n. Philippus Caesar quotes St Bernard on

the legal theft of usury: '*Usury is a legal thief, foretelling aforewhat he doth mind afterward to steal.*' See Caesar, *A General Discourse Against the Damnable Sect of Usurers*, trans. Thomas Rogers (London: John Kyngston, 1578) fol. 6.

32. See *The Death of Usury, or, The Disgrace of Usurers* (Cambridge: John Legatt, 1594) p. 33; my italics for 'thrift' and 'theft'. Cf. also Thomas Lodge, who mentions 'thriftiness' as one euphemism for usury. See Thomas Lodge, *An Alarum against Usurers* [1584], in *The Complete Works of Thomas Lodge*, vol. 1 (New York: Russell & Russell, 1963) sig. F3. The author of *Death of Usury* also has a single instance of usance as a euphemistic term (p. 40).

33. See Wilson, pp. 231, 363. Cf. also, pp. 229, 355; for good intent as non-sinful, see pp. 344, 335. Cf. Mosse, sigs B2–B2ᵛ.

34. See Brown (ed.), 1.3.90 n.; Mosse, p. 110.

35. See Mahood (ed.) 1.3.126 n. Aristotle's objection to the unnatural breeding of money is also founded on its confusion of a means for an end: 'Currency came into existence merely as a means of exchange; usury tries to make it increase [as though it were an end in itself]. This is the reason why usury is called by the word we commonly use [the word *tokos*, which in Greek also means "breed" or "offspring"].' See Aristotle, *The Politics of Aristotle*, trans. Ernest Barker (1946; rpt. Oxford: Clarendon Press, 1948) pp. 28–9. Cf. also, Wilson, p. 313. This philosophical concern with means and ends pervades the play as does the literal and figurative play on the 'generational' motif. Wilson also treats the Greek (*tokos* – 'a birth or born creature') and the Latin (*faenus a faetu* – 'of a birthe or born creature') etymology for the generational wordplay on 'usury'. See Wilson, p. 241.

36. See Mosse, pp. 10–12, 32. In his discussion of the signification of the word 'usury', Mosse clarifies that 'usury' simply signifies the use of a thing, and therefore usury has a proper and improper meaning (legitimate use as opposed to abuse that constitutes the sin of usury).

37. Spenser, *The Faerie Queene*, ed. T. P. Roche, Jr (Harmondsworth: Penguin, 1978) I.iv.27–8.

38. See Wilson, pp. 331–3.

39. Thomas Nashe, *The Works of Thomas Nashe*, ed. R. B. McKerrow, 5 vols (1904–10; rpt. Oxford: Basil Blackwell, 1958) vol. 2, pp. 92–108; Thomas Lodge, *Wits, Misery and the World Madness: Discovering the Devils Incarnate of this Age* (1596), in *The Works of Thomas Lodge*, vol. 4, sigs. E4ʳ–E4ᵛ.

40. Mosse, sig. B3. In Wilson's treatise, on the other hand, the chief user of Scripture is Ockerfoe, the preacher, who argues against usury as sinfully contrary to God's law, and the amateur lawyer, who supports moderate usury, notes the preacher's use of Scripture in an attempt to refute that position, especially with arguments from nature and human law (see p. 235).

41. See Wilson, p. 309. For more references to the commonplace association of usury and the devil, see, e.g., Lodge, sigs. A2, B2ᵛ, B3,

B4, F4^v, *et passim*; Jewel, p. 115; Stubbes, sig. K8; Caesar, fols 6–6^v, 12, 29^v, 33^v–34, 35^v–36; *Death of Usury*, p. 39.

42. Wilson, pp. 178, 272, 279; cf also, pp. 220–1, 229, 248, 258, 270, 272, 309, 328, 338, 354, 373.

43. Ibid., pp. 232, 269.

44. Cf. Mahood (ed.), 1.3.103 n.; 3.3.6 n. on 'dog' and usury. Cf. Noble, p. 97.

45. Mosse, pp. 89–90. While this criticism and its language probably derives from the lending principle of *mutuum* (see Thomas Wilson, p. 276), the typical phrasing is 'his own', 'her own', or 'their own'. See Wilson, pp. 372–3; Jewel, p. 118; Nicolas Sander, *A Brief Treatise of Usury* (Lovanii: Joannem Foulerum, 1568), in *English Recusant Literature 1558–1640*, ed. D. M. Roger, vol. 97 (Menston, England: Scolar Press, 1972) sig. B6^v and for '*mutuum*' see sig. B7. The precise phrase, 'mine own', is much more atypical, but three instances appear in Wilson's lengthy treatise (pp. 236, 248, 276) and one in N. Sander, *A Brief Treatise of Usury*, sig. C1^v.

46. Mosse, p. 133.

47. Ibid., p. 133. This is ultimately the view that will prevail in the revision of English usury law in 1624; only exorbitant usury will be deemed unlawful.

48. Ibid., p. 135. The pro-usury lawyer in Wilson's treatise tries to minimise this argument that usury is a 'monstrous beast' because it is considered 'a kind of biting, as a dog useth to bite or gnaw upon a bone . . . [and] bringeth forth monsters from time to time, by excessive increase of gain' (p. 241).

49. See, e.g., 1.3.39; 2.5.14–15; 4.1.137–8.

50. See, e.g., 3.3.32–3; 4.1.265–7.

51. Wilson, pp. 220, 240–1, 231, 270, 258. Cf. also, for dog imagery, 226, 227; for biting/gnawing/feeding imagery, 208, 219, 232, 236, 257, 266, 270, 284.

52. See Wilson, pp. 232, 254, 290, 357; cf. 240, 253, 358. See Mosse, p. 83. Cf. Brown (ed.), who notes that 'cut throat' appears once in a possible literary source for Shakespeare's play, Anthony Munday's *Zelauto* (1580) p. 166 and 1.3.106 n. Marlowe uses the verb phrase, 'cut thy throat', but not the noun or adjective forms in *The Jew of Malta*, e.g., 2.3.119, 4.1.11, 4.5.5.

53. See Nashe, vol. 3, p. 106. For Shakespeare's probable use of Nashe's *Have with You to Saffron-Walden* in his composition of *Romeo and Juliet*, see G. B. Evans (ed.), *Romeo and Juliet* (Cambridge: Cambridge University Press, 1984) pp. 3–6. Regarding the composition date of *The Merchant of Venice*, see Mahood (ed.), pp. 1–2, where she suggests the likelihood of 1597; cf. also, Brown (ed.), pp. xxvi–vii.

54. See *OED*, 'Spoil', 4., 11.

55. See Marlowe, *The Jew of Malta*, 2.3.20–5. Marlowe uses 'dog(s)' as an opprobrious epithet for Christians, Jews, and infidels in the play. See, e.g., 5.1.19; 5.5.86. 'Dog' is apparently one of the vilest terms in the Elizabethan arsenal of name-calling; Shakespeare uses

it outside of a Jewish or usurious context very effectively in *Richard III*. Nashe, like Shakespeare, would certainly be familiar with Marlowe's play. Nashe perhaps collaborated with Marlowe in the first composition of *Dido Queen of Carthage*, perhaps when they were both at Cambridge around 1586/7. See I. Ribner (ed.), *The Complete Plays of Christopher Marlowe* (New York: Odyssey, 1963) p. xx.

56. Wilson, p. 278.
57. Brown (ed.), 1.3.138 n.
58. For an alternative argument, see Lawrence Danson, who alleges that Antonio is not deceived and that Shylock does not intend to deceive him. L. Danson, *The Harmonies of 'The Merchant of Venice'* (New Haven and London: Yale University Press, 1978) p. 156. But in the *Ballad of Gernutus*, the only source presenting the bond as a 'merry jest', the Jewish usurer intends deception, and the deceived merchant signs the bond 'with right good will'. See the *Ballad of Gernutus*, in Brown (ed.), p. 154. This 'good will' response is similar to Antonio's approval (1.3.173–4), and this deceived merchant does not expect the forfeiture to be of any good to Gernutus, herein paralleling Shylock's argument (1.3.153–63) as well as Salarino's query: 'thou wilt not take his flesh. What's that good for?' (3.1.40–1), Antonio's initial suspicion (1.3.90–4) is later deceived or at least allayed, not merely forgotten, as Brown claims (1.3.95 n.), because the messages of distrust are now assigned to Bassanio (1.3.147–8, 172) to serve as reminders.
59. On the moral necessity for risk in business and concomitant trust in God's providence, see Mosse, pp. 54–7. Cf. Jewel, p. 142; Jones, pp. 4, 11; and S. Barnet, 'Prodigality and Time in *The Merchant of Venice*', *PMLA*, **87** (1972) pp. 28–9.
60. See Mosse, pp. 55–7.
61. This concept appears in almost every sixteenth-century English treatise on usury. See, e.g., Sander, sigs A7, E6, F1, G8; Wolfgang Musculus, *Common Places of Christian Religion. Hereunto are added two other treatises . . . one of Oaths, and an other of Usury*, trans. John Man (London: Henry Bynneman, 1578) p. 22; Henry Smith, *The Examination of Usury, in Two Sermons* (London: R. Field, 1591) pp. 5, 18; *Death of Usury*, pp. 3–5.
62. Wilson, pp. 218–19; my italics.
63. See Mosse, p. 45.
64. See ibid., pp. 72–3; Wilson, pp. 292, 359; Sander, sigs. F1, H6^v–H7, H8^v; and John T. Noonan, Jr, *The Scholastic Analysis of Usury* (Cambridge, MA: Harvard University Press, 1957) pp. 32–3.
65. Mosse, p. 72.
66. Ibid., p. 69.
67. Mahood (ed.), p. 18.
68. See Jones, pp. 118–44.
69. Mosse, p. 18.
70. Ibid., p. 61.

71. See ibid., pp. 64–6.
72. See ibid., p. 59. Cf. p. 60: 'I do not think (saith Aretius) that any man knoweth thoroughly the arts of usury, but only those which are daily conversant in the *practice* of the same' (p. 60, my italics). We realise that Antonio, who neither gives nor takes usury, lacks this conversance in practice. Wilson earlier explained, 'the usurer beareth the *countenance* of an honest man . . . [and] he undoeth as many as he dealeth withal, under the color of *amity* and *law*'. See Wilson, p. 285, my italics.
73. Mosse, p. 58.
74. Ibid., p. 74; my italics.
75. Ibid., p. 75; my italics.
76. Ibid., p. 46; my italics.
77. Ibid., p. 75.
78. See W. Cohen, '*The Merchant of Venice* and the Possibilities of Historical Criticism', *ELH*, **49** (1982) p. 771.
79. Cohen, p. 772.
80. Perhaps an English audience would even hear in the pound of flesh a pun on the English 'pound', despite the foreign currency of ducats native to the play's Venetian setting. The traditional view that usury involved taking an overplus beyond the principal of *anything* that is paid by 'number, weight, or measure' (see Wilson, pp. 276, 291, 326) allows for a pun on 'pound' as a measure of both money and weight.
81. See Harold C. Goddard, '*The Merchant of Venice*', in *The Meaning of Shakespeare* (1951; rpt. Chicago: Chicago University Press, 1960) vol. 1, p. 100.
82. See the Bishops' Bible (1568) and the gloss on Gn 30.31.
83. See Ginsburg, cited in Brown (ed.), pp. 26–7, n. on ll. 87–8.
84. Regarding the problematic patriarch Jacob, cf. Arnold Williams, *The Common Expositor: An Account of the Commentaries on Genesis 1527–1633* (Chapel Hill: University of North Carolina Press, 1948) pp. 169–71; John S. Coolidge, 'Law and Love in *The Merchant of Venice*', *SQ*, **27** (1976) pp. 246–50. For an argument that supports my reading, see Norman Nathan, 'Shylock, Jacob, and God's Judgment', *SQ*, **1** (1950) pp. 257–8, 259 n. 6. For a different argument about identifying the Shylock–Antonio relation in terms of the relation between Jacob and Laban, as well as the possible identifications of Shylock with Jacob, Laban, and Esau, see Engle, pp. 29–32.
85. See esp. the glosses in the Geneva and Bishops' Bibles on these verses.
86. See Mosse, pp. 31–2, for this criterion; see pp. 56–7 for the distinction between adventuring the issue but not the means regarding the principal in usury.
87. W. H. Auden, *The Dyer's Hand and Other Essays* (New York: Random House, 1962) p. 227.
88. M. Shell, 'The Wether and the Ewe: Verbal Usury in *The Merchant of Venice*', *Kenyon Review*, n.s. 1, **4** (Fall 1979) pp. 70, 89.
89. René Girard, '"To Entrap the Wisest": A Reading of *The Merchant*

of Venice', in *Literature and Society*, ed. Edward W. Said, Selected Papers from the English Institute, 1978, n.s. 3 (Baltimore and London: Johns Hopkins University Press, 1980) pp. 103–4.

90. David Bady, 'The Sum of Something: Arithmetic in *The Merchant of Venice'*, *SQ*, **36** (1985) p. 27. Bady, however, offers valuable comments on 'the theology of the devil's overcharge' (pp. 28–9), which amplify the common association of the devil with usury.

91. Engle, pp. 27, 31. Engle suggests that the binding of Antonio as guarantor for Bassanio (1.3.1–5) would convey to an Elizabethan audience that Antonio, as a merchant, is socially inferior to the Lord Bassanio so that Shakespeare's situating Antonio 'in class terms between Bassanio and Shylock' might account for Antonio's extreme negations of Shylock's attempt to draw parallels between them. See Engle, p. 27. Shakespeare, however, 'elevates' Antonio's social rank as merchant to 'royal merchant' or the literary merchant-prince figure of civic heroism that L. Stevenson discusses (p. 107 ff.). Shakespeare, moreover, does not stress Bassanio's social rank as a nobleman other than to have him compete favourably with Portia's other suitors, two of whom are princes and therefore higher in social rank.

92. W. Cohen, pp. 768–9.

93. See Mosse, p. 27.

94. See Wilson, p. 228; Mosse, p. 108.

95. Mosse, p. 108. Mosse claims usurers are compelled to hang down their heads at the very naming of usury (p. 111).

96. See ibid., p. 27; Jewel, p. 135; Wilson, pp. 319–20; Caesar, fols 25–7; and John Blaxton (ed.), *The English Usurer: or, Usury Condemned, By The most learned . . . Divines of the Church of England . . .* (London: John Norton, 1634) pp. 9–10. Cf. also, Noonan, pp. 105–6; Jones, pp. 5, 10 for 'interest' and pp. 22–3, 199, 201–2 for adherence to the rule of charity and virtuous intent as necessary for a positive view of moneylending in sixteenth-century England.

97. See J. Shatzmiller, *Shylock Reconsidered: Jews, Moneylending, and Medieval Society* (Berkeley: University of California Press, 1990) pp. 1–3, 71–118, 123–6 *et passim.*

98. See Bullough, vol. 1, pp. 480–2.

99. Jones, p. 29.

100. Shatzmiller, p. 71.

101. Wilson, pp. 366, 379; Mosse, p. 106. For the view that Shakespeare's family was involved in moneylending, see E. A. J. Honigmann, '"There is a World Elsewhere": William Shakespeare, Businessman', in Werner Habicht, D. J. Palmer and Roger Pringle (eds), *Images of Shakespeare*, Proceedings of the International Shakespeare Association, 1986 (Newark, NJ: University of Delaware Press, 1988) pp. 40–6. But Shylock cannot be designated a 'merchant' (p. 45). Careful legal definition also must be observed: 'Wills' are not 'loans', and legitimate 'interest' (under the extrinsic titles *damnum emergens* and *lucrum cessans*) differs from illegitimate 'interest' as usury. Cf. N. Jones, pp. 4–5.

102. Hazlitt, quoted in J. R. Brown (ed.), p. xxxiv. Girard, p. 107.
103. Mosse, sig. B2ᵛ.
104. Wilson, pp. 204, 222, 232. See Wilson, p. 283: 'And no better do I call them then Jews, yea worse than any infidel, that wittingly live by the only gain of their money.'
105. See G. K. Hunter, 'The Theology of Marlowe's *The Jew of Malta*', *JWCI*, **17** (1964) p. 214; Alan C. Dessen, 'The Elizabethan Stage Jew and Christian Example: Gerontus, Barabas, and Shylock', *MLQ*, **35** (1974) p. 243.
106. See Wilson, p. 309; cf. also, pp. 205–6, 240, 253, 258, 291.
107. See ibid., pp. 362, 315, 347. Cf. also, pp. 283, 333, 361, 374, 375.
108. This passage is cited in Nelson, pp. 99–100.
109. See Bullough, vol. 1, p. 472. Cf. also, the attempt of the 'merchants friends' to rescue the merchant by paying much more than the bond in *The Ballad of Gernutus*, in Brown (ed.), pp. 154–5.
110. For the view that Jessica's elopement causes Shylock's bloodthirstiness, see, e.g., Goddard, pp. 96–100; John H. Smith, 'Shylock: "Devil Incarnation" or "Poor Man . . . Wronged"?', *JEGP*, **60** (1961) pp. 14–19; Morris Carnovsky, 'The Mirror of Shylock', *Tulane Drama Review*, **3** (1958) pp. 35–45.

Notes to Chapter 5

1. See T. Wilson, *A Discourse upon Usury* [1572], ed. R. H. Tawney (New York: Harcourt Brace, 1925) pp. 288, 289, 278, 254, 290. To the best of my knowledge, Wilson is original in using the imagery of the usurer's taking out the hearts of men. Along with other verbal parallels cited herein, it seems likely that Shakespeare knew and used Wilson's treatise. The closest resemblance that I can find to Wilson's idea is Phillip Stubbes's development of Cato's basic idea when he describes the usurer as sucking out the blood of a man's heart. See P. Stubbes, *The Anatomy of Abuses . . .* (London: Richard Jones, 1583) sig. K7ʳ.
2. See N. Coghill, 'The Basis of Shakespearian Comedy: A Study in Medieval Affinities', *E&S*, **3** (1950) p. 21. A shortened, revised version appears in *Shakespeare Criticism: 1935–1960*, ed. Anne Ridler (London: Oxford University Press, 1963).
3. For Declamation 95 from Alexander Silvayn's *The Orator* (1596), trans. by L. P[iot], see G. Bullough (ed.), *Narrative and Dramatic Sources of Shakespeare*, 8 vols (1957); 5th imp. (London & Henley: R&KP and New York: Columbia University Press, 1977) vol. 1, pp. 482–6; quotation is from p. 483.
4. Regarding the avoidance of murder, Silvayn's Jew is motivated by his own self-interest because he does not want to risk subsequent legal liability for causing a death (p. 484). In Silvayn's work the Jew is rhetorically brilliant, even though the Christian merchant dismisses his 'sophistical reasons' (p. 485). The Jew has written the

bond so as to put the debtor in the position of having to *give* his flesh and to *choose* from which part of his body he thinks he can best spare a pound of flesh and not lose his life.

5. G. Midgley, '*The Merchant of Venice*: A Reconsideration', *Essays in Criticism*, **10** (1960) pp. 122–3.

6. Quoted in J. R. Brown (ed.), *The Merchant of Venice* (New Arden Shakespeare) (1955; rpt. London: Methuen, 1969) p. xxxv.

7. Bullough, vol. 1, p. 472.

8. See ibid., vol. 1, pp. 480–2.

9. See ibid., vol. 1, p. 482.

10. The important issue of conversion in both Marlowe's and Wilson's plays will be considered when we examine the nature and purpose of the judgement passed on Shylock.

11. T. Wilson, p. 363.

12. The quotation is from the Geneva Bible. For the use of this idea, see Israel Gollancz, *Allegory and Mysticism in Shakespeare* (London: G. W. Jones, 1931) pp. 38–9. Although Antonio did not sign the bond with any belief that he would forfeit and have to pay a pound of his flesh, he deserves credit for his courageous equanimity and spirit of willingness to suffer the penalty. He does not atttempt to make his friend feel guilty for his death as Mercutio does when he curses the houses of both the Capulets and the Montagues and blames Romeo for his intervention that costs his own life (*Rom.* 3.1.90–108).

13. See L. Danson, *The Harmonies of 'The Merchant of Venice'* (New Haven and London: Yale University Press, 1978) pp. 121–2.

14. In Paul's continuation of the argument for laying up one's treasure in heaven, he explains how those who embrace Christ 'have put off the old man with his works,/And have put on the new, which is renewed in knowledge after the image of Him that created him' (Col 3.9–10). In putting on the new man through baptism, Shylock will be called upon to put on 'love, which is the *bond* of perfectness' (Col 3.12–14, my italics). This same theological idea and image help to explain the 'old man' in Chaucer's *The Pardoner's Tale* (F. N. Robinson (ed.), *The Works of Geoffrey Chaucer* (Cambridge: Riverside Press, 1961) ll. 713–67). There the old man keeps looking for some man who will change his youth for the old man's age. Paul clarifies that the only man who can do that is Christ. Shakespeare probably plays again with this motif in the young man/old man relationship of Hal and Falstaff and the problem of reformation, especially in *Henry IV, Part One*.

15. Baldessaro is a common Italian name (e.g., Baldassare Castiglione), Balthazar is the name of a Portuguese viceroy in Kyd's *The Spanish Tragedy*, and Shakespeare uses the name for characters in three other plays, but I do not agree with Mahood's dismissal of the biblical context for Shakespeare's ingenious use of the names Balthazar and Daniel. See M. M. Mahood (ed.), *The Merchant of Venice*, New Cambridge Shakespeare (Cambridge: Cambridge University Press, 1987) 4.1.153 n. For the biblical source identification of Portia's assumed name, see Norman Nathan, 'Balthasar, Daniel, and Portia', *N&Q*,

n.s. **4** (1957) pp. 334–5. For Portia's assumption of the names Balthazar and Daniel, cf. B. Lewalski, 'Biblical Allusion and Allegory in *The Merchant of Venice*', *SQ*, **13** (1962) pp. 340–1; Harry Morris, 'The Judgment Theme in *The Merchant of Venice*', *Renascence*, **39** (Fall 1986) pp. 304–6.

16. The meaning of this name (like that of Daniel) is easily found in the Geneva Bible's Table of Names. But in Herrey's biblical concordance, the Elizabethan reader could find biographical summaries that reveal at a glance the biblical significance of the person named. In Herrey's concordance, see 'Belshatsar', sig. B1[r]; see 'Daniel', sig. B3[r].

17. See *OED*, 'doctor', 1., 4., 5.b. For a study emphasising Portia's role as 'a born and incorrigible teacher', not as 'a judge administering the law', see Robert Hapgood, 'Portia and *The Merchant of Venice*: The Gentle Bond', *MLQ*, **28** (1967) pp. 19–32, esp. 21.

18. For the scales and sword as a symbol of justice, see Samuel C. Chew, *The Pilgrimage of Life* (New Haven & London: Yale University Press, 1962) pp. 124, 125, 137, 138. For the knife or dagger as an attribute of wrath, see Spenser, *The Faerie Queene*, ed. T. P. Roche, Jr (Harmondsworth: Penguin, 1978) I.iv.33.8 and 35.3–4.

19. See Bullough, vol. 1, p. 472.

20. D. McPherson, 'Lewkenor's Venice and Its Sources', *RenQ*, **41** (1988) p. 459.

21. See David C. McPherson, *Shakespeare, Jonson, and the Myth of Venice*, (Newark: University of Delaware Press and London and Toronto: Associated University Presses, 1990) pp. 51, 62–7. McPherson argues that Shakespeare's insistence in the play on the supposed impartiality of Venetian law is the aspect of the myth of Venice used by Shakespeare to enhance the credibility of his fairy-tale stories of the caskets and the flesh bond. See pp. 63, 118. McPherson considers the wealth and justice aspects of the myth but overlooks the important emphasis on 'wisdom' that Shakespeare cultivates. Another aspect of Venice to be explored further is perhaps her ancient reputation for being a city of great love, free from cupidity. See McPherson, 'Lewkenor's Venice and Its Sources', p. 464. If this is known to Shakespeare, as is possible, he builds on this idea of Venice through the friendship of Antonio and Bassanio as well as the romantic love of Jessica, who leaves behind the mass of her father's wealth to marry the poor and unthrift Lorenzo. Such a 'historical' idea of Venice might qualify the opposite argument ('Love in Venice generally has a poor record') presented by Catherine Belsey in her far-ranging article, 'Love in Venice', *Shakespeare Survey*, **44** (1992) pp. 41–53.

22. See G. K. Paster, *The Idea of the City in the Age of Shakespeare* (Athens: University of Georgia Press, 1985) p. 179. Paster finds 'the biggest difference between the Shakespearean comic city and the cities of Jonson and Middleton [to be] the efficacy Shakespeare is willing to hypothesise for social love, for civic charity' (p. 222).

23. See Mahood (ed.), pp. 16–18, for a concise overview of critical

perspectives on the play's use of law in relation to English law. Critics tend to see Shakespeare's trial as concerned with 'equity' or Chancery, the legal system in Shakespeare's era that based its decrees on equity and conscience. Mahood declares that 'the concept of equity . . . does indeed lie at the heart of the scene' (p. 17). Although E. F. J. Tucker persuasively refutes the idea that Shakespeare is concerned with Chancery in his trial scene, Tucker none the less concludes that Portia's solution is an 'equitable remedy'. See E. F. J. Tucker, 'The Letter of the Law in *The Merchant of Venice*', *ShS*, **29** (1976) pp. 93–101. Upon reconsideration of these arguments for equity, I must now conclude that the concept of equity, regardless of whether we are speaking of equitable decrees in Chancery or principles of equity applied to Common Law statutes, is irrelevant to Shakespeare's use of stage law in Act IV. Danson supports this view; however, like other scholars, Danson tends to equate the different concepts of 'equity' and 'mercy'. See Danson, pp. 83–6, 94–5. For another interpretation that the concept of equity is extralegal in the play, see Richard A. Posner, *Law and Literature: A Misunderstood Relation* (Cambridge, MA and London: Harvard University Press, 1988) pp. 96–7. For a helpful article on the definition of equity and the problematic relationship between equity and law in the Renaissance, see Roger T. Simonds, 'The Problem of Equity in the Continental Renaissance', in *Renaissance Papers 1989*, eds Dale B. J. Randall and Joseph A. Porter (Durham, NC: The Southeastern Renaissance Conference, 1989) pp. 39–49.

24. See A. Benston, 'Portia, the Law, and the Tripartite Structure of *The Merchant of Venice*', *SQ*, **30** (1979) p. 378. Benston discusses the tripartite structure of the play but overlooks the tripartite structure of Portia's and Antonio's judgements and their significance.

25. See Bullough, vol. 1, p. 472. Cf. also, vol. 1, p. 469: 'the Jew had a formal bond drawn up and witnessed, with all due form and ceremony'.

26. See Wilson, p. 340.

27. Cartelli complains that the 'dominant ideological discourse [Portia's mercy speech] . . . serves to suppress the claim to validity of any alternative discourse that dares to dispute its prerogatives', specifically Shylock's refusal to grant mercy. See T. Cartelli, *Marlowe, Shakespeare, and the Economy of Theatrical Experience* (Philadelphia: University of Pennsylvania Press, 1991) p. 153. But Cartelli does not define what constitutes 'validity', as Shakespeare seems so bent on doing in proving Shylock's motive in the trial. Shylock's right to deny the court answers that 'please' and his refusal of the extralegal appeal to mercy are granted within the play as his valid free choices. But Shylock is not simply using Venetian law as his 'only form of social protection' (Cartelli, p. 154). Shylock is primarily misusing the law for unlawful purpose, for murderous revenge. Within Shakespeare's use of stage law for the strict court of Venice this 'alternative discourse' of Shylock's is not judged as 'valid'.

28. See, e.g., H. B. Charlton, 'Shakespeare's Jew', *Shakespearian Comedy*

(London: Methuen, 1938) pp. 123–60; M. J. Landa, *The Jew in Drama*, intro. Murray Roston (1924; New York: Ktav Publishing House, 1969) pp. 76–7.

29. Lewalski sees Portia's final tactic with Shylock as a working out of Paul's metaphor, 'permitting the Law to demonstrate its own destructiveness' (p. 341). Although she furnishes excellent examples of the metaphor as used in the major Christian theological traditions, her argument about the Law's own destructiveness for the play seems overstated because the Law is not presented as 'destructive' but rather as constructively punitive and revelatory. Cf. Gal 3.25, gloss.

30. The pejorative description of Portia's interpretation is almost commonplace. For 'quibble', see, e.g., E. M. W. Tillyard, 'The Trial Scene in *The Merchant of Venice*', *A Review of English Literature*, 2 (1961) pp. 51–9, esp. p. 51. For the 'merest technicality', see, e.g., Lewalski, p. 340. For 'the merest trick', see, e.g., Danson, p. 95.

31. See Bullough, vol. 1, p. 472.

32. The absence of equity as an operative legal principle in this Venetian courtroom needs emphasis to correct the opposite, and currently prevailing, view. In what has proved to be a very influential article, E. F. J. Tucker argues that the so-called 'quibble' over blood is no quibble but rather Portia's legally brilliant, 'equitable remedy' based upon 'Common Law principles of equity, as applied to the interpretation of statutes': the letter or appearance of the law should not be confused with its spirit or reality, 'outward shows' should not mask corrupt pleas, and a judgment that diminishes, expands, or even contradicts the letter of the law is valid so long as it upholds 'the intent of the law'. See Tucker, pp. 98–100. The argument rests on several crucial assumptions that contradict what happens in Shakespeare's play. First, Portia does not interpret the letter of the *law* but the letter of Shylock's *bond*. Shylock's bond, although lawful according to the Venetian system, is no statute. Second, Portia does not use 'Common Law principles of equity' in her interpretation of the bond because her interpretation never 'diminishes, expands, or even contradicts the letter of the law [to uphold] the intent of the law', as Tucker claims. Portia's interpretation is not flexible but strict in upholding the literalism of Venetian law governing written contracts. Third, Tucker concludes that the play shows that the letter and the spirit are not opposed; they are integrated, like body and soul. The opposite is true regarding Venetian law in the play. Cf. Posner, pp. 96–8.

33. See *OED*, 'blood', 3.b., 4., III.8., 9., 10., 11. and b.; 'flesh', 7., 8., 9.

34. Lewalski, p. 339.

35. See 1 Cor 1.24, 30. See esp. the first three chapters of Paul's first epistle to the Corinthians: 1 Cor 1.17–30; 2.5, 9–16; 3.18–20.

36. *Zelauto* is the only posited source where the penalty is not death but the loss of the usurer's eyes.

37. Thomas Marc Parrot and J. R. Brown note the addition of this penalty which has been 'too little regarded by critics'. Both scholars,

however, do not discuss how or why Shakespeare purposefully structures Portia's judgement in three parts, the first two parts devoted
to the judgement of the bond and the third part to the judgement
of the author of the bond. Brown is puzzled by Shakespeare's intention but thinks the Venetian legal penalty is 'perhaps significant . . . added to emphasize Shylock is defeated on his own grounds
of law and justice'. See Brown (ed.), p. li. But Shakespeare goes
beyond this defeat, characteristic of his sources, to moral education
regarding justice and mercy.

38. In *Il Pecorone* the Jew leaves in a furious rage, with the court smugly
satisfied that he got what he deserved. See Bullough, vol. 1, p. 323.
In *The Ballad of Gernutus* the Jewish usurer leaves with 'griped grieved
mind', while the Christians pray that all wretches like him receive
a similar sentence and that the Lord may deliver them from such
evil. See Brown (ed.), p. 155.

39. For the statute's language, see N. Jones, *God and the Moneylenders:
Usury and Law in Early Modern England* (Oxford and Cambridge,
MA: Basil Blackwell, 1989) p. 64.

40. Mahood (ed.), p. 18.

41. Alexander Pope, *An Essay on Criticism*, in *Poetry and Prose of Alexander Pope*, ed. Aubrey Williams (Boston: Houghton Mifflin, 1969)
p. 51, l. 525.

42. G. W. Keeton, *Shakespeare's Legal and Political Background* (New York:
Barnes & Noble, 1968) p. 145.

43. See Henry Campbell Black, *Black's Law Dictionary*, rev. 4th edn (St
Paul, MN: West Publishing, 1968) 'Equity', p. 634. In its broadest
sense equity is 'natural right' or essential justice which gives a person his reasonable due, and in its technical sense, it refers to a system of jurisprudence distinct from common law courts. See *OED*,
'Equity', both the general and legal meanings. In his canon Shakespeare's four uses of 'equity' refer to its meaning of justice.

44. Tucker, p. 97.

45. See G. K. Hunter, 'The Theology of Marlowe's *The Jew of Malta*',
JWCI, **17** (1964) p. 214; A. C. Dessen, 'The Elizabethan Stage Jew
and Christian Example: Gerontus, Barabas, and Shylock', *MLQ*, **35**
(1974) p. 243. Dessen also notes Gratiano's vengeful response as a
foil to Antonio's.

46. Critics frequently misread the facts of Shylock's financial settlement,
wrongly seeing him as 'stripped' of his wealth. For examples, see
J. R. Brown, *Shakespeare and His Comedies*, 2nd edn (London: Methuen,
1962) p. 74; Albert Wertheim, 'The Treatment of Shylock and Thematic
Integrity in *The Merchant of Venice*', *ShakS*, **6** (1970) pp. 85–6; Anne
Barton (ed.), *The Merchant of Venice*, in *The Riverside Shakespeare*, ed.
G. Blakemore Evans *et al.* (Boston: Houghton Mifflin, 1974) p. 252;
Jan Lawson Hinely, 'Bond Priorities in *The Merchant of Venice*', *SEL*,
20 (1980) p. 228; Barbara Tovey, 'The Golden Casket: An Interpre-
tation of *The Merchant of Venice*', in *Shakespeare as Political Thinker*,
eds John Alvis and Thomas G. West (Durham: Carolina Academic
Press, 1981) pp. 233–6. Danson rightly reads the specific terms of

the financial settlement (pp. 124–5) but overlooks its familial significance and its interrelationship with usury as well as Antonio's conversion stipulation.

47. For the legal phrase, 'in use', see *OED*, 'use', 4c. This legal phrase does not refer to usury or the taking of interest, as has been suggested by Richard A. Levin, *Love and Society in Shakespearean Comedy: A Study of Dramatic Form* (Newark: University of Delaware Press; London and Toronto: Associated University Presses, 1985) p. 76. See the legal interpretations by G. W. Keeton, pp. 146–47; Mark Edwin Andrews, *Law Versus Equity in 'The Merchant of Venice': A Legalization of Act IV* (Boulder: University of Colorado Press, 1965) pp. 74–5; John D. Eure, 'Shakespeare and the Legal Process: Four Essays', *Virginia Law Review*, **61** (1975) pp. 402–11, esp. p. 409; Posner, p. 92 n. 31. Keeton and Eure concur about the disposition of Shylock's property, emphasising Antonio's generosity, and Posner suggests the income of the trust could go to Shylock, or it could accumulate for Jessica. These three scholars differ from Andrews, who entitles Antonio to receive the income from one-half of Shylock's estate, but not the principal, which he was to manage responsibly.

48. See Brown (ed.), p. 119, for several different interpretations of Antonio's lines on his trust, and see Mahood (ed.), p. 149. Keeton (pp. 146–7) and Eure (p. 409) support Brown's suggestion about the estate's profits. Cf. also H. H. Furness (ed.), *The Merchant of Venice*, New Variorum Edition, 23 vols (Philadelphia: J. B. Lippincott, 1888) vol. 7, pp. 227–8 notes. The germ for the idea of giving the usurer's wealth to his daughter and new son-in-law Shakespeare may well have found in Munday's *Zelauto*, as noted by Brown (ed.), (pp. xxi, 168) and Muir, *The Sources of Shakespeare's Plays* (p. 88). If so, Shakespeare *changes* the source for the idea from the usurer to his merchant. In *Zelauto* the Christian usurer, of his own volition, decides to accept his son-in-law and settle all his wealth on him after his own decease. Shakespeare's detailed execution of Shylock's financial settlement differs impressively.

49. Posner, p. 92 and n. 31, my italics.

50. See Lewalski, p. 341; Danson, pp. 164–5.

51. See Miles Mosse, *The Arraignment and Conviction of Usury . . .* (London: Widow Orwin, 1595) sig. B4^v, pp. 4–5.

52. See N. Rabkin, 'Meaning in *The Merchant of Venice*', *Shakespeare and the Problem of Meaning* (Chicago: University of Chicago Press, 1981) pp. 12–14.

53. In England Jessica would have to convert for the marriage to be valid. See A. J. Cook, *Making a Match: Courtship in Shakespeare and His Society* (Princeton: Princeton University Press, 1991) p. 217. Whatever may have been the rule in Venice, the reason given for Jessica's conversion through marriage emphasises spiritual salvation, not social or legal validity. The same spiritual emphasis governs the reason for Abigail's conversion in Marlowe's play.

54. Abigail gives no indication that she intends to convert because her beloved, Don Mathias, is a Christian, and Barabas does not foresee

conversion as a possibility. Abigail converts only after the tragedy of her Christian lover's death. Barabas is so shocked and angered to discover she converted (and may know his own role in the killing) that he has her poisoned: 'False and unkind! What, hast thou lost thy father? . . . she is hateful to my soul and me' (3.4.1–33).

55. For these terms, see *Encyclopedia Judaica*, vol. 5, p. 936 and vol. 11, p. 1018. 'Conversos' is a positive term used for true Moorish or Jewish converts (and sometimes their descendants), and the term conveys no derogatory implications, unlike the term 'Marranos'.

56. Cited in S. W. Baron, *A Social and Religious History of the Jews*, 2nd edn, 16 vols (New York: Columbia University Press, 1952–76) vol. 15, p. 128. Baron also cites the more typically popular and ecclesiastical opinion of Catholics, who abhored all 'Jews and Infidels' because they were separated from the Church of Christ, 'and heretics which, although they be christened, yet obstinately defend error against the Catholic faith'. Because New Christians (Jewish converts) could be 'suspected by Catholics of being heretics and by Protestants of being subversive', Baron observes that these converts 'had every incentive to adhere to their ancestral faith'. Noting the anti-alien riots in England in 1588, 1593, and 1595, Baron suggests that for the English 'Shakespeare's *Merchant* may indeed have proposed a solution for the alien problem in Shylock's ultimate conversion to [Protestant] Christianity and Jessica's marriage to Lorenzo; in other words, in the speedy absorption of alien groups by the native majority.' See Baron, vol. 15, p. 135. He then postulates that this sentiment may account for why 'Shakespeare and Marlowe present very attractive Jewesses.' But Marlowe's Abigail converts deliberately and does not get absorbed into the native majority by marriage but only by conversion. Likewise, Jessica deliberately resolves on conversion through marriage, and her reasons for so doing are important.

57. See Chapter 5 for this argument and evidence.

58. See Wilson, pp. 290, 285.

59. See ibid., p. 232; cf. 183–4, 268, 376–7, 379. See *The Market or Fayre of Usurers*, trans. Willaim Harrys (London: Steven Mierdman, 1550) (photostat facsimile reproduced from the copy of STC 17330 in the Henry E. Huntington Library) sig. L7^r.

60. See Wilson, p. 381, my italics.

61. For a valuable interpretation of the judgement of Shylock in terms of 'the symmetrical *aequalitas* of Aristotelian justice', see D. N. Beauregard, 'Sidney, Aristotle, and *The Merchant of Venice*: Shakespeare's Triadic Images of Liberality and Justice', *ShakS*, **20** (1988) pp. 46–7. Beauregard presents helpful analysis, but he misidentifies Shylock as a merchant and underestimates Shylock's conversion in theological terms (p. 47).

62. Analysis of Shakespeare's *interrelation* of the financial and spiritual parts of Shylock's judgement has been rather neglected. The conversion stipulation, however, has received extensive commentary. For interpretations that support my argument, in various ways, see, e.g., Coghill, p. 23; Lewalski, pp. 340–1; Leo Kirschbaum, 'Shylock

in the City of God', in *Character and Characterization in Shakespeare* (Detroit: Wayne State University Press, 1962) p. 30; Wertheim, pp. 85–7; John F. Hennedy, 'Launcelot Gobbo and Shylock's Forced Conversion', *TSLL*, **15** (1973) pp. 405–10; Danson, pp. 164–9; K. Muir, *Shakespeare's Comic Sequence*, p. 58; H. Morris, 'The Judgment Theme in *The Merchant of Venice*', *Renascence*, **39** (Fall 1986) pp. 293, 306–8. For some interpretations that oppose my argument, see, e.g., J. W. Lever, 'Shylock, Portia and the Values of Shakespearian Comedy', *SQ*, **3** (1952) pp. 383–6; A. D. Moody, *Shakespeare: 'The Merchant of Venice'* (London: Edward Arnold, 1964) pp. 43–4; R. Chris Hassel, Jr, 'Antonio and the Ironic Festivity of *The Merchant of Venice*', *ShakS*, **6** (1970) pp. 68–9; Rabkin, pp. 12–14; D. Lucking, 'Standing for Sacrifice: The Casket and Trial Scenes in *The Merchant of Venice*', *UTQ*, **58** (1989) pp. 370–2.

63. Cf. Morris, pp. 293–5.
64. See Baron, *Social and Religious History*, vol. 13, p. 128.
65. W. Cohen, '*The Merchant of Venice* and the Possibilities of Historical Criticism', *ELH*, **49** (1982) p. 780.
66. Before Abigail converts, even Barabas specifically plans to give his wealth to his daughter: 'I have no charge, nor many children, / But one sole daughter ... and all I have is hers' (1.1.134–7).
67. Bishop Gervase Babington, *Certain Plain, Brief, and Comfortable Notes upon every Chapter of Genesis* (London: A. Jeffes and P. Short, 1952) sig. O8ʳ.
68. T. Wilson, p. 362.
69. For the difference between 'enjoyment' and 'use' of things, see St Augustine, *On Christian Doctrine*, trans. D. W. Robertson, Jr (New York: Bobbs-Merrill, 1958) p. 9.
70. See, e.g., Thomas Lodge, *An Alarum against Usurers* (1584) in *The Complete Works of Thomas Lodge* (New York: Russell & Russell, 1963) sig. F4; John Jewel, *An Exposition upon the Two Epistles of the Apostle Saint Paul to the Thessalonians* (London: R. Newberie, 1583) pp. 124, 128–29, 192; Philippus Caesar, *A General Discourse Against the Damnable Sect of Usurers*, trans. T. Rogers (London: John Kyrgston, 1578) fols 5, 6ᵛ, 7ᵛ; R. Porder, *A Sermon of gods fearful threatenings for Idolatry ...: with a Treatise against Usury* (London: Henry Denham, 1570) fols. 87ᵛ–88, 100ᵛ, 104, 105ᵛ, 107ᵛ–08ᵛ.
71. Lewalski, p. 341.
72. Lewalski, pp. 338, 340, 341.
73. Norman Nathan suggests the reason Shylock so readily accepts the Christian faith after his conversion is because he sees God has rewarded the 'Christian state of Venice', not himself as he expected, and thus by his own standard he has been proved the 'infidel', not the chosen one. See N. Nathan, 'Shylock, Jacob, and God's Judgment', *SQ*, **1** (1950) pp. 257–8. The text and glosses on Gn 30.33 in both the Geneva and the Bishops' Bibles bolster this argument that God rewards the righteous.
74. See Danson, pp. 165–7.
75. See Rom 11.15–27, and glosses on verses 16 and 17. Cf. Danson, p. 167.

76. Danson, p. 167.

77. Ibid., pp. 167–8.

78. See Hunter, pp. 216–17; he cites Gal 3.3–16, 29.

79. See Wayne A. Meeks (ed.), *The Writings of St Paul* (New York: W. W. Norton, 1972) p. 118. Meeks uses the text of the Revised Standard Version, which conveys the sense of the biblical glosses of Shakespeare's era: 'God made [you] alive . . . having canceled the bond which stood against us with its legal demands; this he set aside, nailing it to the cross' (Col 2.14). For effective use of the language of 'debt as sin', see the example cited from Launcelot Andrewes' 1609 Christmas sermon, in Lewalski, pp. 339–40.

80. Quotation of the gloss on Eph 2.11 is from the Geneva–Tomson Bible (1590). Although Paul's interpretation of salvation-history needs to be put in some historical perspective because it reflects the pattern of his own life and as such might be seen as more 'personal' and 'polemical', his writings are none the less extremely influential. Peter Morwyng, e.g., does not specify his biblical allusion, but clearly Paul's epistle to the Romans (Chapter 11) furnishes Morwyng with the stock (Jews) and graft (Christians) imagery that he uses so effectively in his epistle to the reader in his translation of Joseph's Jewish history.

81. Paul's learning through hard experience the vanity of arrogant self-righteousness, falsely rooted in the letter of the law, somewhat evokes the broad outlines of Shylock's Pharisaical course in the play. The glossator interprets the fate of the worldly who do not convert or change their ways: 'The vainglory which they seek after in this world, shall turn to their confusion, and shame' (Phil 3.19, gloss).

82. Bullough, vol. 1, p. 482.

83. By contrasting Abigail's true virtue and wisdom with the hypocrisy of the Christian friar to whom Abigail confesses (4.1.40–50), Marlowe continues his savage satire on human vice, whether of Christian, Turk, or Jew.

84. See René Girard, '"To Entrap the Wisest": A Reading of *The Merchant of Venice*', in *Literature and Society*, ed. E. W. Said (Baltimore and London: Johns Hopkins University Press, 1980) pp. 100–19; quotations are from pp. 108–9. See also Cartelli, who assigns to Portia's mercy speech a 'pivotal role . . . in the scapegoating process' so that Shylock is 'mercilessly degraded', but Portia is also 'as much a victim as Shylock of her rhetorical formulation'. See *Marlowe, Shakespeare*, pp. 152–6; quotations are from pp. 155–6. Cartelli does not relate Portia's mercy speech to her own actions in Act V, which serve as another instance in the play when mercy is not just paid lip service as an imaginary, poetic artifact.

85. See *OED*, 'Scapegoat', 1. See the Geneva Bible, Lv 16.8, 10, 21–22, 26.

86. See the Geneva Bible, Lv 16.21, gloss. Cf. Is 53.4; Heb 10.1–9, glosses.

87. Lewalski, p. 341.

88. See Chaucer, *The Parson's Tale*, ed. Robinson, p. 242.

Notes to Chapter 6

1. See G. Bullough (ed.), *Narrative and Dramatic Sources of Shakespeare*, 8 vols (1957); 5th imp. (London and Henley: R&KP and New York: Columbia University Press, 1977) vol. 1, p. 146.
2. See Seneca, *De Beneficiis, The Moral Essays*, trans. J. W. Basore, 3 vols (London: Heinemann, 1933) pp. 9–11: 'what glory would there be in doing good to many if none ever deceived you? . . . No matter what the issue of former benefits has been, still persist in conferring them upon others; this will be better even if they fall unheeded into the hands of the ungrateful, for it may be that either shame or opportunity or example will some day make these grateful.'
3. See ibid., pp. 9–11.
4. See Mt 5.15–16 for this biblical image: 'men light a candle, and put it . . . on a candlestick, & it giveth light unto all. . . . Let your light so shine before men, that they may see your good works, & glorify your Father which is in heaven.' Cf. the gloss in the Geneva Bible on 'let your light shine': 'Because you are seen far off, give good example of life.'
5. The Civilian in Thomas Wilson's treatise objects that according to his knowledge no man is so perfect that he avoids the taking of some small return on a loan, e.g., a farthing or a point on a loan, although Preacher Ockerfoe condemns even the smallest overplus as 'damnation' to him who takes it. See T. Wilson, *A Discourse upon Usury* [1572], ed. R. H. Tawney (New York: Harcourt Brace, 1925) p. 347. Mosse also emphasises that generous Christians have grown rare in his time, but both he himself and John Whitgift, the Archbishop of Canterbury, to whom he dedicates his book, are guiltless of the sin of taking or giving usury. See Miles Mosse, *The Arraignment and Conviction of Usury* . . . (London: Widow Orwin, 1595) sigs A4^{r-v}, B3^{r-v}, p. 45.
6. For this phrase and a discussion of mental usury, see Mosse, pp. 16, 19, 69, 72–3. Cf. Wilson, pp. 292, 275.
7. See J. T. Noonan, Jr, *The Scholastic Analysis of Usury* (Cambridge, MA: Harvard University Press, 1957) pp. 32–3. Noonan explains, 'it is axiomatic in scholastic theology that the intention to perform a sinful act, even though not executed, is a sin in itself. . . . The intention to profit from a loan was as sinful as profiting in fact; no contractual disguise of the loan and no absence of an express contractual provision for the payment of usury freed from guilt the man who desired the usury in his heart. In particular, a special emphasis was placed on intention by the text, "Lend freely, hoping for nothing thereby", and its interpretation given by Urban III in *Consuluit*' (p. 32).
8. For quotations, see T. Wilson, p. 292. Cf. Jan Lawson Hinely, 'Bond Priorities in *The Merchant of Venice*', *SEL*, **20** (1980) p. 229; she first cited Wilson's mention of '"*Mentalis usura*"'. Our arguments, however, disagree regarding Antonio's role in Shylock's judgement, his moral growth, and his mood at the play's end.

9. Regarding the legitimacy of expecting a return of love, see Mosse, pp. 46, 74–5. Regarding the definition of gain in monetary terms, see Mosse, pp. 47–8, 71. Mosse cites one author, Bartholomus Fumus, for a limited definition of mental usury that concurs with the monetary definition of gain (see p. 71). For a fuller analysis of this matter, see Holmer, 'Miles Mosse's *The Arraignment and Conviction of Vsurie* (1595): A New Source for *The Merchant of Venice'*, *ShakS*, **21** (1993) pp. 11–54.

10. See Mosse, pp. 46, 75.

11. Danson argues strongly against the homosexual interpretation; see L. Danson, *The Harmonies of 'The Merchant of Venice'* (New Haven and London: Yale University Press, 1978) pp. 34–40. Danson finds *The Merchant of Venice* closest to *The Winter's Tale* in the spirit in which it treats friendship and marriage (p. 39). But an important difference between the two plays concerns the extent and placement of disruption. Unlike *The Winter's Tale*, no literal disruption of friendship occurs between the males, and the potential disruption between husband and wife is contained through role-playing on the wife's part and no fury (only sincere amendment) on the husband's part. For some studies favouring a homosexual interpretation of Antonio, see Nevill Coghill, 'The Basis of Shakespearian Comedy: A Study in Medieval Affinities', *E&S*, **3** (1950) pp. 1–28; W. I. D. Scott, 'Antonio – the Endogenous Depressive', *Shakespeare's Melancholics* (London: Mills & Boon, 1962) pp. 35–46; Norman Holland, *Psychoanalysis and Shakespeare* (New York: McGraw-Hill, 1964) pp. 231–42, 330–1; Tyrone Guthrie, *In Various Directions: A View of Theatre* (New York: Macmillan, 1965) pp. 97–103; William J. Martz, *The Place of 'The Merchant of Venice' in Shakespeare's Universe of Comedy* (New York: Revisionist Press, 1976); Ralph Berry (ed.), *On Directing Shakespeare: Interviews with Contemporary Directors* (London: Croom Helm, 1977) pp. 29–40; and W. Thomas MacCary, *Friends and Lovers: The Phenomenology of Desire in Shakespearean Comedy* (New York: Columbia University Press, 1985) pp. 167–70.

12. G. Midgley, 'The Merchant of Venice: A Reconsideration', *EIC*, **10** (1960) p. 125.

13. Hurrell, 'Love and Friendship in *The Merchant of Venice'*, *TSLL* **3** (1961) pp. 328–41, esp. 340–1.

14. See Eugene M. Waith, 'Shakespeare and Fletcher on Love and Friendship', *ShakS*, **18** (1986) pp. 235–50; see esp. Waith's quotation of Montaigne's 'rhapsodic' description of his affection for his friend (Étienne de la Boetie) and his note on Montaigne's distinction between honourable male friendship (in which there is no physical passion) and the Greek licence of homosexuality '"justly abhorred by our customes"' (pp. 241, 250 n. 15).

15. See B. R. Smith, *Homosexual Desire in Shakespeare's England: A Cultural Poetics* (Chicago: University of Chicago Press, 1991) pp. 67–8. Smith presents a cultural context in which to examine the male bonding of Antonio and Bassanio, a context which emphasises that 'in early modern England . . . we recognize a *potential* for erotic feeling

in male relationships of all kinds', but that in Shakespeare's plays 'about soldiering and about courtship . . . homosexuality remains only an implicit subject' (pp. 76–7). Our interpretations of the nature and conclusion of Antonio's melancholy differ, as do our interpretations of Antonio's role in Belmont.

16. See MacCary, p. 168. MacCary also bases his interpretation on a typically modern assumption, not generally shared by the Renaissance, that heterosexual marriage represents a naturally mature choice whereas 'adolescent' male friendship does not (p. 168).

17. See S. C. Chew, *The Pilgrimage of Life* (New Haven & London: Yale University Press, 1962) p. 185.

18. This perspective is clarified by E. K.'s gloss on the love of Hobbinol (Gabriel Harvey) for Colin Clout (Edmund Spenser) in the January eclogue (ll. 56–9) of Spenser's *The Shepheards Calender* (1579). E. K. reassures the reader that this love is not 'disorderly', not homosexual, or 'forbidden and unlawful fleshliness', but extraordinary male friendship as exemplified in the classical model of Socrates' love for Alcibiades: 'such love is much to be allowed and liked of, specially so meant, as Socrates used it: who saith, that " . . . he loved Alcibiades extremely, yet not Alcibiades' person, but his *soul*, which is Alcibiades' own self"'. It is in this explicit sense of spiritual friendship that E. K. prefers 'paederastice' over 'gynerastice, that is the love which enflameth men with *lust* toward womankind'. For quotations, see *Spenser: Poetical Works*, eds E. De Selincourt and J. C. Smith (1912; rpt. London: Oxford University Press, 1912) pp. 422–3, my italics. For an opposite reading favouring 'the privileged status of homosexuality' as 'of the highest moral philosophy', a reading that omits E. K.'s emphasis on male love of souls (not bodies), see Stephen Orgel, 'Nobody's Perfect: Or Why Did the English Stage Take Boys for Women?', *SAQ*, **88** (1989) pp. 7–29; quotations are from p. 23. Orgel suggests that the sixteenth-century English stage preferred transvestite boys because 'homosexuality in this culture appears to have been less threatening than heterosexuality' (p. 26) primarily because the association of men with women gave rise to 'the fear of effeminization' (p. 15). However, the wise love of either men or women does not threaten but blesses with 'a heavenly match' (3.5.67). It is only 'lust' which is a perverted, debased form of 'love' that threatens human identity, whether for man or woman.

19. See Waith, pp. 235–6, 241, 250 n. 5 and n. 15.

20. See Leo Rockas, '"A Dish of Doves": *The Merchant of Venice*', *ELH*, **40** (1973) p. 346; R. Berry, 'The Problem of Antonio', *SAP*, **4** (1972) p. 170. M. M. Mahood (ed.), *The Merchant of Venice*, New Cambridge Shakespeare (Cambridge: Cambridge University Press, 1987) also glosses 'wether' as 'castrated ram'; see 4.1.114 n.

21. See *OED*, 'wether', 1.; 1.b.

22. Karen Newman, 'Portia's Ring: Unruly Women and Structures of Exchange in *The Merchant of Venice*', *SQ*, **38** (1987) pp. 19–33; quotations are from pp. 27–9. I agree with Newman's learned emphasis on this play's interrogation of the historical treatment of women as com-

modities, but we differ on how and why the play does so. E.g., Newman argues for Portia's female subversion of the authorised system of gender and power in the Venetian courtroom but curiously overlooks Portia's choice to seek help from her male cousin (see p. 30).

23. For a different reading that does not see Portia's pretence of sexual infidelity as a specific response to male verbal infidelity, but rather generally argues that Portia's response reflects the Renaissance cultural ambivalence towards the educated woman, whose intellectual 'knowingness' could be a sign of her sexual 'knowingness', see Lisa Jardine, 'Cultural Confusion and Shakespeare's Learned Heroines: "These are old paradoxes"', SQ, **38** (1987) pp. 14–18.

24. The virtue of chastity is not to be confused here with physical virginity. Virginity is abstinence from all sexual activity. Paul suggests virginity as the ideal state, because Christ was a virgin, but Paul realistically counsels that if one cannot maintain virginity, it is better to marry than to burn with lust (1 Cor 9). Virginity of spirit (innocence of soul) is always more important than literal virginity of flesh (see Ap 14.4–5 and glosses). Chastity is the *proper* sexual use of one's mind and body; therefore, married couples were expected to be chaste in their relations with one another. For these distinctions, see, e.g., Chaucer's *The Parson's Tale*, in *The Works of Geoffrey Chaucer*, ed. F. N. Robinson (Cambridge: Riverside Press, 1961) pp. 258–60. A good example of the lack of chastity in marriage appears in Chaucer's description of January's wedding night in *The Merchant's Tale* (ll. 1795–1856) and more obviously in May's adultery with Damyan (ll. 2320–53). A good example of chaste marital love may be found in Edmund Spenser's *Epithalamion* (ll. 296–426), and Milton's *Paradise Lost*, ed. M. Y. Hughes (New York: Odyssey, 1962) Book IV, ll. 659–775.

25. See, e.g., H. B. Charlton, 'Shakespeare's Jew', in *Shakespearian Comedy* (London: Methuen, 1938) pp. 123–60.

26. See Mt 23.16–23. This passage is important for several emphases: the emphasis on the Pharisees as false interpreters of oath formulas; the emphasis on folly, blindness, and hypocrisy; and the emphasis on false priorities, elevating what is minor (the precise verbal formulation of an oath) over that which is major (the keeping of 'judgment, and mercy, & fidelity').

27. For 'Sabaoth', see *OED*, Sabaoth; Mahood, 4.1.36 n.; Spenser, *The Faerie Queene*, ed. T. P. Roche, Jr (Harmondsworth: Penguin, 1978) pp. 1243–4 (notes on 'Sabbaoth'). 'Sabaoth' is the Hebrew word for 'armies', rendered as 'hosts' in English (see 1 Sm 17.45; Is 6.3). Shakespeare does seem to be taking this word as 'Sabbath', the holy day of religious observance and rest from labour.

28. See, e.g., Monica J. Hamill, 'Poetry, Law, and the Pursuit of Perfection: Portia's Role in *The Merchant of Venice*', *SEL*, **18** (1978) p. 242.

29. For the view that Bassanio's offer of his wife in the trial causes Portia's subsequent trial of Bassanio, see Anne Barton (ed.), *The Merchant of Venice*, in *The Riverside Shakespeare*, ed. G. Blakemore Evans *et al.* (Boston: Houghton Mifflin, 1974) p. 253.

30. Kenneth Muir, e.g., argues in *The Sources of Shakespeare's Plays* (London: Methuen, 1977) that Bassanio could not honourably refuse Antonio's request (p. 90).

31. See Chaucer, *The Parson's Tale*, ed. Robinson, p. 242.

32. T. Wilson quotes Plutarch on the danger usury poses for those 'as will be unthrifts'; unthrifts (like Bassanio) would be financially better off selling their lands than borrowing at usury (see p. 333).

33. See Lawrence W. Hyman, 'The Rival Lovers in *The Merchant of Venice*', *SQ*, **21** (1970) p. 113.

34. See Barton, p. 253.

35. See Hinely, pp. 236–7.

36. See Waith, p. 235. The quotation is from Lyly's *Endimion*, cited by Waith (p. 235).

37. See Aelred de Rievaulx, *L'Amitié Spirituelle*, ed. J. Dubois, 667 B–S. Cf. C. Belsey, 'Love in Venice', *ShS*, **44** (1992) pp. 46, 48–9, n. 26, 52. Belsey rightly sees Shakespeare's emphasis on Portia as wife and friend, but treats this idea as a 'new model of marriage' (p. 52) as if it were radically new, lacking any prior philosophical basis.

38. J. Taylor, *A Discourse of the Nature, Offices and Measures of Friendship*, in *The Whole Works of the Right Rev. Jeremy Taylor, D. D.*, ed. Reginald Heber, 15 vols (London: William Clowes for C. & J. Rivington, 1828) vol. 11, p. 330.

39. Ibid., vol. 11, p. 331.

40. Ibid., vol. 11, pp. 333–4. Taylor prefaces this discussion of male friendship with the opinion that if both men and women are imperfect, 'we might as well allow women as men to be friends; since they can have all that which can be necessary and essential to friendships' (p. 331). He also quotes Martial and Solomon on the importance of giving gifts to friends (p. 334).

41. See Orgel, p. 22.

42. See ibid., p. 26.

43. See Mosse, p. 13, my italics. Cf. also, Thomas Wilson, who refers to the parable of the talents (Mt 19) as an example of 'spiritual usury, which is the right usury in deed', defining it as the 'multiplication of the gifts and graces of god'. See Wilson, p. 190.

44. A. Fowler, *Spenser and the Numbers of Time* (New York: Barnes and Noble, 1964) pp. 18–19 and n. 3. The number three occurs at least twenty-five times in the play, the second highest frequency for this number in a given work by Shakespeare. See Danson for the play's use of the circle as a figure of harmony, pp. 11, 19–21, 195.

45. Antonio's role is often overlooked. See, e.g., Lynda E. Boose, 'The Comic Contract and Portia's Golden Ring', *ShakS*, **20** (1988) p. 246; H. S. Donow, 'Shakespeare's Caskets: Unity in *The Merchant of Venice*', *SQ*, **4** (1968) p. 92; R. A. Levin, *Love and Society in Shakespearean Comedy: A Study of Dramatic Form* (Newark: University of Delaware Press; London and Toronto: Associated University Presses, 1985) p. 84. Regarding the two usuries, see E. Pearlman, 'Shakespeare, Freud, and the Two Usuries, or Money's a Meddler', *ELR*, **2** (1972) pp. 227, 231, 233. Pearlman, however, overlooks 'inheritance' as the concept that links children and money.

46. See Jardine, p. 16. In this instance, how is mutually chosen sexual fidelity in marriage an act of subordination?

47. I concur with M. Biggs, pp. 157–9, R. F. Hill, pp. 84–5, Hamill, pp. 237, 143, Danson, pp. 192–5, A. Benston, 'Portia, the Law, and the Tripartite Structure of *The Merchant of Venice*', *SQ*, **30** (1979) pp. 379, 383–5), and R. Sharp, 'Gift Exchange and the Economics of Spirit in *The Merchant of Venice*', *MP*, **83** (1986) pp. 256–7, 261–3) on the essentially harmonious thrust of Act V, but they do not examine as I do the various ways in which Shakespeare further unifies his play through this final act, and our arguments include some basic points of disagreement regarding characters and themes. Murray Biggs and R. F. Hill see the ring episode as only a 'jeu d'esprit' (Biggs, p. 156) or 'wholly jesting' in nature (Hill, p. 85), and thus render the soul bond a redundancy by arguing that Portia would 'secretly approve – not regret' Bassanio's action (Biggs, p. 159). See Biggs, 'A Neurotic Portia', *ShS*, **25** (1972) pp. 153–9; R. F. Hill, '*The Merchant of Venice* and the Pattern of Romantic Comedy', *ShS*, **28** (1975) pp. 75–87. Hamill sees the marriage-bond and Portia's cuck-oldry pretence as 'love's possessiveness displac[ing] its generosity' (p. 243). Danson believes that 'Portia's ring must be given in order that charity be kept' (pp. 192, 137). Benston views Antonio not as a best friend but as a father figure involved in the 'parental process of "letting go" . . . by giving Bassanio "away" in ceremony' to Portia (pp. 382–5). Sharp argues that 'Portia arranged the ring trick' (p. 256) so that Bassanio would have the opportunity to risk all for Antonio and to reveal that 'male–male friendship has no equivalent to the institution of marriage for romantic love' (p. 261).

48. Spenser, *The Faerie Queene*, ed. Roche, Book I, cantos IV–V.

49. C. L. Barber, 'The Merchants and the Jew of Venice: Wealth's Communion and an Intruder', in *Shakespeare's Festive Comedy: A Study of Dramatic Form and Its Relation to Social Custom* (Princeton: Princeton University Press, 1959) p. 187. For dissents regarding the harmony of Act V, see, e.g., A. D. Moody, *Shakespeare: 'The Merchant of Venice'* (London: Edward Arnold, 1964) pp. 45–51, 55–6; Marilyn L. Williamson, 'The Ring Episode in *The Merchant of Venice*', *SAQ*, **71** (1972) pp. 587–97, esp. p. 593; Frank Whigham, 'Ideology and Class Conduct in *The Merchant of Venice*', *RenD*, **10** (1979) pp. 112–14; R. Chris Hassel, Jr, *Faith and Folly in Shakespeare's Romantic Comedies* (Athens: University of Georgia Press, 1980) pp. 183, 102–7; Janet Adelman, 'Male Bonding in Shakespeare's Comedies', in *Shakespeare's "Rough Magic": Renaissance Essays in Honor of C. L. Barber*, eds Peter Erickson and Coppelia Kahn (Newark: University of Delaware Press, 1985) p. 91; Newman, p. 32.

50. Thomas Wilson, cited in J. R. Brown (ed.), p. liv.

51. See Guthrie, pp. 97–103.

52. See, e.g., MacCary, pp. 160–70; Belsey, pp. 41–53.

53. As interesting as is Catherine Belsey's use of Lacan's concept of desire, her argument overlooks how Shakespeare has deliberately opposed 'desire' to 'give and hazard' by linking 'desire' to 'gain'

as the operative verbs in the golden casket's motto. Hence, we cannot conclude that 'Western literature presents desire as . . . thrilling precisely because it is hazardous' when Morocco, hoping to gain what many men desire, avoids the hazardous choice of the leaden casket and backs away from how 'this casket threatens' (2.7.18). See Belsey, p. 43.

54. The reference to Denis de Rougemont's *Love in the Western World* is cited in Belsey, p. 43 n. 8.
55. Belsey, p. 53.
56. Dante Alighieri, *The Divine Comedy (Paradiso)*, trans. Louis Biancolli (New York: Washington Square Press, 1966) vol. 3, p. 136.

Bibliography

Adelman, Janet, 'Male Bonding in Shakespeare's Comedies', in *Shakespeare's "Rough Magic"*: *Renaissance Essays in Honor of C. L. Barber*, eds Peter Erickson and Coppelia Kahn (Newark: University of Delaware Press, 1985) pp. 73–103.

Aelred de Rievaulx, *L'Amitié Spirituelle*, ed. J. Dubois (Bruges: Éditions C. Beyaert, 1948).

Andrews, Mark Edwin, *Law Versus Equity in 'The Merchant of Venice'*: *A Legalization of Act IV* (Boulder: University of Colorado Press, 1965).

Anonymous, *The Death of Usury, or, the Disgrace of Usurers* (Cambridge: John Legatt, 1594).

Aristotle, *The Politics of Aristotle*, trans. Ernest Barker (1946; rpt. Oxford: Clarendon Press, 1948).

Auden, W. H., 'Brothers and Others', in *The Dyer's Hand and Other Essays* (New York: Random House, 1962).

Augustine, Saint, *On Christian Doctrine*, trans. D. W. Robertson, Jr (New York: Bobbs-Merrill, 1958).

Babington, Bishop Gervase, *Certain Plain, Brief, and Comfortable Notes upon every Chapter of Genesis* (London: A. Jeffes and P. Short, 1952).

Bady, David, 'The Sum of Something: Arithmetic in *The Merchant of Venice*', *SQ*, **36** (1985) pp. 10–30.

Baker, John R., *Race* (New York and London: Oxford University Press, 1974).

Baldwin, Charles Sears, *Three Medieval Centuries of Literature in England, 1100–1400* (New York: Phaeton Press, 1968).

Baldwin, T. W., *On Act and Scene Division in the Shakespeare First Folio* (Carbondale: Southern Illinois University Press, 1965).

Baldwin, T. W., *William Shakespeare's Five-Act Structure* (Urbana: University of Illinois Press, 1974).

Barber, C. L., 'The Merchants and the Jew of Venice: Wealth's Communion and an Intruder', in *Shakespeare's Festive Comedy: A Study of Dramatic Form and Its Relation to Social Custom* (Princeton: Princeton University Press, 1959).

Barnet, Sylvan, 'Prodigality and Time in *The Merchant of Venice*', *PMLA*, **87** (1972) pp. 26–30.

Baron, Salo W., *A Social and Religious History of the Jews*, 2nd edn, 16 vols (New York: Columbia University Press, 1952–76).

Baron, Salo W., Arcadius Kahan *et al.*, *Economic History of the Jews* (New York: Schocken Books, 1975).

Barroll, J. Leeds, *Artificial Persons: The Formation of Character in the Tragedies of Shakespeare* (Columbia: University of South Carolina Press, 1974).

Baskervill, Charles Read, 'Bassanio as an Ideal Lover', in *The Manly Anniversary Studies in Language and Literature* (Chicago: University of Chicago Press, 1923).

Beauregard, David N., 'Sidney, Aristotle, and *The Merchant of Venice*: Shakespeare's Triadic Images of Liberality and Justice', *ShakS*, **20** (1988) pp. 33–51.

Beckerman, Bernard, *Shakespeare at the Globe, 1599–1609* (New York: Macmillan, 1962).

Belsey, Catherine, 'Love in Venice', *ShS*, **44** (1992) pp. 41–53.

Benston, Alice, 'Portia, the Law, and the Tripartite Structure of *The Merchant of Venice*', *SQ*, **30** (1979) pp. 367–85.

Berger, Harry, 'Marriage and Mercifixion in *The Merchant of Venice*: The Casket Scene Revisited', *SQ*, **32** (1981) pp. 155–62.

Berry, Ralph, (ed.), *On Directing Shakespeare: Interviews with Contemporary Directors* (London: Croom Helm, 1977).

Berry, Ralph, 'The Problem of Antonio', *SAP*, **4** (1972) pp. 161–72.

The Bible (Bishops' version) (London: Richard Jugge, 1568).

The Geneva Bible (a facsimile of the 1560 edition), intro. Lloyd E. Berry (Madison: University of Wisconsin Press, 1969).

The Bible (Geneva version), [bound with] *Two . . . Concordances* (trans. Robert F. Herrey, 1578) (London: Deputies of Christopher Barker, 1594).

The Bible (Geneva–Tomson version) (London: Deputies of Christopher Barker, 1590).

Biggs, Murray, 'A Neurotic Portia', *ShS*, **25** (1972) pp. 153–9.

Black, Henry Campbell, *Black's Law Dictionary*, rev. 4th edn (St Paul, MN: West Publishing, 1968).

Blaxton, John (ed.), *The English Usurer: or, Usury Condemned, By the Most Learned . . . Divines of the Church of England . . .*(London: John Norton, 1634).

Boose, Linda E., 'The Comic Contract and Portia's Golden Ring', *ShakS*, **20** (1988) pp. 241–54.

Boswell, J. C., 'Shylock's Turquoise Ring', *SQ*, **14** (1963) pp. 481–3.

Brown, John Russell, 'Love's Wealth and the Judgment of *The Merchant of Venice*', in *Shakespeare and His Comedies*, 2nd edn (London: Methuen, 1962).

Brown, John Russell (ed.), *The Merchant of Venice* (New Arden Shakespeare) (1955; rpt. London: Methuen, 1969).

Brown, John Russell, 'The Realization of Shylock: A Theatrical Criticism', in *Early Shakespeare*, eds John Russell Brown and Bernard Harris (London: Edward Arnold, 1961) pp. 186–209.

Bullough, Geoffrey (ed.), *Narrative and Dramatic Sources of Shakespeare*, 8 vols (1957); 5th imp. (London and Henley: Routledge and Kegan Paul, and New York: Columbia University Press, 1977) vol. 1, pp. 450–1, 476–82.

Bulman, James C., *The Merchant of Venice*, Shakespeare in Performance (Manchester and New York: Manchester University Press, 1991).

Burckhardt, Sigurd, '*The Merchant of Venice*: The Gentle Bond', *ELH*, **29** (1962) p. 247.

Caesar, Philippus, *A General Discourse Against the Damnable Sect of Usurers*, trans. Thomas Rogers (London: John Kyngston, 1578).

Camden, William, *Annales–Tomus Alter, & Idem: or The History of the Life and Reign of . . . Elizabeth*, trans. Thomas Browne (London: Thomas Harper, 1629).

Cameron, G. W., *Robert Wilson and the Plays of Shakespeare* (Riverton, New Zealand: G. W. Cameron, 1982).

Cardozo, Jacob L., *The Contemporary Jew in the Elizabethan Drama* (Amsterdam: H. J. Paris, 1925).

Carnovsky, Morris, 'The Mirror of Shylock', *Tulane Drama Review*, 3 (1958).

Carrington, Norman, *Shakespeare: 'The Merchant of Venice'* (Bath: Brodie, 1967).

Cartelli, Thomas, *Marlowe, Shakespeare, and the Economy of Theatrical Experience* (Philadelphia: University of Pennsylvania Press, 1991).

Cartelli, Thomas, 'Shakespeare's *Merchant*, Marlowe's *Jew*: The Problem of Cultural Difference', *ShakS*, 20 (1988) pp. 255–60.

Castiglione, Baldassare, *The Book of the Courtier*, trans. Sir Thomas Hoby, ed. Walter Raleigh (London: David Nutt, 1900) Book IV.

Charlton, H. B., 'Shakespeare's Jew', in *Shakespearian Comedy* (London: Methuen, 1938).

Charney, Maurice, 'Jessica's Turquoise Ring and Abigail's Poisoned Porridge: Shakespeare and Marlowe as Rivals and Imitators', *RenD*, 10 (1979) pp. 33–44.

Chaucer, Geoffrey, *The Works of Geoffrey Chaucer*, ed. F. N. Robinson (Cambridge: Riverside Press, 1961).

Chew, Samuel C., *The Pilgrimage of Life* (New Haven & London: Yale University Press, 1962).

Coghill, Nevill, 'The Basis of Shakespearian Comedy: A Study in Medieval Affinities', *E&S*, 3 (1950) pp. 1–28. Shortened and rev. version of Coghill's essay appears in *Shakespeare's Criticism: 1935–1960*, ed. Anne Ridler (London: Oxford University Press, 1963).

Cohen, Derek M., 'The Jew and Shylock', *SQ*, 31 (1980) pp. 53–63.

Cohen, Walter, '*The Merchant of Venice* and the Possibilities of Historical Criticism', *ELH*, 49 (1982) pp. 765–89.

Cook, Ann Jennalie, *Making a Match: Courtship in Shakespeare and His Society* (Princeton: Princeton University Press, 1991).

Coolidge, John S., 'Law and Love in *The Merchant of Venice*', *SQ*, 27 (1976) pp. 243–63.

Cooper, John R., 'Shylock's Humanity', *SQ*, 21 (1970) pp. 117–24.

Crane, Milton, *Shakespeare's Prose*, 2nd imp. (Chicago: University of Chicago Press, 1952).

Danson, Lawrence, *The Harmonies of 'The Merchant of Venice'* (New Haven and London: Yale University Press, 1978).

Dante Alighieri, *The Divine Comedy* (*Paradiso*), trans. Louis Biancolli (New York: Washington Square Press, 1966) 3 vols.

Davis, J. Madison and Sylvie L. F. Richards, 'The Merchant and the Jew: A Fourteenth-Century French Analogue to *The Merchant of Venice*', *SQ*, 36 (1985) pp. 56–63.

De Roover, Raymond, *San Bernardino of Siena and Sant' Antonino of Florence: The Two Great Economic Thinkers of the Middle Ages*, in *The Kress Library of Business and Economics*, ed. James P. Baughman, no. 19 (Cambridge: Harvard University Printing Office, 1967).

Dessen, Alan C., 'The Elizabethan Stage Jew and Christian Example: Gerontus, Barabas, and Shylock', *MLQ*, **35** (1974) pp. 231–45.

Dimock, Arthur, 'The Conspiracy of Dr. Lopez', *English Historical Review*, 9 (1894) pp. 440–72.

Donow, Herbert S., 'Shakespeare's Caskets: Unity in *The Merchant of Venice*', *SQ*, **4** (1968) pp. 86–93.

Doran, Madeleine, *Endeavors of Art: A Study of Form in Elizabethan Drama* (Madison: University of Wisconsin Press, 1954).

Draper, J. W., 'Usury in *The Merchant of Venice*', *MP*, **33** (1935) pp. 37–47.

Eagleton, Terry, *William Shakespeare* (Oxford and New York: Basil Blackwell, 1986).

Ellis, I. P. 'The Archbishop and the Usurers', *Journal of Ecclesiastical History*, **21** (1970) pp. 33–42.

Elze, Karl, '*The Merchant of Venice*', in *Essays on Shakespeare*, trans. L. Dora Schmitz (London: Macmillan, 1874).

Encyclopedia Judaica, 16 vols (Jerusalem: Encyclopedia Judaica, 1972).

Engle, Lars, '"Thrift is Blessing": Exchange and Explanation in *The Merchant of Venice*', *SQ*, **37** (1986) pp. 20–37.

Eure, John D., 'Shakespeare and the Legal Process: Four Essays', *Virginia Law Review*, **61** (1975) pp. 390–433.

Evans, B. Ivor, *The Language of Shakespeare's Plays* (London: Methuen, 1959).

Evans, G. B. (ed.), *Romeo and Juliet* (Cambridge: Cambridge University Press, 1984).

Evans, G. Blakemore (textual ed.), *The Riverside Shakespeare* (Boston: Houghton Mifflin, 1974).

Evans, R. C., 'Shakespeare, Sutton, and Theatrical Satire: An Unreported Allusion to Falstaff', *SQ*, **40** (1989) pp. 493–4.

Faulkner, William, *Light in August* (the corrected text) (New York: Vintage, 1990).

Fiedler, Leslie, 'The Jew as Stranger: or "These be the Christian husbands"', in *The Stranger in Shakespeare* (New York: Stein and Day, 1972) pp. 85–136.

Fleissner, Robert F., 'A Key to the Name of Shylock', *ANQ*, **5** (Dec. 1966) pp. 52–4.

Florio, John, *Queen Anna's New World of Words* (1611; rpt. Menston: Scolar Press, 1968).

Fortin, René E., 'Launcelot Gobbo and the Use of Allegory in *The Merchant of Venice*', *SEL*, **14** (1974) pp. 265–8.

Fowler, Alastair, *Spenser and the Numbers of Time* (New York: Barnes and Noble, 1964).

Fowler, Alastair, *Triumphal Forms: Structural Patterns in Elizabethan Poetry* (Cambridge: Cambridge University Press, 1970).

Freud, Sigmund, 'The Theme of the Three Caskets' (1913), in *Collected Papers*, 4 vols, 5th imp. (London: Hogarth Press and Institute of Psycho-Analysis, 1949) vol. 4, pp. 244–56.

Friedlander, Gerald, *Shakespeare and the Jew* (London: George Routledge & Sons; New York: E. P. Dutton, 1921).

Fujimura, Thomas H., 'Mode and Structure in *The Merchant of Venice*', *PMLA*, **81** (1966) pp. 499–511.

Furness, H. H. (ed.), *The Merchant of Venice*, The Variorum Shakespeare, 23 vols (Philadelphia: J. B. Lippincott, 1888) vol. 7.

Garn, Stanley M., *Human Races* (Springfield, Ill.: Charles C. Thomas, 1961).

Gesenius, William, *A Hebrew and English Lexicon of the Old Testament*, trans. Edward Robinson, eds Francis Brown, S. R. Driver and Charles A. Briggs (1907; rpt. Oxford: Clarendon Press, 1968).

Gesta Romanorum (1595), trans. and rev. R. Robinson, ed. John Weld (Delmar, New York: Scholars' Facsimiles & Reprints, 1973).

Girard, René, '"To Entrap the Wisest": A Reading of *The Merchant of Venice*', in *Literature and Society*, ed. Edward W. Said, Selected Papers from the English Institute, 1978, n.s. **3** (Baltimore and London: Johns Hopkins University Press, 1980) pp. 100–19.

Goddard, Harold, '*The Merchant of Venice*', in *The Meaning of Shakespeare* (Chicago: University of Chicago Press, 1951).

Godshalk, William, *Patterning in Shakespearean Drama* (The Hague: Mouton, 1973).

Goldstein, Gary, 'Edward De Vere's Hebrew', *ShOSN*, **26**, i (1990), pp. 6–11.

Gollancz, Israel, *Allegory and Mysticism in Shakespeare* (London: G. W. Jones, 1931).

Gorelik, Mordecai, 'This Side Idolatry', *Educational Theatre Journal*, **3** (1951) pp. 187–91.

Gosson, Stephen, *The School of Abuse*, in *The English Experience*, no. 523 (1579) (facsimile rpt. Amsterdam: Da Capo Press, 1972).

Graham, Cary B., 'Standards of Value in *The Merchant of Venice*', *SQ*, **4** (1953) pp. 145–51.

Granville-Barker, Harley, 'The Merchant of Venice', in *Prefaces to Shakespeare* (Princeton: Princeton University Press, 1964) vol. 4.

Gray, Richard A., 'Case Studies in Censorship: Censoring *The Merchant of Venice*', *RSR: Reference Services Rev.*, **19**, iii (1991) pp. 55–69.

Grazia, Margreta de, *Shakespeare 'Verbatim': The Reproduction of Authenticity and the 1790 Apparatus* (Oxford: Oxford University Press, 1990).

Greaves, Richard, *Society and Religion in Elizabethan England* (Minneapolis: University of Minnesota Press, 1981).

Greenblatt, Stephen J., 'Marlowe, Marx, and Anti-Semitism', *CI*, **5** (1978) pp. 291–307.

Greenblatt, Stephen, *Renaissance Self-Fashioning: From More to Shakespeare* (Chicago: University of Chicago Press, 1980).

Guthrie, Tyrone, *In Various Directions: A View of Theatre* (New York: Macmillan, 1965).

Hamill, Monica J., 'Poetry, Law, and the Pursuit of Perfection: Portia's Role in *The Merchant of Venice*', *SEL*, **18** (1978) pp. 229–43.

Hammond, G. H. and H. H. Scullard (eds), *The Oxford Classical Dictionary*, 2nd edn (Oxford: Clarendon Press, 1970).

Hapgood, Robert, 'Portia and *The Merchant of Venice*: The Gentle Bond', *MLQ*, **28** (1967) pp. 19–32.

Hardison, O. B., 'Shakespearean Tragedy: The Mind in Search of the

World', *The Upstart Crow*, **6** (1986) pp. 71–83.

Harrys, William (trans.), *The Market or Fayre of Usurers* (London: Steven Mierdman, 1550), (photostat facsimile reproduced from the copy of STC 17330 in the Henry E. Huntington Library).

Hartman, Louis F. (trans. & ed.), *Encyclopedic Dictionary of the Bible*, 2nd rev. edn (New York: McGraw-Hill, 1963).

Hartwig, Joan, *Shakespeare's Analogical Scene* (Lincoln and London: University of Nebraska Press, 1983).

Hassel, R. Chris, Jr, 'Antonio and the Ironic Festivity of *The Merchant of Venice*', *ShakS*, **6** (1970) pp. 67–74.

Hassel, R. Chris, Jr, *Faith and Folly in Shakespeare's Romantic Comedies* (Athens: University of Georgia Press, 1980).

Hawkes, Terence, *Meaning by Shakespeare* (London and New York: Routledge, 1992).

Hennedy, John F., 'Launcelot Gobbo and Shylock's Forced Conversion', *TSLL*, **15** (1973) pp. 405–10.

Hibbard, G. R., *Thomas Nashe: A Critical Introduction* (Cambridge: Harvard University Press).

Hill, R. F., '*The Merchant of Venice* and the Pattern of Romantic Comedy', *ShS*, **28** (1975) pp. 75–87.

Hinely, Jan Lawson, 'Bond Priorities in *The Merchant of Venice*', *SEL*, **20** (1980) pp. 217–39.

Hirsh, James E., *The Structure of Shakespearean Scenes* (New Haven and London: Yale University Press, 1981).

Hobson, Alan, 'With Undiscording Voice', in *Full Circle: Shakespeare and Moral Development* (London: Chatto & Windus, 1972).

Hockey, Dorothy C., 'The Patch is Kind Enough', *SQ*, **10** (1959) pp. 448–50.

Holaday, Allan, 'Antonio and the Allegory of Salvation', *ShakS*, **4** (1968) pp. 109–118.

Holland, Norman, *Psychoanalysis and Shakespeare* (New York: McGraw-Hill, 1964).

Holmer, Joan Ozark, 'Loving Wisely and the Casket Test: Symbolic and Structural Unity in *The Merchant of Venice*', *ShakS*, **11** (1978) pp. 54–60.

Holmer, Joan Ozark, 'Miles Mosse's *The Arraignment and Conviction of Vsurie* (1595): A New Source for *The Merchant of Venice*', *ShakS*, **21** (1993) pp. 11–54.

Holmer, Joan Ozark, 'The Education of the Merchant of Venice', *SEL*, **25** (1985) pp. 307–35.

Honigmann, E. A. J., 'Shakespeare's "Lost Source-Plays"', *MLR*, **49** (1954) pp. 293–307.

Honigmann, E. A. J., '"There is a World Elsewhere": William Shakespeare, Businessman', in Werner Habicht, D. J. Palmer, Roger Pringle (eds), *Images of Shakespeare*, Proceedings of the International Shakespeare Association, 1986 (Newark, NJ: University of Delaware Press, 1988).

Horace, *Ars Poetica*, in *Satires, Epistles, and Ars Poetica*, trans. H. Rushton Fairclough (1926; rev. & rpt. London: William Heinemann, 1929).

Hotine, Margaret, 'The Politics of Anti-Semitism: *The Jew of Malta* and *The Merchant of Venice*', *N&Q*, n.s. **38** (March 1991) pp. 35–8.

Huhner, Max, *Shakespearean Studies and other Essays* (New York: Farrar, Strauss and Young, 1952).

Humphreys, Arthur, '*The Jew of Malta* and *The Merchant of Venice*', *HLQ*, **50** (1987) pp. 279–93.

Hunter, G. K., 'The Theology of Marlowe's *The Jew of Malta*', *JWCI*, **17** (1964) pp. 211–40.

Hurrell, John D., 'Love and Friendship in *The Merchant of Venice*', *TSLL*, **3** (1961) pp. 328–41.

Hyman, Lawrence W., 'The Rival Lovers in *The Merchant of Venice*', *SQ*, **21** (1970) pp. 109–16.

Janson, Horst Noldemar, *Apes and Ape Lore in the Middle Ages and the Renaissance* (London: The Warburg Institute, University of London, 1952).

Jardine, Lisa, 'Cultural Confusion and Shakespeare's Learned Heroines: "These are old paradoxes"', *SQ*, **38** (1987) pp. 1–18.

Jewel, John, *An Exposition upon the Two Epistles of the Apostle Saint Paul to the Thessalonians* (London: R. Newberie, 1583).

Johnson, Samuel, *Johnson on Shakespeare*, ed. Arthur Sherbo, in *The Yale Edition of the Works of Samuel Johnson*, 16 vols to date (New Haven: Yale University Press, 1958–90) vol. 7 (1968).

Jones, Norman, *God and the Moneylenders: Usury and Law in Early Modern England* (Oxford and Cambridge, MA: Basil Blackwell, 1989).

Joseph ben Gorion, *A Compendious History of the Latter Times of the Jews' Common Weal*, trans. Peter Morwyng (London: Richard Jugge, 1561).

Joyce, James, 'The Sisters', in *Dubliners*, eds. Robert Scholes and A. Walton Litz (New York: Viking, 1969).

Kamen, Henry, *The Rise of Toleration* (New York: Weidenfeld and Nicolson, 1967).

Keeton, George W., 'Shylock vs Antonio', in *Shakespeare's Legal and Political Background* (New York: Barnes & Noble, 1968).

Kirsch, Arthur, *Shakespeare and the Experience of Love* (Cambridge: Cambridge University Press, 1981).

Kirschbaum, Leo, 'Shylock in the City of God', in *Character and Characterization in Shakespeare* (Detroit: Wayne State University Press, 1962).

Kofman, Sarah, 'Conversions: *The Merchant of Venice* Under the Sign of Saturn', trans. Shaun Whiteside, in *Literary Theory Today*, eds Peter Collier and Helga Geyer-Ryan (Cambridge: Polity Press, 1990).

Labrousse, Elisabeth, *Pierre Bayle*, 2 vols (The Hague, 1963–4).

Labrousse, Elisabeth, 'Religious Toleration', in *Dictionary of the History of Ideas: Studies of Selected Pivotal Ideas*, ed. Philip P. Wiener, 4 vols (New York: Charles Scribner's Sons, 1968–73).

Landa, Meyer Jack, *The Jew in Drama*, intro. Murray Roston (1924; New York: Ktav Publishing House, 1969).

Leary, William G., *Shakespeare Plain: The Making and Performing of Shakespeare's Plays* (New York: McGraw-Hill, 1977).

Lecler, Joseph, S. J., *Toleration and the Reformation* (London: Association Press, 1960).

Leggatt, Alexander, *Shakespeare's Comedy of Love* (New York: Harper & Row, 1974).

Lelyveld, Toby, *Shylock on the Stage* (1960; rpt. London: Routledge & Kegan Paul, 1961).

Lever, J. W., 'Shylock, Portia and the Values of Shakespearian Comedy', *SQ*, **3** (1952) pp. 383–6.

Levin, Richard A., *Love and Society in Shakespearean Comedy: A Study of Dramatic Form* (Newark: University of Delaware Press; London and Toronto: Associated University Presses, 1985).

Levith, Murray J., *What's in Shakespeare's Names* (Hamden, CT: Shoe String Press, 1978).

Lewalski, Barbara, 'Biblical Allusion and Allegory in *The Merchant of Venice*', *SQ*, **13** (1962) pp. 327–43.

Lewis, C. S., *The Discarded Image: An Introduction to Medieval and Renaissance Literature* (Cambridge: Cambridge University Press, 1970).

Lewis, Cynthia, '"Wise Men, Folly-Fall'n": Characters Named Antonio in English Renaissance Drama', *RenD*, n.s. **20** (Evanston: Northwestern University Press, 1990) pp. 197–236.

Lodge, Thomas, *An Alarum against Usurers* [1584], in *The Complete Works of Thomas Lodge*, vol. 1 (New York: Russell & Russell, 1963).

Lodge, Thomas, *Wits, Misery and the Worlds Madness: Discovering the Devils Incarnate of This Age* (1596), in *The Works of Thomas Lodge*, ed. Edmund W. Gosse, 4 vols (1883; rpt. New York: Russell & Russell, 1963) vol. 4.

Lucking, David, 'Standing for Sacrifice: The Casket and Trial Scenes in *The Merchant of Venice*', *UTQ*, **58** (1989) pp. 355–75.

Lyon, John, *The Merchant of Venice*, Harvester New Critical Introductions to Shakespeare (Hertfordshire: Harvester Wheatsheaf, 1988).

MacCary, W. Thomas, *Friends and Lovers: The Phenomenology of Desire in Shakespearean Comedy* (New York: Columbia University Press, 1985).

Mahood, M. M. (ed.), *The Merchant of Venice*, New Cambridge Shakespeare (Cambridge: Cambridge University Press, 1987).

Mahood, M. M., 'Golden Lads and Girls', *AJES*, **4** (1979) pp. 108–23.

Marcham, Frank, (ed.), *The Prototype of Shylock: Lopez the Jew . . . An Opinion by Gabriel Harvey* (London: Waterlow & Sons, 1927).

Martz, William J., *The Place of 'The Merchant of Venice' in Shakespeare's Universe of Comedy* (New York: Revisionist Press, 1976).

McCombie, Frank, 'Wisdom as Touchstone in *The Merchant of Venice*', *New Blackfriars*, **64** (1982) pp. 113–24.

Mclean, Hugh, 'Bassanio's Name and Nature', *Names*, **25** (1977) pp. 52–62.

McPherson, David C., *Shakespeare, Jonson, and the Myth of Venice* (Newark: University of Delaware Press, and London and Toronto: Associated University Presses, 1990).

McPherson, David, 'Lewkenor's Venice and Its Sources', *RenQ*, **41** (1988) pp. 459–66.

Meeks, Wayne A. (ed.), *The Writings of St Paul* (New York: W. W. Norton, 1972).

Melville, Herman, *Billy Budd, Sailor*, eds Harrison Hayford and Merton M. Sealts, Jr (Chicago and London: University of Chicago Press, 1962).

Midgley, Graham, '*The Merchant of Venice*: A Reconsideration', *EIC*, **10** (1960) pp. 119–33.

Milton, John, *Areopagitica*, in *John Milton: Prose Selections*, ed. Merritt Y. Hughes, Odyssey Series in Literature (New York: Odyssey Press, 1947).

Milton, John, *Paradise Lost*, ed. Merritt Y. Hughes (New York: Odyssey Press, 1962).

Moisan, Thomas, '"Which is the merchant here? and which the Jew?": Subversion and Recuperation in *The Merchant of Venice*', in *Shakespeare Reproduced: The Text in History and Ideology*, eds Jean E. Howard and Marion F. O'Connor (New York and London: Methuen, 1987) pp. 188–206.

Monter, William, *Ritual, Myth and Magic in Early Modern Europe* (Athens, Ohio: Ohio University Press, 1984).

Moody, A. D., *Shakespeare: 'The Merchant of Venice'* (London: Edward Arnold, 1964).

Morris, Harry, 'The Judgment Theme in *The Merchant of Venice*', *Renascence*, **39** (Fall 1986) pp. 292–311.

Moseley, Charles W. R. D., *Shakespeare's History Plays: Richard II to Henry V*, Penguin Critical Studies, ed. Bryan Loughrey (London: Penguin, 1988).

Mosse, Miles, *The Arraignment and Conviction of Usury. That is, The iniquity and unlawfulness of usury, displayed in six Sermons, preached at Saint Edmunds Burie in Suffolke, upon Proverb 28.8* (London: Widow Orwin, 1595).

Mottana, Annibale, Rodolfo Crespie and Giuseppe Liborio, *Simon and Schuster's Guide to Rocks and Minerals*, ed. M. Prinz, G. Harlow, and J. Peters, The American Museum of Natural History (New York: Simon and Schuster, 1978).

Muir, Kenneth, *Shakespeare's Comic Sequence* (New York: Barnes & Noble, 1979).

Muir, Kenneth, *The Sources of Shakespeare's Plays* (Methuen, 1977).

Murry, John Middleton, *Shakespeare* (London: Jonathan Cape, 1936).

Musculus, Wolfgang, *Common Places of Christian Religion. Hereunto are added two other treatises ... one of Oaths and an other of Usury*, trans. John Man (London: Henry Bynneman, 1578).

Nashe, Thomas, *The Works of Thomas Nashe*, ed. Ronald B. McKerrow, 5 vols (1904–10; rpt. Oxford: Basil Blackwell, 1958).

Nathan, Norman, 'Balthasar, Daniel, and Portia', *N&Q*, n.s. **4** (1957) pp. 334–5.

Nathan, Norman, 'Bassanio's Name', *ANQ*, **24** (1986) pp. 1–3.

Nathan, Norman, '"On the Hip"', *N&Q*, **192** (1952) p. 74.

Nathan, Norman, 'Portia, Nerissa and Jessica – Their Names', *Names: Journal of the American Name Society*, **34** (Dec. 1986) pp. 425–9.

Nathan, Norman, 'Shylock, Jacob, and God's Judgment', *SQ*, **1** (1950) pp. 255–9.

Neale, J. E., *Queen Elizabeth I* (1934; rpt. Harmondsworth: Pelican Books, 1971).

Nelson, Benjamin, *The Idea of Usury: From Tribal Brotherhood to Universal Otherhood*, 2nd edn (Chicago: University of Chicago Press, 1969).

Newman, Karen, 'Portia's Ring: Unruly Women and Structures of Exchange in *The Merchant of Venice*', *SQ*, **38** (1987) pp. 19–33.

Noble, Richmond, *Shakespeare's Biblical Knowledge and Use of the Book of Common Prayer* (1935; rpt. New York: Octagon Books, 1970).

Noonan, John T., Jr, *The Scholastic Analysis of Usury* (Cambridge, MA: Harvard University Press, 1957).

Oberman, Heiko Augustinus, *Wurzein des anti-Semitismus* (*The Roots of Anti-Semitism in the Age of Renaissance and Reformation*), trans. James I. Porter (Philadelphia: Fortress Press, 1984).

O'Connor, Flannery, 'The Lame Shall Enter First' and 'A Good Man is Hard to Find', in *The Complete Stories* (1946; rpt. New York: Farrar, Straus and Giroux, 1974).

Orgel, Stephen, 'Nobody's Perfect: Or Why Did the English Stage Take Boys for Women?', *SAQ*, **88** (1989) pp. 7–29.

Oxford Shakespeare Concordances, *The Merchant of Venice: A Concordance to the Text of the First Quarto of 1600* (Oxford: Clarendon Press, 1969).

Painter, William (trans.), *The Palace of Pleasure*, ed. Joseph Jacobs (1890; rpt. New York: Dover Publications, 1966), vol. III.

Palmer, John Leslie, 'Shylock', in *Comic Characters of Shakespeare* (London: Macmillan, 1946).

Parry, Christopher (ed.), *The Merchant of Venice*, The Macmillan Shakespeare (Basingstoke: Macmillan, 1976).

Paster, Gail Kern, *The Idea of the City in the Age of Shakespeare* (Athens: University of Georgia Press, 1985).

Pearlman, E., 'Shakespeare, Freud, and the Two Usuries, or Money's a Meddler', *ELR*, **2** (1972) pp. 217–36.

Perkins, William, *A Golden Chaine*, trans. R. H. (Cambridge: John Legatt, 1590; 2nd edn 1592).

Pettet, E. C., 'The Merchant of Venice and the Problem of Usury', *Essays and Studies*, **31** (1945) pp. 19–33.

Phialas, Peter, *Shakespeare's Romantic Comedies* (Chapel Hill: University of North Carolina Press, 1966).

Pitcairn, Robert, *Criminal Trials in Scotland . . .*, vol. 1, pt 2 (1569–1593) (Edinburgh: William Tail and London: Longman, Rees, Orme, Brown, Green & Longman, 1833).

Pope, Alexander, *An Essay on Criticism*, in *Poetry and Prose of Alexander Pope*, ed. Aubrey Williams (Boston: Houghton Mifflin, 1969).

Popkin, Richard, 'A Jewish Merchant of Venice', *SQ*, **40** (1989) pp. 329–31.

Porder, Richard, *A Sermon of gods fearful threatenings for Idolatry . . .: with a Treatise against Usury* (London: Henry Denham, 1570).

Posner, Richard A., *Law and Literature: A Misunderstood Relation* (Cambridge, MA and London: Harvard University Press, 1988).

Quiller-Couch, Arthur and John Dover Wilson (eds), *The Merchant of Venice* (Cambridge: Cambridge University Press, 1926).

Rabkin, Norman, 'Meaning and The Merchant of Venice', in *Shakespeare and the Problem of Meaning* (Chicago: University of Chicago Press, 1981).

Rackin, Phyllis, 'Androgyny, Mimesis, and the Marriage of the Boy Heroine on the English Stage', *PMLA*, **102** (1987) pp. 29–41.

Ragussis, Michael, 'Representation, Conversion, and Literary Form: Harrington and the Novel of Jewish Identity', *Critical Inquiry*, **16** (1989) pp. 113–43.

Ranald, Margaret Loftus, *Shakespeare and His Social Context* (New York: AMS Press, 1987).

Randall, Lilian, M.C., 'An Elephant in the Litany; Further Thoughts on an English Book of Hours in the Walters Art Gallery (W. 102)', in *Beasts and Birds of the Middle Ages*, eds Willene B. Clark and Meredith T. McMunn (Philadelphia: University of Pennsylvania Press, 1989).

Rasmussen, Eric, 'Shakespeare's *The Merchant of Venice*, III.ii. 63–68, *Explicator*, **44** (Winter 1986) pp. 12–13.

Restak, Richard M., M.D., *The Mind* (New York: Bantam Books, 1988).

Ribner, Irving (ed.), *The Complete Plays of Christopher Marlowe* (New York: Odyssey Press, 1963).

Robertson, D. W. Jr, *A Preface to Chaucer: Studies in Medieval Perspectives* (Princeton: Princeton University Press, 1962).

Rockas, Leo, '"A Dish of Doves": *The Merchant of Venice*', *ELH*, **40** (1973) pp. 339–51.

Rose, Mark, *Shakespearean Design* (Belknap Press of Harvard University Press, 1972).

Rossky, William, 'Imagination in the English Renaissance: Psychology and Poetic', *Studies in the Renaissance*, **5** (1958) pp. 49–73.

Roth, Cecil, *A Short History of the Jewish People*, rev. and enl. edn (London: East and West Library, 1969).

Salingar, Leo, *Shakespeare and the Traditions of Comedy* (London: Cambridge University Press, 1974).

Sander, Nicholas, *A Brief Treatise of Usury* (Lovanii: Joannem Foulerum, 1568), in *English Recusant Literature 1558–1640*, ed. D. M. Rogers, vol. 97 (Menston: Scolar Press, 1972).

Sastri, H. N. L., 'Shylock's Language', *IJES*, **3** (1962).

Saviolo, Vincentio, *Vincentio Saviolo his Practise* (1595), ed. James L. Jackson, in *Three Elizabethan Fencing Manuals* (Delmar, New York: Scholars' Facsimiles & Reprints, 1972).

Scott, W. I. D., 'Antonio – the Endogenous Depressive', in *Shakespeare's Melancholics* (London: Mills & Boon, 1962).

Seneca, *De Beneficiis, The Moral Essays*, trans. John W. Basore, Loeb Library edn, 3 vols (London: W. Heinemann; Cambridge: Harvard University Press, 1935).

Sen Gupta, S. C., 'Tragedy and Comedy: Barabas and Shylock', in *A Shakespeare Manual* (Calcutta: Oxford University Press, 1977) pp. 85–105.

Shaheen, Naseeb, *Biblical References in Shakespeare's Tragedies* (Newark: University of Delaware Press; London and Toronto: Associated University Presses, 1987).

Shaheen, Naseeb, 'Shakespeare's Knowledge of the Bible – How Acquired', *Shakespeare Studies*, **20** (1988) pp. 201–14.

Shaheen, Naseeb, 'Shylock's "Abram" in *The Merchant of Venice*', *N&Q*, 38 (1991) pp. 56–7.

Shapiro, James, *Rival Playwrights: Marlowe, Jonson, Shakespeare* (New York: Columbia University Press, 1991).

Sharp, Ronald A., 'Gift Exchange and the Economics of Spirit in *The Merchant of Venice*', *MP*, **83** (1986) pp. 250–65.

Shatzmiller, Joseph, *Shylock Reconsidered: Jews, Moneylending, and Medieval Society* (Berkeley: University of California Press, 1990).

Shell, Marc, 'The Wether and the Ewe: Verbal Usury in *The Merchant of Venice*', *Kenyon Review*, n.s. **1**, iv (1979) pp. 65–92.

Sider, John W., 'The Serious Elements of Shakespeare's Comedies', *SQ*, **24** (1973) pp. 1–11.

Sidney, Sir Philip, *An Apology for Poetry*, ed. Forrest G. Robinson (Indianapolis: Bobbs Merrill Educational, 1970).

Siegel, P. N., 'Shylock, and the Puritan Usurers', in *Studies in Shakespeare*, eds Arthur D. Matthews and Clark M. Emery (Coral Gables: University of Miami Press, 1953).

Simonds, Roger T., 'The Problem of Equity in the Continental Renaissance', in *Renaissance Papers 1989*, eds Dale B. J. Randall and Joseph A. Porter (Durham, NC: The Southeastern Renaissance Conference, 1989) pp. 34–49.

Sinsheimer, Hermann, *Shylock: The History of a Character* (1947; rpt. New York: Citadel, 1964).

Sisson, C. J., 'A Colony of Jews in Shakespeare's London', *Essays and Studies*, **23** (1937) pp. 38–51.

Slights, Camille, 'In Defense of Jessica: The Runaway Daughter in *The Merchant of Venice*', *SQ*, **31** (1980) pp. 357–68.

Smith, Bruce R., *Homosexual Desire in Shakespeare's England: A Cultural Poetics* (Chicago: University of Chicago Press, 1991).

Smith, Bruce R., 'Parolles's Recitations: Oral and Literate Structures in Shakespeare's Plays', in *Renaissance Papers 1989*, eds Dale B. J. Randall and Joseph A. Porter (Durham, NC: The Southeastern Renaissance Conference, 1989) pp. 75–88.

Smith, Henry, *The Examination of Usury, in Two Sermons* (London: R. Field, 1951).

Smith, John H., 'Shylock: "Devil Incarnation" or "Poor Man . . . Wronged"?, *JEGP*, **60** (1961) pp. 1–21.

Soellner, Rolf, 'Shakespeare's *Lucrece* and the Garnier-Pembroke Connection', *ShakS*, **15** (1982) pp. 1–20.

Spencer, Christopher, *The Genesis of Shakespeare's 'The Merchant of Venice'*, Studies in British Literature, vol. 3 (Lampeter, Dyfed, Wales: Edwin Mellen Press, 1988).

Spencer, Hazelton, *The Art and Life of Shakespeare* (New York: Harcourt Brace, 1940).

Spencer, Theodore, *Shakespeare and the Nature of Man*, 2nd edn (New York: Macmillan, 1949).

Spenser, Edmund, 'A Letter . . . To . . . Sir Walter Raleigh', in *The Faerie Queene*, ed. Thomas P. Roche, Jr (Harmondsworth: Penguin, 1978).

Spenser, Edmund, *The Faerie Queene*, ed. Thomas P. Roche, Jr (Harmondsworth: Penguin, 1978).

Spenser, Edmund, *Spenser: Poetical Works*, eds J. C. Smith and E. De Selincourt (1912; rpt. London: Oxford University Press, 1912).

Stevenson, Laura Caroline, *Praise and Paradox: Merchants and Craftsmen in Elizabethan Popular Literature* (Cambridge: Cambridge University Press, 1984).

Stoll, Elmer Edgar, 'Shylock', in *Shakespeare Studies: Historical and Comparative in Method* (New York: Macmillan, 1927) pp. 255–336.

Stonex, Arthur B., 'Money Lending and Money-Lenders in England During the 16th and 17th Centuries', in *Schelling Anniversary Papers* (New York: Russell & Russell, 1923) pp. 263–85.

Stonex, Arthur B., 'The Usurer in Elizabethan Drama', *PMLA*, **31** (1916) pp. 190–210.

Stubbes, Phillip, *The Anatomy of Abuses: Containing A Discovery . . . of such Notable Vices . . . in a very famous Island called Aligna . . .* (London: Richard Jones, 1583).

Taeusch, Carl F., 'The Concept of "Usury"', *JHI*, **3** (1942) pp. 291–318.

Tawney, R. H., *Religion and the Rise of Capitalism* (1926; rpt. New York: Penguin Books, 1947).

Taylor, Jeremy, *The Whole Works of the Right Rev. Jeremy Taylor*, ed. Reginald Heber, 15 vols (London: William Clowes for C. and J. Rivington, 1828) vol. 11.

Tennenhouse, Leonard, *Power on Display: The Politics of Shakespeare's Genres* (New York and London: Methuen, 1986).

Thompson, Karl F., *Modesty and Cunning: Shakespeare's Use of Literary Tradition* (Ann Arbor: University of Michigan Press, 1971).

Tilley, Morris Palmer, *A Dictionary of Proverbs in England in the Sixteenth and Seventeenth Centuries* (Ann Arbor: University of Michigan Press, 1950).

Tillyard, E. M. W., 'The Trial Scene in *The Merchant of Venice*', *A Review of English Literature*, **2** (1961) pp. 51–9.

Tovey, Barbara, 'The Golden Casket: An Interpretation of "*The Merchant of Venice*"', in *Shakespeare as Political Thinker*, eds John Alvis and Thomas G. West (Durham: Carolina Academic Press, 1981).

Trousdale, Marion, *Shakespeare and the Rhetoricians* (Chapel Hill: University of North Carolina Press, 1982).

Tucker, E. F. J., 'The Letter of the Law in *The Merchant of Venice*', *ShS*, **29** (1976) pp. 93–101.

Tucker, Patrick and Michael Holden (eds), *The Merchant of Venice* (Shakespeare's Globe Acting Edition) (London: M. H. Publications, 1991).

Vickers, Brian, *The Artistry of Shakespeare's Prose* (London: Methuen, 1968).

Waith, Eugene M., 'Shakespeare and Fletcher on Love and Friendship', *ShakS*, **18** (1986) pp. 235–50.

Weber, Max, *The Protestant Ethic and the Spirit of Capitalism*, trans. Talcott Parsons, 2nd imp. (1930; London: G. Allen & Unwin, 1948).

Welles, Orson and Roger Hill (eds), *The Merchant of Venice* (ed. for reading and arranged for staging), The Mercury Shakespeare (New York and London: Harper & Brothers, 1939).

Wertheim, Albert, 'The Treatment of Shylock and Thematic Integrity in *The Merchant of Venice*', *ShakS*, **6** (1970) pp. 75–87.

Wheeler, Thomas, *The Merchant of Venice: An Annotated Bibliography* (New York & London: Garland, 1985).

Whigham, Frank, 'Ideology and Class Conduct in *The Merchant of Venice*', *RenD*, **10** (1979) pp. 93–115.

Whitaker, Virgil K., 'The Romantic Comedies', in *Shakespeare's Use of Learning* (San Marino: The Huntington Library, 1953).

Wilkins, Leah W., 'Shylock's Pound of Flesh and Laban's Sheep', *MLN*, **62** (1947) pp. 28–30.

Willet, Andrew, *Hexapla in Genesin . . . A Sixfold Commentary upon Genesis . . .* (London: Thomas Creede, 1608).

Williams, Arnold, *The Common Expositor: An Account of the Commentaries on Genesis 1527–1633* (Chapel Hill: University of North Carolina Press, 1948).

Williamson, Marilyn L., 'The Ring Episode in *The Merchant of Venice*', *SAQ*, **71** (1972) pp. 587–94.

Wilson, F. P., *The English Drama 1485–1585*, ed. G. K. Hunter, Oxford History of English Literature (Oxford: Clarendon Press, 1969).

Wilson, Robert, *An Edition of Robert Wilson's 'The Three Ladies of London' and 'Three Lords and Three Ladies of London'*, in *The Renaissance Imagination*, vol. 36 (New York: Garland, 1988).

Wilson, Thomas, *A Discourse upon Usury* [1572], ed. R. H. Tawney (New York: Harcourt Brace, 1925).

Withycombe, E. G., *The Oxford Dictionary of English Christian Names*, 2nd edn (Oxford: Oxford University Press, 1959).

Wolf, Lucien, 'Jews in Elizabethan England', *Transactions of the Jewish Historical Society of England*, **11** (1924–7) pp. 8–9.

Wright, Celeste Turner, 'Some Conventions Regarding the Usurer in Elizabethan Literature', *SP*, **31** (1934) pp. 176–97.

Wright, Celeste Turner, 'The Usurer's Sin in Elizabethan Literature', *SP*, **35** (1938) pp. 178–94.

Yachnin, Paul, 'The Powerless Theater', *ELR*, **21** (1991) pp. 49–74.

Index

Abigail, 15, 19, 70, 85–7, 106, 118, 120, 124, 219, 236–8, 304n.67, 311n.63, 331n.53–4, 332n.56, 333n.66, 334n.83

Abrabanel, Judah (*alias* Leone Ebreo), 16

Abraham (Abram), 15, 72, 76, 78–9, 85–7, 90, 92, 150, 158–9, 170, 233–4, 244, 259, 301n.41, 304n.76, 319n.28,30

Act Against Usury (1571), 36, 170, 176, 209, 275, 319n.27; *see also* usury

Act of Uniformity (1559), 17, 205

Adelman, Janet, 340n.49

Aelred de Rievaulx, 117, 267, 310n.45, 339n.37

allegory, 6, 47, 90–2, 95–6, 105, 126, 158, 162, 193, 196, 205, 232–5, 282, 287n.18, 300n.25, 303n.55, 306n.18, 326n.12

Alvares, Ferdinand, 288n.28

Andrews, Mark Edwin, 331n.47

Antonio, xv–xvi, 8–10, 12–13, 19, 25, 30–1, 39–42, 44, 48–9, 52–6, **59–64**, 68, 76–7, 80, 84–5, 95, 98–9, 104–5, 109, 113, 115–17, 122, 126, 129–38, 140, **142–6**, 148–58, **160–92**, 196, 199–203, 205–7, **209–26**, 228–33, **237–55**, 257, **260–73**, 275–6, **278–84**, 298n.16, 299n.17, 310n.43, 315n.6, 318n.18, 319n.25, 322n.58, 323n.72, 324n.91, 326n.12, 327n.21, 328n.24, 330n.45, 331n.47, 335n.8, 336n.11,15, 339n.30,45, 340n.47

  and figurative conversion, 66, 176–8, 218

  and judgment of Shylock, 214–32, 237–8, 244–5

  and law, 153, 156, 168, 182, 186, 199, 201, 214, 219, 222, 237, 239, 242, 331n.47

  and usury, 31, 38–9, 59–60, 62, 80, 133–5, 144, 154–7, 163–4, 166–9, 172, 176–8, 180, 182, 217, 229–30, 248–9, 254, 262, 270, 276, 278, 284, 315n.6, 323n.72, 331n.47

  as friend, 40, 56, 99, 116–17, 128–33, 135–40, 143, 181, 185–6, 192, 214, 216–19, 229–32, 237–8, 246–50, 254, 263–7, 269–71

  as merchant, 39, 116, 137, 142–3, 149, 152, 156, 168, 181–2, 248, 270, 276

  as name, 134–5, 313n.85–91

  as stage Christian, 10, 30–1, 38–9, 61–2, 65–6, 68, 133, 142–5, 152–7, 163, 167–9, 176–8

  as victim, 59–60, 62–3, 143, 181, 184–5, 187, 200–1

  as victimizer, 60, 143–4, 163, 181–2, 192

  homoeroticism of, 250–4, 336n.11–21

  in relation to casket choice, 105, 136, 140, 162, 183, 266, 268

  melancholy of, 12, 130–2, 270, 312n.79, 313n.80–1

  moral growth of, 129, 137, 185, 192, 215, 283

Aristotle, 33, 36, 161–2, 293n.91, 296n.1, 320n.35

Arragon, xvii, 12, 41, 49, 54, 56, 64, **99–106**, **108–9**, **112–14**, 121, 144, 146, 149, 151, 202, **208–9**, 241, 244, 259, 266, 306n.19, 307n.22

Auden, W. H., 95, 174, 296n.1, 305n.2, 323n.87

Babington, Gervase, Bishop, 229, 317n.15, 319n.30, 333n.67

Bacon, Francis, 26, 37, 292n.66
Bacon, Nathaniel, 37
Bady, David, 174, 324n.90
Baldwin, Charles Sears, 304n.65
Baldwin, T. W., 297n.7
Balthazar, 55, 57, 71, 85, 186–7,
    193–5, 211, 215, 218, 233, 235,
    240, 255, 301n.38–9, 304n.71,
    326n.15; *see also* Portia
Barabas, 11, 13, 15, 18, 23, 28, 39, 61,
    66, 70, 84–6, 91, 93–4, 115, 118,
    120, 124, 139–40, 159, 165,
    189–90, 206, 219, 223, 236–8,
    243, 289n.32, 299n.20, 300n.30,
    301n.38, 303n.57, 318n.18,
    319n.30, 325n.105, 330n.45,
    331n.54, 333n.66; *see also*
    Christopher Marlowe
Barabbas (biblical), 11, 14, 76, 119,
    206, 238, 256, 301n.38
Barber, C. L., 272, 296n.1, 340n.49
Barnet, Sylvan, 308n.30, 322n.59
Baron, Salo W., 227, 288n.28,
    290n.42, 292n.80, 294n.107–8,
    322n.56, 333n.64
Barroll, J. Leeds, 306n.19
Baskervill, Charles Read, 306n.19
Bassanio, 9, 19, 27, 40–1, 44, 48–9,
    52–4, 56–7, 59, 62, 65, 71, 82–3,
    87, 97–9, 101–3, **105–19**, 125,
    129– 33, 135–8, 140, 142–6,
    148–52, 154–6, 162–3, 167,
    169– 71, 175, 177, 181, 183, 188,
    191–2, 199–201, 203, 211, 213– 14,
    233, 241, **246 –73**, 278–9, 281,
    283, 298n.16, 299n.17, 305n.4,
    306n.13,19, 308n.27,29,30,
    309n.33,38, 310n.42–3, 311n.51,
    314n.97, 315n.6, 322n.58,
    324n.91, 327n.21, 336n.15,
    338n.29, 339n.30,32, 340n.47
  and Morocco and Arragon, 97– 9,
    102–3, 106, 108– 9, 111– 13, 259,
    306n.19
  and rings episode, 104, 107, 114,
    241, 246, 256–70, 338n.29
  and Shylock, 62, 106, 145, 149,
    155, 200, 262
  as friend, 40, 52, 99, 116, 130–2,
    135–8, 142–3, 145, 149, 156, 181,
    191, 199–200, 203, 247, 253, 255,
    262, 264–6, 279, 310n.43,
    339n.30, 340n.47
  as Lancelot's master, 57, 87, 137
  as lover/husband, 9, 40–1, 49, 52,
    56, 99–103, 106–15, 129, 131,
    138, 140, 183, 241, 248, 253, 255,
    258, 262, 264–9, 279, 306n.13,19,
    308n.27, 308n.29, 310n.43
  as name, 110–13, 118, 309n.33–5
  as too liberal, 130, 136–7, 145, 246,
    256, 264–6, 268, 279, 339n.32
Beauregard, David, 296n.1, 332n.61
Beckerman, Bernard, 46, 297n.9
Bellario, 54, 193, 256; *see also* Portia
Belsey, Catherine, 113, 277, 306n.17,
    309n.39, 310n.46, 327n.21,
    339n.37, 340n.52–3, 341n.54–5
Benston, Alice, 198, 328n.24, 340n.47
Berger, Harry, 306n.14
Berry, Ralph, 253, 336n.11, 337n.20
Bible
  Old Testament (Hebrew Bible)
    references: Genesis, 15, 73, 76,
    78, 80–1, 90–2, 127, 157–61,
    173–4, 205, 229, 254, 302n.43,
    303n.53–4, 315n.3, 317n.14–15,
    323n.82, 333n.73; Exodus, 70,
    206, 303n.56, 317n.16; Leviticus,
    35, 64, 153, 205, 239, 304n.85–6;
    Deuteronomy, 35, 89, 123, 128,
    153–4, 168, 180, 189, 259,
    300n.24, 317n.16; Joshua, 81;
    Judges, 81; 1 Samuel, 81, 85,
    110, 206, 338n.27; 2 Samuel,
    206; 1 Chronicles, 79, 86; Job,
    66, 69, 110; Psalms, 35, 67, 79,
    82, 89, 92, 133, 196, 205;
    Proverbs, 12, 69, 157, 173, 205,
    225, 271, 319n.25; Ecclesiastes,
    196, 230; Isaiah, 76, 86, 91,
    233–4; Ezekiel, 35; Daniel,
    194–5; Micah, 146
  Apocrypha references: Tobit, 153;
    The Wisdom of Solomon, 68;
    Ecclesiasticus, 12, 67, 312n.69;
    Susanna, 194-5; 2 Maccabees,
    223

Bible – *cont.*
New Testament references:
  Matthew, 9–10, 35, 65–7, 85,
  117, 150, 152–4, 189, 206, 227,
  232–3, 235, 242, 260, 315n.4,
  335n.4, 338n.26, 339n.43; Mark,
  10, 147; Luke, 8–10, 33, 35, 78,
  85, 123, 133, 150, 154–5, 206,
  231, 248, 313n.82, 317n.17; John,
  128; Acts of the Apostles, 69,
  338n.24; Romans, 19, 65, 81, 86,
  119, 159, 188–9, 207, 228, 234,
  278, 333n.75; 1 Corinthians, 15,
  65, 69, 110, 196, 206, 300n.24,
  329n.35, 338n.24; Galatians, 19,
  67, 90–2, 117, 188, 200, 207, 212,
  232, 242, 244, 329n.29, 334n. 78;
  Ephesians, 15, 117, 121, 123,
  235, 334n.80; Philippians, 163,
  334n.81; Colossians, 235,
  326n.14, 334n.79; Philemon,
  236; Hebrews, 90–1, 127,
  334n.86; James, 19, 67–8, 93,
  140, 188–9, 192, 221, 242, 260; 1
  Peter, 91, 141, 157; 2 Peter, 93; 1
  John, 7, 154, 186, 205, 300n.25
Biel, Gabriel, 169, 249
Biggs, Murray, 340n.47
Bishops' Bible, 11, 15, 71, 73, 76,
  80–1, 86, 127, 153, 159, 160, 173,
  301n.41, 303n.54,56, 304n.76,
  315n.3, 317n.15–16, 323n.82,85,
  333n.73; *see also* Figure 2, 74–5,
  301n.41
Black, Henry Campbell, 303n.43
Blaxton, John, 313n.87, 324n.96
blessing, 8, 9, 12, 53, 58, 68, 72–3,
  80–3, 96, 119, 121, 124, 158–9,
  174–5, 234, 236, 247, 259, 273,
  303n.54, 310n.48
Boethius, 128
Bondavid, *see* Joseph Shatzmiller
bonds, 33, 36, 124, 168, 171, 198–9,
  201, 229, 235, 246, 265, *passim*
Boose, Linda, 339n.45
Boswell, Jackson Campbell, 125,
  311n.60–1, 312n.72
Brown, John Russell, 10, 33, 44, 68,
  159, 167, 216, 285n.1, 287n.21,
  293n.92, 294n.101, 297n.6,

298n.10, 300n.26–7, 302n.51,
  303n.52–3,61–2,64, 306n.15,
  307n.22, 308n.27, 309n.37,
  310n.50, 314n.96, 316n.9,
  318n.23, 319n.27,29,31, 320n.34,
  321n.52–3, 322n.57–8, 323n.83,
  325n.102,109, 326n.6, 329n.37,
  330n.38,46, 331n.48
Bullough, Geoffrey, 289n.33,
  290n.38, 295n.128, 310n.50,
  311n.54,62, 312n.71,77–9,
  314n.1, 315n.6, 324n.98,
  325n.109, 326n.7–9, 327n.19,
  328n.25, 329n.31, 330n.38,
  334n.82, 335n.6
Bulman, James C., xi, 285n.1
Burckhardt, Sigurd, 306n.19

Caesar, Philippus, 319n.31, 320n.41,
  324n.96, 333n.70
Camden, William, 26, 292n.71,74,76
Cameron, G. W., 289n.33, 293n.93
Cardozo, Jacob L., 78, 302n.46–7
Carnovsky, Morris, 325n.110
Carrington, Norman, 308n.27
Cartelli, Thomas, xvi, 286n.15,
  299n.20, 328n.27, 334n.84
casket plot, *see* unity
Castiglione, Baldassare, 106,
  308n.24,31, 326n.15
Cato, 33, 36, 89, 162, 184
Charlton, H. B., 308n.27, 328n.28,
  338n.25
Charney, Maurice, 311n.63,65
Chaucer, Geoffrey, 243, 295n.111,
  308n.31, 312n.73, 334n.88,
  339n.31
Chew, Samuel C., 327n.18, 337n.17
choice, 47, 240–1, 264, *passim*
  see also language; structure; unity
Chus (Chush, Cush), 71, 73, 76, 78,
  89–90, 182
Cicero, 162, 253, 268
Cinthio, Giambattista Giraldi, 67
Coghill, Nevill, 185, 325n.2, 332n.62,
  336n.11
Cohen, D. M., 28, 292n.85
Cohen, Walter, xiii–xv, 30, 171–2,
  174–5, 228, 285n.6,7,9,11–13,

289n.34, 293n.90, 296n.1, 323n.78–9, 324n.92, 333n.65
Coke, Sir Edward, 26
consequence, 21, 246, 261, *passim*
    see also language, structure; unity
conversion, **15–19**, 21, 26, 29, 53, **55–6**, 66, 80, 85, 88, **114–15**, 122–3, 136, 143, 178, 191, 197, **219–38**, 240–2, 245, 276, **280**, **283**, 290n.37,38, 309n.38, 326n.10, 330n.46, 331n.53–4, 332n.56,61–2, 333n.73
conversos, 221, 332n.55
Cook, Ann Jennalie, 107, 308n.26, 310n.50, 311n.57, 331n.53
Coolidge, John S., 305n.79, 323n.84
Cooper, John R., 299n.22
Crane, Milton, 314n.2
Cromwell, Oliver, 14, 180, 290n.40

Danson, Lawrence, 4, 13, 81, 132, 193, 217, 233–4, 238, 286n.10, 288n.27, 290n.38, 293n.93, 303n.55, 306n.19, 313n.81, 322n.58, 326n.13, 327n.23, 329n.30, 330n.46, 331n.50, 332n.62, 333n.74–5, 334n.76–7, 336n.11, 339n.44, 340n.47
Dante, Alighieri, 270, 341n.56
Davis, J. Madison, 318n.18
Death of Usury, The, 159, 222n.61, 320n.32,41
De Grazia, Margreta, 286n.16
De Roover, Raymond, 134–5, 293n.91, 295n.115, 313n.86, 314n.88–90
Dessen, Alan C., 14, 215, 289n.32, 325n.105, 330n.45
Dimock, Arthur, 292n.71
Donow, Herbert S., 296n.1, 311n.52, 339n.45
Doran, Madeleine, 2–3, 46, 286n.5–6
Draper, J. W., 288n.30
Duke of Venice, 48–9, 52, 133, 156, 177–8, 181–2, 186–8, 200, 203, 208, 210–15, 221–3, 225–6

Eagleton, Terry, 309n.40

Ebreo, Leone, *see* Judah Abrabanel
Eccles, Ambrose, 318n.23
education, 5,8, 31, 69, 161, 168, 170, 185, 199, 200, 210, 215, 231, 235, 242, 247, 260, 279, 284, 329n.37
Elizabeth I, 12, 25, 27, 38, 205, 292n.71,77
Ellis, I. P., 295n.123
Elze, Karl, 78–9, 302n.46,49, 303n.64
Encyclopedia Judaica, 288n.29, 294n.107–8, 295n.110,113, 332n.55
Engle, Lars, 174, 315n.6, 323n.84, 324n.91
Esau, 80–1, 127, 158, 174, 303n.54, 323n.84
Essex, Earl of, 26, 288n.28, 292n.77
Eure, John D., 331n.47–8
Evans, B. Ivor, 314n.2
Evans, G. Blakemore, 321n.53, 338n.29
Evans, R. C., 295n.125

Faulkner, William, 20, 69, 94, 130, 300n.31, 312n.76
Fian, Dr (*alias* John Cunningham), 23, 291n.64
Fiedler, Leslie, 305n.9
Fleissner, Robert F., 303n.61
flesh-bond plot, *see* unity
Florio, John, 70, 304n.68, 311n.65
Fortin, René, 303n.55
Fowler, Alastair, 270, 311n.57, 339n.44
Freud, Sigmund, 112, 277, 309n.38, 339n.45
Friedlander, Gerald, 147, 294n.106, 295n.114, 315n.5
Furness, H. H., 299n.18, 311n.63, 318n.23, 331n.48

Ganz, Joachim, 288n.28
Geneva Bible, 8, 11–12, 65, 71, 73, 76, 78, 80, 86, 87, 89–90, 92, 127, 147, 153, 158, 193, 232–3, 235, 287n.20, 301n.36,38, 303n.56, 312n.72, 313n.82, 315n.3–4, 317n.15–16, 323n.85, 326n.12, 327n.16, 333n.73, 334n.85–6, 335n.4

360

Index

Geneva–Tomson Bible, 11, 70–1, 139, 235, 301n.38, 334n.80
genre, 5, 40–2, 233, 246
Gernutus, Ballad of, 39, 70, 79, 198–9, 201, 302n.51, 318n.18, 322n.58, 325n.109, 330n.38; *see also* J. R. Brown (ed.)
Gerontus, 16, 18–19, 70, 180, 189–91, 289n.32, 295n.128, 325n.105, 330n.45; *see also* H. S. D. Mithdal; Robert Wilson
Gesta Romanorum, 6, 46–7, 95–7, 122, 158, 298n.12, 306n.13,18
Ginsburg, Christian David, 173, 323n.83
Giovanni Ser, Fiorentino; *see Il Pecorone*
Girard, René, 174, 176, 239, 323n.89, 325n.102, 334n.84
Gobbo, Lancelot, 9, 12, 15, 41, 49, **53–5**, 58, 62, 64, 77, 81–2, 87, **91–4**, 99, 105, **117–21**, 126, 137, 139, 142, 149, 161, 179, 205, 211, 219, **225–8**, 273, 280, 303n.55, 305n.82, 307n.23, 310n.48, 314n.96
Gobbo (Lancelot's father), 81, 94, 97, 119, 139, 149, 282
Goddard, Harold, 323n.81, 325n.110
Godshalk, William, 298n.11
golden fleece, myth of, 114–15, 141, 314n.97
Goldstein, Gary, 72, 301n.40
Gollancz, Israel, 83, 191, 303n.62, 326n.12
Gorelik, Mordecai, 308n.27
Gosson, Stephen, 300n.25, 307n.22
Graham, Cary B., 189, 251, 306n.19
Granville-Barker, Harley, 96, 296n.1, 305n.4
Gratiano, 12–14, 25, 27, 41, 48–9, 52, 57, 62, 65, **70**, 72, 114, 131–2, **136–7**, 156, 161, 184, 194, 196, 200, 203, 211, 215, 219, 221, 224, 225, 240, 243, 245, 252, 255, 256, **258–61**, 263, **268–71**, 280, 282, 298n.16, 299n.17, 330n.45
Gray, Richard A., 286n.14
Greaves, Richard, 295n.123, 315n.6

Greenblatt, Stephen, 286n.18, 299n.20
Greene, Robert, 21, 288n.27
Guthrie, Tyrone, 276, 336n.11, 34n.51

Hagar (Agar), 71, 81, 90–3, 301n.38
Hamill, Monica J., 338n.28, 340n.47
Hammond, G. H., 304n.70,75
Hapgood, Robert, 327n.17
Hardison, O. B., Jr, 2, 286n.4
Harrys, William (trans.), *see The Market or Fayre of Usurers*
Hartman, Louis F., 316n.10
Hartwig, Joan, 297n.8
Harvey, Gabriel, 26, 292n.75, 337n.18
Hassel, R. Chris, Jr, 332n.62, 340n.49
Hawkes, Terence, xiii–xv, 285n.4
Hawthorne, Nathaniel, 227
hazard, 49, 54, 58, 97, 100–1, 104, 112, 114, 123, 128, 130, 135–7, 140, 149, 183, 207–8, 256–6, 266, 268, 270, 277, 306n.17, 340n.53
Hazlitt, William, 176, 325n.102
Hennedy, John F., 332n.62
Herrera, Alonso Nuñez de, 288n.28
Herrey, Robert F., 71, 76, 79–80, 87–8, 90, 282, 301n.37–8, 303n.53, 327n.16
Hibbard. G. R., 23–4, 291n.58–9,63
Hill, R. F., 340n.47
Hinely, Jan Lawson, 262, 330n.46, 335n.8, 339n.35
Hirsh, James E., 297n.7
Hobson, Alan, 296n.1
Hockey, Dorothy, 303n.55
Holaday, Allan, 296n.1
Holland, Norman, 336n.11
Holmer, Joan Ozark, 294n.96, 296n.1, 305n.3, 306n.13, 336n.9
Honigmann, E. A. J., 307n.22, 324n.101
Horace, 4–5, 287n.11
Hotine, Margaret, 292n.70
Huhner, Max, 308n.27
Humphreys, Arthur, 299n.20
Hunter, G. K., 14, 22, 27, 70, 165, 206, 215, 289n.31,35, 304n.69, 325n.105, 330n.45, 344n.78

Hurrell John D., 252, 336n.13
Hyman, Laurence W., 339n.33

Il Novellino, see Masuccio
　　Salernitano
Il Pecorone, 30, 46–7, 67, 70, 96,
　　130–1, 142, 144, 156, 160, 181,
　　190, 193, 196, 198–9, 201–2, 205,
　　207, 214, 220, 247, 252, 257, 269,
　　279, 282, 288n.28, 293n.93,
　　295n.128, 312n.78, 314n.1,
　　315n.6, 330n.38
inheritance, 15, 72, 81, 89, 92, 122,
　　137, 145, 58–9, 216–17, 219,
　　229–30, 234–6, 265, 339n.45
irony, 42–3, 60, 65, 81, 91, 93–4,
　　103–4, 106, 136, 145–7, 149–51,
　　153, 159, 165, 167–8, 173, 187–8,
　　191, 201–2, 211, 215, 235, 260,
　　264, 279, 300n.30, 315n.3
Irving, Sir Henry, 28, 189
Isaac, 78–9, 92, 158, 303n.54
issues, comparison of
　　appearance and reality, 44, 110,
　　　162, 179, 181, 183, 277, 329n.32
　　faith and wealth, 31, 111, 133, 222,
　　　224–5, 229, 236, 280
　　fidelity and infidelity, 101, 111,
　　　114, 122–3, 125, 168, 258–9,
　　　264–6, 269, 272–3
　　friendship and romance, 6, 56,
　　　128, 140, 253, 270, *passim*
　　Jew and Christian, 10, 14, 16, 18,
　　　28, 35, 65–6, 69, 93, 124, 147,
　　　151, 176, 178, 218, 226–7, 238,
　　　241, 280, 289n.31–2,35
　　justice and mercy, 5, 35, 44, 55,
　　　57–8, 67–9, 113, 178–9, 183–5,
　　　196, 199–200, 202, 208, 210–14,
　　　216, 223, 225, 231, 243, 245, 259,
　　　262, 266, 269, 279–80, 329n.37
　　knowing and doing, 4, 8, 45, 117,
　　　143, 167, 242–3, 248, 260
　　life and death, 25, 42, 69, 77,
　　　96–7, 112, 140, 192, 201, 205,
　　　210, 213, 221, 223, 236–8, 268,
　　　280
　　life and living, 9, 25, 142, 184, 210,
　　　213, 217–18, 223, 230–2, 239,

　　　269–70, 280
　　love and hate, 9, 140, 143, 148,
　　　150, 153–4, 178, 180, 183–6,
　　　191, 236
　　money and love, 10, 30, 135, 148,
　　　166, 171
　　old and young, 58, 119, 122, 193,
　　　310n.50, 326n.14
　　Old Law and New Law, 5, 15–16,
　　　35, 90, 153, 185, 212, 232–3, 242;
　　　see also law (biblical)
　　sight and insight, 58, 62, 67, 69,
　　　90–1, 98, 100–1, 104–5, 109–10,
　　　113
　　spirit and flesh, 10, 14, 55, 58,
　　　67–8, 92–3, 119, 127, 188, 205,
　　　211–12, 219, 226, 228, 235–6,
　　　338n.24
　　spirit and letter, 102, 186, 202–4,
　　　226, 329n.32
　　wisdom and folly, 12–13, 179–80,
　　　183, 206, 228, 245, 277
　　see also individual characters; law
　　　(biblical); unity; usury
Ithamore, 70, 94, 115; *see also*
　　Christopher Marlowe

Jacob, 9, 12, 15, 71–2, 78–83, 91,
　　119, 121, 125–7, 150–3, 157–61,
　　167, 173–4, 229, 233–4, 244, 254,
　　259, 301n.38, 303n.54,57,
　　310n.48, 312n.70, 315n.3,
　　317n.14–15, 319n.30, 323n.84,
　　333n.73
Jardine, Lisa, 338n.23, 340n.46
Jessica, 9, 11, 14–15, 19, 28, 41, 44,
　　49, **53–7**, 59, 61–2, 71, 76, 78,
　　81–3, **85–94**, 97, 99, 102, 106,
　　115, 117, **118–29**, 131, 140, 142,
　　148, 159, 161, 177, 179, 180, 182,
　　197, 203, 205, 211, 213, **216–19**,
　　226–9, 236, 269, **272– 4**, 279–80,
　　282–3, 289n.35, 301n.38,
　　303n.64, 304n.65–6, 310n.50,
　　311n.51,63, 312n.72, 325n.110,
　　327n.21, 331n.47,53, 332n.56
Jewel, John, Bishop, 79, 302n.50,
　　319n.31, 320n.41, 321n.45,
　　322n.59, 324n.96, 330n.70

Jews, *passim*
Elizabethan views of, 13–16, 19–28, 31, 38–9, 289n.31–3,35, 290n.36,39, 291n.46,48,50–7, 60–2, 292n.70,72–83, 294n.95
in England, 14, 34, 38, 180, 288n.28, 290n.38, 295n.110
in Venice, 17–18, 34, 290n.41–2, 294n.108
livelihoods, 34–5, 294n.106–7,109, 295n.111–14
see also religious tolerance *and* intolerance
Johnson, Samuel, 5, 287n.16
Jones, Norman, 14, 30, 36, 176, 285n.8, 288n.30, 293n.89, 294n.100,104, 295n.121–3,126, 298n.14, 315n.6, 319n.27, 322n.59,68, 324n.96,99,101, 330n.39
Joseph ben Gorion, ha-Kohen, 19, 20–2, 27, 78, 84–5, 291n.48,55,60, 303n.63, 334n.80
Joyce, James, 312n.68
Judah, Nathaniel, 288n.28

Kahn, Michael, 220
Kahneman, Daniel, Dr, xiv, 285n.5
Kamen, Henry, 290n.43
Keeton, George W., 212, 330n.42, 331n.47–8
Kirsch, Arthur, 5–6, 287n.17–18
Kirschbaum, Leo, 322n.62
Kofman, Sarah, 309n.38

Laban, 71, 83, 126, 153, 157–60, 173–4, 229, 254, 301n.38, 312n.70, 317n.15, 318n.23–4, 319n.27, 323n.84
Labrousse, Elisabeth, 19, 290n.43–4
Lancelot, *see* Lancelot Gobbo
Landa, Meyer Jack, 15, 289n.34, 328n.28
language, 3, 30, 32, 47, 57–69, 104–5, *passim*
and Shylock, 32, 55, 60–1, 202–6, 314n.2
literalism, 53, 55, 64, 146, 149, 199, 202, 203–4, 206–7, 225, 227–8,

233, 245, 282, 329n.32
Portia's mercy speech, 67–9
Shylock's revenge speech, 58–66
verbal clues, 97, 99–102, 145, 149, 201–3, 214, 226, 306n.13
wordplay, 58, 71, 76, 80, 86, 89, 101, 114–15, 148, 164, 167, 183, 202, 212, 258, 266, 271, 281, 292n.69, 304n.65,67, 320n.35, 323n.80
law, 11, 58, 92, 98, 106, 276, 278, 290n.40, 329n.29,32, 330n.43
and equity, 202, 212–13, 327n.23, 329n.32, 330n.43
and usury, xiv, 33–8, 156, 160, 170–1, 180, 184, 187, 275, 285n.8, 298n.14, 317n.16, 319n.27, 320n.40, 321n.47, 323n.72
biblical (Old Testament and New Testament), 5, 9–10, 15–16, 35, 64–5, 72, 77, 80–1, 90, 92, 150, 156, 163, 173, 177, 185–6, 189, 200, 204, 206–7, 212, 219, 226, 232–5, 242, 259–60, 300n.24, 305n.79, 316n.10, 317n.16, 329n.29, 334n.81
divine and human, 34, 37, 47, 64, 170, 188, 191, 196, 211, 235, 275, 278, 317n.16, 320n.40
English, 17, 24, 33, 36, 38, 212, 216, 319n.27, 321n.47, 327n.23, 329n.32,37
literalistic legalism, 92, 197–8, 201–4, 232–3, 236, 282, 329n.32
literary stage law, 197–9, 202, 204, 214, 222, 282, 329n.37
Venetian, 182–4, 187, 191, 198–9, 201–2, 207–13, 222, 239–40, 282, 327n.21, 329n.32,37
Leah, 24, 71–2, 77, 83, 87, 90–1, 124–6, 142, 174, 243, 301n.38, 303n.57, 305n.78–9
Leary, William G., 299n.18
Lecler, Joseph, S. J., 290n.43
Leggatt, Alexander, 296n.1
Lelyveld, Toby, 285n.1
Lever, J. W., 332n.62
Levin, Richard A., 331n.47, 339n.45

Levith, Murray J., 70, 300n.33–4, 303n.64, 304n.73, 305n.81, 309n.33, 310n.46, 313n.85

Lewalski, Barbara, 12, 206, 217, 232, 240, 287n.18,24, 296n.1, 306n.19, 326n.15, 329n.29–30,34, 331n.50, 332n.62, 333n.71–2, 334n.79,87

Lewis, C. S., 1, 286n.1, 299n.23, 308n.31

Lewis, Cynthia, 313n.85

Lewkenor, *see* David C. McPherson

Lodge, Thomas, 21, 31, 137, 162, 294n.97, 313n.80, 314n.93, 320n.32,39,41, 333n.70

Lombards, 34, 295n.111

Lopez, Roderigo (Ruy), 14, 16, 19–20, 23–7, 212, 292n.69–70,75

Lord of Belmont (Portia's father), xvii, 6, 9, 100, 107–8, 110, 113–14, 116, 120, 230, 252, 257

Lorenzo, 9, 14–15, 41, 48–9, 53–8, 77, 82, 86, 88, 90, 106, 115, **117–23**, 125, 128–32, 140, 213, 216–19, 224, **227–9**, 252, 269, **271–4**, 281–2, 298n.16, 307n.23, 310n.46,50, 327n.21, 332n.56

love, 3, 6–9, 30, 33, 44–5, 109–10, 112–13, 117, 128–9, 132–3, 140–1, 230–1, 246, 264, 267, 270, 276–7, 284, *passim*
see also individual characters; issues; law (biblical); usury; unity

Lucking, David, 308n.29–30, 314n.97, 332n.62

Lyly, John, 270, 339n.36

Lyon, John, 295n.120, 296n.1

MacCary, W. Thomas, 336n.11, 337n.16, 340n.52

Machiavelli, N., 139, 190, 243, 318n.18

Mahood, M. M., 3, 6, 12, 24, 28, 43–4, 154, 161, 170, 178, 210, 212, 216, 221, 285n.1, 286n.9, 287n.23, 288n.29, 291n.47, 292n.66, 293n.86, 294n.106, 295n.128, 296n.1, 297n.5, 316n.7, 326n.15

Marcham, Frank, 292n.75

Marlowe, Christopher, xii, 11, 13, 15, 18, 23, 39, 45, 61, 66, **70–1**, **84–8**, 90–1, **93–4**, 106, **115**, 120, 124, 139, 159–60, **165–6**, **189–90**, 219, 223, **236–8**, 251, 281, 283, 286n.15, 288n.27, 289n.31, 292n.70,84, 299n.20, 301n.38, 303n.60, 304n.67, 311n.63, 318n.18, 321n.52,55, 326n.10, 328n.27, 331n.53, 332n.56, 334n.83–4

The Market or Fayre of Usurers, 223, 332n.59

marranos, 34, 221, 239, 332n.55

Martz, William J., 336n.11

Marx, Karl, xiv–xv

Masuccio Salernitano, 90, 122–3, 127, 310n.50

McCombie, Frank, 12, 287n.23–5, 306n.12, 319n.25

McKerrow, Ronald B., 23, 291n.48,60,64, 294n.103

Mclean, Hugh, 309n.33

McPherson, David C., 197, 290n.41, 294n.108, 327n.21

Meeks, Wayne A., 334n.79

Melville, Herman, 126, 312n.66

Menasseh ben Israel, Rabbi, 180

Mercadore, 191, 237; *see also* Robert Wilson

merchantry, xii, 29, 34, 38–9, 135, 137, 143, 149, 152, 156, 172, 190, 270, 276, 288n.28,30, 314n.88, 315n.6; *see also* Antonio

Middleton, Thomas, 11

Midgley, Graham, 189, 251–2, 326n.5, 336n.12

Miller, Jonathan, 28, 225

Milton, John, 4, 7, 110, 254, 286n.3, 287n.13,19, 308n.31, 309n.32, 310n.44, 314n.94, 338n.24

Mithdal, H. S. D., 290n.38

Moisan, Thomas, 13–4, 293n.93, 295n.120, 313n.84

Monter, William, 17–18, 290n.38,40,42–3

Moody, A. D., 332n.62, 340n.49

Morocco, xvii, 8, 12, 29, 41, 49, 53–4, 56, 64, 77, **97–100**, **102–6**, 108–9, **111–14**, **119–21**, 126, 144, 146, 149, 151, 161, 193, 202, 208, 241, 243–4, 259, 266, 276, 288n.28, 305n.4, 306n.16–19, 307n.22, 308n.29, 309n.41, 340n.53
Morris, Harry, 326n.15, 332n.62, 333n.63
Morwyng, Peter, 20–3, 27, 78, 84, 291n.48,50–6, 302n.45, 334n.80
Mosley, Charles W. R. D., 1, 286n.2
Mosse, Miles, 31–3, 134, 151, 156–7, 162, 164, 169–71, 175–7, 217–19, 249–50, 282, 287n.25, 293n.89, 294n.95, 295n.117,127, 313n.83,87, 317n.12,16, 318n.18,21–2,24, 319n.25–6,31, 320n.33–4,36,40, 321n.45–8,52, 322n.59–60,63–6, 69–70, 323n.71–7,86, 324n.93–6, 101, 325n.103, 331n.51, 335n.5–6, 336n.9, 339n.43
Mottana, Annibale, *et al.*, 309n.34
Muir, Kenneth, 43, 297n.3, 331n.48, 332n.62, 339n.30
Munday, Anthony, *see Zelauto*
Murry, John Middleton, 296n.1
Musculus, Wolfgang, 302n.50, 322n.61
music, 56, 99, 101, 108–9, 126, 274, 306n.13, 308n.29

Nashe, Thomas, 4–5, 11, 19–27, 31, 33, 84, 160, 162, 164–6, 287n.14, 290n.36, 291n.60–1,64, 292n.72, 294n.103, 311n.64, 320n.39, 321n.53,55
Nathan, Norman, 83, 89, 152, 303n.58,64, 304n.66,71–2,74, 309n.33, 317n.14, 323n.84, 326n.15, 333n.73
Neale, J. E., 292n.77
Nelson, Benjamin, 138, 295n.114, 313n.82, 314n.95, 319n.31, 325n.108
Nerissa, xvii, **6**, 8, 41, 48, 49, 52, 56–7, 71, 88–9, **98–100**, 113–14, 116, 118, 128, 136, 140, 193, 246, 247, 252, 255–8, 268–9, 271–2, 282,

303n.64, 304n.66,71
Newman, Karen, 256, 337n.22, 340n.49
Noble, Richmond, 151, 287n.22
nomenclature, 69–94; *see also* individual characters; language
Noonan, John T., Jr, 34, 134–5, 295n.111, 313n.82, 314n.88,91, 322n.64, 324n.96, 335n.7

oaths, 9, 41, 52, 55–6, 58, 72, 103, 114, 116, 180, 186, 186, 205, 209, 256–7, 259–60, 262–3, 265, 268, 271, 278, 282, 338n.26
Oberman, Heiko Augustinus, 15, 17, 23, 289n.35, 290n.39, 291n.62, 293n.87
O'Connor, Flannery, 129, 290n.45, 312n.75
Olivier, Sir Laurence, 28, 239
Orgel, Stephen, 269, 337n.18, 339n.41,42

Painter, William, 113, 306n.16
Palmer, John Leslie, 314n.2
paradox, xvi–xvii, 10, 108, 112–13, 142, 184, 193, 241, 248, 279
Parry, Christopher, 296n.1
Parsons, Robert, 222, 332n.56
Paster, Gail Kern, 197, 327n.22
Paul IV, Pope (Cardinal Carafa), 18
Pearlman, E., 339n.45
Perkins, William, 36, 295n.118
Pettet, E. C., 288n.30
Phialas, Peter, 296n.1
Pitcairn, Robert, 291n.64
Plutarch, 151, 162, 339n.32
Pope, Alexander, 29, 211, 330n.41
Popkin, Richard, 288n.28, 294n.109
Porder, Richard, 302n.50, 317n.13, 333n.70
Portia, xvii, 6, 8–9, 12, 29, 40–2, 44, 48–9, 52–5, 56–9, **67–9**, 77, 85, 88–9, 95, **97–111**, **113–18**, 120, 112–23, 125, 127–9, 131–3, 136, 138, 140–3, 181, **183–7**, **192–6**, **199–203**, **206–10**, 213–16, 221, 225, 230–1, 233, 237, 240–2, **246–8**, 250, **252–73**, **278–82**,

299n.17, 303n.64,
304n.66,69,71–2, 306n.12,14,
307n.23, 308n.29, 310n.42,43,
316n.8, 324n.91, 326n.15,
327n.17, 328n.24, 329n.30,32,
334n.84, 337n.22, 338n.23,28–9,
339n.37, 340n.47
and Jessica, 88, 118, 120, 122–3,
125, 127–8
and law, 59, 193–4, 196–9, 200,
204, 233, 256, 327n.17, 328n.24,
329n.29,32, 338n.28
and Morocco and Arragon, 29, 53,
99, 102–5
and rings episode, 44, 246, 256–69,
337n.22, 338n.29, 340n.47
as Balthazar/Daniel, 85, 186–7,
193–6, 255
as daughter, 6, 9, 12, 56–7, 97–101,
107–10, 113, 116, 120, 127, 133,
183, 193, 230, 241, 252, 278, 282
as friend, 9, 52, 56, 116–17, 129,
132, 140, 246–8, 250, 253, 255,
262–3, 267–70, 272, 288,
310n.43, 339n.37
as lover/wife, 9, 41, 49, 53, 101–2,
107–8, 114, 116, 122–3, 131, 136,
252–3, 255–6, 258, 265–6, 269,
272–3, 310n.42–3, 339n.37
as name, 88–9, 109, 184, 267,
303n.64, 304n.66,69,71, 326n.15
as woman and heroine, 9, 12, 40,
42, 48–9, 52, 55–6, 67–9, 97–9,
101, 106, 109, 114, 116–18, 120,
129, 140–3, 185, 193, 200–3,
207–8, 214, 231, 237, 241, 260–2,
265–9, 273, 278–80, 282, 306n.12,
310n.43, 334n.84, 338n.23
Posner, Richard A., 216, 327n.23,
331n.47,49
props, 12, 57, 98, 104, 196, 281–2

Quiller-Couch, Arthur, 296n.1,
308n.27

Rabkin, Norman, 43, 218, 297n.4,
331n.52, 332n.62
Rachel, 82, 90, 126–7, 174, 301n.38,
305n.79, 312n.70, 317n.14

Rackin, Phyllis, 308n.27, 310n.43
Ragussis, Michael, 290n.37
Ranald, Margaret Loftus, 310n.50
Randall, Lilian M. C., 304n.65
Rasmussen, Eric, 308n.29
Rebecca, 121, 158, 303n.64
religious tolerance and intolerance,
16–19, 220–1, 241, 290n.40,43–4,
293n.87
Restak, Richard M., M.D., 285n.5
reversal, 12, 55, 68, 94, 115, 142, 151,
153, 168, 177, 181, 202, 207,
209–10, 225–6, 242, 244, 259,
279–80, 283
Ribner, Irving, 292n.84, 321n.55
Robertson, D. W., Jr, 285n.3,
308n.31, 333n.69
Robinson, Richard, 298n.12; *see
Gesta Romanorum*
Roche, Thomas P., 338n.27
Rockas, Leo, 253, 337n.20
Rose, Mark, 46, 297n.9
Rossky, William, 286n.3
Roth, Cecil, 294n.107
Rowe, Nicholas, 45

St Antonino (Antonio), 134–5,
293n.91, 313n.85–6, 314n.88
St Augustine, 18, 308n.31, 333n.69
St Paul, 15, 67, 69, 86, 91–2, 117, 119,
163, 188, 193, 200, 206, 212, 219,
277–8, 232–5, 242, 244, 278,
300n.25, 302n.50, 316n.10,
326n.14, 329n.29,35, 334n.80–1
Salarino, 41, 49, 59, 62, 65, 130–2,
138, 140, 149, 177, 179, 181,
186–7, 204, 251–2, 273, 282,
298n.16, 322n.58
Salerio, 49, 115, 181–2, 282
Salingar, Leo, 300n.26
Sander, Nicholas, 321n.45,
322n.61–4
Sara, 24, 90–2, 301n.38
Sastri, H. N. L., 314n.2
Saviolo, Vincentio, 294n.96, 311n.51
Seltzer, Daniel, xi
Seneca, 67, 129, 248, 312n.74,
335n.2,3
Sen Gupta, S. C., 299n.20

Scott, W. I. D., 336n.11
Shaheen, Naseeb, 12, 287n.22–3,25, 319n.28
Shakespeare, William, *passim*
  All's Well That Ends Well, 42
  As You Like It, xvi, 110
  Coriolanus, 294n.98
  Cymbeline, 294n.98
  Hamlet, ix, xvi–xvii, 39–40, 84, 132, 268
  Henry IV, Part One, 143, 295n.125, 326n.14
  Julius Caesar, 88, 267
  King Lear, 3, 283–4
  Love's Labor's Lost, 256
  Measure for Measure, 41, 214–15, 230, 237, 278, 284
  The Merchant of Venice, passim
  The Merry Wives of Windsor, 41
  A Misummer Night's Dream, 1, 7, 41
  Much Ado About Nothing, 41, 121, 253, 283
  Othello, 7, 13, 29, 66, 96, 102–3, 124, 160, 265, 284, 312n.78
  Pericles, 110–11
  Richard III, 160, 190, 322n.55
  Romeo and Juliet, 45, 90, 116, 121, 129, 132, 144, 213, 244, 254, 259, 277, 281, 283, 294n.96,98, 321n.53, 326n.12
  The Taming of the Shrew, 41
  Timon of Athens, 33, 294n.98,102
  Titus Andronicus, 13
  The Tempest, 273, 282
  Troilus and Cressida, 251
  Twelfth Night, 41
  Two Gentlemen of Verona, 41, 98, 123
  The Winter's Tale, 42, 268, 298, 336n.11
Shapiro, James, 106, 303n.60, 307n.23
Sharp, Ronald A., 313n.82, 340n.47
Shatzmiller, Joseph, 34, 175–6, 295n.112,128, 324n.97,100
Shell, Marc, 174, 323n.88
Shylock, xi, xv, 9–14, 18–19, 24–5, 28–32, 34–5, 38–42, 44, 46, 48, 49, **52–73**, **76–84**, 87, 89–95, 97–8,
  100, 103–6, 115, **118–27**, 129, 132–4, **136–40**, **142–96**, **198–249**, 254–7, 259–60, 262, 266, 269–71, 273–4, **278–82**, 284, 285n.2, 288n.28, 289n.34–5, 292n.75, 295n.128, 296n.129, 298n.16, 299n.22, 303n.53,57,61, 304n.71, 305n.9, 311n.51, 314n.1,2, 315n.3, 316n.7, 318n.23, 319n.25,27,30, 322n.58, 323n.84, 324n.91,101, 325n.110, 326n.10,14, 328n.27, 329n.29,32,37, 331n.47, 332n.56,61–2, 333n.73, 334n.81,84
  and conversion, 19, 29, 55, 143, 176–8, 219–24, 226–8, 232, 239–42
  and law, 34, 52, 64, 69, 90, 106, 150, 168, 173, 180, 184, 187–8, 190, 196, 199, 201–2, 205–6, 208–12, 222, 239–40, 242–3, 259, 276, 296n.129, 328n.27, 329n.32
  and Marlowe's Barabas, 18, 39, 91, 94, 159, 165, 189, 223, 238
  and revenge, 49, 53, 60, 63–6, 69, 83, 159–60, 169, 173–4, 179, 183, 201, 231
  and usury, xi, xv, 9, 30–1, 34, 59, 62, 64, 80, 106, 121, 133, 143–4, 148–9, 151–2, 157, 160, 162, 166–9, 170, 172–7, 179, 180, 182–4, 189, 209–11, 213, 217, 229–30, 239, 249, 284
  and wealth, 24–5, 30, 76, 80, 120, 138–9, 148, 174, 178, 188, 208, 218, 223, 226, 228, 240–1, 244, 311n.51
  and Wilson's Gerontus, 18, 180, 189, 191, 295n.128
  as father, 14, 49, 55, 92, 97, 120–1, 124, 159, 174, 211, 219, 226, 228
  as friend, 63, 138–9, 189, 231
  as husband, 24, 83, 124–6, 142, 174
  as master, 91–3, 211, 228
  as stage Jew: for an Elizabethan audience, 11, 14, 19, 24–5, 30, 35, 39, 62–3, 65, 91, 144, 146–7, 151, 153, 165, 177–8, 188–9, 191,

206, 220, 223, 234, 241, 289n.32;
  in Venice, 10, 13–14, 24, 91, 147,
  222; Pharisee, 188–9, 150–1,
  168, 226, 244, 260, 296n.129
  as victim, 19, 28, 60, 62, 65, 153,
  156, 177–8, 189, 202
  as victimizer, 60, 62–3, 65–6, 69,
  140, 143–4, 160, 174, 176–7, 184,
  187, 189–90, 201, 203
  in relation to casket choice, 27, 95,
  98, 104–6, 140, 144, 146, 158,
  209, 226, 243–4
Sider, John W., 296n.1
Sidney, Sir Philip, xii, xvii, 4–5, 69, 93,
  148, 186, 246, 279, 287n.12,15,
  300n.32
Siegel, P. N., 39, 296n.129
Silvayn, Alexander, *see The Orator*
Sinsheimer, Hermann, 295n.114
Sisson, C. J., 288n.29
Slights, Camille, 126, 312n.67
Smith, Bruce R., 46, 252, 297n.9,
  298n.15, 336n.15
Smith, Henry, 322n.61
Smith, John H., 325n.110
Soellner, Rolf, 304n.69
Solanio, 41, 49, 59, 62, 65, 76, 120,
  130–32, 134, 138, 140, 149, 177,
  179–81, 186, 251–2, 273, 282,
  298n.16
sources, 6, 71, 281, *passim*
  see under individual entries: Bible;
  *Gernutus, Gesta Romanorum, Il
  Pecorone*; Christopher Marlowe;
  Masuccio; Miles Mosse; *The
  Orator*; Robert Wilson; Thomas
  Wilson; *Zelauto*
Spencer, Christopher, 24, 78, 82,
  292n.67,69, 293n.94, 302n.46–7,
  303n.58
Spencer, Hazelton, 305n.4
Spencer, Theodore, 308n.31
Spenser, Edmund, 3–4, 162, 272,
  280, 287n.12, 299n.21, 310n.49,
  327n.18, 329n.37, 337n.18,
  338n.27, 340n.48
Stevenson, Laura Caroline, 288n.30,
  295n.118, 318n.19–20, 324n.91
Stewart, Patrick, xi, 221, 240, 285n.2

Stoll, Elmer Edgar, 312n.68
Stonex, Arthur B., 71, 288n.30,
  300n.35, 315n.6, 318n.19
structure, 40, 45–57, 223, 238–9,
  297n.7, 328n.24; *see also*
  Figure 1
Stubbes, Phillip, 319n.31, 320n.41,
  325n.1
Suchet, David, xi
Sutton, Thomas, 37, 295n.125
Swift, Jonathan, 29
symbol, xvii, 8, 45, 48, 57, 81–2, 96, 98,
  104–5, 110–14, 121, 123–4, 127,
  133, 140–1, 161, 173, 183, 185,
  196, 201, 205–6, 224–6, 232, 235,
  239, 246, 256–7, 261, 265, 269,
  270–2, 282

Taeusch, Carl, 294n.104
Tawney, R. H., 37, 286n.10, 295n.124
Taylor, Jeremy, 267–8, 339n.38–40
Tennenhouse, Leonard, 29, 108,
  293n.88, 308n.28
The Orator, 187, 198, 201, 325n.3–4
Thompson, Karl, 296n.1
Tilley, Morris Palmer, 311n.55
Tillyard, E. M. W., 329n.30
Tindale, William, 239
Tomson, Lawrence, 11, 29
Tovey, Barbara, 289n.34, 330n.46
Trousdale, Marion, 287n.17
Truculento, 68, 300n.25, 318n.18;
  see also Zelauto
Tubal, 49, 52, 60–2, 64–5, 71, 73, 76,
  78, 83, 90, 119, 126, 138–40, 142,
  154, 160, 166, 181–2, 184, 189,
  201, 222, 282, 301n.38, 303n.57
Tucker, E. F. J., 214, 327n.23,
  329n.32, 330n.44
Tucker, Patrick and Michael
  Holden (eds), 285n.1, 306n.13

unity, ix–x, 2–3, 31, 46–8, 57, 71,
  95, 151, 209, 236, 259, 275–6,
  281, 296n.1, 297n.9, 298n.11,
  311n.52, *passim*
  of plots, ix, xi, 3, 6, 30, 46, 53, 55,
  57, 71, 90, 129, 150, 244, 257,
  276, 281, 307n.22

Unity – *cont.*
  through idea of wise love, 3, 7–9,
    33, 43–5, 55, 57, 95–6, 106, 110,
    113, 129, 133, 140–1, 182–3, 185,
    193, 206, 230, 236, 244, 248, 277,
    284, 337n.18
  see also issues; language; structure
usury, xii, xiv, 29, 31, 281–2, 285n.2,
    287n.25, 288n.30, 289n.33,
    293n.89,91, 294n.104,
    295n.111,113,118, 295n.128,
    298n.14, 302n.50, 307n.22,
    313n.82,86, 316n.8, 317n.13,16,
    318n.19,23, 319n.27,31,
    320.36,40, 321n.45, 322n.61,64,
    323n.88, 324n.101, 331n.47,
    339n.32
  and Christians, 31, 34–5, 38, 170,
    177–8, 224, 280, 294n.105,
    317n.16, 318n.21, 335n.5
  and Jews, 31, 34–5, 38, 160, 163,
    166, 177–8, 180, 224, 280,
    294n.105, 316n.8
  associations with, avarice, 162;
    deception, 79, 170, 323n.72;
    destruction, 80, 302n.50;
    devil/hell, 35, 162, 320n.41;
    dogs, 163–4, 180, 321n.44,48;
    injustice, 35, 121; labourless
    profit, xv, 161; mercilessness,
    35, 179, 184; murder, 79, 184;
    pirates, 148; publicans, 151–2;
    risklessness, 35, 149, 161, 207;
    theft, 35, 79, 121, 159–60, 184,
    319n.31, 320n.32;
    unnaturalness, 36, 161–2,
    320n.35; worldliness, 126,
    156–7, 162, 180, 300n.25
  classical views of, 36, 320n.35,
    339n.32
  condemnation of, 30, 33–5, 38,
    126, 134–5, 148, 159, 162, 166,
    176, 179, 184, 244
  definition of, 30, 32–3, 35, 160–2,
    169, 174–5, 249, 270, 275,
    293n.91, 320n.36, 323n.80,86,
    324n.101
  Elizabethan views of, xiv, 30,
    33–4, 38, 162, 172, 174, 176, 217,

    224, 231, 249, 276, 294n.105,
    302n.50, 314n.92, 316n.8,
    318n.21, 319n.27,31,
    320n.40,41, 324n.95–6,
    330n.32, 335n.5
  in England, xiv, 31–3, 36–8, 48,
    162, 170, 172, 217, 224, 275,
    294n.96, 294n.105, 315n.6,
    319n.27, 321n.47, 324n.96,
    335n.5
  in Venice, xiv, 34, 184
  reassessment of, 33, 36–7, 176,
    275, 321n.47, 324n.96
  Shakespeare's use of, 30, 32–3,
    38–9, 45, 151–2, 154–6, 166,
    170–2, 176, 183, 209, 217, 221,
    224, 248–9, 270, 275, 280, 282,
    294n.102, 316n.8, 318n.18,23,
    319n.25
  see also law
Vickers, Brian, 314n.2, 316n.7

Waith, Eugene M., 267, 336n.14,
    337n.19, 339n.36
Weber, Max, 37, 295n.124
Welles, Orson and Roger Hill (eds),
    285n.1
Werthheim, Albert, 330n.46, 332n.62
Wheeler, Thomas, 42, 285n.1, 297n.2
Whigham, Frank, 340n.49
Whitaker, Virgil K., 314n.2
Wilkins, Leah W., 319n.27
Willet, Andrew, 89, 127, 305n.77–8,
    312n.70, 319n.30
Williams, Arnold, 323n.84
Williamson, Marilyn L., 340n.49
Wilson, F. P., 304n.69
Wilson, Robert, 14, 16, 18, 70, 125,
    175, 180, 189, 236, 288n.27,
    289n.33, 290n.38, 295n.128,
    311n.62
Wilson, Thomas, 15, 21, 32, 39, 47,
    68, 126, 134, 137, 148, 160,
    162–4, 166, 169, 175–6, 178–9,
    184, 198, 224, 230, 236, 281–2,
    286n.10, 289n.33, 291n.57,
    294n.105, 295n.115, 298n.13,
    300n.29, 312n.69, 313n.83,87,
    314n. 92, 316n.8, 317n.13,17,

Wilson Thomas – *cont.*
  318n.21, 319n.27,31,
  320n.33,35,38,41, 321n.42,45,
  51–2, 322n.56,62,64, 323n.72,80,
  324n.94, 96,101, 325n.104,106–7,
  326n.11, 328n.26, 332n.58–60,
  333n.68, 335n.5–6,8, 339n.32,43,
  340n.50
Withycombe, E. G., 304n.66, 305n.82

Wolf, Lucien, 288n.29
Wölfflin, Heinrich, 2–3, 286n.7, 297n.9
Wright, Celeste Turner, 288n.30

Yachnin, Paul, 286n.18

Zelauto, 67–8, 198–9, 300n.25,28,
  318n.18, 321n.52, 329n.36,
  331n.48